Caregiver Education Guide for Children with Developmental Disabilities

Aspen Reference Group

Sara Nell Di Lima

Managing Editor

Suzanne Niemeyer

Senior Editor

Jennifer R. Carson

Assistant Research Editor

AN ASPEN PUBLICATION
Aspen Publishers, Inc.
Gaithersburg, Maryland
1998

Caregiver education guide for children with developmental disabilities/Aspen Reference Group; Sara Nell Di Lima, manager; Suzanne Niemeyer, senior editor; Jennifer R. Carson, research editorial assistant.

p. cm.

Includes bibliographical references and index.

ISBN 0-8342-1034-7

1. Developmentally disabled children—Care. I. Di Lima, Sara N. II. Niemeyer, Suzanne. III. Carson, Jennifer R. IV. Aspen Reference Group (Aspen Publishers)

RJ135.C37   1997

362.1'9892—dc21

97-13393

CIP

Editorial Resources: Ruth Bloom

Printing and Manufacturing: Terri Miner

About Aspen Publishers ¢ For more than 35 years, Aspen has been a leading professional publisher in a variety of disciplines. Aspen's vast information resources are available in both print and electronic formats. We are committed to providing the highest quality information available in the most appropriate format for our customers. Visit Aspen's Internet site for more information resources, directories, articles, and a searchable version of Aspen's full catalog, including the most recent publications: **http://www.aspenpub.com**

Aspen Publishers, Inc. ¢ The hallmark of quality in publishing

Member of the worldwide Wolters Kluwer group

Library of Congress Catalog Card Number: 97-13393

ISBN: 0-8342-1034-7

Printed in the United States of America

1 2 3 4 5

Table of Contents

For a detailed listing of chapter contents,
please see the first page of each chapter.

Editorial Board

Rosemary Manago, MSN, RN
Assistant Director
Division of Specialized Care for Children,
    Home Health Care
The University of Illinois at Chicago
Chicago, Illinois

Guy L. McCormack, MS, OTR
Professor
Occupational Therapy Department
San Jose State University
San Jose, California

Patricia Meinhold, PhD
Department of Psychology
Western Michigan University
Kalamazoo, Michigan

Lu Merrick
Program Coordinator/Behavioral Specialist
Ivymount School
Rockville, Maryland

James A. Mulick, PhD
Professor
Department of Pediatrics, Division of
    Psychology
The Ohio State University
Columbus, Ohio

Maurine Packard, MD
Fellow in Child Neurology
Children's Medical Center
Dallas, Texas

Yvonne Perret, MA, MSW, LCSW
Social Worker
Coauthor, *Children with Disabilities:
    A Medical Primer*
Baltimore, Maryland

Adele Proctor, ScD
Associate Professor
Speech and Hearing Science
University of Illinois at Urbana-Champaign
Champaign, Illinois

Lynn Rosenfeld, PhD, MSW
Author and Consultant
Birmingham, Alabama

Susan S. Russell, MS, CCC
Arkansas Children's Hospital/Department of
    Pediatrics, University of Arkansas for
    Medical Sciences
Little Rock, Arkansas

Eldon G. Schulz, MD
Department of Pediatrics
University of Arkansas for Medical Sciences
Little Rock, Arkansas

Caryl Semmler, PhD, OTR
Private Practice
Dallas, Texas

**Ronald T. Smolarski, MA, CLCP, CCM,
    CVE, LPC, CDE II, CRV, ABVE, ABMP**
Director/Certified Rehabilitation Counselor
Beacon Rehabilitation Services, Inc.
Ann Arbor, Michigan

Marjorie Szor, MA, MS, RNC
Clinical Nurse Specialist—Spina Bifida
Medical College Hospitals—Medical College
    of Ohio
Toledo, Ohio

Shayne Tokita, CCC-SLP
Easter Seal Society of Hawaii
Lihue, Kauai, Hawaii

**Symme Trachtenberg, MSW, ACSW,
    LSW**
Clinical Affiliate of Social Work in Pediatrics
University of Pennsylvania Medical School
    Lecturer
University of Pennsylvania School of Social
    Work
Philadelphia, Pennsylvania

R. Franklin Trimm, MD
Developmental/Behavioral Pediatrics
University of South Alabama
Mobile, Alabama

Christine M. Wallin, BSN, MA
Consultant
Arlington, Virginia

Josie Woll, RN
Director
Sultan Easter Seal School
Honolulu, Hawaii

Preface

Advances in medicine, technology, and civil rights have opened up a whole new world of opportunities for children with developmental disabilities. In order for children to take full advantage of these opportunities, effective care coordination, family-professional collaboration, and caregiver education are paramount.

Care coordination is a complex prospect. A wide spectrum of professionals serve children with disabilities, including physicians, physical therapists, occupational therapists, social workers, speech/language pathologists, dietitians, and nurses. And of course families, teachers, day care providers, and others who may be unfamiliar with developmental disabilities play crucial roles in shaping a child's development. Ensuring optimal, family-centered care requires extensive and effective communication between an interdisciplinary professional team and nonprofessional caregivers, among members of the professional team, and among multiple nonprofessional caregivers. Based on this premise, the *Caregiver Education Guide for Children with Developmental Disabilities* presents materials covering the many diverse components of caring for children with developmental disabilities.

As a comprehensive caregiver education resource, the *Caregiver Education Guide for Children with Developmental Disabilities* addresses the immense need for specific, hands-on instructions and guidelines for parents and other caregivers. Designed for distribution by the health care professional, the guide's patient information sheets comprise guidelines, instructions, checklists, and other tools to facilitate caregiving and enhance treatment. Primary caregivers can in turn disseminate relevant information to other caregivers—teachers, babysitters, day care providers, and other family members. Professionals can also use the manual as a quick reference in areas outside their field of expertise.

The guide presents patient education materials culled from hospital departments, surveys of private practices and clinics, rehabilitation centers, support organizations, health associations, and extensive review of both professional and lay literature. Guided by our editorial board of experts, we honed in on the most relevant topics and the highest quality materials.

Beginning with concise overviews of some of the most common disabilities, the materials here address a broad spectrum of concerns: behavior management and psychosocial issues, physical management, home care issues/activities of daily living, care coordination and family-professional collaboration, nutrition and feeding, oral health, technology for communication, and educational issues. Within these broad subject areas, we've packed the guide with a full range of materials. In addition to hands-on items, the guide offers assessment tools and communication tips and techniques to aid the professional in counseling families.

The Appendix groups the guide's patient information sheets by type of disability for ready reference.

Suzanne Niemeyer,
Senior Editor, Aspen Reference Group
Jennifer R. Carson,
Assistant Research Editor,
Aspen Reference Group

Acknowledgments

Creating a large reference volume such as *Caregiver Education Guide for Children with Developmental Disabilities* demand tremendous effort during the development period—shaping the focus on the manual, collecting and evaluating materials, and ensuring that the format is practical and easy to use.

Foremost among the people who help us fulfill these responsibilities are the editorial board members. By answering queries, providing contacts, sharing their patient education tools, and reviewing materials, they are instrumental to the development of a high quality resource. I would particularly like to thank Christine M. Wallin, BSN, MA, Consultant, Arlington, Virginia; Toby M. Long, MA, PT, Director, Physical Therapy, Georgetown University Child Development Center, Washington, D.C.; Allan K. Bird, PhD, CCC-SLP, Program Director of Speech Pathology, Texas Woman's University, Denton, Texas; Jean L. Blosser, EdD, Director, Speech and Hearing Center, Professor Communicative Disorders, The University of Akron, Akron, Ohio; Roberta DePompei, PhD, School of Communicative Disorders, The University of Akron, Akron, Ohio; A. Mervyn Fox, MB, BS, FRCP(C), DCH, Thames Valley Children's Centre and Children's Hospital of Western Ontario, London, Ontario, Canada; Carla Jurgensmeyer, MA, Psychological Examiner, University of Arkansas for Medical Sciences/Arkansas Children's Hospital, Little Rock, Arkansas; Melody Kinney, LCSW, Maternal-Child Social Worker, Good Samaritan Hospital, San Jose, California; Kant Lin, MD, Division of Craniofacial Surgery, University of Virginia Health Sciences Center, Charlottesville, Virginia;

Patricia Meinhold, PhD, Department of Psychology, Western Michigan University, Kalamazoo, Michigan; Lu Merrick, Program Coordinator/Behavioral Specialist, Ivymount School, Rockville, Maryland; James A. Mulick, PhD, Professor, Department of Pediatrics, Division of Psychology, The Ohio State University, Columbus, Ohio; Caryl Semmler, PhD, OTR, Private Practice, Dallas, Texas; Shayne Tokita, CCC-SLDP, Easter Seal Society of Hawaii, Lihue, Kauai, Hawaii; R. Franklin Trimm, MD, Developmental/Behavioral Pediatrics, University of South Alabama, Mobile, Alabama; and Josie Woll, RN, Director, Sultan Easter Seal School, Honolulu, Hawaii.

I am grateful to all the health care facilities, organizations, individual professionals, and others who generously shared their patient education materials with us—special thanks to Laura Barnes, RN, MSN, CNAA, Director, Child Health Education Center, East Tennessee Children's Hospital, Knoxville, Tennessee; Robert H. Parrot, MD, Director Emeritus, Project CHAMP, Children's National Medical Center, Washington, D.C.; Mary Boland, RN, MSN, Children's Hospital AIDS Program, Children's Hospital of New Jersey, Newark, Jew Jersey; and Michelle R. Girard, Coordinator of Support Services, Muscular Dystrophy Association National Headquarters, Tucson, Arizona.

Suzanne Niemeyer,
Senior Editor, Aspen Reference Group
Jennifer R. Carson,
Assistant Research Editor,
Aspen Reference Group

1
Common Diagnoses

Parent's Assessment of Learned Skills Form

USES OF THIS FORM

This Parent's Assessment of Learned Skills (PALS) form can be used for parent training about child development or for part of a team evaluation with parents as the informants. Using the PALS, parents are able to assess their own child in relation to skills that they see in the natural environment. This process of parent assessment of their own child empowers parents to become important members of the multidisciplinary treatment team. It also gives a realistic, functional look at what babies do and what they need to be able to do to be "successful" in their home and future environments.

NOTE TO PARENTS

Everything that babies do is important and can be seen as a learning opportunity. Infant development is divided into 7 major domains, which are described below.

This assessment tool will enable you to look at your infant's activities, decide what skills your baby has achieved, and understand what comes next so that you can foster or enhance your child's developmental potential. Please remember that most babies exhibit scattered development across several months' range. For example, a typical 8-month-old baby may display different skills ranging from 7 to 9 months on a developmental scale. It is very unlikely that your child will display solid development for his or her chronological age level without showing some degree of scattered skills.

One factor to consider when looking at an infant's development is the baby's true "gestational age." If your child is 8 months old but was born 2 months before the expected due date, he or she should be performing activities roughly at the 6-month level.

Because this tool was designed to be used by parents, it has been written in "functional language" that describes behaviors and activities that actually occur in a baby's home environment. This assessment has been cross-referenced with 5 standardized evaluations currently being used by professional early interventionists. These reference codes appear beneath each activity or skill. Each skill is also coded by the developmental domain or domains that the skill represents.

This form alternates in referring to the baby as "he" or "she." All skills listed, however, apply to both boys and girls.

DESCRIPTION OF DEVELOPMENTAL DOMAINS

Cognition (C)

Cognitive skills represent the way a baby observes, understands, and learns from his or her environment. Cognition includes understanding cause and effect, the means to obtain desired ends (the ability to "make things happen"), imitation skills (the ability to copy what the baby sees and hears), spatial relationships, and schemes for relating objects to each other and to people. Concept development and memory tasks are also examples of cognitive skills.

continues

continued

Social/Emotional (SE)

Socialization skills represent the way a baby interacts with other people and expresses and responds to human emotions. Crying, smiling, laughing, cuddling, and game playing are all examples of infant social skills.

Fine Motor (FM)

Fine motor skills represent activities that primarily involve the smaller hand muscles. Object manipulation, eye-hand coordination, and bilateral hand movements are all fine motor skills.

Gross Motor (GM)

Gross motor skills involve the larger body muscles and include such activities as balancing, sitting, crawling, and walking.

Self-Help (SH)

Self-help skills represent feeding activities (such as nursing and finger feeding), toileting activities, and dressing and undressing tasks. Bathing and personal hygiene activities (such as brushing teeth and combing hair) are also included in the self-help domain.

Expressive Language (EL)

Expressive language represents the way an infant uses voice and gestures to communicate his or her needs and desires to others. Crying, cooing, babbling, and gesturing are all expressive language tools.

Receptive Language (RL)

Receptive language skills represent the ability to hear and understand what others are trying to communicate to the infant. Early receptive skills include attending to and locating the source of sounds. These skills develop into the ability to understand and respond to verbal and gestural cues or verbal statements.

USE OF DEVELOPMENTAL DOMAINS

You will notice that many of the assessment tasks fall under more than one developmental domain. Infant development is interrelated and interdependent, and any attempt to categorize developmental skills is somewhat artificial. It is, however, useful to understand the concept of developmental domains when trying to communicate your child's abilities to professionals.

continues

continued

ASSESSMENT FORM

Child's Name _____   Date _____

Activity	Domain	Date	Date	Comments
Newborn				
Stops crying when picked up (ELAP) (HELP) (CAR)	C, SE, EL, RL			
Opens eyes wide—or becomes very still—to listen to sounds (HELP) (ELAP) (CAR)	C, RL			
Startles to loud noises—sometimes cries (ELAP) (CAR)	C, SE, EL, RL			
Head and arms droop when you hold baby across your lap (ELAP) (PEA)	GM			
Held under his arms, facing you, he raises his feet alternately (ELAP) (PEA)	GM			
When placed on her stomach, she curls up in a ball and turns head to the side (PEA) (HELP)	GM			
Grabs your finger when placed in his palm (U&H) (ELAP) (CAR)	FM			
When resting, keeps one elbow bent with hand fisted and close to face (ELAP) (HELP) (PEA)	GM			

continues

Reference Code: ELAP—Early Learning Accomplishment Profile; HELP—Hawaii Early Learning Profile; CAR—The Carolina Curriculum for Handicapped Infants and Infants at Risk; U&H—Uzgiris and Hunt Scales of Infant Psychological Development; PEA—Peabody Scales of Motor Development.
   Developmental Domain Code: C—Cognition; SE—Social/Emotional; FM—Fine Motor; GM—Gross Motor; SH—Self-Help; EL—Expressive Language; RL—Receptive Language.
   Note: For flexibility, this form includes two date columns to meet your individual needs. You may want to use one column to show when the parent first observed a behavior and the other to show when the health care professional first observed the behavior.

continued

Activity	Domain	Date	Date	Comments
1 Month				
Moves arms and legs excitedly when he hears your voice but can't see you (CAR) (HELP)	C, SE, RL			
Makes small throaty "ooh" and "aah" sounds as you change her position (ELAP) (HELP) (U&H)	SE, EL			
Becomes quiet and stares at your face for 5 to 10 seconds when you speak to him (ELAP) (HELP)	C, SE, RL			
Stares momentarily at a crib mobile or overhead lights (U&H) (CAR) (HELP)	C			
Head falls completely back when you pull him by his arms from his back to a sitting position (ELAP) (PEA)	GM			
Turns her head from one side to the other when lying on her stomach (HELP) (ELAP)	GM			
When held sitting on your lap, he raises his head momentarily and then drops it back down (PEA)	GM			
Kicks her legs in and out from under herself when lying on stomach (HELP) (ELAP) (PEA)	GM			
Straightens out his leg momentarily when you press on the bottom of his foot (ELAP) (PEA)	GM			

continues

continued

Activity	Domain	Date	Date	Comments
Occasionally lifts her head off your shoulder when you hold her on your chest (HELP) (ELAP)	GM			
When lying on his back with his head turned to the right side, his right arm and left leg are straight while his left arm and right leg are bent (Opposite reaction if head is facing left.) (ELAP) (PEA)	GM			
Smiles "accidentally"—not as a direct result of anything you do (CAR) (HELP)	SE			
Turns in the direction of bottle or breast when you touch his cheek with the nipple (CAR) (HELP)	C, SE, SH			
Squirms or nuzzles in when held close to your body (HELP)	SE			
2 Months				
Kicks his legs and waves his arms excitedly when you hold a toy over him (U&H) (ELAP)	C, GM			
While lying on her stomach, lifts her chin completely off the bed (ELAP) (PEA)	GM			
Kicks legs "bicycle style" in the bath water (ELAP) (PEA)	GM			
While lying on her side, she occasionally flips over to her back (ELAP)	GM			
Holds both hands together resting on his chest (HELP) (ELAP)	FM			

continues

continued

Activity	Domain	Date	Date	Comments
Holds a rattle or blanket for a few seconds (PEA) (CAR)	FM			
Smiles as a direct result of your touch or your face and voice (CAR)	C, SE, RL			
Smiles more readily for Mom or Dad than for other people (ELAP) (HELP)	C, SE			
Has fussy periods during which only Mom can soothe him (HELP)	C, SE			
Tries to talk back to you with coos and gurgles (U&H) (HELP)	C, EL			
Makes open "fussy noises" that are not quite crying (U&H)	EL			
3 Months				
Her eyes follow you as you move from one side of the crib to the other or across the room (HELP)	C			
Holds his hands up in front of his face and stares at them (U&H) (HELP) (CAR)	C			
When you hold her up in the air, she arches her head and legs (playing "airplane") (ELAP) (PEA)	GM			
When on his stomach, he rises up on his forearms and elbows to look at you (ELAP) (PEA)	GM			

continues

continued

Activity	Domain	Date	Date	Comments
When you hold her standing on your lap, she makes little steps with her legs (ELAP) (PEA)	GM			
While resting or sleeping, his hands are usually open (ELAP)	FM			
Shakes a rattle placed in her hand and hits her face with it (CAR)	FM			
When you talk to him, he turns his head to find your face (CAR) (U&H)	C, RL			
Is more interested in watching your face than in looking at objects or toys (ELAP)	C, RL			
Smiles and chuckles when you tickle him or blow on his tummy (HELP)	C, EL			
Babbles and coos consistently when you talk to her (U&H) (CAR)	C, EL			
When you take him out of your home, he becomes wide-eyed and watches his surroundings (HELP) (ELAP)	C			
Doesn't cry as often and is able to wait for you when you call to her and she hears you coming (ELAP) (HELP)	C, SE, RL			
4 Months				
If he is lying on his back and you pull him up to sitting by his hands, his head and neck remain stiff and do not fall back (PEA)	GM			

continues

continued

Activity	Domain	Date	Date	Comments
While lying on her back, she can roll to either side to reach for a toy (CAR) (PEA)	GM			
Able to sit propped up in the corner of the couch and hold his head up straight for 1 to 2 minutes (HELP)	GM			
When you hold her standing on your lap, she bounces her legs up and down momentarily (ELAP)	GM			
Intentionally shakes a rattle and stops occasionally, as if listening to the sound (U&H) (CAR)	C, FM, RL			
Puts her fingers in her mouth (ELAP)	FM			
Pulls his blanket up and down over his face (CAR)	C, GM			
Grabs at her clothes or a toy placed on her chest (CAR) (ELAP)	C, FM			
Sometimes reaches up to touch your face or bat at a toy (HELP) (ELAP) (U&H)	C, FM			
Cries or frowns when she hears an angry voice (ELAP)	C, SE, RL			
Talks or coos to himself when he is alone (ELAP)	C, EL			
Coos, smiles, or reaches for a familiar person (CAR) (ELAP)	C, SE, EL			

continues

continued

Activity	Domain	Date	Date	Comments
Smiles, opens his mouth, and kicks excitedly when he sees his bottle (HELP) (ELAP)	C, EL			
Turns her head to the sound of the television or a favorite toy (CAR) (U&H)	C, RL			
Laughs aloud when you tickle or play with him (ELAP) (HELP)	C, SE, EL			
5 Months				
While on her stomach, she lifts her head and chest completely off the floor to look around (PEA) (ELAP)	C, GM			
When you hold him on your lap and bounce him, his head and neck are steady with little or no wobble (ELAP) (PEA) (CAR)	GM			
While you hold her sitting on your lap, her back is completely straight (ELAP) (CAR)	GM			
Grasps and holds onto a toy while sitting (CAR)	FM, GM			
While holding one toy, she watches or looks at a second toy (U&H) (ELAP)	C, FM			
Turns head to look for a toy he sees you drop (U&H) (CAR)	C			
Makes high-pitched squealing sounds when she is happy (ELAP)	SE, EL			

continues

continued

Activity	Domain	Date	Date	Comments
Can find his bottle or a toy that is hidden halfway under a diaper (U&H) (CAR)	C			
When reaching for an object, she opens her hand in anticipation of grabbing it (U&H)	C, FM			
Likes to "play games" (If you make a funny face or play peek-a-boo, he bounces excitedly or does something to let you know he wants the "trick" repeated) (CAR) (U&H)	C			
Likes to bang a toy or a spoon on her high-chair tray (U&H) (ELAP)	C, FM			
6 Months				
Rolls completely over from back to stomach and stomach to back (PEA) (ELAP)	GM			
Sits well in a high-chair or stroller and does not slump or fall to the side (ELAP) (PEA)	GM			
Stands up in your lap with his legs straight when you hold him under his arms (ELAP) (PEA)	GM			
While having her diaper changed, she sometimes lifts her legs out straight and holds them up high in the air (ELAP) (PEA)	GM			

continues

continued

Activity	Domain	Date	Date	Comments
Rakes up small things from the floor using all of his fingers to close into his palm (ELAP) (PEA) (CAR)	C, FM, SH			
Tries to make the same sound that you make (U&H) (CAR)	C, SE, EL,			
Reaches out for everything you put in front of him (ELAP) (CAR)	RL			
Fusses by crying or frowning when you take away a toy (ELAP) (CAR) (HELP)	C, FM			
Looks at, talks to, and reaches for himself in a mirror (ELAP) (HELP) (CAR)	C, SE, EL			
Stares at new people; does not go readily to them but turns head toward parent (HELP) (ELAP) (CAR)	C, SE, EL			
Looks down to find a toy that he has dropped while playing (ELAP) (U&H) (CAR)	C, SE			
Explores toys by turning them over and over in her hands and then putting them in her mouth (ELAP) (CAR)	C			
Begins to "fret" or look around the room anxiously when Mom leaves (ELAP) (HELP)	C, FM			
7 Months				
While playing on her tummy, holds herself up with one arm and reaches for a toy with the other (ELAP) (PEA)	C, SE, EL C, GM			

continues

continued

Activity	Domain	Date	Date	Comments
Sits alone on the floor with no external support and uses both hands to play with a toy (ELAP) (PEA)	FM, GM			
She bounces up and down when you hold her standing in your lap and sometimes watches her feet as she is bouncing (ELAP) (PEA)	GM			
When lying on his tummy, pushes up on his hands and knees and rocks back and forth several times (CAR) (ELAP) (PEA)	GM			
While holding a toy, passes it back and forth from one hand to the other (CAR) (ELAP) (PEA)	C, FM			
When holding a toy in each hand, drops one toy to reach out for a third toy (U&H) (CAR)	C			
Often throws toys when she is no longer interested in them, but she does not watch to see where the toy goes (U&H) (CAR)	C, FM			
Tries to imitate the pitch of your voice as it rises and falls when you talk to him (CAR) (HELP)	C, EL			
Shouts or yells a loud noise to get your attention (not crying) (HELP)	SE, EL			
Can reach for his bottle, bring it to his mouth, and hold it for himself (CAR) (HELP)	FM, SH			

continues

continued

Activity	Domain	Date	Date	Comments
Uses her fingers to feed herself small pieces of food (ELAP) (CAR)	FM, SH			
Sometimes sleeps through the night (8 to 10 hours) without waking for a feeding (HELP)	SE, SH			
Daytime sleeping usually consists of 1 or 2 short naps and 1 long (2- to 3-hour) nap each day (HELP)	SE			
8 Months				
Pushes himself up to a sitting position from his tummy by holding onto the crib rail or other furniture (ELAP) (CAR) (PEA)	C, GM			
Crawls around the floor on her stomach (combat style) to get to toys (ELAP) (CAR) (PEA)	C, GM			
Can find a toy that is completely hidden under a blanket or diaper (ELAP) (U&H)	C, FM			
Pushes one toy out of the way to get to another toy (U&H)	C, FM			
Pulls on a scarf or tablecloth to get to a toy or food that is out of reach (U&H)	C, FM			
Bangs toys together in each hand or hits them on a table (ELAP) (HELP)	C, FM			
Copies banging a toy after you bang a similar toy (U&H) (ELAP)	C, SE			

continues

continued

Activity	Domain	Date	Date	Comments
After shaking a rattle or object that makes a noise, she stops, listens, and then shakes it again (U&H) (ELAP)	C, FM, RL			
Lifts his arms to "come up" and looks at the floor to "get down" (U&H) (CAR)	C, RL			
Says "ma-ma," "ba-ba," or "da-da," but not as names for specific people (CAR)	EL			
Shows a distinct preference for certain foods, toys, or places by smiling and making sounds (HELP)	C, SE, EL			
Drinks from a cup that you hold for her (ELAP) (HELP)	SH			
9 Months				
Pulls himself from sitting to standing using a crib rail or other furniture and remains standing for several minutes (ELAP) (PEA) (CAR)	GM			
Sits on the floor alone, playing with toys for at least 10 minutes without falling (PEA) (ELAP)	GM			
Moves across the floor by creeping on his hands and knees (CAR) (PEA) (ELAP)	GM			
Can hold and purposely bite off pieces of a cookie or cracker (Does not simply suck on the cracker) (ELAP) (HELP)	FM, SH			

continues

continued

Activity	Domain	Date	Date	Comments
Enjoys soft table foods, such as mashed potatoes or carrots (CAR)	SH			
Picks up strings or small objects using only her thumb and 1 forefinger (ELAP) (PEA)	FM			
Claps his hands together when you clap yours (CAR) (U&H)	C, FM			
Enjoys putting small objects into and out of a container (such as blocks in a bowl) (HELP) (CAR)	C, FM			
Can find toys that he sees you hide in at least 3 different places (U&H)	C			
Imitates playful sounds that you make, such as coughing or lip popping (ELAP)	C, EL			
While playing alone, often "practices" saying "ba-da-ma" or other sound combinations (CAR) (HELP)	EL			
Appears to understand a lot of what you say to her, either by looking at the toy you name or by shaking her head "no" to some questions (ELAP) (HELP)	C, RL			
When you call his name, he stops playing, turns to you, and smiles (ELAP)	C, SE, RL			

continues

continued

Activity	Domain	Date	Date	Comments
Likes to play turn-taking games, such as pulling a toy back and forth (HELP) (CAR)	C, SE			
Displays a very definite dislike for certain foods by spitting them out, or for certain toys by throwing them as soon as you present them to him; may also refuse to be cared for by anyone but mother (HELP)	C, SE			
10 Months				
While standing and holding onto furniture, momentarily lets go and tests her balance standing alone (PEA) (CAR)	C, FM, GM			
Intentionally lowers himself from standing to sitting and does not fall (ELAP) (PEA)	GM			
When standing, able to hold on to furniture with one hand and bend down to pick up toy with other hand (ELAP) (CAR)	FM, GM			
Sidesteps around the furniture, holding onto it for support (PEA) (ELAP)	FM			
Walks short distances (up to 10 steps) with one or both hands being held for support (PEA) (ELAP)	GM			
Uses his index finger to explore holes such as those on a phone dial (ELAP) (PEA)	C, FM			

continues

continued

continues

Activity	Domain	Date	Date	Comments
Bangs pots and pans or blocks together using both hands (ELAP) (HELP)	C, FM			
Specifically uses his thumb and index finger to pick up small bits of food or paper (CAR) (PEA) (ELAP)	FM			
Plays "pat-a-cake," "bye-bye," "so big," or other nursery games when asked (ELAP) (CAR) (HELP)	C, SE			
Can obtain a toy by pulling on an attached string, or he pulls on parents' clothing to make them come closer (U&H) (ELAP) (CAR)	C, FM			
Copies with her hands new games that you begin (such as tickling or patting your tummy) (U&H) (CAR)	C, FM			
Touches or pulls at your hand and looks at you to make a toy work again (he wants you to make the toy play) (U&H)	C, SE			
Likes to look at pictures in a book instead of eating the paper or shaking the pages (ELAP) (HELP)	C			
Usually ceases his activity when you tell him "no-no" (HELP) (ELAP)	C, SE, RL			
Calls either parent by name (Mama or Dada) (HELP) (ELAP)	C, EL			

continued

Activity	Domain	Date	Date	Comments
If left alone, he "gets into everything" and is very excited by environment or new situations (HELP)	C, SE			
Helps with dressing, by pushing her arm through a sleeve (HELP)	SH			
12 Months				
Takes 3 to 5 steps from one person to another (no hands held) (PEA) (ELAP)	GM			
Crawls on hands and knees very rapidly across the room (ELAP)	GM			
Can stack one toy on top of another (CAR) (HELP)	C, FM			
Turns to either side to reach for a toy she hears but does not see (CAR)	C, FM			
Brings a phone receiver to his ear and listens or pretends to talk (CAR)	C, SE, EL			
Hits a paper with a crayon in an attempt to make marks (PEA) (ELAP)	C, FM			
Can find a toy that he has dropped and pick it up again (ELAP) (U&H)	C, FM			
Can put a toy in your hand and release it when you say "give it here" (ELAP) (CAR)	C, RL			

continues

continued

Activity	Domain	Date	Date	Comments
Likes to put his hands in food and squish it between his fingers (HELP)	C, FM			
Wants to feed herself and fights to bring the spoon to her mouth (usually turning it upside down) (HELP) (CAR)	SE, SH			
Likes to hold and drink from his own cup (with much spilling) but may still prefer his bottle at naptime or bedtime (HELP) (CAR)	SE, SH			
Enjoys "showing off" tricks or teasing, by repeating things that make you laugh (HELP) (ELAP)	C, SE			
Follows simple commands, such as pointing to specific people or toys or coming to you when you call (ELAP) (CAR) (HELP)	C, SE			
Says at least two words besides "ma-ma" and "da-da" (CAR) (ELAP) (U&H)	C, EL			
During play he "talks" in a string of jabbering, using various pitches and intonations (not real words) (ELAP) (HELP) (U&H)	EL			
Pulls off her socks or hat and throws them down (ELAP) (HELP)	SH			
May be more difficult to put to bed at night. (He may cry and rock or bang his head) (HELP) (CAR) (ELAP)	SE			

continues

continued

Activity	Domain	Date	Date	Comments
14 Months				
Throws a ball overhand to you using a definite forward fling of the wrist (ELAP) (HELP)	GM			
Walks, independent of any support, across the room with few falls (ELAP) (HELP)	GM			
Is able to stand up from the center of a room without using the furniture or your help (ELAP) (PEA) (HELP)	GM			
Crawls up the steps on hands and knees but needs your help to come down (HELP) (ELAP)	GM			
Able to stoop over and pick up toys in the middle of the floor without falling (May squat or use one hand for support) (HELP) (PEA) (CAR)	GM			
Brings a toy to you that he wants activated or brings you his cup when he wants a drink (U&H) (CAR)	C, SE			
Likes to put blocks or small objects into a plastic bowl and then dumps them out (May seem preoccupied with this game and repeat it many times) (U&H)	C, FM			
When given a crayon and paper, scribbles large strokes back and forth (HELP) (ELAP)	FM			

continues

continues

continued

Activity	Domain	Date	Date	Comments
Can place paper muffin cups into a muffin tin or eggs into an egg carton (ELAP) (HELP)	C, FM			
Uses sounds (vocalizations) along with pointing or other gestures to tell you what he wants (CAR) (ELAP)	C, EL			
Tries to imitate almost any word she hears; although "words" may not be clear, you can tell what she is trying to say (CAR) (ELAP)	C, EL, RL			
16 Months				
Says "hi" or "bye-bye" when people come in or leave or when you ask him to (HELP)	SE, EL, RL			
Says "no" to everything, even when you're sure she means yes (HELP)	SE, EL			
Gets mad, yells, and resists when you try to correct him or stop him from doing something (such as when it's time to stop playing and go somewhere) (HELP)	SE, EL			
Walks up stairs holding on to the rail, wall, or your hand, taking one step at a time and not alternating her feet (ELAP) (PEA)	GM			
Removes his own hat, shoes, and socks when you ask or during play (CAR) (HELP)	SH			

continued

Activity	Domain	Date	Date	Comments
Walks very quickly (almost a stiff run), especially when trying to get away from a "chaser" (HELP) (CAR)	GM			
Bends over while standing and looks between his legs at you upside down (HELP)	GM			
Climbs up on a chair to reach food or a toy on the table (U&H) (CAR)	C, GM			
Points to his nose or other body parts when you ask him (CAR)	C, SH, RL			
Can put 6 or more pennies into a piggy bank, 1 at a time, without being distracted midtask (CAR) (ELAP) (PEA)	C, FM			
When he sees you writing, he wants to "write" too; his marks consist of random scribbling from side to side (PEA) (CAR)	C, FM			
Can hold a cup with both hands and drink with a little spilling (ELAP) (HELP)	SH			
Likes to "help" with household jobs, such as putting trash in the garbage can or pulling clothes out of the dryer (ELAP) (HELP)	SH			
Is able to pick up several toys and return them to the toy box when asked (ELAP) (HELP)	SE, EL			
Shows affection by giving kisses and hugs on request to adults or dolls (CAR)	SE			

continues

continued

Activity	Domain	Date	Date	Comments
Indicates a messy diaper by pulling on it or telling you verbally (ELAP) (HELP)	SH, EL			
18 Months				
Pushes large boxes or chairs across the floor (ELAP) (HELP)	GM			
Walks down the steps by placing both feet on each step (does not use alternate feet) (PEA) (CAR)	GM			
Kicks a ball several feet without losing his balance (PEA) (HELP)	GM			
Can pull a toy behind her by a string while walking (HELP)	FM, GM			
Can back into and seat himself in a small (child-size) chair (HELP)	GM			
Enjoys looking at picture books and turns the pages one at a time (PEA) (ELAF)	C, FM			
While looking at pictures, he can point to and name at least 3 pictures (ELAP) (CAR)	C, EL			
Imitates animal sounds or car sounds while playing (CAR) (HELP)	C, EL			
Imitates body games like beeping his nose or stomping his feet (U&H) (CAR)	C			
Feeds herself with a spoon and hands the empty dish to you when fin shed (ELAP) (HELP)	SH			

continues

continued

Activity	Domain	Date	Date	Comments
Plays independently all over the house, running back to check on you every few minutes (ELAP) (CAR)	SE			
Can unzip her own jacket and untie her shoes (CAR) (HELP)	SH			
Plays well alongside other children, sometimes stealing their toys (CAR) (ELAP)	SE			
Stomps her feet, cries, and throws herself on the floor when she doesn't get her way (HELP) (ELAP)	SE			
Can eat almost any solid food (such as hot dogs, toast, and peeled apples) (CAR) (ELAP)	SH			
21 Months				
Walks down a sidewalk curb with 1 foot on and 1 foot off for several feet (PEA) (ELAP)	GM			
Jumps down from a bottom step or a small stool (PEA) (ELAP)	GM			
Can play with toys on the floor while in a squat position rather than sitting down for several minutes (HELP) (CAR)	GM			
Can stack as many as 6 pennies or cans (HELP) (PEA)	C, FM			
Can match like toys (blocks to blocks, cars to cars) (CAR)	C			

continues

continued

Activity	Domain	Date	Date	Comments
Follows simple 1-step directions ("Take this to Daddy," "Put this on the table") (ELAP) (HELP)	C, RL			
Looks for a lost toy or bottle in at least 3 different places (U&H) (CAR)	C			
Can copy a single horizontal and vertical line that he watches you make (CAR) (PEA)	C, FM			
Knows how to turn on the television or radio, and wind up a musical toy (U&H) (PEA)	C, FM			
Drinks primarily from a cup and no longer nurses or requires a bottle (HELP) (CAR)	SH			
Tries to comfort other children (with hugs and patting) when they cry (CAR)	SE			
Washes his own hands and tries to brush teeth (may still need help to get the job done) (ELAP) (HELP)	SH			
Takes 1 long daytime nap (2 to 3 hours) and sleeps 10 to 12 hours at night (HELP)	SE			
Completes simple 3- to-4-piece puzzles (CAR)	C, FM			

continues

continued

Activity	Domain	Date	Date	Comments
May cry or pull on you when you show attention to other children (HELP)	SE			
Says at least 20 different words clearly enough that you can understand what he means (ELAP) (HELP)	EL			
24 Months				
Jumps up and down when she is excited (PEA) (HELP)	SE, GM			
Can pull a toy on a string by walking backwards (PEA) (ELAP)	GM			
Can run faster than you can catch her (PEA) (CAR)	GM			
Can draw a ball or a circle with a crayon (ELAP) (CAR) (PEA)	FM			
Understands the difference between big/little and inside/outside (CAR) (HELP)	C, RL			
Can say his first name when asked (HELP) (ELAP)	C, EL			
Can put 2 words together into meaningful phrases like "Daddy work" or "Doggie gone" (ELAP) (CAR) (U&H)	C, EL			
Can use household objects in pretend play (a spoon for a telephone, or a towel for a cape) (ELAP) (CAR)	C, SE			

continues

continued

Activity	Domain	Date	Date	Comments
Shares toys with other children or gives you a bite of her cookie (CAR)	SE			
Sits on a potty chair for 2 to 3 minutes before getting up (ELAP) (HELP)	SH			
Shows you objects that belong to her and says the word "mine" (ELAP)	C, SE, EL			
Enjoys pretending to feed a doll and to cook with a play stove (HELP) (CAR) (U&H)	C, SE			

Source: May Insley-Seale, *PALS: Parent's Assessment of Learned Skills*, © 1993.

Genetics

PRINCIPLES OF HUMAN GENETICS

Genes are the basic units of inheritance. Genes come in pairs. One member of each pair of genes is inherited from each parent. Because the parents' genes also come in pairs, each parent contributes one of two possible genes to the child. Different pairs of genes determine various characteristics of the child, ranging from eye color to blood type.

Genes line up in a pattern to form chromosomes. Chromosomes also come in pairs. Humans have 46 chromosomes, or 23 chromosome pairs. Twenty-two pairs of chromosomes are identical in males and females. These are called autosomes. The twenty-third pair of chromosomes determines the sex of the individual, and so these two chromosomes are called the sex chromosomes. There are two types of sex chromosomes, known as X and Y chromosomes. Females have two X chromosomes, while males have one X and one Y chromosome.

Genetic Causes of Disabilities

There are many reasons why a child might be born with a disability. There are genetic reasons, which include chromosome abnormalities and single gene disorders. There are environmental reasons. There are also combinations of genetic and environmental reasons—such a combination of reasons results in disorders known as multifactorial disorders.

Autosomal Dominant Disorders

Autosomal dominant disorders are caused by a single altered gene along one of the autosomes. The disorder may have been present for several generations, passed on from parent to child, or it may be caused by a new mutation (change) in the gene. An individual affected with an autosomal dominant disorder who parents children with someone who does not have the disorder has a 50 percent chance of passing the gene on to each of his or her offspring.

Examples of autosomal dominant disorders include achondroplasia, Apert's syndrome, distal muscular dystrophy, facioscapulohumeral muscular dystrophy, Huntington chorea, Marfan's syndrome, myotonic dystrophy, neurofibromatosis, Noonan's syndrome, oculopharyngeal muscular dystrophy, Tourette syndrome,[†] and Treacher-Collins' syndrome.

[†]*Note:* Children may inherit genetic vulnerability for Tourette syndrome yet show few, if any, noticeable symptoms. This is called *incomplete penetrance*. Penetrance for Tourette syndrome is more likely in males than in females; that is, males are more likely to exhibit symptoms.

continues

continued

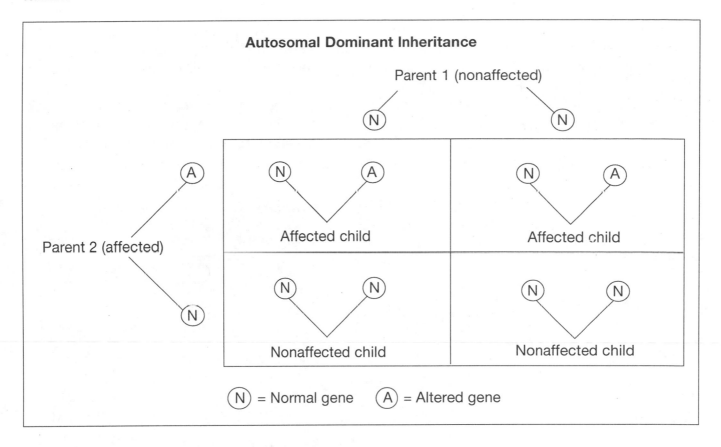

Autosomal Dominant Inheritance

Parent 1 (nonaffected)

Parent 2 (affected)

Affected child

Affected child

Nonaffected child

Nonaffected child

(N) = Normal gene   (A) = Altered gene

In the diagram showing *autosomal dominant inheritance*, parent 1 is not affected by the disorder in question and will therefore pass on one of two normal genes to each offspring. Parent 2 is affected by the disorder and may contribute either an altered or a normal gene to each offspring. Thus there is a 50 percent chance that each of this couple's offspring will inherit the disorder. It is important to remember that the 50 percent chance applies to each child. That is, if the couple's first child is affected by the disorder, this does not mean that the second child will be nonaffected—the second child still has a 50 percent chance of inheriting the disorder.

Autosomal Recessive Disorders

Autosomal recessive disorders result when both members of an autosomal gene pair are altered. It is estimated that every human carries 4 percent to 8 percent recessive altered genes. These genes, when present in a single dose, usually do not cause any significant health problems. Individuals who have a single dose of the altered recessive genes are called carriers. They are not affected by the altered gene because it is paired with a normal gene that takes precedence. The problem arises when two carriers of the same recessive altered gene by chance pass on the

continues

continued

altered gene to their offspring. When both members of a couple are carriers of an autosomal recessive disorder, they have a 25 percent risk of passing on the disorder to each offspring. Thus, in a family with an autosomal recessive disorder, affected individuals will usually be observed in one generation in one immediate family.

Examples of autosomal recessive disorders include congenital muscular dystrophy, cystic fibrosis, Friedreich's ataxia, galactosemia, Gaucher's disease, hypothyroidism, limb-girdle muscular dystrophy, maple syrup urine disease, Niemann-Pick disease, phenylketonuria (PKU), sickle cell anemia, spinal muscular atrophy, and Tay-Sachs disease.

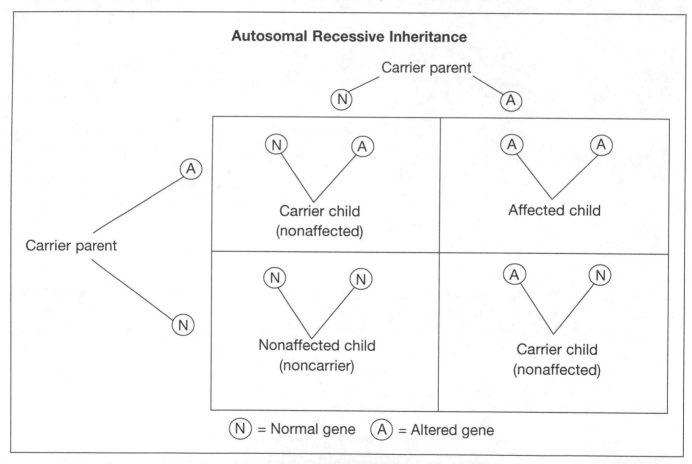

In the diagram showing *autosomal recessive inheritance*, both parents have an altered gene but are not affected by a disorder because the altered gene is paired with a normal gene that offsets its effects. There is a 25 percent chance for each offspring that both parents will pass on the altered gene, in which case the child will be affected by the disorder. It is important to remember that the 25 percent chance applies to each child. That is, if the couple's first child is affected by the disorder, this outcome does not mean that the next three children will not be affected—each child still stands a 25 percent chance of inheriting the disorder.

continues

continued

X-Linked Disorders

X-linked disorders occur when there is a gene abnormality along the X sex chromosome. X-linked recessive disorders are much more common than X-linked dominant disorders. They occur much more frequently in males than in females. Because males have just one X chromosome, if they have the gene in a single dose, they display the disorder. Females have two X chromosomes; therefore, they must have the gene present in a double dose in order to be affected with the disorder. A female who is a carrier of an X-linked recessive disorder has a 25 percent risk of having an affected son. A male who is affected with an X-linked recessive disorder will most likely have no affected children. But all of his daughters (since they receive his X chromosome) will be carriers of the disorder.

Examples of X-linked recessive disorders include Becker muscular dystrophy, Duchenne muscular dystrophy, and fragile X syndrome.[†]

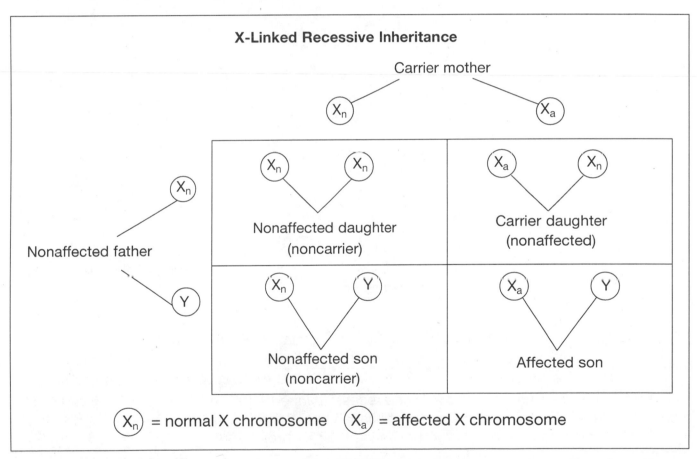

[†]*Note:* Males may inherit genetic vulnerability for fragile X syndrome yet show few, if any, noticeable symptoms. This condition is called *incomplete penetrance*.

continues

continued

In the first diagram showing *X-linked recessive inheritance*, the mother is a carrier of an affected X chromosome. She is not affected by the disorder because the affected X chromosome is with a normal X chromosome. There is a 25 percent chance she will have a son who inherits the disorder. It is important to remember that the 25 percent chance applies to each pregnancy. That is, if the couple's first child is a son who inherits the disorder, there is still a 25 percent chance that their second child will be a son who inherits the disorder.

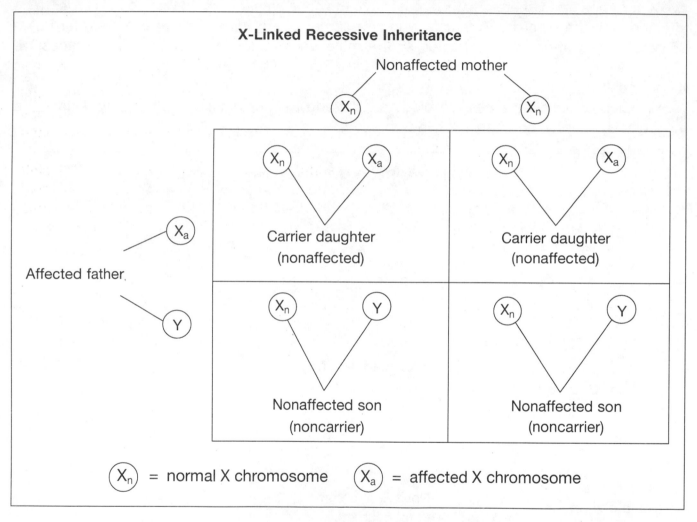

In the second diagram showing *X-linked recessive inheritance*, the father is affected with the disorder. His daughters will all be carriers because one of their X chromosomes is inherited from him. None of his sons will be affected because their X chromosome will be inherited from their mother.

continues

continued

Chromosome Abnormalities

Chromosome abnormalities result when a child receives either too many or too few genes or chromosomes, or when genes or chromosomes are rearranged. This condition usually results in alterations in growth and development of the child. Some chromosome abnormalities may be inherited, but most occur from an error in cell division in either the egg or sperm cell that contributed to the formation of the child. Down syndrome is one of the most common disabilities resulting from a chromosome abnormality.

Multifactorial Disorders

Disabilities that are multifactorial in origin occur as a result of many genetic and environmental influences working together. These disabilities are by far the most common type of congenital disabilities. Multifactorial disorders tend to cluster in families; that is, they occur more frequently than one would expect by chance and yet not frequently enough to be attributed to a single gene inheritance pattern.

Examples of multifactorial birth defects include neural tube defects (such as spina bifida), cleft lip/palate, many forms of congenital heart defects, club foot, pyloric stenosis, and situs inversus. Examples of disorders that are often multifactorial and that show up later in life are many forms of cancer, diabetes, adult onset heart disease, seizure disorders, and familial mental retardation.

Detection of Genetic Disorders

Some genetic disorders may be detected early in life, even prenatally (before birth). Prenatal diagnosis involves techniques such as ultrasound, amniocentesis, chorionic villus sampling (CVS), and maternal blood tests. Examples of disorders that are detectable prenatally are:

- Down syndrome
- neural tube defects (including spina bifida)
- Tay-Sachs disease

Examples of disorders that are detectable soon after birth are:

- PKU
- sickle cell anemia
- hypothyroidism
- galactosemia
- biotinidase deficiency
- homocystinuria

Sources: Elizabeth J. Thomson, "A Genetics Primer for Early Service Providers," *Infants and Young Children*, Vol. 2:1, Aspen Publishers, Inc., © 1989; Aspen Reference Group.

Diagnosis of Autism: Questions Parents Ask

BACKGROUND

The diagnosis of autism was added to the psychiatric literature almost 50 years ago. Since that time a large body of literature has developed that catalogues literally thousands of clinical and experimental studies of the syndrome. It is only recently, however, that clinicians and researchers throughout the world have reached a consensus concerning the nature and the essential diagnostic criteria for autism.

These definitions typically follow a standard medical model. Autism is considered to be a syndrome that is diagnosed by the appearance of characteristic symptoms and developmental delays early in life, usually prior to 30 months of age. These symptoms are the result of a disorder of the central nervous system, which in turn may have multiple causes. Researchers still have not reached a consensus regarding specific evaluations necessary for identifying the syndrome nor have they agreed on the symptoms that must present to establish it. This lack of diagnostic specificity has resulted in confusion for parents and professionals responsible for the day-to-day management of individuals with autism.

Currently, it is generally agreed that:

- Autism is a spectrum disorder. Its expression ranges from the very severely involved to those who are only mildly affected.
- Autism is a developmental diagnosis (that is, expression of the syndrome varies with age and the developmental level of the person affected). As with any other child, the child who has autism will change as he or she grows older.
- Autism is a retrospective diagnosis. The diagnosis cannot be made without taking a careful developmental history from parents and persons involved in the child's life.
- Autism can coexist with any other condition that the child may have. The most common coexisting condition is mental retardation. Just because a child has autism does not mean that he or she cannot have other diagnosable conditions.

Parents, when confronted with the diagnosis, typically have many questions. It is crucial to find someone who is willing to take the time to listen to and answer these questions. The purpose of this patient information sheet is to answer some of the questions most commonly asked by parents who are receiving the diagnosis for the first time.

COMMON QUESTIONS

What Is Autism?

This question is by far the most frequently asked one. In brief, autism is an incapacitating, lifelong developmental disability that typically appears within the first three years of life. It is the result of a neurological disorder that affects functioning of the brain. Autism and its behavioral

continues

continued

symptoms occur in approximately 2 to 4 children per 10,000 births. Autism is four times more common in boys than girls. It is found throughout the world, in families of all racial, ethnic, and social backgrounds. There are no known factors in the psychological environment of the child that can cause autism. Autism usually manifests itself by the appearance of typical behavioral symptoms in the following four areas:

1. disturbances in the rate of appearance of physical, social, and language skills
2. abnormal responses to sensations (any one or a combination of senses or responses is affected—sight, hearing, touch, balance, reaction to pain, or in the way the child holds his or her body)
3. speech, language, and nonverbal communication
4. abnormal ways of relating to people, objects, and events in the environment

Autism can occur in association with other disorders that affect the functioning of the brain (for example, viral infections, metabolic disturbances, and seizure disorders). It is important to distinguish autism from mental retardation or mental disorders because diagnostic confusion may result in inappropriate and ineffective treatment.

How Do You Know My Child Is Autistic?

There are no medical tests used to diagnose autism. Autism is diagnosed by the presence or absence of certain behaviors as evidenced both by personal history and examination. As noted, a child must exhibit behaviors in four areas. The first area is the way a child develops. For example, in the first year of life a child without a disability learns to walk, talk, and interact with you, so that by the end of the first year the child is a "little person." A child who exhibits a developmental delay learns those skills, but learns them at a slower rate. A child with autism has very inconsistent development. He or she may start to develop normally and then seem to stop; may start to talk and then stop; may have very good motor skills or be very good in some areas and very poor in others. It is this *inconsistency in development* that is important to making the diagnosis of autism.

The second area is the way in which a child sees the world. People with autism perceive the world like an FM radio station that is not exactly tuned in when you are driving down the freeway. Sometimes the world comes in clearly and at other times it does not. Therefore, people with autism tend to respond inconsistently. For example, sometimes the person with autism will appear to hear and at other times he or she will not. Sometimes the child will appear nondisabled and at other times very withdrawn. *Inconsistency* is a hallmark of autism. Children with autism may or may not exhibit the behaviors thought of as indicative of the syndrome at any one time.

The third area in which a child with autism has problems involves speech, language, and nonverbal communication. The problem is not that the child does not talk (although some children never develop speech), but rather that the child does not communicate. Even when language

continues

continued

development follows established milestones, a child with autism has difficulty initiating conversations and volunteering information. Thus, another hallmark of autism is an inability to communicate. Often the young child does not use the speech and language capabilities present. The child may repeat everything heard but never use words to request things.

The final area of symptoms concerns the way that the child with autism relates to people, objects, and events in his or her environment. A child with autism often has difficulty initiating and sustaining relationships with children of a similar age but can relate to adults without a problem. Adults can figure out what the child wants or needs. Wanting to communicate and interact with other children is critical to development. It is not that a child with autism does not relate, it is that the child relates in peculiar ways. It is not that the child with autism does not want to make friends, but that the child does not know how. Thus, it is critical to teach the child social skills. However, social problems remain a lifelong difficulty even in those people who do the best. Social deficits are the most difficult to overcome.

What Causes Autism?

The cause of autism is not known. However, current research indicates that anything that can produce structural or functional damage in the central nervous system can also produce the syndrome of autism. Certain viruses and genetic conditions are known to be associated with autism. In addition, in rare cases there is more than one autistic child in a family. At this point, it is believed that about 10 percent of the incidence of autism is attributable to genetic causes. It is not possible to explain specifically why your child is autistic or why you have an autistic child and your neighbor does not.

Is There a Cure for Autism?

Because the specific causes of autism are unknown, there is no way to fix (cure) what is wrong with your child's brain. However, people with autism can and do get better. They can lead happy, productive lives when appropriate treatment is begun.

What Is the Treatment for Autism?

Parents of a child with autism must educate themselves about new treatments. There is more misinformation about autism than any other disorder. Parents are constantly bombarded by people who claim to have a cure. Yet, there is only one treatment that has passed the test of time and is known to be effective: *structured educational programs geared to the child's developmental level of functioning*. Other treatments might be helpful at different points in the child's life, but structured educational programs should be a constant. Nevertheless parents should keep an open mind and be knowledgeable about new treatments as they become available. Parents should remember, however, that the majority of other treatments are not scientifically proven. Treatment decisions should always be made individually after studying the treatment, assessing the

continues

continued

child, and determining its appropriateness for the child and his or her family. Remember, you as a parent know your child better than anyone else and also the type of program that is going to be best.

How Do I Know If a Treatment Program Is Appropriate?

This question is a difficult one to answer. Eight general guidelines for evaluation of various treatment approaches are as follows:

1. Approach any new treatment with hopeful skepticism. Remember the goal of any treatment should be to help the child with autism become a fully functioning member of society.
2. *Beware* of any program or technique that is touted as effective or desirable for every child with autism.
3. *Beware* of any program that thwarts individualization and potentially results in harmful program decisions.
4. *Be aware* that any treatment represents one of several options for a child with autism.
5. *Be aware* that treatment should always depend on individual assessment information that points to it as an appropriate choice for a particular child.
6. *Be aware* that no new treatment should be implemented until its proponents can specify assessment procedures necessary to determine whether it will be appropriate for a child with autism.
7. *Be aware* that debate over use of various techniques is often reduced to superficial arguments over who is right, moral, and ethical and who is a true advocate for the child. This approach can lead to results that are directly opposite to those intended including impediments to maximizing programs.
8. *Be aware* that often new treatments have not been validated scientifically.

Here are five questions you as a parent should ask yourself prior to initiating a new treatment:

1. Will the treatment result in harm to my child?
2. How will failure of the treatment affect my child and family?
3. Has the treatment been validated scientifically?
4. Are assessment procedures specified?
5. How will the treatment be integrated into my child's current program? (Do not become so infatuated with a given treatment that functional curriculum, vocational life, and social skills are ignored.)

Will My Child Regress?

The answer to this question generally is "no." Everyone has good days and bad days. However, people with autism have more extreme swings. Generally, in a well-structured program after early diagnosis, people with autism continue to improve throughout life.

continues

continued

What Is My Child's IQ?

IQ scores as measured on cognitive tests are important in assessing a child with autism. However, it is important not to assign too much significance to a score on a test. People with autism often have very good cognitive skills, but they are unable to use them. In general, people with autism can be divided into three groups by the age of 5 or 6 years. In approximately 50 percent of people with autism, retardation will also be present, affecting both verbal and nonverbal skills. Another 25 percent will have average nonverbal skills but poor language skills; the remaining 25 percent will have average language and nonverbal skills. It is very difficult when a child is young to determine which of these three groups he or she will fall into.

It is important to remember that a child's score on an IQ test is not as important as his or her ability to function independently in society. Assessment of social adaptive skills is much more important than intellectual functioning. It does not matter how smart a child is if he or she cannot get across the street. Likewise, it does not matter if a child can do calculus if he or she cannot make change.

If the goal is to help integrate people with autism into society, then it becomes crucial to focus on the development of social and adaptive rather than cognitive and academic skills.

How Autistic Is My Child?

This question is the most difficult to answer. Currently, there is no objective measure of the severity of autism in the individual child. Typically, a child is considered to have mild autism when intelligence is not affected. However, there are children who score well on intelligence tests who possess many of the symptoms of autism and thus are considered to have severe autism. There are still other children who score lower on intelligence tests but have fewer symptoms and have milder forms of the disorder. At this point in time, there is no objective way of determining how severe the autism is. Time will tell. It is very important that autism be viewed developmentally and as a lifetime disorder. Long-term planning and periodic reassessments are essential to monitor people with autism and alter their programs as needs change.

What Can I as a Parent Do?

There are many things parents can do. One of the most important is to educate themselves about autism and to become advocates for their child and family. Service organizations often listen more readily to parents than to professionals. It is also important for parents to identify a professional who can help in navigating the system initially. Moreover, it is critical for parents to meet other parents of children with autism. Parents are generally the most helpful to other parents. Other parents can tell you how to handle certain problems that may arise for your child and family.

continues

continued

   Finally, it is most important that you love your child. Remember that he or she is a child first and needs to be treated like any other child. Recognizing that he or she is a child with autism is important. Understanding the origins of the difficulties makes them easier to deal with and ensures that appropriate services are obtained. After that, every child is different. The more a child with autism is treated like a nondisabled child, the better he or she is going to do. While it is important to recognize that this approach is the ideal, it may take the child with autism longer to learn the things necessary to function independently in society as an adult. However with love, early intervention, and education, people with autism can and do lead happy, productive lives and can be integrated into society. The problem is that society is not always tolerant of people who are different. Parents and professionals must educate society and increase understanding and appreciation of these very special individuals.

Notes:

Courtesy of B.J. Freeman, Professor, Medical Psychology, University of California, Department of Psychiatry and Biobehavioral Sciences, Los Angeles, California.

Autism Diagnostic Checklist Form E-2

NAME OF CHILD _____ BIRTHDATE _____
      first   *last*

NAME OF PERSON COMPLETING THIS FORM _____

ADDRESS _____ CITY _____ STATE _____ COUNTRY _____ ZIP _____

RELATIONSHIP TO CHILD ____ Mother ____ Father ____ Other _____ PHONE (____) _____

FATHER'S OCCUPATION(s) (past and current) _____

MOTHER'S OCCUPATION(s) (past and current) _____

HAS THIS CHILD BEEN DIAGNOSED BEFORE? ___ Yes ___ No If yes, what was diagnosis? _____

ANY OTHER DIAGNOSIS? _____ DIAGNOSED BY _____ WHERE? _____

PURPOSE: This checklist, Form E-2, is designed for completion by parents of children who have been, or who may be, diagnosed as children with autism, pervasive developmental disorder (PDD), children with autistic-like symptoms, or similar designations. Form E-2 is intended to clarify the diagnosis of such children. Completed forms will be computer scored and the result sent to the person or agency submitting the Form E-2.

INSTRUCTIONS: Please mark an X next to one answer for each question. Additional information is welcome; write it near the question, or copy the question number on a blank sheet of paper and add the information there. Please try to answer all questions.

PLEASE USE AN "X" TO MARK ONE ANSWER FOR EACH QUESTION. PLEASE DO NOT SKIP QUESTIONS.

---

1. **Present age of child:**
   - ___1 Under 3 years old
   - ___2 Between 3 and 4 years old
   - ___3 Between 4 and 5 years old
   - ___4 Between 5 and 6 years old
   - ___5* Over 6 years old (Age: ____ years)

(*Note:* This checklist is designed primarily for children 3 to 5 years old. If child is over 5, answer as well as you can by recall of child's behavior.)

2. **Indicate child's sex:**
   - ___1 Boy
   - ___2 Girl

3. **Child's birth order and number of mother's other children:**
   - ___1 Child is an only child
   - ___2 Child is first born of ____ children
   - ___3 Child is last born of ____ children
   - ___4 Child is middle born; ____ children are older and ____ are younger than this child
   - ___5 Foster child, or don't know

4. **Were pregnancy and delivery normal?**
   - ___1 Pregnancy and delivery both normal
   - ___2 Problems during both pregnancy and delivery

continues

continued

___3   Pregnancy troubled, routine delivery

___4   Pregnancy untroubled; problems during delivery

___5   Don't know

5. **Was the birth premature (birth weight under 5 lbs)?**

___1   Yes (about ___ weeks early; ___ lbs)

___2   No

3   Don't know

6. **Was the child given oxygen *in the first week*?**

___1   Yes

___2   No

___3   Don't know

7. **Appearance of child during first few weeks after birth:**

___1   Pale, delicate looking

___2   Unusually healthy looking

___3   Average, don't know, or other

8. **Unusual conditions of birth and infancy (check only one number in left-hand column):**

___1   Unusual conditions (indicate which: blindness____, cerebral palsy___, birth injury____, seizures____, blue baby____, very high fever____, jaundice____, other _____)

___2   Twin birth (identical___, fraternal___)

___3   Both 1 and 2

___4   Normal, or don't know

9. **Concerning baby's health in first 3 months:**

___1   Excellent health, no problems

___2   Respiration (frequent infections___, other_____)

___3   Skin (rashes___, infection___, allergy___, other_____)

___4   Feeding (learning to suck___, colic___, vomiting___, other_____)

___5   Elimination (diarrhea___, constipation___, other_____)

___6   Several of above (indicate which: 2__, 3__, 4__, 5__)

10. **Has the child been given an electroencephalogram (EEG)?**

___1   Yes, it was considered normal

___2   Yes, it was considered borderline

___3   Yes, it was considered abnormal

___4   No, or don't know, or don't know results

11. **In the first year, did the child react to bright lights, bright colors, unusual sounds, etc.?**

___1   Unusually strong reaction (pleasure____, dislike____)

___2   Unusually unresponsive

___3   Average, or don't know

12. **Did the child behave normally for a time before his abnormal behavior began?**

___1   Never was a period of normal behavior

___2   Normal during first 6 months

___3   Normal during first year

___4   Normal during first 1½ years

___5   Normal during first 2 years

___6   Normal during first 3 years

___7   Normal during first 4–5 years

continues

continued

13. **(Age 4–8 months) Did the child reach out or prepare himself to be picked up when mother approached him?**
    ___1　Yes, or I believe so
    ___2　No, I don't think he did
    ___3　No, definitely not
    ___4　Don't know

14. **Did the child rock in his crib as a baby?**
    ___1　Yes, quite a lot
    ___2　Yes, sometimes
    ___3　No, or very little
    ___4　Don't know

15. **At what age did the child learn to walk alone?**
    ___1　8–12 months
    ___2　13–15 months
    ___3　16–18 months
    ___4　19–24 months
    ___5　25–36 months
    ___6　37 months or later, or does not walk alone

16. **Which describes the change from crawling to walking?**
    ___1　Normal change from crawling to walking
    ___2　Little or no crawling, gradual start of walking
    ___3　Little or no crawling, sudden start of walking
    ___4　Prolonged crawling, sudden start of walking
    ___5　Prolonged crawling, gradual start of walking
    ___6　Other, or don't know

17. **During the child's first year, did he seem to be unusually intelligent?**
    ___1　Suspected high intelligence
    ___2　Suspected average intelligence
    ___3　Child looked somewhat dull

18. **During the child's first 2 years, did he like to be held?**
    ___1　Liked being picked up; enjoyed being held
    ___2　Limp and passive on being held
    ___3　You could pick child up and hold him only when and how he preferred
    ___4　Notably stiff and awkward to hold
    ___5　Don't know

19. **Before age 3, did the child ever imitate another person?**
    ___1　Yes, waved bye-bye
    ___2　Yes, played pat-a-cake
    ___3　Yes, other (_____)
    ___4　Two or more of above (which? 1__, 2__, 3__)
    ___5　No, or not sure

20. **Before age 3, did the child have an unusually good memory?**
    ___1　Remarkable memory for songs, rhymes, TV commercials, etc., in words
    ___2　Remarkable memory for songs, music (humming only)
    ___3　Remarkable memory for names, places, routes, etc.
    ___4　No evidence for remarkable memory
    ___5　Apparently rather poor memory
    ___6　Both 1 and 3
    ___7　Both 2 and 3

continues

continued

21. **Did you ever suspect the child was very nearly deaf?**
    ___1 Yes
    ___2 No

22. **(Age 2–4) Is child "deaf" to some sounds, but hears others?**
    ___1 Yes, can be "deaf" to loud sounds, but hears low ones
    ___2 No, this is not true of him

23. **(Age 2–4) Does child hold his hands in strange postures?**
    ___1 Yes, sometimes or often
    ___2 No

24. **(Age 2–4) Does child engage in rhythmic or rocking activity for very long periods of time (like on rocking horse or chair, jump-chair, swing, etc.)?**
    ___1 Yes, this is typical
    ___2 Seldom does this
    ___3 Not true of him

25. **(Age 2–4) Does the child ever "look through" or "walk through" people, as though they weren't there?**
    ___1 Yes, often
    ___2 Yes, I think so
    ___3 No, doesn't do this

26. **(Age 2–5) Does child have any unusual cravings for things to eat or chew on?**
    ___1 Yes, salt or salty foods
    ___2 Yes, often chews metal objects
    ___3 Yes, other
    (_____)

    ___4 Yes, more than 2 above
    (which? _____)
    ___5 No, or not sure

27. **(Age 2–4) Does child have certain eating oddities such as refusing to drink from a transparent container, eating only hot (or cold) food, eating only one or two foods, etc.?**
    ___1 Yes, definitely
    ___2 No, or not to any marked degree
    ___3 Don't know

28. **Would you describe your child around age 3 or 4 as often seeming "in a shell," or so distant and "lost in thought" that you couldn't reach him?**
    ___1 Yes, this is a very accurate description
    ___2 Once in a while he might possibly be like that
    ___3 Not an accurate description

29. **(Age 2–5) Is he cuddly?**
    ___1 Definitely, likes to cling to adults
    ___2 Above average (likes to be held)
    3 No, rather stiff and awkward to hold
    ___4 Don't know

30. **(Age 3–5) Does the child deliberately hit his own head?**
    ___1 Never, or rarely
    ___2 Yes, usually by slapping it with his hand
    ___3 Yes, usually by banging it against someone else's legs or head

continues

continued

___4   Yes, usually by hitting walls, floor, furniture, etc.

___5   Several of above (which? 2__, 3__, 4__)

31. (Age 3–5) How well physically coordinated is the child (running, walking, balancing, climbing)?

___1   Unusually graceful

___2   About average

___3   Somewhat below average, or poor

32. (Age 3–5) Does the child sometimes whirl himself like a top?

___1   Yes, does this often

___2   Yes, sometimes

___3   Yes, if you start him out

___4   No, he shows no tendency to whirl

33. (Age 3–5) How skillful is the child in doing fine work with his fingers or playing with small objects?

___1   Exceptionally skillful

___2   Average for age

___3   A little awkward, or very awkward

___4   Don't know

34. (Age 3–5) Does the child like to spin things like jar lids, coins, or coasters?

___1   Yes, often and for rather long periods

___2   Very seldom, or never

35. (Age 3–5) Does child show an *unusual* degree of skill (much better than normal child his age) at any of the following:

___1   Assembling jigsaw or similar puzzles

___2   Arithmetic computation

___3   Can tell day of week a certain date will fall on

___4   Perfect musical pitch

___5   Throwing and/or catching a ball

___6   Other (_____)

___7   More than one of above (which? _____)

___8   No unusual skill, or not sure

36. (Age 3–5) Does the child sometimes jump up and down gleefully when pleased?

___1   Yes, this is typical

___2   No or rarely

37. (Age 3–5) Does child sometimes line things up in precise, evenly spaced rows and insist they not be disturbed?

___1   No

___2   Yes

___3   Not sure

38. (Age 3–5) Does the child refuse to use his hands for an extended period of time?

___1   Yes

___2   No

39. Was there a time before age 5 when the child *strongly* insisted on listening to music on records?

___1   Yes, insisted on only certain records

___2   Yes, but almost any record would do

___3   Liked to listen, but didn't *demand* to

___4   No special interest in records

continues

continued

40. **(Age 3–5) How interested is the child in mechanical objects such as the stove or vacuum cleaner?**
    ___1   Little or no interest
    ___2   Average interest
    ___3   Fascinated by certain mechanical things

41. **(Age 3–5) How does child usually react to being interrupted at what he is doing?**
    ___1   Rarely or never gets upset
    ___2   Sometimes gets mildly upset; rarely very upset
    ___3   Typically gets very upset

42. **(Age 3–5) Will the child readily accept new articles of clothing (shoes, coats, etc.)?**
    ___1   Usually resists new clothes
    ___2   Doesn't seem to mind, or enjoys them

43. **(Age 3–5) Is child upset by certain things that are not "right" (like crack in wall, spot on rug, books leaning in bookcase, broken rung on chair, pipe held and not smoked)?**
    ___1   Not especially
    ___2   Yes, such things often upset him greatly
    ___3   Not sure

44. **(Age 3–5) Does child adopt complicated "rituals" which make him very upset if not followed (like putting many dolls to bed in a certain order, taking exactly the same route between two places, dressing according to a precise pattern, or insisting that only certain words be used in a given situation)?**
    ___1   Yes, definitely

    ___2   Not sure
    ___3   No

45. **(Age 3–5) Does child get very upset if certain things he is used to are changed (like furniture or toy arrangement, or certain doors which must be left open or shut)?**
    ___1   No
    ___2   Yes, definitely
    ___3   Slightly true

46. **(Age 3–5) Is the child destructive?**
    ___1   Yes, this is definitely a problem
    ___2   Not deliberately or severely destructive
    ___3   Not especially destructive

47. **(Age 3–5) Is the child unusually physically pliable (can be led easily; melts into your arms)?**
    ___1   Yes
    ___2   Seems normal in this way
    ___3   Definitely not pliable

48. **(Age 3–5) Which single description, or combination of two descriptions, best characterizes the child?**
    ___1   Hyperactive, constantly moving, changes quickly from one thing to another
    ___2   Watches television quietly for long periods
    ___3   Sits for long periods, staring into space or playing repetitively with objects, without apparent purpose
    ___4   Combination of 1 and 2

continues

continued

___5   Combination of 2 and 3

___6   Combination of 1 and 3

49.   (Age 3–5) Does the child seem to want to be liked?

___1   Yes, unusually so

___2   Just normally so

___3   Indifferent to being liked; happiest when left alone

50.   (Age 3–5) Is child sensitive and/or affectionate?

___1   Is sensitive to criticism and affectionate

___2   Is sensitive to criticism, *not* affectionate

___3   Not sensitive to criticism, is affectionate

___4   Not sensitive to criticism, *not* affectionate

51.   (Age 3–5) Is it possible to direct child's attention to an object some distance away or out a window?

___1   Yes, no special problem

___2   He rarely sees things very far out of reach

___3   He examines things with fingers and mouth only

52.   (Age 3–5) Do people consider child especially attractive?

___1   Yes, very good-looking child

___2   No, just average

___3   Faulty in physical appearance

53.   (Age 3–5) Does the child look up at people (meet their eyes) when they are talking to him?

___1   Never, or rarely

___2   Only with parents

___3   Usually does

54.   (Age 3–5) Does the child take an adult by the wrist to use adult's hand (to open door, get cookies, turn on television, etc.)?

___1   Yes, this is typical

___2   Perhaps, or rarely

___3   No

55.   (Age 3–5) Which set of terms best describes the child?

___1   Confused, self-concerned, perplexed, dependent, worried

___2   Aloof, indifferent, self-contented, remote

56.   (Age 3–5) Is the child extremely fearful?

___1   Yes, of strangers or certain people

___2   Yes, of certain animals, noises or objects

___3   Yes, of 1 and 2 above

___4   Only normal fearfulness

___5   Seems unusually bold and free of fear

___6   Child ignores or is unaware of fearsome objects

57.   (Age 3–5) Does the child fall or get hurt in running or climbing?

___1   Tends toward falling or injury

___2   Average in this way

___3   Never, or almost never, exposes self to falling

___4   Surprisingly safe despite active climbing, swimming, etc.

continues

continued

58. **(Age 3–5) Is there a problem in that the child hits, pinches, bites or otherwise injures *himself* or *others*?**
    ___1 Yes, self only
    ___2 Yes, others only
    ___3 Yes, self and others
    ___4 No (not a problem)

59. **At what age did the child say first words (even if later stopped talking)?**
    ___1 Has never used words
    ___2 8–12 months
    ___3 13–15 months
    ___4 16–24 months
    ___5 2–3 years
    ___6 3–4 years
    ___7 After 4 years
    ___8 Don't know

59a. **On lines below list child's first six words (as well as you can remember them)**

    _____ _____ _____
    _____ _____ _____

60. **(Before age 5) Did the child start to talk, then become silent again for a week or more?**
    ___1 Yes, but later talked again (age stopped _____, duration _____)
    ___2 Yes, but never started again (age stopped _____)
    ___3 No, continued to talk, or never began talking

61. **(Before age 5) Did the child start to talk, then stop, and begin to whisper instead, for a week or more?**
    ___1 Yes, but later talked again (age stopped _____, duration _____)

    ___2 Yes, still only whispers (age stopped talking _____)
    ___3 Now doesn't even whisper (stopped talking _____, stopped whispering _____)
    ___4 No, continued to talk, or never began talking

62. **(Age 1–5) How well could the child pronounce his first words when learning to speak, and how well could he pronounce difficult words between 3 and 5?**
    ___1 Too little speech to tell, or other answer
    ___2 Average or below average pronunciation of first words ("wabbit," etc.), and also poor at 3 to 5
    ___3 Average or below on first words, unusually good at 3–5
    ___4 Unusually good on first words, average or below at 3–5
    ___5 Unusually good on first words, and also at 3–5

63. **(Age 3–5) Is the child's vocabulary (the number of things he can name or point to accurately) greatly out of proportion to his ability to "communicate" (to answer questions or tell you something)?**
    ___1 He can *point* to many objects I name, but doesn't speak or "communicate"
    ___2 He can correctly *name* many objects, but not "communicate"
    ___3 Ability to "communicate" is pretty good—about what you would expect from the number of words he knows
    ___4 Doesn't use or understand words

continues

continued

64. **When the child spoke his first sentences, did he surprise you by using words he had not used individually before?**

___1   Yes (Any examples? _____)

___2   No

___3   Not sure

___4   Too little speech to tell

65. **How did child refer to *himself* on first learning to talk?**

___1   "[John] fall down," or *"Baby* [or *Boy*] fall down"

___2   *"Me* fall down," or *"I* fall down"

___3   "[*He, Him, She,* or *Her*] fall down"

___4   *"You* fall down"

___5   Any combination of 1, 2, and/or 3

___6   No speech or too little speech as yet

66. **(Age 3–5) Does child repeat phrases or sentences heard in the past (maybe using a hollow, parrot-like voice), what is said having little or no relation to the situation?**

___1   Yes, definitely, except voice not hollow or parrot-like

___2   Yes, definitely, including peculiar voice tone

___3   Not sure

___4   No

___5   Too little speech to tell

67. **(Before age 5) Can child answer a simple question like "What is your first name?" "Why did Mommy spank Billy?"**

___1   Yes, can answer such questions adequately

___2   No, uses speech, but can't answer questions

___3   Too little speech to tell

68. **(Before age 5) Can the child understand what you say to him, judging from his ability to follow instructions or answer you?**

___1   Yes, understands very well

___2   Yes, understands fairly well

___3   Understands a little, if you repeat and repeat

___4   Very little or no understanding

69. **(Before age 5) If the child talks, do you feel he understands what he is saying?**

___1   Doesn't talk enough to tell

___2   No, he is just repeating what he has heard with hardly any understanding

___3   Not just repeating—he understands what he is saying, but not well

___4   No doubt that he understands what he is saying

70. **(Before age 5) Has the child used the word "Yes"?**

___1   Has used "Yes" fairly often and correctly

___2   Seldom has used "Yes," but has used it

___3   Has used sentences, but hasn't used word "Yes"

___4   Has used a number of other words or phrases, but hasn't used word "Yes"

___5   Has no speech, or too little speech to tell

continues

continued

71. **(Age 3–5) Does the child typically say "Yes" by repeating the same question he has been asked? (Example: You ask "Shall we go for a walk, Honey?" and he indicates he does want to by saying, "Shall we go for a walk, Honey?" or "Shall we go for a walk?")**
    ___1   Yes, definitely, does not say "yes" directly
    ___2   No, would say "Yes" or "OK" or similar answer
    ___3   Not sure
    ___4   Too little speech to say

72. **(Before age 5) Has the child asked for something by using the same sentence you would use when you offer it to him? (Example: The child wants milk, so he says: "Do you want some milk?" or "You want some milk?")**
    ___1   Yes, definitely (uses "You" instead of "I")
    ___2   No, would ask differently
    ___3   Not sure
    ___4   Not enough speech to tell

73. **(Before age 5) Has the child used the word "I"?**
    ___1   Has used "I" fairly often and correctly
    ___2   Seldom has used "I," but has used it correctly
    ___3   Has used sentences, but hasn't used the word "I"
    ___4   Has used a number of words or phrases, but hasn't used the word "I"
    ___5   Has used "I," but only where word "you" belonged

___6   Has no speech, or too little speech to tell

74. **(Before age 5) How does the child usually say "No" or refuse something?**
    ___1   He would just say "No"
    ___2   He would ignore you
    ___3   He would grunt and wave his arms
    ___4   He would use some rigid meaningful phrase (like "Don't want it!" or "No milk!," "No walk!")
    ___5   Would use phrase having only private meaning like "Daddy go in car"
    ___6   Other, or too little speech to tell

75. **(Before age 5) Has the child used one word or idea as a substitute for another, for a prolonged time? (Example: always says "catsup" to mean "red," or uses "penny" for "drawer" after seeing pennies in a desk drawer)**
    ___1   Yes, definitely
    ___2   No
    ___3   Not sure
    ___4   Too little speech to tell

76. **Knowing what you do now, at what age do you think you could have first detected the child's abnormal behavior? That is, when did detectable abnormal behavior actually begin? (Under "A," indicate when you *might* have; under "B" when you *did*.)**
    A. *Might* have noticed   B. Actually *did* notice
    ___1 In first 3 months   ___1
    ___2 4–6 months   ___2
    ___3 7–12 months   ___3
    ___4 13–24 months   ___4

continues

continued

   ___5 2–3 years   ___5

   ___6 3–4 years   ___6

   ___7 After 4th year ___7

been in a mental hospital or who were known to have been seriously mentally ill or retarded. Consider parents, siblings, grandparents, uncles, and aunts.

If none, check here h

**Parents' highest educational level
(77 for father, 78 for mother)**

77. Father

___1 Did not graduate high school

___2 High school graduate

___3 Post–high school technical training

___4 Some college

___5 College graduate

___6 Some graduate work

___7 Graduate degree (_____)

78. Mother

___1

___2

___3

___4

___5

___6

___7

79. Indicate the child's nearest blood relatives, including parents, who have

	Relationship	Diagnosis (if known)
___1	_____	Schizophrenia___
	Depressive___	Other___
___2	_____	Schizophrenia___
	Depressive___	Other___
___3	_____	Schizophrenia___
	Depressive___	Other___
___4	_____	Schizophrenia___
	Depressive___	Other___
___4	_____	Schizophrenia___
	Depressive___	Other___

Please answer the following questions by writing 1 if very true, 2 if true, and 3 if false on the line preceding the question. Except for the first two questions, which pertain to the child before age 2, answer very true (1) or true (2) if the statement described the child any time before his 10th birthday. If the statement is not particularly true of the child before age 10, answer false (3).

Remember: 1 = VERY TRUE 2 = TRUE 3 = FALSE

80.___ Before age 2, arched back and bent head back, when held

81.___ Before age 2, struggled against being held

82.___ Abnormal craving for certain foods

83.___ Eats unusually large amounts of food

84.___ Covers ears at many sounds

85.___ Only certain sounds seem painful to him

86.___ Fails to blink at bright lights

87.___ Skin color lighter or darker than others in family (which: lighter___ darker___)

88.___ Prefers inanimate (nonliving) things

89.___ Avoids people

90.___ Insists on keeping certain object with him

91.___ Always frightened or very anxious

92.___ Inconsolable crying

93.___ Notices changes or imperfections and tries to correct them

94.___ Tidy (neat, avoids messy things)

95.___ Has collected a particular thing (toy horses, bits of glass, etc.)

continues

continued

96.___ After delay, repeats <u>phrases</u> he has heard

97.___ After delay, repeats <u>whole sentences</u> he has heard

98.___ Repeats <u>questions</u> or <u>conversations</u> he has heard, over and over, without variation

99.___ Gets "hooked" or fixated on one topic (like cars, maps, death)

100.___ Examines surfaces with fingers

101.___ Holds bizarre pose or posture

102.___ Chews or swallows nonfood objects

103.___ Dislikes being touched or held

104.___ Intensely aware of odors

105.___ Hides skill or knowledge, so you are surprised later on

106.___ Seems not to feel pain

107.___ Terrified at unusual happenings

108.___ Learned words useless to himself

109.___ Learned certain words, then stopped using them

Please use the rest of this sheet for supplying additional information that you think may be relevant to understanding the cause or diagnosis of the child's illness.

Questions and Answers about PDD

WHAT DOES PDD MEAN?

PDD stands for pervasive developmental disorders. Children with PDD have some or all of these 3 developmental features in common:

1. **Social skills.** Children with PDD often have difficulty forming everyday "give and take" relationships with the people in their lives. Doctors call this "qualitative impairment in reciprocal social interaction."
2. **Communication skills.** Children with PDD may have trouble communicating both with words and without words. They also tend not to take part in the "make-believe" play that is common for most children. Doctors call these features "qualitative impairment in verbal and nonverbal communication and in imaginative activity."
3. **Interests and activities.** Children with PDD tend to have a limited range of interests and activities. They might repeat the same body movement over and over again, become very upset about minor changes in their environment, show an unusual fascination with seemingly ordinary objects, or insist on following exact routines. Doctors call this a "markedly restricted repertoire of activities and interests."

WHAT ARE THE DIFFERENT TYPES OF PDD?

Doctors divide PDD into 5 different types:

1. autistic disorder
2. Rett's disorder
3. childhood disintegrative disorder
4. Asperger's disorder
5. pervasive developmental disorder not otherwise specified (PDDNOS)

Autistic Disorder

Children with autistic disorder have significant impairments in all 3 of the developmental domains involved in PDD: social skills, communication skills, and range of interests and activities. Before the age of 3 years, they show a noticeable delay in at least one of the following areas: social skills, communication, or imaginative play. About 75 percent of children with autism also have mental retardation. Most children with autism (75 to 80 percent) are boys.

Rett's Disorder

Rett's disorder occurs only in girls and is believed to be caused by a genetic disorder. Girls with Rett's disorder experience no developmental delays until they are about 5 months old.

continues

continued

Then head growth slows down, the child's skills in using her hands are lost and replaced with repetitive motions such as hand wringing, the child's interest in social interaction decreases, and the child's motor and language development are impaired. Children with Rett's disorder tend to regain some interest in social activities after a few years, but their difficulties with communication usually persist. Children with Rett's disorder usually have severe mental retardation.

Childhood Disintegrative Disorder

Childhood disintegrative disorder is very rare. Children with this disorder experience no developmental delays until they are at least 2 years old, but between the ages of 2 and 10 years they lose the skills they have developed in at least 2 of the following areas: language skills, social skills, bladder or bowel control, play, and motor skills. Childhood disintegrative disorder differs from autism in that children with autism usually show signs of delayed development in their first year, while children with childhood disintegrative disorder demonstrate normal development for the first 2 to 10 years and then lose the skills that they gained earlier.

Asperger's Disorder

Children with Asperger's disorder have significant social impairment and a restricted range of interests, but they do not show cognitive or language delays. Motor milestones may be delayed in children with Asperger's disorder. Children are usually older than 3 years of age when Asperger's disorder is diagnosed, because this is when their social difficulties become obvious.

PDDNOS

PDDNOS is diagnosed when a child has a severe impairment in social skills, language skills, or range of interests and activities, but the child's symptoms do not fulfill the requirements for a diagnosis of other types of PDD. This may happen, for example, when a child's developmental delays are not severe enough to warrant a diagnosis of another PDD or when a child has autistic-like symptoms that do not appear until the child is older than 3 years of age.

WHAT IS THE DIFFERENCE BETWEEN PDD AND MENTAL RETARDATION?

It is important to understand that children with PDD may also have mental retardation. In fact, 70 to 80 percent of children with autism also have mental retardation. Their degree of mental retardation, though, is not severe enough to account for their difficulties with social, communication, and play behaviors.

continues

continued

WHAT CAUSES PDD?

PDD is a diagnosis that describes a **set of behaviors**. This set of behaviors probably arises from a variety of causes. PDD occurs in all parts of the world, in all races and colors, and in all types of families. Research shows that, as a group, families with children who have PDD are the same as families with nondisabled children, except that families of children with PDD have to deal with the unique stress of having a child with a disability.

Doctors believe that PDD often results from problems with a person's central nervous system. Researchers estimate that 15 to 20 percent of people diagnosed with autism have an identifiable nervous system disorder. There are probably many causes for the types of social and communication difficulties seen in children with PDD. But researchers have associated several developmental disorders with autistic-like behavior. These developmental disorders include disturbances of the metabolic system, such as phenylketonuria (PKU); progressive dysfunctions of the nervous system, such as Lesch-Nyhan syndrome; and certain genetic disorders, such as fragile X syndrome and tuberous sclerosis.

WHY IS PDD DIFFICULT FOR HEALTH CARE PROFESSIONALS TO DIAGNOSE?

Children with PDD often display some symptoms at an early age. But many behaviors associated with PDD (such as repetitive movements and preoccupation with the sensory aspects of objects) are also seen in very young children with other disabilities, such as severe mental retardation or language disorders. Doctors must rule out several other possibilities before making a diagnosis of PDD. These other possibilities include sensory disabilities (such as hearing or visual impairment), a variety of known nervous system and genetic disorders, specific language disorders, and mental retardation.

Also, individual children reach developmental milestones at different times. It would be quite typical, for example, for a nondisabled child to lag behind in certain developmental areas while being ahead of his or her peers in other areas. As children grow older, however, failure to reach developmental milestones becomes more of a concern.

WHAT DOES A DIAGNOSIS OF PDD MEAN FOR MY CHILD?

Development of a functional communication system is a first priority for a child with PDD. Teaching strategies for enhancing the child's communication skills can be formulated, once the professional has completed a careful evaluation. As people with PDD become adults, some have serious functional limitations and will require constant support in many life activities. Others will need supervision in living situations but will be able to function in supported employment. Still others—mainly those without an accompanying diagnosis of mental retardation—will be able to live and work independently and, in rare cases, may marry and have children.

Source: Ann E. Wagner and Sharon L. Lockwood, "Pervasive Developmental Disorders: Dilemmas in Diagnosing Very Young Children," *Infants and Young Children*, Vol. 6:4, Aspen Publishers, Inc., © 1994; B.J. Freeman, "The Syndrome of Autism: Update and Guidelines for Diagnosis," *Infants and Young Children*, Vol. 6:2, Aspen Publishers, Inc., © 1993; *DSM-IV*, American Psychiatric Association, © 1994; Aspen Reference Group.

Introduction to Mental Retardation

WHAT IS MENTAL RETARDATION?

According to the new definition by the American Association on Mental Retardation (AAMR), an individual is considered to have mental retardation based on the following three criteria: intellectual functioning level (IQ) is below 70 to 75; significant limitations exist in two or more adaptive skill areas; and the condition is present from childhood (defined as age 18 years or less).

WHAT ARE THE ADAPTIVE SKILLS ESSENTIAL FOR DAILY FUNCTIONING?

Adaptive skill areas are those daily living skills needed to live, work, and play in the community. The new definition includes ten adaptive skills: communication, self-care, home living, social skills, leisure, health and safety, self-direction, functional academics, community use, and work.

Adaptive skills are assessed in the person's typical environment across all aspects of life. A person with limits in intellectual functioning who does not have limits in adaptive skill areas may not be diagnosed as having mental retardation.

HOW MANY PEOPLE ARE AFFECTED BY MENTAL RETARDATION?

Various studies have been conducted in local communities to determine the prevalence of mental retardation. A review of these prevalence studies in the early 1980s concluded that 2.5 percent to 3 percent of the general population has mental retardation. A recent review of prevalence studies generally confirms this distribution.

Based on the 1990 census, an estimated 6.2 to 7.5 million people have mental retardation. Mental retardation is 12 times more common than cerebral palsy and 30 times more prevalent than neural tube defects such as spina bifida. It affects 100 times as many people as total blindness.

Mental retardation cuts across the lines of racial, ethnic, educational, social, and economic backgrounds. It can occur in any family. One out of ten American families is directly affected by mental retardation.

HOW DOES MENTAL RETARDATION AFFECT INDIVIDUALS?

The effects of mental retardation vary considerably among people, just as the range of abilities varies considerably among people who do not have mental retardation. About 87 percent will be mildly affected and will be only a little slower than average in learning new information and skills. As children, their mental retardation may not be readily apparent and may not be identified until they enter school. As adults, many will be able to lead independent lives in the community and will no longer be viewed as having mental retardation.

continues

continued

The remaining 13 percent of people with mental retardation—those with IQs under 50—will have serious limitations in functioning. However, with early intervention, a functional education, and appropriate supports as an adult, all can lead satisfying lives in the community.

AAMR's new definition no longer labels individuals according to the categories of mild, moderate, severe, and profound mental retardation based on IQ level. Instead, it looks at the intensity and pattern of changing supports needed by an individual over a lifetime.

HOW IS MENTAL RETARDATION DIAGNOSED?

The AAMR process for diagnosing and classifying a person as having mental retardation contains three steps and describes the system of supports a person needs to overcome limits in adaptive skills.

The first step in diagnosis is to have a qualified person give one or more standardized intelligence tests and a standardized adaptive skills test, on an individual basis.

The second step is to describe the person's strengths and weaknesses across four dimensions. The four dimensions are:

1. intellectual and adaptive behavior skills
2. psychological/emotional considerations
3. physical/health/etiological considerations
4. environmental considerations

Strengths and weaknesses may be determined by formal testing, observations, interviewing key people in the individual's life, interviewing the individual, interacting with the person in his or her daily life, or a combination of these approaches.

The third step requires an interdisciplinary team to determine needed supports across the four dimensions. Each support identified is assigned one of four levels of intensity: intermittent, limited, extensive, pervasive.

- *Intermittent* support refers to support on an as-needed basis. An example would be support that is needed to find a new job in the event of a job loss. Intermittent support may be needed occasionally by an individual over his or her life span, but not on a continuous daily basis.
- *Limited* support may occur over a limited time span such as during transition from school to work or in time-limited job training. This type of support has a limit on the time that is needed to provide appropriate support.

continues

continued

- *Extensive* support in a life area is assistance that an individual needs on a daily basis that is not limited by time. This assistance may involve support in the home and/or support in work. Intermittent, limited, and extensive supports may not be needed in all life areas.
- *Pervasive* support refers to constant support across environments and life areas and may include life-sustaining measures. A person requiring pervasive support will need assistance on a daily basis across all life areas.

WHAT DOES THE TERM "MENTAL AGE" MEAN WHEN USED TO DESCRIBE THE PERSON'S FUNCTIONING?

The term mental age is used in intelligence testing. It means that the individual received the same number of correct responses on a standardized IQ test as the average person of that age in the sample population.

Saying that an older person with mental retardation is like a person of a younger age or has the "mind" or "understanding" of a younger person is incorrect usage of the term. The mental age only refers to the intelligence test score. It does not describe the level and nature of the person's experience and functioning in aspects of community life.

WHAT ARE THE CAUSES OF MENTAL RETARDATION?

Mental retardation can be caused by any condition that impairs development of the brain before birth, during birth, or in the childhood years. Several hundred causes have been discovered, but in about one-third of the people affected, the cause remains unknown. The three major known causes of mental retardation are Down syndrome, fetal alcohol syndrome, and fragile X syndrome.

The causes can be categorized as follows:

- **Genetic conditions.** These conditions result from abnormality of genes inherited from parents, errors when genes combine, or from other disorders of the genes caused during pregnancy by infections, overexposure to X-rays, and other factors. Inborn errors of metabolism that may produce mental retardation, such as phenylketonuria (PKU), fall in this category. Chromosomal abnormalities have likewise been related to some forms of mental retardation, such as Down syndrome and fragile X syndrome.

- **Problems during pregnancy.** Use of alcohol or drugs by the pregnant mother can cause mental retardation. Malnutrition, rubella, glandular disorders and diabetes, cytomegalovirus, and many other illnesses of the mother during pregnancy may result in a child being born with mental retardation. Physical malformations of the brain and HIV infection originating in prenatal life may also result in mental retardation.

continues

continued

- **Problems at birth.** Although any birth condition of unusual stress may injure a baby's brain, prematurity and low birth weight predict serious problems more often than any other conditions.

- **Problems after birth.** Childhood diseases such as whooping cough, chicken pox, measles, and Hib disease, which may lead to meningitis and encephalitis, can damage the brain, as can accidents such as a blow to the head or near drowning. Substances such as lead and mercury can cause irreparable damage to the brain and nervous system.

- **Poverty and cultural deprivation.** Children in poor families may become mentally retarded because of malnutrition, disease-producing conditions, inadequate medical care, and environmental health hazards. Also, children in disadvantaged areas may be deprived of many common cultural and day-to-day experiences provided to other children. Research suggests that such under-stimulation can result in irreversible damage and can serve as a cause of mental retardation.

Notes:

Courtesy of The Arc, National Headquarters, Arlington, Texas, September 1993.

General Information about Down Syndrome

DEFINITION

Down syndrome is the most common and readily identifiable chromosomal condition associated with mental retardation. It is caused by a chromosomal abnormality: for some unexplained reason, an accident in cell development results in 47 instead of the usual 46 chromosomes. This extra chromosome changes the orderly development of the body and brain. In most cases, the diagnosis of Down syndrome is made according to results from a chromosome test administered shortly after birth.

INCIDENCE

Approximately 4,000 children with Down syndrome are born in the United States each year, or about 1 per 1,000 live births. Although parents of any age may have a child with Down syndrome, the incidence is higher for women over the age of 35 years. Most common forms of the syndrome do not usually occur more than once in a family.

CHARACTERISTICS

There are over 50 clinical signs of Down syndrome, but it is rare to find all or even most of them in one person. Some common characteristics include:

- poor muscle tone
- slanting eyes with folds of skin at the inner corners (called epicanthal folds)
- white ("Brushfield") spots in the iris of the eye
- short, broad hands with a single crease across the palm on one or both hands
- broad feet with short toes
- flat bridge of the nose
- short, low-set ears
- short neck
- small head
- small oral cavity
- short, high-pitched cries in infancy

Individuals with Down syndrome are usually smaller than their nondisabled peers, and their physical as well as intellectual development is slower.

Besides having a distinct physical appearance, children with Down syndrome frequently have specific health-related problems. A lowered resistance to infection makes these children more prone to respiratory problems. Visual problems such as crossed eyes and far- or nearsightedness are higher in those with Down syndrome, as are mild to moderate hearing loss and speech difficulty.

continues

continued

Approximately one-third of babies born with Down syndrome have heart defects, most of which are now successfully correctable. Some children are born with gastrointestinal tract problems that can be surgically corrected.

Some people with Down syndrome also may have a condition known as atlantoaxial instability, a misalignment of the top two vertebrae of the neck. This condition makes these individuals more prone to injury if they participate in activities that overextend or flex the neck. Parents are urged to have their child examined by a physician to determine whether or not their child should be restricted from sports and activities that place stress on the neck. Although this misalignment is a potentially serious condition, proper diagnosis can help prevent serious injury.

Children with Down syndrome may have a tendency to become obese as they grow older. Besides having negative social implications, this weight gain threatens health and longevity. A supervised diet and exercise program may help reduce this problem.

EDUCATIONAL AND EMPLOYMENT IMPLICATIONS

Shortly after a diagnosis of Down syndrome is confirmed, parents should be encouraged to enroll their child in an infant development or early intervention program. These programs offer parents special instruction in teaching their child language, cognitive, self-help, and social skills, and specific exercises for gross and fine motor development. Research has shown that stimulation during early developmental stages improves the child's chances of developing to his or her fullest potential. Continuing education, positive public attitudes, and a stimulating home environment have also been found to promote the child's overall development.

Just as in the general population, there is a wide variation in mental abilities, behavior, and developmental progress in individuals with Down syndrome. Their level of retardation may range from mild to severe, with the majority functioning in the mild to moderate range. Due to these individual differences, it is impossible to predict future achievements of children with Down syndrome.

Because of the range of ability in children with Down syndrome it is important for families and all members of the school's education team to place few limitations on potential capabilities. It may be effective to emphasize concrete concepts rather than abstract ideas. Teaching tasks in a step-by-step manner with frequent reinforcement and consistent feedback has been proven successful. Improved public acceptance of persons with disabilities, along with increased opportunities for adults with disabilities to live and work independently in the community, have expanded goals for individuals with Down syndrome. Independent living centers, group shared and supervised apartments, and support services in the community have proven to be important resources.

Source: "General Information about Down Syndrome," Fact Sheet #4, National Information Center for Children and Youth with Disabilities (NICHCY), Washington, DC, June 1992.

About Fragile X Syndrome

BACKGROUND

Until the early 1980s, the most common hereditary cause of mental retardation was rarely diagnosed. Second only to Down syndrome as a genetic cause of mental retardation, fragile X, or Martin-Bell syndrome, results from an abnormal gene on the X sex chromosome commonly causing moderate to severe mental retardation, delayed speech and language development, and subtle differences in physical features such as a long, narrow face and prominent ears.

Also associated with fragile X syndrome are behavior problems (for example, hyperactivity) and poor sensory perception and integration of information.

Fragile X syndrome occurs in at least 1 in 1,000 males. However, it is estimated that 90 percent of those with fragile X syndrome are undiagnosed.

LEARNING ABILITIES

The learning abilities of individuals with fragile X syndrome vary widely and range from severe mental retardation to mild learning disabilities to no learning problems. Because females have two X chromosomes, their learning problems typically are less severe. The second X chromosome seems to mask the effects.

Delayed speech and language development are often the first indications of a problem that leads to a diagnosis of fragile X syndrome. Compared to males with Down syndrome, males with fragile X have more jargon (unintelligible strings of syllables), perseveration (frequent and inappropriate repetition of words, phrases, or a specific topic), and echolalia (repetition of verbalizations of a previous speaker; usually indicates lack of understanding).

Their language is more inappropriate (off the subject), and they talk to themselves more. They also use fewer appropriate nonverbal gestures, such as face and head movements and pointing. These language patterns of males with fragile X syndrome are more characteristic of the language of individuals with autism. In fact, approximately 14 percent of males diagnosed with autism are known to have fragile X syndrome.

Special education services and small classroom settings are typically recommended for individuals with fragile X syndrome. An interdisciplinary approach, involving a speech-language pathologist, occupational therapist, teachers, parents, and others, as necessary, is generally considered the most effective plan for treatment.

Source: *Let's Talk . . . for People with Special Communication Needs*, No. 21, American Speech-Language-Hearing Association, Rockville, Maryland.

Introduction to Fetal Alcohol Syndrome

Fetal alcohol syndrome (FAS) is a specific pattern of abnormalities seen in children exposed to high amounts of alcohol during pregnancy. Children with FAS are small, usually in the lowest 10th percentile of all children in height and weight. They have unusual facial features including a wide nose bridge, small eye openings, flattened midsection (from the eyebrows to the mouth), smooth philtrum (the groove from the base of the nose to the upper lip), and thin upper lip. They have abnormalities or delays in their central nervous system (CNS) or brain, which may result in severe learning disabilities, mental retardation, language delays, perceptual dysfunction, developmental lags, and neurobehavioral disorders. Children with fetal alcohol effects (FAE) have some, but not all, of the problems seen in FAS.

Children with FAS are not all alike. Some are more severely affected than others; none will have all the characteristics described here. However, as a group, children with FAS display more developmental and behavioral problems than other children. Parents who recognize the reasons for their child's problems can plan the most effective treatment and educational strategies.

FAS is present at birth, although its signs may not be obvious until a child is 1 or 2 years old. Many children are not diagnosed until they enter school and their disabilities become more evident. Diagnosis is difficult because the problems seen in children with FAS are also seen in children with other disabilities.

An accurate diagnosis is important in understanding your child. If you do not have a diagnosis and think your child may have FAS/FAE, consult a pediatrician or a pediatric neurologist who has experience with alcohol-related birth defects or a willingness to learn.

Whether your child receives a diagnosis of FAS or not, all children with developmental concerns will benefit from evaluation and educational planning such as early intervention, special needs schooling, occupational therapy, and other specialized services.

Notes:

Source: Barbara A. Morse and Lyn Weiner, "FAS: Parent and Child," Fetal Alcohol Education Program, Boston University School of Medicine, Brookline, Massachusetts, © 1992.

Developmental Stages of Children with Fetal Alcohol Syndrome/Fetal Alcohol Effects

Fetal alcohol syndrome (FAS) can be diagnosed at any time during the life of the child by clinicians experienced in identification. The following sections describe the most relevant characteristics of FAS at each period of development.

INFANCY

For babies, the most distinguishing characteristic of FAS is their small, scrawny appearance. At birth, these babies are often tremulous and irritable, have a weak sucking reflex, and hypotonia (weak muscle tone). They often have "failure to thrive" (meaning that they may continue to lose weight longer than usual after delivery) and may need a continued period of hospitalization after birth in order to stabilize their weight. It is also usual for these newborns to be readmitted to the hospital during the first few months of life for failure to thrive, pneumonia, and evaluation of heart defects, hip dysplasia, and developmental delay. Feeding difficulties are a concern to caregivers during this period. Sleep patterns may be erratic, with poor differentiation of sleep-wake cycles.

Neglect, abandonment, and abuse are often reported during this stage, particularly when the babies remain in the care of biological mothers who continue to drink. Family members and friends often come to the rescue but custody issues need to be dealt with.

As the babies mature, they may be slow to master motor milestones, slow to start to say words, and slow to combine words. Adjusting to solid food is often difficult, and caregivers continue to complain of poor appetites and disinterest in food. During this period, the babies are often described as "very good." They are usually very oriented toward people and often show no stranger anxiety.

PRESCHOOL YEARS

During this period, children with FAS are usually short and elf-like in manner and appearance. They flit from one thing to another, moving with butterfly-like movements. They seem alert, outgoing, excessively friendly, and more interested in people than objects. Their needs for bodily contact often seem insatiable; they like to touch, fondle, pat, and kiss, and usually they have a happy disposition. However, they can be stubborn and unyielding in their demands.

During this period, children with FAS begin talking, but expressive speech may be delayed. They may talk a lot and ask a lot of questions, but they often lack richness of speech, thought, and grammatical complexity. They are often excessively talkative and intrusive, which gives the superficial appearance that speech is not impaired.

Hyperactivity is most pronounced during the preschool years. At home these children may be "into everything," and their first preschool experience is often difficult because they "can't sit still

continues

continued

a minute." They also are often fearless and do not respond well to verbal restrictions. They tend to wander away, go into the street, and need closer supervision than nondisabled children. Problems with coordination, fine motor control, and gross motor control become apparent as they try to draw and to ride a tricycle.

Sometimes one sees a preschool child with FAS who is fearful, withdrawn, and excessively passive. Such behaviors, which are not typical of young children with FAS, may reflect emotional problems associated with adverse living conditions. Such behaviors often diminish as the living conditions improve.

Child abuse, both physical and sexual, may occur during this stage, particularly among those children remaining with mothers who continue to abuse alcohol and other drugs. Custody issues continue to be a problem, particularly because many of the natural mothers are deceased from alcohol-related causes by the time the children are ready for school.

Many caregivers find these children endearing during this period, and their slow development and poor performance are often excused on the basis of their small size. "Oh, he or she will outgrow it" is a commonly expressed hope at this age, and developmental delays are often not taken seriously by the family. Children with serious hyperactivity are usually diagnosed at this age. Alert preschool and Headstart teachers are an important part of the community screening team, often being the first to recommend a diagnostic evaluation.

EARLY SCHOOL YEARS

School may be delayed a year with the idea that the child will catch up, or kindergarten may be repeated with the hope that motor skills will develop and hyperactivity will subside. Referrals for special education occur during this stage for those children with FAS with obvious mental disabilities and they usually continue in a special classroom or a special school for the rest of their school years. However, those children with FAS who have lesser disabilities often continue in regular classrooms during their early school years. Reading and writing skills during the first two years may not be noticeably delayed, particularly for children who have repeated kindergarten and are not hyperactive. Arithmetic is usually more of a problem for children with FAS than spelling and reading. When one compares their achievement test scores to their IQ test scores at this stage, they may appear to be achieving quite well relative to their IQ scores.

Attentional deficits become more manifest during the early school years as the demands for classroom attention increase. Emotional lability is also more pronounced at this time, and poor impulse control, memory deficits, and social intrusiveness are also observed. Poor peer relations and social isolation may be noted in the more functional children. Excessive demands for bodily contact often continue during this period, and interest in sexual exploration with other children may get them into trouble. Hostility and destructiveness are sometimes seen, but appear to be related to the living situation (current or previous) rather than a typical manifestation of FAS per se.

continues

continued

MIDDLE SCHOOL YEARS

During the middle school years, academic achievement usually reaches the maximum point, with reading and spelling often being superior to arithmetic skills. Increased difficulty maintaining attention, completing assignments, and mastering new academic skills converge to make school attendance increasingly stressful. However, good verbal skills, a superficially friendly social manner, and good intentions often continue to mask the seriousness of the situation. Increased stress and decreased classroom satisfaction can lead to lack of motivation and poor school attendance during this period, particularly for children without a strong and supportive family. A psychological evaluation and remedial placement are usually necessary at this time, even for the most functional children. Without proper evaluation and educational or vocational placement during the middle school years, they are at risk for increased truancy and school dropout. This problem is of particular concern because their low adaptive living skills and poor intellectual development do not make children with FAS good candidates for employment or independent living.

Notes:

Source: Ann Pytkowicz Streissguth, Robin A. LaDue, and Sandra P. Randels, *A Manual on Adolescents and Adults with Fetal Alcohol Syndrome with Special Reference to Native Americans*, Indian Health Service, Public Health Service, U.S. Department of Health and Human Services, 1988.

Needs Associated with Fetal Alcohol Syndrome: Practical Guidelines

INFANCY AND EARLY CHILDHOOD (AGES 0–5 YEARS)

Problems and Concerns

- Poor habituation
- Exaggerated startle response
- Sleep disturbances
- Poor sleep-wake cycle
- Poor sucking response
- Failure to thrive
- Delays in walking, talking, toilet training
- Distractibility and hyperactivity
- Irritability, temper tantrums, disobedience
- Difficulty following directions
- Inability to adapt to changes and environment

Recommendations

- Early identification of at-risk children
  — important for implementing needed services
  — important for maximizing the potential outcome for the child
  — important for identifying women and families at risk
  — important for providing needed services for families at risk and maximizing the chances for the family to remain intact
- Careful monitoring of physical development and health
- Placement of child in preschool
  — Help child to begin appropriate socialization and communication skills and behavior
  — Provide respite care for parents and caregivers
- Intervention with and education of birth, foster, and adoptive parents
  — referral for alcohol treatment, if appropriate
  — referral for subsidized adoption
  — referral for parenting skills, if appropriate
  — education regarding normal development
  — education regarding possible health concerns and developmental delays
- Intervention to ensure safe, stable, structured home
  — Help child learn appropriate behavior
  — Help parents and caregivers (for example, support with sobriety, accessing social and health services)
  — Set appropriate goals and expectations
  — Help parents and caregivers to better understand the child's methods of communication

continues

continued

- Adaptation of the environment to the child
  — low to moderate level of stimulation
  — simple, concrete directions
  — consistent, limited rules
- Assignment of case manager to coordinate services for the child and family

LATENCY PERIOD (AGES 6–11 YEARS)

Problems and Concerns

- Continued delays in physical and cognitive development
- Temper tantrums, lying, stealing, disobedience, and defiance of authority
- Hyperactivity and distractibility
- Memory deficits
- Impulsivity
- Inappropriate sexual behavior, often with animals
- Difficulty separating fact from fantasy
- Easily influenced by others
- Difficulty predicting and understanding the consequences of their own or others' behavior
- Poor comprehension of social rules and expectations
- Difficulty in abstracting abilities

Recommendations

- Monitor health issues
- Ensure safe, stable, structured home or place in residential facility
- Help caregivers and teachers establish realistic goals and expectations
- Help the child make healthy choices appropriate to his or her emotional and cognitive level
- Use clear, concrete, predictable, and immediate consequences in response to behavior
- Give simple, clear, and concrete directions for daily chores and activities along with positive consequences for appropriate behavior, listed in writing
- Structure leisure time
  — participation in organized sports (for example, Special Olympics)
  — participation in clubs for children with disabilities
- Administer psychological, academic, and adaptive evaluations on a regular basis
- Educate parents and caregivers regarding age-appropriate sexual development
- Provide respite care for parents and caregivers
- Give continued support for parent's sobriety, if needed
- Ensure appropriate educational placement
  — activity-based curriculum
  — focus on communication skills

continues

continued

   — focus on appropriate behavior
   — basic academic skills embedded within functional skills
- Expand case manager's role to include schools, mental and physical health providers, and social service agency personnel
- Document health impairment and deficits in adaptive behavior to aid in acquiring Supplemental Security Income (SSI) and other funding

ADOLESCENCE (AGES 12–17 YEARS)

Problems and Concerns

- Academic ceiling is often reached, usually by fourth grade for reading, third grade for spelling and arithmetic
- Increasing social difficulties and isolation
- Low motivation
- Egocentric, difficulty comprehending and responding to others' feelings, needs, and desires
- Lying, stealing, and passivity in responding to requests
- Faulty logic
- Impulsive, aggressive, unpredictable, and violent behavior
- Involvement in vandalism or other criminal activity
- Pregnancy or fathering a child
- Loss of residential placement
- Low self-esteem and mental health issues
   — depression
   — suicidal ideation and attempts
   — substance abuse
   — sexual or emotional abuse and trauma

Recommendations

- Change focus from academic skills to vocational and daily living skills
- Structure and monitor leisure time and activities
- Involve in structured social and sport group activities
- Anticipate transition or crisis situations along with appropriate planning and early interventions
- Help the child make healthy choices and to build on existing skills
- Educate parents, caregivers, and child regarding sexual development, birth control options, and protection against sexually transmitted diseases (STDs)
- Educate parents, caregivers, and child to help protect against sexual exploitation
- Implement planning for future residential placement, financial needs, and vocational or educational training

continues

continued

- Expand case manager's role to include acting as a liaison between child, family, schools, vocational programs, health care providers, and court services, if necessary
- List daily chores with increasing responsibility
- Provide respite care for families
- Advise of availability of caregiver's support groups

ADULTHOOD (AGES 18+ YEARS)

Problems and Concerns

- Increased expectations of others
- Increased dissatisfaction toward the person by others
- Unpredictable and impulsive behavior
- Aggressive and violent behavior
- Depression and suicidal ideation and attempts
- Poor comprehension of social expectations
- Withdrawal and social isolation
- Social, sexual, and financial exploitation
- Economic support and protection
- Job training and placement
- Medical care
- Birth control, pregnancy, or fathering a child
- Child care
- Legal issues or incarceration

Recommendations

- Guardianship for funds
- Subsidized residential placements, including special monies for biological and adoptive parents to help defray costs for special needs
- "Homebuilders" support to help the person live as independently as possible and to help in teaching parenting skills if the person becomes a parent
- Specialized vocational training and job placement
- Medical coupons and care
- Case manager support in accessing services
  — drug and alcohol treatment for person, if needed
  — liaison with court and other legal concerns, if necessary
- Patient advocates to ensure recommendations are acknowledged and implemented
- Acknowledgment of the person's limitations, strengths, and skills
- Acceptance of the person's "world"

Courtesy of Robin A. LaDue, Fetal Drug & Alcohol Unit, University of Washington, School of Medicine, Seattle, Washington.

Prader-Willi Syndrome

Prader-Willi syndrome is an uncommon condition detected by genetic testing. The syndrome's indicator is missing genetic material on the 15th chromosome. Either there is material missing (deletion) or material normally supplied by the mother is doubled (maternal dysomy). It is still not known what causes the loss of the father's 15th chromosome material to the child.

PHYSICAL SYMPTOMS

Intelligence and Muscle Strength

The brain and the central nervous system (CNS), which control the body and intelligence, are affected. The CNS effects include a range of mental retardation present in 95 percent of all cases. IQ typically is slightly lower than normal, usually ranging from 70 to 79 but can be below 40 or above 100 (100 is considered average for the general population). Generally, people with Prader-Willi syndrome do not function at their IQ level. In addition, an impairment of balance, less large muscle strength, and poor coordination characterize the syndrome. Another common problem is strabismus ("lazy eye").

Behavior

The temperament of babies and children with Prader-Willi syndrome is angelic. Subtle changes often occur after about 5 years of age. Later in life behavior ranges from stubbornness to destructive temper tantrums. Behavior, linked to the CNS, cannot automatically be controlled.

An Insatiable Appetite

An insatiable appetite is also linked to the CNS. It is important to note that Prader-Willi syndrome is not an eating disorder that can be psychologically treated. If food intake is uncontrolled this condition can be a critical problem. An additional complicating factor is that those affected usually seem to require considerably fewer calories than the average person in order to gain weight. Obesity generally becomes prominent about 2 or 3 years of age if food intake is not controlled, or this behavior may not set in until later years. These people have an overwhelming preoccupation with food and will become obese if their environment is not adequately controlled. Controlling food intake is extremely difficult, because people with Prader-Willi syndrome often are adept at finding ways of obtaining food. Early deaths have occurred because of lack of control of food intake.

continues

continued

Compulsive Behaviors

Compulsive behavior, including scratching and picking at sores or insect bites, is also common. If not controlled, infection may result from this behavior. The compulsive personality also manifests itself in the desire for routine, self-centeredness, and lack of logical and abstract thoughts.

Hypotonia

Hypotonia, or poor muscle tone, is at its worst during infancy. Children usually get stronger as they grow older. Babies with hypotonia often lack the ability to control their heads, arms, or legs; have a weak cry; and have a poor sucking ability.

Abnormal Growth

Abnormal growth usually results in short stature, both as a child and as an adult. The typical adult height averages 5 feet. Small hands and feet, narrow forehead, and downturned mouth can be detected. Developmental milestones, typically delayed, occur in all stages of life. Less frequently, scoliosis may be present, more so in cases where weight is inadequately controlled.

Hypogenitalism

Hypogenitalism, or incomplete sexual development, is most obvious with males due to their external genitalia, but this condition affects nearly all people with Prader Willi syndrome. Sexual development may begin at an earlier age, but stops before reaching a nondisabled adult level.

Diabetes and Heart Problems

Diabetes and heart problems pose little difficulty except in those cases where, like scoliosis, excessive weight is uncontrolled.

continues

continued

TREATMENT

Research is currently being conducted on Prader-Willi syndrome. Presently, there is no known cure or medical treatment for the syndrome. Only a few medications are helpful in managing its characteristics.

The effects of the syndrome can be minimized through controlled living environments, psychological and sociological guidance, special schooling, and proper genetic counseling. Nonetheless, the effects continue throughout the child's lifetime.

The team approach is best in the treatment of a child with Prader-Willi syndrome. The team should include

- parents
- pediatrician or family physician
- physiatrist
- nutritionist or dietitian
- psychologist/psychiatrist
- endocrinologist
- special education teachers
- county case worker

Notes:

Courtesy of Prader-Willi Syndrome Association, St. Paul, Minnesota.

Questions and Answers about Tourette Syndrome

WHAT IS TOURETTE SYNDROME?

Tourette syndrome (TS) is a neurological disorder characterized by tics—involuntary, rapid, sudden movements that occur repeatedly in the same way. The symptoms include

- both multiple motor and one or more vocal tics present at some time during the illness although not necessarily simultaneously
- the occurrence of tics many times a day (usually in bouts) nearly every day or intermittently throughout a span of more than one year
- periodic change in the number, frequency, type, and location of the tics and in the waxing and waning of their severity; symptoms can sometimes disappear for weeks or months at a time
- onset before the age of 21

The term "involuntary," used to describe TS tics, is sometimes confusing since it is known that most people with TS do have some control over their symptoms. What is not recognized is that the control, which can be exerted from seconds to hours at a time, may merely postpone more severe outbursts of symptoms. Tics are experienced as irresistible and (as the urge to sneeze) eventually must be expressed. People with TS often seek a secluded spot to release their symptoms after delaying them in school or at work. Typically, tics increase as a result of tension or stress and decrease with relaxation or concentration on an absorbing task.

HOW ARE TICS CLASSIFIED?

Two categories of TS tics and several of the more common examples are

1. *Simple:*
   - Motor—eye blinking, head jerking, shoulder shrugging, and facial grimacing
   - Vocal—throat clearing, yelping and other noises, sniffing, and tongue clicking
2. *Complex:*
   - Motor—jumping, touching other people or things, smelling, twirling about, and only sometimes self-injurious actions including hitting or biting oneself
   - Vocal—uttering words or phrases out of context, coprolalia (vocalizing socially unacceptable words), and echolalia (repeating a sound, word, or phrase just heard)

The range of tics or tic-like symptoms that can be seen in TS is very broad. The complexity of some symptoms often is perplexing to family members, friends, teachers, and employers, who may find it hard to believe that the actions or vocal utterances are *involuntary*.

continues

continued

DO ALL PEOPLE WITH TS HAVE OTHER ASSOCIATED BEHAVIORS IN ADDITION TO TICS?

No, but many have additional problems, which may include the following:

- **Obsessive-compulsive and ritualistic behaviors** are when the person feels that something must be done over and over. Examples include touching an object with one hand after touching it with the other hand to "even things up" or repeatedly checking to see that the flame on the stove is turned off. Children sometimes beg their parents to repeat a sentence many times until it "sounds right."
- **Hyperactivity with or without Attention Deficit Disorder (ADHD)** occurs in many people with TS. Children may show signs of hyperactivity before TS symptoms appear. Indications of ADHD may include difficulty with concentration, failing to finish what is started, not listening, being easily distracted, often acting before thinking, shifting constantly from one activity to another, needing a great deal of supervision, and general fidgeting. Adults too may exhibit signs of ADHD, such as overly impulsive behavior and concentration difficulties.
- **Learning disabilities**, such as reading and writing difficulties, arithmetic disorders, and perceptual problems, occur in many children with TS.
- **Difficulties with impulse control** may result, in rare instances, in overly aggressive behaviors or socially inappropriate acts. Also, defiant and angry behaviors can occur.
- **Sleep disorders** are fairly common among people with TS. These include frequent awakenings or walking or talking in one's sleep.

WHAT ARE THE FIRST SYMPTOMS?

The most common first symptom is a facial tic, such as rapidly blinking eyes or twitches of the mouth. However, involuntary sounds, such as throat clearing and sniffing, or tics of the limbs may be the initial signs. For some, the disorder begins abruptly with multiple symptoms of movements and sounds.

WHAT CAUSES THE SYMPTOMS?

The cause has not been established, although current research presents considerable evidence that the disorder stems from the abnormal metabolism of at least one brain chemical (neurotransmitter) called dopamine. Undoubtedly, other neurotransmitters (e.g., serotonin) also are involved.

IS IT INHERITED?

Genetic studies indicate that TS is inherited as a dominant gene that causes varying symptoms in different family members. A person with TS has about a 50 percent chance with each separate

continues

continued

pregnancy of passing on the gene to one of his or her children. However, that genetic predisposition may express itself as TS, as a milder tic disorder, or as obsessive-compulsive symptoms with no tics at all. A higher-than-normal incidence of milder tic disorders and obsessive compulsive behaviors occurs in the families of TS patients.

The sex of the child also influences the expression of the gene. The chance that the gene-carrying child of a person with TS will have symptoms is at least three to four times higher for a son than for a daughter. Yet only about 10 percent of the children who inherit the gene will have symptoms severe enough to ever require medical attention. In some cases TS may not be inherited and is identified as sporadic TS. The cause in these cases is unknown.

HOW IS TS DIAGNOSED?

The diagnosis is made by observing the symptoms and by evaluating the history of their onset. No blood analysis or other type of neurological testing exists to diagnose TS. However, some physicians may wish to order an EEG, MRI, CAT scan, or certain blood tests to rule out other ailments that might be confused with TS. Rating scales are available for assessment of tic severity.

IS THERE A CURE?

Not yet.

IS THERE EVER A REMISSION?

Some people experience marked improvement in their late teens or early twenties. Many of the people with TS get better, not worse, as they mature, and those diagnosed with TS can anticipate a normal life-span. There are several reports of a complete remission of symptoms.

HOW WOULD A TYPICAL CASE OF TS BE DESCRIBED?

The term "typical" cannot be applied to TS. The expression of symptoms covers a spectrum from very mild, which is true of most people, to quite severe.

HOW IS THE SYNDROME TREATED?

The majority of people with TS are not significantly disabled by their tics or behavioral symptoms and therefore do not require medication. However, there are medications available to help control the symptoms when they interfere with functioning. The drugs include haloperidol (Haldol), clonidine (Catapres), pimozide (Orap), fluphenazine (Prolixin, Permitil), and clonazepam (Klonopin). Stimulants, such as Ritalin, Cylert, and Dexedrine, that are prescribed for hyperactivity

continues

continued

may increase tics. Their use is controversial. For obsessive-compulsive traits that interfere significantly with daily functioning, fluoxetine (Prozac) and clomipramine (Anafranil) are prescribed.

The dosage necessary to achieve maximum control of symptoms varies for each individual and must be gauged carefully by a doctor. The medicine is administered in small doses, with gradual increases to the point where there is a maximum alleviation of symptoms with minimal side effects. Some of the undesirable reactions to medications are weight gain, muscular rigidity, fatigue, and motor restlessness, most of which can be reduced with specific medications. Side effects that include depression and cognitive impairment can be alleviated with dosage reduction or a change of medication.

Other types of therapy may also be helpful. Psychotherapy can assist a person with TS and help his or her family cope, and some behavior therapies can teach the substitution of one tic for another that is more acceptable. The use of relaxation techniques and/or biofeedback can serve to alleviate stress reactions that cause tics to increase.

HOW MANY PEOPLE IN THE UNITED STATES HAVE TS?

Since many people with TS have yet to be diagnosed, there are no absolute figures. The official estimate by the National Institutes of Health is that 100,000 Americans have full-blown TS. Some genetic studies suggest that the figure may be as high as one in two hundred if those with chronic multiple tics and transient childhood tics are included in the count.

DO CHILDREN WITH TS HAVE SPECIAL EDUCATIONAL NEEDS?

Although schoolchildren with TS as a group have the same IQ range as the population at large, many have special educational needs. It is estimated that many may have some kind of learning problem. That condition, combined with attention deficits and the problems inherent in dealing with the frequent tics, often calls for special educational assistance. The use of tape recorders, typewriters, or computers for reading and writing problems; untimed exams (in a private room if vocal tics are a problem); and permission to leave the classroom when tics become overwhelming are often helpful. Some children need extra help, such as access to tutoring in a resource room.

When difficulties in school cannot be resolved, an educational evaluation may be indicated. A resulting identification as "other health impaired" under federal law will entitle the student to an Individual Education Plan (IEP) to address specific educational problems in schools. Such an approach can significantly reduce the learning difficulties that prevent the young person from performing at his or her potential. The child who cannot be adequately educated in a public school with special services geared to his or her individual needs may be served best by a special school.

IS IT IMPORTANT TO TREAT TOURETTE SYNDROME EARLY?

Yes, especially in those instances when the symptomatology of the condition is viewed by some people as bizarre, disruptive, and frightening. Not infrequently, TS symptoms provoke

continues

continued

ridicule and rejection by peers, neighbors, teachers, and even casual observers. Parents may be overwhelmed by the strangeness of their child's behavior. The child may be threatened, excluded from activities, and prevented from enjoying normal interpersonal relationships. These difficulties may become greater during adolescence—an especially trying period for young people and even more so for a person coping with a neurological problem. To avoid psychological harm, EARLY DIAGNOSIS AND TREATMENT ARE CRUCIAL. Moreover, in more serious cases, it is possible to control the symptoms with medication.

WHAT KINDS OF FAMILY SERVICES EXIST?

Local Tourette Syndrome Association support groups allow families to exchange ideas and feelings about their common problems. Often family therapy is helpful. Parents of a child with TS have to walk a fine line between understanding and overprotection. They are constantly faced with deciding whether or not certain actions are the expression of TS or are just poor behavior. Parents then must determine the appropriate response. For socially unacceptable behavior, a child should be encouraged to control what he or she can whenever possible and to try to substitute what is more socially acceptable. Parents are urged to give their children with TS the opportunity for as much independence as possible, while gently but firmly limiting attempts by some children to use their symptoms to control those around them.

Notes:

Source: *Questions and Answers about Tourette Syndrome*, Tourette Syndrome Association, Bayside, New York, 1992.

Overview of Phenylketonuria

Phenylketonuria (PKU) is an inherited disorder of protein metabolism. Children with PKU do not have a functioning enzyme to metabolize, or break down, an amino acid called phenylalanine, which is found in all food proteins.

Protein in foods is important for building and repairing the body's tissues. Amino acids are often called the "building blocks" of protein. Twenty-two amino acids can be joined together in various combinations to form all the different kinds of proteins in foods. Enzymes are special substances in the body that work to separate the amino acids in food proteins and recombine them to form the different proteins the body needs.

All humans need a certain amount of phenylalanine for normal growth and tissue repair. Most of the time the unused phenylalanine is converted to another amino acid and eventually used by the body in different ways. Because the person with PKU lacks the enzyme that breaks down the extra phenylalanine, the excess builds up in the body tissues, including the blood. This excess can prevent normal brain development and result in mental retardation.

By law, 48 states check a newborn's blood during the first week of life to determine if the baby has PKU. The other states check for PKU also, although it is not mandated. The baby with PKU can then be put on a carefully controlled diet that allows enough phenylalanine for growth but prevents the flood of phenylalanine that can interfere with normal brain development. Blood tests are then done on a regular basis. With proper dietary control initiated early in life, normal physical and intellectual development can proceed in a person with PKU.

Because phenylalanine is found in all foods that contain protein, children with PKU must limit their intake of protein-containing foods. Foods that contain a large amount of protein should not be eaten. Food with a small amount of protein can be eaten only in controlled amounts. Some foods are "free" foods because they contain no protein and are free of phenylalanine. They are eaten to help boost the child's intake of calories needed for energy.

A child with PKU is given a special drink that contains most of the protein, vitamins, and minerals needed for growth. The drink provides almost all of the nutrients that other children get from their food. It has a taste and smell that may seem objectionable to someone not used to it, but children with PKU acquire the taste for the drink at an early age and grow up with it.

The amount of drink and food the child consumes in a day is carefully calculated by the child's family, doctor, and dietitian. All foods must be carefully measured to control the amount of phenylalanine the child eats. These amounts are adjusted to the child's changing needs as he or she grows. A child with PKU learns at an early age that his or her diet is restricted and to ask a parent if a new food is allowed. By school age, children with PKU know a good deal about their own diet.

Source: Marcia Nardella and Mimi Kaufman, *A Teacher's Guide to PKU*, Office of Nutrition Services, Children's Rehabilitative Services, Arizona Department of Health Services, Phoenix, Arizona, 1985.

Galactosemia Basics

THE FACTS ABOUT GALACTOSEMIA

Galactosemia is an inherited disorder of carbohydrate metabolism that affects the body's ability to utilize certain sugars from food. Galactose is a sugar that may be found alone in foods, but it is usually found as part of another sugar called lactose.

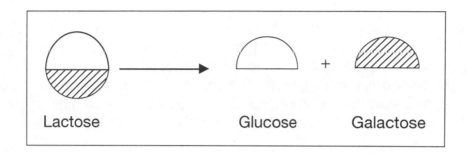

Lactose   Glucose   Galactose

Lactose, which is sometimes called milk sugar, is made of equal parts of the simple sugars galactose and glucose. The simple sugars can be absorbed directly into the bloodstream after digestion.

Children with galactosemia are missing the enzyme to convert galactose to glucose for energy in the body. If galactosemia is left untreated, galactose will accumulate in the blood and body tissues and will cause damage. A newborn with untreated galactosemia may develop vomiting and diarrhea and fail to gain weight. The buildup of galactose can eventually lead to jaundice, an enlarged liver, cataracts, mental retardation, and possibly death.

THE GOOD NEWS

Many states routinely check a newborn's blood during the first week of life to see if the baby has galactosemia. The baby with galactosemia can then be put on a galactose-free formula to prevent any dietary galactose from entering the bloodstream. The immediate response to dietary treatment is excellent, and the effects of the disorder are greatly alleviated. Blood monitoring is then done on a regular basis.

QUESTIONS AND ANSWERS ABOUT GALACTOSEMIA

Is Galactosemia the Same as Lactose or Milk Intolerance?

No, galactosemia should not be confused with lactose intolerance. People with galactosemia usually have no problems digesting lactose or absorbing galactose. The problems occur after

continues

continued

galactose has entered the bloodstream. People who are lactose intolerant must avoid large amounts of lactose in foods but can usually still digest and metabolize galactose. Commercial enzymes that are available to break down lactose in foods do not alter the amount of galactose in the food, and therefore are of no help to people with galactosemia. Strict avoidance of foods with lactose and galactose is the only known treatment for galactosemia.

If My Child with Galactosemia Eats a Food with Galactose, Will He or She Feel Sick?

If a child with galactosemia eats a food with galactose in it, he or she may not feel sick or different in any way. However, some children with galactosemia are more sensitive than others and may experience discomfort. It is the elevated blood levels over time from the continued ingestion of galactose that leads to serious complications. The changes may not be seen for several weeks or months. Because of this slow and subtle effect, it sometimes makes it difficult for a child with galactosemia to understand that milk products and other foods with galactose are harmful.

Without Dairy Products, Does the Child with Galactosemia Grow Like Other Children?

The child with galactosemia grows just like other children. The important protein, vitamins, and minerals that other children get from dairy products are provided in the prescribed milk substitute that children with galactosemia drink. Without a milk substitute, the child with galactosemia needs to take a daily vitamin and mineral supplement.

How Can I Explain the Galactosemia Diet to Other Children?

Young children can understand the concept that cars with different engines use different fuels (gas, diesel, and so forth). Thus, it can be understood by analogy that some children have bodies that work in different ways, and they need different food. Older children can understand the concept of a food allergy.

Do not hide the fact that the child's dietary needs are different if asked, but do not give a long explanation. Speak privately to the child and his or her teacher about the best way to explain galactosemia to classmates to determine how best to answer this question.

When Can the Diet Be Discontinued?

In the past, some children with galactosemia stayed on the diet only through infancy and early childhood. Most physicians today are advising families to continue with the diet indefinitely. The child with galactosemia will never be able to metabolize galactose in the normal way and will always be at risk for the associated medical complications.

Source: Maria Nardella, *A Teacher's Guide to Galactosemia*, Office of Nutrition Services, Children's Rehabilitative Services, Arizona Department of Health Services, Phoenix, Arizona, 1992.

Maple Syrup Urine Disease

DEFINITION

Maple syrup urine disease (MSUD) is a rare inherited disorder of protein metabolism. Patients with MSUD do not have a functioning enzyme to metabolize or break down a group of three amino acids called the branched chain amino acids (BCAAs). They are leucine, isoleucine, and valine. These BCAAs are found in all food proteins.

All children need a certain amount of BCAAs for normal growth and tissue repair. In the general population, extra BCAAs are broken down and eventually used by the body in different ways. But in people with MSUD, extra BCAAs and their byproducts are not broken down and can build up in the blood, spinal fluid, and urine, producing a distinctive sweet smell that gives the disease its name. Left untreated, excess BCAAs can interfere with normal brain development, causing mental retardation and other life-threatening complications.

Many states have newborn screening programs that check a baby's blood during the first week of life to determine if the baby has MSUD. The baby with MSUD can then be put on a carefully controlled diet that allows just enough BCAAs for growth. Blood monitoring of BCAAs with dietary adjustments is then done on a regular basis. Early diagnosis and continued dietary treatment are essential for normal growth and development in a child with MSUD.

TREATMENT

Because BCAAs are found in all foods that contain protein, children with MSUD must limit their intake of protein-rich foods. Foods that contain a large amount of protein are also high in BCAAs and should not be eaten. Foods with a small amount of protein and BCAAs can be eaten only in controlled amounts. Some foods are "free" foods because they contain no protein and are free of BCAAs. They are eaten to help boost the child's intake of calories needed for energy.

A child with MSUD is given a special drink that has most of the protein, vitamins, and minerals needed for growth with little or no BCAAs. The drink provides almost all of the nutrients that other children get from their food. It has a taste and smell that may seem objectionable to someone not used to it, but children with MSUD acquire a taste for the drink at an early age and grow up with it.

The amount of drink and food the child consumes in a day is carefully calculated by the child's family, physician, and dietitian. All foods must be carefully measured to control the amount of BCAAs the child eats, specifically the amino acid leucine. The amount is adjusted according to the child's changing needs as he or she grows. A child with MSUD learns at an early age that his or her diet is restricted and to ask a parent if a new food is allowed. By school age, children with MSUD know a great deal about their own diet.

Source: Maria Nardella, *A Teacher's Guide to MSUD*, Office of Nutrition Services, Children's Rehabilitative Services, Arizona Department of Health Services, Phoenix, Arizona, 1988.

Homocystinuria

WHAT IS HOMOCYSTINURIA?

Homocystinuria (HCU) is an inherited disorder of protein metabolism. People with HCU do not have the proper enzymes to metabolize or break down a group of amino acids. One of these amino acids is called methionine (MET) and is found in all food proteins.

All children need a certain amount of MET for normal growth and tissue repair. In most people, any unused MET is converted to another amino acid and eventually used by the body in different ways. But, in people with HCU, unneeded MET in the body can lead to an abnormal buildup of other amino acids, including homocystine. High levels of homocystine can be found in the blood and urine, and hence the name, homocystinuria. With untreated HCU, these abnormal levels of amino acids interfere with normal brain development, causing mental retardation and other serious side effects.

Many states check a newborn's blood during the first week of life to determine if the child has HCU. The baby with HCU can then be put on a carefully controlled diet that allows enough MET for growth but prevents the flood of MET that can lead to associated problems. Blood tests are then done on a regular basis. With proper dietary control initiated early in life, normal physical and intellectual development can proceed in a child with HCU.

TREATMENT

Since MET is found in all foods that contain protein, children with HCU must limit their intake of protein-containing foods. Foods that contain a large amount of protein are also high in MET and should not be eaten. Foods with a small amount of protein and MET may be eaten only in controlled amounts. Some foods are "free" because they contain no protein and are free of MET. They are eaten to help boost the child's intake of calories needed for energy.

A child with HCU is given a special drink that has most of the protein, vitamins, and minerals a child needs for growth with little or no MET. The drink provides almost all of the nutrients that other children get from their food. It has a taste and smell that may seem objectionable to someone not used to it, but children with HCU acquire the taste for the drink at an early age and have grown up with it.

The amount of food and drink the child consumes in a day is calculated by the child's family, physician, and dietitian. All foods must be measured to control the amount of MET the child eats. These amounts are adjusted to the child's changing needs as he or she grows. A child with HCU learns at an early age that his or her diet is restricted and to ask a parent if a new food is allowed. By school age, children with HCU know a good deal about their own diet.

Source: Maria Nardella, *A Teacher's Guide to HCU*, Office of Nutrition Services, Children's Rehabilitative Services, Arizona Department of Health Services, Phoenix, Arizona, 1985.

What Are Mitochondrial Disorders?

MITOCHONDRIA

Mitochondria are tiny thread-like or bead-like objects that are present in all the cells of the body. These structures contain many different substances that are necessary for the biochemical work of the particular tissue in which they are found, and for the activity of the body as a whole. The chief energy-making chemical reactions in any cell occur in the mitochondria. The contents of the mitochondria are almost entirely inherited from our mothers. The genetic material (DNA) in the mitochondria can suddenly change and these "mutations" are often what is passed on.

METABOLISM

Metabolism is the process of biochemical activity that generates energy and is responsible for keeping cells, tissues, and individual people alive. Without proper metabolism, the body will not work properly. Many different metabolic "assembly lines" or "pathways" come together in the mitochondria. For example, the metabolism of carbohydrates (starches and sugars), amino acids (the "building blocks" of protein), and fatty acids, all join up in the metabolism of tricarboxylic acid and a very basic energy-release process called the *electron transfer chain*. The "respiratory chain" within the mitochondria regulates the burning of fuels and the generation of energy, acting as a sort of "cruise control" or governor on the body's activity.

MITOCHONDRIAL DISORDERS

Mitochondrial disorders are a group of diseases that can interfere with muscle or brain activity or development in childhood. In fact, almost any tissue or function of the body can be involved. Even though all the disorders share some disturbance of the mitochondrial metabolism or respiratory chain of energy regulation, they can cause very different problems for the child. One mitochondrial disorder may seem to have nothing in common with another, unless their common biochemical disturbance inside the little energy bag or mitochondrion in each cell is understood.

Diagnosis

Diagnosis of this group of disorders can be very difficult. There is no simple test that always tells whether such a disorder is present. Each different condition has to be looked for individually within the child's own tissues, and this most often involves taking out a small sample of living tissue (or a *biopsy*) and doing difficult biochemical and genetic (DNA) testing on that material. Some of the biochemical and genetic testing can be done on blood cells, but these tests are far more complicated than any routine blood test. Although some of the mitochondrial disorders have fairly typical symptoms that may lead your doctor to suspect that they are present, many of the conditions seem quite vague and the symptoms might have any number of other explanations.

continues

continued

There are many other causes for muscle weakness or for disturbances in brain function that cause child development to be very slow or even go backward.

Suspicion that such a disorder might underlie your child's problem is the first step along the path to making a diagnosis. Your pediatrician will consider this group of diseases with any child whose progress or symptoms are in any way unusual or seem to involve an unusual mixture of different systems of the body. A history of similar problems in the family—or even of other children who have died young with no known cause—will be very important, especially if these cases have been on the mother's side. Help your pediatrician by asking about such things in the mother's family; remember that in the past people did not like to talk about children who developed slowly or died young.

One test that may indicate your child may have one of these disorders is a measurement of the levels of lactic and pyruvic acids in your child's blood or in the cerebrospinal fluid removed at a spinal tap. However, there are many other causes for raised levels of these chemicals in the blood (difficulty taking the blood from the child is the most common), and unfortunately, these levels are normal in many of these disorders. In other disorders, the levels may sometimes be normal, and so if the symptoms seem to "come and go," repeated blood tests may be needed to catch the levels when they are high.

Symptoms

What are the symptoms? In order of frequency, the symptoms may include muscle weakness (myopathy); delayed motor development or exercise intolerance, including intermittent paralysis, heart muscle disease (cardiomyopathy and heart block), and very typically eyelid muscle weakness (ptosis); visual problems leading to blindness; stroke-like episodes; particular types of seizures; and developmental delay. Because mitochondria are found in all parts of the body, other problems may occur, which can include nerve deafness, cataracts, a particular type of kidney problem (renal tubular defects), anemia (sideroblastic anemia), diabetes and other hormone disorders, bowel problems, vomiting spells, and liver failure. So, almost anything *might* be due to one of these serious diseases. Many of these diseases occur only in adults.

What are these disorders called? Because these disorders were discovered at different times, and because the names refer to the most typical or obvious surface sign rather than to the basic biochemical upset, the names are complicated and often seem very odd or unusual. Some of the names of the individual diseases are:

- **Neurological disorders:** MELAS (mitochondrial encephalopathy with lactic acidosis and stroke-like episodes) syndrome, MERRF (myoclonic epilepsy with ragged red fibers) syndrome, NARP (neurogenic weakness, ataxia, and retinitis pigmentosa) syndrome, chronic progressive external ophthalmoplegia, Leigh's disease, Kearns-Sayre syndrome, Alpers-Huttenlocher disease, and sensorineural deafness

continues

continued

- **Muscle disorders:** various types of myopathy ranging from benign to fatal
- **Disorders of other systems:** Barth syndrome (heart, anemia) and other types of cardiomyopathy, Fanconi syndrome, Pearson syndrome (liver, pancreas, blood), other liver diseases and anemias, partial villous atrophy (bowel), and hormone disorders, including diabetes, thyroid, and parathyroid problems

Genetics

Are these diseases inherited? Yes, but in a number of different ways. Mitochondrial DNA is passed on by the mother to both boy and girl children. A small mutation may be quite harmless and seem to cause no trouble, but as mutations build up, one or another of the disorders may cause symptoms. If your child is diagnosed as having a definite mitochondrial disorder, a visit to a genetic clinic will be very helpful.

Treatment

What about treatment? There is an enormous amount of research going on to find ways of treating these diseases. The first thing is to make an accurate diagnosis. Then discuss both treatment and rehabilitation with your pediatrician.

Notes:

Courtesy of A. Mervyn Fox, MB, BS, FRCP(C), DCH, Developmental Paediatrician, London, Ontario, Canada.

Cerebral Palsy

WHAT IS CEREBRAL PALSY?

Cerebral palsy is a condition caused by damage to specific areas of the brain, usually occurring during fetal development or before, during, or shortly following birth. Damage to the brain during infancy can also cause cerebral palsy. *Cerebral* refers to the brain and *palsy* refers to muscle weakness or poor control, usually resulting in disorders of movement or posture. It is neither progressive nor communicable. It is not curable either, in the accepted sense, although training and therapy can help restore function. It is not a disease and should never be referred to as such.

WHAT ARE THE EFFECTS?

Cerebral palsy is characterized by an inability to control motor function fully. Depending on which part of the brain has been damaged and the degree of involvement of the central nervous system, one or more of the following may occur: spasms; involuntary movement; disturbance in gait and mobility; seizures; abnormal sensation and perception; impairment of sight, hearing, or speech; and mental retardation.

WHAT ARE THE CAUSES?

Any damage to the brain, whether caused by genetic disorder, defective development, injury, or disease, may produce cerebral palsy. An important cause is an insufficient amount of oxygen reaching the fetal or newborn brain. Oxygen supply can be interrupted by premature separation of the placenta from the wall of the uterus, an awkward birth position, labor that goes on too long or is too abrupt, or interference with circulation in the umbilical cord. Other causes may be associated with premature birth, low birth weight, Rh or A-B-O blood type incompatibility between parents, infection of the mother with German measles or other virus diseases in early pregnancy, and micro-organisms that attack the newborn's central nervous system. Most causes of cerebral palsy are related to the developmental and childbearing processes and, because the condition is not inherited, the condition is often called congenital cerebral palsy. A less common type is acquired cerebral palsy: head injury is the most frequent cause, usually the result of motor vehicle accidents, falls, or child abuse.

ARE THERE DIFFERENT TYPES OF CEREBRAL PALSY?

There are three main types of cerebral palsy: spastic (stiff and difficult movement), athetoid (involuntary and uncontrolled movement), and ataxic (disturbed sense of balance and depth perception). There may be a mixture of these types for any one individual. Other types do occur, although infrequently.

continues

continued

HOW PREVALENT IS CEREBRAL PALSY?

It is estimated that 500,000 to 700,000 children and adults in the United States manifest one or more of the symptoms of cerebral palsy. It is roughly estimated that currently about 5,000 to 7,000 babies are born with the condition each year and, in addition, some 1,200 to 1,500 preschool-age children acquire cerebral palsy annually.

CAN CEREBRAL PALSY BE PREVENTED?

Yes. Measures of prevention are increasingly possible today. Pregnant women are tested routinely for the Rh factor and, if Rh negative, they can be immunized within 72 hours after the pregnancy terminates and prevent adverse consequences of blood incompatibility in a subsequent pregnancy. If the woman has not been immunized, the consequences of blood incompatibility in the newborn can be prevented by exchange transfusion in the baby. If a newborn has jaundice, this condition can be treated effectively by phototherapy in the hospital nursery. The increased use of neonatal intensive care units, particularly for high-risk babies, has helped to decrease the occurrence of cerebral palsy. Other preventive programs are directed toward reducing exposure of pregnant women to viruses and other infections; unnecessary exposure to X-rays, drugs, and medications; and the control of diabetes, anemia, and nutritional deficiencies. Of great importance are optimal well-being prior to conception, adequate prenatal care, and protecting children from accidents or injury.

CAN CEREBRAL PALSY BE TREATED?

"Management" is a better word than treatment. Management consists of helping the child achieve maximum potential in growth and development. This effort should be started as early as possible with identification of the very young child who may have developmental disorders. A management program can then be started promptly to include attention to the child's movement, learning, speech, hearing, and social and emotional development. Such programs utilize physicians, therapists, educators, nurses, social workers, and other professionals to assist the family as well as the child. Certain medications, surgery, and braces are sometimes used to improve nerve and muscle coordination or to prevent and correct deformity.

As a child grows up, he or she may require support services such as attendant care, continuing therapy, special education, vocational training, living accommodations, counseling, transportation, recreation and leisure programs, and employment opportunities. Above all, people with cerebral palsy need the opportunity to live as normally as possible in society.

Courtesy of United Cerebral Palsy Associations, Inc., 1522 K Street, NW, Suite 1112, Washington, DC 20005-1202; 1–800–872–5827.

Cleft Palate

ANATOMY OF THE ROOF OF THE MOUTH*

Hard Palate

The hard palate is the hard, bony part of the roof of the mouth. It arches over the front of the tongue and holds the teeth.

Soft Palate

The soft palate is the muscular extension of the hard palate that lies at the back of the mouth. Movement of the muscles in this soft tissue is essential to clear speech.

The hard and soft palates separate the nasal cavity from the mouth.

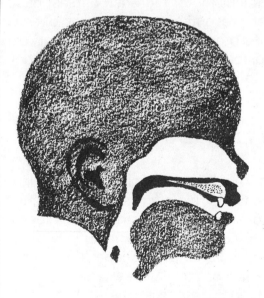

Soft palate open.
Muscles relax for breathing and making certain speech sounds.

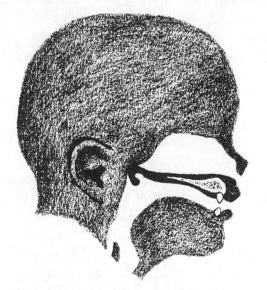

Soft palate closed.
Muscles in the soft palate and throat seal off the nasal cavity for swallowing foods and liquids and making certain speech sounds.

continues

continued

TYPES OF CLEFTS**

A cleft lip is a condition that creates an opening in the upper lip between the mouth and nose. It looks as though there is a split in the lip. A cleft palate occurs when there is an opening in the roof of the mouth. Cleft lip and palate can occur separately or together.

The type and severity of clefts vary from child to child. A cleft lip can range from a slight notch in the colored portion of the lip to complete separations on both sides extending up and into the nose.

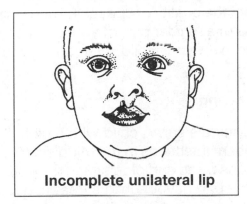

Incomplete unilateral lip

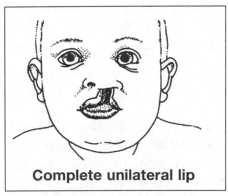

Complete unilateral lip

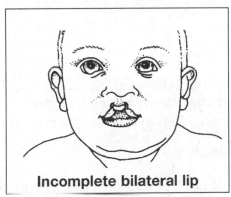

Incomplete bilateral lip

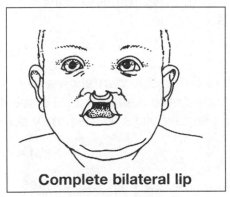

Complete bilateral lip

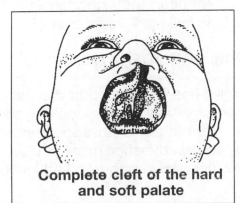

Complete cleft of the hard and soft palate

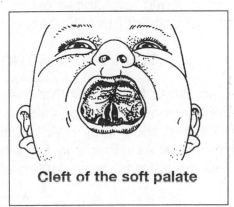

Cleft of the soft palate

continues

continued

MAJOR AREAS OF DIFFICULTY FOR CHILDREN WITH CLEFTS**

The major areas of difficulty for children with a cleft lip or palate are speech, hearing, dental care, and orthodontics.

Speech

Clear speech depends on the condition of the palate. A cleft palate may make it difficult for the child to say words clearly, and it may also affect the quality of speech (giving it a nasal sound, for example). Speech evaluations will therefore form a regular part of your child's treatment plan. A variety of treatments has been developed to help your child overcome problems in speech development.

Hearing

The condition of the palate also affects the middle ear. A child with a cleft palate may suffer some hearing loss as a result of severe or frequent infections in the middle ear, and this situation may contribute to speech difficulties. Evaluations by an audiologist and an otolaryngologist (ear, nose, and throat specialist) will also be a routine part of your child's treatment plan. Your child's hearing will need to be carefully monitored to ensure that he or she is responding to sound at a level appropriate to age.

Dental Care

Your child should receive dental care to ensure that teeth and gums are healthy. Dental care is important because all the teeth must be present and free from cavities for an orthodontist to proceed with treatment. Regular visits to the family dentist should begin when the child is 3 years old.

Orthodontics

Problems with the alignment of the teeth and jaws almost always occurs, but they can be corrected by orthodontic appliances or braces. Although the orthodontist will see your child regularly, treatment does not usually begin until the child is 7 years of age.

SOCIAL AND EMOTIONAL CONSIDERATIONS**

For parents, adjusting to the fact that their child has this condition may take some time. All members of the team are aware of these issues, particularly the social worker. Parents are particularly concerned about their child's adjustment to his or her appearance. Some children may experience difficulties in this area, but with sensitive direction most children and families are able to cope well. Also, family associations offer parental support and education.

*Source: *Looking Forward: A Guide for Parents of the Child with Cleft Lip and Palate*, Mead Johnson & Company, Evansville, Indiana, © 1991.
**Courtesy of The Hospital for Sick Children Foundation, Toronto, Ontario, Canada.

General Information on Microtia

WHAT IS MICROTIA?

Microtia is the absence or lack of normal outer ear configuration. It usually involves one side and rarely involves both. The severity varies, and is sometimes classified from stage I through V. Stage I is anotia or absence of the outer ear and stage V is a prominent ear. Microtia may present as a feature of a syndrome that involves the soft tissue and bones of the cheek and jaw region. This syndrome may be referred to as craniofacial microsomia, hemifacial microsomia, or brachial arch syndrome. The craniofacial surgeon and geneticist can describe your child's condition in detail.

WHAT IS THE CAUSE?

It is estimated that microtia occurs once every 6,000 births. The exact cause is unknown, however, factors such as rubella during the first trimester of pregnancy, and certain drugs have been linked to microtia. The geneticist can discuss your child's individual situation.

WHAT TYPE OF TREATMENT DOES MY CHILD NEED?

An early evaluation by the craniofacial team is important. This evaluation allows you the opportunity to meet with the various members and have your questions answered.

The evaluation by the surgeon and geneticist determines the extent of involvement and allows a plan of care to be tailored to meet your child's needs. Many parents' immediate concern involves hearing. Your child's hearing is evaluated, if it has not already been done by the audiologist and otolaryngologist (ear, nose, and throat specialist). Children with microtia often have atresia (closure) of the ear canal and conductive hearing loss. Typically children maintain 40 percent of normal hearing on the affected side. If both sides are affected, a hearing aid is most always needed.

Most children with microtia develop normal speech patterns. If a concern about speech does arise, the speech pathologist can provide an evaluation and assist with appropriate therapy.

If surgery is indicated, reconstruction will begin when the child is approximately 5 years old. Almost 85 percent of ear growth has occurred by this time. Also, this timing allows intervention before school age. Prior to surgery, the surgeon may wish to obtain an X-ray or CT scan to more fully evaluate the bony development. The reconstructive process is completed in stages. The first stage generally involves creating the ear framework with cartilage from the rib. The steps following this stage are aimed of defining and projecting the ear for a more normal appearance. Every child is unique, and each surgical step will be described carefully by your surgeon.

continues

continued

PREOPERATIVE AND POSTOPERATIVE CARE

Preoperative care mandates no aspirin-containing medicines for 2 weeks prior to surgery so as not to interfere with blood clotting. Tylenol (acetaminophen) may be given. Parents should consider donating blood for their child for possible transfusion during surgery.

Children are admitted to the hospital the day of surgery. They must not have any solid food after midnight, and liquids are allowed only per the instruction of the anesthesiologist.

Following surgery, a bandage will cover your child's ear. The dressing generally remains until the time of suture removal. An IV will be placed during the operation so that your child can receive nourishment until he or she is able to tolerate food and fluids by mouth. Pain medication is available for your child. Special instructions for positioning include avoid lying on the affected side. Your child is discharged once he or she is eating and drinking well and the surgeon is pleased with the healing process. Discharge instructions include provisions for returning for suture removal and for giving any medications required.

Notes:

Courtesy of Kant Lin, MD, Division of Craniofacial Surgery, Department of Plastic Surgery, University of Virginia Health Sciences Center, Charlottesville, Virginia.

General Information on Craniosynostosis

WHAT IS CRANIOSYNOSTOSIS?

In normal skull development the brain is protected by plates of bone. These plates are separated by seams (or sutures) so that the brain can expand beneath the bone. All skull sutures and fontanelles are usually open in the newborn (see the diagram below). Closure of the sutures occurs within the first few years of life. The metopic suture closes in early childhood, while the sagittal, coronal, and lambdoid close in early adulthood. When a suture closes prematurely, it is called craniosynostosis. The majority of brain growth (80 percent) will occur by the age of 3 years, so early detection and intervention are recommended to prevent permanent damage to the brain. A baby with craniosynostosis generally has a misshapen (asymmetric) skull. Keep in mind that immediately after delivery most babies have skull asymmetries due to molding, but this asymmetry will resolve spontaneously by the second to third month of life. It is when these asymmetries persist that the pediatrician may request an evaluation for craniosynostosis. To determine if this condition is present, a thorough examination is performed by the craniofacial surgeon as well as careful radiological evaluation (X-rays and CAT scans).

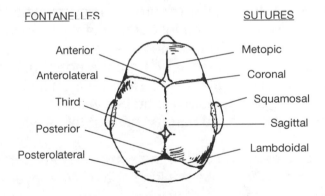

WHAT IS THE CAUSE?

The exact cause is not known, and there may be more than one factor involved.

continues

continued

HOW IS CRANIOSYNOSTOSIS TREATED? IS SURGERY NEEDED?

Each child is unique, and specific treatment plans are tailored to meet individual needs. Your child's care will be discussed with you in detail by the child's surgeon. Not all children with craniosynostosis require surgery. However, surgery is indicated when there is increased pressure within the skull as the brain grows. The ophthalmologist can help determine whether there is increased pressure by an eye examination. The CAT scan also gives valuable information. If surgery is indicated, the operation is usually completed before the child reaches the age of 12 months. The purpose of the surgery is to decrease the pressure and allow the brain to grow unimpeded by releasing the closed suture and reshaping the skull.

PREOPERATIVE AND POSTOPERATIVE CARE

Preoperative care includes no aspirin-containing medicines for 2 weeks prior to surgery so as not to interfere with blood clotting. Tylenol (acetaminophen) may be given. Parents should consider donating blood for their child for possible transfusion during surgery.

Children are admitted to the hospital the day of surgery. They must not have any solid food after midnight, and liquids are allowed only per the instruction of the anesthesiologist.

The child will stay overnight in the pediatric intensive care unit (PICU) so that he or she may be closely watched. After surgery there is usually a great amount of swelling around the eyes, and the head itself, but this swelling will gradually go away. Often there will be a bandage on the child's head covering the stitches or staples. The stitches will start at one ear and go across the top of the head to the other ear (like a head band). These stitches will be removed 1 week after surgery.

Your baby may be fussy or sleepy the day of the surgery. An IV will be attached to provide needed nourishment until the child feels like drinking again. Whenever your baby does wish to resume eating, however, he or she can be fed by whatever method was used before the surgery (bottle or breastfeeding). If your baby experiences discomfort after the operation, medication (such as Tylenol) is given.

Special instructions on positioning in bed are given to protect your baby. Once the swelling has decreased, and the child is eating and drinking, he or she is discharged.

Courtesy of Kant Lin, MD, Division of Craniofacial Surgery, Department of Plastic Surgery, University of Virginia Health Sciences Center, Charlottesville, Virginia.

Auditory Brainstem Response Testing

An auditory brainstem response (ABR) test is a relatively simple procedure used in conjunction with other hearing tests to determine a child's hearing sensitivity. The ABR test measures the response of the auditory nerve and lower brain to sound. This patient information sheet answers some of the questions parents may have about the test. Other questions, or information not understood, should be directed to the child's physician or other staff member, as appropriate.

HOW IS THE PROCEDURE DONE?

The ABR test is performed in a soundproof room and takes about 1 hour to complete. Your child is sedated and placed on a bed next to the testing equipment. Once asleep, electrodes are pasted to the child's skin on the forehead and behind each ear. Series of click-like sounds are presented through headphones. Each ear is tested separately, and the response to sounds of varying loudness is determined. As your child "hears" the click sounds, the electrodes pick up the electrical responses from the auditory nerve and lower brain and translate them into wave patterns. The audiologist conducting the test records and interprets these wave patterns and discusses the results either during or following the test. The procedure is not painful, and your child sleeps peacefully throughout the test.

WHY MUST MY CHILD BE SEDATED?

Your child must remain very still during the test. Any movement of the head, neck, or jaw causes false wave patterns that interfere with an accurate interpretation of the results. It is difficult for a child to stay completely still for a few minutes let alone an hour. Therefore, the nurse gives the child a mild sedative, as ordered by the child's physician, about one-half hour prior to the test. The sedative is most effective if your child is already sleepy before he or she takes it.

PRETEST INSTRUCTIONS

There are four instructions to follow:

1. Ensure that the child is as sleepy as possible when brought for the ABR test. Keep your child awake late the night before and waken him or her early the morning of the test. Try to book the test for the time of day your child normally has a nap. This timing will make it easier for your child to fall asleep.
2. Give your child a light meal or feeding 1 hour before the test.

continues

continued

3. Bring a favorite drink for your child to take after the sedative is given.
4. Bring a favorite blanket or toy that may help your child feel more comfortable and fall asleep quickly.

> If your child has a cold, fever, diarrhea, or recent contact with communicable disease (for example, measles), please call the day before the test, if possible, for a decision as to whether or not the test can be performed.

DOES MY CHILD NEED ANY SPECIAL CARE AFTER THE TEST?

As the procedure is finishing, your child gradually awakens. You may take your child home as soon as your appointment is completed. Your child may be a little sleepier than usual for the rest of the day, but no other side effects of the medication should be evident. Once home, if there are any concerns about your child's post-test condition, contact your child's physician.

Notes:

Courtesy of British Columbia's Children's Hospital, Vancouver, British Columbia, Canada.

Hearing Impairment

AUDIOLOGICAL AND MEDICAL INFORMATION ABOUT HEARING LOSS

There are four types of hearing loss, each of which can result in different problems and different possibilities for medical and nonmedical remediation.

1. *Conductive hearing losses* are caused by diseases or obstructions in the outer or middle ear (the conduction pathways for sound to reach the inner ear). Conductive hearing losses evenly affect all frequencies of hearing and do not result in severe losses. A person with a conductive hearing loss usually is able to use a hearing aid well, or can be helped medically or surgically.
2. *Sensorineural hearing losses* result from damage to the delicate sensory hair cells of the inner ear or the nerves that supply it. These hearing losses can range from mild to profound. They often affect certain frequencies more than others. Thus, even with amplification to increase the sound level, the person with a hearing loss perceives distorted sounds. The distortion accompanying some forms of sensorineural hearing loss is so severe that successful use of a hearing aid is impossible.
3. *Mixed hearing losses* involve problems in both the outer or middle and the inner ear.
4. *Central hearing losses* result from damage or impairment to the nerves or nuclei of the central nervous system, either in the pathways to the brain or in the brain itself.

Among the causes of hearing loss are heredity, accident, and illness. An unborn child can inherit hearing loss from his or her parents. In about 50 percent of all cases of hearing loss, genetic factors are the probable cause. Environmental factors (accident, illness, ototoxic drugs, and so forth) are responsible in the remaining cases. Rubella or other viral infections contracted by the pregnant mother may cause hearing loss in an unborn child. Hazards associated with the birth process (for example, a cut-off in the oxygen supply), may affect hearing. Illness or infection may cause a hearing loss In young children. Constant high noise levels can cause progressive and eventually severe sensorineural hearing loss, as can tumors, exposure to explosive sounds, heavy medication, injury to the skull or ear, or a combination of these factors.

Central hearing loss may result from congenital brain abnormalities, tumors or lesions of the central nervous system, strokes, or some medications that specifically harm the ear.

The detection and diagnosis of hearing impairment have come a long way in the last few years. It is now possible to detect the presence of hearing loss and evaluate its severity in a newborn child. While medical and surgical techniques of correcting conductive hearing losses have also improved, medical correction for sensorineural hearing loss has been more elusive. Current research on a cochlear implant, which provides electrical stimulation to the inner ear, may lead to important improvements in the ability to medically correct profound sensorineural hearing loss.

continues

continued

COMMUNICATION: SOME CHOICES FOR PEOPLE WITH HEARING LOSS

Communication is an important component of everyone's life. The possible choices for communication involve a variety of symbol systems. For example, communication in English can occur through speaking and writing. Despite your skills, it would be impossible to communicate with someone whose only language is Chinese, even though that person also speaks, reads, and writes quite fluently.

In the United States, people who are deaf also use a variety of communication systems. They may choose among speaking, speechreading, writing, and manual communication. Manual communication is a generic term referring to the use of manual signs and fingerspelling.

American Sign Language

American Sign Language (ASL) is a language whose medium is visible rather than aural. Like any other language, ASL has its own vocabulary, idioms, grammar, and syntax, which are different from English. The elements of this language (the individual signs) consist of the handshape, position, movement, and orientation of the hands to the body and each other. ASL also uses space, direction and speed of movements, and facial expression to help convey meaning.

Fingerspelling

In essence, fingerspelling is "writing in the air." Instead of using an alphabet written on paper, a manual alphabet consisting of handshapes and positions corresponding to each of the letters of the written alphabet are used.

Conversations can be entirely fingerspelled. Among people who are deaf, however, fingerspelling is more typically used to augment American Sign Language. Proper names and terms for which there are no signs are usually fingerspelled. In the educational setting, the use of fingerspelling as the primary mode of communication in combination with spoken English is known as the Rochester method.

Manual English

When the vocabulary of the American Sign Language and fingerspelled words are presented in English word order, a "pidgin" results. Pidgin Sign English (PSE) is neither strictly English nor ASL, but combines elements of both.

A number of systems have recently been devised to assist children who are deaf in learning English. These systems supplement some ASL signs with invented signs that correspond to elements of English words (plurals, prefixes, and suffixes, for example). There is usually a set of

continues

continued

rules for word (sign) formation within the particular system. These systems are generically known as manually coded English or manual English systems. The two most commonly used today are Signing Exact English and Signed English. While each of these systems was devised primarily for use by parents and teachers in the educational setting, many of the invented and initialized signs from their lexicons are filtering into the vocabulary of the overall community of people who are deaf.

Oral Communication

This term denotes the use of speech, residual hearing, and speechreading as the primary means of communication for people who are deaf.

The application of research findings and technological advances through the years has led to refinements in the rationale for and approach to teaching speech to children who are deaf. Several findings are pertinent here. Some children may actually have functional residual hearing. The speech signal is redundant. Because it carries excess information, it is not necessary to hear every sound to understand a message. For language learning to be successful with children who are deaf (no matter what the educational approach), programs of early intervention must take place during the critical language-learning years of birth through 6 years. Hearing screening procedures that accurately detect hearing impairments in very young children make it possible to fit hearing aids and other amplification devices and to introduce auditory and language training programs as soon as the problem is detected.

Almost all auditory approaches today rely heavily on the training of residual hearing. The traditional auditory/oral approach trains the child with hearing loss to acquire language through speechreading (lipreading), augmented by the use of residual hearing, and sometimes vibrotactile cues. The auditory/verbal approach (also called unisensory or acoupedic method) teaches children to process language through amplified residual hearing, so that language is learned through auditory channels.

Speechreading

Recognizing spoken words by watching the speaker's lips, face, and gestures is a daily challenge for all people with hearing loss. Speechreading is the least consistently visible of the available communication choices; only about 30 percent of English sounds are visible on the lips, and 50 percent are homophonous, that is, they look like something else. For example, looking in a mirror and "saying" without voice the words "kite," "height," and "night," almost no changes in the lips distinguish the three words. Then, saying the words "maybe," "baby," "pay me," and they look exactly alike on the lips, too.

Some people who are deaf become skilled speechreaders, especially if they can supplement what they see with some hearing. Many do not develop great skill at speechreading, but most do speechread to some extent. Because speechreading requires guesswork, very few people who are deaf rely on speechreading alone for exchanges of important information.

continues

continued

Cued Speech

Cued speech is a system of communication in which eight hand shapes in four possible positions supplement the information visible on the lips. The hand "cue" signals a visual difference between sounds that look alike on the lips—such as /p/, /b/, /m/. These cues enable the person with hearing loss to see the phonetic equivalent of what others hear. It is a speech-based method of communication aimed at taking the guesswork out of speechreading.

Simultaneous Communication

This term denotes the combined use of speech, signs, and fingerspelling. Simultaneous communication offers the benefit of seeing two forms of a message at the same time. The individual who is deaf speechreads what is being spoken and simultaneously reads the signs and fingerspelling of the speaker.

Total Communication

Total communication is a philosophy that implies acceptance and use of all possible methods of communication to assist the child who is deaf in acquiring language and the person who is deaf in understanding language.

Historically, proponents of particular systems have often been at odds with proponents of other systems or modes. There is increasing consensus that whatever system or systems work best for the individual should be used to allow access to clear and understandable communication.

Notes:

Source: National Information Center on Deafness and the National Association of the Deaf, "Deafness: A Fact Sheet," Gallaudet University, Washington, DC, © 1989.

General Information about Speech and Language Disorders

DEFINITION

Speech and language disorders refer to problems in communication and related areas such as oral motor function. These delays and disorders range from simple sound substitutions to the inability to understand or use language or use the oral-motor mechanism for functional speech and feeding. Some causes of speech and language disorders include hearing loss, neurological disorders, brain injury, mental retardation, drug abuse, physical impairments such as cleft lip or palate, and vocal abuse or misuse. Frequently, however, the cause is unknown.

INCIDENCE

One-quarter of the children served in the special education programs of public schools (almost 1 million children in the 1988–1989 school year) were categorized as having speech or language impairments. This estimate does not include children who have speech and language problems secondary to other conditions such as deafness. Language disorders may be related to other disabilities such as mental retardation, autism, or cerebral palsy. It is estimated that communication disorders (including speech, language, and hearing disorders) affect 1 of every 10 people in the United States.

CHARACTERISTICS

A child's communication is considered delayed when the child is noticeably behind his or her peers in the acquisition of speech and language skills. Sometimes a child will have greater receptive (understanding) than expressive (speaking) language skills, but this situation is not always the case.

Speech disorders refer to difficulties producing speech sounds or problems with voice quality. They might be characterized by an interruption in the flow or rhythm of speech, such as stuttering, which is called dysfluency. Speech disorders may be problems with the way sounds are formed, called articulation or phonological disorders, or they may be difficulties with the pitch, volume, or quality of the voice. There may be a combination of several problems. People with speech disorders have trouble using some speech sounds, which can also be a symptom of a delay. They may say "see" when they mean "ski" or they may have trouble using other sounds like "l" or "r." Listeners may have trouble understanding what someone with a speech disorder is trying to say. People with voice disorders may have trouble with the way their voices sound.

continues

continued

A language disorder is an impairment in the ability to understand or use words in context, both verbally and nonverbally. Some characteristics of language disorders include improper use of words and their meanings, inability to express ideas, inappropriate grammatical patterns, reduced vocabulary, and inability to follow directions. One or a combination of these characteristics may occur in children who are affected by language-learning disabilities or developmental language delay. Children may hear or see a word but not be able to understand its meaning. They may have trouble getting others to understand what they are trying to communicate.

Notes:

Source: *General Information about Speech and Language Disorders*, National Information Center for Children and Youth with Disabilities (NICHCY), Washington, DC, 1990.

Types of Speech and Language Disorders

COMMON SPEECH DISORDERS

- *Phonological impairment* (also called misarticulation). Here the child says the sounds wrong, or omits or duplicates certain sounds within a word. The problem may reflect poor neurological motor skills, a learning error, or difficulty in identifying certain speech sounds. Examples of common errors are "wabbit" for rabbit," "thnake" for "snake," "dood" for "good," and "poo" for "spoon."

    Another phonological impairment is unstressed syllable deletion in which a child simply skips over a syllable in a long word, as in "nana" for "banana or "te-phone" for "telephone." Many of these misproductions are a part of normal development and are expected in the speech of very young children, but when they persist past the expected age they are considered abnormal and usually indicate brain dysfunction.

- *Verbal dyspraxia.* This term is used by some scientists and clinicians to describe the inability to produce the sequential, rapid, and precise movements required for speech. Nothing is wrong with the child's vocal apparatus, but the child's brain cannot give correct instructions for the motor movements involved in speech. This disorder is characterized by many sound omissions. Some verbally dyspraxic children, for instance, speak only in vowels, making their speech nearly unintelligible. One little boy trying to say "My name is Billy" can only manage "eye a eh ee-ee." These children also have very slow, halting speech with many false starts before the right sounds are produced. Their speech errors may be similar to those of children with phonological impairment.

- *Dysarthria.* Here muscle control problems affect the speech-making apparatus. Dysarthria most commonly occurs in combination with other nervous system disorders such as cerebral palsy. A child with dysarthria cannot control the muscles involved in speaking and eating, so the mouth may be open all the time or the tongue may protrude.

COMMON LANGUAGE DISORDERS

- *Form errors.* These errors are present when the child cannot understand or use the rules of grammar. A child with this problem might say "We go pool" instead of "We went to the pool."

    Children with language disorders seem to have particular difficulty with complex sentence constructions such as questions and negative forms.

continues

continued

Examples of Form Errors	
Correct sentence	**Disordered sentence**
They won't play with me.	They no play with me.
I can't sing.	I no can sing.
He doesn't have money.	He no have money.
When will he come?	When he will come?
What is that?	What that?

- *Content errors.* This language disorder is involved when the semantics, or what the child understands or talks about, is limited or inaccurate. The child may have a limited vocabulary or may fail to understand that the same word—match, for example—can have multiple meanings.

- *Use errors.* This term concerns what linguists call pragmatics, the ability of the child to follow the rules of communication: when to talk, how to request information, how to take turns. A child with a use error might be unable to ask an adult for help, even though he or she knows that help is needed and the adult can provide it. Children with autism who have difficulty communicating with people may have use errors.

Notes:

Source: *Developmental Speech and Language Disorders*, Office of Scientific and Health Reports, National Institute of Neurological and Communicative Disorders and Stroke, National Institutes of Health, Public Health Service, U.S. Department of Health and Human Services, 1988.

Categorizing Speech and Language Disorders

If children with a speech or language problem are to benefit from different treatment approaches now available, they must be accurately subgrouped according to the type of impairment. In categorizing children with speech and language impairments, experts tend to ask two questions. First, is the disorder expressive, receptive, or a mixture of both? Second, is the child simply delayed in speech or language development, or is the child not only delayed but abnormal in speech and language when these skills begin to develop?

EXPRESSIVE OR RECEPTIVE?

Some children with language disorders have primarily expressive (speaking) disorders; others have mainly receptive (understanding) disorders. Most have a combination of both.

Clinicians often encounter children who may be unable to communicate effectively, but nonetheless show signs of understanding others quite well. Consider Becky, a 6-year-old girl seen at a speech clinic. Her conversation with a clinician goes like this:

Clinician: What is your favorite game?
Becky: Doctor.
Clinician: How many can play that game?
Becky: Two four.
Clinician: Two or four?
Becky: Or three.
Clinician: How do you play doctor?
Becky: One has to be doctor.
Clinician: Anything else?
Becky: One operation man.
Clinician: Anything else?
Becky: No.
Clinician: What do you want to be?
Becky: A nurse.
Clinician: Oh, you need a nurse?
Becky: No, you don't.

Becky has an expressive language disorder. Her responses are limited to incomplete sentences that may be inappropriate to the question, and they reveal Becky's inability to use verbs, conjunctions, or any of the subtleties of language. Like some children with expressive language problems, Becky has a good vocabulary, but she has difficulty connecting words. Even though she is 6 years of age, she talks at a 2-year-old level.

Children with expressive language problems may or may not have articulation problems. But even if their speech is perfectly articulated, communication is impaired because language remains ungrammatical, reduced, and babyish.

continues

continued

Paul, who is 7 years of age, is Becky's opposite, a child with a receptive language disorder who has difficulty understanding language. Receptive language problems rarely occur alone; usually they are accompanied by at least some degree of expressive language disorder. The condition often is misdiagnosed as attention problems, behavioral problems, or hearing problems. Standardized language tests may reveal, though, that a child with a receptive language disorder is trying to cooperate but simply cannot understand the instructions.

Paul, for instance, cannot point to a picture that best reveals his understanding of single vocabulary words or of grammatical associations between words. When asked to point to a picture of "the ball under the table," Paul might just as readily point to a picture of a ball *on* the table. When asked to point to the picture of "the boy running after the girl," he might instead choose the one of a girl running after a boy.

DELAY OR DISORDER?

Scientists have not agreed on whether children with language disorders acquire language normally—but more slowly—than other children or whether they develop language in an abnormal way when they begin to talk and understand. If any consensus has been reached in the past decade, it is that both sides may be right. There may be two quite separate conditions, one in which speech or language is delayed, and another in which speech or language is not only delayed but also incorrect.

The general consensus is that many children with language impairments seem to be merely delayed, but a sizable number also develop language in an abnormal way. The distinction is important, because it can help clinicians recognize that some children should be treated aggressively and others should be left alone.

Notes:

Source: *Developmental Speech and Language Disorders*, Office of Scientific and Health Reports, National Institute of Neurological and Communicative Disorders and Stroke, National Institutes of Health, Public Health Service, U.S. Department of Health and Human Services, 1988.

Tracking Your Child's Speech and Hearing

Child's Name _____ Date _____

BIRTH

Hearing and Understanding

YES NO
☐   ☐   Does your child listen to speech?
☐   ☐   Does your child startle or cry at noises?
☐   ☐   Does your child awaken at loud sounds?

Talking

YES NO
☐   ☐   Does your child make pleasure sounds?
☐   ☐   When you play with your child, does he or she look at you, look away, and then look again?

0–3 MONTHS

Hearing and Understanding

YES NO
☐   ☐   Does your child turn to you when you speak?
☐   ☐   Does your child smile when spoken to?
☐   ☐   Does your child seem to recognize your voice and quiet down if crying?

Talking

YES NO
☐   ☐   Does your child repeat the same sounds a lot (cooing, gooing)?
☐   ☐   Does your child cry differently for different needs?
☐   ☐   Does your child smile when he or she sees you?

4–6 MONTHS

Hearing and Understanding

YES NO
☐   ☐   Does your child respond to "no"? To changes in your tone of voice?
☐   ☐   Does your child look around for the source of new sounds, such as a doorbell, a vacuum, or a dog barking?
☐   ☐   Does your child notice toys that make sounds?

Talking

YES NO
☐   ☐   Does your child's babbling sound more speech-like with lots of different sounds, including *p*, *b*, and *m*?
☐   ☐   Does your child tell you (by sound or gesture) when he or she wants you to do something again?
☐   ☐   Does your child make gurgling sounds when left alone? When playing with you?

continues

continued

7 MONTHS–1 YEAR

Hearing and Understanding

YES NO

☐ ☐ Does your child recognize words for common items like "cup," "shoe," "juice"?

☐ ☐ Has your child begun to respond to requests ("Come here," "Want more")?

☐ ☐ Does your child enjoy games like peek-a-boo and pat-a-cake?

☐ ☐ Does your child turn or look up when you call his or her name?

☐ ☐ Does your child listen when spoken to?

Talking

YES NO

☐ ☐ Can your child say 1 or 2 words (bye-bye, dada, mama, no) although they may not be clear?

☐ ☐ Does your child's babbling have both long and short groups of sounds such as "tata upup bibibibi"?

☐ ☐ Does your child imitate different speech sounds?

☐ ☐ Does your child use speech or noncrying sounds to get and keep your attention?

1–2 YEARS

Hearing and Understanding

YES NO

☐ ☐ Can your child point to pictures in a book when they are named?

☐ ☐ Does your child point to a few body parts when asked?

☐ ☐ Can your child follow simple commands and understand simple questions ("Roll the ball," "Kiss the baby," "Where's your shoe?")?

☐ ☐ Does your child listen to simple stories, songs, and rhymes?

Talking

YES NO

☐ ☐ Is your child saying more and more words every month?

☐ ☐ Does your child use some 1 to 2 word questions ("Where kitty?" "Go bye-bye?" "What's that?")?

☐ ☐ Does your child put 2 words together ("More cookie," "No juice," "Mommy block")?

☐ ☐ Does your child use many different consonant sounds at the beginning of words?

continues

continued

2–3 YEARS

Hearing and Understanding

YES NO

☐ ☐ Does your child understand differences in meaning ("go-stop," "in-on," "big-little," "up-down")?

☐ ☐ Does your child notice sounds (telephone ringing, television, knocking at the door)?

☐ ☐ Can your child follow 2 requests ("Get the ball and put it on the table")?

Talking

YES NO

☐ ☐ Does your child have a word for almost everything?

☐ ☐ Does your child use 2 to 3 word "sentences" to talk about and ask for things?

☐ ☐ Do you understand your child's speech most of the time?

☐ ☐ Does your child often ask for or direct your attention to objects by naming them?

3–4 YEARS

Hearing and Understanding

YES NO

☐ ☐ Does your child hear you when you call from another room?

☐ ☐ Does your child hear television or radio at the same loudness level as other members of the family?

☐ ☐ Does your child answer simple "who," "what," "where," and "why" questions?

Talking

YES NO

☐ ☐ Does your child talk about what he or she does at school or at friends' homes?

☐ ☐ Does your child say most sounds correctly except a few, like *r*, *l*, *th*, and *s*?

☐ ☐ Does your child usually talk easily without repeating syllables or words?

☐ ☐ Do people outside your family usually understand your child's speech?

☐ ☐ Does your child use a lot of sentences that have 4 or more words?

continues

continued

4–5 YEARS

Hearing and Understanding

YES	NO	
☐	☐	Does your child hear and understand most of what is said at home and in school?
☐	☐	Does everyone who knows your child think he or she hears well (teacher, baby sitter, grandparent, etc.)?
☐	☐	Does your child pay attention to a story and answer simple questions about it?

Talking

YES	NO	
☐	☐	Does your child's voice sound clear like other children's?
☐	☐	Does your child use sentences that give lots of details (e.g., "I have two red balls at home")?
☐	☐	Can your child tell you a story and stick pretty much to the topic?
☐	☐	Does your child communicate easily with other children and adults?
☐	☐	Does your child say all sounds correctly except maybe 1 or 2?
☐	☐	Does your child use the same grammar as the rest of the family?

Source: "How Does Your Child Hear and Talk?" American Speech-Language-Hearing Association, Rockville, Maryland.

Verbal Dyspraxia

DEFINITION

Dyspraxia is defined as difficulty or inability in making purposeful movements in the absence of paralysis, loss of sensation, or a persistent loss of coordination apparent in all activities. Usually, the term describes people who have difficulty getting their hands to carry out such tasks as combing their hair, buttoning, or printing, even though they can do other fine motor activities well.

The terms *verbal dyspraxia* and *speech dyspraxia* are used to describe very severe communication problems that interfere with an individual's ability to speak clearly or to get words in the right order, even though individual sounds can be produced accurately, the muscles of speech work perfectly normally when they are used for eating and swallowing activities, and there is no basic learning disorder in regard to grammar.

SYMPTOMS

Children with these dyspraxias are sometimes described as having "garbled speech." They may be difficult or even impossible for their parents to understand. In speech dyspraxia, others cannot recognize what word the child is trying to say; in verbal dyspraxia, the words themselves may be all in the wrong order so that even if others can understand single words, they still cannot make sense of what the child is trying to say.

No single cause for these conditions is known. It has long been recognized that boys are much more likely to have these problems than girls. A child diagnosed with this type of problem has normal intelligence, and usually there are no indications of any other neurological disorder such as cerebral palsy, autism, or any type of mental retardation. Unfortunately, one characteristic of children with these problems is that they do not respond to speech therapy.

DIAGNOSIS AND ALTERNATIVE COMMUNICATION

Because of the poor response to therapy, health care professionals are reluctant to make this diagnosis very early. Once the diagnosis is made, however, the search should begin for alternative methods of communication, such as handwriting, typewriters or word processors, or even electronic speech synthesizers, which are now available. Although the provision of such augmentative communication aids does not mean that speech therapy has to be stopped, it does provide a "safety net" for the child if later on it is clear that therapy is not helping.

Although your speech-language pathologist may well suspect the diagnosis, and there are a number of tests used to identify the disorder, none of the tests is absolutely reliable. Eventually the diagnosis has to be made at a clinical level, that is to say on the basis of experience and the exclusion of various other conditions that might produce the same sort of difficulties for a child.

continues

continued

For this reason, it is important that when this diagnosis is made your child should be seen by a developmental/behavioral pediatrician or a pediatric neurologist. Although neurological investigations do not usually show anything, the physician involved may want to discuss with you genetic testing, magnetic resonance neuroimaging (a picture of the brain, requiring general anesthetic), a brain wave test [electroencephalogram (EEG)], and possibly other biochemical tests, as well.

You may want to contact the National Organization for Apraxia and Dyspraxia at 7675 Charter Oak Drive, Pensacola, Florida 32154. Their telephone number is (904) 478-4895.

Notes:

Courtesy of A. Mervyn Fox, MB, BS, FRCP(C), DCH, Developmental Paediatrician, London, Ontario, Canada.

General Information about Visual Impairments

DEFINITION

The terms *partially sighted, low vision, legally blind*, and *totally blind* are used in the educational context to describe people with visual impairments. They are defined as follows:

- *Partially sighted* indicates that some type of visual problem has resulted in a need for special education.
- *Low vision* generally refers to a severe visual impairment, not necessarily limited to distance vision. Low vision applies to all individuals with sight who are unable to read the newspaper at a normal viewing distance, even with the aid of eyeglasses or contact lenses. They use a combination of vision and other senses to learn, although they may require adaptations in lighting, the size of print, and, sometimes, Braille.
- *Legally blind* indicates that a person has less than 20/200 vision in the better eye or a very limited field of vision (20 degrees at its widest point).
- *Totally blind* refers to people who learn via Braille or other nonvisual media.

Visual impairment is the consequence of a functional loss of vision, rather than an eye disorder itself. Eye disorders that can lead to visual impairments include retinal degeneration, albinism, cataracts, glaucoma, muscular problems that result in visual disturbances, corneal disorders, diabetic retinopathy, congenital disorders, and infection.

INCIDENCE

The rate at which visual impairments occur in children under the age of 18 is 12.2 per 1,000. Severe visual impairments (legally or totally blind) occur at a rate of 0.06 per 1,000.

CHARACTERISTICS

The effect of visual problems on a child's development depends on the severity, type of loss, age at which the condition appears, and overall functioning level of the child. Many children who have multiple disabilities may also have visual impairments resulting in motor, cognitive, and social developmental delays.

A young child with visual impairments has little reason to explore interesting objects in the environment, and thus may miss opportunities to have experiences and to learn. This lack of exploration may continue until learning becomes motivating or until intervention begins.

continues

continued

Because the child cannot see parents or peers, he or she may be unable to imitate social behavior or understand nonverbal cues. Visual impairments can create obstacles to a growing child's independence.

EDUCATIONAL IMPLICATIONS

Children with visual impairments should be assessed early to benefit from early intervention programs, when applicable. Technology in the form of computers and low-vision optical and video aids enable many children who are partially sighted, have low vision, or are blind to participate in regular class activities. Large print materials, books on tape, and braille books are available.

Children with visual impairments may need additional help with special equipment and modifications in the regular curriculum to emphasize listening skills, communication, orientation and mobility, vocation and career options, and daily living skills. Children with low vision or who are legally blind may need help in using their residual vision more efficiently and in working with special aids and materials. Children who have visual impairments combined with other types of disabilities have a greater need for an interdisciplinary approach and may require greater emphasis on self-care and daily living skills.

Notes:

Source: *General Information about Visual Impairments*, National Information Center for Children and Youth with Disabilities (NICHCY), Washington, DC.

General Information about Spina Bifida

DEFINITION

Spina bifida means cleft spine, which is an incomplete closure in the spinal column. In general, the three types of spina bifida (from mild to severe) are:

1. **Spina bifida occulta.** There is an opening in one or more of the vertebrae (bones) of the spinal column without apparent damage to the spinal cord.

2. **Meningocele.** The meninges, or protective covering around the spinal cord, has pushed out through the opening in the vertebrae in a sac called the "meningocele." However, the spinal cord remains intact. This form can be repaired with little or no damage to the nerve pathways.

3. **Myelomeningocele.** This form is the most severe, in which a portion of the spinal cord protrudes through the back. In some cases, sacs are covered with skin; in others, tissue and nerves are exposed. Generally, the terms "spina bifida" and "myelomeningocele" are used interchangeably.

INCIDENCE

Approximately 40 percent of all Americans may have spina bifida occulta, but because they experience little or no symptoms, very few of them ever know that they have it. The other two types of spina bifida, meningocele and myelomeningocele, are known collectively as "spina bifida manifesta," and occur in approximately 1 out of every 1,000 births. Of the babies born with spina bifida manifesta, about 4 percent have the meningocele form, while about 96 percent have the myelomeningocele form.

CHARACTERISTICS

The effects of myelomeningocele, the most serious form of spina bifida, may include muscle weakness or paralysis below the area of the spine where the incomplete closure (or cleft) occurs, loss of sensation below the cleft, and loss of bowel and bladder control. In addition, fluid may build up and cause an accumulation of fluid in the brain (a condition known as hydrocephalus). Many children (70 percent to 90 percent) born with myelomeningocele have hydrocephalus. Hydrocephalus is controlled by a surgical procedure called "shunting," which relieves the fluid buildup in the brain. Hydrocephalus may occur without spina bifida, but the two conditions often occur together. If a drain (shunt) is not implanted, the pressure buildup from hydrocephalus can cause brain damage, seizures, or blindness.

continues

continued

Although spina bifida is relatively common, until recently most children born with myelomeningocele died shortly after birth. Now that surgery to drain spinal fluid and protect children against hydrocephalus can be performed in the first 48 hours of life, children with myelomeningocele are much more likely to live. Quite often, however, they must have a series of operations throughout their childhood.

Many children with myelomeningocele need training to learn to manage their bowel and bladder functions. Some require catheterization, or the insertion of a tube to permit passage of urine.

EDUCATIONAL IMPLICATIONS

Most children with spina bifida do not have learning disabilities. But in some cases, children with spina bifida who also have a history of hydrocephalus experience learning problems. They may have difficulty with paying attention, expressing or understanding language, and grasping reading and math. Early intervention with children who experience learning problems can help considerably to prepare them for school.

Mainstreaming, or successful integration of a child with spina bifida into a school attended by nondisabled children, sometimes requires changes in school equipment or the curriculum. Although student placement should be in the least restrictive environment, the day-to-day school pattern also should be as "normal" as possible.

Children with myelomeningocele need to learn mobility skills, and they often use crutches, braces, or wheelchairs. It is important that all members of the school team and the parents understand the child's physical capabilities and limitations. Physical disabilities like spina bifida can have profound effects on a child's emotional and social development. To promote personal growth, families and teachers should encourage children, within the limits of safety and health, to be independent and to participate in activities with their nondisabled classmates.

Notes:

Source: *General Information about Spina Bifida*, National Information Center for Children and Youth with Disabilities (NICHCY), Washington, DC.

General Information about Hydrocephalus

WHAT IS HYDROCEPHALUS?

Hydrocephalus is an abnormal accumulation of fluid—cerebrospinal fluid (CSF)—within cavities called ventricles inside the brain. CSF is produced in the ventricles, circulates through the ventricular system, and is absorbed into the bloodstream. CSF is in constant circulation and has many important functions. It surrounds the brain and spinal cord and acts as a protective cushion against injury. CSF contains nutrients and proteins that are needed for the nourishment and normal function of the brain. It also carries waste products away from surrounding tissues. Hydrocephalus occurs when there is an imbalance between the amount of CSF that is produced and the rate at which it is absorbed. As the CSF builds up, it causes the ventricles to enlarge and the pressure inside the head to increase.

WHAT CAUSES HYDROCEPHALUS?

Hydrocephalus that is congenital (present at birth) is thought to be caused by a complex interaction of genetic and environmental factors. Aqueductal stenosis, an obstruction of the cerebral aqueduct, is the most frequent cause of congenital hydrocephalus. Acquired hydrocephalus may result from spina bifida, intraventricular hemorrhage, meningitis, head trauma, tumors, and cysts. Hydrocephalus affects about 1 in every 500 children born.

HOW IS HYDROCEPHALUS TREATED?

There is no known way to prevent or cure hydrocephalus. To date, the most effective treatment is surgical insertion of a shunt. A shunt is a flexible tube placed into the ventricular system that diverts the flow of CSF into another region of the body where it can be absorbed. A valve within the shunt maintains the CSF at normal pressure within the ventricles. This procedure is performed by a neurosurgeon, preferably one who specializes in pediatrics.

WHAT ARE THE EFFECTS OF HYDROCEPHALUS?

In most cases, shunting successfully controls hydrocephalus. In many children, hydrocephalus does not affect intelligence or physical development, but some children with hydrocephalus are slower in acquiring such skills as eye-hand coordination and in learning to walk. Shunt malfunctions and infections, developmental delays, and learning disabilities are not uncommon. Families need to be aware of the complexities of hydrocephalus to ensure their child receives comprehensive, ongoing care.

Courtesy of Hydrocephalus Association, San Francisco, California.

Surgery—Back Closure

Call the neurosurgeon if you notice any of the following:

- Problems at the site of surgery (on the back)

  - Redness

  - Fluid leaking

  - Bulging

- Fever

- Irritability

- Sleeping more than usual

Notes:

Source: Marjorie Szor, MA, MS, RNC, Myelomeningocele Clinical Nurse Specialist, Spina Bifida Center, Medical College Hospitals, Toledo, Ohio, © 1990.

Guidelines for Detecting Shunt Malfunction or Infection

SHUNT MALFUNCTION

Call your doctor if you notice any of the following signs or symptoms lasting longer than a few days. These may be <u>subtle</u>, very slight changes.

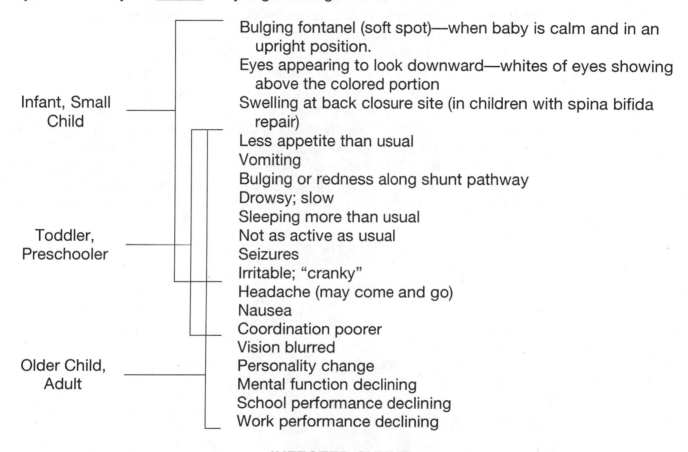

Infant, Small Child
- Bulging fontanel (soft spot)—when baby is calm and in an upright position.
- Eyes appearing to look downward—whites of eyes showing above the colored portion
- Swelling at back closure site (in children with spina bifida repair)

Toddler, Preschooler
- Less appetite than usual
- Vomiting
- Bulging or redness along shunt pathway
- Drowsy; slow
- Sleeping more than usual
- Not as active as usual
- Seizures
- Irritable; "cranky"

Older Child, Adult
- Headache (may come and go)
- Nausea
- Coordination poorer
- Vision blurred
- Personality change
- Mental function declining
- School performance declining
- Work performance declining

INFECTED SHUNT

- Call your neurosurgeon immediately if you notice any of the following skin conditions:
  Along the shunt pathway
  - –Redness
  - –Tenderness
  - –Skin opening, ulceration, or a sore

  At either incision site
  - –Drainage
- Call your neurosurgeon if fever (above 99° axillary) occurs within two weeks after your surgery.

Source: Marjorie Szor, MA, MS, RNC, Myelomeningocele Clinical Nurse Specialist, Spina Bifida Center, Medical College Hospitals, Toledo, Ohio, © 1990.

Tethered Cord

WHAT IT IS

The spinal cord becomes tethered when it adheres to the surrounding tissue at the bottom of the spinal column. Normally, the cord floats freely in the surrounding CSF (cerebrospinal fluid). This could happen because the cord adheres to scar tissue from the back closure surgery done shortly after birth, or it could come from small cysts or fatty tumors such as lipomeningocele. This progressive scarring (adhesions) ties down the spinal cord so that when the person bends over, moves about, or grows, the cord is stretched. The small blood vessels supplying nourishment to the cord are stretched, too. This interferes with the blood supply to the cord.

While all persons who have had their backs closed because of spina bifida are at risk for tethered cord, not all will show symptoms. It could mean the difference between walking without the need for bracing or crutches and needing aid for ambulating. Symptoms are most likely to occur at times of rapid growth, though they can occur at any time. It is very important to notice any slight decreases in function and to bring these to the attention of the medical team. A myelo clinic appointment needs to be made when you notice the following signs and they cannot be attributed to something else.

SIGNS

Watch for the following signs in your child:

- increased difficulty in walking
- less strength in feet and/or legs
- pain in the back, down the leg, or around the back and abdomen
- spasticity in lower extremities
- worsening scoliosis
- decrease in bowel and/or bladder control

There can be other reasons for the above signs. Therefore, it is important that your child be examined on a regular basis in the clinic. Manual muscle testing by the physical therapist aids in a diagnosis. The neurosurgeon, orthopedist, urologist, and physical therapist may confer to determine a diagnosis. The changes may be subtle and could be missed by you or other caregivers.

TREATMENT

If it has been determined that tethering of the spinal cord is causing loss of function, the neurosurgeon may recommend untethering surgery. This releases the tether but may not bring back all of the function that has disappeared, especially if there has been a long period of

continues

continued

deterioration and much function loss before surgery. It should relieve any pain, however, and should prevent continued decrease in function. Because other problems, such as bladder infection, weight gain, hip dislocation, poorly fitting shoes and braces, and hydromyelia (water-filled cord) can also cause signs of function loss, regular evaluation by the myelo team is helpful. This is true not only in noticing slight changes but also in determining whether tethered cord is the likely cause.

Notes:

Source: Marjorie Szor, MA, MS, RNC, Myelomeningocele Clinical Nurse Specialist, Spina Bifida Center, Medical College Hospitals, Toledo, Ohio, © 1993.

Chiari II Malformation

WHAT IT IS

Chiari II malformation, an abnormality of the back part of the brain (hindbrain), is associated with spina bifida. In fact, most neurosurgeons believe that almost all persons with spina bifida have this malformation; however, only about 25 percent of persons with spina bifida have symptoms and are affected by it. Possible causes have been debated and much discussion has taken place, but there is still no agreement on why this occurs. In the past it was called Arnold-Chiari malformation (ACM), and you still may hear references to that name, though Chiari II is now considered the correct term.

Several features are included in this condition. The area housing the hindbrain or the back part of the brain is too small. This forces the lower part of the cerebellum (part of the hindbrain) downward through the opening in the skull into the upper neck area. A portion of the brainstem (another part of the hindbrain) is also squeezed downward into a very tight area of the spine. The fourth ventricle is lengthened and also enters the cervical (neck) canal.

This means that several important structures are compressed into a small space. It also means that the lower cranial nerves that extend from the brainstem have to stretch back upward to find their usual route, and thus their function may be disturbed. The portion of the brainstem that is lengthened may become kinked; this can occur with the fourth ventricle as well.

Chiari II is a condition that is poorly understood but can be a complicating factor in spina bifida. Usually, it does not cause symptoms—which seems surprising—and when it does, rarely are they serious. The lower into the upper spine area the portions of the hindbrain go, the more likely the person is to have symptoms. The occurrence of symptoms seems to bear no relationship to the level of the myelomeningocele lesion, however.

WHAT TO LOOK FOR

The symptoms of Chiari II come from abnormalities in one or all of the following areas: the cerebellum, the fourth ventricle, the lower part of the brainstem, and/or the neck area of the spinal cord. Each area produces different symptoms. The age of the child is another factor that influences the type of symptoms. Below is a partial listing. Those found, for the most part, in newborns, infants, and very young children are listed first; whereas, farther down the list are symptoms generally found in older children:

- weak cry
- noisy breathing, especially when breathing in and when crying (could be confused with croup)
- apnea—periods of not breathing
- unusual breathing patterns
- blue lips or blue tinge around mouth
- poor sucking

continues

continued

- gagging
- difficulty swallowing
- drooling
- choking
- spitting up—regurgitation through mouth or nose
- vomiting
- reflux—backing up of stomach contents, some of which may go into the lungs causing pneumonia
- pneumonia—frequent bouts
- backward arching of neck
- eye jerking
- loss of some head control
- arm weakness, stiffness
- tingling in arms, hands
- facial weakness
- hoarseness (voice changes)
- neck pain
- headaches starting in the neck area
- vision disturbances
- balance problems

DIAGNOSIS

In infants these symptoms can increase quickly in a period of a few days. In older children they are more likely to progress slowly. The symptoms can be caused by problems other than Chiari II; however, the neurosurgeon needs input from the parents and from the other members of the myelo team to determine a diagnosis. Observations from the pediatrician and physical therapist are of particular importance.

An MRI (magnetic resonance imaging) is valuable as it can provide an accurate image of the base of the skull; however, a person who has very abnormal findings on the MRI may not show any symptoms. Manual muscle testing of the arms performed by the physical therapist is also helpful. A shunt malfunction or a cyst in the spinal cord both need to be ruled out as the cause of the symptoms. A diagnosis is not always easy to make.

TREATMENT

In many cases, if the symptoms are not serious, close follow up with the myelo team is all that is required. If the symptoms are serious and are progressing, decompression surgery will be considered; however, not all patients with symptoms will require surgery. Opinions often vary on whether or not to operate. Of course, the clearer it is that the symptoms are related to Chiari II,

continues

continued

the more generally accepted is the opinion to operate. Surgery slows the progression of symptoms, and, in some cases where the symptoms are light, there may even be some improvement. Older children and those with less severe symptoms seem to benefit the most from the surgery. Most children with spina bifida, however, do not show a rapid progression of symptoms.

Decompression surgery relieves the pressure on the part of the brain that has been squeezed downward. A laminectomy is performed in the upper neck region. A portion of one or more vertebrae is removed to unroof the area over the abnormally low-positioned hindbrain. This opens the area, creates more space, and allows CSF (cerebrospinal fluid) to flow more normally. After surgery, care must be taken for a few days to support the neck muscles. This prevents stress on the incision and reduces discomfort. A soft cervical collar is worn until the neck muscles are strong enough to hold the head well. Physical therapy helps to improve head control and strengthen the upper body.

OUTLOOK

The leading cause of death and serious disability in spina bifida is the Chiari II malformation. Most children will not show symptoms, but it is important for parents of children with spina bifida to be aware of the potential for developing symptoms. In the first few weeks of life, symptoms can progress quickly with fatal outcomes. Babies can die, even with treatment. Therefore, it is necessary that parents understand the condition and provide careful monitoring of symptoms. Regular follow up throughout life for evaluation by the myelo team is required. Though some persons need surgery, others will be able to adapt, to manage the difficulties, and in time the problem may resolve.

UNDERSTANDING

To increase your awareness of this condition, it is helpful to read more in-depth material about it. The SBAA (Spina Bifida Association of America) and the myelo clinic are sources for written information as well as video- and audiotapes. Attending regional and national conferences is an excellent way to learn the latest information on spina bifida. Talking with other parents or persons with spina bifida is another opportunity for gaining insight into this condition. Nationally, there is a parent network that has proved helpful to many families. There is no fee for joining. You may write to:

> Chiari Family Network
> 67 Spring St.
> Weymouth, MA 02188 (or call 617-337-2368)

In addition, write down questions for the myelo team doctors, especially the neurosurgeon and pediatrician. Go over the information with them until you feel comfortable with your understanding

continues

continued

of it. It is a good idea to repeat to them, in your own words, your understanding. This is a complex condition. In the past it was poorly understood, but now can be explained somewhat better. If you need access to material, talk with the myelo clinical nurse specialist.

SUMMARY

It is important that you learn what you can about Chiari II, that you are alert to the development of any symptoms, and that you are aware of progression of these symptoms. Notify the neurosurgeon of your observations. Regular follow up in the clinic for evaluation by the team is essential.

It is especially important that parents of newborns pay close attention to the development of symptoms. In infancy this condition can be the most serious. Although most persons with spina bifida do not have symptoms of Chiari II, if they do and the symptoms are progressive, surgery may be considered.

Notes:

Source: Marjorie Szor, MA, MS, RNC, Myelomeningocele Clinical Nurse Specialist, Spina Bifida Center, Medical College Hospitals, Toledo, Ohio, © 1993.

Latex Allergy

Many children with spina bifida are sensitive to products made of latex rubber. Contact with these items can cause serious reactions in certain children. In some instances, death has occurred.

WHO IS AT RISK?

When these deaths and reactions were investigated, it was found that the group of children to be at highest risk were those with spina bifida. Those who had several surgeries and/or a history of allergies themselves or in the family were most at risk.

WHY IS IT OCCURRING?

Only in the last few years has this become a widespread problem. Latex products, such as rubber gloves and condoms, are used much more now than in the past, due to the need for protection against HIV infection. Also, some experts believe that something has changed either in the raw material or in the processing of latex, and that is why now more people have developed reactions.

WHAT IS LATEX?

Latex is natural rubber—the milky sap from the Hevea brasiliensis tree. After the sap is drained from the tree, it is treated with chemicals to make it durable and pliable. Often it is a tan, natural color and is thin and stretchy. Examples of items made of latex are exam gloves, balloons, and condoms. To form hard rubber, latex is processed further. Latex can be found everywhere.

WHY THOSE WITH SPINA BIFIDA?

Persons with spina bifida are more likely than others to have reactions to latex. Why this is so is not really known, but medical professionals have suggested that it may be because these people have more surgeries, are hospitalized more often and, in the past, were catheterized regularly using rubber catheters.

WHAT IS A REACTION?

An allergic reaction is a response by the body to a certain substance (the allergen, e.g., latex, pollen, dust). When the body comes in contact with this substance, it releases a chemical that causes symptoms. If the item made of latex (or even of harder rubber) touches a mucous membrane (lining of the mouth, urethra, vagina, rectum), there is a greater likelihood of a reaction. Wet or damp skin coming in contact with latex also increases the chance of a reaction. The

continues

continued

symptoms listed below could indicate an allergic response to an allergen. Keep in mind that these symptoms could occur with an allergic response to any substance. They are not specific just to latex. If the symptoms occur after exposure or contact with something made of latex, then it is more likely that latex is the culprit. Be careful when trying to pin down the cause of the reactions. Certainly, if these occur every time contact with latex is made, it is easier to assume the cause. Also, these symptoms can be caused by many things other than an allergic response, such as a cold or other infection.

Signs and Symptoms of Allergic Response

- Itching of lips after blowing up a balloon, after dental work
- Swelling of lips after blowing up a balloon, after dental work
- Swelling of penis or genital area after catheterization, after an exam
- Redness
- Blistering
- Itching of eyes (child rubs them)
- Sneezing
- Nasal drip
- Rash
- Hives
- Redness, itching, swelling of any part of body
- Difficulty breathing (tightness in chest, hard to catch breath)
- Sudden, serious drop in blood pressure; fast pulse
- Unconsciousness
- Death

Important: Someone who has never had a reaction could change at any time to being a positive reactor. Having a negative response in the past does not ensure that child of remaining negative.

PREVENTION

Repeated exposure to items made of latex is thought to contribute to developing an allergic reaction to it. Therefore, it is important to limit such contact, starting when your child is a newborn. You cannot eliminate it totally, but with exposure cut to a minimum, you may be able to *prevent* an allergy. With limited exposure, your child may never develop reactions to latex. If your child with spina bifida receives care at a hospital, make sure his or her care will include latex precautions, which means that the environment will be free of latex. This protection is advisable for those who

continues

continued

have never had a reaction as well as for those who have. For negative reactors, it will reduce the amount of exposure and possibly prevent their ever becoming positive. For those with a positive history, it will help to prevent possible serious reactions.

Eliminating exposure to latex is important not only in the hospital but also in the home, the school, the dentist's office, therapy areas, and so forth. Caregivers in these areas need to be informed.

In addition to items made of latex, bananas and avocados should be avoided. They do not contain any latex, but there is a cross-sensitivity. Some children who have had reactions to latex also react to these fruits. Two other foods that have shown this are kiwi fruit and chestnuts. Latex paint does *not* have natural latex in it, according to the Sherwin Williams Company. Chewing gum, according to the Wrigley Company, does *not* contain natural latex. Often it is difficult to tell if a product is made of latex. Recently, some companies have agreed to label their products, but labeling is still rare.

RECOMMENDATIONS

If your child has **not** had symptoms in the past:

- **Avoid all products made of latex. Use substitutes.**
- Inform all medical and dental caregivers, therapists, teachers, and babysitters. Inform lab technicians when blood is drawn that cloth (a sleeve) needs to cover the skin under the tourniquet. Persons who draw blood do not always know a child has spina bifida.
- Teach your child to recognize latex and to communicate with his or her caregivers about the need to avoid it.

If your child **has** had symptoms in the past:

- **Do not have contact with latex. Use substitutes.**
- Inform all medical and dental caregivers, therapists, and babysitters. Inform lab technicians when blood is drawn that cloth (a sleeve) needs to cover the skin under the tourniquet. Persons who draw blood do not always know a child has spina bifida.
- Teach your child to recognize latex and to communicate with his or her caregivers about the need to not come in contact with it.
- Share with caregivers a list of substitutes for latex items.
- Whenever questioned about any allergies, inform the questioner about the need for latex precautions.
- Carry vinyl gloves with you. Supply them in an emergency.
- Carry a letter with you (from the myelo team) to explain the problem of latex sensitivity to caregivers, if they should ask for more information. You could show them a copy of this handout, as well.

continues

continued

- Learn to recognize products made of latex quickly. If unsure, ask questions. Call the company who makes the product, if necessary.
- Request a private room for your child when he or she is hospitalized, if this is possible. Particles of latex from items used in the care of a roommate may become airborne and cause difficulties (especially with breathing). Balloons are of particular concern. If a private room is not available, request that all rubber items be removed from the roommate's side as well.
- Be sure signs are placed over your child's hospital bed and on the chart stating "latex precautions."
- Request that surgery be scheduled as the first case of the day in a particular operating room. This will reduce the amount of airborne latex particles present. The operating room needs to be latex free.
- Discuss with the surgeon and/or anesthesiologist prophylaxis by medication 24 hours before surgery. The drugs used are an antihistamine and a steroid.
- Keep an antihistamine on hand at home to use in case of a mild reaction.
- Discuss with the medical director of the myelo team the advisability of having injectable epinephrine also on hand to use in case of a severe reaction.
- Have your child wear a medical alert necklace or bracelet. Order forms are available from the clinic or can be found at pharmacies.
- Report any reactions to the medical director of the myelo team. Latex reactions are being recorded at the Centers for Disease Control (a U.S. government health agency).

Keep watching for new developments in this area. It is possible that changes will be made and that latex will be processed differently, products will be labeled more fully, or a more reliable, yet safe method of testing for the allergy will be developed. In the meantime, be quick to recognize latex items, keep your child from contacting it, substitute with other materials, and inform other people as needed.

It may be impossible to eliminate all contact with latex completely, since it is found everywhere, but it is most important, indeed imperative, that exposure be so low that the risk of an allergic reaction is minimal.

Source: Marjorie Szor, MA, MS, RNC, Myelomeningocele Clinical Nurse Specialist, Spina Bifida Center, Medical College Hospitals, Toledo, Ohio, © 1993.

Products Made of Latex and Suggested Substitutes

Contain LATEX—Do NOT Use	Use
Baby bottle nipples	Silicone or vinyl nipples: Clear and Soft (Gerber) Soft Flex (MAM) (Evenflo)

Pacifiers	Silicone or vinyl pacifiers:
	Clear and Soft (Gerber)
	Pur (Infa)
	Soft Flex (MAM)
	                  (Kip)
	                  (Binky)

Teething toys	Cloth, plastic, vinyl
Changing pad (rubber)	Cloth pad
Mattress cover (rubber)	Cloth pad
Latex gloves	Vinyl gloves, Baggies
Finger cots	Vinyl gloves, Baggies
Tape—Cloth adhesive, Band Aids, butterfly closures, moleskin, Coban	Plastic, silk, paper, steri strips, Dermicel hypoallergenic cloth tape, J&J waterproof tape, 3M tape, Microfoam, Micropore, Blenderm, Durapore, Transpore
Band Aids	Gauze with the above tape
Catheters, red rubber	PVC, clear plastic, Argyle Rob Nel
Diapers with elastic	Velco closure diapers, cloth
Toys (rubber)	Vinyl, plastic, cloth, wood
Balloons	Mylar (foil) balloons
Balls—rubber, tennis, Koosh	Vinyl, plastic balls, Throton sports ball
Water toys—swim and scuba equipment, goggles, rubber ducky	Plastic, vinyl
Bathing cap	
Playdough from McDonald's Happy Meal	
Racquet handles	Vinyl or leather handles—wrap handle with another material

continues

continued

Contain LATEX—Do NOT Use	Use
Zip in Ziploc Bag (some)	Baggies
Wheelchair cushion (rubber, Roho)	Cover with cloth
Wheelchair tires	Touch only the metal ring, wear gloves
Crutch arm pads, hand pads	Cover with cloth, terry cloth "footies"
Foam lining (some) of braces, shells	Cloth, felt over lining
Milkweed plant	Do not touch
Bananas, avocados, kiwi fruit, water chestnuts	May by a cross-sensitivity
Rubber cement	Glue
Erasers	Do not put end in mouth, use "whiteout" correction fluid
Rubber bands	String, ties
Condoms	Natural skin (lambskin) condom *under* latex condom, if male is sensitive to latex Natural skin (lambskin) over latex condom if female is sensitive to latex
Diaphragm for birth control	Use another birth control form
Cleaning/kitchen gloves	Vinyl, cotton liners
Sneakers	Wear sox
Rubber boots, raincoats	Vinyl raincoat, boots
Elastic—sox, bra	Sox without elastic or may be worn if elastic covered with cloth
Spandex stretch fabric	Clothing without it
Air mattress	Plastic air mattress
Foam pillow	Poly-fill, Dacron, feather, down

Source: Marjorie Szor, MA, MS, RNC, Myelomeningocele Clinical Nurse Specialist, Spina Bifida Center, Medical College Hospital, Toledo, Ohio, © 1993.

Developmental Strategies for Children with Spina Bifida— Birth through 2 Years

- Regular evaluation by myelo team at least every 3 months
- Mother and father emotional bonding established with infant
- Immunizations begun
- Recordkeeping system begun
- Infant stimulation techniques used
- Community early intervention opportunities used to promote development
- Changes in food textures accepted
- Developmental milestones monitored
- Parental understanding of bowel management begun:
  - soft, well-formed stool consistency maintained
  - effects of certain foods, medicines, fluids noted
  - regular timing established
- Playing alongside other children begun
- Mobility begun (self and by others)
- Occasional separation from parents occurring
- Can comfortably discuss child's abilities and disabilities

Notes:

Source: Marjorie Szor, MA, MS, RNC, Myelomeningocele Clinical Nurse Specialist, Spina Bifida Center, © Medical College Hospitals, Toledo, Ohio.

Developmental Strategies for Children with Spina Bifida— 3 through 6 Years

In addition to items listed in birth to 2 years handout:

- Attends myelo clinic at least every 6 months for regular checkups by the myelo team
- Hygiene managed to some extent by child:
  - washes own hands, face (entire body later on)
  - brushes teeth (however, an adult needs to brush child's teeth afterward)
  - asks for assistance as soon as soiled (if still in diapers)
- Feeds self; does not snack excessively
- Skin checks done daily with parental supervision; understands why skin needs to be protected
- Regular bedtimes established
- Dental visits begun
- Immunization schedule followed
- Developmental milestones monitored
- Proper weight maintained
- Dressing self mastered
- Mobility managed by self:
  - stands by self or in parapodium
  - propels self if in wheelchair
  - applies braces by self
  - transfers self to and from wheelchair
- Bowel management completed by entry to kindergarten
- Clean intermittent catheterization (CIC) (if necessary) performed by child, with timing reminders from adult; if help required, it is preferred that same-sex parent provide assistance
  - modesty, privacy maintained
  - out of diapers by entry to kindergarten
- Is physically active on a daily basis
- Socializes with friends through play
- Verbalizes basic understanding of spina bifida
- Is encouraged to talk openly with empathetic parents about his or her feelings relating to being "different"
- Is expected to make simple decisions and is held to the outcomes
  - (e.g., choice of clothing to wear for the day, choice of flavor of ice cream, choice of bedtime story)
- Is allowed experiences in which problem solving is necessary
  - (e.g., how to retrieve an out-of-reach toy, how to get from one place to another when obstacles are in the way)

Source: Marjorie Szor, MA, MS, RNC, Myelomeningocele Clinical Nurse Specialist, Spina Bifida Center, © Medical College Hospitals, Toledo, Ohio.

Developmental Strategies for Children with Spina Bifida— 7 through 12 Years

In addition to items listed in 3 to 6 year handout:

- Attends myelo clinic at least every 6 months for regular checkups by the myelo team
- Can discuss health concerns with team members with appropriate input from a parent
- Cares for own hygiene needs—bathing, brushing teeth, etc.
- Appropriate bathroom adaptations made to encourage privacy and independence
- Dresses self completely; applies own braces
- Has regular bedtime
- Is out of diapers
- Manages bowel routine successfully:
  – can state three influences on bowel activity
  – can state specifically what he or she does to aid bowel management
- Catheterizes self (if needed), and does so with minimal prompting
- Completes toileting by leaving self and bathroom clean
- Maintains modesty and privacy when toileting
- Initiates self-care routines with little prompting
- Eats foods with regard to the sections of the "food group pyramid"
- Keeps weight within normal range
- Participates in vigorous physical activity daily
- Can state three symptoms of an allergic response to latex; reminds caregivers of latex precautions
- Knows what medicines he or she takes and why
- Does own daily skin checks with occasional supervision; knows why they are needed
- Does pressure releases and small shifts of body weight (if in wheelchair) every 15 minutes
- Can explain to others, in his or her own words, what spina bifida is
- Can state three possible symptoms of a urinary tract infection
- Can state three possible symptoms of a shunt malfunction
- Plays frequently with friends; belongs to a peer group (e.g., Scouts, 4H, church group)
- Spends periods of time away from parents easily
- Is developing special interests, activities
- Is responsible for a share of household tasks
- Manages own money—allowances, gifts, etc.
- Can state what he or she would like to be when grown up
- Participates in family decision making
- Makes an increased number of decisions for which he or she is held accountable
- Solves problems with greater skill

Source: Marjorie Szor, MA, MS, RNC, Myelomeningocele Clinical Nurse Specialist, Spina Bifida Center, © Medical College Hospitals, Toledo, Ohio.

Developmental Strategies for Teenagers with Spina Bifida

In addition to items listed in 7 to 12 year handout:

- Attends myelo clinic for regular evaluation at least once a year; understands importance of follow-up care in preventing complications; can discuss concerns with team members with parent out of room by age 16
- Manages own care: dressing, bracing, bathing, etc.
- Monitors and maintains physical appearance and body hygiene
- Manages bowels effectively: stools easy to pass on the toilet, stools occurring once a day or no less than once every 3 days, accidents less often than once a month
- Can list five possible ways to regulate bowels
- Practices four techniques that will help to prevent skin breakdown
- Can state the importance of folic acid in the diet
- Can state names of all medicines he or she takes, their actions, doses, and schedule; remembers to take own medications with little supervision
- Can state five products made of latex and alternatives to these
- Can explain what spina bifida is in more depth than previously
- Knows how to order own supplies and medicines
- Cleans own room, cooks occasionally, shares household cleaning tasks; kitchen adaptations have been made
- Has developed special interests/hobbies/activities and participates in these
- Takes advantage of social opportunities
- Increases circle of friends; has two or three close friends
- Socializes with members of the opposite sex
- Has increasing understanding of sexual functioning and is able to discuss this with family members, doctors, and other team members
- Understands role of genetics in occurrence of spina bifida and the personal risk factor involved
- Expresses goals for the future; is developing plans to achieve these
- Explores career options through school career fairs, library, resource people in the community
- Explores college programs; takes high school courses required for a selected college program
- Understands vocational assistance available
- Is involved with BVR (Bureau for Vocational Rehabilitation) at age 16
- Begins process at age 16 to obtain driver's license
- Becomes involved in early work experiences—volunteering, summer jobs, part-time work
- Experiences earning money
- Manages own finances, including saving
- Increases time spent away from parents; manages safely at home alone for much of a day and feels secure; performs self-care adequately; handles emergencies
- Is involved in situations and activities requiring more complex decision making and problem solving

Source: Marjorie Szor, MA, MS, RNC, Myelomeningocele Clinical Nurse Specialist, Spina Bifida Center, © Medical College Hospitals, Toledo, Ohio.

Goals for Adult Self-Care for Spina Bifida

In addition to items listed in the handout for teenagers:

- Has established self with a primary adult care physician and visits myelo clinic as well, at least once a year
- Performs self-care, requiring no reminders or supervision
- Does own laundry and complete care of clothes
- Does share of grocery shopping, meal preparation, and cleanup
- Cleans and maintains living unit
- Does own banking and controls own finances
- Makes own decisions, but knows when to seek input from others in order to make an informed choice
- Solves problems with increasing skill
- Makes own appointments and keeps them
- Makes use of transportation services, if needed
- Takes multivitamin containing folic acid daily and understands reason for this (females)
- Orders own supplies and medicines; renews prescriptions before last dose
- Has developed assertiveness skills and can express self effectively
- Is able to advocate for self with confidence
- Is acquainted with community resources and uses them appropriately, when needed
- Has long-range goals; can express detailed steps for achieving goals
- Has employment or has entered college or a training program (after high school) to prepare for a vocation
- Is developing job search skills
- Is improving knowledge of important employee behavior
- Maintains ongoing satisfying relationships with family and friends
- Is aware of ability to participate in intimate, sexual relationships; can discuss potential concerns about sexual functioning with doctors and team members
- Is familiar with genetics counseling resources, if planning to have a family in the future
- Is aware of and sensitive to community issues; participates in community affairs

Notes:

Source: Marjorie Szor, MA, MS, RNC, Myelomeningocele Clinical Nurse Specialist, Spina Bifida Center, © Medical College Hospitals, Toledo, Ohio.

Preventing Skin Breakdown

Skin breakdown can be *very serious*. But the good news is that it does not have to happen. You *can* prevent it, if you do certain things on a daily basis. Responsibility for preventing skin sores is yours.

Nerves send messages of pain or discomfort to the brain. If they are working well, we receive in the brain those signals coming from the skin by way of the nerves and spinal cord. We then can act on this information (such as pain from coming in contact with something hot or discomfort from sitting too long in one spot) by changing our position or removing the source of discomfort. Because children with spina bifida lack normal sensation (nerve supply) in the lower part of the body, they do not feel everything that comes in contact with it or puts pressure on it. For this reason, they are at great risk for serious skin breakdown. They also are at risk because movement of their feet and legs is limited. This decreases blood circulation which, in turn, decreases nourishment of the skin. Scars from a previous sore are particularly weakened tissue as well. Even if such children have never been bothered with skin breakdown in the past, they are still at risk. In fact, as they become older, skin breakdown can become even more of a problem.

Skin ulcers (sores) can be caused by *pressure, burns, bumps, cuts, shearing, scrapes, friction,* and *stepping on something sharp*. If an area of skin, especially over a bony part, has something pressing against it, that area is deprived of an adequate blood supply. Not enough oxygen and nutrients can get to it, so it becomes weakened (unhealthy). The longer the pressure continues, the more weakened the skin becomes. A reddened area means there is pressure and should be cause for concern.

Keep in mind the following recommendations:

- Check skin daily for any of the following: redness; dry, cracked skin; and open, moist, or draining areas.
- Check everything that comes in contact with the skin and applies undue pressure.
- Use a mirror to check the child's buttocks and back.
- Shift the child's weight from side to side every 20 to 30 minutes while sitting and hold for 15 seconds—small shifts of weight.
- Lift the child up from the sitting position every 20 to 30 minutes and hold for 15 seconds—wheelchair pushups, pressure releases.
- Note if a reddened area does not go away 20 minutes after pressure is relieved, is dusky colored, or does not blanch (turn white) when pressed with a finger, and keep all pressure off that area. If the area is not gone in two to three days or worsens (red area enlarges, it is black in the center, there is blistering or drainage, or skin comes off), call the doctor.
- When the child receives a new brace, slowly increase the amount of time that it is worn. At first, have the child wear it for only 15 to 20 minutes. If no reddened areas are seen when removed, gradually increase the time period of wearing. Call the orthotist if red areas develop, so modifications may be made. Check skin frequently. Have the child continue to wear it only if the skin is clear.

continues

continued

- Have the child wear a clean, thin, close-fitting (with no seams or wrinkles) cotton shirt under a back brace. *Fabric softener (and certain laundry soaps) can be irritating. Rinse laundry well.*
- Ensure that the child exercises vigorously every day.
- Wash any open area with antibacterial soap (Dial, Safeguard, etc.).
- Cover any open area with a sterile dressing.
- Use a good cushion for a wheelchair.
- Use a good cushion when riding in a car.
- Remember to do weight shifts and pressure releases every 20 to 30 minutes while the child is in the car.
- Ensure that the child uses a properly fitted wheelchair. *Legs should not be higher than hips.*
- Lay the child on the abdomen (prone) as much as possible.
- Spread the child's weight evenly while sitting.
- Give special attention to the child's feet.
  - Wash feet daily. Dry well.
  - Avoid dry, cracked skin. Massage feet with lotion, but avoid overuse as feet should not remain damp.
  - Have the child wear clean, cotton (or wool) socks. Change daily.
  - Keep blisters from opening.
  - Check for long nails or sharp edges.
  - Trim nails only after soaking feet. Trim straight across to prevent hangnails.
  - Check feet after being outside in cold weather. Look at the bottom of the feet too. See that the child wears wool or polypropylene socks and lined boots in cold weather.
  - Prevent the child from dragging the feet or legs along a concrete pool bottom when swimming.
  - Have the child wear footwear when in a swimming area.
  - Check for wrinkles in socks or foreign objects in shoes.
  - Check for proper fit of shoes and braces.

Normally, there are many bacteria on the skin. When a break in the skin occurs, germs will get into the area and delay healing. If stool or urine gets into the area, it is very likely a sore will have a difficult time healing.

- Wash daily (use antibacterial soap). Dry well.
- Change diapers as soon as they are wet or soiled. Keep stool or urine from an open area.
- Ensure that the child is wearing clean clothes.
- Wash braces regularly.
- Call the doctor if swelling, warmth, or pus develops in a sore.

Skin ulcers also can be caused by shearing (rubbing), which happens when the skin moves in one direction and the underlying bone in another. To prevent shearing, be careful when making transfers. Avoid dragging the child. Lifting up and over is better.

continues

continued

Trauma is another cause of skin breakdown. Cuts, bumps, burns, or scrapes can all cause skin ulcers.

- Have the child wear shoes at all times.
- Avoid sharp objects.
- Avoid hot water bottles, electric blankets, heating pads, or being close to a radiator.
- Check bath water temperature.
- Check the temperature of metal seat belt buckles, vinyl upholstery, and other objects in the car when the car is hot. Park in the shade.
- Avoid leaving a wheelchair in the sun or near a fireplace. The frame can get hot.
- Have the child wear shoes at the beach. The sand can be very hot.
- Avoid placing hot cups or plates on the lap. Be careful of hot food, drinks, steam, and grease.
- Do not let the child carry hot liquids when walking.
- Do not let the child come too close to a campfire or fireplace.
- Do not let the child sit on something cold or hot, such as bleachers, the curb, steps, or a swing.
- Avoid staying outside in very cold weather (snow, ice, wind) for more than 30 minutes. Check the child's feet after coming in.
- Avoid cigarettes. Fallen ashes can cause serious burns; nicotine makes blood vessels smaller, and skin will not be well nourished.

Finally, a word about nutrition. Skin needs good nourishment to stay healthy. If the right foods are not eaten, a sore may develop from slight pressure or trauma, and it may become infected, taking a long time to heal. Be sure to include foods high in vitamin C in the daily diet. This vitamin—present especially in citrus fruits (oranges, grapefruits), tomatoes, broccoli, cantaloupe, collards, and potatoes—helps keep skin elastic, so if the skin is pulled, it stretches and goes back into shape without bruising or tearing. Protein—from meat, legumes (dried peas, beans, lentils), milk, and cheese—promotes tissue repair. Several glasses of water and other fluids are needed daily as well to keep the skin healthy.

It is easy to get a skin ulcer but difficult to get rid of it. Skin breakdown affects many aspects of a person's life—school attendance, work, involvement in activities, and the quality of lifestyle. It can really hold a person back. It could also mean many doctor visits, lengthy treatments, lengthy hospitalizations, and possible amputations. Treatment for skin breakdown results in financial hardship too. A study of 75 people with spina bifida showed they required 202 hospital admissions

continues

continued

for a total of 6,000 days. This resulted in spending $2,000,000 just to cover hospital costs (in the 1970s).

The magnitude of the problem should be kept in mind always. As soon as you notice a reddened area that does not go away or an open area, call the doctor for early attention. A small area of skin breakdown is hard to heal and can become serious quickly. But it is not inevitable.

Notes:

Source: Marjorie Szor, MA, MS, RN, C, Clinical Nurse Specialist—Myelomeningocele, © Medical College Hospitals, Toledo, Ohio.

General Information about Seizure Disorders

DEFINITION*

A seizure is a physical condition that occurs when there is a sudden, brief change in how the brain works. When brain cells are not working properly, a person's consciousness, movement, or actions may be altered for a short time. These physical changes are called seizures. Seizure disorders, which affect people in all nations and of all races, used to be called epilepsy.

Some people can experience a seizure and not have a seizure disorder. For example, many young children have convulsions from fevers. These febrile convulsions are one type of seizure. Other types of seizures not classified as seizure disorders include those caused by an imbalance of body fluids or chemicals or by alcohol or drug withdrawal. A single seizure does not mean that the person has a seizure disorder.

INCIDENCE*

About 2 million Americans have seizure disorders; of the 100,000 new cases that develop each year, three-quarters of them are in children and adolescents.

CHARACTERISTICS*

Although the symptoms listed below are not necessarily indicators of seizure disorders, it is wise to consult a physician if a child experiences one or more of them:

- "blackouts" or periods of confused memory
- episodes of staring or unexplained periods of unresponsiveness
- involuntary movement of arms and legs
- "fainting spells" with incontinence or followed by excessive fatigue
- odd sounds, distorted perceptions, or episodic feelings of fear that cannot be explained
- rapid eye blinking**
- swinging movements of the head**
- repetitive and purposeless sounds and body movements (handrubbing, pacing)**
- sagging of the head**
- lack of response**
- eyes rolling upward**
- lip smacking, chewing movements of the mouth**
- irregular breathing**

Seizures can be generalized, meaning that all brain cells are involved. One type of generalized seizure consists of a convulsion with a complete loss of consciousness. Another type looks like a brief period of fixed staring.

Seizures are partial when those brain cells not working properly are limited to one part of the brain. Such partial seizures may cause periods of "automatic behavior" and altered conscious-

continues

continued

ness. This seizure is typified by purposeful-looking behavior, such as buttoning or unbuttoning a shirt. Such behavior, however, is unconscious, may be repetitive, and is usually not recalled.

EDUCATIONAL IMPLICATIONS*

Children with seizure disorders are eligible for special education and related services under the Individuals with Disabilities Education Act (IDEA), formerly the Education of the Handicapped Act (Public Law 94-142). Seizure disorders are classified as "other health impaired" and an Individualized Education Program (IEP) would be developed to specify appropriate services. Some children may have additional conditions such as learning disabilities along with the seizure disorders.

Seizures may interfere with the child's ability to learn. If the child has the type of seizure characterized by a brief period of fixed staring, he or she may be missing parts of what the teacher is saying. It is important that the teacher observe and document these episodes and report them promptly to parents and to school nurses.

Depending on the type of seizure or how often they occur, some children may need additional assistance to help them keep up with classmates. Assistance can include adaptations in classroom instruction, first aid instruction on seizure management for teachers, and counseling, all of which should be written in the IEP.

It is important that the teachers and school staff be informed about the child's condition, possible effects of medication, and what to do in case a seizure occurs at school. Most parents find that a friendly conversation with teachers at the beginning of the school year is the best way to handle the situation. Even if a child has seizures that are largely controlled by medication, it is still best to notify the school staff about the condition.

School personnel and the family should work together to monitor the effectiveness of medication as well as any side effects. If a child's physical or intellectual skills seem to change, it is important to tell the child's physician. There may also be associated hearing or perception problems caused by the brain changes. Written observations of both the family and school staff will be helpful in discussions with the child's physician.

Children and youth with seizure disorders must also deal with the psychological and social aspects of the condition. These aspects include public misperceptions and fear of seizures, uncertain occurrence, loss of self-control during the seizure episode, and compliance with medications. To help children feel more confident about themselves and accept their seizure disorders, the school can assist by providing seizure disorder education programs for staff and students, including information on seizure recognition and first aid.

Children can benefit the most when both the family and school are working together. There are many materials available for families and teachers so that they can understand how to work most effectively as a team.

*Source: *General Information about Epilepsy*, National Information Center for Children and Youth with Disabilities (NICHCY), Washington, DC, 1992.
**Source: "Epilepsy," Indiana Department of Health, Indianapolis, Indiana.

Charcot-Marie-Tooth Disorder

WHAT IS CHARCOT-MARIE-TOOTH DISORDER?

Charcot-Marie-Tooth (CMT) disorder is the most common inherited neurological disorder, affecting approximately 125,000 Americans. CMT disorder is found worldwide, in all races and ethnic groups. Although discovered in 1886 by three physicians, Jean-Marie Charcot, Pierre Marie and Howard Henry Tooth, the disorder has remained a mystery to the general public and medical community. Children with CMT disorder slowly lose normal use of their feet and legs and hands and arms as nerves to the extremities degenerate. The muscles in the extremities become weakened because of the loss of stimulation by the affected nerves. There is a corresponding loss of sensory nerve function. Unlike the muscular dystrophies, in which the defect is in the muscles, the CMT disorder is in the nerves that control the muscles. CMT disorder is not fatal, and people with CMT enjoy a normal life expectancy.

Medical Alert

Certain Drugs TOXIC to the Peripheral Nervous System

This list contains drugs that could be harmful to the child with CMT disorder. Before using any medication, please discuss it fully with the child's physician for possible side effects.

Alcohol	Adriamycin
Amiodarone	Chloramphenicol
Cis-platinum	Dapsone
Diphenylhydantoin (Dilantin)	Disulfiram (Antabuse)
Gold	Glutethimide (Doriden)
Isoniazid (INH)	Hydralazine (Apresoline)
Megadose of vitamin D	Megadose of vitamin A
Nitrofurantoin (Furadantin, Macrodantin)	Metronidazole (Flagyl)
	Nitrous oxide (chronic repeated inhalation)
Perhexiline (Pexid)	Penicillin (large IV doses only)
Pyridoxine (vitamin B6)	Vincristine

WHAT ARE ITS CHARACTERISTICS?

A high arched foot is one of the first signs of this disorder. As the disease progresses, structural foot deformities take place. The child develops a pes cavus foot, characterized by foot drop and

continues

continued

hammer toes. Ankle sprains are frequent. The progressive muscle wasting leads to problems with walking, running, and balance. The knees have to be raised higher off the ground, and the child develops high steppage gait. In some children muscle weakness may also occur in the upper legs.

Hand function is also affected because of progressive muscle atrophy, making fine manipulatory acts like writing more difficult.

The loss of nerve function in the limbs and extremities leads to sensory loss as well. The ability to distinguish hot and cold is diminished as well as the sense of touch.

The degree of severity can vary greatly from person to person, even within the same family. A child may or may not be more severely disabled than his or her parent.

HOW IS IT INHERITED?

CMT disorder is generally inherited in an autosomal dominant pattern. That is, if one parent has the disease (either the father or the mother), there is a 50 percent chance of passing it on to each child. CMT disorder can also be inherited in a recessive or in an X-linked pattern. To determine the pattern of inheritance, each child with CMT disorder should be evaluated by a genetic counselor, neurologist, or other medical authority familiar with the disease to define the pattern of inheritance in the family.

HOW IS IT DIAGNOSED?

Careful diagnosis of CMT disorder involves clinical evaluation of muscle atrophy, testing of muscle and sensory responses, nerve conduction and electromyographic studies, as well as a thorough review of the child's history. Even within the same family group, some people with CMT disorder may exhibit more disability than others. Some people who carry the CMT genetic trait show no apparent physical symptoms. This variation in degree of physical disability, together with a lack of physician awareness, has often led to misdiagnosis.

HOW IS IT TREATED?

At present there is no cure for CMT disorder, although physical therapy and moderate activity are often recommended to maintain muscle strength and endurance. Leg braces and custom-made shoes can help improve the quality of life for most children. Corrective orthopedic foot surgery is available to help maintain mobility when medically indicated. Splinting, specific exercises, adaptive devices, and sometimes surgery will help maintain hand function.

Courtesy of the Charcot-Marie-Tooth Association, Upland, Pennsylvania.

Facts about Muscular Dystrophy

WHAT IS MUSCULAR DYSTROPHY?

Muscular dystrophy refers to a group of inherited diseases marked by progressive weakness and degeneration of the skeletal, or voluntary, muscles that control movement.

DOES MUSCULAR DYSTROPHY AFFECT CHILDREN EXCLUSIVELY?

No. Contrary to widespread belief, muscular dystrophy can affect people of all ages. While some forms first become apparent in infancy or childhood, others may not appear until middle age or later.

WHAT ARE THE FORMS OF MUSCULAR DYSTROPHY IN ORDER OF PREVALENCE?

- myotonic
- Duchenne
- Becker
- limb-girdle
- facioscapulohumeral
- congenital
- oculopharyngeal
- distal
- Emery-Dreifuss

HOW DO THE FORMS OF MUSCULAR DYSTROPHY DIFFER?

They differ in severity, age of onset, muscles first and most often affected, and the rate at which symptoms progress.

IS MUSCULAR DYSTROPHY ANYONE'S FAULT?

No. All forms of muscular dystrophy are genetic disorders—inherited diseases that can be passed down from one generation to the next—making them beyond the control of parents and children.

IS MUSCULAR DYSTROPHY CONTAGIOUS?

No. Inherited diseases are not contagious.

continues

continued

IS A FAMILY MEDICAL HISTORY IMPORTANT?

Yes. Because the muscular dystrophies are inherited disorders, it is important for the physician to know if anyone in the family ever had a similar disorder.

HOW IS MUSCULAR DYSTROPHY DIAGNOSED?

An experienced physician makes a diagnosis by evaluating the child's medical history and by performing a thorough physical examination. Essentials to diagnosis are details about when weakness first appeared, its severity, and which muscles were affected. Diagnostic tests may also be used to help the physician distinguish between different forms of muscular dystrophy, or between a type of muscular dystrophy and other neuromuscular disorders.

WHAT ARE SOME COMMON DIAGNOSTIC TESTS?

Studying a small piece of muscle tissue taken from an individual during a muscle biopsy often enables a physician to determine whether or not the disorder is muscular dystrophy and which form of the disease it is.

Another diagnostic test is the electromyogram (EMG). Placing small electrodes into muscle helps create a graph indicating the health of the body's muscles and nerves.

Blood tests are helpful because degenerating muscles leak enzymes that can be detected in the blood. The presence of these enzymes in the blood at greater than normal levels may be a sign of muscular dystrophy.

CAN SOMETHING BE DONE TO ALLEVIATE THE SYMPTOMS OF MUSCULAR DYSTROPHY?

Yes. Exercise programs and physical therapy minimize contractures, a common condition associated with muscular dystrophy that causes muscle shortening around joints. In addition, exercise may prevent or delay scoliosis, or curvature of the spine. Rehabilitative devices, ranging from canes to electric wheelchairs, help maintain mobility and independence as long as possible. Surgical procedures can also be helpful in relieving muscle shortening caused by some forms of muscular dystrophy.

WHAT CAUSES MUSCULAR DYSTROPHY?

Each form of muscular dystrophy is caused by a defect in a gene. Genes are the body's basic units of heredity, determining inherited physical characteristics such as height, hair color, and muscle development. Scientists estimate that human beings have between 50,000 and 100,000 genes, which together form the blueprints for the individual's development, growth, and functioning.

Courtesy of the Muscular Dystrophy Association, Tucson, Arizona.

Facts about Friedreich's Ataxia

WHAT IS FRIEDREICH'S ATAXIA?

Friedreich's ataxia is an inherited, progressive disease of the nervous system. The most prominent characteristic of the disease is ataxia—shaky movements and unsteadiness. Ataxia results from the brain's failure to regulate the body's posture and the coordination of muscle movements.

Other common symptoms include loss of tendon reflexes, weakness of muscles, clubfoot, and a gradual loss of sensation. In addition, some medical problems not related to the nervous system often develop as a result of the disease.

WHEN DO SIGNS OF THE DISEASE FIRST BECOME APPARENT?

Friedreich's ataxia appears in both boys and girls, usually between the ages of 7 and 13 years. It can, however, occur as late as 20 years of age.

WHAT ARE THE EARLY SYMPTOMS OF FRIEDREICH'S ATAXIA?

The first symptom that usually appears is clumsiness in walking. Jerky and poorly controlled movements of the arms and legs often follow as the disease progresses. Weakness in the legs and unsteadiness in standing are among other early symptoms.

HOW FAST DOES FRIEDREICH'S ATAXIA PROGRESS?

Friedreich's ataxia differs markedly from one individual to another, although generally the rate at which the disease progresses is gradual.

As a rule, within a few years after walking becomes recognizably difficult, ataxia appears in the arms in the form of shaky, unsteady movements. In time, a person's ability to walk may become sufficiently impaired for him or her to require the use of a wheelchair. In the disease's later stages, dysarthria, a speech disorder manifested by unclear pronunciation, usually develops. Curvature of the spine (scoliosis) also occurs in many cases.

IS FRIEDREICH'S ATAXIA CONTAGIOUS?

No. Genetic diseases are not contagious.

HOW IS FRIEDREICH'S ATAXIA DIAGNOSED?

A diagnosis is reached after a thorough physical examination and a careful evaluation of the child's symptoms by a physician. The child's medical history and family history are also evaluated. Then the clinical diagnosis may be confirmed by a series of laboratory tests.

continues

continued

WHAT ARE SOME COMMON DIAGNOSTIC TESTS?

Common diagnostic tests that help confirm a clinical diagnosis of Friedreich's ataxia include:

- electromyogram, measuring electrical activity of muscle cells
- nerve conduction velocity, measuring how fast nerves are transmitting impulses
- electrocardiogram or echocardiogram, to determine if heart abnormalities exist

It is anticipated that research aimed at finding the gene responsible for Friedreich's ataxia will lead to diagnostic tests based on genetics. Such genetic testing promises to make possible diagnosis of Friedreich's ataxia even before symptoms appear. This early diagnosis should enhance prospects for successful treatment as physicians will be able to start therapy earlier in the course of the disease.

IS THERE ANY TREATMENT FOR FRIEDREICH'S ATAXIA?

Many of the symptoms of Friedreich's ataxia can be treated. At present, however, there is no specific treatment or cure for the disease. Continuous supervision by a physician is recommended to treat complications associated with the disease.

Heart problems and diabetes can be treated with medication. Orthopedic intervention, which may include surgery, can alleviate scoliosis, and orthopedic appliances and physical therapy can prolong the ability to walk.

WHAT OTHER SERVICES ARE HELPFUL?

Psychological counseling can help the child and family adjust to living with a progressively disabling disease. Genetic counseling can clarify the inherited nature of the disease and its potential effect on the family as a whole.

Notes:

Courtesy of Muscular Dystrophy Association, Tucson, Arizona.

Facts about Spinal Muscular Atrophy

WHAT IS SPINAL MUSCULAR ATROPHY?

Spinal muscular atrophy is a term for a group of inherited neuromuscular diseases. All forms of the disease attack specialized nerve cells called motor neurons, which control the movement of voluntary muscles. Spinal muscular atrophy causes lower motor neurons in the base of the brain and the spinal cord to disintegrate gradually, preventing them from delivering electrical and chemical signals that muscles depend on for normal function.

WHAT ARE THE NAMES OF THE FOUR FORMS OF THE DISEASE?

1. infantile progressive spinal muscular atrophy
2. intermediate spinal muscular atrophy
3. juvenile spinal muscular atrophy
4. adult spinal muscular atrophy

HOW DO THE FORMS OF THE DISEASE DIFFER?

They differ in the age of onset, severity and rate of progression, and, in the case of the adult type, muscles affected.

WHICH TYPES OF THE DISEASE AFFECT CHILDREN?

Infantile progressive spinal muscular atrophy, intermediate spinal muscular atrophy, and juvenile spinal muscular atrophy affect both boys and girls.

WHAT ARE THE SYMPTOMS OF THE INFANTILE FORM?

Newborns with the infantile type cannot roll over, raise their heads, or sit without support. They also have trouble swallowing and sucking. By 3 months of age, most are unable to move because of paralysis in their arms, legs, and lower and upper torso. Because of breathing distress and respiratory infection, the life span rarely exceeds 2 years of age.

FORM	AGE OF ONSET	PROGRESSION
infantile progressive	before birth to 3 months	rapid
intermediate	6 months to 3 years	moderate to rapid
juvenile	1 to 15 years	moderate
adult	18 to 50 years	slow

continues

continued

HOW IS THE INTERMEDIATE FORM DIFFERENT?

Babies with intermediate spinal muscular atrophy appear to progress normally until the age of 6 to 18 months. After that, symptoms include progressive muscle weakness in the arms, as well as the legs and upper and lower torso, making standing difficult. Most children survive through early childhood. Some, however, live longer, depending on the extent to which respiratory muscles are weakened.

WHAT ARE THE SYMPTOMS OF JUVENILE SPINAL MUSCULAR ATROPHY?

Children with the juvenile form can show symptoms as early as the age of 1 year. The disease, which causes weakness in the leg and hip muscles, makes it difficult to climb stairs and stand up, and it turns the child's walk into a waddle. In addition, calf muscles become enlarged and respiratory muscles may be weakened. Children with this type can walk, although with difficulty, at least ten years after symptoms become apparent. The child's life span is unaffected.

DO ALL CHILDREN OR ADULTS WITH THESE SYMPTOMS HAVE SPINAL MUSCULAR ATROPHY?

Not necessarily. A thorough neurological examination is required to establish a diagnosis and confirm that the symptoms indicate spinal muscular atrophy and not another condition with similar symptoms.

HOW ARE THE SPINAL MUSCULAR ATROPHIES DIAGNOSED?

An experienced physician makes a diagnosis by carefully evaluating the child's medical history and by performing a thorough physical examination. The clinical diagnosis is then confirmed by a series of laboratory tests.

IS A FAMILY MEDICAL HISTORY IMPORTANT?

Yes. The spinal muscular atrophies are genetic disorders—inherited diseases that can be passed down from one generation to the next. That is why it is important for the physician to know if there is a family history of these disorders.

WHAT IF THE DIAGNOSIS IS UNCLEAR?

It is sometimes difficult to distinguish between spinal muscular atrophy and other neuromuscular disorders. In these cases, physicians use tests to help them arrive at a diagnosis.

continues

continued

WHAT ARE SOME COMMON DIAGNOSTIC TESTS?

Studying a small piece of muscle tissue taken from an individual during a muscle biopsy often enables a pathologist to determine whether a disorder is one of the spinal muscular atrophies.

Another diagnostic test is the electromyogram (EMG). By placing small electrodes in muscle, this test creates a graph that indicates the health of the body's muscles and nerves.

Blood tests are administered to evaluate the levels of certain enzymes, helping to distinguish the spinal muscular atrophies from other neuromuscular diseases.

IS THERE ANY TREATMENT FOR SPINAL MUSCULAR ATROPHY?

At present, there is no known treatment that will stop or reverse any form of spinal muscular atrophy.

IS THERE A CARRIER-DETECTION TEST FOR SPINAL MUSCULAR ATROPHY?

No. There is currently no method to detect nonaffected carriers.

ARE THERE OTHER NAMES FOR THE DIFFERENT FORMS OF SPINAL MUSCULAR ATROPHY?

Yes. Infantile progressive spinal muscular atrophy is also referred to as Type 1, or Werdnig-Hoffmann disease. Intermediate spinal muscular atrophy is also known as Type 2. Juvenile spinal muscular atrophy is often called Type 3, or Kugelberg-Welander disease. Adult spinal muscular atrophy may be referred to as Aran-Duchenne type.

Notes:

Courtesy of Muscular Dystrophy Association, Tucson, Arizona.

Facts about Polymyositis and Dermatomyositis

WHAT ARE POLYMYOSITIS AND DERMATOMYOSITIS?

In polymyositis and dermatomyositis, voluntary muscle deteriorates and becomes inflamed. The major characteristic of these diseases is muscular weakness, which usually gets progressively worse and may become severely disabling. The pattern of muscle weakness and wasting is similar in polymyositis and dermatomyositis, but the conditions differ in other ways.

ARE THERE OTHER NAMES FOR POLYMYOSITIS AND DERMATOMYOSITIS?

Yes. Both of these conditions can be called inflammatory myopathies, which means they involve muscle problems associated with inflammation.

HOW DO POLYMYOSITIS AND DERMATOMYOSITIS DIFFER?

The most obvious difference is that people with dermatomyositis usually have a patchy, dusky, reddish, or lilac rash on the eyelids, cheeks, and bridge of the nose, and on the back or upper chest, elbows, knees, and knuckles. In severe cases, all of the individual's skin may take on a reddish hue. People with dermatomyositis may also develop calcified nodules, or hardened bumps, under the skin, which may become uncomfortable. Polymyositis does not involve a rash or nodules.

In addition, there may be a slightly increased incidence of malignancy in adults with dermatomyositis. This association does not hold for children with dermatomyositis, and there is no apparent increase in malignancies among individuals with polymyositis.

Many investigators have found that polymyositis progresses more slowly than dermatomyositis. Recent research indicates that what goes wrong in the immune system may be different in the two diseases.

WHAT ARE THE EARLY SIGNS AND SYMPTOMS OF THESE DISEASES?

Muscular weakness, sometimes accompanied by pain and tenderness, usually shows up first in the large muscles around the hips and shoulders. Typically, the onset is gradual and the weakness occurs symmetrically, or on both sides of the body.

The person may then experience difficulty in rising from a chair, climbing stairs, or holding up the arms. Excessive fatigue may develop after prolonged standing or walking. In some cases, the early effects include impairment of the voluntary components of the muscles used in swallowing and breathing.

continues

continued

AT WHAT AGE DO THESE DISEASES USUALLY BEGIN?

Polymyositis is usually a disease of adults, generally beginning after the age of 18 years. Dermatomyositis can occur at any age from childhood to adulthood.

ARE THE TWO SEXES AFFECTED EQUALLY?

Dermatomyositis appears to be more common in females than in males. Polymyositis affects both sexes in approximately equal numbers.

IS THERE A TYPICAL PATTERN OF PROGRESSION?

The course of polymyositis and dermatomyositis varies widely in rate of progression, symptoms, severity, and complications. In general, weakness develops in a matter of weeks or months. Spontaneous remissions occasionally occur in which the symptoms diminish or stop. But, most often, if polymyositis or dermatomyositis is untreated, more muscle groups are gradually affected, and weakness becomes increasingly severe.

As either disease advances, a child's gait may become clumsy and waddling, and he or she may have a tendency to fall or difficulty lifting the head from a pillow when reclining. In severe cases, the child may become bedridden or require the use of a wheelchair. Some physicians have found that the more rapid the onset, the better the prognosis, or chance of recovery. Approximately 50 percent of people with polymyositis or dermatomyositis improve with treatment. Without treatment, these conditions may lead to permanent disability or even death.

WHAT CAUSES POLYMYOSITIS AND DERMATOMYOSITIS?

It is believed that these diseases result from a disturbance of the immune system. Most experts consider polymyositis and dermatomyositis to be autoimmune conditions. Normally, the immune system produces specialized cells and proteins called antibodies to fight infection. In autoimmune disease, for some unknown reason the antibodies instead injure the body's own tissues.

Why such abnormal immunological activity occurs is not clearly understood. It is possible that viral infections trigger the autoimmune reaction and the onset of some cases of polymyositis and dermatomyositis.

Both polymyositis and dermatomyositis are sometimes seen in conjunction with the so-called connective tissue disorders, some of which are thought to be autoimmune, and with other autoimmune conditions. An underlying malfunction of the immune system, resulting in an attack on several different tissues in the body, including muscle and, in the case of dermatomyositis, blood vessels, has been proposed as a cause.

continues

continued

ARE POLYMYOSITIS AND DERMATOMYOSITIS HEREDITARY DISEASES?

These are not considered to be hereditary diseases. However, some research suggests that the immune systems of certain individuals may be more prone to autoimmune dysfunction than those of others and that heredity may play a role in this tendency.

The Search for a Cause

Research has uncovered many clues about the immune system malfunctions in polymyositis and dermatomyositis. Physicians now believe that polymyositis probably results in large part from an attack on the muscles by specialized immune system cells called T cells.

In dermatomyositis, the main autoimmune attack appears to involve antibodies and a group of proteins known as complement. In this disease the small blood vessels that supply the muscles with blood are attacked early in the disease. The muscle damage comes later and probably results from the reduced blood supply rather than from direct destruction of muscle cells.

A better understanding of the immune system and of autoimmune disease in general will probably have the greatest effect on the treatment of polymyositis and dermatomyositis. The goal is to find medications that can suppress specific parts of the immune system while leaving the rest intact for its crucial task of fighting disease.

ARE POLYMYOSITIS AND DERMATOMYOSITIS CONTAGIOUS?

No. There is no evidence that autoimmune diseases are contagious.

HOW ARE POLYMYOSITIS AND DERMATOMYOSITIS DIAGNOSED?

Dermatomyositis is easy to recognize. Physicians diagnose it by the distinctive reddish skin rash and the typical distribution and onset of muscle weakness, although laboratory tests may be used to confirm the diagnosis. Polymyositis, especially in its slowly progressive form, may be difficult to distinguish from other neuromuscular or autoimmune conditions.

A muscle biopsy may be ordered for confirming the diagnosis in both diseases. In this test, a small piece of muscle is removed and then examined under a microscope. A biopsy showing widespread degeneration and regeneration of muscle fibers, extensive inflammation, and no enlarged muscle fibers provides strong support for a diagnosis of inflammatory myopathy.

Other tests that may be done to confirm the diagnosis of either polymyositis or dermatomyositis include measurements of the serum creatine kinase level, an electromyogram, and nerve conduction studies.

continues

continued

The serum creatine kinase (CK) test requires a blood sample and measures the level of a chemical substance that leaks out of degenerating muscle cells into the bloodstream. A higher than normal level of CK indicates the presence of muscle cell destruction.

In an electromyogram, tiny needle-shaped electrodes are inserted into the muscles to measure the muscle cells' electrical activity. Certain changes in the electrical activity of muscle cells occur in different diseases.

Nerve conduction studies measure the speed at which an electrical impulse travels along a nerve. In this test, an external shock is applied to one part of the nerve and measured by an electrode inserted at another point along the nerve. These studies may also be used during diagnosis to differentiate one neuromuscular condition from another.

IS THERE ANY TREATMENT FOR POLYMYOSITIS OR DERMATOMYOSITIS?

Two types of treatment have proven very effective in both conditions. With either or both of these treatments, many individuals have been freed of the most crippling symptoms and have been able to lead nearly symptom-free lives.

Most people respond to medications that inhibit inflammation and suppress the immune system. Prednisone is the most commonly prescribed. Other immunosuppressants, such as azathioprine and methotrexate, may also be used. Unfortunately, these drugs can have serious side effects, such as high blood pressure and edema, or fluid retention, especially after prolonged use.

A blood-filtering procedure known as plasmapheresis, pioneered in the 1970s, has sometimes been successful in treating those who are seriously ill from the inflammatory myopathies as well as other conditions such as myasthenia gravis and Lambert-Eaton syndrome. In this process, antibodies that are attacking the muscle tissue are removed from the blood plasma.

The procedure involves drawing the child's blood through a tube, usually from a vein in the arm. The blood enters a machine where blood cells are separated from the plasma by a membrane filter or by centrifugation. The blood cells are then reconstituted in a plasma substitute and returned through another vein.

In some cases, plasmapheresis may help to bring polymyositis or dermatomyositis under control and reduce the amount of time that high doses of toxic medications are necessary. However, there are few studies of the effectiveness of this procedure in these diseases.

The intravenous administration of immunoglobulins (immune system proteins) may also be of benefit in some children with polymyositis or dermatomyositis. The exact mechanism by which this treatment works is not yet understood.

Physical therapy is of benefit early in either disease. The proper exercises can help to preserve function in muscles and joints and partially prevent muscle wasting.

Courtesy of Muscular Dystrophy Association, Tucson, Arizona.

When a Child Tests Positive for HIV

When your child tests "positive" for HIV antibody, it is both frightening and confusing. There are so many questions: "What does the test mean?" "Who should be told?" "What happens next?" Each is an important question and warrants a closer look. (HIV stands for human immunodeficiency virus.)

WHAT DOES THE TEST MEAN?

It is important to know that:

- This test does not mean that your child has AIDS. (AIDS stands for acquired immune deficiency syndrome.)
- It does reveal that your child may be carrying the virus that can cause AIDS.
- It indicates that other family members may need to be tested.
- It means that some special steps should be taken to support your child's health and prevent the spread of the virus (which is found mainly in blood and semen).

THINGS TO REMEMBER

Because your child may be susceptible to illness:

- Wash your hands frequently.
- Try to avoid crowds and sick people as much as possible.
- Tell the child's physician immediately if your child is exposed to chicken pox.

Because your child may be carrying a bloodborne virus, be especially careful if your child bleeds.

- Keep open sores covered.
- Do not share toothbrushes, pierced earrings, or razors.
- Wear disposable gloves when cleaning up blood and soiled surfaces. (Because diarrhea frequently contains tiny amounts of blood, it is a good idea to wear gloves when changing messy diapers.)
- Dispose of diapers in plastic garbage bags or wrap in newspaper before throwing them away.
- Clean blood-soiled surfaces thoroughly and rinse with a solution of 1 cup bleach per 1 gallon water.
- Keep a separate bucket and sponge just for this purpose, and flush unused solution down the toilet.

WHO SHOULD BE TOLD?

Unfortunately, there is still much prejudice associated with being HIV positive. Therefore, it is important to think about those with whom this information should be shared. Presently, only

continues

continued

children with AIDS (not just positive for the HIV antibody) must be reported to the local department of health.

What Should You Say to Your Child?

Think about talking with your child, especially if he or she is old enough to know that "something is going on." Reassure the child that he or she has done nothing wrong and answer questions in language that can be understood.

For example, telling a child that his or her body's defenses are not quite as strong as they should be, and that the physician and nurse are going to work with Mommy and Daddy to keep him or her healthy is a concept most children can understand. Older children can understand the concept of a germ being present without making them "sick."

Simple truth, warmth, and reassurance are the best way to relieve fear. The child's physician or nurse can also be helpful resources in responding to the child's questions.

What Caregivers Should Be Told

Other health care providers, such as physicians, dentists, or laboratory technicians, need to know so that they can use care when handling your child's blood.

Consider telling the principal, teacher, or school nurse about your child's condition. Parents have the right to an assurance that this information will be kept confidential.

Nonprofessional caregivers, such as babysitters, need to be informed about special care needs, but do not necessarily need to be told the diagnosis.

The child's physician, nurse, or social worker can discuss your particular needs and circumstances as they arise.

Should Family and Friends Be Told?

You may find it comforting to confide in those trusted friends or family members whom you usually rely on for support. Know that casual family contact (living in the same household) has not been shown to be a means of transmitting the virus—so don't worry about hugging your child. In fact, it will do you both a world of good.

WHAT HAPPENS NEXT?

Regular medical care is very important; it is also important to keep your child in as normal a routine as possible. A physician should monitor your child's health to prevent or minimize other kinds of infection. Every 1 to 3 months the child should have a physical examination and blood tests that measure the strength of the immune system. Sometimes medications may be used. These might be antibiotics (for infection) or monthly doses of intravenous (by vein) gamma globulin (to "boost" immunity). The doctor will explain exactly what is needed for your child.

Source: *When a Child's Test Is HIV Positive*, Children's National Medical Center, Special Immunology Service, Washington, DC.

HIV and Your Child

THE IMMUNE SYSTEM AND HIV

The body's health is defended by its immune system. White blood cells, called lymphocytes (B cells and T cells), protect the body from germs such as viruses, bacteria, parasites, and fungi. When germs are detected, B cells and T cells are activated to defend the body.

This process is hindered in the case of the acquired immune deficiency syndrome (AIDS). AIDS is a disease in which the body's immune system breaks down. AIDS is caused by the human immunodeficiency virus (HIV). When HIV enters the body, it infects special T cells, where the virus grows. The virus kills these cells slowly. As more and more of the T cells die, the body's ability to fight infection weakens.

A child with HIV infection may remain healthy for many years. Children with HIV infection are said to have AIDS when they are sick with serious illnesses and infections that can occur with HIV. The illnesses tend to occur late in HIV infection, when few T cells remain.

WHERE DID HIV AND AIDS COME FROM?

We may never know where or how HIV and AIDS began. Many experts believe that AIDS was present in the United States, Europe, and Africa for several decades or longer before the earliest cases appeared in 1980 and 1981.

HIV was first identified in 1984 by French and American scientists, but the human immunodeficiency virus did not get its name until 1986.

PURPOSE OF THIS HANDOUT

Even before HIV causes AIDS, it can cause health problems. Learning about how the virus can affect your child's body and getting care early, before health problems worsen, can help your child live a longer and healthier life.

This handout is a guide to understanding HIV and getting the right care for your child. It gives you questions to ask your doctor, nurse, or other medical care provider. What you learn about HIV and AIDS will help you become more involved in your child's health care.

HIV affects everyone in a family, whether only one or several family members are infected. Babies with HIV and their infected parents need to be followed very closely by a medical care provider such as a doctor, nurse, or other medical professional.

Babies who may have HIV infection should be tested for HIV as soon as possible after birth and have regular follow-up exams. This is very important to help your baby stay as healthy as possible.

continues

continued

FACTS ABOUT HIV IN BABIES AND CHILDREN

- A mother can pass HIV to her baby during pregnancy or at birth.
- The chance that a woman with HIV will pass the virus to her baby is one in four for each pregnancy (that is, 25%).
- Just like adults, children and adolescents can become infected through contact with blood or body fluids, or by having sexual relations.
- Your child needs to be cared for by a doctor with experience in treating HIV infection in babies and children.
- HIV can be passed to a baby through breast milk from an HIV-infected mother.
- Bathing, kissing, feeding, and playing with your child are not risky and do not cause the spread of HIV.
- In the past, some babies and children became infected through blood transfusions. Today the blood from all donors is screened for the virus, and HIV infection from this source is unlikely.
- Special blood tests can show whether your infant is infected with HIV.
- Early immunizations (shots) can help protect your child from other HIV-related diseases.

HOW WILL I KNOW IF MY BABY HAS HIV?

Before a baby is born, it shares its mother's blood supply. If you are infected with HIV, you can transmit HIV to your child through your blood before birth. The baby also can become infected during delivery.

For the first few months, your baby may test positive for HIV infection because it still has some parts of your blood, so early tests are not accurate. After several months, the child's own system takes over. Test results then become accurate for your child and can indicate HIV infection.

When your child is less than two years old, his or her blood should be tested every two to three months until the system matures. After age two, a single blood test can show if your child is infected with HIV.

WHAT WILL HAPPEN TO MY BABY?

Some babies who have HIV infection may become ill in the first year of life. Others remain healthy for many years. Regular medical checkups and blood tests will help your doctor keep track of how your child is doing and decide whether special medicines are needed. Ask your health care provider how you can help protect your child.

HOW CAN I HELP MY CHILD STAY HEALTHY?

It is very important to seek medical care as soon as you know that your child has HIV. Although there is no cure as yet for HIV, there are things you can do to help your child stay as healthy as possible.

continues

continued

Because your child has HIV infection, you will want to learn as much as you can about the virus. You can prevent many illnesses by:

- keeping your home safe and clean
- observing and listening to your child
- telling your health care provider right away about unusual behavior or symptoms
- working with the doctor, nurse, or other health care provider to plan your child's care
- making sure your child gets all recommended baby shots and booster shots
- trying to keep a positive outlook

Hope is very important. Every day, there are new drugs and treatments for HIV that may help your child. Each time you take your child for health care, be sure to ask about new treatments or clinical trials that might be right for your child.

STEPS TO HELP YOUR CHILD STAY HEALTHY

1. Prevent Illness

Immunize against Infection

With HIV infection, your child is more likely to get common childhood illnesses, and these may be more serious. You can protect your child by making sure all the baby shots are given on time. These shots include:

- diphtheria, pertussis (whooping cough), and tetanus (DPT)
- polio (IPV)
- mumps, measles, rubella (MMR)

Your health care provider may recommend other immunizations, depending on the results of medical tests. These include:

- *Haemophilus influenzae* type B (HIb)
- hepatitis B (HepB)
- pneumococcal infection (after two years of age)
- influenza (yearly)

Avoid Common Illnesses

Some infections cannot be prevented by shots. Infections from the bacteria and viruses that cause sores, colds, and influenza (flu) can weaken your child and make it harder to resist the more serious HIV-related diseases.

Keep your child away from people who are sick, and tell the doctor or nurse if you think your child has been near someone with tuberculosis (TB) or other infections.

continues

continued

2. Provide a Healthy Home Life

As the parent or guardian of a child who has HIV infection, you will want to take special care of yourself so that you can care for your child. The advice that follows can help both you and your child to stay as healthy as possible.

Teach Personal Care

Wash your hands often, and teach your child to do the same as soon as he or she is able. Keep your child away from human or animal waste.

Brush your child's teeth until he or she is able. Your child will need to visit the dentist twice a year. Ask the dentist to help you teach your child proper mouth care. The first sign of your child's HIV infection may be sores in the mouth. At each visit, the doctor or nurse will examine your child's mouth.

Eat Healthy Foods

Your child needs healthy foods in order to grow and to help fight infections. A proper diet will also help you and your child have strength and energy. Your child's health care provider can help you decide which foods are best. Ask how to help a "picky eater" learn to enjoy healthy foods.

Get Regular Exercise

Most children with HIV infection are active; however, some need encouragement to get physical exercise (in fresh air and sunshine, if possible). Regular exercise is important to help you and your child keep up your strength.

Get Plenty of Sleep

Children with HIV infection need rest. Sleep will renew your child's energy for the next day, especially for going to day care or school, where there may be little time for rest during the day.

Play with, Talk to, and Hug Your Child Often

Spending time together will help you spot problems that should be reported to your child's health care provider.

Give Medication Correctly and on Time

Your child needs medicines to slow the HIV infection and prevent other infections, such as pneumonia, that can occur when the immune system is weak.

Your doctor or nurse will tell you exactly what medicine your child should have. Giving your child the right amount of medicine, and giving it on time, can mean the difference between staying healthy and becoming severely ill.

Do not allow your child to take any other medicines, alcohol, or illegal (street) drugs.

continues

continued

See the end of this handout for some helpful hints on giving medicine to a young child. Your child's health care provider can show you how to hold the baby and use medicine droppers or syringes correctly.

Help Your Child Lead a Normal Life

Playing with other children in your home and in the neighborhood is good for your child. It is not dangerous for your child or for the other children. HIV infection is not spread by touching or being in close contact with a friend.

3. Report Symptoms Promptly

Watch your child carefully. Report any of the following to your health care provider right away:

- fever
- cough
- fast or difficult breathing
- loss of appetite and poor weight gain
- white patches or sores in the mouth
- diaper rash that won't go away
- blood in the diaper or bowel movements
- diarrhea (frequent loose, watery bowel movements)
- vomiting
- contact with a person who has chicken pox, measles, TB, or other diseases that can spread

4. Be Sure Your Child Gets Medical Treatment

Your child may stay strong and healthy for a long time, but to be sure, regular blood tests will be needed to show how well the immune system is working.

Special T cells, called *CD4 cells*, in the blood help the body defend itself from attackers, such as viruses. But CD4 cells can be destroyed as your child's HIV infection worsens, leaving your child unable to fight off other infections and illnesses.

Your child's health care provider will do a CD4 cell count every few months. This test shows the number of CD4 cells in your child's blood and lets the doctor know when special medicine is needed.

The doctor will probably prescribe medicine such as AZT (now known as ZDV), didanosine (ddl), or dideoxycitidine (ddC) to try to slow the advance of the HIV infection.

Another drug, trimethoprim-sulfamethoxazole or TMP-SMX (Bactrim, Septra, and generic products), may be given to prevent *Pneumocystis carinii* pneumonia (PCP). PCP is the most common serious pneumonia in children with HIV. Your child may need other medicines to prevent "opportunistic" infections that can take advantage of a weakened immune system.

These treatments are strong and can cause problems. Watch for and report side effects such as problems in sleeping, headaches, vomiting, muscle or belly pain, numbness in hands or feet, or hyperactivity.

continues

continued

Your health care provider will take blood tests regularly to see how well your child can resist infections. Be sure to ask your doctor about new HIV drugs or vaccines. New medicines are tested on people to see if they are safe or helpful. This is called a clinical trial. Usually, new HIV medicines must be tested in a clinical trial before a doctor can give them to patients who are not part of the clinical trial.

Also ask your doctor about other tests and treatments your child may need, including:

- special X-rays and other tests for growth, development, and nervous system function
- special feedings or formulas
- physical, occupational, or speech therapy

SIGNS AND SYMPTOMS OF HIV INFECTION IN BABIES

- Swelling in the lymph glands in the neck, under the arms, and in the diaper area
- Swollen belly, sometimes with diarrhea (frequent loose, watery bowel movements)
- Itchy skin rashes
- Frequent lung infections (pneumonia)
- Frequent ear and sinus infections
- Problems with gaining weight or growth
- Inability to do the kinds of things healthy babies do (such as sitting alone, crawling, walking)
- Crankiness, irritability, and constant crying

Most important, talk with your health care provider right away about anything you notice that seems unusual for your baby.

TELLING OTHERS ABOUT YOUR CHILD'S HIV INFECTION

Talking about Your Child's HIV Infection

Possible Benefits:

Telling others may have benefits:

- more support from family and friends
- in some states, better health and welfare benefits
- more acceptance of the child's infection

Possible Risks:

- rejection by family, friends, or day care, school, or social programs
- changes in health benefits

continues

continued

Although it is risky, sharing information about your child's HIV infection can be helpful in a number of ways. Telling others may help you seek the medical care your child needs and apply for other kinds of help. You can begin actively planning for your child's care and your family's future.

Your doctor, nurse, social worker, or other members of the health care team can help you plan how and when to share information about your child's HIV infection. They can help you tell others. Your list of people to tell may include:

- the child, if he or she is old enough to understand
- family members
- day care workers or babysitters
- teachers, classmates, and other people at school
- health professionals who work with your child or your family, including your family doctor and dentist, nurses, social workers, nutrition counselors, and pharmacists

Your doctor may be required by law to report your child's HIV infection to the state or local health department. Ask about the laws, confidentiality, and anonymous HIV testing in your state.

Talking with Your Child about HIV Infection

Consider your child's age. Talk with your child about HIV when he or she seems ready, possibly around age five. The way you talk with an older child about HIV infection depends on whether the child has had HIV since infancy or is newly diagnosed.

Young Children

Children born with the virus have learned a lot about living with HIV infection by the time they reach the age when they can understand what it means to have HIV. Your child will have had regular visits to doctors and other health care providers and will have experienced blood drawing and shots. Taking medicines may be routine. Perhaps your child knows or can say the name of the infection, too.

Young children are usually content with knowing only a little about HIV. You can give short, simple answers to most of the questions your young child asks.

School-Age Children

Older children can understand much more. It is very important to give your child correct information and honest answers about your feelings. Otherwise the child may get the wrong information from someone else.

A child who has HIV infection that is kept secret may suffer silently because of shame or fear. An older child who is having trouble coping with HIV infection may:

- have problems sleeping
- pull away from friends and family

continues

continued

- be depressed or sad
- have problems at school

Even a young child may have many of the same problems that adults do when dealing with HIV infection. Counselors and health care providers who work with children with HIV can help you recognize changes in your child's behavior. They can help the child, and you, find ways to talk about these problems.

Older Children

The older child—from 12 to 21 years of age—who has recently become infected with HIV may feel and express many of the same emotions as an adult in the same situation: disbelief, fear, sadness, depression, shame. At the same time, the child may behave in some of the same ways as a younger child.

He or she may have many concerns:

- Am I going to get sick? When?
- What will happen to me?
- Will I have to go to the hospital or see the doctor more often?
- How will HIV affect my family, friends, and people at school?
- How can I prevent giving HIV to others?

It is important to talk with older children who have HIV about using condoms for safe sex, as well as the dangers of sharing needles. It may be very hard to stay calm and neutral when talking with your older child about HIV infection. You may want to arrange for your child to meet privately with an HIV/AIDS health counselor who knows how to interact with teenagers. Ask your child's health care provider to help you find a counselor who can meet with your child.

Talking with your older child in an open and friendly way will do much to ease fears about rejection by other family members and friends. You may decide together whom to tell about the HIV infection and when.

HOW CAN WE GET THE SUPPORT OUR FAMILY NEEDS?

A child or family with HIV may need many kinds of support. Your child's health care provider and your local health and social services departments can assist you in finding the help you need. Help may include someone who can:

- answer your questions about HIV and AIDS
- help you find health care providers and make health care decisions
- provide transportation to and from health care appointments

continues

continued

- assist in planning ways to meet financial and daily needs
- arrange home nursing care or rehabilitation services
- refer your child and family members to support groups
- represent your family in legal matters

Sometimes it helps to talk with others who have HIV or who have a child with HIV. Here are some ways of finding them:

- Read HIV newsletters.
- Join a support group for friends and family.
- Volunteer to help others.
- Attend social events to meet other families living with HIV.

ADDITIONAL RESOURCES

There are many information sources for persons with HIV. You may find it helpful to read about HIV and to learn about how others deal with the infection and care for themselves and their children:

- You can get information from your local health department about HIV, including where to get tested for the virus and the kinds of services available to your child and your family.
- Your local or state medical society can help you find a doctor.
- Your library may have information that you can share with your child. Ask your librarian if there is a special directory that lists groups for families whose children have HIV.
- Some hospitals and churches offer programs and support groups.

National hotlines and information clearinghouses can send you free publications and give you the latest news about drug testing and clinical trials. Below are some telephone numbers to help you get the information you need:

- **General Information**
  - National AIDS Hotline
    English   (800) 342-AIDS (2437)
    Spanish   (800) 344-SIDA (7432)
    Daily, 8:00 A.M. to 2:00 A.M. (ET)
  - TDD Service for the Deaf   (800) 243-7889
  - National AIDS Clearinghouse   (800) 458-5231
  - National Pediatric Resource Center   (800) 362-0071

continues

continued

- **HIV/AIDS Treatment Information**
  - American Foundation for AIDS Research   (800) 39AMFAR (392-6327)
  - AIDS Treatment Data Network   (212) 268-4196
  - Project Inform   (800) 822-7422
- **Clinical Trials Conducted by the National Institutes of Health or Food and Drug Administration–Approved Trials**
  - AIDS Clinical Trials Information Service   (800) TRIALS-A (874-2572)
- **Social Security Disability Benefits:** For confidential assistance in applying for Social Security disability benefits, call the Social Security Administration at (800) 722-1213. You also may request a personal earnings and benefit estimate statement (PEBES) to help you estimate the retirement, disability, and survivor benefits payable on your Social Security record.

Start your own list of services, support groups, and where to get information now:

_____

_____

_____

HINTS FOR GIVING MEDICINE TO BABIES AND TODDLERS

Giving medicine to your baby or young child does not have to be a chore for either of you. Just follow these steps:

1. Prepare the medicine and place it and other things you will need on a table within reach of the hand you will use to feed your child.
2. Hold the baby on your lap. If you are right handed, hold the baby on your left (if left handed, on your right).
3. With your left hand, hold baby's left arm; baby's right arm should go under your left arm, around your back.
4. Support the baby's head and shoulder firmly between your left arm and chest, and tilt the head back a little bit.
5. Squirt small amounts of medicine into the side of the baby's mouth alongside the back of the tongue on the side closest to your body (baby will have a hard time spitting and will not choke).
6. Keep the baby's mouth closed and hold baby's body upright until the medicine is swallowed.

Helpful Hints

- For liquids, use a soft plastic dropper or syringe.
- Try mixing medicine in food for spoon-feeding.

continues

continued

- Sit in a firm, comfortable chair.
- Put a bib or towel on the baby.
- Stay calm and use a soft voice.
- Reward baby with juice or water to rinse the mouth.

Notes:

Source: "HIV and Your Child," U.S. Department of Health and Human Services, Public Health Service, Agency for Health Care Policy and Research, AHCPR Publication No. 94-0576, January 1994.

General Information about Attention Deficit Disorder

WHAT IS ATTENTION DEFICIT DISORDER?

Attention deficit disorder (ADD), also called attention deficit hyperactivity disorder (ADHD), is a developmental disability estimated to affect between 3 percent and 5 percent of all children. The disorder is characterized by three predominant features: inattentiveness, impulsivity, and in many but not all cases, restlessness or hyperactivity. The disorder is most prevalent in children and is generally thought of as a childhood disorder. Recent studies, however, show that ADD can and does continue throughout the adult years. Current estimates suggest that approximately 50 percent to 65 percent of the children with ADD will have symptoms of the disorder as adolescents and adults.

WHAT CAUSES ADD?

Scientists and medical experts do not know precisely what causes ADD. Scientific evidence suggests that the disorder is genetically transmitted in many cases, and it is caused by a chemical imbalance or deficiency in certain neurotransmitters (chemicals that regulate the efficiency with which the brain controls behavior). Even though the exact cause of ADD remains unknown, it is known that ADD is a neurologically based medical problem and is not caused by poor parenting or diet.

WHAT ARE THE SIGNS OF ADD?

Inattention

A child with ADD is usually described as having a short attention span and as being distractible. The child will have difficulty concentrating (particularly on tasks that are routine or boring), listening, beginning or finishing tasks, and following directions (especially when three or more steps are given at one time). The child may appear to hear but not listen. Parents and teachers find that they often have to repeat directions and redirect the child to tasks such as getting ready for school, putting away toys or materials, completing worksheets, or finishing meals. Some children with ADD wander about, while others appear to daydream.

Attention is a skill that can be applied or directed in a variety of ways. The inattentiveness of a child with ADD, then, can take several forms. The child may have difficulty with selective attention (figuring out where his or her attention needs to be), focusing attention (the child knows where attention needs to be, but has difficulty zeroing in on the relevant task), sustaining attention (difficulty in maintaining attention through distractions), and dividing attention (difficulty doing two or more tasks at the same time). The child can have difficulty with one or all of these attention skills.

continues

continued

Impulsivity

A child with ADD often acts without thinking and has great difficulty waiting for his or her turn. The child may rush through assignments, shift excessively from one task to another, or frequently call out or ask irrelevant questions in class. This child will often interrupt others and have outbursts of inappropriate responses such as silliness or anger. When this child gets a case of "the giggles" or flies into a temper tantrum, he or she has great difficulty regaining emotional control.

Impulsivity often leads the child into physical danger and disapproval. He or she may engage in what looks like risk-taking behavior, such as running across a street without looking, climbing on or jumping from roof tops or tall trees, shooting a rubber band at a classmate, and so on. This child is not really a risk-taker but rather a child who has great difficulty controlling impulse. Often, the child is surprised to discover that he or she has gotten into a dangerous situation and has no idea how the situation developed or why.

Hyperactivity (Poor Motor Control)

Many (but not all) children with ADD are hyperactive. The child is often described as "always on the go" or "motor driven." This child runs or climbs excessively, has difficulty sitting still, fidgets, and engages in physical activity not related to the task, such as frequent pencil sharpening, falling out of his or her chair, finger tapping, or fiddling with objects. The child may also make excessive vocalizations, noises, or talk in a loud voice. It is important to realize, however, that some children are more hyperactive than others, and that a child with hyperactivity may have periods of calm as well.

In contrast to children who have ADD with hyperactivity, some children with ADD are underactive and often called "lazy" or "spacey." Children with ADD—those with hyperactivity and those without—are often "accident prone."

Disorganization

Inattentiveness and impulsivity often cause the child with ADD to be very disorganized. This child frequently forgets needed materials or assignments, loses his or her place, and has difficulty following sequences, such as directions with three or more steps. When given multiple worksheets or directions, the child often does not know where to begin or overlooks part of the assignment.

Social Skill Deficits

The child with ADD is often described as immature, lacking in self-awareness and sensitivity, and demanding of attention. The child may frustrate easily and be inconsiderate, overly sensitive, or emotionally overreactive. He or she may have difficulty expressing feelings, accepting

continues

continued

responsibility for behavior, or avoiding fights or arguments. This child often reacts to a social situation without first determining what behavior is desirable. For example, he or she may interrupt a game in progress or crack a "joke" during a serious moment. Though this child has social problems, it is important to understand that the social skills deficits stem from the disorder. This child wants to be liked and accepted, but usually goes about it in an inappropriate style.

DON'T ALL CHILDREN SHOW THESE SIGNS OCCASIONALLY?

From time to time all children will be inattentive, impulsive, and exhibit high energy levels. But, in the case of ADD, these behaviors are the rule, not the exception. This child is often described as experiencing difficulty "getting with the program" at home, in school, or with peers. Keep in mind, however, that the degree of difficulty varies with each child.

Many parents spend years wondering why their child is difficult to manage. They may blame themselves, thinking they are "bad" parents or feeling guilty and ashamed of the way they respond to the child. As the child grows older, the "out of step" behavior is often misunderstood as a deliberate choice to be noncompliant, and the child is blamed. When the child enters school and experiences difficulty in that environment, teachers with knowledge of this disability may recognize the behaviors as possible indicators of ADD. Teachers without knowledge of ADD may blame the child, the parents, or both.

HOW IS IT DETERMINED IF MY CHILD HAS ADD?

There is a big difference between suspecting a child has ADD and knowing for certain. Parents are cautioned against diagnosing this disorder by themselves. ADD is a disability that, without proper identification and treatment, can have serious and long-term complications.

Unfortunately, there is no simple test, such as a blood test or urinalysis, that will determine if a child has this disorder. Diagnosing ADD is complicated and much like putting together a puzzle. An accurate diagnosis requires an assessment conducted by a well-trained professional, usually a developmental pediatrician, child psychologist, child psychiatrist, or pediatric neurologist.

WHAT DOES AN ADD ASSESSMENT INVOLVE?

The evaluation for diagnosing ADD usually includes the following six elements:

1. a thorough medical and family history
2. a physical examination
3. interviews with the parents, child, and child's teacher
4. behavior rating scales
5. observation of the child
6. psychological tests (which measure IQ and social and emotional adjustment, as well as screen for learning disabilities)

continues

continued

Sophisticated medical tests such as EEGs (to measure the brain's electrical activity) or MRIs (an X-ray that gives a picture of the brain's anatomy) are not part of the routine assessment. Such tests are usually given only when the diagnostician suspects another problem, and those cases are rare. Positron emission tomography (PET) scans have recently been used for research purposes but they are not part of the diagnostic evaluation.

The professional evaluating the child will look at all the information collected and decide whether or not the child has ADD. This professional will base this decision in part on whether the child exhibits at least eight of the behaviors (called criteria) listed in the American Psychiatric Association's (APA) *Diagnostic and Statistical Manual* (DSM).

It is useful to know that in recent years the description of ADD in the DSM has been revised as a result of research and the opinions of experts in the field. While prior editions of the DSM referred to the disorder as "ADD with hyperactivity" and "ADD without hyperactivity," the latest edition of the DSM uses the acronym ADHD, which stands for attention deficit hyperactivity disorder. This change in terminology shows the predominance of hyperactivity as one characteristic of the disability. Yet, many children with attention deficit disorder are not hyperactive. The latest DSM acknowledges this fact by stating that impulsiveness and hyperactivity are not always evident in undifferentiated attention deficit disorder. Thus, while professionals may assess a child according to the criteria listed in the DSM, they will take into consideration that hyperactive or impulsive behavior may not necessarily be present in all children with ADD.

In general, then, for a child to be diagnosed as having ADD, behavioral signs must be evident in early childhood (prior to age seven), inappropriate for the child's age, and present for at least six months.

All children with ADD do not have the disorder to the same degree or intensity. ADD can be mild with the child exhibiting few symptoms in perhaps only the home or school environment. Other children may have moderate to severe degrees of ADD and experience difficulty in all areas of their lives.

HOW IS ADD TREATED?

There is no cure or "quick fix" when treating ADD. Widely publicized cures such as special diets have, for the most part, proven ineffective.

Effective treatment of ADD generally requires the following basic components: education about the disorder, training in the use of behavior management, medication when indicated, and an appropriate educational program.

Parents and teachers need to be aware of the symptoms of ADD and how those symptoms impact the child's ability to function at home, in school, and in social situations. Once the adults in the child's life understand that the child cannot help many of his or her problematic behaviors, they will be able to structure situations to enable the child to behave appropriately and achieve success. Remember, the child who has difficulty with attention, impulse control, and regulation of physical activity needs help and encouragement to overcome these problems.

Source: Mary Fowler, *Attention Deficit Disorder*, National Information Center for Children and Youth with Disabilities (NICHCY), Washington, DC, September 1991.

Learning Disabilities

DEFINITION OF LEARNING DISABILITIES*

The regulations for Public Law 94-142 (The Individuals with Disabilities Education Act) define a learning disability as a "disorder in one or more of the basic psychological processes involved in understanding or in using spoken or written language, which may manifest itself in an imperfect ability to listen, think, speak, read, write, spell, or to do mathematical calculations."

The federal definition further states that learning disabilities include "such conditions as perceptual handicaps, brain injury, minimal brain dysfunction, dyslexia, and developmental aphasia." According to the law, learning disabilities do not include learning problems that are primarily the result of visual, hearing, or motor handicaps; mental retardation; or environmental, cultural, or economic disadvantage. Definitions of learning disabilities also vary among states.

Having a single term to describe this category of children with disabilities reduces some of the confusion, but there are many conflicting theories about what causes learning disabilities and how many there are. The label "learning disabilities" is all-embracing; it describes a syndrome, not a specific child with specific problems. The definition assists in classifying children, not teaching them. Parents and teachers need to concentrate on the individual child. They need to observe both how and how well the child performs, to assess strengths and weaknesses, and invent ways to help each child learn. It is important to remember that there is a high degree of interrelationship and overlap among the areas of learning. Therefore, children with learning disabilities may exhibit a combination of characteristics.

These problems may mildly, moderately, or severely impair the learning process.

OVERVIEW OF LEARNING DISABILITIES**

Does My Child Have a Learning Disability?

All children do not learn in the same way or at the same pace. Most children, however, can master basic skills in speaking, reading, writing, spelling, and math in the early grades of school or before. For the child with a learning disability, however, it is extremely difficult to progress in one or more of these basic skills without special help.

The child with a learning disability has a cluster of difficulties in one or more of these four categories:

1. speaking and listening
2. reading, writing, and spelling
3. reasoning skills
4. arithmetic concepts and computation

continues

continued

Other symptoms that may help identify a child with a learning disability include:

- short attention span
- poor memory
- difficulty following directions
- problems in telling the difference between letters, numbers, or sounds
- eye-hand coordination problems
- difficulties with sequencing
- disorganization
- day-to-day performance differences
- impulsiveness
- late or immature speech development
- difficulty telling time and telling right from left
- late motor development
- difficulty with discipline
- difficulty naming familiar people or things

Dyslexia

Dyslexia (a term used to describe specific language difficulties) and other types of learning disabilities can affect a child's ability to read, write, spell, and do math.

A child with dyslexia may have one or more of these problems:

- difficulty in learning and remembering a printed word or symbol
- reversals of letters or improper letter sequencing
- unusual spelling errors
- illegible handwriting
- poor composition of written work

How Many People Have Learning Disabilities?

It is estimated that as many as one out of every seven children and adults has some form of learning disability. Some recent studies have even suggested figures as high as 10 percent to 15 percent of the population may be seriously affected by learning disabilities.

What Causes Learning Disabilities?

There is probably no single cause of learning disabilities, but some of the causes that scientists are investigating include:

- *Genetic predisposition.* The family of a child with a learning disability will often report that other family members have had similar problems.

continues

continued

- *Brain differences.* A recent study found differences in the size and shape of parts of the brains of children with dyslexia compared to the brains of children who do not have dyslexia.
- *Toxic substances.* Exposure to high levels of toxic substances such as lead can cause hyperactivity and learning problems that may contribute to a learning disability.
- *Prenatal exposures.* Researchers are studying the effects of substances (drugs, chemicals, alcohol, additives) that may be toxic to the central nervous system of the developing fetus.

TYPES OF LEARNING DISABILITIES***

The present model of learning disabilities distinguishes four stages of information processing used in learning: input, integration, memory, and output. *Input* is the process of recording in the brain information that comes from the senses. *Integration* is the process of interpreting this information. *Memory* is storage of this information for later retrieval. *Output* of information is achieved through language or motor (muscular) activity. Learning disabilities can be classified by their effects at one or more of these stages. Each child has individual strengths and weaknesses at each stage.

Stage 1: Input

The first major type of problem at the input stage is a visual perception disability. Some children have difficulty in recognizing the position and shape of what they see. Letters may be reversed or rotated. For example, the child might confuse the letters d, b, p, q, and g. The child might also have difficulty distinguishing a significant form from its background. Children with this disability often have reading problems. They may jump over words, read the same line twice, or skip lines. Other children have poor depth perception or poor distance judgment. They might bump into things, fall over chairs, or knock over drinks.

The other major input disability is auditory perception disability. Children may have difficulty understanding because they do not distinguish subtle differences in sounds. They confuse words and phrases that sound alike—"blue" with "blow" or "ball" with "bell." Some children find it hard to pick out a sound from its background; they may not respond to the sound of a parent's or teacher's voice, and it may seem that they are not listening or paying attention. Others process sound slowly and therefore cannot keep up with the flow of conversation, inside or outside the classroom. Suppose a parent says, "It's getting late. Go upstairs, wash your face, and get into your pajamas. Then come back down for a snack." A child with an auditory perception disability might hear only the first part and stay upstairs.

Stage 2: Integration

Integration disabilities take several forms, corresponding to the three stages of sequencing, abstraction, and organization.

continues

continued

Sequencing

A child with a sequencing disability might recount a story by starting in the middle, going to the beginning, and then proceeding to the end. The child might also reverse the order of letters in words, seeing "dog" and reading "god." Such children are often unable to use single units of a memorized sequence correctly. If asked what comes after Wednesday, they have to start counting from Sunday to get the answer. In using a dictionary, they must start with "A" each time.

Abstraction

The second type of integration disability involves abstraction. Children with this problem have difficulty inferring meaning. They may read a story but not be able to generalize from it. They may confuse different meanings of the same word used in different ways. They find it difficult to understand jokes, puns, or idioms.

Organization

Once recorded, sequenced, and understood, information must be organized—integrated into a constant flow and related to what has previously been learned. Children with an organization disability find it difficult to make bits of information cohere into concepts. They may learn a series of facts without being able to answer general questions that require the use of these facts. Their lives inside and outside of the classroom reflect this disorganization.

Stage 3: Memory

Disabilities also develop at the third stage of information processing: memory. Short-term memory retains information briefly while attending to it or concentrating on it. For example, most people can retain the ten digits of a long-distance telephone number long enough to dial it, but forget it if interrupted. When information is repeated often enough, it enters long-term memory, where it is stored and can be retrieved later. Most memory disabilities affect short-term memory only; children with these disabilities need many more repetitions than usual to retain information.

Stage 4: Output

At the fourth stage, output, there are both language and motor disabilities.

Language Disabilities

Language disabilities almost always involve what is called "demand language" rather than spontaneous language. Spontaneous language occurs when initiating speech—selecting the

continues

continued

subject, organizing thoughts, and finding the correct words before uttering a word. Demand language occurs when someone else creates the circumstances in which communication is required. A question is asked, and the child must simultaneously organize his or her thoughts, find the right words, and answer. A child with a language disability may speak normally when initiating conversation but respond hesitantly in demand situations—pause, ask for the question to be repeated, give a confused answer, or fail to find the right words.

Motor Disabilities

Motor disabilities are of two types: poor coordination of large muscle groups, which is called gross motor disability, and poor coordination of small muscle groups, which is called fine motor disability. Gross motor disabilities make children clumsy. They stumble, fall, and bump into things. They may have difficulty in running, climbing, riding a bicycle, buttoning shirts, or tying shoelaces. The most common type of fine motor disability is difficulty in coordinating the muscles needed for writing. Children with motor disabilities write slowly, and their handwriting is often unreadable. They may also make spelling, grammar, and punctuation errors.

Notes:

*Source: "General Information about Learning Disabilities," National Information Center for Children and Youth with Disabilities (NICHCY), Washington, DC, September 1992.

**Source: "Learning Disabilities," NIS Information Sheet, National Information System for Vietnam Veterans and Their Families, The University of South Carolina, Columbia, South Carolina.

***Source: Larry Silver, "A Look at Learning Disabilities in Children and Youth," November 1991. Reprinted with permission of Learning Disabilities Association of Montgomery County, Inc., PO Box 623, Rockville, Maryland 20848-0623; 301–933–2510.

General Information about Brain Injuries

A brain injury is any trauma to the head that results in brain damage. Damage can be very mild to severe. Brain injuries are classified into three types: blunt, penetrating, and compression.

BLUNT INJURIES

Blunt injuries are the most common type of brain injury. These injuries occur in two ways:

1. when a moving head hits a fixed object (for example, head hits the windshield in a car accident)
2. when the head is stationary and is suddenly hit by a blunt moving object (for example, head hit by a baseball bat)

The skull may or may not be fractured at the site of the blunt injury. Brain damage may occur at the site of the injury even when there is no fracture of the skull. Often the most damage occurs on the surface of the brain immediately *opposite* the site of the injury. This damage is caused by the "jarring" of the soft tissue against the opposite side of the bony skull.

This movement causes diffuse, widespread damage to the nerve cells and nerve fibers in the brain. Diffuse damage results in the loss of consciousness.

PENETRATING INJURIES

A common example of a penetrating injury is a gunshot wound. Damage to the brain is local and occurs along the path the penetrating object has traveled. Diffuse damage to brain cells does not occur and, therefore, there is usually no loss of consciousness.

COMPRESSION INJURIES

Compression injuries occur when the head is crushed. These injuries usually produce multiple skull fractures, often without loss of consciousness. Additionally, brain damage may be produced after the initial injury by several means:

- intracranial hemorrhage, or bleeding in the brain, due to severing or shearing of blood vessels
- infection due to open fractures
- brain swelling inside the skull
- hypoxia, or lack of oxygen to the brain cells, from all of the above and also from a severe drop in blood pressure from shock and bleeding in any part of the body

Courtesy of Pediatric Rehabilitation Institute, Cardinal Glennon Children's Hospital, St. Louis, Missouri.

How the Brain Works

WHAT IS THE BRAIN?

The brain is the central organ of the nervous system. It controls all functions of the body including thinking, moving, and breathing. Messages are sent to, and received from, other parts of the body through the spinal cord and the nerves. The brain uses sensory information (taste, smell, sight, touch, and hearing) to control and coordinate movement. The brain has three major parts, the cortex (sometimes called the cerebrum), the cerebellum, and the brainstem. It looks something like the diagram below.

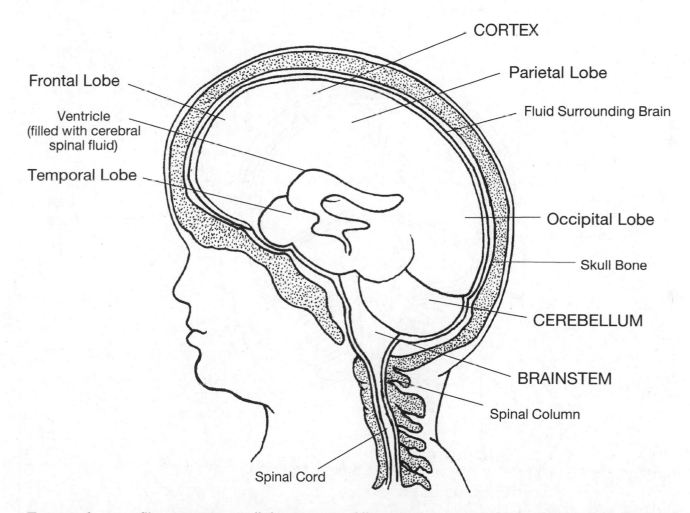

Tracts of nerve fibers connect all three parts. All messages *enter* the brain through the brainstem, and all messages to the body *exit* through the brainstem. At the lower end of the brainstem, where it leaves the skull, the spinal cord begins. Because everything is so compact in the brainstem, a small area of damage can have a great effect.

continues

continued

THE CORTEX

The largest part of the brain, the cortex, is divided into hemispheres (two halves). Each hemisphere controls activity on the opposite side of the body. If, for example, there is damage on the left side of the brain, the right hand or leg may be affected. In each hemisphere there are four lobes: the frontal, parietal, temporal, and occipital.

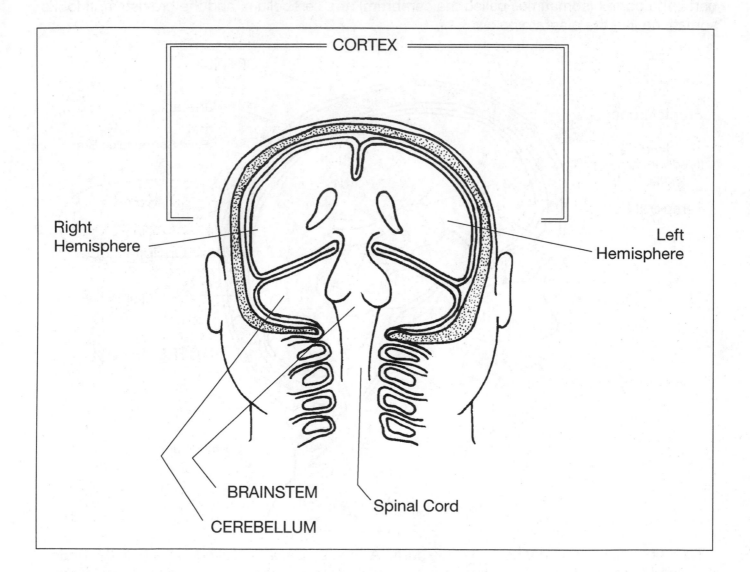

Parts of the brain control different functions. Examples of these functions follow.

continues

continued

Functions of the Frontal Lobe

continues

continued

Functions of the Parietal Lobe

READING **INTERPRETATION OF SENSATION** **SPATIAL RELATIONSHIPS**

Functions of the Temporal Lobe

MEMORY **UNDERSTANDING OF LANGUAGE** **HEARING**

Functions of the Occipital Lobe

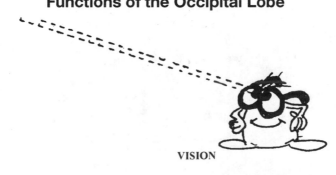

VISION

continues

continued

THE CEREBELLUM

BALANCE

COORDINATION OF MOVEMENT

THE BRAINSTEM

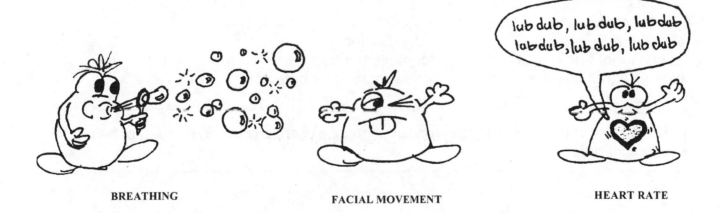

BREATHING   **FACIAL MOVEMENT**   **HEART RATE**

Source: KCRC TBI Team; Editors, Judy Gary, M.Ed., and Pat Morris, R.N.; Illustrator for Functions of the Brain, Peter Shibuya, R.N.; *Traumatic Brain Injury: A Guide for Families*, Kluge Children's Rehabilitation Center, Children's Medical Center of the University of Virginia, Charlottesville, Virginia, 1992.

Changes after Traumatic Brain Injury

Your child's traumatic brain injury will cause changes in many areas. Some of these areas are discussed below.

COGNITION (THINKING)

Traumatic brain injury (TBI) may cause general loss of overall thinking functions. Or, it may cause specific deficits (problems) in understanding, in judgment, or in being able to pay attention or concentrate. Memory problems, especially short-term memory problems, are very common after head injury. Sometimes a child may repeat a movement or word over and over. This behavior is called perseveration. Even after recovery, some children may have learning problems.

> Calm, structured surroundings help your child "sort" thoughts. Speaking in simple sentences may help the child better understand communication.

MOTOR (MOVEMENT)

The body is controlled by messages from the brain. When there is a brain injury, the muscles and joints are usually affected. Some of the common words related to muscles and joints include:

- tone
  — spasticity (tight or stiff muscle tone)
  — hypotonia (loose or floppy muscle tone)
- ataxia (problems with unsteadiness and balance)
- apraxia (not being able to plan motor movements)
- paralysis (not being able to move one or more arms or legs)

> Splinting, casting, therapy, and medicine may be used to prevent, correct, or help physical deformities.

PERSONALITY (EMOTIONS AND BEHAVIOR)

Personality may be very different after brain injury. Changes are not always permanent. Most of the time when people are recovering from brain injury they go through stages of agitation. An agitated child seems to be bothered by everything. He or she may be irritable, combative,

continues

continued

impatient, and rude. Some children even have emotional outbursts. This behavior may be very hard to cope with, but it is expected. It can last a few days or a few weeks.

Sometimes too much activity, loud noises, television, and visitors may trigger agitated behavior. This agitation occurs because the child's brain is having trouble dealing with all of this information the way it might have before the TBI. Your child may say words and do things very differently than before the injury.

> Ways to help an agitated child include avoiding sudden changes and praising efforts for self-control. Being consistent, predictable, and structured helps children feel less confused and safer. Seeing familiar faces is comforting. It is important for all caregivers, including the family, to use the same approaches. Parents and schools may have to learn new skills for managing behavior, helping the child learn, and getting along with others.

PERCEPTION (SENSING, TOUCH, SIGHT, SMELL, TASTE)

There may be a loss or change in the way a child with a brain injury senses information. Tactile defensiveness, for example, is an oversensitive reaction to touch. A touch on the arm, for instance, may feel like "pins and needles." Food may taste or smell differently. Bright lights may be troubling.

> Remembering these sensory changes helps meet your child's needs.

SEIZURES (CONVULSIONS)

Seizures can occur at the time of the accident, or they may happen weeks or months later when the brain is healing. If there is a seizure at the time of injury, an anticonvulsant (medicine) is almost always given.

> Children who have had a brain injury may continue to take these drugs for many years after the injury to prevent seizures. They should be watched carefully for seizures, drug levels, and changes.

Source: KCRC TBI Team; Editors, Judy Gary, M.Ed., and Pat Morris, R.N.; *Traumatic Brain Injury: A Guide for Families*, Kluge Children's Rehabilitation Center, Children's Medical Center of the University of Virginia, Charlottesville, 1992.

Recovery from Traumatic Brain Injury

Children and young adolescents often recover from a traumatic brain injury (TBI) to a greater degree than adults with a similar injury. Their recovery, though, tends to take longer. For older adolescents it is hard to say whether they will recover more like an adult or more like a child.

RECOVERY

Children and adolescents usually recover from TBI in spurts (quick gains in function). These spurts may alternate with plateaus (periods of very little change). It is just like going up a mountain: climbing a small hill, stopping for rests, or maybe even going down a few steps to gain momentum to get up the mountain.

While recovery is happening in many areas at one time (including motor, cognition, communication, and emotion), the *rate* of recovery in one area may not equal the *rate* of recovery in another. For example, a child may make motor gains so quickly that his or her therapy may be changed daily to keep up with the gains. At the same time, he or she may make only small gains in memory or communication. Later, the language skills may improve at a faster rate than the motor skills.

Recovery from TBI is a long process. Parents usually want to know how much damage there is and how much recovery to expect. Tests like MRI and CAT scans provide part of the picture. The best answers to those questions, however, come from examining and assessing the child.

Your child will go through many stages during rehabilitation. Knowing these stages, or levels, will enhance understanding of the child's behavior. Remember: *All children with TBI recover at different rates*.

The Rancho Los Amigos Scales will be mentioned often. These scales are *guides* to understanding the recovery process. If your child is between infancy and school age, your therapist will speak in terms of consciousness (alertness) levels. Your child's health care team can increase understanding of how these scales apply to your child.

CHILDREN IN A COMA

A child who is in a coma will have physical needs met first. Physical needs include skin care, respiratory care, and splinting and casting of arms or legs. Children in comas are usually fed by a small tube through the nose to the stomach (nasogastric tube) or a gastrostomy tube placed through the stomach wall.

Family and team health care members work together to provide sensory stimulation (using touch, taste, smell, vision, and hearing) to try to organize and reorient brain function. To help with this stimulation, families might bring pictures, tapes, and favorite objects that the child may recognize. As with all stages of recovery, rest is important to prevent over-stimulation.

continues

continued

INPATIENT REHABILITATION

Inpatient rehabilitation is needed as long as the child is making rapid gains in functioning. Treatment will change continuously. When recovery begins to plateau, or level off, discharge to output therapy and school may be the plan. It is important to remember that recovery from TBI can continue as long as 2 to 5 years, though the most rapid gain occurs in the first year.

Notes:

Source: KCRC TBI Team; Editors, Judy Gary, M.Ed., and Pat Morris, R.N.; *Traumatic Brain Injury: A Guide for Families*, Kluge Children's Rehabilitation Center, Children's Medical Center of the University of Virginia, Charlottesville, 1992.

Spinal Cord Injury

WHAT IS THE SPINAL CORD?

The backbone is the number one support for the body. It has many bones stacked on top of each other like building blocks. The bones stacked on top of each other are called vertebrae. The spinal cord runs through these stacked bones. The bones help protect the spinal cord.

The spinal cord is part of the nervous system. The spinal cord acts like a telephone cable. It sends messages to and from the brain to all parts of the body. The brain is like a computer and sorts all the messages. The spinal cord goes from the brain, down the middle of the back, to the buttocks. The adult spinal cord is about 18 inches long. It contains many nerves that are like the wires in a telephone cable. With a spinal cord injury (SCI), the spinal cord can be hurt any place between the neck and the buttocks.

WHAT HAPPENS WHEN A SPINAL CORD INJURY OCCURS?

When a spinal cord injury occurs all of the nerves above the injury keep working like they always have. Below the injury, things are not working right. The spinal cord nerves cannot send messages to and from the brain to parts of the body like it did before the injury. If the child cannot move his or her legs, but movement and use of the arms are like always, the spinal cord is hurt in the "back" area. A child who cannot use his or her legs has paraplegia. If the child cannot move his or her arms and legs, the spinal cord is injured in the neck area. A child who cannot use his or her legs and also cannot use his or her arms as he or she did before the injury has quadriplegia or tetraplegia.

The closer the injury of the spinal cord is to the brain, the higher the level of injury. Fewer parts and systems of the body work normally when there is a higher level of injury.

WILL THE CHILD BE ABLE TO MOVE AGAIN?

The answer to this question depends on how damaged the nerves in the spinal cord were when the injury occurred. The child's physician will stick pins in the legs and arms and also ask the child to try to move. This examination tells the physician how the nerves are working.

The nerves that go from the brain and down the spine go to other parts of the body, too. The lungs (to help you breathe), the bladder, and the bowels are some parts of the body that may not work the same as before the spinal cord injury.

continues

continued

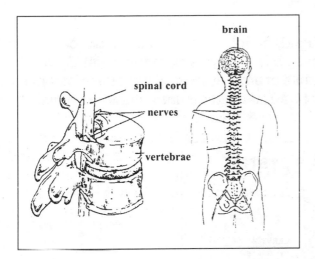

The spinal cord is protected by the vertebrae (backbone).

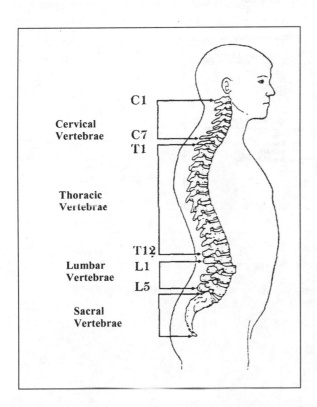

This picture shows the place and names of the vertebrae. A physician or nurse can explain where the level of injury is.

Source: *Learning about Spinal Cord Injury*, Medical Rehabilitation Research and Training Center in Prevention and Treatment of Secondary Complications of Spinal Cord Injury, Training Office, Spain Rehabilitation Center, University of Alabama at Birmingham, © 1991.

Paralysis

When nerve fibers from the spinal cord are damaged, quadriplegia or paraplegia can result. Quadriplegia is paralysis below the neck, and paraplegia is paralysis from the waist down. The level of injury determines whether a person loses the use of arms, hands, and legs. A person may also experience renal and respiratory failure, loss of sexual function, intractable pain, incontinence, and a variety of other disabling conditions.

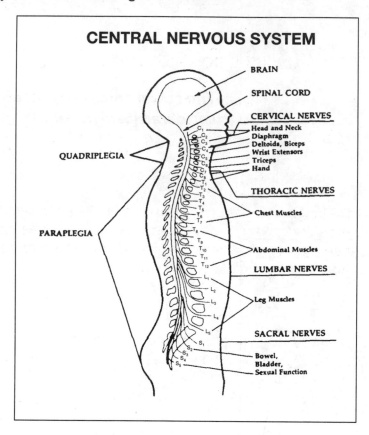

Courtesy of American Paralysis Association, Springfield, New Jersey.

Prematurity

DEFINITION

The usual gestational age—the length of time the fetus is carried in the uterus—ranges from 37 to 42 weeks. (Two techniques for determining gestational age are assessing the newborn's neuromuscular and physical characteristics and counting from the first day of the mother's last menstrual period.) Babies with a gestational age of less than 37 weeks are considered premature, or preterm.

POSSIBLE COMPLICATIONS

A preterm baby may be physically healthy at birth—though immature—and then develop serious problems after birth. These complications may, to varying degrees, damage the brain and other tissues, affecting the baby's future health and development.

Respiratory Distress Syndrome

Normally, the air sacs of the lungs are opened by the newborn's first breaths; they are kept open by a chemical coating called surfactant. If the premature infant does not produce enough surfactant, the lungs collapse after each breath. The result is too little oxygen in the blood and body tissues and a disruption of the acid-base balance.

Infection

The child's immature defense mechanisms are sometimes unable to combat bacteria that are in the environment or that are introduced through IV lines, chest tubes for collapsed lungs, or other equipment. This may result in an infection of the blood (sepsis) or an inflammation of the membranes surrounding the brain or spinal cord (meningitis).

Intracranial Hemorrhage

There may be bleeding into the brain substance or, more commonly, around or into the fluid-filled chambers of the brain (peri- or intraventricular hemorrhage). This may result in the spastic type of cerebral palsy (stiff and difficult movement).

Malnutrition

Because many premature infants have difficulty tolerating oral feeding, they may suffer temporary malnutrition. At times, these babies must receive their total caloric and fluid needs by IV feeding or through a tube.

continues

continued

Jaundice

Jaundice is a yellowish color of the skin and whites of the eyes, caused by an accumulation of bilirubin in the body. Bilirubin, a product of the breakdown of red blood cells, normally is removed by the liver and excreted into the intestines. In preterm babies, the liver may not eliminate the bilirubin from the blood quickly enough. While moderate levels usually are inconsequential (except in sick or very premature babies), high levels may damage the brain permanently, particularly parts called the basal ganglia. Such damage, called kernicterus, may result in athetoid cerebral palsy (involuntary and uncontrolled movement).

Apnea

Apnea is a prolonged pause between breaths, often accompanied by a slowing of the heart rate (bradycardia) or a blue color to the skin (cyanosis). While this condition may occur in full-term infants, it is particularly common in those who are premature. Apnea is different from periodic breathing, typical in premature infants, in which a period of rapid breathing alternates with a short period (five seconds, or so) of no breathing.

The sudden onset of apnea may indicate a serious illness, such as sepsis, meningitis, pneumonia, intracranial hemorrhage, or low blood sugar (hypoglycemia).

Physical stimulation is often adequate to restart breathing. In the absence of serious illness, apnea is treated by environmental stimulation, such as a change in temperature or gentle rocking on a water bed. Medical therapy includes theophylline and caffeine; at times, cardiopulmonary resuscitation is necessary. Occasionally, babies are sent home from the hospital with apnea monitors, which sound an alarm when there is a prolonged period of no breathing.

Necrotizing Enterocolitis

Inflammation, and sometimes death (necrosis), of intestinal wall tissue is a life-threatening complication, the exact cause of which is unknown (though it seems to be related to other problems that beset the preterm infant). In mild cases, conservative medical management is adequate; if a segment of the intestine dies, however, it must be removed surgically, and the shortened bowel may result in temporary—but prolonged—malabsorption of nutrients and diarrhea.

Congestive Heart Failure

During intrauterine life, fetal circulation bypasses the lungs by means of a small blood vessel called the ductus arteriosus. This vessel normally closes at the time of birth. However, in some preterm infants or infants with heart defects, it may remain open, leading to enlargement of the heart and backup of blood in the lungs (congestive heart failure). In some cases, this vessel closes on its own or is closed by the administration of certain drugs; in other instances, it must be tied off surgically.

Source: James A. Blackman, MD, *Medical Aspects of Developmental Disabilities in Children Birth to Three*, ed. 2, Aspen Publishers, Inc., © 1990.

Respiratory Distress Syndrome

DESCRIPTION

Respiratory distress syndrome (RDS) is a pulmonary disorder commonly encountered in premature infants. It is among the most frequent causes of death in premature infants and the most common illness in many neonatal intensive care units. The usual signs are labored, grunting breathing, poor oxygenation of body tissues in room air, and characteristic findings on chest X-ray examinations.

CAUSE

RDS is caused by a deficiency of a material called surfactant, which is needed to keep the air sacs (alveoli) in the lungs open. When surfactant is absent or when it is present in inadequate amounts, the air sacs collapse, and hence the entire lung collapses (a condition known as atelectasis). The tremendous energy then required to breathe leads to exhaustion and the above-mentioned signs of RDS.

A fetus seldom produces adequate amounts of surfactant before 36 weeks of gestation. RDS is therefore common among premature infants. This condition rarely occurs in full-term infants unless the lungs are particularly immature, as they may be, for example, in infants born to women with diabetes.

INCIDENCE

RDS occurs in 1 percent of newborns, making it the most common severe respiratory problem in the first few days after birth. The incidence of RDS varies greatly with gestational age; it is rare in full-term infants and extremely common in infants born prior to 32 weeks of gestation.

SYMPTOMS

Usually within a few hours after birth, the premature baby with RDS audibly grunts on expiration, breathing frequently and with great effort, flaring the nostrils and retracting the muscles between the ribs and just below the rib cage. The infant is also lethargic and has a bluish color due to decreased oxygen concentration in the blood.

COURSE

Depending on the prematurity of the infant, the duration of RDS may be one to two days, or it may last more than a week. This condition usually improves when the infant begins producing adequate amounts of surfactant.

continues

continued

ACCOMPANYING HEALTH PROBLEMS

Premature infants suffering from RDS are vulnerable to other health problems associated with prematurity. One of the most important of these is bleeding into the fluid-filled spaces of the brain (intraventricular hemorrhage), a condition often associated with later disabilities.

Infants with very severe RDS, especially those who are on mechanical ventilators for prolonged periods or those who receive high concentrations of oxygen, are at risk for developing a chronic lung disorder known as bronchopulmonary dysplasia.

MEDICAL MANAGEMENT

Neonatal intensive care units, anticipating RDS in premature infants, routinely monitor pulse and respiration, along with the amount of oxygen in the blood. At the first clinical sign of RDS, treatment is begun. Initially this may take the form of increasing the concentration of inspired oxygen. Often, constant distending pressure through the nose or mouth (continuous positive airway pressure) is applied to keep the alveoli and lungs from collapsing. Some infants require a mechanical ventilator, which essentially breathes for them. Infants with RDS usually are not able to nurse or drink formula from a bottle; they must be either fed intravenously or given formula or breast milk through a tube that is passed through the mouth or nose and into the stomach.

IMPLICATIONS FOR EDUCATION

Today, approximately 90 percent of infants with RDS survive. Of these, the majority will develop normally and do well in regular classes. A small group, however, particularly those who have experienced intraventricular hemorrhage or other medical complications during the early days of life, may have developmental disabilities including cognitive and/or physical impairment. Some may have continuing problems with respiratory illness, especially during the first year. Breathing difficulties, cough, or fever should always be evaluated by a health provider.

Source: James A. Blackman, MD, *Medical Aspects of Developmental Disabilities in Children Birth to Three*, ed. 2, Aspen Publishers, Inc., © 1990.

Bronchopulmonary Dysplasia

DESCRIPTION

Bronchopulmonary dysplasia (BPD), sometimes called chronic lung disease of the premature infant, is a condition characterized by chronic lung changes in infants who have had respiratory distress syndrome and/or have required prolonged mechanical ventilation and high concentrations of oxygen. Full-term infants with meconium aspiration, pneumonia, or other causes of respiratory distress may develop BPD. Infants with BPD require oxygen for at least 28 days, and their chest X-rays show abnormalities.

CAUSE

BPD results both from the initial injury to the lungs and from its treatment. Irritation to the lungs from inflammation is compounded by the repeated pounding pressures delivered by a ventilator. Extra oxygen, while needed to maintain adequate blood levels, can itself further damage the lungs. Mechanical ventilation and supplemental oxygen are necessary but further contribute to the disease. Nevertheless, these treatments must continue until the infant's lungs heal and new, normal air sacs grow.

DETECTION

The most common symptom of BPD is an increased respiratory effort and rate. Listening to the lungs, one hears wheezing, honking, and crackling. Infants on ventilators have periodic episodes of blue spells that require increases in oxygen delivery and respiratory support. They tend to retain carbon dioxide in the blood and need supplemental oxygen, often for long periods after hospital discharge. Chest X-rays show signs of chronic inflammation and scarring, overexpansion because of air trapping, and sometimes an enlarged heart because of the extra work it has to do to pump blood through damaged lungs.

COURSE

BPD, by definition, is a chronic disease lasting many months to years with symptoms that can be mild to severe. An infant with mild disease may be discharged from the hospital when other problems, such as feeding, have resolved. In severe cases, the child may remain in the hospital for over a year. With moderate disease, the child may go home but require a high level of medical support, sometimes provided by the parents alone or with home nursing assistance. Improvement is very gradual and setbacks are common.

ACCOMPANYING HEALTH PROBLEMS

BPD is one of the most complex health conditions because so many body systems are affected by the disease and its treatments. In addition to the complications of prematurity, there are health problems specifically related to BPD.

continues

continued

Infection

Infants with BPD are particularly susceptible to lower respiratory tract infections. Recurrent ear infections may lead to hearing loss.

Kidney Stones

BPD is treated commonly with medicines such as furosemide (Lasix), which lead to calcium deposits and stone formation in the kidneys.

Fragile Bones

Because of feeding problems and some of the medications used, the bones may not mineralize as they should and thus are more likely to fracture. Rickets, a bone disease caused by insufficient calcium and vitamin D, is common.

Abnormalities of the Trachea

Infection and irritation from the tube placed in the trachea to ventilate the infant mechanically may cause the trachea to narrow and collapse. A tracheostomy (an opening through the tissues of the neck into the trachea) is placed if the child has difficulty moving air through the damaged trachea or if it is anticipated that the child will need prolonged ventilator support.

Vomiting and Feeding Problems

Infants with BPD often have gastroesophageal reflux; that is, the highly acid stomach contents back up abnormally into the esophagus, causing irritation, pain, and the risk that they will back up far enough to spill into the trachea, producing aspiration pneumonia. Treatments include positioning, thickened feedings, or at times a gastrostomy and other treatment to prevent reflux. Infants who have been fed for long periods by tube (either nasogastric or gastrostomy) and have had unpleasant oral experiences (such as suctioning and tubes) frequently resist attempts at oral feedings.

Poor Growth

Because of feeding problems, food intolerance, repeated setbacks from infections or respiratory complications, and excessive caloric needs for increased energy expenditures and "catch up" growth, infants with BPD tend to fall and remain well below the fifth percentile on weight and weight-for-length growth charts. Persistent attention to growth is needed to avoid possibly permanent injury to tissues, especially those of the central nervous system.

continues

continued

High Blood Pressure

Damage to the kidneys and lungs can lead to high blood pressure. This should be monitored on a regular basis.

Delayed Development

A child with BPD may lag in development. Creative ways must be sought to allow a child tied to a ventilator to move and interact with people, to provide a variety of experiences outside the hospital room, and to provide opportunities for attachment and healthy emotional development. It is in this area where the most regrettable, avoidable damage can be done if heroic efforts are not made to normalize the environment as much as possible.

MEDICAL MANAGEMENT

Parents need to learn about nutrition, respiratory status, oxygen therapy, medications, cardiopulmonary resuscitation, and routine health maintenance.

Notes:

Source: James A. Blackman, MD, *Medical Aspects of Developmental Disabilities in Children Birth to Three*, ed. 2, Aspen Publishers, Inc., © 1990.

Failure To Thrive

DAILY WEIGHTS

It is important to weigh your baby every day to make certain that the weight has stabilized or is increasing. Some tips for weighing your baby include:

- Weigh at the same time every day.
- Weigh the baby in the nude on the same scale.

Report a weight loss to the nurse or physician as soon as possible on the day it is discovered.

NUTRITIONAL INTAKE

Your baby's physician has prescribed the following special diet for your baby:

_____

_____

_____

_____

_____

_____

Maintain a daily log for the nurse to review when he or she returns. Write the time of day and type and amount of nutrients ingested. You may use ounces or cup measurements. (Be certain to use a measuring cup for accuracy if you are using this type of measurement.)

WHEN TO NOTIFY THE DOCTOR

It is very important that the baby's doctor be notified of a:

- decrease in the baby's weight
- fever greater than 100°F (rectal) or 102°F (under the arm)
- ongoing episodes of vomiting
- inability to swallow nutrients
- continual crying

MEDICAL APPOINTMENT FOLLOW-THROUGH

It is very important that you schedule and keep the baby's doctor appointments. Your doctor has ordered home care to *supplement* his or her care, not to replace it. Your doctor is the

continues

continued

only person who can make changes in the medication and order tests that may be indicated. Discuss any transportation problems you may have with the nurse—there may be ways to help you.

WHAT IS FAILURE TO THRIVE?

Failure to thrive is diagnosed when a baby's weight and height are in the lower third of the normal developmental scale. There are two causes of failure to thrive: (1) physical reasons or (2) emotional reasons. Some physical reasons may be related to a swallowing problem or cardiac problems, while emotional reasons may be a result of lack of knowledge by the significant other or parents.

SIGNS AND SYMPTOMS OF FAILURE TO THRIVE

The signs and symptoms of failure to thrive are:

- measured in lower third percentile for weight and height
- poor muscle tone
- delay in development for age group
- reluctant to interact with others (does not respond to person changing diapers or engaging in play)
- glares into your eyes
- unable to develop a relaxed posture when being held

WHAT ARE SOME OF THE SPECIAL EMOTIONAL NEEDS OF MY BABY?

It would be helpful if babies could speak, but babies speak through actions not words.

- A crying baby may be saying;
  – "I'm wet. Please change me."
  – "I'm hungry. Please feed me."
  – "I'm lonely. Please cuddle me and talk to me."
- When you talk to your baby and he or she stops momentarily and looks toward you, your baby is saying, "I know this person. This is _____." You can respond by holding and talking to your baby.
- Babies say thank you for spending your time cuddling and talking with them by relaxing their posture. They seem to mold themselves into the shape of your body as you hold them. They are saying, "I feel good right now. Thanks!"

continues

continued

A child with failure to thrive needs extra attention. Be aware of this fact, and spend extra time with your baby. He or she will soon start to tell you how happy he or she is by expressing the emotions discussed above, eating more, and gaining weight.

The baby's doctor has prescribed nursing visits at home. Ask the nurse to help you learn about your baby. Caring for a baby is something that we all learn. It doesn't just come naturally.

WHAT ABOUT ME?

You also have special needs. It can become emotionally draining to care for a baby.

- Communicate your feelings and needs. Do you have someone with whom to talk? Is that person available all of the time for you? Is that person available at a moment's notice?
- Contact the United Way in your area or talk with your nurse about available support groups or parent/infant workers especially trained to help you.
- Recognize any special needs you may have. Your situation may require special services. Become aware of *all* your options and consider which one is the best for your health and that of your baby.
- Set aside some time every day to be kind to yourself. Make certain that the baby is in good hands, and do something frivolous such as taking a leisurely bubblebath or a nap.

Notes:

Source: Susan-Jane E. Rossi, "Maternal-Child," in *Clinical Pathways for the Multidisciplinary Home Care Team,* Barbara Stover Gingerich and Deborah Anne Ondeck, eds., Aspen Publishers, Inc., © 1995.

Developmental Coordination Disorder—20 Questions

1. What is developmental coordination disorder?

Developmental coordination disorder (DCD) is the name now used to describe children who used to be called "clumsy kids," "awkward," or "minimally brain damaged." We now know that their clumsiness is not their fault, but is caused by a disorder of the movement control systems of the body.

2. All children are clumsy. How do I know my child has DCD?

Children with DCD are not just a bit clumsy or late in learning to do some everyday tasks. They have an extreme difficulty in learning various motor skills. Even when they have learned, say, to fasten buttons or tie knots, they often do so very slowly and sometimes get it wrong. These are the children who may cry or show anger when you try to teach them to cut with a knife, draw a straight line, or catch a ball, or who always seem to avoid certain tasks, even running away and hiding when you offer to show them how.

3. What sort of activities are we talking about?

Any motor activity may be involved; some children have difficulty with almost everything, others with just a few particular jobs. Motor activities can be divided into two groups:

- Gross motor activities include walking, running, using stairs, jumping, hopping, kicking a ball, skating, throwing and catching, and sports.
- Fine motor activities include using a spoon, fork, or knife; brushing teeth and hair; getting undressed and dressed, especially doing buttons, zips, and knots; wiping self on the toilet; cutting with scissors; threading needles, and using tools.

Some children seem to show no interest in scribbling or have great difficulty drawing a straight line or circle or keeping within the lines when they draw or copy, and they go on to have real problems with printing and writing.

4. Is this disorder a disease? What causes it?

Children with DCD are healthy. They are of normal intelligence, and they do not have any known neurological (brain or muscle) disorder. The cause is not known; probably there are many causes. DCD seems to be more like a motor learning disability than a difference in the brain, spine, nerves, muscles, or joints themselves. Sometimes DCD runs in families, and often one parent is still not well coordinated. Not enough is yet known about how we control the movements of our body to be sure what has gone wrong in every case.

5. I think my child has DCD. Who can tell me for sure?

The first step is to see your family doctor to make sure your child is healthy and free of neurological diseases. Then you may be sent to a children's specialist (pediatrician) to make

continues

continued

sure. An occupational therapist may do some tests on your child to measure the degree of difficulty and also to find out what tasks can be done well.

6. My doctor said my child was normal and would grow out of it. I'm still worried. What do I do?

There are children who are just a bit late, or not very well coordinated, without having DCD, so the doctor may be right, but if you are still worried you should insist on seeing either a pediatric neurologist (specialist in children's brain and muscle diseases) or a developmental pediatrician (children's doctor trained in child development and learning problems) for a proper assessment. If your child is in day care or school, you should request an assessment by an occupational therapist.

7. Don't most children grow out of it?

Some do, but research has shown that more than half the children with DCD still have difficulties as teenagers.

8. What is a proper assessment?

A good medical assessment makes sure your child is in good health; some medical problems can cause a child to be clumsy. Then the doctor or a therapist will watch your child doing some of the things he or she is good at and enjoys and some of the things he or she finds difficult or avoids. It is important to know how well your child is doing in all areas of development, so speech and language, concentration and behavior, getting along with other people, and school work should all be reviewed. If there are problems in these areas, which seem to have nothing to do with clumsiness or coordination, they should be studied further, perhaps by a speech pathologist, psychologist, or special educator. If the gross motor problems are severe, a physical therapist or a kinesiologist may be helpful.

9. Do children with DCD usually have other problems?

Some children just have motor difficulties as described above.

Many children develop other problems as they get older. These may be any other type of learning disability. Problems with concentration and written language are common. Some children have problems with behavior or getting along with others, or are unhappy or anxious.

The progress of all children with DCD should be followed carefully for other problems by their parents, teachers, and doctors. Knowing about these problems early on makes it much easier to help the child and keep the problems small.

10. Do children with other problems have DCD?

Yes. Sometimes when children have a severe speech problem, their difficulties with other motor activities will hardly be noticed, or will have been thought less important. Some

continues

continued

"hyperactive" children have motor difficulties even when they are concentrating well. Some children with disturbed behavior, poor social skills, or school problems have DCD. Sometimes their motor difficulties cause them the greatest unhappiness, but parents and teachers seem more worried about the other difficulties.

11. Do both girls and boys get DCD?

Yes. Probably DCD is slightly more common in boys.

12. How common is DCD?

The most widely accepted figure is 6 percent of school children, so there will be one child with DCD in most elementary school classes.

13. My son or daughter has DCD. What do we do now?

First, it is important to explain to everyone who knows your child—the family, teachers at day care or school, and especially your son or daughter—that DCD is *real* and *not anyone's fault*. Clumsiness is not due to being lazy, or stupid, or bad. People with DCD have usually tried harder to succeed than most people ever have to. It is sensible to avoid what seems to be impossible—it's something we all do! Your child needs to know that he or she is well and normal, and that things will get easier now that people understand something about his or her difficulties and frustrations.

Next, there are a number of nonspecific interventions that may be helpful. "Bypass strategies" can be very important. There may be a place for therapy.

14. What are the helpful nonspecific interventions?

By the time they are recognized as having DCD, many children have poor self-esteem and may be physically unfit or overweight although they are quite healthy.

It is important to boost self-esteem, to help the child look forward to the future, and to decrease feelings of hopelessness ("I'll never learn it," "I wish I was dead") and incompetence ("I'm stupid," "I can't do that," or even "I can't do *anything*"). Find out what being clumsy means to your child as an individual. If you were clumsy, too, make sure your child knows! It is important to find things the child does well, appreciate these, and help your child to do them even better. Children who really enjoy an activity should be encouraged to feel comfortable with their ability even if maybe they are not stars. Give more attention to strengths than to weaknesses. Reward each small effort and tiny step toward success. Indoor hobbies and interests are very important even if they have nothing to do with motor tasks. However, many youngsters watch too much television.

Don't force the child to practice motor activities that he or she hates and in which there has been no progress. The great football coach Vince Lombardi said, "Only perfect practice

continues

continued

makes perfect." Doing something badly lots of times does not help one do it better, it just makes one hate it more. Practice is great once one *can* do the task—it helps one to do it right each time—but without special teaching, children with DCD cannot force themselves to get it right at all. For the child with DCD, practice usually becomes very frustrating and destructive. If the child enjoys it, it's probably helping.

Pay attention to exercise and nutrition. Give up sports that frustrate your child; try to find noncompetitive exercise that he or she enjoys. Karate helps build self-confidence and ease frustration. Some DCD children are very good at swimming, horseback riding, target sports, running, or dancing. An overweight child should see a nutritionist.

15. What are bypass strategies?

Some children with DCD will simply never learn to do particular tasks well, or they get into so much trouble because of their problem that something has to be done immediately.

Some everyday activities are just too important for frustration to continue, or for the child to get further and further behind. Doing something badly time and time again destroys the child's interest and motivation.

When we cannot "drive through" the problem, it is right to "get around it." Most parents have discovered that a child who cannot tie knots is very happy when given shoes with Velcro fasteners. Most parents avoid difficult fasteners, or use training wheels for the child who is slow to ride a bike. It is important to help your child to avoid embarrassment or repeated failure. Try to avoid pushing your child into activities just because you enjoyed them when you were young, or because your friends' children are good at them. It is sensible to "give up" on the impossible!

16. What about the child with difficulties in school?

Children with difficulties in speed or neatness of written work should be encouraged to use a typewriter or word processor on long assignments or projects. Some children can print well but can't manage cursive handwriting. They should be allowed to print. Others can write better than they print—encourage them! The teacher should avoid long tests. If the child can show what he or she knows by getting five out of five, there may be no need to test with 20 questions. If the child takes an hour to do well what others can do in 20 minutes, he or she should be allowed an hour without being marked down.

Some parents and teachers think bypass strategies are wrong, and will keep the child from learning the tasks. They do keep the child from giving up, allow the student to show what he or she knows, and are no more wrong than is a cane for a person with a disability. If your child really has DCD, and is becoming hopeless about or far behind in some activity, it is *right* to bypass the problem and get back to progress.

Children who just have difficulties in writing are sometimes said to have *dysgraphia* rather than DCD.

continues

continued

17. What can occupational therapy do?

Most occupational therapists (OTs) are familiar with DCD and can give helpful advice to parents, day care staff and teachers.

OTs can give standardized tests that allow the severity of the DCD, and the individual child's pattern of strengths and weaknesses, to be measured. Such tests can be very helpful in measuring whether there is an improvement.

OTs can help to advise on bypass strategies and on equipment (such as special spoons, pencil grips, clothing) that may make things easier for the child. OTs may also try to help your child's coordination with *therapy*.

18. Will therapy help my child with DCD?

Most occupational therapy has *not* helped children to become better coordinated. It *can* often help a child to do better on a particular task, especially a simple one. Unfortunately, helping children with simple tasks does not seem to help them to do more complicated and important ones. Such learning is said not to "generalize." Getting better at putting pegs into holes can be taught, but has nothing to do with catching, knots, or writing, so time spent on such tasks is usually wasted. Teaching a preschool child to use scissors may be useful in its own right, but does not seem to help with printing later on.

Before starting your child on therapy, you should be sure that the focus of the task is important to you. Ask the therapist for the evidence that the task will generalize.

Important tasks include dressing, feeding, and self-care. For school children, printing or writing are very important. Children in trouble because of poor printing or writing should be seen by an OT. Some sports, games, or other activities may be very important to the child, and it may be worthwhile asking the OT for direct help with these.

Occupational therapy works best when the task is chosen *by the child* because it is very important *to the child*. One child chose "eating spaghetti with a fork," another "doing up my watch strap." The most effective therapy helps children to "talk their way" through the task, with the OT breaking the task down into simple steps and providing intense encouragement for each sign of progress. Therapy using such "verbal self-guidance" (VSG) may generalize to other tasks.

19. What about drugs?

Drugs are not useful for children with DCD. If a child with DCD also has an attention deficit disorder, clinical depression, or a seizure disorder, drugs may be medically prescribed.

20. What about curing DCD?

There is no known cure. Early identification should help to limit the effects.

continues

continued

RECOMMENDED READING

1. "Helping Clumsy Children," edited by Neil Gordon and Ian McKinlay. Churchill-Livingstone, 1980.
2. "Management of Children with Developmental Coordination Disorder at Home and in the Classroom," by Cheryl Missiuna, Carolyn Busby, and Christine Rupert. Cheryl Missiuna, NCRU, Chedoke-McMaster Hospitals, P.O. Box 2000, Station "A", Hamilton, Ontario L8N 3Z5. Published 1992.

Notes:

Courtesy of A. Mervyn Fox, MB, BS, FRCP(C), DCH, Developmental Paediatrician, London, Ontario, Canada.

What Is Asthma?

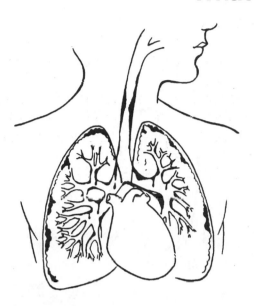

Asthma is a chronic lung disease that lasts a long time. It cannot be cured—only controlled.

- Airways are inflamed. That is, airway linings are swollen.
- Airways narrow, and breathing becomes hard to do. This narrowing gets better (but not all the way in some children), sometimes by itself and sometimes with treatment.
- Airways are super sensitive. They react to many things, such as cigarette smoke, pollen, or cold air. Coughing, wheezing, tight chest, difficult breathing, or an asthma episode may result. A more complete list of things that can cause some people's airways to react is given later (see the section, "What Causes Asthma Episodes").

WHAT ARE THE SYMPTOMS OF ASTHMA?

The main symptoms of asthma are

- shortness of breath
- wheezing
- tightness in the chest
- cough lasting more than a week

Not all children with asthma wheeze. For some, coughing may be the only symptom of asthma. Coughing often occurs during the night or after exercise.

It's important to know that treatment can reverse asthma symptoms. And it's important to treat even mild symptoms of asthma so that you can keep the symptoms from getting worse.

NORMAL BREATHING

When you breathe in, air is taken in through the nose and mouth. It goes down your windpipe, through your airways, and into the air sacs. When you breathe out, stale air leaves the lungs in the reverse order.

What Happens During an Episode of Asthma?

Asthma affects the airways in the lungs. During an episode of asthma

- The lining of the airways become swollen (inflamed).

continues

continued

- The airways produce a thick mucus.
- The muscles around the airways tighten and make the airways narrower.

These changes in the airways block the flow of air, making it hard to breathe.

You need to know the ways that asthma affects the airways so you can understand why it often takes more than one medicine to treat the disease. Very simply, some medicines relax the airways, and others reduce (and even prevent) the swelling and mucus.

WHAT CAUSES ASTHMA?

The basic cause of asthma is not yet known. What we do know is that asthma is not caused by emotional factors, such as a troubled parent-child relationship. In short, asthma is not "all in one's head." It is instead a chronic lung disease.

WHAT CAUSES ASTHMA EPISODES?

Children with asthma have airways that are super sensitive to things that do not bother children who do not have asthma. These things are called triggers because when a child is near or comes in contact with them, they may start an asthma episode. The airways may become swollen, produce too much mucus, and tighten up. Common triggers for asthma episodes include the following:

- dander (or flakes) from the skin, hair, or feathers of all warm-blooded pets (including dogs, cats, birds, and small rodents)
- house dust mites
- cockroaches

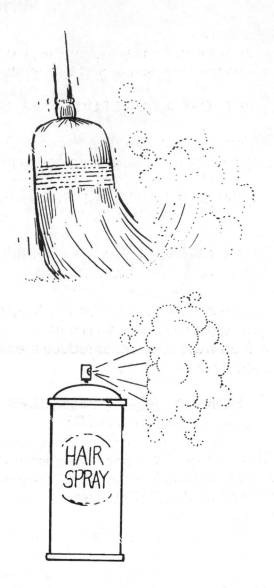

- pollens from grass and trees and mold
- molds (indoor and outdoor)
- cigarette smoke; wood smoke; scented products, such as hair spray, cosmetics, and cleaning products; strong odors from fresh paint or cooking; automobile fumes; and air pollution
- infections in the upper airway, such as colds (a common trigger for both children and adults)

continued

- exercise
- showing strong feelings (crying, laughing)
- changes in weather and temperature

IS THERE A CURE FOR ASTHMA?

Asthma cannot be cured, but it can be controlled. You should expect nothing less.

HOW CAN ASTHMA EPISODES BE PREVENTED?

To prevent asthma episodes, you will have to work closely with your doctor to

- Develop a medicine plan that keeps your child from getting symptoms.
- Plan ways to avoid or reduce the child's contact with triggers.

HOW ARE ASTHMA EPISODES CONTROLLED?

To control asthma episodes when they occur, you will have to work out a medicine plan with your doctor that includes

- treating symptoms early
- doing the right things for any changes in symptoms
- knowing when a doctor's help is needed and seeking help right away

WHAT CAN A CHILD WITH ASTHMA EXPECT FROM TREATMENT?

With proper treatment most children with asthma will be able to

- Be active without having asthma symptoms. This includes participating in exercise and sports.
- Sleep through the night without having asthma symptoms.
- Prevent asthma episodes (attacks).
- Have the best possible peak flow number—lungs that work well (peak flow described in "About Peak Flow Meters")
- Avoid side effects from asthma medicines.

Source: *Teach Your Patients about Asthma*, National Heart, Lung, and Blood Institute, October 1992.

About Peak Flow Meters

A PEAK FLOW METER CAN BE USED AT A CLINIC OR AT HOME TO MEASURE HOW WELL A PERSON IS BREATHING.

- It helps the doctor decide if someone has asthma.
- It helps to see how bad an asthma episode is.
- It helps the doctor see how well asthma is controlled over time.

If a peak flow meter is used every day at home, you can detect breathing problems even before a child with asthma starts to wheeze or cough. Then you will know when more asthma medicine is needed.

There are many kinds of peak flow meters.

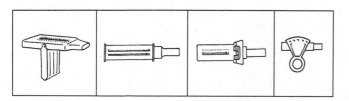

HOW TO USE A PEAK FLOW METER

1. Slide the little marker down as far as it will go. This sets the meter to zero.

2. Have the child stand and take a big breath with the mouth open. Hold the meter in one hand. Keep fingers away from the numbers.

3. Have the child quickly close his or her lips firmly around the tube, without putting the tongue in the hole. Have the child blow one time as fast and hard as possible.

continues

continued

4. The marker will then go up and stay up. Do not touch the marker. Find the number where the marker stopped.

6. Have the child blow two more times. Push the button down each time. Write the number down each time.

5. Write the number on a piece of paper or on a chart.

Notes:

Source: *What You and Your Family Can Do About Asthma*, Global Initiative for Asthma, National Heart, Lung, and Blood Institute, December 1995.

Peak Flow Chart

Name: _____

Doctor: _____

Date: _____

HOW TO USE A PEAK FLOW CHART AT HOME.

1. Find the peak flow number in the morning and evening.
2. Each morning and each evening, have the child blow three times.
3. After each blow, mark the spot where the marker stopped.
4. Put the meter next to the peak flow chart to help you find the spot to mark.
5. Circle the highest of the three numbers. That is the child's peak flow number.

Sample Day		Day 1		Day 2		Day 3		Day 4		Day 5		Day 6		Day 7	
morning	evening	morning	evening	morning	evening	morning	evening	morning	evening	morning	evening	morning	evening	morning	evening

Source: *What You and Your Family Can Do About Asthma*, Global Initiative for Asthma, National Heart, Lung, and Blood Institute, December 1995.

How To Keep Children with Asthma Away from Things That Make Their Asthma Worse

The airways of a child with asthma are very sensitive. They may react to things that can cause asthma attacks or episodes. Keeping the child away from such things will help you keep the asthma from getting worse.

- Ask the doctor to help you find out what makes the child's asthma worse. Discuss ways to keep the child away from these things. The tips listed below will help you.
- Ask the doctor for help in deciding which actions will do the most to reduce the child's asthma symptoms. Carry out these actions first. Discuss the results of your efforts with the doctor.

TIPS FOR HELPING CHILDREN WHO ARE ALLERGIC TO OR BOTHERED BY ANY ITEM LISTED BELOW

House-Dust Mites

The following actions should help you control house-dust mites:

- Encase the child's mattress and box spring in an airtight cover.
- Either encase the child's pillow or wash it in hot water once a week.
- Wash the bed covers, clothes, and stuffed toys once a week in hot water (130°F).

The following actions will also help you control dust mites—but they are not essential:

- Reduce indoor humidity to less than 50 percent. Use a dehumidifier if needed.

- Remove carpets from the child's bedroom.
- Do not have the child sleep or lie on upholstered furniture. Replace with vinyl, leather, or wood furniture.
- Remove carpets that are laid on concrete.
- Keep the child out of a room while it is being vacuumed.
- If you must vacuum when the child is nearby, one or more of the following things can be done to reduce the amount of dust he or she breathes in: (1) Have the child wear a dust mask. (2) Use a central vacuum cleaner with the collecting bag outside the home. (3) Use double-wall vacuum cleaner bags and exhaust-port HEPA (high-efficiency particulate air) filters.

Animals

Some children are allergic to the dried flakes of skin, saliva, or urine from warm-blooded pets. Warm-blooded pets include ALL dogs, cats, birds, and rodents. The length of a pet's hair does not matter. Here are some tips for those allergic to animals:

- Remove the animal from the home or school classroom.
- Choose a pet without fur or feathers (such as a fish or a snake).
- If you must have a warm-blooded pet, keep the pet out of the child's bedroom at all times. Keeping the pet outside of the home is even better.
- If there is forced-air heating in the home with a pet, close the air ducts in the child's bedroom.

continues

continued

- Wash the pet weekly in warm water.
- Do not visit homes that have pets. If you must visit such places, take asthma medicine (cromolyn is often preferred) before going.
- Do not buy or use products made with feathers. Use pillows and comforters stuffed with synthetic fibers like polyester. Also do not use pillows, bedding, and furniture stuffed with kapok (silky fibers from the seed pods of the silk-cotton tree).
- Use a vacuum cleaner fitted with a HEPA filter.
- Have the child wash hands and change clothes as soon as he or she can after being in contact with pets.

Cockroaches

Some children are allergic to the droppings of roaches.

- Insect sprays may be used, but have someone else spray when the child is not at home. Air out the home for a few hours after spraying. Roach traps may also help.
- All homes in multiple-family dwellings (apartments, condominiums, and housing projects) must be treated to get rid of roaches.

Tobacco Smoke

- Do not smoke
- Do not allow smoking in the home. Have household members smoke outside.
- Encourage family members to quit smoking. Ask the doctor or nurse for help on how to quit.

- Choose no-smoking areas in restaurants, hotels, and other public buildings.

Wood Smoke

- Do not use a wood-burning stove to heat the home.
- Do not use kerosene heaters.

Strong Odors and Sprays

- Keep the child out of the home when it is being painted. Use latex rather than oil-based paint.
- Keep the allergic child away from perfume, talcum powder, hair spray, and similar products.
- Use household cleaning products that do not have strong smells or scents.
- Reduce strong cooking odors (especially frying) by using an exhaust fan and opening windows.

Colds and Infections

- Talk to the doctor about flu shots.
- Stay away from people with colds or the flu.
- Do not give the child over-the-counter cold remedies, such as antihistamines and cough syrup, unless you speak to the doctor first.

Exercise

- Make a plan with the doctor that allows the child to exercise without symptoms. For example, he or she should take inhaled beta$_2$-agonist or cromolyn less than 30 minutes before exercising.

continues

continued

- Do not have the child exercise during the afternoon when air pollution levels are highest.
- Have the child warm up before doing exercise and cool down afterward.

Weather

- Have the child wear a scarf over his or her mouth and nose in cold weather or pull a turtleneck or scarf over the nose on windy or cold days.
- Dress the child warmly in the winter or on windy days.

Pollens

During times of high pollen counts

- Keep the child indoors during the midday and afternoon when pollen counts are highest.

Notes:

- Keep windows closed in cars and homes. Use air conditioning if you can.
- Keep pets either outdoors or indoors. Pets should not be allowed to go in and out of the home. This prevents your pet from bringing pollen inside.

Mold (Outdoor)

- Avoid sources of molds (wet leaves, garden debris, stacked wood).
- Avoid standing water or areas of poor drainage.

REMEMBER: Making these changes will help keep asthma episodes from starting. These actions can also reduce the child's need for asthma medicines.

Source: *Nurses: Partners in Asthma Care*, National Asthma Foundation and Prevention Program, National Heart, Lung, and Blood Institute, NIH Publication No. 95-3308, 1995.

Medicines for Asthma

MOST CHILDREN WITH ASTHMA NEED TWO KINDS OF ASTHMA MEDICINE.

1. Everyone with asthma needs a quick-relief medicine to stop asthma attacks.

2. Many children also need a preventive medicine every day to protect the lungs and keep asthma episodes from starting.

ASK THE DOCTOR TO WRITE DOWN WHAT ASTHMA MEDICINES TO GIVE AND WHEN TO GIVE THEM.

- The doctor may use a medicine plan like the following "Asthma Medicine Plan."

- Use the medicine plan to know what quick-relief medicines to give when the child is having an asthma episode.

- Use the medicine plan to help remember what preventive medicines to give to the child every day.

- Use the medicine plan to see if the child should take asthma medicine just before sports or working hard.

continues

continued

PREVENTIVE MEDICINES FOR ASTHMA ARE SAFE TO USE EVERY DAY.

- A child cannot become addicted to preventive medicines for asthma even if he or she uses them for many years.
- Preventive medicine makes the swelling of the airways in the lungs go away.

- The doctor may tell the child to take preventive medicine every day if he or she
  - coughs, wheezes, or has a tight chest more than once a week
  - wakes up at night because of asthma
  - has many asthma episodes
  - has to use quick-relief medicine every day to stop asthma episodes

TELL THE DOCTOR ABOUT ANY PROBLEMS THAT THE CHILD IS EXPERIENCING WITH ASTHMA MEDICINES.

- The doctor can change the asthma medicine or change how much the child takes. There are many asthma medicines.
- Take the child to the doctor two or three times a year for checkups so the doctor can see how well the asthma medicine works.
- Asthma may get better or it may get worse over the years. The doctor may need to change the asthma medicines.

continues

continued

ASTHMA MEDICINE CAN BE TAKEN IN DIFFERENT WAYS.

When asthma medicine is breathed in, it goes right to the airways in the lungs where it is needed. Inhalers for asthma come in many shapes. Most are sprays. Some use powder.

Asthma medicine also comes as pills and syrups.

BE PREPARED. ALWAYS HAVE ASTHMA MEDICINE.

Set aside money for asthma medicine. Buy more before you run out.

Always carry quick-relief asthma medicine when the child leaves home.

Notes:

Source: *What You and Your Family Can Do About Asthma*, Global Initiative for Asthma, National Heart, Lung, and Blood Institute, December 1995.

Asthma Medicine Plan

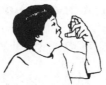

You can use the colors of a traffic light to help learn about the child's asthma medicines.

1. **Green** means **Go.** Use preventive medicine.
2. **Yellow** means **Caution.** Use quick-relief medicine.
3. **Red** means **Stop.** Get help from a doctor.

Name: _____

Doctor: _____ **Date:** _____

Phone for doctor or clinic: _____

Phone for taxi or friend: _____

---

1. Green - Go

- Breathing is good
- No cough or wheeze
- Can work and play

Peak Flow Number
_____ to _____

Use preventive medicine.

Medicine	How much to take	When to take it

20 minutes before sports, use this medicine:

_____

---

2. Yellow - Caution

Cough

Wheeze

Tight chest

Wake up at night

Peak Flow Number
_____ to _____

Give the child quick-relief medicine to keep an asthma episode from getting bad.

Medicine	How much to take	When to take it

continues

continued

3. Red - Stop - Danger

- Medicine is not helping
- Breathing is hard and fast
- Nose opens wide
- Can't walk
- Ribs show
- Can't talk well

Peak Flow Number

_____ to _____

Get help from a doctor now!

Give these medicines until you talk with the doctor.

Medicine   How much to take   When to take it

_____

_____

_____

_____

Notes:

Source: *What You and Your Family Can Do About Asthma*. Global Initiative for Asthma, National Heart, Lung, and Blood Institute. December 1995.

The Metered-Dose Inhaler: How To Use It

Using a metered-dose inhaler is a good way to take asthma medicines. There are few side effects because the medicine goes right to the lungs and not to other parts of the body. It takes only 5 to 10 minutes for inhaled beta$_2$-agonists to have an effect compared to the liquid or pill form, which can take 15 minutes to 1 hour. Inhalers can be used by all asthma patients aged five and older. A spacer or holding chamber attached to the inhaler can help make taking the medicine easier.

The inhaler must be cleaned often to prevent buildup that will clog it or reduce how well it works.

- The guidelines that follow will help the child use the inhaler the correct way.
- Ask the doctor or nurse to show you how to use the inhaler.

USING THE INHALER

1. Remove the cap and hold the inhaler upright.
2. Shake the inhaler.
3. Tilt the child's head back slightly, and have the child breathe out.
4. Use the inhaler in any one of these ways. (A and B are the best ways. B is recommended for young children, older adults, and those taking inhaled steroids. C is okay if the child is having trouble with A or B.)
    - A. Open mouth with inhaler 1 to 2 inches away.
    - B. Use spacer (ask for the handout on spacers).
    - C. Put inhaler in the child's mouth and seal lips around the mouthpiece.
5. Press down on the inhaler to release the medicine as the child starts to breathe in slowly.
6. Tell the child to breathe in *slowly* for three to five seconds.
7. Have the child *hold* his or her breath for 10 seconds to allow the medicine to reach deeply into the lungs.
8. Repeat puffs as prescribed. Waiting one minute between puffs may permit the second puff to go deeper into the lungs.

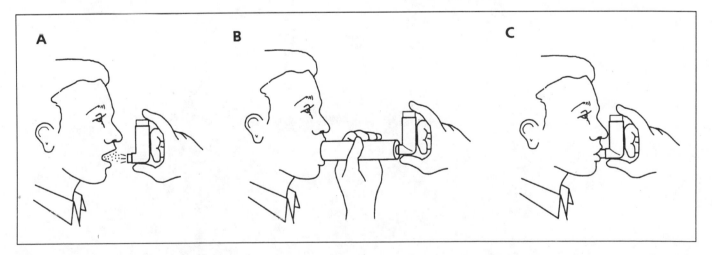

continues

continued

Note: Dry powder capsules are used differently. To use a dry powder inhaler, close the mouth tightly around the mouthpiece and inhale very fast.

CLEANING

1. Once a day clean the inhaler and cap by rinsing it in warm running water. Let it dry before using again. Have another inhaler to use while it is drying. Do not put the canister holding cromolyn or nedocromil in water.
2. Twice a week wash the L-shaped plastic mouthpiece with mild dishwashing soap and warm water. Rinse and dry well before putting the canister back inside the mouthpiece.

Notes:

CHECKING HOW LONG A CANISTER WILL LAST

1. Check the canister label to see how many "puffs" it contains.
2. Figure out how many puffs the child will take per day (e.g., 2 puffs, 4 times a day = 8 puffs a day). Divide this number into the number of puffs contained in the canister. That tells you how long the canister should last.

Example:

- Canister contains 200 puffs.
- The child takes 2 puffs, 4 times a day, which equals 8 puffs/day.
- $200 \div 8 = 25$. The canister will last 25 days.

Source: *Nurses: Partners in Asthma Care*, National Asthma Foundation and Prevention Program, National Heart, Lung, and Blood Institute, NIH Publication No. 95-3308, 1995.

Spacers: Making Inhaled Medicines Easier To Take

Unless the child uses the inhaler the right way, much of the medicine may end up on the tongue, on the back of the throat, or in the air. Use of a spacer or holding chamber can help prevent this problem.

A spacer or holding chamber is a device that attaches to a metered-dose inhaler. It holds the medicine in its chamber long enough for the child to inhale it in one or two slow deep breaths.

The spacer makes it easy to use the medicines the right way (especially if the child is young or is having a hard time using just an inhaler). It helps the child not cough when using an inhaler. A spacer will also help prevent a yeast infection in the mouth (thrush) when taking inhaled steroid medicines.

There are many models of spacers or holding chambers that you can purchase through your pharmacist or a medical supply company. Ask the doctor about the different models.

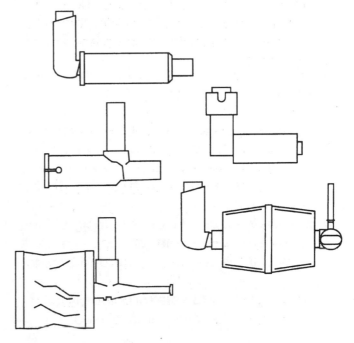

There are a variety of spacers.

HOW TO USE A SPACER

1. Attach the inhaler to the spacer or holding chamber as explained by the doctor or by using the directions that come with the product.
2. Shake well.
3. Press the button on the inhaler. This will put one puff of the medicine in the holding chamber.
4. Place the mouthpiece of the spacer in the child's mouth, and have the child inhale slowly. (A face mask may be helpful for a young child.)
5. Tell the child to hold his or her breath for a few seconds and then exhale. Repeat steps 4 and 5.
6. If your doctor has prescribed two puffs, wait between puffs for the amount of time he or she has directed and repeat steps 2 through 5.

Source: *Nurses: Partners in Asthma Care*, National Asthma Foundation and Prevention Program, National Heart, Lung, and Blood Institute, NIH Publication No. 95-3308, 1995.

Summary of Steps To Manage Asthma Episodes

- **Know the child's warning signs** and peak flow zones so you can begin treatment early.
- **Give the correct amount of medicine** at the times the doctor has stated. If the asthma control plan includes increased dosage or a second medicine to be used during episodes, give it as prescribed. **Always call the doctor if you need to give more medicine than the doctor ordered.**
- **Remove the child from the trigger** if you know what it is. Treatment does not work as well if the child stays around the trigger.
- **Keep calm and relaxed.** Family members must stay calm and relaxed too.
- **Rest.**
- **Observe the child** by noting changes in body signs, such as wheezing, coughing, trouble breathing, and posture. If you have a peak flow meter, measure peak flow number 5 to 10 minutes after each treatment to see if peak flow is improving.
- **Review the list below for signs to seek emergency medical care for asthma.** They include
  - **The child's wheeze, cough, or shortness of breath gets worse, even after the medicine has been given and had time to work.** Most inhaled bronchodilator medicines produce an effect within 5 to 10 minutes. Discuss the time the medicines take to work with the doctor.
  - **The child's peak flow number goes down or does not improve after treatment with bronchodilators,** or drops to 50 percent or less of personal best. Discuss this peak flow level with the doctor.
  - **The child's breathing gets difficult.** Signs of this are
    - The child's chest and neck are pulled or sucked in with each breath.
    - The child is hunching over.
    - The child is struggling to breathe.
  - **The child has trouble walking or talking.**
  - **The child stops playing or working and cannot start again.**
  - **The child's lips or fingernails are gray or blue.** If this happens, **go to the emergency department now!**
- **Keep important information for seeking emergency care handy.**
- **Call a family member, friend, or neighbor to help you** if needed.
- **Immediately call a clinic, doctor's office, or hospital for help** if needed.

The Child Should Not Do the Following:
- drink a lot of water; he or she should just drink normal amounts
- breathe warm moist air from a shower
- rebreathe into a paper bag held over the nose
- use over-the-counter cold remedies without first calling the doctor

Source: *Teach Your Patients about Asthma*, National Heart, Lung, and Blood Institute, October 1992.

Sample Patient Asthma Management Plan

ASTHMA ACTION PLAN

Name: _____   Issue Date _____

		PEAK FLOW		**TREATMENT**
1	BEST	=	☐	⇨ Continue regular treatment
2	<80%	=	☐	⇨ Double dose of:_____
3	<60%	=	☐	⇨ Start prednisone & ring Doctor
4	<40%	=	☐	⇨ Call emergency Dr. or Dial 911 for ambulance

	SYMPTOMS		**TREATMENT**
1	Asthma under control	⇨	Continue regular treatment
2	Waking with asthma at night	⇨	Double dose of
3	Increasing breathlessness or poor response to	⇨	Start prednisone & ring your Doctor
4	Severe attack	⇨	Call emergency Dr. or Dial 911 for ambulance

Contact Dr. _____ Tel. _____

Source: *Asthma Management and Prevention*, Global Initiative for Asthma, National Heart, Lung, and Blood Institute, NIH Publication No. 96-3659A, December 1995.

2
Behavior Management and Psychosocial Issues

Discipline and Managing Behavior Problems in Children with Disabilities

HOW CHILDREN LEARN BEHAVIOR

Initially, all children learn the limits of acceptable behavior from the adults who care for them. Their sense of what is right and wrong is built up over the years as a result of the consequences of their own behavior, the direct effects of their actions and the reactions they receive from other people, and the things they observe the important people around them doing.

Usually, parents are the first teachers of appropriate social behavior through the vehicle of discipline within the family. Later, brothers and sisters, classmates, friends, teachers, and the extended family provide additional information to the child in the form of approval or disapproval that depends on the child's social actions. Thus, the feedback given to children is an important teaching tool; it functions as either positive reinforcement or punishment.

A child is a keen observer of the things others do. Children frequently learn new actions by trying out ways of acting that seem to work for others. Because children tend to imitate the actions of successful people and of people who seem to be in control, the things that parents and older brothers and sisters do (or get away with) are especially apt to be imitated. For this reason, consistency between words and actions is so often stressed. The need to set a good example is an important principle to keep in mind.

BEHAVIOR PROBLEMS

Behavior problems do occur. Children with a disability do not differ from other children in this respect. All children lack the judgment to understand the effects their behavior may be having on the other people around them. They require the corrective feedback that parents and those who care for them can provide.

There is, unfortunately, a tendency for many people to treat children with a disability as exempt from discipline. This belief stems from the improper view of them as "sick" and therefore not covered under normal standards of behavior. Unlike a temporary illness that may be associated with understandable lapses in conduct, a disability represents a condition to which the child must learn to adapt. Like all of us, they ultimately will be judged by most people outside of the family according to widely shared values regarding public actions. To the extent that it is possible, they should learn to act and react as any child would under similar circumstances. When children with a disability learn to behave in ways similar to other children, they are more readily accepted into social and recreational opportunities that lead to lasting relationships and enhance personal growth.

Developmental disabilities complicate the task of judging whether or not a child is behaving appropriately. On the one hand, delayed development of many skills and abilities may be associated with physical development that is quite close to average for the child's chronological

continues

continued

age. Such children might be socially rejected because of the behavioral immaturity they exhibit or the obvious gaps in their knowledge in comparison to children who look similar but who have developed skills at a rate corresponding to their chronological age. On the other hand, marked physical disabilities and altered patterns of bodily growth do not necessarily indicate that a child's rate of intellectual development has been affected. Initially, strangers are likely to make mistakes about how to act around children with a disability based on either of these possibilities. The important thing is to help others to correct their misunderstanding with a minimum of stress.

MANAGING BEHAVIOR PROBLEMS

Behavior problems can be extremely stressful for everyone concerned. Even the parents of a child with a disability are not sure how to view some of the behavior patterns exhibited by their child. They often ask, "Is this behavior something I should be concerned with? Is this behavior normal?" Many parents are concerned about how others will perceive them when their child misbehaves. These concerns are quite natural and in no way unique to parents of children with a disability.

The truth is, behavior problems are normal. Managing behavior problems is much easier if they are understood one at a time and are viewed as an opportunity for parental teaching. Most behavior problems fall into the category of normal problems of childhood. This category includes understanding and following family rules, using toys and household materials properly, learning safety matters, and resolving issues involving self-care responsibilities, bedtime, mealtime, and chores. A problem in these areas usually means that the child is only just learning the way such basic matters are handled within the family. Another set of problems may be related to a child's developmental disability, in that few nondisabled children of the same age exhibit similar problem behavior. This type of problem includes emotional difficulties that appear to be a reaction to the disability or to the way the child is treated as a result of the disability, and some behavior patterns that are characteristic of some of the more severe developmental disorders.

It is helpful to think of behavior problems as indicative of teaching problems in which there may be behavioral deficits, behavioral excesses, or a combination of the two. A behavioral deficit indicates that the child lacks a skill that would be called for in a particular situation, and the child is behaving inappropriately because of a lack of knowledge. A good example of this deficit would be a child who eats without using silverware, but who has never been properly taught how to do so. A behavioral excess indicates that a child is doing something too often or too intensely to be tolerated. An example of this excess might be the child who cries excessively or has tantrums in order to get his or her way. In most cases of behavior problems, it is likely that both of these teaching problems are present. For example, a child may engage in disruptive behavior in the classroom when the work is completely new and some necessary prior learning is lacking and the other children laugh at and seem to enjoy the disruptive behavior. This child cannot do what the teacher expects because of a lack of some critical prior learning, and the child performs an excessive number of disruptive acts that are strengthened by the positive reinforcement of other children's attention.

continues

continued

SELECTING AN APPROACH TO MANAGING PROBLEM BEHAVIOR

Managing problem behavior, then, becomes a matter of setting the stage for effective teaching. The problem behavior must be well defined, because poorly described behavior is hard to handle in a consistent manner. It is usually a good idea to count or measure a problem behavior for some time before trying to change it. This preliminary measure makes it possible to tell whether or not the behavior management strategy selected is working. If the behavior problem happens less often or lasts for less and less time after the management strategy is used, then the strategy can be said to have been successful.

Selecting the strategy is a little more tricky. Behavior problems that are the result of skill deficits are handled by teaching the required skills. Sometimes the child really possesses the necessary skills, but appropriate behaviors are not consistently followed by satisfying consequences (that is, they are not positively reinforced). Behavioral deficits of this kind can be turned around by seeing that good behavior is always rewarded. Parental attention, approval, hugs, and other ways of expressing appreciation and love are among the most universal positive reinforcers. Behavior that is followed by this kind of attention usually is strengthened rapidly. Parents should always consider using their attention and praise to increase desirable behavior before settling on other forms of nonsocial or material reinforcers.

Similarly, sometimes the skills are there and would be followed by reinforcing consequences if the child performed them, but there is no opportunity to perform the appropriate skills in the setting where the problem occurs. This situation happens when not enough time is available for the desired behavior to be completed, and when, for example, tools necessary for completing the desired behavior are lacking, inaccessible, or too hard for the child to use.

Unfortunately, misbehavior is more likely to be followed by parental attention. There is a tendency to "let well enough alone" when things are going along as desired and to intervene only when problems develop. But because parental attention is such a strong reinforcer of children's behavior—even when the parent feels anger—the attention lavished on problem behavior may actually strengthen it. When no longer followed by attention, many annoying problem behaviors, such as tantrums or even some mild forms of aggressive behavior, are eventually abandoned by children.

For this reason many parents have been told to ignore problem behavior. However, this advice is usually insufficient. Many misbehaviors (behavioral excesses) cannot be ignored without risk to the child or others. Further, even if parental attention had been accidentally strengthening the problem behavior, there may have been additional sources of positive reinforcement for the child's actions. For example, aggressive behavior may result in material gain or temporary resolution of the conflict. A misbehavior may actually feel good to the child when it is performed, or other people besides the parents—people who do not realize that attending to misbehavior often just serves to make it more persistent—may continue to provide attention following the misbehavior even though the parents have stopped. Finally, even if the original form of problem behavior decreases, there is no guarantee that the child will behave appropriately thereafter.

continues

continued

There is still the question as to whether the child possesses the necessary skills to behave in a desirable or more effective manner. The child may not know how to do the right thing.

A better approach is always to ask, "What would I like to see the child doing at this time instead of the problem behavior?" Then, go about making the desired behavior more likely under similar circumstances in the future by teaching the appropriate behavior, seeing that it is rewarded, and doing everything possible to make the misbehavior less likely to occur in the future.

Increasing desirable behavior sometimes serves to displace undesirable behavior, simply because nobody can do two things at the same time. Another way to make misbehavior less likely is to change the environment so that it is harder to do anything "bad." For example, placing breakable objects out of reach of small children is an environmental change that decreases the likelihood of problems. Parents are less likely to think of a child who actively explores a child-proofed environment as hyperactive or destructive. Such precautions provide an opportunity to introduce the child to potential problems in a controlled fashion over a longer period of time.

PUNISHMENT

When circumstances dictate that ignoring, displacing, or avoiding excess behavior represents an incomplete solution, methods are available to decrease the strength of a misbehavior directly. Self-stimulatory behavior or repetitive self-injurious acts, although relatively unusual, do occur in children with developmental delays and tend to be highly resistant to change. Punishment can have fairly rapid effects on such misbehavior. If punishment is immediate, always follows the misbehavior, and is truly something that the child dislikes, it will function as expected.

However, there are several drawbacks to using punishment to change behavior. Parents tend to dislike using punishment so much that they delay its use too long after the misbehavior occurs to affect the behavior at all ("Wait till your father comes home!"), are inconsistent in its use ("You're gonna get it next time!"), and feel so bad about using punishment that it is followed by giving in to whatever it was that motivated the child's misbehavior in the first place. Giving in after punishing a child can be very dangerous. Giving in afterward can teach the child to endure, and possibly even to seek, punishment because it represents a signal to the child that the parents are ready to comply with his or her wishes. Another practical consideration is that the things selected as punishment simply may not be that undesirable from the child's point of view. These are all patterns in the use of punishment that make punishment fail to act as expected in stopping problem behavior.

Other drawbacks include the fact that punishment does not teach anything new. It only stops or discourages behavior that it follows consistently. If no alternative action is available to the child, either because of a lack of skill or a lack of opportunity, the improvement will be temporary at best. Punishment can also create fear in the child, and fear can distract the child from the learning situation or disrupt relationships in the family. Finally, punishment that is given in anger can become excessive and even harmful.

continues

continued

These drawbacks can be overcome by never punishing without a plan to reward desirable behavior and by calmly planning the use of undesirable consequences at a time and place other than that of the problem situation. Punishing without a plan, in anger, or impulsively can lead to an injury, lingering bad feelings, and learning failure. In addition, many techniques have been developed to avoid the need to use physical punishment. One of the best known of these is called time-out from positive reinforcement. An example of a time-out procedure would be leading a child to a seat in the corner immediately following a misbehavior such as a tantrum, and not allowing the child to get up until 2 or 3 minutes of quiet behavior has occurred. This approach is based on the fact that withdrawing something pleasant—in the example, a chance to be free and up and around doing things—is equivalent to providing something unpleasant in terms of its effect on the behavior that it follows. That is, time-out is like punishment in terms of its effect on behavior. Time-out in various forms has been used with great success by many parents and teachers to decrease undesirable behavior, but one must be quite sure that the exact nature of the time-out experience truly represents the temporary withdrawal of something that the child values. As with many of the teaching strategies discussed here, additional readings are available to help adapt these approaches to specific needs. It might be advisable to consult with a psychologist before planning to use punishment in a systematic way with any child. A professional analysis of the behavior problem and the context in which it occurs may reveal more lasting and less unpleasant ways of teaching the child to behave differently.

Discipline is important to all children. A structured approach sometimes is needed to deal with particularly difficult problems, and many professional psychologists and special educators can give needed advice at such times. There is a role for structure in every family, although the majority of situations can be handled through firm limit setting, giving enthusiastic attention and appreciation when behavior is as we wish it to be, and by setting a good example.

Notes:

Courtesy of James A. Mulick, Ph.D., Professor, Department of Pediatrics, Division of Psychology, College of Medicine, The Ohio State University, and The Children's Hospital, Columbus, Ohio.

Empowered Parenting

CLASSIFYING BEHAVIORS

Fill in at least five behaviors in each of the columns below. Use one form for each child.

Behaviors you like and want to see more of: ☺	Behaviors you don't like but can live with: 😐	Behaviors you find totally unacceptable: ☹
Positive Reinforcement	Ignore	Effective Punishment

RECOMMENDED RESPONSES

Courtesy of R. Franklin Trimm, III, MD, Developmental/Behavioral Pediatrics, University of South Alabama, Mobile, Alabama.

Family Problem Solving

GOALS

- Deal with behavior problems that occur frequently, do not respond to other behavior management techniques, or seem to have no other solution.
- Have a tool that can be used to prevent problem behaviors from developing into family crises.
- Establish a forum that is safe and productive for all family members.
- Enable compromise: a settlement of differences in which each side makes concessions.

STEPS

- Make an appointment to talk at a time agreeable to all involved.
- Call the meeting—meet at a place where you can have good eye contact and no distractions. Turn off the radio and the television.
- State the problem in the first person and how you feel.
- Ask if there is agreement that there is a problem.
- Ask for suggestions to help resolve the problem. Praise any suggestions. Do not judge answers.
- Poll each family member on each suggested resolution.
- Agree on or contract for the resolution that is most acceptable to everyone involved.
- Ask for a promise to implement the resolution.
- Promise to notice the child's progress.
- Have the child restate agreement in his or her own words.
- Set appointment in a few days to see how things are going.
- Praise child for working things out.

Suggested Resolutions	Person 1	Person 2	Person 3
TOTALS:			

Courtesy of R. Franklin Trimm, III, MD, Developmental/Behavioral Pediatrics, University of South Alabama, Mobile, Alabama.

Why Children Misbehave

SOCIAL LEARNING THEORY

Of all the theories that attempt to explain human development and learning, one stands out for its usefulness in understanding human behavior. Social learning theory has survived the rigors of scientific investigation. It has proven itself helpful in handling behavior problems for several decades.

This theory tells us that most behaviors are learned. These behaviors can be learned by observing others and by pure accident. A specific behavior that gets reinforced repeatedly becomes a habit. Behaviors that have become learned can also be weakened or unlearned by withholding these reinforcers.

REINFORCERS

A reinforcer is something that strengthens or supports a behavior. It is easy to recognize rewards (a positive reinforcer). There are also negative interactions that can act as reinforcers as well. These are often more difficult to recognize.

When a behavior is reinforced, it is strengthened. Repeated reinforcement will increase both the frequency and intensity of the behavior. Ignoring (the absence of a reinforcer) or punishing (removal of a normal privilege as a consequence) will decrease the frequency and intensity of the behavior.

Behavior can be compared to a seesaw: whichever side has the most weight (or reinforcement) is the side that is going to prevail.

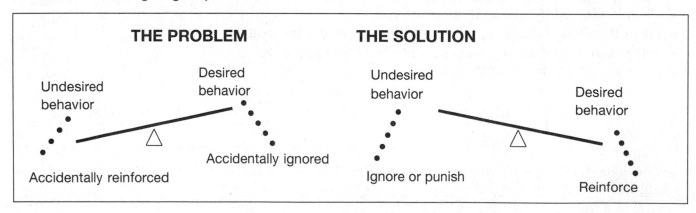

One reinforcement will not accomplish change! Change requires dozens of reinforcers. Once a desired behavior becomes a habit, it usually requires intermittent reinforcement to maintain it. As seen above, ignoring a behavior weakens it.

continues

continued

ACCIDENTAL TEACHING

The following story is an example of accidental teaching:

It's time to go grocery shopping. Mom is home alone with Joey, her three-year-old son. They get into the car and head to the store. Upon arrival, Mom gets out her shopping list and sets out to try to get everything as quickly as possible. She hopes she'll finish before Joey gets too bored and throws one of his tantrums. Joey starts out quietly following his mother down the aisles. She is busy selecting items and putting them into the cart. After a while, a particularly bright can catches Joey's attention and he starts to pull it off the shelf. Mom sees this out of the corner of her eye. She turns to Joey and reminds him not to touch anything. This scenario repeats itself several times with Joey becoming progressively more difficult to manage.

Families do not usually plan to teach their children undesirable behaviors, but through lack of understanding often do just that. Let's use the principles of social learning theory to see how Joey was being taught to misbehave in public.

In this story, the desired behavior would be for Joey to follow along without touching things. The undesired behaviors consist of touching things as well as whining and crying when corrected. Whenever Joey was exhibiting the desired behaviors he was ignored (while Mom was trying to get her shopping done). Only when he did something unacceptable did he get his mom's attention, and the way he did this got progressively more intense.

More than anything else, most children want their parents' attention. They prefer negative attention to no attention at all. Joey got reinforced every time he did something unacceptable by getting his mother's attention. The fact that the attention was negative did not make it punishment. In addition to this accidental reinforcement of the undesired behavior, the desired behavior was systematically ignored.

IGNORING

As humans, we have limited amounts of energy to reinforce and weaken our children's behaviors. It is therefore very important to choose which behaviors to work on and which behaviors to let ride. Many instances of "accidental teaching" occur because parents are trying to deal with too many behavioral problems at once.

The bad news of parenting is that there is no middle ground. Whenever we respond to a behavior we either strengthen it or weaken it. The good news is that reinforcing and punishing are not the only two options! For behaviors that are not a danger to persons or property and do not have severe long-term consequences, ignoring is the response of choice. Ignoring is an effective way of weakening an undesired behavior. Furthermore, it provides a way of preventing accidental reinforcement that would result from dealing poorly with the situation.

Courtesy of R. Franklin Trimm, III, MD, Developmental/Behavioral Pediatrics, University of South Alabama, Mobile, Alabama.

Time-In

· GOALS

- Reinforce children in a consistent fashion for good behaviors.
- Enhance the development and maintenance of a healthy self-esteem.
- Create an environment so enriching that any separation from it would be a significant loss.
- Avoid the use of ineffective "positive attention."
- Avoid being negative (if you don't have anything nice to say, don't say anything at all).

EFFECTIVE TOOLS OF POSITIVE ATTENTION

- verbal praise
  — Praise immediately following the desired behavior.
  — Get the child's attention.
  — Use short, specific praise.
  — Catch the child being good.
  — Praise effort more than product.
- physical praise
  — Use 1–2 second contacts (love pats).
  — Keep in mind the advantages of physical praise: less distracting than verbal praise, less energy consuming for parents, can be given more frequently.
  — Use for any acceptable behavior.
- "piece of the pie" approach
  — Give positive attention to any portion of expected behavior in beginning.
- frequent praise
  — Praise 50+ times per day to maintain positive environment.
  — Praise 75+ times per day when problem behaviors are present.

INEFFECTIVE TOOLS OF POSITIVE ATTENTION (PRAISE SPOILING)

- Attaching the praise to future expectation: "What a good grade you got on your spelling test. Do you think you can do this well next week too?"
- Attaching the praise to previous disappointments: "Your bed looks so nice today. Why couldn't you have made it this nicely yesterday?" or "What a good job you did cleaning up your room. Now aren't you ashamed that you put up such a fuss about doing it?"
- Being too lengthy when giving verbal praise: "You were so good at the party today. Mommy is so happy when you are a good girl. I like it when you are so good. I'm sure you have more fun at parties when you are good. Daddy will be so happy too when he hears what a good girl you were today."

continues

continued

- Mixing positive words with negative body language: "Well, you sure look nice today." (Said while crossing your arms and rolling your eyes up toward the ceiling.)
- Employing praise that diminishes the value of the performance: "What a good job you did on the dishes. See, that wasn't such a big deal, was it?"
- Using nonspecific or lazy praise: "Nice job!" or "Good boy."

> *Every time you miss a chance to catch your child being good, you miss a chance to teach your child how you would like him or her to behave.*

Notes:

Courtesy of R. Franklin Trimm, III, MD, Developmental/Behavioral Pediatrics, University of South Alabama, Mobile, Alabama.

Giving Effective Commands

GOALS FOR EFFECTIVE COMMANDS

- Improve compliance of child.
- Avoid triggering "flight-fight" response in child.
- Be efficient in use of time and energy.
- Set up parent and child for success.

STEPS FOR EFFECTIVE COMMANDS

- Go to your child or have your child come to you.
- Place your hand firmly on child's back. Lean your upper body toward your child, get down to his or her eye level.
- Say your child's name, pausing, then repeating until he or she looks at you. Use an assertive, firm, but nonhostile tone. Praise child for successful eye contact.
- State your command while maintaining eye contact. Commands should:
  — be a *statement*, never a question, unless you intend to give the child a choice.
  — be clear, short, and specific. (Don't lecture or make negative comments while your child is trying to comply.)
- Ignore everything your child says and does after you give a command that is not a move toward obedience. These diversionary tactics are learned behaviors that need to be weakened. If an unacceptable diversionary tactic is used, deal with it after you have completed the current task.
- Praise all efforts that are a move toward obedience.
- Use the "broken record" technique of repeating the command over and over with pauses in between until the child complies.

ADDITIONAL GUIDELINES

- Use this extended technique only when you know you can follow through.
- Practice this technique at home and when you are rested. Do not practice in public or in front of your in-laws!
- If you are sure you will not receive much resistance from your child, only an abbreviated approach should be necessary.
- If you start losing your self-control, put the current command on hold and return to it after you have calmed down. (This is very unnerving for children and often promotes hasty obedience.)

continues

continued

OUTLINE OF SIX STEPS

1. Go to child.

2. Get child's attention.
   - physical contact
   - call name

3. State command.

4. Ignore diversionary tactics.

5. Use "broken record" technique.

6. Praise obedience.

Notes:

Courtesy of R. Franklin Trimm, III, MD, Developmental/Behavioral Pediatrics, University of South Alabama, Mobile, Alabama.

Warnings and Consequences

GOALS FOR USING WARNINGS AND CONSEQUENCES

- Use in instances where a behavior may deserve punishment.
- Give children the "last chance" signal to get their behavior under control.
- Give parents a tool to keep from losing their self-control when "backed against the wall."
- Provide buffer against parental inconsistencies.

EFFECTIVE WARNINGS AND CONSEQUENCES

A warning reflects an in-control parent who is stating clearly what he or she wants from the child and the consequences for the child not getting back in control. The consequence is also clear and believable, and always occurs if the child does not obey. Effective warnings may not get immediate compliance. The child has to be convinced that you mean what you say and that you will follow through without losing control. The steps for using effective warnings are:

- Give a clear, effective command (for example, "Stop hitting your brother."). Praise if child obeys.
- If the child does not obey, repeat the command and add the consequence for disobedience (for example, "Stop hitting your brother now or you will have to go to time-out."). Praise if child obeys.
- If your child does not get back in control after the warning is given, you must follow through with the consequence as stated in the warning. Choose your consequences carefully.

INEFFECTIVE WARNINGS

- Multiple warnings and consequences before following through are ineffective.
- A threat usually reflects an out-of-control parent who, not knowing what to do next, tries to scare the child into compliance. A threat is usually something the parent says but does not really mean or has no intention of carrying out (for example, "If you touch that again I'll beat you within an inch of your life." Or, "If you do that again, I'll knock a hole in your head.").
- A bribe is another sign of an out-of-control parent who does not feel powerful enough to be taken seriously by the child. The parent does not know what to do if the child does not comply so an attempt is made to try to buy obedience from the child with a favor. This usually is a one-to-one exchange (for example, "If you pick up your toys like a good girl, I'll give you an ice cream bar." Or, "If you take your nap without crying, we'll go to the park."). Parents who bribe often feel victimized by their children. Their children learn not to obey until they get something out of it and consequently have a high rate of noncompliance.

continues

continued

REWARDS AND BRIBES ARE DIFFERENT

- Rewards are coupled with expected behaviors by parents who have self-control (for example, "We're going into the store now, Joey. Remember to keep your hands to yourself and not touch things. If you remember to do that, then we'll go home and read a story together when I'm done shopping."). This approach is likely to yield several positive results:

  1. You have an opportunity to teach your child what behavior is expected while shopping.
  2. You have created a situation where the child is likely to succeed.
  3. You will probably have the opportunity to reward, and therefore strengthen, the desired behavior.
  4. You have a much higher chance of having a positive shopping experience.

- Bribes are used by an out-of-control parent who is trying to get out of a specific out-of-control situation (for example, "Joey, I've told you a hundred times not to touch anything. Now look what you've done. [Joey starts crying loudly.] I'll buy you a toy if you just calm down."). This approach is likely to result in several negative results:

  1. The child is reinforced for out-of-control behaviors.
  2. The parent has lost his or her own self-control.
  3. The shopping experience has been far from positive.
  4. The child has learned nothing about self-control in public.

Notes:

Courtesy of R. Franklin Trimm, III, MD, Developmental/Behavioral Pediatrics, University of South Alabama, Mobile, Alabama.

Effective Punishment

GOALS OF PUNISHMENT

- Prevent avoidance behaviors and escape from the punisher.
- Undo or prevent teaching the child a hateful attitude toward the punisher.
- Reduce the need for punishment later.
- Provide a model of nonaggressive behavior.

USE OF PUNISHMENT

- Use when a behavior is of physical danger to the child, another person, or to property.
- Use when the consequences of the behavior are serious.
- Use when a problem behavior occurs so often there is no good behavior to reinforce.

RULES OF EFFECTIVE PUNISHMENT

- Give punishment immediately.
- Use only one punishment per crime.
- Use the least amount that will be effective.
- Take away reinforcers.
- Provide a clear-cut method for earning reinforcers back.
- Use warnings.
- Carry out in a calm, matter-of-fact way.
- Give punishment along with reinforcement for behaviors incompatible with the punished behavior.
- Give punishment consistently. Reinforcement is not given for the punished behaviors.

CORPORAL PUNISHMENT

Corporal punishment includes spanking with your hand or another object, pinching, squeezing, pushing, tickling in excess, and a number of other variants. Corporal punishment can be effective but has several major limitations in fulfilling the criteria for effective punishment.

- It is only in the small child that you can guarantee that the child cannot avoid the punisher. In the older child, this situation can easily go out of control for both parent and child, leading to abuse.
- Instead of undoing or preventing a hateful attitude toward the punisher, corporal punishment reinforces this hate.

continues

continued

- Decreasing the frequency of the undesired behavior is the one goal of punishment it does achieve.

- Corporal punishment provides a model for aggression.

It has often been stated that punishment is best used when safety is concerned. However, in reviewing the examples cited, what is often being used is negative reinforcement. *Negative reinforcement* is the withdrawal of a noxious stimuli when the desired behavior is performed. The classic example of this is nagging. When teaching safety, the parent often starts yelling and screaming at the child while he or she is approaching or in the midst of danger (near a fire, running into the street). When the child is back on safe ground, the parent often stops the screaming and instead holds and hugs the child. This approach is negative reinforcement. If, however, the scolding and perhaps spanking continued after the child was safe, that would be punishment.

In reviewing the four goals of punishment, spanking generally meets one goal, while causing side effects that have to be dealt with separately by not meeting the other three goals. It is like taking a medicine that has a 25 percent chance of cure and a 75 percent chance of causing side effects that will need additional treatment.

Notes:

Courtesy of R. Franklin Trimm, III, MD, Developmental/Behavioral Pediatrics, University of South Alabama, Mobile, Alabama.

Time-Out

Time-out can be used as early as 18 to 24 months of age in most children. The upper age range depends on emotional maturity but is often between 10 and 12 years of age. Children who are learning self-control often respond to the warning and do not get sent to time-out as opposed to time-out no longer working.

STEPS FOR TIME-OUT

- Select a suitable place in the home for time-out. Use a chair in the hall or the corner. The space should be well lighted, not too closed off, but without any "fun potential." The location should also be without any dangerous materials such as glass, medicine, and so forth.
- Determine a specific time period for time-out. One minute per year of age with a maximum of 5 minutes is usually effective. Many situations may require even less time.
- Use a timer. Show it to the child to indicate the beginning of punishment period. The timer alarm will indicate the end of the period.
- Time-out should be preceded by a warning. If intolerable behavior stops, praise the child. If behavior continues, proceed with the time-out.
- Tell the child to go to time-out. Parents must show displeasure and firmness without excessive emotional responses in a matter-of-fact way, keeping physical distance (that is, avoid physical force in getting child to time-out).
- Start timer when child has gone to the designated place (and becomes quiet).
- Allow the child to return to previous or new activity when timer alarm sounds. Praise as soon as possible after time-out episode. If the child went to time-out because of noncompliance with an action command, return to an effective command routine to get that task finished.
- Use the skills of positive attention and ignoring at every phase of time-out. The ability to ignore diversions is crucial.
- Explain and practice time-out to the child before using it. The younger the child, the longer the training period will need to be.

COMMON PITFALLS

- *Child does not comply with command to go to time-out.* If the child has been adequately trained in time-out, this situation is not likely to happen more than once or twice. An additional warning with an appropriate consequence may need to be given. If the child does not comply, drop the time-out and follow through with alternate consequence.
- *Child will not get quiet after going to designated place.* Again, this situation is not likely to happen persistently if the child thoroughly understands time-out. Remind the child that the timer does not start until quiet occurs.
- *Child seems to "enjoy" going to time-out.* Make sure surroundings for selected location are appropriate. This response may be seen when a child outgrows time-out as well.

Courtesy of R. Franklin Trimm, III, MD, Developmental/Behavioral Pediatrics, University of South Alabama, Mobile, Alabama.

Temper Tantrums: Six General Guidelines

1. Ensure the child is safe physically and emotionally.
2. Pay no attention, positive or negative, to the child.
3. Do not reason with the child during the tantrum.
4. Do not restrain or spank the child; these actions generally do not help.
5. Reunite after tantrum.
6. Do not give in.

Notes:

Courtesy of Brad D. Berman, MD, Child Development Center, Children's Hospital Oakland, Oakland, California.

Dos and Don'ts of Behavior and Weight Management for Children with Prader-Willi Syndrome

DO

- Keep food inaccessible at all times. Children with Prader-Willi syndrome cannot fight their compulsion to get it. Put food away and lock the cupboards and refrigerator.
- Keep the child's life structured. Children need structure; preplan changes.
- Praise and recognize good performances. A lot of mileage can be obtained with a few words, smiles, and hugs.
- Listen when the child needs to talk. The time it takes to listen may alleviate or prevent unpleasantness later.
- Include the child with Prader-Willi syndrome in planning and programming. Children feel a need for some control and will cooperate 100 percent if they feel the idea was their own.
- Keep sight of the fact that the hand of the child with Prader-Willi syndrome is quicker than the eye of the parent or caregiver.
- Snack in private. It is very hard for a child with Prader-Willi syndrome to watch others enjoy goodies.
- Use smaller plates and cups, spread the food out, and add extra nonfattening items. Using carrots, dill pickles, or diet jello makes the amount on the plate look larger.
- Inform neighbors, relatives, teachers, babysitters, classmates, everyone with whom the child comes in contact of guidelines. Inform them more than once.
- Be consistent. Children thrive on routines and knowing exactly what the guidelines are.
- Remember that logic and reason will not prevail. When a child with this syndrome gets upset or "stuck" on an idea or position, logic or reason will not help.

DON'T

- Use food as a reward or punishment except on a very limited basis.
- Assume, if the child has lost weight, that the problem is now "cured."
- Nag. (Once a behavior has been dealt with, do not bring it up again; discuss temper tantrums and then forget it.)
- Argue. (Make the statement, allow the child one more comment, warn that the discussion is over—and stick to it! You will never win an argument.)
- Tease, be sarcastic, or even use subtle humor. (Children with Prader-Willi syndrome do not respond well to such tactics.)

continues

continued

- Ignore bad behavior. (Try interventions to prevent it.)
- Lose your temper. (Easier said than done, but do whatever it takes to keep cool because nothing will be gained from loss of self-control.)
- Promise anything that you cannot or will not do. The child will not accept any reason for change.
- Ignore poor table manners. (The child is capable of using utensils; slowing down; and staying until the meal is finished without additional food.)
- Try to talk things out. (This tactic does not work.)
- Lose sight of the humorous aspects of all this. (Hang on to a sense of humor while figuring out how to lock up the apple tree.)
- Hesitate to ask for professional help.
- Forget that this situation is a life-threatening one.

Notes:

Courtesy of Prader-Willi Syndrome Association, St. Paul, Minnesota.

Behavior Management and Attention Deficit Disorder

BEHAVIOR MANAGEMENT

Children with attention deficit disorder (ADD) respond well to rewards and structure. The child does best in an organized environment where rules and expectations are clear and consistent, and when consequences for meeting the demands of a given situation are set forth ahead of time and delivered immediately. Thus, the child's environment needs to be ordered and predictable. Frequent and consistent praise and rewards for appropriate behavior such as completing tasks on time or being polite and courteous encourage the child to repeat such desirable behavior.

The main principle behind all behavior management strategies is to increase the child's appropriate behavior and decrease inappropriate behavior through the use of consequences. The best way to influence any behavior is to pay attention to it. The best way to increase a desirable behavior is to reward it. Ignoring an undesirable behavior will decrease its frequency.

There are many books on behavior management written for the lay person. Below are some guidelines for behavior management.

GUIDELINE 1: BEHAVIOR MODIFICATION CHARTS

Children with ADD usually require a formal program for managing their behavior. Most often, such a program centers around behavior modification charts. Parents, teachers, and other important adults in the child's life will need training in how to implement and use these charts effectively.

Charts are designed to provide the child with a clear picture of what behaviors are expected. The child then has the choice of meeting those expectations. Parents or teachers provide feedback to the child about his or her choices by delivering consequences. Charts tend to motivate and enable the child to develop an internal sense of self-control—specifically, that he or she can behave appropriately.

There are two basic types of chart programs.

1. *Token Economy.* The child earns tokens (chips, stickers, stars) for appropriate behavior. Tokens can be exchanged for various rewards.
2. *Response Cost.* The child is given tokens for free. Tokens are withdrawn for inappropriate behavior (for example, out of seat, off-task, and so forth).

The most effective programs use both types of chart systems and work on a give-and-take basis. In this combination system, the child is given a token for behaving appropriately and loses a token when misbehaving.

continues

continued

When creating and implementing a behavior modification chart, keep these suggestions in mind:

- Make a list of problematic behaviors or ones that need improving.
- Select the behaviors to be modified. The parents (or teachers), with input from the child, review the list of problematic behaviors and select three, four, or five to work on at a given time. The behaviors charted should be ones that occur daily, such as going to bed on time, doing homework, or getting ready for school on time.
- Design a reward system (token economy, response cost, or a combination). The parents (or teachers) need to pay attention to the child's behavior throughout the course of a day and provide frequent rewards when the child behaves appropriately. At the end of the day, tokens can be exchanged for rewards, such as going to bed later, playing a game, or getting a favorite snack. Remember, a reward is only effective when it has value to the child. Rewards might have to be changed frequently.

GUIDELINE 2: PUNISHMENT

Children with ADD respond best to motivation and positive reinforcement. It is best to avoid punishment. When punishment is necessary, use it sparingly and with sensitivity. It is important for parents and teachers to respond to the child's inappropriate behavior without anger and in a matter-of-fact way. The child needs to be taught to replace inappropriate behavior with appropriate behavior.

GUIDELINE 3: TIME-OUT

When the child is misbehaving or out of control, time-out is an effective way to manage the problem. Time-out means the child is sent to a predetermined location for a short period of time. A place out of the mainstream of activity is best (for example, one particular chair may be specified as the "time-out chair"). The time-out location should not be a traumatic place, such as a closet or dark basement. The purpose of time-out is to provide the child with a cooling-off period wherein he or she can regain control.

An important aspect to time-out is that the child no longer has the privilege to choose where he or she would like to be and how time is spent. In general, the child stays in time-out and must be quiet for 5 minutes. Preschool-aged children are usually given 2 or 3 minutes in time-out. For toddlers, 30 seconds to a minute is appropriate.

Source: Mary Fowler, "Attention Deficit Disorder," National Information Center for Children with Disabilities (NICHCY), Washington, DC, September 1991.

Living with a Child with Hyperactivity

1. **Accept your child's limitations.** A parent must accept the fact that the child is active and energetic and possibly always will be. The hyperactivity is not intentional, or designed to aggravate. A parent should not expect to eliminate hyperactivity but just keep it under reasonable control. Any undue criticism or attempts to change the energetic child into a quiet child will cause more harm than good. Nothing is more helpful for the child with hyperactivity than having a tolerant and patient parent.

2. Provide outlets for the release of excess energy. Your child's energy cannot be "bottled up" and stored. The child needs daily outside activities such as running, sports, or long walks. In bad weather the child needs a place to act freely without undue criticism.

3. **Keep the home existence organized.** Household routines help the child with hyperactivity accept order. Mealtimes, chores, and bedtimes should be kept as consistent as possible. Predictable responses by the parents help the child become more predictable. Parents must share their duties and chores for the child's good. Such activities build self-discipline and a sense of responsibility. Be prepared for the fact that it will take time, effort, goodwill, and many calm reminders to get these chores done. Withholding a desired privilege for a short time may be necessary if the child fails to do assigned chores.

4. **Avoid fatigue.** When the child is exhausted, self-control often breaks down and the hyperactivity becomes worse.

5. **Maintain firm discipline.** The child with hyperactivity is unquestionably difficult to manage. More careful, planned discipline is needed. Establish clear ground rules when the child is young, and keep these rules (with whatever amendments are necessary) into adolescence. As the child improves in judgment, give more leeway. Aggressive behavior and attention-getting behavior should not be accepted. Unnecessary rules should be avoided. The child with hyperactivity tolerates fewer rules than children without this condition. Avoid "getting after" the child all the time with negative comments such as "Don't do that" and "Stop that."

6. **Enforce discipline with nonphysical punishment.** The family should have a time-out place. A corner is probably best, but wherever it is, it should be free of distractions (for example, toys, television, and so forth). Punishment should follow immediately after the offense so that the association between the undesirable behavior and the punishment that follows such action will be strengthened. Punishment should be of short duration. It must clear the air—a parent should not continue to accuse and grumble, but the child may be allowed to grumble a bit. A kitchen timer is an excellent way to set the time-out period. It should be placed in the child's view, but out of reach. Length of time depends on the child's age, but should not be longer than 5 minutes.

continues

continued

7. **Do not flood the child with petty decisions.** Petty decisions would involve what to eat, what to wear, and so forth. If the child dawdles or shows indecision, make these decisions for the child. On the other hand, consider the child's opinion in larger matters. For example, let the child decide whether or not to go to a friend's birthday party. If there is no real reason to deny the child, then allow the option of deciding. Give the child time to picture the situation and think it through.

8. **Be prepared to accept absentmindedness.** The child with hyperactivity often needs to be reminded again, and again, but without "nagging." Try to avoid the usual escalation of irritation when directions or reminders need to be given over and over. Be alert to your child's absentmindedness in regard to care of tools, toys, and other implements. Give calm reminders to put things away. Short lists of tasks are excellent ways to help a child remember.

9. **Remember that the child may seem to never hear or to ignore parental directions and commands.** Often the child cannot "process" multiple requests quickly or accurately. First, get the child's attention—stand in front of the child, touch the child, and make eye contact. State the direction in simple, clear, one-concept commands, then ask the child to repeat what was said. Speak in a clear, slow voice.

10. **Recognize that the child may have difficulty waiting for his or her turn.** Some interruptions when adults are talking may be allowed, understanding the impulsivity of a child with hyperactivity. However, having permitted an infraction on good manners with a gentle correction, do not allow the child to persist in interrupting. Send the child from the table or discipline the child if this behavior continues.

11. **Do not permit the child to be unduly loud or rowdy in a public place.** Do something about the behavior quickly (remember "cause and effect"), even if it means embarrassment for all concerned. It may be necessary to avoid shopping or eating out with the child initially, until behavior is better controlled. Again, time-out in the car or in a corner of the store can be most effective.

Notes:

Source: John C. King, MD.

Suggestions for Parents: Helping Children Achieve Self-Determination

Being aware of the significance of self-esteem and decision-making and problem-solving skills in a child's overall development does not necessarily mean that parents and professionals know how to encourage the growth of these skills. The following suggestions for how parents and others can help children with disabilities develop a sense of self-worth and self-sufficiency have been developed from readings in literature on disability and from conversations with individuals with disabilities.

- Treat your child with a disability as a capable human being by encouraging and supporting his or her efforts to explore, take healthy risks, and try out new situations.

- Provide opportunities for self-awareness by focusing on your child's strengths and the qualities that make him or her special and unique.

- Let your child know that you enjoy spending time with him or her. Try to really listen when your child shares thoughts and experiences.

- Share your family stories, histories, and traditions with your child to help the child understand that he or she is a member of a family circle, with a permanent place in the larger scheme of things.

- Provide opportunities for interaction with others of different ages and backgrounds to help your child develop social confidence.

- Help your child experience success by encouraging him or her to build on known strengths and abilities.

- Acknowledge your child's efforts toward a goal, not just the final product or accomplishment.

- Have realistic expectations; do not expect so much that your child is set up for failure or frustration, or so little that a lack of faith is communicated.

- Let your child take responsibility for his or her own actions.

- Acknowledge your child's presence. Include your child in discussions with family and friends. Do not interfere unnecessarily to answer questions that were directed at the child.

- Give your child a chance to grow into a unique adult. Avoid using labels such as "shy," "lazy," or "clumsy" to describe your child.

- Respect your child's need for privacy and time alone. Do not intrude unless it is absolutely necessary.

- Promote your child's assertive (not aggressive) behavior as well as respect for others. Being assertive is an excellent way for your child to avoid being exploited or taken advantage of.

continues

continued

- Encourage your child to practice and use basic coping statements to handle difficult emotions, such as anger, jealousy, or fear, but by all means, encourage their expression. (An example of a coping statement might be: "I can do this. I'll be just fine." Or, "I really feel upset, but I need to stay calm.")
- Acknowledge your own sense of self-worth, when appropriate. Your healthy self-image will be a good model for your child.

As a parent, a teacher, or a professional who is helping a child with disabilities achieve self-sufficiency, remember that learning to be independent is a difficult task for all children. Likewise, it is sometimes difficult to encourage a child's independence earnestly: letting go is one of the most difficult tasks that parents face. What is important to realize is that all children, regardless of their strengths and weaknesses, have to try many times—and sometimes fail— before they can gain the self-assurance and sense of personal worth that comes with adulthood.

Notes:

Source: "Self-Determination," *NICHCY Transition Summary*, No. 5, National Information Center for Children and Youth with Disabilities (NICHCY), Washington, DC, 1988.

Encouraging Independence in Children with Spina Bifida

PROBLEMS INTERFERING WITH INDEPENDENCE

Children with spina bifida may experience several kinds of problems that interfere with independence. Remember, however, that children are born with courage. They want to do for themselves. Parents (or teachers) want to *encourage* them to do for themselves, too. If parents and teachers do things for children that they can do themselves, they will become discouraged. Problems that interfere with achieving independence include:

- **Physical problems.** This category includes problems with walking and moving around as well as bladder and bowel incontinence.

- **Social problems.** A basic problem is not having as much opportunity to be with other children.

- **Emotional dependence.** Often, your child becomes dependent on you for doing things, for making decisions, and for solving problems.

- **Learning disabilities.** Often, the child experiences problems when trying to learn how to do things. These problems may include difficulty:
  — paying attention (distractibility)
  — staying still (restlessness or hyperactivity)
  — thinking before acting (impulsivity)
  — remembering instructions or steps in doing something (short-term memory)
  — putting ideas in order (sequencing)
  — keeping things in order (organization)
  — solving problems

Because the child may experience several of these barriers, achieving independence will be an ongoing challenge.

WHAT PARENTS NEED TO ENCOURAGE INDEPENDENCE

Before talking about your child, you need to find and use qualities in yourself. These include:

- **Creativity.** Finding different ways to meet developmental tasks often requires using creative energies.

- **Patience.** When attempting new tasks, time must be allowed for the child to learn and do.

continues

continued

- **Determination.** Parents need to stay after the task, so that independent behaviors become commonplace.

- **Vigilance.** It is easy to stay in the role of doing for the child, but it is important to look for things that can be performed by the child. Always be aware of the small tasks performed for the child that he or she could do without assistance.

- **Wisdom.** Continue to distinguish what the child can do alone and what the child needs help with.

- **Support.** A parent cannot do all this alone. Emotional support is needed from family and friends, including other parents of children with spina bifida.

- **Guidance.** Sometimes information or specific ideas about particular problem areas are needed. Professionals are available to help and should be included as resources.

Notes:

Courtesy of Donald J. Lollar, EdD, Health and Rehabilitation Psychologists of Atlanta, Shepherd Spinal Center, Atlanta, Georgia

Encouraging Independence in Girls with Disabilities

How do stereotypes of male and female behavior and potential affect children with disabilities? To begin with, many adults feel that children with disabilities need more help. Boys with disabilities can often escape the disability stereotype of helplessness or dependence by aspiring to such traditional male characteristics as competence, autonomy, and work. Girls with disabilities, however, confront two stereotypes—the "passive, dependent" female and the "helpless and dependent" person with a disability. As a result, they often get a double dose of assistance that can lead to a kind of a dependence called *learned helplessness.*

What can parents do, in practical terms, to foster greater independence and self-sufficiency in their child? Perhaps the single, most important thing parents can do to help their child is to expect her to *aspire*. If parents truly want their daughter to realize her potential for independence, they must make this their expectation from day one. From infancy on, they should allow her as much autonomy as possible, stretching her vision rather than limiting it. She should be encouraged to go out and meet the world. This is a common thread running through the stories of women with disabilities who have strived for and gained independence and self-sufficiency— their parents expected and encouraged them to aspire and achieve.

Here are some ideas that parents can put to use in their home and in their parenting style.

- **Start early.** Don't wait until your daughter is 16. Independence and self-determination are built one day at a time. Encouraging a child's learning, growth, and achievement should be a part of the daily consciousness and activities of the household.
- **Recognize that *your* behavior, as a family, may need to change.** It may need to change because you have come from a different culture with societal expectations that place limitations on women's achievement and self-determination. Or perhaps change is indicated because you do not know, or have not considered, the options available to your daughter in today's society due to new education programs and work opportunities.
- **Take a personal assessment.** Identify the expectations you have, the assistance you routinely offer your daughter, and the motivation she has or is given to develop her capabilities. For example, if she is in a family with all female siblings, do you expect as much from your daughter with a disability? If she is in a family with male siblings, how are your expectations for her different? Families need to have the same expectations for their female and male children and provide their daughters with the same opportunities they would give a male child with the same disabilities.

The following suggestions are limited by the great variety of disabilities to be addressed. Probably the most beneficial advice is to really assess your daughter's abilities and examine your thoughts about what you expect of your other children and of her. Think of ways she can become a more integral and contributing member of the family.

continues

continued

EXPECTATIONS

How much do you expect your daughter to do for herself? Take a look at your girl's day: Where can you expect her to do more for herself? Where can you expect her to do more within the household?

ASSISTANCE

How much assistance do you offer your daughter? To achieve greater independence, she has to do things without constant help, reminders, and suggestions. And she *can* do these things, although it may take longer and be more difficult than if you do it for her.

Many caregivers speak of the pain of watching their child's laborious efforts to perform what, to most of society, are routine tasks. And while it is natural to want to step in and help and to spare your child the struggle, it is often better to let her do the task in her own time and in her own way. Then the achievement is hers. So look closely at the assistance you give and decide when and how it can be faded over time. Parents too must let go at their own pace and in their own way— no one would say that letting go of any child is an easy task. It may involve taking risks that you find disquieting.

MOTIVATION

Your daughter may very well want no part of being self-sufficient. It's much more convenient to have you! So you need to develop a system of rewards, such as attention, praise, tokens, or permitting her to do something she likes once the task has been completed successfully. Focus on her positive behaviors and reinforce these.

DECISION MAKING

Another vital component of independence is *decision making*. How do parents teach this complex skill? First, consider how it feels when you are told what to do, instead of being allowed to act according to your own preferences and judgment. Also, ponder how you learned to make decisions and how you taught your nondisabled children to be good decision makers. As much as possible, apply the same methods to your daughter with a disability.

The reasons we make decisions, of course, cover a spectrum of daily and life choices. Knowing when to put on a jacket is a decision that a child who is deaf will not long find difficult; it may be a much more complex decision for a child with severe disabilities to make. Much modeling and repetition may be necessary to help such a child learn to make decisions herself.

For children who have difficulty learning to perform a task from beginning to end, you may need to break the task into its component parts and teach each part separately. Then, when your

continues

continued

daughter can successfully perform each part, expect her to begin combining parts. Foster her ability to make these decisions about sequence by asking her, "What's next?" Through your modeling and repetition, she will learn to ask herself, "What's next?" Eventually she will be able to perform the task herself, from start to finish.

Self-Awareness

An essential part of good decision making is *self-awareness*. Having insight into what your daughter's strengths and weaknesses are, given her disability and her motivation, will help you help her in all facets of her life. Her ability, through your help, to assess herself—how she feels, what she believes about herself and others, what she wants in life—provides a central point around which to make decisions. Realism, of course, is important in self-appraisal. You can foster your daughter's self-awareness and her ability to make honest self-appraisals by being honest yourself, by allowing her to make decisions that require her to identify her preferences and desires, and by engaging her in conversations that lead her to examine herself. It is especially important that your daughter realize her strengths and learn to emphasize them.

Consequences and Risk-Taking

Another intrinsic part of decision making is the ability to consider consequences.

Sometimes, making decisions and acting upon them involve taking physical, emotional, or intellectual risks. For parents, allowing their much-loved child to take risks is disquieting, even more so when that child is a daughter. "She might get hurt," "She can't protect herself," and "I can't stand to watch her try and fail," are reasons parents of girls commonly give for wanting their daughter to go slow, be careful, and hold back. The problem is, girls then *learn* to hold back and will "play it safe" in the kinds of decisions they make. This results in self-limiting thinking and behavior.

Teaching your daughter that it's okay to take risks may mean that you have to teach yourself as well, gritting your teeth and crossing your fingers.

Teaching that it's okay to take a risk involves teaching that it's okay to try and fail. In fact, in learning a new skill, even the most adept person generally has many failures on the road to mastery. This is an important message to give your daughter. Understanding that learning may involve repeated attempts to do something before one is successful places initial failures in their proper context and illustrates that immediate success is not essential, but the willingness to try and try again *is*.

Encourage your daughter to try new things, even if this means she has to struggle and swallow initial failure. Be understanding, too, if she shows a range of emotional reactions. We all have felt the fear, frustration, anger, and occasional despair that can accompany trying something new and difficult. Your daughter is as entitled to these human reactions as any other person. Praise

continues

continued

her attempts and honor the courage it takes her to keep on trying. Your encouragement will be a powerful validation of her effort and will reinforce the message that only in striving do we achieve.

In short, whether the decision is a small one, such as what to wear or what to eat, or a far-reaching one, such as what career track to follow, encourage your daughter to identify her preferences and act upon them, even if this means taking a chance and risking failure. In this way, she develops her sense of self and the ability to take action that expresses that self. The skills of decision making are learned in many ways: modeling, discussion, risk-taking, consideration of consequence, and practice. The more decisions you allow her to make, the better equipped she will be to determine her own way in the world outside your home.

Notes:

Source: "Having a Daughter with a Disability: Is It Different for Girls?" *NICHCY News Digest*, No. 14, National Information Center for Children and Youth with Disabilities (NICHCY), Washington, DC, October 1990.

Shaken Baby Syndrome

One of the most hazardous experiences for a baby or young child to endure is being shaken. It is estimated that 10 percent of all reported incidents of child abuse can be attributed to severe shaking. Of those with shaken baby syndrome, 15 percent die and 50 percent suffer long-term or permanent disability.

The shaken baby syndrome describes a possible group of consequences of severe shaking in young children, the most serious of which is death. It may also cause blindness; spinal cord or skeletal injuries; psychological disturbances; and brain damage, which can result in coma, mental retardation, cerebral palsy, behavioral disorders, and seizure disorders.

Adults and sometimes older children may shake babies in anger or out of frustration with the child's behavior, for example, when trying to get the baby to stop crying. Babies are also injured by being shaken in play, for example when a baby is tossed in the air and caught.

While shaken baby syndrome is often a form of intentional abuse, there are many cases in which the person shaking a baby does not realize the possible damage that can result, because there is no external sign of injury. It is important for everyone to know that it is never all right to shake a baby. Many children are injured by their parents, babysitters, and relatives in rough play or in one uncharacteristic moment of anger. Parents do not generally spank children until they are 9 months of age or older. A tired, frustrated parent trying to quiet a baby can very easily resort to shaking without realizing the harm. Not surprisingly, boys are twice as likely to incur abuse, whether intentional or unintentional. Even as babies, boys are expected to be brave and tough and enjoy being tossed into the air and caught. This mode of play is just another form of shaking.

Despite the identification of shaken baby syndrome in 1972, many child pediatric health professionals failed to recognize shaken baby syndrome, especially because of the absence of external injury and because the symptoms produced from severe shaking may mimic other conditions. Advances in medical technology such as the CT scan and MRI have greatly enhanced the ability to diagnose shaken baby syndrome.

Brain injury, which is the most frequent result of shaking babies up to approximately one year of age, occurs because the baby's head is disproportionately larger than the body and the neck is not strong enough to support the head when shaking occurs. The result is a whip-lash–like injury, in which the brain literally bounces against the skull, causing bruising and tearing of veins. The bruising and bleeding inside the brain can cause permanent physical and mental disability and even death.

Courtesy of Casa Colina Children's Services Center, Casa Colina Centers for Rehabilitation, Pomona, California. Individuals wishing to receive free copies of shaken baby syndrome materials may contact Casa Colina Children's Services Center at 909–593–7521.

Suggestions about Handling Sibling Issues

Parents set the tone for sibling interactions and attitudes by example and by direct communications. In any family, children should be treated fairly and valued as individuals, praised as well as disciplined, and each child should have special times with parents. Thus, parents should periodically assess the home situation. Although important goals for a child with special needs are to develop feelings of self-worth and self-trust, to become as independent as possible, to develop trust in others, and to develop to the fullest of his or her abilities, these goals are also important to nondisabled siblings.

To every extent possible, parents should require their children with disabilities to do as much as possible for themselves. Families should provide every opportunity for a normal family life by doing things together, such as cleaning the house or yard; or going on family outings to the movies, the playground, museums, or restaurants. Always, the child with a disability should be allowed to participate as much as possible in family chores, and should have specific chores assigned as do the other children.

Caregiving responsibilities for the child with a disability or chronic illness should be shared by all family members. It is especially important that the burden for caregiving does not fall onto the shoulders of an older sibling. If there is an older sister, there is a tendency in some families to give her the primary responsibility, or an excessive amount of it. Today, however, more communities are providing resources to ease the family's caregiving burdens. Examples include recreation activities, respite care, and parent support groups.

Here are several strategies suggested by nondisabled siblings for parents to consider in their interactions with their nondisabled children. These siblings suggest that parents should:

- Be open and honest.
- Limit the caregiving responsibilities of siblings.
- Use respite care and other supportive services.
- Accept the disability.
- Schedule special time with the nondisabled sibling.
- Let siblings settle their own differences.
- Welcome other children and friends into the home.
- Praise all siblings.
- Recognize that they are the most important, most powerful teachers of their children.
- Listen to siblings.
- Involve all siblings in family events and decisions.
- Require the child with a disability to do as much for himself or herself as possible.

continues

continued

- Recognize each child's unique qualities and family contribution.
- Recognize special stress times for siblings and plan to minimize negative effects.
- Use professionals when indicated to help siblings.
- Teach siblings to interact.
- Provide opportunities for a normal family life and normal family activities.
- Join sibling-related organizations.

Children with special needs, disabilities, or chronic illness may often need more help and require more attention and planning from their parents and others in order to achieve their maximum independence. Brothers and sisters can give parents some of the extra help and support they need; the special relationship of brothers and sisters, disabled and nondisabled, is often lifelong. This special and unique bond among siblings can foster and encourage the positive growth of the entire family.

Notes:

Source: "Children with Disabilities: Understanding Sibling Issues," *NICHCY News Digest*, No. 11, National Information Center for Children and Youth with Disabilities (NICHCY), Washington, DC, 1988.

The Importance of Developing Social Skills

LEARNING SOCIAL SKILLS

In order to build gratifying human relationships, it is vital that children with disabilities learn and have the opportunity to practice the social skills considered appropriate by society. Many will find this process more difficult than their peers without disabilities, because of learning or other cognitive disabilities, visual or hearing impairments, or a physical disability that limits their chances to socialize. Most, however, are capable of learning these important "rules."

Consider how you learned society's social rules. You made mistakes when you were a child. You were corrected by your parents or others; sometimes you were punished. Sometimes friends got mad at things you did or said. And, given this feedback, you gradually learned. Unfortunately, all too often, this important feedback on performance is denied those with disabilities. For some, there is a presumption that they cannot learn the basics of social behavior. For others, social isolation plays a key role. How can there be feedback on one's social skills when little socializing takes place?

Acquiring socialization skills does not happen overnight. These skills are developed across years of observation, discussion, practice, and constructive feedback. Some of the most important aspects of socializing that individuals with disabilities may initially have difficulty grasping include turn-taking during conversations, maintaining eye contact, being polite, maintaining attention, repairing misunderstandings, finding a topic that is of mutual interest, and distinguishing social cues (both verbal and nonverbal). These subtleties, however, are not impossible for individuals with disabilities to learn. This training can begin at home, with you as parents playing a vital role in helping your child learn how to socialize. For example, when you entertain, you should not have your child with a disability safely tucked into bed before guests arrive. Instead, make sure your child has a part to play in the festivities. This part might be greeting people at the door, taking their coats, showing them where the chairs are, or offering them food. You may find it helpful to take one aspect at a time and practice it with your child in advance (for example, how and when to shake hands). Even those with severe disabilities can be creatively included. Remember, these early interactions lay the foundation for interactions in the future, many of which will take place outside of the home.

As most children grow older, they interact more and more with people in situations where direct supervision by parents is not possible. Drawing from what they have learned at home about socializing, children make friends within their peer group and soon learn more about socializing, hopefully refining their social skills as they grow and mature. These friendships are important for all children to develop, not only because contact, understanding, and sharing with others are basic human needs. Friends also satisfy other needs for children as well as contribute to the shaping of a child's social skills and sense of identity.

Unfortunately, many children with disabilities are socially isolated. They may have great difficulty building a network of friends and acquaintances with whom to share their feelings, opinions, ideas, and selves. A number of factors may contribute to their becoming isolated. The

continues

continued

presence of a disability may make peers shy away, may make transportation to and from social events difficult, may require special health care, or may make the individual with a disability reluctant to venture out socially. A lack of appropriate social skills may also contribute to a person's social isolation.

WHAT CAN FAMILIES AND CAREGIVERS DO?

Families and caregivers can help children with disabilities widen their social circle in a number of ways. As has been said, the first action involves laying the foundations of socializing at home, from early childhood on. (This process includes emphasizing good grooming and personal hygiene, and teaching children the basics of self-care.) Another way you can help is by discussing and exploring with your child what makes a good friendship, how friendships are formed and maintained, and some reasons why friendships may end. Children with disabilities need to be aware that they may have to be the initiator in forming friendships. In the beginning, this role may be difficult for children with disabilities. You may wish to model important social behaviors for your child and then have your child role-play with you or other family members any number of typical friendly interactions. Such interactions might include telephone conversations, how to ask about another person's interests or describe one's house, or how to suggest or share an activity with a friend. Other suggestions you may want to consider are:

- *Help your child to develop hobbies or pursue special interests.* Hobbies are not only gratifying in themselves, but shared hobbies or interests bring people together and provide opportunities for friendships to develop.
- *Encourage your child to pursue recreational and leisure activities in the community.* Activities might include scouting, the 4-H Club, a church group, and activities through the parks and recreation department, local community centers, or the YMCA/YWCA. These groups provide healthy outlets for youthful energy, build self-esteem through developing competence, and provide occasions for the young person to interact with peers of the same age.
- *Encourage your child to participate in extracurricular activities at school.* Most schools have special-interest activities or clubs that bring together students with similar interests. Even after-school daycare programs offer many opportunities for socialization.
- *Be alert to opportunities for your child to become involved creatively at school.* One mother of a teenaged boy with multiple disabilities talked with the high school football coach about how her son could contribute managerially to the team's activities. Alex became waterboy for the varsity football team and currently travels to all games with the team. He now knows all the football players, the cheerleaders, and their friends, a major social "coup" at his school.
- *Help your teenager find employment or volunteer positions in the community.* Working after school or on the weekends in the community offers opportunities for social interaction and certainly enhances self-esteem.

continues

continued

- *Try not to overprotect your child.* Although it is natural to want to shield your child from the possibility of failure, hurt feelings, and others' rejection, you must allow your child the opportunity to grow and stretch socially. Be available to talk about difficulties your child is having socially and about his or her fears, questions, and feelings. When attempts to build a friendship don't work out, encourage your child to try again.

COMMON SOCIAL MISTAKES

Beyond developing basic interpersonal skills, there are two types of social mistakes that many individuals with disabilities will need special help to avoid. These are: stranger-friend errors and private-public errors. A stranger-friend error occurs when the person with a disability treats acquaintances or total strangers as if they were dear and trusted friends. Individuals with mental retardation are particularly vulnerable to making these kinds of mistakes (for example, hugging or kissing a stranger who comes to the family home). Private-public errors generally involve doing or saying something in public that society considers unacceptable in that context, such as touching one's genitals or undressing in plain view of others. Committing either type of error can put the person with a disability into a vulnerable position in terms of breaking the law or opening the door to sexual exploitation.

The majority of individuals with disabilities who are likely to commit stranger-friend errors or private-public errors can learn to avoid them, but it is important to start this type of training when children are quite young.

Most individuals with disabilities can learn fairly early in life how to avoid private-public errors. The difference between public and private, however, may be a difficult notion for some individuals with disabilities to grasp, particularly those with moderate or severe mental retardation. It is well recognized that many people with disabilities have virtually no privacy so it is not surprising that they may not initially understand that society considers a behavior inappropriate in one location (for example, undressing in a public park) but appropriate in another (for example, undressing in the privacy of the bathroom).

You can teach the distinction between public and private most effectively through modeling, explanation, and persistence. When you teach the skills of personal grooming, for example, do so in a private place. When your child commits public-private errors, such as touching his or her genitals, immediately and calmly say, "No, that's private. We don't touch ourselves in public." If possible, allow the child to go to a private place, but if this is not possible, focus the child's attention on something else and discuss appropriate behavior later at home. It is also important that children and youth be given privacy. Having privacy allows them to understand the difference between public and private and acknowledges their right as individuals to have and enjoy time alone.

Source: "Sexuality Education for Children and Youth with Disabilities," *NICHCY News Digest*, Vol. 1:3, National Information Center for Children and Youth with Disabilities (NICHCY), 1992.

Teaching Children and Youth about Sexuality: Overview

The vast majority of parents want to be—and, indeed, already are—the primary sex educators of their children. Parents communicate their feelings and beliefs about sexuality continuously. Parents send messages to their child about sexuality both verbally and nonverbally, through praise and punishment, in the interactions they have with their child, in the tasks they give the child to do, and in the expectations they hold for the child. Children absorb what parents say and do not say, and what they do and do not do, and children learn.

Of course, a great deal of education about socialization and sexuality takes place in settings outside the home. The school setting is probably the most important, not only because most students take classes in sexuality education, but also because it is there that children and youth encounter the most extensive opportunities to socialize and mix with their peers. Thus, both parents and the school system assume responsibility for teaching children and youth about appropriate behavior, social skills, and the development of sexuality. Parents are strongly encouraged to get information about what sexuality education is provided by the school system and to work together with the school system to ensure that the sexuality education their child receives is as comprehensive as possible.

Although physical development is not much delayed for most individuals with disabilities, a child may not show certain behaviors or growth at the usual times. Depending on the nature of the disability, emotional maturity may not develop in some adolescents at the same rate as physical maturity. This does not mean that physical development will not occur. It will. Parents can help their child to cope with physical and emotional development by anticipating development and talking openly about sexuality and the values and choices surrounding sexual expression. This approach will help prepare children with disabilities to deal with their feelings in a healthy and responsible manner. It is important to realize that discussing sexuality will not create sexual feelings in young people. Those feelings are already there, because sexuality is a part of each human being throughout the entire life cycle.

Notes:

Source: "Sexuality Education for Children and Youth with Disabilities," *NICHCY News Digest*, Vol. 1:3, National Information Center for Children and Youth with Disabilities (NICHCY), Washington, DC, 1992.

Teaching about Sexuality: Infancy through 3 Years Old

Babies and young children find great pleasure in bodily sensations and exploration. Fascination with genitals is quite normal during this period and should not be discouraged or punished by parents or caregivers. Similarly, "accidents" during toilet training should not be punished or shamed, for that is all they are—accidents, in the process of learning. When a young child holds or fondles his or her genitals, parents need not react with harshness, for the child is merely curious and the sensation may very well be a pleasant one. (Of course, if may also be that the child merely has to go to the bathroom or that his or her pants are uncomfortable!) When a child of 3 years of age holds his or her genitals in public, parents may wish to move the child's hand and say quietly but firmly, "We don't do that in public." Then offer diversion—"Look at that!" or play a game such as peek-a-boo or "chase"—to change the child's focus.

Most children 3 or 4 years of age are capable of understanding the basic difference between "public" and "private." You can put the concepts in understandable terms such as "being with others" or "being alone." Children with cognitive impairments may not be able to understand the public and private concept as yet. For these children, parents can begin making concrete distinctions between public and private situations, for this is how the children will eventually learn the difference.

Notes:

Source: "Sexuality Education for Children and Youth with Disabilities," *NICHCY News Digest*, Vol. 1:3, National Information Center for Children and Youth with Disabilities (NICHCY), Washington, DC, 1992.

Teaching about Sexuality: Preschool
(Ages 3 through 5 Years)

Parents are usually teaching their children the names of body parts during this period, although the process may start earlier for some children and later for others, depending on the nature of the child's disability and his or her facility for language acquisition. When you are teaching the names of body parts, it is important not to omit naming the sexual organs. Take advantage of the natural learning process to teach your child what the sexual organs are called. It is a good idea to be accurate about the names, too, just as you are when you teach your child the names for eyes, nose, arms, and legs. Boys have a penis, for example, not a "pee-pee." Being accurate and matter-of-fact now saves having to reteach correct terminology later, and avoids communicating that the sexual organs are somehow taboo or must be referred to in secretive, nonspecific ways. Remember that children do not interpret the world from the same perspective as adults. They will not spontaneously invest the sexual organs with values or hidden meanings; these are reactions they learn from others.

During this period, most children also become intensely curious not only about their own bodies but also those of others. While exploration and "show me" games may be unsettling to you, remember that healthy curiosity prompts these games. The messages you send in your reaction, and how strong and emotional your reaction is, teach your child a great deal about the acceptability of the body and curiosity itself. It is important not to overreact. Calm remarks such as "Please put your clothes back on and come inside" give you a more positive message than "Shame on you! Come in here this minute!" Soon afterwards, talk to your child in simple, basic terms about his or her body and appropriate behavior. Detailed discussions of anatomy or reproduction are not necessary and, when offered to a young child, are generally met with boredom.

A great concern of parents and professionals is that children with disabilities are more vulnerable to sexual exploitation. Therefore, one message that is important to start mentioning when children are young is that their body belongs to them. There are many good reasons for some adults to look at or touch children's bodies (such as a parent giving a child a bath), but beyond that, children have the right to tell others not to touch their body when they do not want to be touched. Likewise, your child should hear from you that he or she should not touch strangers. Children of this age should also be taught that if a stranger tries to persuade them to go with him or her, they should leave at once and tell a parent, neighbor, or other adult.

Source: "Sexuality Education for Children and Youth with Disabilities," *NICHCY News Digest*, Vol. 1:3, National Information Center for Children and Youth with Disabilities (NICHCY), Washington, DC, 1992.

Teaching about Sexuality: Ages 5 through 8 Years

During the early school years, many children tend to lose interest in the opposite sex but may still continue to explore the body with same-sexed friends. While this practice may concern some parents, again, they should try to control the severity of their reaction, for such exploration is an expression of curiosity and is natural and normal. The child's need for information about all kinds of topics—not just the body—increases. Socialization skills are important to emphasize and practice during this period. Children with disabilities can also benefit from activities that bolster self-esteem as they grow and develop. For example, children with disabilities should have household responsibilities that they are capable of performing or learning to perform, given their disability, because accomplishment and a sense of competency build self-esteem.

It is important during this age period to become more specific in teaching about sexuality. Up to this point, training has focused more on the social self, avoiding negative messages about the body and its exploration and communicating positive messages ("Your body is good, It's yours, Your feelings about yourself and your body are good"). Some topics that may need to be addressed during this age are:

- the correct names for the body parts and their functions
- the similarities and differences between girls and boys
- the elementals of reproduction and pregnancy
- the qualities of good relationships (friendship, love, communication, respect)
- decision-making skills, and the fact that all decisions have consequences
- the beginnings of social responsibility, values, and morals
- masturbation can be pleasurable but should be done in private
- the need to avoid and report sexual exploitation

Notes:

Source: "Sexuality Education for Children and Youth with Disabilities," *NICHCY News Digest*, Vol. 1:3, National Information Center for Children and Youth with Disabilities (NICHCY), Washington, DC, 1992.

Teaching about Sexuality: Ages 8 through 11 Years

Pre-teens are usually busy with social development. They are becoming more preoccupied with what their peers think of them and, for many, body image may become an issue. Recognizing the emphasis placed on physical beauty within our society—"perfect bodies," exercise, sports, make-up—it is not difficult to imagine why many pre-teens with disabilities (and certainly teenagers) have trouble feeling good about their bodies. Those with disabilities affecting the body may be particularly vulnerable to low self-esteem in this area.

There are a number of things parents and professionals can do to help children with disabilities improve self-esteem in regards to body image. The first action parents and professionals can take is to listen to the child and allow the freedom and space for feelings of sensitivity, inadequacy, or unhappiness to be expressed. Be careful not to wave aside your child's concerns, particularly as they relate to his or her disability. If the disability is one that can cause your child to have legitimate difficulties with body image, then you need to acknowledge that fact calmly and tactfully. The disability is there; you know it and your child knows it. Pretending otherwise will not help your child develop a balanced and realistic sense of self.

What can help is encouraging children with disabilities to focus on and develop their strengths, not what they perceive as bad points about their physical appearance. This approach is called "refocusing." Many parents have also helped their child with a disability improve negative body image by encouraging improvements that can be made through good grooming, diet, and exercise. While it is important not to teach conformity for its own sake, fashionable clothes can often help any child feel more confident about body image.

One of the most important things that parents can do during their children's prepubescent years is to prepare them for the change that their bodies will soon undergo. No female should have to experience her first menses without knowing what it is; similarly, boys should be told that nocturnal emissions (or "wet dreams," as they are sometimes known) are a normal part of their physical development. To have these experiences without any prior knowledge of them can be very upsetting to a child, a trauma that can easily be avoided by timely discussions between parent and child. Tell your child that these experiences are a natural part of growing up. Above all, do so *before* they occur. Warning signs of puberty include a rapid growth spurt, developing breast buds in girls, and sometimes an increase in "acting out" and other emotional behaviors.

In addition to the topics mentioned above, other topics of importance for parents to address with children approaching puberty are:

- sexuality as part of the total self

- more information on reproduction and pregnancy

- the importance of values in decision making

continues

continued

- communication within the family unit about sexuality
- masturbation
- abstinence from sexual intercourse
- the need to avoid and report sexual abuse
- sexually transmitted diseases, including HIV and AIDS

Notes:

Source: "Sexuality Education for Children and Youth with Disabilities," *NICHCY News Digest*, Vol. 1:3, National Information Center for Children and Youth with Disabilities (NICHCY), Washington, DC, 1992.

Teaching about Sexuality: Adolescence
(Ages 12 to 18 Years)

During this period it is important to let the child assume greater responsibility in terms of decision making. It is also important that adolescents have privacy and, as they demonstrate trustworthiness, increasingly greater degrees of independence. For many teenagers, this period is an active social time with many school functions and outings with friends. Many teenagers are dating; statistics show that many become sexually involved. For children with disabilities, there may be some restrictions in opportunities for socializing and in their degree of independence. For some, it may be necessary to continue to teach distinctions between public and private. Appropriate sexuality means taking responsibility and knowing that sexual matters have their time and place.

Puberty and adolescence are usually marked by feelings of extreme sensitivity about the body. Your child's concerns over body image may become more extreme during this time. Let your adolescent voice these concerns, and reinforce ideas you have introduced about refocusing, good grooming, diet, and exercise. Without dismissing the feelings as a "phase you are going through," try to help your child understand that some of the feelings are a part of growing up. Parents may arrange for the child to talk with the family physician without the parent being present. If necessary, parents can also talk to the physician in advance to be sure he or she will be clear about the adolescent's concerns. If, however, your child remains deeply troubled or angry about body image after supportive discussion within the family unit, it may be helpful to have your child speak with a professional counselor. Counseling can be a good outlet for intense feelings, and often counselors can make recommendations that are useful to adolescents in their journey toward adulthood.

One topic that many parents find embarrassing to talk about with their children is masturbation. You will probably notice an increase in self-pleasuring behavior at this point in your child's development (and oftentimes before) and may feel in conflict about what to do, because of personal beliefs you hold. However, beliefs about the acceptability of this behavior are changing. The medical community, as well as many religious groups, now recognize masturbation as normal and harmless. Masturbation only becomes a problem when it is practiced in an inappropriate place or is accompanied by strong feelings of guilt or fear.

How can you avoid teaching your child guilt over a sexual behavior? First, you may wish to talk to your family physician, school nurse, or clergy. You may be surprised to find that what you were taught as a child is no longer being approached in the same way. In dealing with your child, recognize that you communicate a great deal through actions and reactions, and have the power to teach your child guilt and fear, or that there are appropriate and inappropriate places for such behavior.

Teach your child that touching one's genitals in public is socially inappropriate and that such behavior is only acceptable when one is alone and in a private place. Starting from very early in

continues

continued

your child's life when you may first notice such behavior, it is important to accept the behavior calmly. When young children touch themselves in public, it is usually possible to distract them. During adolescence (and sometimes before), masturbation generally becomes more than an infrequent behavior of childhood, and distracting the child's attention will not work. Furthermore, it denies the real needs of the person, instead of helping him or her to meet those needs in acceptable ways.

There are many other topics that adolescents will need to know about. Among these topics are:

- health care, including health-promoting behaviors such as regular checkups, and breast and testicular self-exam
- sexuality as part of the total self
- communication, dating, love, and intimacy
- the importance of values in guiding one's behavior
- how alcohol and drug use influence decision making
- sexual intercourse and other ways to express sexuality
- birth control and the responsibilities of child-rearing
- reproduction and pregnancy (more detailed information than what has previously been presented)
- condoms and disease prevention

Notes:

Source: "Sexuality Education for Children and Youth with Disabilities," *NICHCY News Digest*, Vol. 1:3, National Information Center for Children and Youth with Disabilities (NICHCY), Washington, DC, 1992.

Sexual Orientation

Sexual orientation refers to whether a person is heterosexual, bisexual, or homosexual. First, it is not uncommon for children of the same gender to play "show me" games with one another. This is a normal part of development, for as children grow, their curiosity about their bodies grows as well. Experts caution parents against overreacting to this type of exploration, which often has much more to do with normal curiosity and with the availability and security of same-sexed friends than with homosexuality per se.

Researchers do not know what causes a person to have one sexual orientation versus another. Theories about what determines sexual orientation include factors such as genetics, prenatal influences, sociocultural influence, and/or psychosocial factors. Parents may find it useful to realize that, in spite of the controversies that surround homosexuality and bisexuality, sexual orientation is not something that a person can change. When discussing their own social-sexual development, for example, gay men and women seem to report two basic types of personal stories. Many individuals report that they "always knew" what their sexual orientation was, from adolescence on and sometimes before. In contrast, others struggled for years trying to live up to society's expectations of heterosexuality. The realization that their sexual orientation was not heterosexual but, rather, homosexual was a gradual one ending in the awareness that they would not be able to bring their internal feelings into line with what society, their parents, their religion, or their culture wanted them to do.

Because sexual orientation is something that a person has, rather than something a person chooses, parents and professionals should be aware that strong, emotional messages against homosexuality or bisexuality will not change the orientation a person has. Such messages can—and do—create an impossible situation for the young person who feels one way but who is expected to feel and act another way. Thus, if you suspect that your young person is struggling with his or her own sexual orientation, you may want to:

- Read some books and familiarize yourself with the range of thinking and research on homosexuality, bisexuality, and heterosexuality.

- Share books on the subject with your young person.

- Consider carefully the messages you send your young person about homosexuality or bisexuality, because hostile, negative signals can do a great deal of harm to a person genuinely seeking to clarify sexual orientation.

- Be open to discussion with your child. Should your child tell you that he or she is homosexual or bisexual, do not withdraw your love and support.

- Seek outside assistance (for example, counseling, or call the National Federation of Parents and Friends of Lesbians and Gays, Inc.) if you are having difficulties accepting your child's sexual orientation.

Source: "Sexuality Education for Children and Youth with Disabilities," *NICHCY News Digest*, Vol. 1:3, National Information Center for Children and Youth with Disabilities (NICHCY), Washington, DC, 1992.

Sexual Exploitation

VULNERABILITY TO SEXUAL EXPLOITATION

One of the greatest fears of parents and caregivers is that their child with a disability will be sexually exploited. A number of factors may make individuals with disabilities more susceptible to sexual exploitation or abuse than their peers without disabilities. Several of these factors are:

- physical limitations that make self-defense difficult
- cognitive limitations that make it difficult to determine if a situation is safe or dangerous
- vulnerability to suggestion, because of limited knowledge of sexuality and human relations, including public and private behavior
- lack of information about exploitation and what to do if someone attempts to victimize them
- impulsivity, low self-esteem, and poor decision-making skills
- lack of social opportunities that results in loneliness and vulnerability

The fact that many individuals with disabilities are vulnerable to sexual exploitation makes it all the more imperative for parents and caregivers to address this issue with their child with a disability. Many child abuse prevention programs teach children to identify sexual abuse based on the concept of "good touch" and "bad touch." Recently, this approach has raised concern among many professionals, for a number of reasons. Perhaps the most critical concern is that, from a developmental perspective, young children are not necessarily capable of interpreting with accuracy the distinctions between a good and bad touch. Although most children lack understanding of appropriate expressions of sexuality, they must nonetheless make distinctions about inappropriate expressions.

STEPS TO PROTECT CHILDREN

Because young children (preschoolers and early elementary school children) are not cognitively, emotionally, or socially able to protect themselves against sexual exploitation or abuse, there are a number of steps that parents and professionals can take to help protect children. These steps include:

- Closely supervise the whereabouts and activities of children.
- Carefully scrutinize the backgrounds and references of daycare providers and other caregivers.

continues

continued

- Be informed about sexual abuse, including knowing what physical and behavioral signs a child may show if abuse has occurred.
- Distinguishing between teaching the child to be polite (for example, saying hello to adults) versus compliant (for example, requiring the child to kiss or be kissed by relatives, friends, or acquaintances when the child does not want to do so).

Closely supervising young children (and older children as well) does *not* mean that parents or professionals should strictly limit children's activities (that is, deny opportunities to participate in play groups, social groups, or community activities). Shielding persons with disabilities from the outside world may limit their contact with strangers, but it will not protect them from exploitation by friends, family members, or caregivers. Parents need to be aware that, in most cases, the abuser is someone the child knows.

There is also concern that young children may be receiving their first messages about sexuality in the negative, frightening terms associated with discussing sexual abuse. What impact this message will have on the later development of healthy sexuality is unknown. Parents need to lay a foundation of understanding in terms that are positive about sexuality, then give information about identifying, avoiding, and reporting sexual abuse. Beyond that, parents need to emphasize self-reliance. Building self-reliance includes:

- Telling children that they have the right to say "no" to touches or behaviors that hurt or make them uncomfortable. (Children should also know there are a few exceptions to this rule, such as getting a shot from the physician.)
- Teaching children decision-making and self-advocacy skills, which provide a good foundation for saying "no."
- Letting children know that they should always tell someone when another person attempts to victimize them or when a situation makes them feel uncomfortable.

Notes:

Source: "Sexuality Education for Children and Youth with Disabilities," *NICHCY News Digest*, Vol. 1:3, National Information Center for Children and Youth with Disabilities (NICHCY), Washington, DC, 1992.

Suggestions for Approaching Discussions of Sexuality with Your Child

- Not all discussions need to be lectures or situations where you sit your child down "to talk about sex." There are many daily "teachable moments" that you can take advantage of to initiate a relaxed discussion. Such moments can range from a situation on a television show, a pregnancy of a friend or relative, diapering a baby, or a question about sex that a child or youth suddenly asks.
- Bring home books about sexuality from the public library, and share them with your child, much as you would any other type of book. Curl up together and read, look at the illustrations, and talk about the content in a relaxed manner.
- When you wish your child to learn a particular value or behavior about sexuality, make sure you give your reasons for that value or behavior. This enables the child to understand why the value or behavior is important.
- You can help your child become aware of the appropriateness of the different word systems that can be used when talking about sexuality. Share your feelings about different terms, and give your child the language you prefer. For example, you can say, "The correct word is . . ." or "I prefer . . ." and give a reason why.
- Tailor information to the needs of your child. For children with mental retardation, for example, a small amount of information should be given at a time, in simple, concrete terms, perhaps supported by illustrations.

Notes:

Source: "Sexuality Education for Children and Youth with Disabilities," *NICHCY News Digest*, Vol. 1:3, National Information Center for Children and Youth with Disabilities (NICHCY), Washington, DC, 1992.

Reproduction and Birth Control

Any education about the development and expression of sexuality must include information about reproduction, the responsibilities of childbearing, and how to protect oneself against unwanted pregnancy.

Although there are disabilities that make it difficult or impossible for an individual to become pregnant or to impregnate another, most individuals with disabilities can have children and therefore need to understand the basics of reproduction and how pregnancy occurs. Remember that discussing the basics of reproduction and pregnancy may require adapting materials or the presentation of information to the particular learning characteristics of the young person.

COMPREHENSIVE SEX EDUCATION

Comprehensive sexuality education does not end with providing information about how babies are conceived. It also involves providing information about the responsibilities of child-bearing and the importance of delaying sexual intercourse until the young person is mature enough emotionally to deal with its many responsibilities and consequences.

PROVIDING INFORMATION ABOUT BIRTH CONTROL

Information about the various methods of birth control (natural, condom, IUD, pill, diaphragm, etc.) can play an important part in helping the person prevent unwanted pregnancies when sexual intercourse is finally chosen. In some families, birth control may be controversial, given personal, cultural, or religious beliefs. Yet, the decision to have children and *when* to have children is very much a personal one. Many individuals with disabilities will want to have children. Others may choose not to. Still others may be undecided or have specific concerns such as the possibility that their disability may be passed on genetically to offspring. Information on birth control and family planning is, therefore, essential for young people with disabilities to make responsible decisions about sexual health and behavior.

FORMS OF BIRTH CONTROL

It is important to realize that some forms of birth control may be suitable for a person with a certain disability, whereas other forms may not. For example, young women who have difficulty with impulsivity, memory, or with understanding basic concepts may have difficulty understanding and using the rhythm method. Remembering to take a birth control pill every day would also be difficult, making both of these methods ineffective means of controlling against unwanted pregnancy.

An alternate method of birth control, such as a time-released implant in the arm (known as NORPLANT), might be indicated. Similarly, for many young people with disabilities, learning to use a particular birth control method properly may involve more than just reading about the method or talking with their parents or doctor. For example, learning how to use a condom may require more than a simple instruction such as "you put it on."

Some demonstration and practice may be needed before the person knows how to use the method effectively. It may be useful for parents to talk with the family physician about

continues

continued

methods of birth control and how suitable each method is when the young person's disability is taken into consideration.

Sterilization

Sterilization might be considered as an effective and pragmatic birth control option for some individuals with disabilities, particularly those who do not wish to have children and those who are incapable of understanding the consequences of sexual activity or of assuming the responsibilities of parenthood. All the people involved in making such a decision should be aware that there are strict laws regarding sterilization. These laws vary from state to state, but in most cases, the person in question must give his or her informed consent to such a procedure. (This requirement is intended to protect individuals with disabilities against involuntary sterilization.) For some individuals who are severely disabled, however, it may be impossible to determine whether or not the consent is truly "informed." If sterilization is being considered as an option for the young person with disabilities, all persons involved in making such a decision will need to find out what the laws regarding sterilization are in their state.

Of course, many individuals with disabilities will want to have children at some point in their lives. For those who choose to have a child, conception may be more or less difficult, depending on the nature of the disability. Similarly, carrying and delivering the baby may present considerations unique to the disability. Many women with physical disabilities, for example, have difficulty finding an obstetrician who is willing to assume medical responsibility for a person who requires different treatment and consideration. Yet there are many stories of women who have successfully birthed and parented children in spite of such obstacles. To the young person looking into the future and the possibility of a family, it may be helpful to learn about the responsibilities involved in raising children and to meet, read about, or see on video individuals with disabilities who have successfully done so. These provide positive role models for young people who may feel that because of their disability, they will never have children of their own.

For many, however, there may be concern that the disability might be inherited. Parents may wish to discuss genetic counseling with their child with a disability and with other children in the family as well.

Source: "Sexuality Education for Children and Youth with Disabilities," *NICHCY News Digest*, Vol. 1:3, National Information Center for Children and Youth with Disabilities (NICHCY), 1992.

Special Concerns about Children with Cleft Lip/Palate

PARENTAL ADJUSTMENT

Many parents of children with cleft lip and/or palate worry about emotional damage to the child because of the defect. Actually, studies of children with clefts indicate that as a group they are as well adjusted as other children. The key to a healthy personality appears to be the way parents work out their feelings of disappointment and whether they relate to the child in positive, loving ways.

When you take your baby home from the hospital, you may have a hard time dealing with the reactions of close family members and friends. Their questions and expressions of sympathy may embarrass you or even make you angry. Many parents have found that the best approach is to handle overly sympathetic or inquisitive individuals in a straightforward, positive manner, indicating that the child is expected to be quite normal after treatment.

HOSPITALIZATIONS

Certainly some aspects of the child's infancy and childhood may be a little difficult. It is no fun for a child to make frequent visits to a clinic. Hospitalizations may be especially hard to face. It is a challenge for parents to be firm about what needs to be done and at the same time sympathetic to their child's fears. Most cleft palate clinics offer professional counseling services for families who request it.

REACTIONS OF OTHER CHILDREN

Many parents become concerned that as their child gets older, other children will ask questions, make remarks, or tease. A child with a cleft cannot be shielded from this behavior. Most children's reactions will arise from curiosity, not meanness, and your child will sense this fact. If your child has an understanding of the cleft that is appropriate to his or her age, the child can cope better with questions asked by friends.

GIVING YOUR CHILD INFORMATION

Children with cleft lip and/or palate should be given facts as they ask for them in words they can understand. When you give your child information in a truthful but reassuring way, he or she is able to handle things better. Encourage your child to ask questions of health professionals on the cleft palate team, too. Most of them are good at talking with young patients. And this discussion will make your child feel more like an active participant in treatment.

continues

continued

YOUR CHILD'S INTELLIGENCE

Will your child develop normal intelligence? Many parents ask whether cleft lip and/or palate are related to problems with mental development.

Children with clefts may be bright, average, or slow, just like other children. They grow up and become scientists, physicians, artists, actors, secretaries, and mechanics. If you have concerns about your child's mental development at any time, the cleft palate team can arrange to have a psychologist do an evaluation.

Notes:

Source: *Looking Forward: A Guide for Parents of the Child with Cleft Lip and Palate*, Mead Johnson & Company, Evansville, Indiana, © 1991.

What To Tell Your Child with HIV

What you tell your child about HIV depends on your child's age and what the child can understand. How you feel about HIV is also important because a child can feel when an adult does not like to talk about something. (HIV stands for human immunodeficiency virus.)

CHILDREN LESS THAN 5 YEARS OLD

The child who is less than 5 years old will be mostly concerned about what will happen during clinic visits. He may be worried about the "shot," or having blood drawn, or being examined by the physician. You may want to tell the child ahead of time that a checkup at the clinic is scheduled. But parents should wait until right before a painful procedure, such as blood drawing, before telling the child. The staff will help by telling the child what will happen and how it will feel and by doing the procedure as quickly as possible. After a procedure, give your child lots of hugs and comfort. You can say things like, "You held your arm so still." Do not reprimand the child if he or she cried or was upset. Be sure to tell the child that procedures are never punishment. Reading a book to your child about going to the physician or letting the child play "pretend" with a medical kit can help your child express feelings about going to the clinic.

Even young children may ask questions about why they are going to a clinic. Don't lie. Answer questions in a simple way. For example, if your child wants to know why he or she has to go to the clinic every month, answer that "The physician needs to check on how big you're growing," or "The physician wants to listen to your lungs and heart." Don't give more information than the child can understand. Answer the specific question. Many young children think they are sick because they were "bad" and that needles and medicine are punishment. Don't threaten your child with needles or staying at the hospital.

SCHOOL-AGE CHILDREN

School-age children between 5 and 12 years of age will need help coping with medical procedures and answers to their questions. The older child can use different ways to cope with painful procedures. Distractions like watching a video, listening to the radio, or simply thinking about a favorite television show can help the child get through a difficult procedure. You can help the child remember those times when the child coped well with a similar situation and can encourage the child to think positively, "I did fine the last time and I know I can do it again."

You will want to think about what to tell your child about HIV. Some parents do not feel comfortable telling the child that he or she is HIV positive. Even if you choose not to use the term "HIV," it is very important to give your child an honest explanation of what is happening. Many children hear bits of information and will make up their own explanations if no

continues

continued

information is given to them. If this happens, a child can feel lonely and afraid. Children cope better if they have information about their health condition and a trusted adult to talk to about it. You should try to answer your child's questions simply and clearly without giving the child more detailed information than necessary. Reassure your child that people with HIV can often stay well for a long time. There are many medicines and treatments to help your child stay well and to treat problems if sickness occurs. If you need assistance in telling your child the diagnosis, ask someone you trust such as the physician, social worker, or nurse.

Talk with the staff if a drastic change occurs in your child's behavior since telling him or her about this health problem. Difficulty sleeping, school problems, withdrawing from others, or other behavior problems may mean that the child is having difficulty coping. Counseling can help a child talk about any concerns and feel and act more positively.

SIBLINGS AND OTHER FAMILY MEMBERS

You will also want to think about the other children in your family and what they should know about HIV. They may have questions about their brother or sister's illness. If no one explains things to them they may make up their own explanations based on incorrect information. It is important to talk with your child's siblings. Think about what you want to tell them based on how old they are. Think about how you will answer their questions. For example, they may ask "Will my brother (or sister) ever get well?" You could answer, "The physicians and nurses are doing everything they can to help him (her) get well, and hopefully he (she) will be better soon."

Families need to talk about what is happening so that children can ask questions. Talking can help everyone feel better about HIV and what it is doing to the family.

Remember, sometimes children ask questions that seem silly or stupid to an adult. The question is the child's way of trying to figure things out. Don't laugh or yell. Answer the question and try to find out why the child asked. Talking it over with people you love and trust can help everyone—children and adults—deal with difficult questions and keep a positive attitude.

Notes:

Source: *What Should I Tell My Child about HIV?*, Children's Hospital AIDS Program, Children's Hospital of New Jersey, Newark, New Jersey.

When a Child with AIDS Is Dying

At this time it is normal to feel helpless and unsure of what to do. Parents can still help their children in very important ways.

BEFORE THE CHILD DIES

- Keep communication with your child, spouse, or partner, and other family members open. Death is hard to talk about, but children can handle it when they know their parents are being honest and truthful with them. They feel better when they know what is happening. Secrets and silence increase their fear and loneliness. Don't be afraid to cry and show feelings to them. Older children may want to make their own funeral arrangements. Your social worker can help you talk to your child and other family members.

- Make your wishes and your child's wishes about treatment decisions known to the physicians. Only you and your child know what is best for you and your family.

- Spend as much time with your child as you can but try to take breaks. Eat and sleep in order to remain strong for your child. Hold your child. Holding is wonderful because children fear being alone and get comfort in being held by a parent. Parents have said that being able to hold and comfort their child right to the end helped them a lot.

- Realize that young children see death differently than adults. Your social worker and nurse can help you understand how your child sees death.

- Accept help from others. Friends, family, and professionals will reach out. It is good to lean on others and get support from them. It is important to talk to others about how you feel. Though it may take some time for you to be ready to share your feelings with others, it is important to try. A clergy person might be of help to you now.

WHEN YOUR CHILD HAS DIED

- Shortly before or immediately after your child dies the physicians will ask your permission to do an autopsy. In this procedure, small pieces of each organ (like the heart, lungs, kidney) are taken to be studied. Autopsies are extremely important in helping to fight HIV infection. So much information about the disease is learned from each autopsy that it is like striking another blow at the virus itself. Although your child has died, the information from an autopsy will help other children and families. If you and your family have time to think about this choice ahead of time, it can make the decision easier. To have an autopsy done or not is your decision.

- Your social worker can help you work out funeral arrangements. The social worker knows funeral homes that have cared for children with HIV in a kind and dignified manner and how

continues

continued

to handle the financial aspect. It is important to know that the physician must put your child's HIV status on the death certificate. It is recommended that you tell the funeral director. Funeral directors are bound by rules of confidentiality and cannot tell others the cause of death. Your child's funeral can be planned to reflect the child's life. Favorite toys, songs, and so forth can be included in the ceremonies. Flowers can be chosen to reflect the child's personality. People who were important in the child's life can be a part of the funeral services. Some parents allow friends and family to plan funeral services. They find this support most helpful during a difficult time.

LIVING WITH THE UNBEARABLE

There are no words, no magical ways to make this time easier. Your pain and sorrow will seem unbearable. You will feel many different feelings: anger, shock, disbelief, sorrow, pain, and confusion to name just a few. One thing is very important to know: You will survive this loss. Talking to another parent who has been through the experience helps you see that you will survive also.

Life will never be the same, but it will get better. It will take time and you will need the help and support of others. Your social worker will be available to help you sort out these feelings and guide you to any help you may need. "Letting go" takes time. It may begin when your child dies. But deciding what to do with clothes, toys, and other things that belonged to your child is also a part of "letting go." You may want to keep something special that belonged to your child.

- Lean on people and take the support offered from loved ones.
- Take one day at a time and take care of yourself.
- Remember always, that you did everything you could for your child and that is all that any parent can ever do. From this terrible experience you and your family can grow stronger and closer. Hold on to hope, because someday this disease will be beaten.

Source: *Your Family and HIV/AIDS*, Children's Hospital AIDS Program, Children's Hospital of New Jersey, Newark, New Jersey.

Learning Disabilities and Family Coping

The effects of learning disabilities can ripple outward from the child to family, friends and peers at school or work.

SELF-IMAGE

Children with learning disabilities often absorb what others thoughtlessly say about them. They may define themselves in light of their disabilities, as "behind," "slow," or "different."

Sometimes they don't know how they're different, but they know how awful they feel. Their tension or shame can lead them to act out in various ways—from withdrawal to belligerence. They may get into fights. They may stop trying to learn and achieve and eventually drop out of school. Or they may become isolated and depressed.

MAKING FRIENDS

Children with learning disabilities and attention disorders may have trouble making friends with peers. For children with attention deficit hyperactivity disorder, this may be due to their impulsive, hostile, or withdrawn behavior. Some children with delays may be more comfortable with younger children who play at their level. Social problems may also be a product of their disability. Some children with learning disabilities seem unable to interpret tone of voice or facial expressions. Misunderstanding the situation, they act inappropriately, turning people away.

Without professional help, the situation can spiral out of control. The more that children or teenagers fail, the more they may act out their frustration and damage their self-esteem. The more they act out, the more trouble and punishment it brings, further lowering their self-esteem. The harmfulness of this cycle is illustrated by one boy who lashed out when teased about his poor pronunciation and was repeatedly suspended from school.

EMOTIONAL EFFECTS ON FAMILY

Having a child with a learning disability may also be an emotional burden for the family. Parents often experience a range of emotions: denial, guilt, blame, frustration, anger, and despair. Brothers and sisters may be annoyed or embarrassed by their sibling, or be jealous of all the attention the child with the learning disability gets.

Counseling can be very helpful to people with learning disabilities and their families. Counseling can help affected children and teenagers develop greater self-control and a more positive attitude toward their own abilities. Talking with a counselor or psychologist also allows family members to air their feelings and get support and reassurance.

Many parents find that joining a support group also makes a difference. Support groups can be a source of information, practical suggestions, and mutual understanding. Self-help books written by educators and mental health professionals can also be helpful.

continues

continued

BEHAVIOR MODIFICATION

Behavior modification also seems to help many children with hyperactivity and learning disabilities. In behavior modification, children receive immediate, tangible rewards when they act appropriately. Receiving an immediate reward can help children learn to control their own actions, both at home and in class. A private or school counselor can explain behavior modification and help parents and teachers set up appropriate rewards for the child.

Parents and teachers can help by structuring tasks and environments for the child in ways that allow the child to succeed. They can find ways to help children build on their strengths and work around their disabilities. This may mean deliberately making eye contact before speaking to a child with an attention disorder. For a teenager with a language problem, it may mean providing pictures and diagrams for performing a task. For students with handwriting or spelling problems, a solution may be to provide a word processor and software that checks spelling. A counselor or school psychologist can help identify practical solutions that make it easier for the child and family to cope day by day.

Every child needs to grow up feeling competent and loved. When children have learning disabilities, parents may need to work harder at developing their children's self-esteem and relationship-building skills. But self-esteem and good relationships are as worth developing as any academic skill.

Notes:

Source: "Learning Disabilities," National Institutes of Health, National Institute of Mental Health, NIH Publication No. 93-3611, September 1993.

Inclusive Play Activities

CHILDREN UP TO AGE 6

Goals

The general goal of inclusive play is to provide children from birth to 6 years old, who have various disabilities, the opportunity to participate in various play settings and activities involving nondisabled peers. More specific objectives include:

- To increase the number and variety of interactive social activities between children.
- To provide role models demonstrating age-appropriate social and interpersonal skills for children.
- To foster an awareness and acceptance of all children.
- To promote self-confidence and self-esteem of children through interactive play.

Guidelines for Choosing Play Options

- Observe other children, with and without disabilities, as they participate in activities. Allow your child the same opportunity to observe.
- Ask for your child's input. "What looks like fun?"
- Encourage your child to sample a variety of activities.
- Focus on the interests of your child. Observe your child's responses and ask for his or her input. "What was fun?" "What was difficult?"
- Be selective. "More" is not better.

Be careful not to overprogram. Family involvement is most important especially at the younger ages. As your child grows, the circle enlarges.

CHILDREN AGES 6 TO 12

Children 6 to 12 years of age have many new opportunities to become involved with their peers outside of school. Activities such as scouts, church groups, athletic teams, camps, park and recreation programs, and group lessons are available. This is a wonderful time to develop talents. For example, learning to play a musical instrument can be the foundation for future membership in the high school band. (Band can provide an opportunity for many close friendships to develop in an inclusive setting.)

Parents still need to play a major role in helping their child find those activities that seem most appropriate and enjoyable, depending on the nature of the child's disability. Parents also may choose to be directly involved in helping to arrange opportunities for friendships to develop.

continues

continued

TEENS

The teen years offer new challenges. Children usually want to spend more time with their peers and less time with their families. This can pose real problems for parents who want independence for their teen, yet are aware of obstacles to that independence. Explore the possibilities with teachers, therapists, and staff. Talk with other parents of teens, both with and without disabilities. (You may be surprised to discover how much you have in common.) Observe your teen's peer group. Then try to determine what avenues may allow your teen access to friendships and positive experiences. There are numerous clubs, groups, and activities offered to high schoolers. Most teens with disabilities can attend athletic events, participate in school dances, join clubs, serve on various committees, and participate in school government. Inclusion at this level may be the greatest challenge.

Source: "Inclusion: Enlarging the Circle through Out-of-School Play Options," Metcalf Laboratory School, College of Education, Illinois State University, Normal, Illinois, March 1993.

Inclusion in Family Activities

EVERYDAY ACTIVITIES

A child with a disability can become so involved in therapy that he or she has little time to be just a member of the family. Time spent going to the zoo with Mom, making alphabet pancakes with Dad, or sharing a library book with a brother or sister is valuable time spent. It affirms the child as a valuable member of the family. For the young child, love is usually spelled T-I-M-E.

Part of being a member of a family is sharing the work. Be sure that the child with a disability has household responsibilities that are tailored to his or her age and abilities. Even participating in a shopping trip can fulfill a household responsibility and provide an experience that is both educational and inclusive.

VACATIONS

Family vacations, outings, and trips can be challenging when trying to include a child with a disability. A few resources may be of assistance in planning family vacations. The "State-by-State Directory of Accessibility Offices," *Exceptional Parent*, Third Annual Mobility Guide 1992 (Psy-Ed Corp.), provides a directory of offices that will give advice and guidance about services, facilities, attractions, and destinations in the United States that are accessible to individuals with disabilities. See "Accessible Theme Parks," *Exceptional Parent*, April/May 1992, for specific information about popular theme parks in the United States and their accessibility to visitors with disabilities. The resource, "Wheelchair Accessible National Parks," *Exceptional Parent*, Annual Guide to Products and Services 1992, provides a directory of national parks with wheelchair access to campsites, restrooms, and visitor centers.

THE EXTENDED FAMILY

For many children, extended families are scattered across the country and, perhaps, around the globe. If your extended family is available, make the time for relationships to develop. Going fishing with a favorite uncle and cousins, seeing a movie with Grandpa, going shopping with an aunt, or attending a children's theatrical performance with Grandma can link the generations. Rituals and traditions at holidays, birthdays, and other special events can help the child feel part of a larger network.

In these situations, parents have opportunities to involve others in the care of their child. For example, parents can show, explain, and demonstrate equipment, and they can suggest methods for dealing with behavior. Parents can observe what works best as they enlist the support of extended family.

Source: "Inclusion: Enlarging the Circle through Out-of-School Play Options," Metcalf Laboratory School, College of Education, Illinois State University, Normal, Illinois, March 1993.

Inclusion in Neighborhood Activities

- What do the other children in the neighborhood do? What do the children of friends do for fun? If other young children are riding trikes on the sidewalk, is there a walker, scooter, or adapted trike that your child could use? Work with therapists, teachers, and other consultants to determine the best way to encourage participation by your child.

- Organize or join a play group (daytime, after school, weekends, school holidays, or early-dismissal days).

- Provide activities in your yard that attract other children over to play. A supervised wading pool with water balloons, water toys, a sprinkler, and a hose can be very attractive on a hot summer day. Be sure to get parental permission, and you might even end up with additional assistance. Providing a big box of colorful chalk might attract a cluster of sidewalk artists. Rakes and leaves or sleds and shovels may invite the participation of others.

- Organize or join a Mom's/Dad's Day/Night Out. Get several children together in one home and give parents some time away while children from the neighborhood play together.

- If you're on your way to the playground, pool, or park, invite another child and parent along.

- Share a particular interest you have with the kids in the neighborhood. A few possibilities are: making pretzels, making and flying kites, grooming a dog, demonstrating pet care or pet obedience, or allowing the children to plant and tend a small portion of your garden.

- Invite neighbors over for a potluck dinner or a cookout, followed by a game of ball in the backyard. Or keep it simple and meet at a fast-food restaurant and allow the children to explore the play areas.

Source: "Inclusion: Enlarging the Circle through Out-of-School Play Options," Metcalf Laboratory School, College of Education, Illinois State University, Normal, Illinois, March 1993.

Inclusion in the School Group and Community

SCHOOL

What are the other children at school doing?

If they are Daisy Scouts or Tiger Cubs and this is an interest for your child, then consider getting involved.

If there are after-school activities that appeal to your child, investigate them and consider how your child might participate. Children with disabilities were included in an after-school "circus" group that included gymnastics, tumbling, juggling, and clown acts. One student with disabilities perfected the act of juggling two sheer scarfs.

Attending school plays, concerts, and sports events as a family shows young children that the family values these school activities. Parents meet other parents. Children see other children and have opportunities to interact.

By participating in parent-teacher organizations and attending their functions (picnics, carnivals, and so forth) as a family, a sense of "school family" can develop.

Even walking home from school with the neighborhood children can be a significant inclusive experience.

COMMUNITY

What's available in your community?

Ask other parents, check the newspaper, listen to the local radio station, and even thumb through the yellow pages of the phone book. You may find:

- Library programs
  - story hours
  - summer reading programs
- Parks and recreation programs
  - movement play groups
  - arts and crafts
- Zoo programs
- Museum programs
- Lessons
  - art and music
  - gymnastics and swimming

Letting go of our children is one of the hardest things for parents to do. Sometimes, with the best of intentions, we deny them opportunities to try something new. We claim that we are keeping them safe.

Remember the words of Helen Keller: "Life is either a daring adventure or nothing."

Source: "Inclusion: Enlarging the Circle through Out-of-School Play Options," Metcalf Laboratory School, College of Education, Illinois State University, Normal, Illinois, March 1993.

Problem Solving Techniques for Parents

TAKING ONE DAY AT A TIME

Some parents become overwhelmed if they focus on the future. Thinking too far ahead gets them into trouble because the years seem endless, while taking things one day at a time is more workable. Try to focus on what needs to be done today, what can be put off until tomorrow, what can be done by someone else, and what doesn't need to be done at all if you play your cards right.

USING A PROBLEM-SOLVING SYSTEM

It is important to have a system for problem solving. Unless organized problem solving is already a natural part of how you operate, consider initially writing out your problem-solving approach. The following guidelines are suggested as a possible method:

1. **Identify the problem.** Be sure to include the following:

   - Who is directly affected by the problem?
   - What is the undesirable effect?
   - Who, what, where, and how does the problem occur? (That is, who is doing what, how often, and under what circumstances?)

2. **Identify all the possible ways**—both acceptable and unacceptable—to resolve the problem. Be as specific as possible, and be sure to think in terms of a minimum standard as well as an ideal. For example, if there is a communication problem between spouses, the following possible solutions are listed in order of acceptability:

   - Unacceptable: Stay away from home all night.
   - Minimum: Come home at night.
   - Acceptable: Tell your spouse that you are upset about something but are not ready to talk about it yet.
   - Ideal: Talk with your spouse.

3. **Formulate a problem-solving plan.** If other input is needed, identify who needs to be involved in discussing how to resolve the problem and formulate a plan for getting all the relevant people together.

4. **Meet with other people, if necessary.** Keep an open mind to alternative solutions that may not have occurred to you. Stay firm on what is unacceptable to you, but be ready to negotiate on the rest—provided that the solution is at least minimally acceptable.

continues

continued

5. **Identify the appropriate resolution.** Formally identify and write out how the problem will be resolved, especially when nonfamily members are involved. Who needs to do what, in what manner, under what circumstances, and for how long?

6. **Plan for evaluation.** Identify what will be done if the problem is not resolved as expected. Formulate a plan for re-evaluating the success or failure of the proposed solution. This is the most frequently neglected step. Yet it is the most critical, because it lets everyone know that the situation will be monitored and that everyone will have to keep at it until a solution that works is identified.

HANDY HINTS TO REMEMBER ABOUT PROBLEM SOLVING

- It takes time for everyone in the family and those not in the family to learn how to get along in an intense home care situation.
- There has to be give and take on everyone's part. However, it does not always have to be the family who gives (or one spouse, or the other children, etc.) and others who take. There has to be a willingness to negotiate that is based on an honest appraisal of everyone's abilities, roles, and responsibilities.
- Those who live in the home have the priority over others in deciding how a problem will be solved, because they live in the situation on a full-time basis and the others do not.
- A well thought out, logically derived plan for addressing problems can develop into a constructive system of communication that is a two-way street between health care professionals and family, husband and wife, parents and children. It is worth the effort, even if it seems tedious at first.

Courtesy of Rosemary Manago, MSN, RN, Assistant Director for Home Health Care, Division of Specialized Care for Children, The University of Illinois at Chicago, Chicago, Illinois.

Handling Stress When You Feel Out of Control

There will be times when everything seems to pile up at once and you feel out of control. The following suggestions may help you feel back in control:

1. Slow down and breathe deeply. Close your eyes, and tell yourself that this is temporary and that you can survive this. Then get paper and pencil.

2. Make a list of all the stressors (feelings, people, services, and so forth). Try to be as specific as possible and sort your list into categories. For example, are all the home care nurses getting on your nerves, or is it just one nurse in particular? Is it waiting around for the physician to return your call or is it just waiting around for anything in general that is stressful? Next to each concrete stressor, write down the feelings that you associate with it (anger, loss, frustration, sadness, and so forth). You may have more than one feeling associated with each stressor, so don't stop with just the first one that occurs to you. If a "feeling" is getting you down (such as feeling depressed), then write out what might be the sources of your feelings. Once you have done this, put that piece of paper aside.

3. On a new piece of paper, write down all that is going right for you and your family and all that you have accomplished that is good since you began to feel like things were getting out of control. Next to each "good," write down your feelings about these accomplishments. Put that paper aside.

4. On a new paper, write out the worst possible scenario you can imagine of what your home and family would be like if everything possible went wrong. Put that page aside.

5. Write on a different piece of paper what your home and family would look like under the best possible circumstances, given the constraints of your situation. What is actually going on is probably somewhere between the worst and the best pictures you have described.

6. Take all your papers, and put the "best" with "what is going right" and the "worst" with "what is going wrong." Focus on what is going right, in order to energize yourself for the work ahead. Look over both sets of papers and compare what is working well with what is not. Focusing on one problem at a time, do the following:

   - Decide whether this is something that needs to be dealt with now, within the next week or month, or can be put off for a while.

   - Prioritize the problems. "Immediate" takes priority over "later," but sometimes it is better to start with the smallest and easiest situations instead of tackling something that is and always will be a problem. When you feel like everything is out of control, you need some successes to energize yourself for the bigger issues.

   - Decide whether this is something you have to be in charge of doing, or if you can take some of the pressure off of yourself by delegating the responsibility to someone else. If so, decide who and give it to them.

continues

continued

- For problems that are immediate and for which you have to be responsible for the work, identify the source of the problem and what can be done to change it using the problem-solving technique detailed above.

7. Once you have sorted through the problems and circumstances that have added to your feeling of being out of control, take action. The action you take may be to rest for a while before tackling anything, or it may be to enlist the help of others to start implementing the problem-solving strategies.

8. It is important to remember that it is perfectly okay to tell whoever else is involved that you are feeling out of control. Enlisting the help of others for moral support as well as action can help to spread the responsibility and decrease anxiety. You do not have to be alone in the home care situation. Although you may feel like others won't understand, if you pick your friends and helpers carefully, they will try to help.

9. You don't need to feel like a bleeding heart any more than you need to feel guilty for having to ask for help. The home care situation is generally bigger than any one person can handle. Help others to understand, so they can help in ways that are truly helpful. You don't have to put up with the well-meaning friend, family member, or health care professional who tries to help in ways that only compound the problem. Tell people what you need and what you don't need, and most will be able to rise to the occasion.

Notes:

Courtesy of Rosemary Manago, MSN, RN, Assistant Director for Home Health Care, Division of Specialized Care for Children, The University of Illinois at Chicago, Chicago, Illinois.

Child Abuse

Child abuse is a hidden, serious problem. It can happen in any family. The scars, both physical and emotional, can last for a lifetime. Because children can't protect themselves, we must protect them.

WAYS TO PREVENT CHILD ABUSE

- Teach your child not to let anyone touch his or her private parts.
- Tell your child to say "No" and run away from sexual touches.
- Take any reports by your child of physical or sexual abuse seriously. Report any abuse to your local or state child protection agency.
  Local Hotline: _____
- If you feel angry and out of control, leave the room, take a walk, take deep breaths, or count to 100. Don't drink alcohol or take drugs. These can make your anger harder to control.
- If you are afraid you might harm your child, get help now! Call someone and ask for help. Talk with a friend or relative, other parents, or your health care professional. Take time for yourself. Share child care between parents, trade babysitting with friends, or use day care.

Notes:

Source: "Put Prevention into Practice," U.S. Department of Health and Human Services, Public Health Service, June 1994.

Principles Underlying Substitute Care for Abused and Neglected Children

The approach to helping abused and neglected children is based on the following principles:

- A child's basic needs are best met within safe, stable, nurturing families.
- Since a child is genetically, biologically, and historically a part of his or her birth family, a child who has been legally adopted will always belong to two families.
- Society's efforts should be directed first toward strengthening and preserving a birth family that can adequately meet the child's needs.
- A child may require substitute family care arranged by the child welfare system when neither the birth parents nor the extended birth families can meet the child's developmental needs.
- Foster care must be focused on meeting the child's immediate needs, preserving the integrity of the birth family for the child while he or she is in care, and returning the child to the parents whenever possible.
- Because they become a part of their foster child's extended family, foster families must negotiate relationships that support the birth parents and the goals of placement.
- Every family is different—moving to a new family is always a cultural shock for children.
- Ethnic and cultural similarities as well as ongoing relationships between families make the move easier for both the child and the families.
- Each child has the right to receive culturally competent care and services and to be prepared for self-sufficiency and independent living.
- Every child needs continuity of care. When the birth family cannot be helped enough to meet their child's ongoing developmental needs, the child should be legally adopted by a family that can provide a greater sense of belonging and permanence.

Notes:

Source: Kenneth Watson, "Substitute Care Providers: Helping Abused and Neglected Children," U.S. Department of Health and Human Services, Administration for Children and Families, Administration on Children, Youth, and Families, National Center on Child Abuse and Neglect, 1994.

Basic Needs of All Children

Early childhood developmental theorists speculate that newborn babies, protected and nurtured in utero, enter the world with the expectation that this kind of care and protection will continue. Birth brings about a sudden change in environment. Because humans are born virtually helpless, they require a longer period of dependent caregiving than do the young of any other species. Very quickly, the baby begins to develop an awareness that the meeting of its needs depends on someone independent from him- or herself. If its basic needs are not met by its caregivers, the baby soon becomes anxious about what will happen to him or her.

If a child is to survive and achieve satisfaction during adulthood, the following six basic needs must be met during infancy and childhood:

1. Security
2. Nurturance
3. Stimulation
4. Continuity
5. Reciprocity
6. Value orientation

It is critical that the child has *all* of these needs met. Although it is difficult to arrange these needs hierarchically, the need for security is clearly the most important.

HIERARCHY OF HUMAN NEEDS

Abraham Maslow, one of the first of the humanistic psychologists, is perhaps best remembered for his theory of the hierarchy of human needs. He postulated that people could not focus on meeting their important individual growth needs until after their more basic universal needs were met. Maslow diagrammed his theory as a pyramid, with the most fundamental needs as a base supporting all the other needs. On the lowermost level of the pyramid, he placed the physiological needs—air, water, food, shelter, sleep, and sex. At the second level, he put safety and security; at the third level, he included love and belongingness; and at the fourth level, he placed self-esteem as reflected by others. At the top of these four levels, he placed all of the individual growth needs.

Security

Although having his or her nurturing needs met is essential to a child's survival, it is noteworthy that a child who is in care or at imminent risk of placement, and who is old enough to be conscious of his or her needs, is often more concerned about protection and security than about any of the basic physiological needs. Whether he or she will be fed, clothed, or sheltered is frequently of less

continues

continued

immediate concern than whether or not the child feels safe. Positive caregiving during infancy and early childhood not only meets the child's physiological needs but also serves as the medium through which caregivers transmit the message that other needs will be met.

Stimulation

Babies need stimulation as well as protection and good nurturing. Those babies who are adequately nurtured but insufficiently stimulated may suffer from infant marasmus (i.e., infantile atrophy) and die. As the child grows and attempts to master appropriate developmental tasks, the need for stimulation continues rather than dissipates.

Consistency

Consistent caregiving is another basic need. From birth to age three, if a sound level of care and stimulation is missing, provided intermittently, or offered by a number of different caregivers, the child's capacity to trust may develop inadequately or be seriously damaged. This sense of trust forms the basis for learning to make attachments, and it is not unusual that children who suffer a loss of consistent caregiving usually demonstrate attachment disorders.

Reciprocity

Reciprocity is yet another basic need. In this context, reciprocity means caregiver-child relationships that are characterized by mutual give and take and that are significant to both individuals. It is important that as he or she grows up the young child should realize that not only are adults important in meeting his or her needs, but the child is also important in meeting the needs of the adults. Because of the transitory nature of foster care, all too often children feel that they are interchangeable pieces in the lives of caregiving adults. Children who are adopted, often after the couple's prolonged attempts to achieve pregnancy, may view themselves as just one of any number of children who could have easily fulfilled the adult's need to be a parent.

Value System

Last, children need a value system to anchor and guide them. An important function of a family in any society is the acculturation of its children. Adults pass along values and beliefs by setting rules that reflect expectations of behavior, by determining what children come to view as important in terms of relationships to others and to their environment, and by reflecting their own values and modeling for children what they consider important. The value base established for children in their families is extremely difficult to alter or change in adulthood.

Source: Kenneth Watson, "Substitute Care Providers: Helping Abused and Neglected Children," U.S. Department of Health and Human Services, Administration for Children and Families, Administration on Children, Youth, and Families, National Center on Child Abuse and Neglect, 1994.

Special Needs of Children in Substitute Care

Foster and adopted children are in care because they have lost, at least on a temporary basis, the family that gave them birth. A child comes into substitute care because of his or her parents' inability to meet some of these basic needs, or because of the wish of the birth parents to have someone else meet those needs. Because he or she is a foster or adopted child, a child in substitute care has special needs in addition to the basic needs of all children. Substitute parents must meet not only the normal developmental needs of the child placed in their care, but these other special needs as well.

TWO FAMILIES

These needs originate from the fact that every child in family foster care or adoption is a member of at least two families. The child belongs to its family of origin. No other family can ever take the place of the birth family. Through substitute care, however, the child has become a member of another family. This second family provides everyday care and meets the child's ongoing developmental needs for as long as the child lives with the new family. It is not unusual for a child in care to have lived in several families. In this case, the child may feel that he or she belongs to many families, including relatives, family friends, or other strangers who have provided care before the child was placed in his or her current home.

Loss and Stress

Whether coming into care for the first time or moving to yet another substitute family, the child arrives suffering the pain of a devastating loss, the loss of being taken away from his or her birth family. Placement away from the birth family means more than the physical loss of living with the family. It also means having to deal with the loss of relationships and the sense of loss of control over one's own life. There can be no greater blow to a child's self-esteem than to be abandoned or rejected by the people who brought him or her into the world. "Why did my parents give me away?" is a question that haunts all children in care.

Children coming into care suffer from the loss of their families and from damaged self-images. They are under a great deal of stress. Like anyone under stress, they try to find ways to behave that are easier for them and that relieve some of the stress. Generally, that means they regress and function in ways inappropriate for their age. They defend against their emotional pain, usually through denial or projection, or they consciously use learned behaviors to protect themselves, attempting to manipulate their environment without investing in new relationships.

THE SPECIAL NEEDS OF FOSTER CHILDREN

Normally, foster care is viewed as temporary, while a more permanent plan for the care of the child is being developed. Thus, all children in foster care suffer from a system-derived tension

continues

continued

about where they are going to live and whether their needs are going to be met, *tomorrow*. No matter how good or loving the foster family, the child is aware that the stay is usually for a limited duration. Although the child has usually been told and retold that planning is underway to ensure long-range security and well-being, most children in foster care are aware that a move is imminent. For most foster children, there is little opportunity for planned input or control over where and when that move will occur. Therefore, it is not unusual for the child to feel anxious and helpless; he or she may resort to behavior that, from his or her perspective, will have some influence on the decision to change placement. The child may somatize illness, run away, or act out in some other way.

Children in foster care are usually ambivalent about leaving their foster homes. Their individual histories, the current case plans, and the tie to their birth families all affect their feelings. Regardless of the family's past behavior or the quality of relationships with family members, it is the fantasy of every child in foster care to return to his or her birth family and grow up safely in his or her original home. Even children who clearly state a preference for continuing in foster care or moving into adoption harbor the fantasy that they will "go home." Because it is a fantasy, the foster child often imagines that everything will work out at home, despite the circumstances that first brought him or her into care. If the parents were abusive, the child may imagine that the parents have changed, will never abuse him or her again, and will somehow make up for the past.

Foster parents must meet their child's basic needs, yet be sensitive and responsive to the special anxieties that are inherent in foster care. A child in foster care is often anxious about being a foster child. He or she is, after all, trying to cope with a new situation and the loss of the birth family while struggling to learn how to fit into a family of strangers, and worrying about the plans that are being made for "permanent" care. Although the foster parents must try to help the child manage his or her behaviors, attempts to reduce the child's anxiety may not be in his or her best interest. It is natural for the foster child to be anxious—his or her status is unsettled, and unfortunately, foster parents cannot offer any promises or reassurances about the future.

THE SPECIAL NEEDS OF ADOPTED CHILDREN

An adopted child does not have to deal with the fantasy about returning home. The good news is that if he or she is adopted, the future seems secure, and the child will not have to move again. The bad news is that if the child is adopted, and the future secured with the adoptive family, the child will not be *able* to move again. That means that the hidden fantasy of returning to a reconstructed, now perfectly functioning birth family is no longer viable. The cost of the security and permanence of an adoptive family is the permanent loss of the birth family as possible nurturing parents. This is similar to what happens to children of divorced parents. Until the final decree, it is not unusual for the child to fantasize that the parents will reconcile and that the family will be reunited. Even after the decree is granted, the fantasy may persist. The child knows it is still possible for the parents to get back together and remarry. If either parent marries someone

continues

continued

else, however, the child must acknowledge that it is highly unlikely that the birth family will ever be reconstructed. For an adopted child, the adoption conveys the same message—the birth family will never be reconstructed. Adoptive parents must help their adopted children deal with the death of the dream that they will ever go home again.

Increasingly, open adoptions are making it possible for children to have ongoing access to information and, in some instances, contact with their birth parents. Open adoptions can help resolve many of the conflicts that adopted children have about their status and the reasons for their adoption.

Notes:

Source: Kenneth Watson, "Substitute Care Providers: Helping Abused and Neglected Children," U.S. Department of Health and Human Services, Administration for Children and Families, Administration on Children, Youth, and Families, National Center on Child Abuse and Neglect, 1994.

Special Needs of Abused and Neglected Children

Being a successful parent to any child is a challenging task, and caring for children in substitute care can be truly complicated and demanding. Foster and adoptive parents assume responsibility for meeting the needs of the children they accept into their homes. To parent a child in foster care or in adoption is more challenging, especially when the child comes into care as a result of neglect or abuse. To meet the needs of these children, substitute parents must clearly understand the following:

- Abused and neglected children have the same basic needs as all children.
- As members of a group of children who are being cared for outside the home, abused and neglected children also bring a special group of needs.
- The needs of children in foster care are different from those of children in adoption.
- The effects of abuse and neglect usually create additional needs that may require special therapeutic interventions.
- Each child brings into care a unique set of individual needs that are a result of that child's genetic heritage, birth experiences, cultural identity, and past life experiences.

Today, most children entering substitute care have been abused or neglected. The majority of these children have suffered deprivation or trauma in having even their basic needs met. It is especially important that child welfare professionals and substitute care providers understand the following:

- Abused and neglected children have *not* been kept safe; thus their capacity to trust and form meaningful relationships has been jeopardized.
- In almost all instances, abused and neglected children have *not* had their basic physical needs adequately met.
- Abused and neglected children may have been ignored and understimulated, or they may have been stimulated inappropriately through sexual abuse.
- Many abused and neglected children have experienced multiple, inadequate caregivers prior to, or perhaps while in, the formal child welfare system.
- Abused and neglected children have not been valued in their own right—they have been ignored, used for adult gratification, or treated as pawns in dysfunctional adult relationships.
- Abused and neglected children have often been exposed to values that society does not accept or hold in high esteem and that will not help them cope successfully in adulthood.

DEVELOPMENTAL REGRESSION

Most children with histories of abuse and neglect enter foster care at regressed developmental levels. Babies who are born addicted or with medical problems may come into care with physical and neurological problems and developmental lags. Older abused and neglected children enter care because their environment has failed to meet their needs. Because critical basic needs were not met, the children have been unable to master age-appropriate developmental tasks. These

continues

continued

children may have had to expend considerable emotional energy surviving hostile or withholding environments, leaving little time to invest in routine developmental growth.

SEPARATION FROM BIRTH FAMILY

In addition to the trauma of the events that brought them into care, all foster children are subjected to the pain of separation from and the possible permanent loss of their birth families. This is more difficult for children who have been abused or neglected as well as for their foster and adoptive parents. Although society sees the separation of a child from abusing or seriously neglectful parents as an act of protection that is clearly in the best interests of the child involved, the child may perceive the placement as just one more traumatic event in his or her sad life. As one child arriving at her first foster home said through her tears, "Don't leave me here. I'd rather be beaten by my mama than by strangers."

As the abused or neglected child adapts and begins to feel more secure and comfortable in his or her foster home, new issues arise. The child is caught between the longing to return to the birth parents and the fear of what could happen if this actually occurred. The ache of separation from the families of birth is especially intense because of the relative comfort and security of the foster homes in which the child now lives.

An abused or neglected child placed in adoption has a more difficult time integrating the two families than do other adopted children. All children in adoption struggle to bring into their lives with their adoptive families the parts of themselves that belong to their pasts. For a child who has been abused or neglected, that includes the history and trauma of those experiences. It is also difficult for adoptive families to allow the child to "bring in" the abusive parents by responding to the child's questions or by sharing the child's earlier experiences. Adoptive families want to deny the impact of those experiences to protect the child from painful memories and to protect themselves from facing the reality of those experiences.

One of the paradoxes of adoption, however, is that the more the adoptive family allows the child to bring in memories of experiences with the birth family, the more the adopted child will belong to the adoptive family. By accepting the whole child, including an abusive or neglectful past, the adoptive family reaffirms acceptance and love of the child.

SCHOOL PROBLEMS

It is not unusual for an abused and neglected child in substitute care to have problems in school. The placement circumstances and the energy needed to cope with feelings of loss, a poor self-image, and the trauma that brought the child into care leave limited energy for learning. In addition, many children in care have learning disabilities, often the result of deprivations that occurred prenatally or in earlier childhood. Many abused and neglected children also choose school as the arena in which to act out their feelings. Misbehaving at school puts the child in less jeopardy than misbehaving at home.

Source: Kenneth Watson, "Substitute Care Providers: Helping Abused and Neglected Children," U.S. Department of Health and Human Services, Administration for Children and Families, Administration on Children, Youth, and Families, National Center on Child Abuse and Neglect, 1994.

Sexually Abused Children in Foster/Adoptive Care

It is estimated that from 75 to 85 percent of the children currently in foster care have experienced some form of sexual abuse. Although many children may enter care because of known sexual abuse, increasing numbers are disclosing sexual abuse after entering care for other reasons. Once secure in the foster or adoptive home, it is not unusual for a child to reveal his or her earlier victimization.

DEFINING SEXUAL ABUSE

Both statutory definitions and public perception vary about what constitutes sexual abuse of children. For the purposes of this handout, sexual abuse is defined as "any activity or interaction where the intent is to arouse and/or control the child sexually." One researcher identified the following three differential factors that can help to distinguish abusive from nonabusive acts and that can provide some guidelines for assessment and treatment:

1. a *power* differential that implies that one party exerts some control over the other and that the encounter is not mutually conceived and undertaken
2. a *knowledge* differential that stems from the fact that the offender is chronologically older, more developmentally advanced, or more intelligent than the victim
3. a *gratification* differential that recognizes that the purpose of the encounter is the satisfaction of the offender and that any gratification of the victim is in the interests of, or incidental to, the offender's pleasure

TYPES OF SEXUAL ABUSE

Although there are several categories of sexual abuse, incest and systemic family sexual abuse are the most common. Most of the sexually abused children coming into substitute care report having experienced either or both of these forms of abuse. Other types of sexual abuse include rape, ritualistic sexual abuse, and sexual exploitation for profit (e.g., prostitution, sex rings, and pornography).

In both incest and systemic family abuse, there is some relationship between the abuser and the victim, and the abuse can be viewed as fulfilling some dynamic function within the family system.

Incest

Incest is the best known type of abuse. It usually involves an immediate family member or paramour as the abuser, generally lasts for a period of time within an established trust relationship, and often occurs with the knowledge and covert approval of other family members.

continues

continued

Systemic Family Sexual Abuse

This is probably the most prevalent type of sexual abuse among children coming into foster care. It is usually only one symptom of family dysfunction that may also include alcohol and drug abuse and the physical neglect and abuse of the child. The family system casts the child in the role of victim; the abuse takes place within the family; and there may be multiple abusers. Usually, the parents participate in or encourage the abuse; at a minimum, they fail to offer the necessary supervision and protection and allow the abuse to continue. Sexual activity is often initiated in infancy, and the child may grow into adulthood without recognizing the behavior as abusive. Such abuse is often not disclosed by the foster or adopted child until after he or she is safely in care.

THE IMPACT OF SEXUAL ABUSE ON THE ABUSED CHILD

Sexual abuse makes most people very uncomfortable. It upsets them to think that adults inflict physical and psychological pain on a child to gratify their own pleasures, especially when the adults are trusted family members or friends.

Although the reactions of family and society surely have some impact on the long-term impact of sexual abuse, especially of very young children, research findings from 40 studies clearly indicate that sexual abuse causes real and profound problems for most abused children and their families. These problems can be classified as falling into one of the following major areas:

- Sexual abuse can undermine the child's ability to trust adults.
- Sexual abuse can lead to an altered view of sexuality.
- Sexual abuse can cause reactive or protracted emotional states (such as depression, anxiety, or fear).
- Sexual abuse can generate behavioral problems reflecting the above (e.g., poor adult relationships, sexual dysfunction, substance abuse, or suicide).

A review of the current literature recently added the following to the list of possible problems: the weakening of the child's will as a result of a sense of powerlessness, the negative connotations that may be incorporated into the developing self-image of the abused child, and role confusion as a result of unclear parental boundaries.

THE IMPACT OF SEXUAL ABUSE ON FOSTER AND ADOPTIVE PARENTS

Sexual abuse brings to the surface strong feelings on the part of those who care about the well-being of children. Most prospective foster and adoptive parents are shocked that such terrible things can happen to a child and are enraged at the parents who participated in the abuse or allowed it to happen. Foster and adoptive parents must reconcile their own feelings before they

continues

continued

can help the child victim. The foster and adoptive parents cannot, of course, condone the behavior of the abusive parents, and they must generate an environment in which the sexually abused child is not only safe from harm, but also feels secure enough to share and recover from the trauma of the abusive experience. Neither the foster and adoptive parents nor the abuse victim can ever forget that the parents who sexually abused the child (or allowed the abuse to take place) are still the birth parents of that child. A sexually abused child must come to terms with that reality. The child can only do so if the foster or adoptive parents are able to accept that part of their child's previous life experiences.

Because most sexual abusers are intrafamily perpetrators, helping the child overcome the effects of the abuse within a family setting seems to be the best approach. Therefore, a child welfare agency has an especially important responsibility in recruiting and developing appropriate and caring foster and adoptive homes for children. That responsibility is threefold:

1. to ensure that prospective substitute parents understand and confront the likelihood that most children coming into foster care and most special needs children available for adoption have suffered from sexual abuse
2. to assist prospective foster and adoptive parents in clarifying and understanding their own feelings about child sexual abuse and the impact of those feelings on their capacity to be effective parents to a sexually abused child
3. to provide the training and support that foster and adoptive parents need to deal with the implications and problems of rearing a sexually abused child

Notes:

Source: Kenneth Watson, "Substitute Care Providers: Helping Abused and Neglected Children," U.S. Department of Health and Human Services, Administration for Children and Families, Administration on Children, Youth, and Families, National Center on Child Abuse and Neglect, 1994.

Helping Foster/Adopted Children Who Have Been Sexually Abused

TRAINING FOR SUBSTITUTE PARENTS

A secure, stable family in which sexual behavior is appropriate and sexual boundaries are clear is the best foundation for the treatment of child sexual abuse. For prospective substitute parents, specialized training in helping children who have been sexually abused is essential. Currently, most preservice foster and adoptive training programs are directing attention to this subject.

Training is important not only for the content and the skills that can be imparted, but because of the highly emotional nature of sexual abuse. The behavior of a sexually abused child affects foster and adoptive parents in at least four critical areas: the parent's own sexuality, the child's sexuality, the act of molestation, and the child's response to the molestation. Sound training aids foster and adoptive parents become more comfortable in discussing sexual abuse and accepting that part of a child's history. At the same time, training programs provide instruction in practical ways to deal with a child who has been sexually abused.

BASIC GUIDELINES

The following are some basic guidelines for substitute parents to keep in mind when they attempt to discuss the abuse with their child:

- Use a private setting.
- Use informal body posture and sit at a level to ensure eye contact with the child.
- Control your emotions.
- Use the child's vocabulary, especially sexual terms.
- Give the child permission to express his or her feelings.
- Reassure the child verbally.
- Give the child permission to talk openly about the experience.
- Universalize the experience.
- Ask specific questions in response to what the child tells.
- Believe the child.

The nature, frequency, onset, perpetrator, and duration of the sexual abuse all make a difference in terms of the meaning of the experience to the child. To the extent that foster or adoptive parents know about these circumstances, they can enhance their therapeutic endeavors. Frequently, details are not completely known or acknowledged. Because sexual abuse of most children takes place within the family setting, placement in a new family provides a healing milieu.

continues

continued

There are some general principles about what that milieu needs to be to help most sexually abused children:

- The family must offer a secure environment, and the safety of the child needs to be of obvious paramount concern to the parents.
- The structure and organization of the family must be apparent and frequently articulated, and family roles and rules must be clear.
- Generational boundaries must be clearly delineated, and parental roles, responsibilities, and behavior distinguished from that of the child.
- Communication among family members must be open.
- Punishment should be immediate, consistent, and of short duration, and threats and promises should be avoided.

SAFETY AND THE SEXUALLY ABUSED CHILD

Providing a safe environment for children coming into care is of primary importance. This is especially important for a child who has been sexually abused, because those adults who were responsible for protecting the child in the past have harmed him or her instead. The child must learn to understand that he or she is valued and that he or she can trust the adults in this new family to keep this a "safe home." This message should be emphasized verbally and behaviorally.

FAMILY STRUCTURE AND THE SEXUALLY ABUSED CHILD

A sexually abused child has usually lived either in a chaotic, dysfunctional family or in a family with unclear parental boundaries. The clearer and more reliable the structure in the new family, the greater the probability that the child will feel safe. Foster and adoptive parents should be able to explain clearly to the child the role each family member plays. They should reiterate this message any time the child seems confused or tries to blur the roles. It is likely that the rules that govern family behavior will also have to be repeated. A few simple, reasonable rules will make it easier for the child to adjust to the new family while developing a sense of safety.

In particular, generational boundaries must be clearly drawn. Nothing offers a sexually abused child more protection than the reassurance that there are parental, child, and family activities. Only the latter activities are meant to include all family members. Parents should not try to participate with the child in all of his or her daily activities, and the child should not be allowed to participate with the adults in all of their activities.

COMMUNICATION AND THE SEXUALLY ABUSED CHILD

A child who has been sexually abused has usually experienced situations in which communication was limited and in which a premium was placed on secrecy. In cases of incest, the child

continues

continued

victim has been told to keep the sexual activity secret within the family structure, and in chaotic families, the child has been told to keep family secrets from the outside world. The child has been taught that open communication is harmful. Indeed, for some sexually abused children, their disclosure has actually resulted in the loss of their families. These children must learn that open communication offers opportunities both to resolve problems and to examine the pain of past experiences.

GUILT AND THE SEXUALLY ABUSED CHILD

There are two particularly sensitive areas in working with a sexually abused child in placement—one is the child's guilt, and the other involves the complications of helping the child resolve being separated from the birth family. Guilt is a common response for victims of sexual abuse. They often feel that they share responsibility for the abuse and for what happens to the adult abuser. All too often, however, the response to a child who acknowledges this guilt is to simply reassure him or her that the adult perpetrator is responsible for the abuse. The intent is to cognitively and verbally explain the adult responsibility and thereby relieve the child of guilt. Unfortunately, such a response is seldom, if ever, very effective. Although the child is not legally or morally responsible for the abuse, he or she may *feel* responsible for what happened. Any reassurances to the contrary will not be heeded until the child's feelings of guilt have been accepted.

A paradox central to treatment is that individuals cannot become anything other than what they are until they can accept what they are. The task of therapeutic intervention is to allow people to accept themselves at their worst so they can initiate change. To offer verbal reassurances to a victim of sexual abuse that he or she is not responsible for what happened is to deny the pain that the victim feels because he or she feels responsible. Before reassurance will have any impact, the child victim must feel that the helping adult understands his or her feelings of responsibility and guilt. That does not mean that the adult agrees with the child's perception, only that the adult validates it as the victim's perception. When the victim relates that he or she feels "dirty" and responsible for what has happened, the helping adult can respond by saying, "What a terrible feeling that must be for you." Once the feeling has been validated (often, after considerable repetition), the adult can introduce the cognitive "truth" with a comment such as, "I know that must be a very uncomfortable feeling for you. But children are not responsible for the actions of the adults with whom they live. You were sexually abused by an adult (or with the permission of the adult who should have been protecting you) and that is not your fault."

RECONCILING SEXUAL ABUSE VICTIMS WITH THEIR FAMILIES

Because most sexual abuse involves a family member as the perpetrator, or at least as the responsible adult who condones such abuse, the reconciliation of an abused child with the birth family can be extremely difficult. This resolution involves the feelings of both the adults and the child. Again, adults must understand that the child who is placed in care always lives in at least

continues

continued

two families and that it is necessary for the child to integrate these two families before the child can develop a sense of completeness and have a feeling of peace with him- or herself. Thus, the child must make some sort of reconciliation with the birth family despite the child's abusive experience. The reconciliation does not have to include face-to-face contact, although this is often the best way for the feelings generated by the abuse to be settled. The foster or adoptive parent of the sexually abused child walks a fine line between acknowledging the ambivalent or angry feelings that the child has toward the family abuser while not condemning that parent as a person. It is essential that foster and adoptive parents resolve their own feelings about the adults who have abused the child; it is often necessary for them to seek support in accomplishing this difficult task.

Special training concerning the issues involved in caring for a sexually abused child is essential for foster and adoptive parents. Such content is now a standard part of most foster parent training programs. In many communities, special programs directed by qualified trainers deal solely with the subject of sexual abuse. Increasingly, comprehensive training materials on sexual abuse have become readily available.

Notes:

Source: Kenneth Watson, "Substitute Care Providers: Helping Abused and Neglected Children," U.S. Department of Health and Human Services, Administration for Children and Families, Administration on Children, Youth, and Families, National Center on Child Abuse and Neglect, 1994.

Medically Fragile Children in Foster/Adoptive Care

A growing number of children are beginning life already the victims of parental neglect. Because their mothers did not obtain proper prenatal care, these babies are born suffering from the effects of their mothers' addictions, illnesses, youth, or poor general health. Included in this group are low birth weight babies, alcohol- or other drug-affected babies, and babies whose mothers may have transmitted infectious diseases to the babies in utero (e.g., mothers who have AIDS or who are HIV-positive).

These children, as well as children who suffer from genetic difficulties or birth injuries, are medically fragile. Whatever the nature of the medical problem, these children make great demands on their caregivers and on all of the members of the families in which they live. Many medically fragile children come into foster care, and some are available for adoption. Most of these children have special medical needs that complicate their care and place increased stress and responsibility on their caregivers. Many medically fragile children are developmentally delayed because of their physical condition, and all are suffering from the impact of the placement itself. Thus, the foster and adoptive families who will care for these children must be selected carefully. Social service agencies must also provide the additional training and support that these families will require.

PRENATAL SUBSTANCE ABUSE

There are a number of unanswered questions about the impact of a mother's use of drugs on a developing fetus. In some instances, such as in fetal alcohol syndrome, the problems the child will face have been clinically determined. The long-term impact of other drugs, such as crack cocaine or "ice," is not fully understood. The full extent of possible neurological damage cannot be assessed until the child reaches later developmental stages. This problem is further compounded because newer "designer drugs" are constantly appearing and because many mothers are addicted to more than one drug.

Within broad limits, however, there are some behaviors of babies associated with prenatal substance abuse. For instance, babies prenatally exposed to drugs may alternate between periods of irritability and lethargy, may frantically suck their hands, become tremulous, or engage in prolonged or high-pitched crying. They may suffer seizures, fever, sweating, diarrhea, or excessive regurgitation. If their mothers have abused stimulants, the babies tend to be easily overstimulated, and they may move from periods of sleep to loud crying within seconds. Whatever the specific symptoms, children prenatally exposed to drugs will require patience and special nurturing skills; they often need close medical supervision and monitoring. Thus, these children require a special kind of foster or adoptive parent.

continues

continued

CAREGIVING CONSIDERATIONS FOR MEDICALLY FRAGILE CHILDREN

In addition to the usual qualities required for foster or adoptive parenting, individuals who accept a medically fragile child must cope with the following:

- a greater number of unknowns (e.g., unpredictable behaviors resulting from the uncertainty of the prenatal drugs involved, lack of knowledge about the developmental impact of newer drugs, and uncertainty about whether an HIV-positive child will develop AIDS, etc.)
- a new focal point in their lives that will assuredly alter their lifestyle and limit their mobility
- multiple appointments with medical and rehabilitative personnel
- working with a complex interdisciplinary team
- the use of medical techniques and equipment that are essential for the monitoring or care of the babies (e.g., apnea monitors, cardiopulmonary resuscitation, suctioning, etc.)
- advocating for the services the child may need
- stress on all family members because of the amount of caregiving that the fragile child demands
- the possibility of deterioration or death after heroic efforts to maintain the child's life

Notes:

Source: Kenneth Watson, "Substitute Care Providers: Helping Abused and Neglected Children," U.S. Department of Health and Human Services, Administration for Children and Families, Administration on Children, Youth, and Families, National Center on Child Abuse and Neglect, 1994.

Coping with Regressive Behavior in Foster/Adoptive Care

Assume that any child coming into foster care or adoption will manifest some reaction to the new home and that the most obvious sign will be some regression. The older the child and the more trauma that is associated with the placement, the greater the developmental regression. In addition, many of the children coming into care are already developmentally delayed. Therefore, many substitute parents are dealing with a child who may already manifest developmental delays and who is probably experiencing some developmental regression as a result of the placement.

AGE-INAPPROPRIATE BEHAVIOR

It can be no surprise, then, that a child placed in foster or adoptive care is likely to exhibit immature behavior. One of the first things that substitute parents must learn is how to accept age-inappropriate behavior. They must learn how to respond to the child as the child presents him- or herself; yet, the substitute parents must provide the child with what he or she requires to begin to recover from any developmental delays. If a child is developmentally disabled or severely developmentally delayed, parents must also adjust their expectations to realistic levels.

The therapeutic process for helping a child with developmental problems begins with accepting the child in his or her current developmental stage. It also includes allowing or encouraging further regression to fill in earlier developmental gaps and then meeting the child's developmental needs in symbolic ways that do not inappropriately stimulate the child or encourage more infantile behavior.

There is a natural tendency for all of us to expect people to respond according to their chronological age or their physical size. "Act your age" is a common admonition that adults use with children. Telling a child that he or she is "too big" to be acting in a certain way is also common. Often, a child in foster or adoptive care does not behave as expected for the child's chronological age. This is usually difficult for the adults helping the child, whereas such behavior may actually be beneficial to the child. The child needs an environment in which he or she can regress, both to feel safe and cared for and to recapture some of the experiences the child may have missed earlier in life.

ACCEPTING AND CONTROLLING BEHAVIOR

The first task of the substitute parent is to accept the behavior that the child presents. That does not mean to accept behavior that is harmful to the child or to others or that is otherwise violent or destructive. The substitute parent should keep in mind that the first need of a child is to feel safe. What is required is that substitute parents carefully and clearly establish the limits of acceptable behavior (as generous an interpretation as possible), while reassuring the child that any behavior that jeopardizes the security of the child or of others is not acceptable. Such behavior

continues

continued

must be controlled by the parents until the child has the ability to control it. But even in controlling the child's behavior, the parents must accept it as part of the child. They must convey to the child that limiting the behavior is not denigrating the child. The limits are necessary for the child's or others' protection until such time that the behavior is altered into a less dangerous form or is no longer necessary.

For example, a 6-year-old child who is angry with his foster mother may grab a butcher knife and threaten to stab her. The mother must disarm the child and protect herself and the child from serious harm. She must try to convey the message that such violent behavior is not acceptable yet recognize in her response the legitimacy of the child's anger and the need to express it. Necessary external control of a child's behavior should be followed as soon as possible by an opportunity for the child to act at a regressed age level in some way that is not harmful. This might be achieved by playing some game that is "younger than the child" or engaging in some childish activity that is developmentally related to the age at which the child was acting.

When a 12-year-old expresses rage through behavior that is appropriate for a 3-year-old, the child should not be encouraged to express rage in some other way. Rather, it is important that the adult try to meet the child's needs at the 3-year-old level of development. The focus should be on the child's developmental age, not on the child's rage. If the behavior would be "normal" for a 3-year-old, what are the developmental needs of a 3-year-old? Can they be met symbolically? Temporary regression is often necessary before the child can move on to more age-appropriate behavior.

Notes:

Source: Kenneth Watson, "Substitute Care Providers: Helping Abused and Neglected Children," U.S. Department of Health and Human Services, Administration for Children and Families, Administration on Children, Youth, and Families, National Center on Child Abuse and Neglect, 1994.

Helping Foster/Adopted Children with Feelings of Loss

Because the most important concern of a child in care is loss, this topic has occupied a significant amount of attention from therapists and authors. Numerous techniques that are easy to learn, but not always easy to implement, have been developed to help a child deal with loss.

Loss is a universal experience. As children mature, they learn ways of dealing with feelings about being temporarily separated from those who are important to them as well as feelings about permanently losing loved ones. Any loss is always painful because of its immediate impact and because it awakens feelings and memories of earlier losses.

Because loss is a universal experience, parents already have the tools to help a child with his or her losses. Adults can draw from their own experiences to understand and empathize with the child. What is necessary is a framework within which to understand loss and practice therapeutic intervention.

When children suffer a loss, they grieve. The feelings of grief are strong, painful, and difficult to sort out. Although they never come one at a time or in perfect order, there are several stages common to the grieving process. The stages are identified by the feeling that is strongest at a given time. There are several theories about the grieving process. The one presented here identifies the following five stages:

1. **Denial.** At first, the individual doesn't want to believe the loss. He or she cannot endure the pain. So he or she pretends it is not true, or that it does not really matter. Sometimes children use excessive activity to keep the pain away, or they may withdraw and sleep a lot.
2. **Guilt.** This is the second step once a person breaks through the denial. Surely, there was something the person did that caused the loss or something that he or she could have done to prevent it. The person thinks of all the unfulfilled plans and the promises that cannot be fulfilled. A child always feels responsible for a loss that he or she experiences, and for children older than age four or five, guilt is usually a part of the grieving process.
3. **Anger.** This stage usually follows guilt. The person questions why the loss occurred, feels it is not fair, and seeks some other person to hold accountable for the pain. Sometimes the fear that one's anger will hurt someone causes a person to block its expression and turn it inward, resulting in depression. Most children are usually quite open with their anger when they have permission to "own" this feeling.
4. **Sadness.** This is the fourth stage of the grieving process. The denial, guilt, and the anger are all ways that people use to keep from feeling the sad impact of a loss. When an individual realizes that the loss has, indeed, occurred and that the impact of the loss cannot be undone by guilt or anger, there is an intense awareness of how much the lost person(s) will be missed, particularly during moments that had been shared and treasured (mealtimes, bed time, holidays, etc.). This sadness is so overwhelming and the pain so acute that it cannot be endured for long. Each person allows it to come and go by retreating to one of the earlier stages. The sadness returns again, and in time a person is able to move through to the final stage.

continues

continued

5. **Acceptance.** This final stage is never fully realized. Acceptance of a significant loss is never *total* acceptance. With acceptance, a child is able to focus energy on other aspects of life. Acceptance, however, resembles denial, and a child starts through the process again or goes back to one of the earlier stages. Each time we work through the process it becomes a little easier, a little quicker. Any new loss, of course, generates a new round of feelings, and pushes a child back toward denial.

The only way out of the pain of a loss is to experience the grieving process. It is almost impossible to get through the process alone. To help a child through this process, adults must first reach within themselves to find and touch their feelings about a loss they have experienced. Then, the adults can try to identify what they think the child may be feeling, giving permission for the child to have that feeling, whatever it is. After accepting and sharing the child's feeling, the adult can very gently try to encourage the child to move on to the next level in the grieving process. The child may move on, refuse to budge, or retreat to an earlier stage. Whatever the child does is all right. If the move is forward, the adult again accepts and shares the feeling. If there is no movement or the child retreats, that too is accepted. There will be other opportunities. If the adults acknowledge that it is acceptable behavior, a child will allow him- or herself to grieve.

The problem is that no adult likes to see a child in pain. The adults tend to join the child at the denial stage, argue the child out of the guilt stage, or fight back at the child in the anger stage. Thus, the adults do not have to endure the child's pain. They tell the child "Don't worry about the past," "Everything will be all right now," "It wasn't your fault you were moved," or "Don't talk to us that way because we're not responsible for what happened to you in the past." Again, the technique for helping is easy to learn but less easy to implement. The adults must allow the child to feel pain, quietly accept the child's pain, and through this sharing and support, make it somewhat easier for the child.

Notes:

Source: Kenneth Watson, "Substitute Care Providers: Helping Abused and Neglected Children," U.S. Department of Health and Human Services, Administration for Children and Families, Administration on Children, Youth, and Families, National Center on Child Abuse and Neglect, 1994.

Helping Drug-Exposed Babies in Foster/Adoptive Care

Infant drug exposure is a subject in which foster and adoptive parents require special training. The drug scene is growing and constantly changing, and little is currently known about the long-range impact on babies prenatally exposed to drugs. However, most social service professionals are aware of many of the immediate consequences of drug exposure, and they can help foster and adoptive parents learn to care effectively for drug-exposed babies. Be aware of the following general rules for the care of such babies:

- Caregivers need to view the baby as a child with medical problems, not as the medical problem itself. Essential medical procedures should never prevent the caregiver from providing the social stimulation and affection that all babies require.
- Whenever possible, caregivers should visit the hospital before the child's discharge and always obtain a written summary of the baby's diagnosis, the treatments provided, and the necessary follow-up care.
- Caregivers should follow exactly as directed any procedures regarding care and medications.
- Caregivers should take special precautions to prevent the already vulnerable baby from the risk of further compromised health from other infectious diseases as well as take care to limit the spread of infectious diseases that the baby might have.
- Caregivers should learn to use and be comfortable with medical or rehabilitative equipment, such as monitors or aspirators, that could be required for the baby's care.
- Caregivers should be consistent and prompt in responding to symptoms and meeting the needs of a drug-exposed baby. Meeting the baby's needs will not make the child more demanding or "spoil" him or her, but it will help the baby begin to develop a sense of trust and instill a sense of structure in the baby's everyday routine. It may even save the child's life.
- Caregivers should seek and use respite care, especially when caring for a child whose care routinely interferes with the parents' sleep.
- Caregivers need to know whom to contact in event of an emergency.
- Caregivers will require readily available support services from the agency that originally placed the child.

Many drug-exposed babies will present special medical or developmental problems, depending on the type of prenatal substance abuse. The rates of preterm deliveries (birth at less than 37 weeks' gestation) for substance-exposed babies are significantly higher than for the general population. The care of some of these babies can be quite technically complex (e.g., a child with gastrointestinal problems that necessitate intravenous feedings), and specially trained foster or adoptive parents may be necessary.

continues

continued

During the first 15 months of life, some drug-exposed babies may present feeding problems. Caregivers may find the following practices helpful:

- Swaddle and hold the baby during feeding; never prop the bottles.
- Use bottles for feeding liquids only; use spoons for solid food.
- Burp the baby frequently if he or she spits up after feeding (some babies need to be burped after each ounce).
- Feed an irritable baby in a quiet place, away from other children and distractions, and avoid sudden movements.
- Allow more time for feeding an unusually sleepy baby and, to keep the baby awake, provide extra encouragement, such as massaging the infant's back or rubbing the soles of the baby's feet while talking softly.
- Offer a pacifier for babies who have an intense need to suck, even after their stomachs are full, to avoid overfeeding.

For drug-exposed babies who are irritable or easily overstimulated, caregivers can also do the following:

- Swaddle the baby, with the baby's hands exposed.
- Walk and hold the baby close to the body, using a front carrier (the combination of swaddling, body contact, and gentle motion helps many fussy babies fall asleep).
- Bathe the baby in warm water, followed by a gentle massage.
- Place the baby face down on the caregiver's abdomen and gently massage the baby's back.
- Offer a pacifier.
- Speak softly.
- Gently rock the baby in a wind-up cradle or swing, but be sure that the baby's head is well supported.
- Play soft music in a quiet room and avoid bright lights, jostling, or loud noises.

In addition to preservice training and involvement with the professional team serving the child in their care, foster and adoptive parents of a drug-exposed child require additional agency support. Ongoing agency training designed especially for these parents is a good way to meet this need. This approach enables the parents to regularly learn new techniques and skills for helping the child and allows the parents to gain support from others who also care for children with special needs.

Finally, it is important that foster and adoptive parents understand that sudden infant death syndrome (SIDS) can occur among drug-exposed babies in spite of excellent care and appropriate monitoring. Recent studies show that the incidence of SIDS is greater when young babies are placed face down in their cribs.

Source: Kenneth Watson, "Substitute Care Providers: Helping Abused and Neglected Children," U.S. Department of Health and Human Services, Administration for Children and Families, Administration on Children, Youth, and Families, National Center on Child Abuse and Neglect, 1994.

Helping Medically Vulnerable Children in Foster/Adoptive Care

Some children are born with congenital anomalies, disabilities, or susceptibilities to chronic illness; infections transmitted prenatally; low birth weights (perhaps as a result of the mother's young age or the failure of the mother to obtain adequate prenatal care); or birth injuries. Other children may become disabled as a result of an illness or accident later in childhood.

Some children who are medically vulnerable, chronically ill, or developmentally disabled come into foster care or adoption in infancy because their birth parents voluntarily seek alternate care arrangements because they feel unable to parent their children. Other medically vulnerable older children are placed in care because the demands of their care cannot be met by their birth parents, some of whom may have abused or neglected these children.

CHALLENGES

A substitute care provider for a child who is disabled and who has also been abused or neglected faces the difficult challenge of meeting the child's basic needs, helping the child master tasks and feelings related to his or her disability, helping the child overcome the trauma of abuse or neglect, and meeting the issues of substitute care.

Foster and adoptive parents are the best resource for most children who are medically vulnerable, chronically ill, or developmentally disabled and who cannot be reared by their birth families. In all but the most serious situations, meeting the child's special needs and managing his or her medical regimen can be handled in a home situation if the caregiver is trained and supported and if community resources are available on an outpatient basis. Success depends on committed and capable foster or adoptive parents and a range of ancillary services offered by qualified, trained providers who are part of a well-managed, comprehensive plan.

Establishing Trust

A child with disabilities who enters foster care or adoption after infancy usually has difficulty trusting his or her caregiver and developing a positive self-image. Many of these children have experienced placement in other homes, institutions, or hospitals. As a result of these earlier placements, the child's mastery of those developmental tasks that are possible within the limits of his or her disability have been delayed. For some children, the capacity to form trusting relationships has been severely damaged. Most perceive that their disability is the reason for their placement, and for many that may actually be a precipitating factor. Even more troubled is the child who knows that he or she has come into substitute care because he or she has been disabled due to an abusive act by his or her parents.

Foster and adoptive parents caring for a child with a disability must help the child feel safe, well cared for, and valued. Many of these children entering care may require immediate medical

continues

continued

attention. A thorough assessment of the child's physical condition is essential both for planning and for helping the new family understand and accept the child's unique needs and limits. Each disabling condition brings its own set of complications for the child and his or her caregivers. For example, a child with cerebral palsy or spina bifida usually requires assistance with routine daily tasks such as eating, toileting, or mobility, and should benefit from physical, occupational, and speech therapy. In contrast, usually a child with Down syndrome can be trained to manage routine care tasks quite well but will require frequent medical attention as a result of one or more congenital abnormalities.

Enhancing Self-Image

Whatever the nature of their particular condition, a number of concerns are shared in common among children who are medically vulnerable, chronically ill, or developmentally disabled. Most of these children must learn to cope with pain and to deal with some degree of incapacitation. Many have experienced hospital environments that generally were not geared toward children, and they have likely been subjected to intrusive and often unpleasant medical procedures. Some of these children must deal with the side effects of medication. All face the future with uncertainty related to the issues of independence, self-care, social acceptance, further impairment, and possible early death. They must develop a self-image that can withstand inner doubts and external pressures.

A person's self-image begins to form in infancy. The first view of self a child has is the reflection of his or her image in the eyes of caregiving adults. A child begins to perceive him- or herself as worthwhile in response to the respect, love, and value the caregiver offers. Although a child's self-image continues to be influenced by the perceptions of others, as the child matures, this image is based less on those external perceptions and more on his or her own sense of achievement and competence. A healthy self-image depends on the child's ability to feel that he or she has the capacity to cope both with current life situations and with future events—by relying on internal resources and by making use of external resources when needed.

Because a child who is medically vulnerable, chronically ill, or developmentally disabled soon learns to see that his or her body does not work as well as that of most other children, it is important that the adult caregiver reflects back to the child how much he or she is valued and loved. It is important, also, for the caregiver to teach the disabled child ways to manage his or her environment and feelings in order to help the child gain a growing sense of his or her own competence.

Perhaps the hardest part of being a caregiver for a child who is medically vulnerable, chronically ill, or developmentally disabled is finding the balance between helping the child accept his or her limitations and achieving the maximum within the restrictions imposed by his or her disabling condition. The caregiver must support the development of self-worth and the child's capacity to act in his or her best interests, yet manage not to place so great an emphasis on achievement that the child feels his or her value is determined by the capacity to please the adult caregiver.

continues

continued

CONCERNS OF SUBSTITUTE CARE PROVIDERS

Just as there are a number of issues that are common among the wide range of children with disabilities, there are issues and concerns that are common among those who provide services to children who are medically vulnerable, chronically ill, or disabled. Unless they have had prior experience caring for a child with a similar condition, most prospective parents experience the following:

- anxiety about their own competence
- confusion and anxiety about the complexities of managing the care of the child and the amount of time this will take
- insecurity about how the care of this child will affect the family routine and other family members
- concern about assuming a financial and emotional burden that may stretch beyond the limits of the family's resources
- worry about the child's prognosis and the capacity to handle the situation should the problems become worse or should the child die
- concern about preparing the child to be self-sufficient by adulthood, or how to arrange for care throughout adulthood
- worry about what would happen to the child in care should they die or themselves become incapacitated

GUIDING PRINCIPLES FOR SUCCESS

All of these concerns are valid and must be addressed in the recruitment, training, and ongoing support of foster and adoptive parents serving this group of children. The following guiding principles may help such parents succeed:

- There is a difference in viewing a child as a whole child who is disabled and in viewing him or her as a disabled child.
- A child with severe disabilities still has the capacity for growth.
- Although parental love cannot overcome a child's physiological weakness or abnormality, it can help that child achieve his or her potential and live a satisfying life.
- The success of caring for a child who is medically vulnerable, chronically ill, or developmentally disabled is related less to the child's special needs than to the family's flexibility and coping mechanisms.

Source: Kenneth Watson, "Substitute Care Providers: Helping Abused and Neglected Children," U.S. Department of Health and Human Services, Administration for Children and Families, Administration on Children, Youth, and Families, National Center on Child Abuse and Neglect, 1994.

Assessing Children in Foster/Adoptive Care

DEVELOPMENTAL FUNCTIONING

The level of a child's development is usually assessed in five areas. First is physical development. The child welfare staff must determine whether the child has developed within the normal range of physical growth and is in good health, or whether there are delays in physical development or special medical concerns. Second is social development. The caseworker must assess how the child interacts with the environment, particularly with other people. Third concerns the child's emotional responses. Are they appropriate for a child of that age? Fourth is cognition. The chronological age and physical development of the child are especially important here because cognitive capacity is more difficult to measure for a preschool-aged child or for a child whose physical development may be slower than the norm. Fifth is the degree of congruence among the other four areas of development. Although all children develop somewhat unevenly, most children develop in the above areas at about the same rate. A child coming into care usually shows greater discrepancies among the various developmental areas or even significant lags in one or more of these areas.

ATTACHMENT

The capacity to make meaningful attachments is important throughout life. It is especially important to assess this capacity for a child in care because attachment capacity can influence the success of care or can be therapeutically strengthened as a result of care.

Attachment is a learned skill. If a child's basic needs are met from infancy to age three, the child will also learn to trust and become affectually involved—first with the primary caregiver and then with others. Many children coming into substitute care have not experienced a stable, nurturing, consistent relationship with an adult during their first three years. As a result, these children come into care with various forms of attachment disorders.

Attachment Disorders

Nonattachment

During assessment, the caseworker must discern the child's capacity to make attachments or identify the nature of any attachment disorder. Attachment disorders fall into three categories. Those children who have been severely deprived of nurture and affection during their first years may be children who are *nonattached*. Simply put, they have never experienced a meaningful attachment; further, these children do not know how to form such a relationship.

Inadequate Attachment

The second type of attachment disorder, more common to children in foster care or adoption, is that of *inadequate attachment*. These children have had their basic needs met at various points

continues

continued

during their early years, but their primary attachment was interrupted by the necessity of having multiple or intermittent caregivers. A child demonstrating inadequate attachment might have had several placements between infancy and age three, or the child may have had a primary caregiver who was a substance abuser who took good care of the child when not under the influence. An inadequately attached child responds well to substitute care that is consistent, allows for regressive behavior, and makes no immediate demands for affectual closeness with other family members. In time, the child can learn how to become affectually involved, though not always to the degree that might have occurred if he or she had an opportunity for consistent early care.

Trauma-Based Attachment Disorder

A third type of attachment disorder is demonstrated by a *traumatized* child. In this situation, a child had been experiencing sound caregiving and was developing a positive view of the world and of relationships when some traumatic event interfered. The young child might have been sexually abused by a trusted adult, or the child might have had to deal with the sudden loss of a primary caregiver because of death or placement in care. Although such attachment disorders are serious, they are the most easily treated. In the case of anticipated death or placement, the trauma can be mitigated by explanation, preparation, sensitivity, and postplacement contact. If the caregiver's loss is unexpected, or the trauma is due to sexual abuse, treatment based on the post-traumatic syndrome model can be effective. In assessing the impact on a child who suffers from an attachment disorder caused by trauma, it is important to consider the child's age when the trauma occurred, the nature of the trauma, and the capacity and stability of the substitute home to which the child is moved.

Learning Attachment Skills

A child who learns attachment when older never learns as well as if it was learned at a more age-appropriate stage of development; however, subsequent interventions can help mitigate these attachment disorders. Trust is a key element in the child's recovery. Trust can be learned, and it is the beginning of the healing process. A preschool-aged child can learn attachment if he or she is placed in an environment in which the child has an opportunity to form a significant primary attachment by regressing to an infantile level and having his or her needs met by a consistent caregiver over a prolonged period of time.

Between the ages of 5 and 11, a child can learn attachment if adult caregivers can create opportunities for the child to have earlier caregiving needs met symbolically. Caregivers must design ways to interact with the child just as a mother would interact with a baby or toddler while discouraging infantile behavior and without inappropriately stimulating the child. Examples include an adoptive mother who structured regular, intimate parental touching by washing and combing her daughter's hair, or a foster mother who put sunscreen on her 10-year-old son's back as a safeguard against exposure to the sun when he was swimming in an outdoor pool.

continues

continued

Adolescents can be helped to learn attachment by demonstrating appropriate behavioral skills, such as how to hold eye contact or how to hug. Young adults may learn attachment if they become involved in a relationship with someone who is a competent caregiver, or they may learn attachment techniques in the process of helping their own children learn how to attach.

LOSS

The assessment of losses in the lives of children relates directly to their capacity to make attachments and is a critical factor in planning and implementing successful substitute care. The loss of family is a core issue in the placement of any child. The child's earlier experiences determine how he or she reacts to that loss and what interventions can be most helpful. In addition, any other losses the child might have sustained, the circumstances and timing of those losses, how the child managed those losses, and the extent to which those losses have been resolved are factors that should be assessed.

Losses are resolved successfully by experiencing a grieving process; that process takes time and support. Any new loss during the grieving period means the process must start anew, and a series of successive losses may stall the process completely. Because they want to ease a child's grief, adults respond by trying to block the child's grief or by speeding up the process. Adults involved with a child in substitute care need to understand the child's past experiences with loss, and they need to be comfortable with helping the child grieve.

IDENTITY

"Identity" is a sense of one's self and of one's boundaries and values. Identity includes knowing who we are and how we fit into our surroundings. Because we spend all of our lives becoming who we are, our identities are never fully formed. There are, however, critical components to one's identity that evolve throughout the normal development of children:

- **Origins.** The base of a person's identity is his or her origins. Who a person is and who he or she becomes is initially shaped by the individual's genetic heritage. One's gender, physical attributes, intellectual capacity, and a predisposition to certain illnesses are determined at conception and provide a foundation on which a person bases a sense of self. Each person is also born with ancestors. Who they were and what they did are also a part of one's identity.
- **Reflections.** A child's image of him- or herself is reflected from the child's caregivers and provides the next layer of his or her developing identity. This includes an awareness of how the child is viewed by his or her caregivers and other family members, the similarities between the child and other family members, and the value that is attached to the child through the pride that others take in the child's appearance or achievements.
- **Autonomy.** In addition to how the child feels that he or she is viewed by others, a young child also begins to develop an awareness of autonomy and a sense of the limits of his or her body.

continues

continued

As the child begins to perceive him- or herself as an individual, the child masters the use of personal pronouns (I, me, my, mine) and an image of his or her body. The child distinguishes him- or herself as a separate entity, and as the child recognizes the differences in the appearance of body parts, including sexual parts, he or she takes another step in defining him- or herself.

- **Belonging.** One of the first external boundaries that a young child learns is that of family membership. One of the characteristics of a family system is the way in which boundaries are established and the permeability of those boundaries. A young child quickly learns that he or she belongs to a family and the identity of the other members of that family. Family membership also establishes the child's identity within the broader community. Before a child is known as Mary Smith, she is known as "the youngest Smith girl" or as "Bobby Smith's little sister."
- **Conscious choices.** As a child matures, he or she observes people who are important to the child and begins to decide if he or she wants to grow up to be like those people. The child often consciously imitates others' behavior and then, perhaps unconsciously, incorporates certain characteristics into his or her own identity. The child can also decide to accentuate one aspect of his or her life experience or a particular role he or she has played in the family or in the community and make it the basis of his or her identity. For instance, if it serves his or her purpose, the child may present him- or herself as a clown, victim, or foster child. That image can be internalized and serve as the organizing principle that shapes the way the child perceives the world and views him- or herself.
- **Self-image.** At the center of the developing identity is a person's internal image of self. The value that one attaches to that self is of critical importance to one's sense of identity. Identity suggests that one has defined oneself and drawn boundaries around what one has defined. One does not define and draw boundaries around something that has no value.

The identity of a child in foster care or adoption is often shaped by the circumstances that initially brought him or her into care and by the experience of being in foster care. The child usually faces difficulties with every component of identity mentioned above:

- **Origins.** Information about the child's origins may be limited, lost, blurred, confused, or deliberately withheld or distorted.
- **Reflections.** From infancy or early childhood, the child might have had inadequate or multiple caregivers and thus has no experience in seeing him- or herself as a whole, valuable, and loved individual.
- **Autonomy.** Because of inadequate caregiving, the sense of autonomy for the child coming into care might not be fully developed. Even a child who has had positive early care experiences suffers from an acute sense of helplessness as a result of the placement. A child coming into care usually regresses to a much more dependent level of functioning, and,

continues

continued

depending on subsequent experiences, the child may experience continued impairment in developing a sense of identity.

- **Belonging.** By definition, adoption or foster care makes it less clear to a child to whom he or she "belongs." Some foster parents, in an effort to deal with their own pain about the plight of the child in care, encourage their foster child to use the foster family name or to call them "Mom" and "Dad." Some foster and adoptive parents discourage the child from talking about his or her experiences and feelings about the birth family. A child with special needs often experiences several placements (to relatives, foster parents, hospitals, residential institutions, or adoptive homes). These experiences add to the inherent confusion that a child in care has about belonging and to the difficulty the child may have in developing his or her own identity.

- **Conscious choices.** A child who has been exposed to numerous role models has a harder time sorting out what it is he or she *wants* to be or feels he or she *can* be. This is especially true if any exposure to a role model has been traumatic. An adopted or foster child may also cling to his or her role as a foster or adopted child and attempt to build a sense of identity around that core.

- **Self-image.** An adopted child has suffered enormous negative impacts on his or her self-esteem by being "given away" by the birth parents. *The success of the care can temper the impact of this blow, but it can never fully compensate for it.* Even a newborn adopted directly from the hospital and reared by a family who meets all of the child's developmental needs must deal with the impact of what may be perceived as rejection by the birth family. Although the circumstances of the situation may make foster or adoptive care the most logical and appropriate solution, even the best explanation does not eliminate the perception by the child that his or her parents did not want the child.

COPING MECHANISMS

Children are remarkably resilient. Whatever their early experiences, most develop ways to manage their lives. Children are not always aware of what mechanisms they use or just how they learned them. Some of these ways are unconscious defense mechanisms, which will probably never be identified. Other responses, however, are conscious techniques that a child has learned from his or her own experience or from observation. For some children, these behaviors (or coping mechanisms) have become habitual, although most children are not usually aware when they use them. Other children, however, very consciously and deliberately use these techniques.

It is useful for substitute parents to have some sense of the types of coping mechanisms a child is likely to employ so they can better understand the child and respond appropriately when the child exhibits such coping mechanisms. It is also important for child welfare staff to identify these behaviors and evaluate whether they are likely to work to the child's long-term advantage or whether efforts should be made to alter or replace the behaviors.

continues

continued

Testing

A child coming into substitute care needs to determine the "dimensions" of the setting. The child needs to learn such things as family boundaries and roles, the important rules of the household, the expectations that are being placed on him or her, and the tolerance for and the consequences of misbehavior. Children determine boundaries in several different ways. Some children immediately engage in testing behavior; that is, they quickly push to the limits to learn what those limits are. Other children need a period of acclimation before they do their testing; and still others learn what they need to know from observation alone and never engage in direct testing behavior.

Manipulation

Often, a child who has been moved frequently learns to cope through manipulation. The child may become a practiced liar, able to persuade foster parents, caseworkers, teachers, and strangers of the truth of false statements. Another child may learn how to "play off" the other members in the family to his or her advantage. Yet another child may carefully observe the kinds of behavior and expressions of feelings that seem to work for others and mimic these behaviors in his or her relationships. Such a child may lack the capacity to feel as deeply as another person or be unable to express that feeling in a genuine way, but he or she will pretend to have the feeling if he or she thinks that it is expected or that it will be to his or her advantage.

Repetition

A third kind of coping behavior is the repetition of patterns of behavior that are based on the child's past experiences. Sometimes the behavior appears bizarre or self-defeating unless its roots and the reasons for its repetition are understood. For instance, if a child has experienced trauma in the birth family or in a previous placement, the child may try to recreate the experience in an attempt to master residual feelings from the earlier experience. If the child has experienced rejection in the past because of his or her behavior, he or she may repeat the same behavior to see if it will elicit a similar response, or the child may engage in similar behavior but try to stop before suffering such dire consequences. This is an attempt to master the behavior or manage the trauma more than to test the new family. The child is trying to gain greater control over the circumstances of his or her life.

SITUATIONAL NEEDS AND RESPONSES

One important, but often overlooked, area that child welfare staff will assess is a child's situational needs and responses. A child's behavior is not always distinct from the environment in which the child lives. What appear to be character traits can in fact be spontaneous responses.

continues

continued

What may appear to be negative character traits can be a healthy reaction to an unhealthy situation. A change of environment can solve many problems. It is, therefore, extremely important for the caseworker to assess what needs and behavior are situational by becoming familiar with the child's total environment.

UNDERSTANDING OF STATUS AND EXPECTATIONS OF FUTURE

Another factor in assessing a child in substitute care, or a child for whom such care is being considered, is to observe the child's understanding of his or her situation and what substitute care entails. How a child perceives care and what that child views as its best and worst resolutions are significant factors in case planning. A child's understanding will be limited by age, by past experience, and by the degree of the child's involvement in the planning. That understanding will also be shaped by what the child perceives as actually happening. This can be best assessed through interpersonal interaction with the child. An older child can usually articulate what placement and care mean to him or her; however, for a child who lacks cognitive or verbal skills, drawing and play may provide relevant clues.

RELATIONSHIP TO AND MEANING OF BIRTH FAMILY

Because a child in foster care and adoption always also belongs in part to the birth family, it is important to assess what the current relationship is between a child and the birth family and the significance that family has to the child. The meaning and importance of the birth family will depend on the age and developmental level of the child; the current membership, integrity, and level of functioning of the family; the circumstances and timing that led to the child's placement; the history of the child's experiences with the birth family; the child's understanding of care; and the goals of the placement.

Visits with Birth Parents

Visits between a child in care and his or her birth parents are often sources of concern and tension. Although they provide an opportunity for a child to understand and resolve his or her foster care or adoptive status, such visits also provide opportunities for acting out feelings or for manipulation. To make visits a positive and valuable experience, all parties should clearly understand the goals of care and the meaning of foster care or adoption.

If foster parents are viewed as a substitute extended family and the goal is the reunification of the birth family, most foster parents can comfortably support the birth parents' attempts to learn to become better parents. Foster parents do this by modeling positive parenting skills, encouraging the birth parents to perform parenting tasks when they visit (e.g., shopping with the child or helping with homework), and by teaching the birth parents parenting skills (such as grandparents might in a well-functioning extended family).

continues

continued

If foster parents are viewed as a substitute extended family and the goal is termination of the parental rights and adoption of the child, the role of the foster parents during visits depends on whether they intend to adopt the child. Most adopted special needs children are adopted by their foster parents. Often, the birth parents voluntarily release the child because they have come to know and trust the foster parents through visits, and the birth parents want the foster parents to adopt the child.

If some other family is to adopt the child, the foster parents can facilitate the adoption placement by using visits with the birth family to allow the birth parents and the child to come to terms with the fact that they will not be reunited. The foster parents' commitment to the adoption plan and the positive relationship they have established with the birth parents can serve as a bridge to the new family for the child. Such a process helps the child feel free to form new attachments without guilt and to adapt to the new situation.

Dual Heritage

One of the developmental tasks of an adopted child is to accept and resolve his or her dual heritage. The nature of the relationship between the adoptive family and the birth family can make a significant contribution to the success of the adoption. When the adoptive parents can figuratively accept the child's birth family into their home, much of the trauma of the adoption is alleviated, and a firmer basis for the child's identity is laid. Recently, there has been a trend toward a more literal acceptance of each other by the birth family and the adoptive family.

Open Adoption

When there is an opportunity for some sort of relationship between the two families, the adoption is called an "open adoption." Because most older children enter adoption with a history of living with their birth families or with memories of the family, and because many of these children are in contact with the birth family when they are adopted, there is usually no choice about whether such adoptions will be open. Increasingly, however, infant adoptions are also becoming open. Birth and adoptive families may engage in a mutual selection process, may meet each other at the time of placement, and may agree to some contact following the placement. Although it is too early to assess the long-range effects of openness, such adoptions provide the adopted person with easier access to the birth family and a greater opportunity to get information and work out concerns about the reason for adoption. Open arrangements can be complicated and must be implemented very carefully, with all parties aware of the consequences.

PERSONAL STYLE

Finally, it is important to assess the personal lifestyle of an older child in order to understand that child's needs and how best to ensure that placement in a substitute family will be successful.

continues

continued

Lifestyle includes all of the idiosyncratic variables that make children so different from each other. Lifestyle is not necessarily related to a child's developmental level, his or her experiences with placement or loss, or any of the other factors already listed. Often, the unique characteristics of a child cannot be measured objectively. It may be some unusual trait or characteristic, or it may just be the way that a child approaches life or the responses he or she engenders in others. For instance, some children have such infectious smiles that whenever they smile they alter their surroundings. Further, some children possess some inner determination that enables them to achieve far beyond their apparent capacity.

Although they are difficult to catalog or analyze, lifestyle behaviors are extremely important. Lifestyles frequently determine the compatibility of strangers. Relationships work best when people cherish each other's unique qualities and approach to life.

MAKING USE OF THE ASSESSMENT

Assessment is an ongoing process that can serve several purposes in helping abused and neglected children in family foster care or adoption:

- to determine the capacity of a potential foster or adoptive family to meet the needs of a child who has been abused or neglected
- to determine the specific strengths and weaknesses of a potential foster or adoptive family in order to make the most optimal match for a child with particular needs
- to organize information about a particular child's needs so that the family can make an informed choice about whether it is willing to attempt to parent that child
- to anticipate the network of treatment and support services that should be used to make a placement helpful to a particular child and rewarding to the substitute care provider(s)

Notes:

Source: Kenneth Watson, "Substitute Care Providers: Helping Abused and Neglected Children," U.S. Department of Health and Human Services, Administration for Children and Families, Administration on Children, Youth, and Families, National Center on Child Abuse and Neglect, 1994.

Parent-Child Drug Discussion Guidelines

When you discuss alcohol and other drugs with young children, concentrate on these points:

- Some drugs will look like candy but they are definitely not to be tasted or handled. Crack cocaine will often look like hard, white rock candy.
- Some drugs look like sugar, baby powder, or flour. Cocaine is a white powdery substance. Don't handle or taste it. Always tell a responsible adult (parent, teacher, police officer, clergy person, bus driver, or utility worker, for example) if you find any unknown substance.
- Never pick up discarded hypodermic needles, plastic bags, burned bottle caps, or other objects. These items are often found on playgrounds, on the streets, in bathrooms, in hallways, near gutters, near grates, under trash piles, in trash bags, or just about anywhere. These things are dangerous. Find a responsible adult and take the adult to the dangerous items.
- There are licit and illicit drugs. Licit drugs that are often used include alcohol (liquor), cigarettes (nicotine), and caffeine (coffee, tea, chocolate, cola drinks).

Notes:

Source: Sylvia Carter and Ura Jean Oyemade, *Parents Getting a Head Start against Drugs*, U.S. Department of Health and Human Services, National Head Start Association and Center for Substance Abuse Prevention, DHHS Publication No. (SMA) 93-1972.

ABCs of Drug Abuse Prevention for Families

A—ACTION. Become actively involved in your children's world. It's a magical place to be. Be ready to speak up for them when the time is right.

B—BONDING. Do special things with your children. This involvement is the glue that holds families together.

C—COMMITMENT, CELEBRATION, COMMUNICATION. Your children are unique. Find ways to tell your children just how much they mean to you and why it is important to do fun things with them.

D—DISCIPLINE. It takes a long time for children to learn to get along with others and to control their own behavior. Explain how you expect children to act. Use words to solve problems with each other. Be patient.

E—EDUCATION. Model the importance of education for your children. Show them how much the school and community mean to your family. Participate in their activities and communicate with teachers.

F—FAMILY. There are all kinds of families and each one is special. Share some funny things, historical facts, hobbies, celebrations, and values. Develop a family tree. All of these things help children understand and appreciate their families.

G—GROWTH. Spread your wings and expand your tomorrows with your children. Reach toward new experiences and embrace the impossible. Everyone can grow and learn today and through all of the tomorrows.

H—HOPE. Never give up on yourself or your children. Keep trying to strengthen the family. Remember that your children represent the future. Invest in them.

I—INVOLVEMENT. No one can give your children the stimulation and hope that you can. Get involved in everything your children do. Let them know how important their activities are. Stay abreast of their friends, activities, hobbies, dreams, fears, feelings, and strengths.

J—JOY. Find the joy in parenting. There is a great amount of fun to be had with your children. Laugh with them when things are funny. Tell a joke or listen to theirs. Do fun things together, such as blowing bubbles, flying a kite, rolling down a grass-covered hill, having a pillow fight, playing hopscotch, jumping rope, playing horseshoes, or making mud pies.

K—KINDNESS. Always be ready to show your concern for your children. Remember that they are not always aware of how they make you feel. Kiss a bump or be there when they need you most.

L—LOVE. All children and adults need large doses of love. Show your love in many special ways. Say it, show it with hugs and kisses, smile, and be ready to understand their special needs.

continues

continued

M—MISTAKES. Everyone makes mistakes. Adults as well as children can learn from mistakes. Learn to forgive yourself and your children. No one is perfect. Pick up the pieces and give support to each other in order to continue growing.

N—NURTURANCE. Parents can provide a warm and safe environment for their children. Let your family know that they are valued and worthy of being treated as special people. Set up special small places for your children at home.

O—OPEN. Keep lines of communication open between you and your children. Keep your eyes open for changes in their behavior. Keep your ears open for signals of need, concern, fear, confusion, problems, and successes. Keep your arms open and ready to give a big hug whenever it's needed or you feel like it.

P—PATIENCE. Was there ever a parent who did not need an extra amount of patience at some point? No! All parents need patience in order to raise their children. Practice using time-outs for yourself when you are about to lose your temper. Remember that little ones are busy exploring their world and are not always aware of all the rules.

Q—QUIET. Find time for yourself. Take a time-out when things seem to be getting the best of you. Find a quiet place, close your eyes, and think about something that is pleasant and relaxing. Be good to yourself.

R—RESOURCES. Find all the resources you need to do your parenting job. There are many different kinds of resources available to you and your family. These resources could help strengthen your family.

S—STRESS. Recognize the stress in your life. Everyone experiences stress at some point. It is important to find ways to cope with stress and recognize it for what it is. Doing fun things with your family is one way to reduce stress.

T—TEACHER. Remember that you are your children's first teacher and most important model. Little children watch all that adults do. Try to model positive actions for them. By observing you, they learn to cope, solve problems, play, and handle stress.

U—UNDERSTANDING. Children need understanding and acceptance. Parents must find ways to communicate these concepts. When children feel understood and accepted, their self-esteem grows.

V—VALUES. Try to understand the values that your family lives by. Share these values with your children. Does your family value education? communication? freedom? individual accomplishments?

W—WISDOM. Parents learn by doing. Acquire as much information as possible about raising children. Use a commonsense approach.

continues

continued

X—TRA. Give yourself and your family extra time to do things together. Plan activities that bring the family together for meals, for talking, for problem solving, for loving, and for sharing small and large successes.

Y—YESTERDAY. Our futures are woven with strands of fabric from the past. Keep a family history and build on it for the future. Remember kinfolk and ancestors, and share their history with your children. Share photos, stories, travels, recipes, customs, and values.

Z—ZEALOUS. Adopt a CAN DO attitude!

OTHER ACTIVITY

On each day of your calendar, write a word from the "ABCs of Drug Abuse Prevention for Families" to practice with your children and yourself. Keep these words and actions in mind as you move through your daily activities.

Notes:

Source: Sylvia Carter and Ura Jean Oyemade, *Parents Getting a Head Start against Drugs*, U.S. Department of Health and Human Services, National Head Start Association and Center for Substance Abuse Prevention, DHHS Publication No. (SMA) 93-1972.

The Parent-Child Relationship: Learning To Communicate

Children are special people, and interacting with them is a special skill that some parents have trouble learning or understanding. Perhaps these pointers will lead to ways of communicating effectively with your child.

Can you think of times and places to use the pointers set out below? Use this exercise to set up some situation in your mind, and think how you could use a group of these pointers in that situation. Then find another situation in which to use other pointers. After you complete this exercise, find out which one of the pointers you used the most, and which the least. Does that tell you something about your personal style with your child?

- Show yourself as a good person worthy of being looked up to.
- Pay careful attention to what your children are trying to tell you. Let them know that what they say is important and valuable to you.
- Use a gentle voice and touch to show acceptance and love.
- Don't intervene when a child makes an error that can be the source of important firsthand information about the world. Let children make mistakes that are harmless and instructive.
- Avoid "talking down" to children, making them feel you have no regard for their capacity to understand or appreciate what you know.
- Try not to say things that will make children feel guilty about things over which they have little or no control.
- Appreciate both the limitations and the special gifts of each stage of development in the child.
- Keep scorn or sharp words that would humiliate the child from your speech, and keep any violent emotions in check. Size and physical strength are never excuses for physical abuse.
- Use reason as your principal tool in dealing with older children. They will respond to it much better than just the silent application of discipline.
- If a child continues to have problems in some task, it may be a sign of a cognitive or motor problem unrelated to the will of the child to succeed. Examine all alternatives. Are you expecting too much too soon?
- Set time aside to be with each child on a one-to-one basis. Every child deserves some time to be with a parent alone, without having to compete with a sibling.
- Study any special skills or interests your child may have. By encouraging individual efforts, the parent may give the child an early opportunity to excel.
- Don't force your child into your own image. Each child comes into this world with special gifts that often do not correspond with the parents' agenda. Children have their own agendas.

Source: Sylvia Carter and Ura Jean Oyemade, *Parents Getting a Head Start against Drugs*, U.S. Department of Health and Human Services, National Head Start Association and Center for Substance Abuse Prevention, DHHS Publication No. (SMA) 93-1972.

Guidelines for Discipline

These techniques are likely to increase children's self-discipline and encourage positive behaviors:

- Ensure that care is given by people who model appropriate behaviors and who remain calm and in control of themselves even when children misbehave.
- Praise good behavior, ignoring any behaviors that are not dangerous.
- Help children figure out solutions to their own problems.
- Consistently enforce clear, age-appropriate rules that spell out what the child is expected to do (rather than what is forbidden).
- Allow children to experience the real, natural consequences of their behavior when it is safe.
- Be patient.
- Encourage cooperation.

These techniques are likely to reduce children's misbehavior.

- Prepare the environment and make schedules to accommodate children's needs (trust, love, attention, safety, learning).
- Give children reasons for your rules.
- Distract children from potential trouble.
- Gently remind children of the rules.
- Discuss misbehavior in private.

Notes:

Source: Sylvia Carter and Ura Jean Oyemade, *Parents Getting a Head Start against Drugs*, U.S. Department of Health and Human Services, National Head Start Association and Center for Substance Abuse Prevention, DHHS Publication No. (SMA) 93-1972.

3
Home Care Issues/ Activities of Daily Living

Positioning

INTRODUCTION

Many children with developmental disabilities exhibit movement problems. Their muscle tone is often either:

- too high (hypertonic), where they show muscle tightness, stiffness, and spasticity
- too low (hypotonic), where they are floppy and lack control
- fluctuating from high to low in varying degrees (athetoid or ataxic), resulting in a lack of controlled movements and often showing excessive amounts of movement
- any combination of the above

WHY POSITION THE CHILD?

As a result of lack of balance and motor control, some children are unable to use their muscles to move about freely, which prevents them from exploring or interacting with their environment. Therefore, positioning becomes a very important aspect of the routine for the following reasons:

- Positioning prevents the development of contractures. (A contracture is a shortened muscle that limits the amount of motion that can occur at a joint.) Contractures may result from the habitual use of only one muscle group without ever using the opposite muscle group or stretching it out. Contractures may also result from habitually positioning a muscle in its shortened range. For example, if a child only sits in a chair or lays curled up on one side all day, the muscles of the hips and behind the knees begin to tighten up very quickly.
- Positioning prevents decubiti (pressure sores) from developing. Whenever sitting or laying in any position for any period of time, frequent shifts of body weight help to take the pressure off of different areas of the body. If shifts are not made the pressure prevents the blood from flowing to that area and a sore results. These sores (decubiti, decubitus ulcers, bed sores) are often very difficult to heal and, therefore, should be prevented. Children with movement disorders often cannot efficiently and effectively shift their weight to relieve the pressure; therefore, shifts must be done for them. Only by frequently changing a child's position can the development of bed sores be prevented.
- Position changes prevent another complication that can arise when children cannot change their own position in their environment: limited sensory input. Frequent position changes afford them the opportunity to view their world from many different perspectives, which is critical for learning and cognitive growth.
- Frequent position changes allow children to interact more with the people around them (especially their peers). This opportunity fosters the development of better communication skills.

continues

continued

WHEN ARE CHILDREN POSITIONED?

The next likely question is, "How often should children be repositioned?" The answer is very individualized. To prevent pressure sores, a child's weight must be shifted (even slightly) at least once every half-hour. However, as far as changing positions, a variety of positions should be available to the child throughout the day. These positions include: prone (belly-lying); supine (back-lying); side-lying; sitting in an adapted wheelchair; sitting in other types of seats; possibly standing; and so forth. Then, position should be changed as there are changes from one activity to the next throughout the day (for example, breakfast, watching television, reading a book, interacting with peers, lunchtime, bathtime, toileting, and so forth). An example of five different positions that can easily be incorporated into the daily routine follows:

1. Feed in a sitting position in the adapted wheelchair with the lap tray on.
2. Place the child in a semi-reclined position on some pillows with pillows under the knees to digest the food while watching television.
3. Position the child in a side-lying position while relaxing.
4. Place the child in a prone position over a wedge or towel roll while reading a book.
5. Position the child in a standing position while assisting with activities such as washing hands, brushing hair, and so on.

HOW ARE CHILDREN PROPERLY POSITIONED?

Prone (Belly-Lying)

In the prone position, children very often do not have enough control in the head, neck, and shoulder girdle region to support themselves fully. Therefore, the child may not be able to lift the head and look around. If the child can lift his or her head, he or she may lift it too high, arch the whole body, and show increased stiffness throughout the truck, arms, and legs. The arms may be caught under the body, and the shoulders may be held high by the ears. The legs may be stiff, very straight, and very tight together. The opposite is also possible, where the child is very "floppy." The legs may be very wide apart and bent at the hips and knees. Neither extreme position is good for the child.

To position the child properly, assist by raising the head. To prevent the child from becoming too stiff or too floppy, use a wedge or towel roll placed under the chest. The towel should be rolled up so that it is thick enough to support the chest at a height approximately the same as the length of the upper arm. Bring the child's elbows forward so they are directly under the shoulders and place the towel under the chest with arms forward. If the lower back arches too much, roll up another smaller towel and place it under the lower chest and abdomen to give support to this area. Another smaller pillow should be placed between the knees to keep legs apart. Finally, a small

continues

continued

towel roll can be placed under both ankles to allow knees to bend slightly and prevent feet from pointing stiffly. It also provides added comfort.

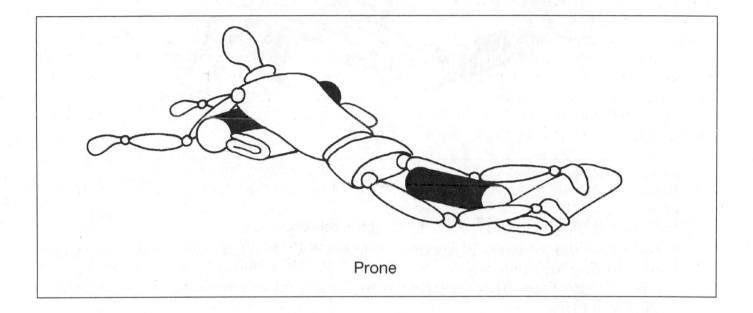

Prone

Supine (Back-Lying)

When placed on their backs, children tend to push back into the floor with their head, elbows, and feet and arch their backs. This position tends to cause them to stiffen up. The other extreme is that they will be very floppy with their hips and knees bent up next to their body. Again, neither extreme position is good.

To correct this problem, a small pillow should be placed under the head (not at the back of the neck). A large towel roll or pillow should be placed under the knees so that the hips and knees are bent. (By bending the hips and knees in all positions, spasticity and tightness throughout the lower trunk and legs will decrease.) Two small towel rolls can also be placed under the shoulders and lengthwise along the trunk. This action will help decrease the tone in the shoulder girdle, prevent children from pushing back with their elbows and shoulders, and allow for the movement of bringing hands together in front of the body.

continues

continued

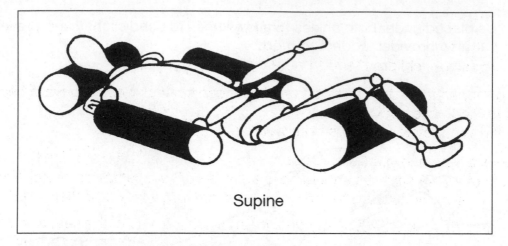

Supine

Side-Lying

Side-lying is a very good position for three reasons:

1. It decreases the influence of abnormal reflexes and, therefore, decreases spasticity or increased tone and stiffness.
2. It makes it easier to bring head and hands to midline, which in turn makes it easier for children to play with toys.
3. It helps stretch out tight trunk muscles that may otherwise lead to scoliosis.

In side-lying, a small flat pillow should be placed under the head to keep it in line with the body. A large towel roll or pillow can be tucked behind the back to keep the child from rolling onto his or her back. A small pillow may also be placed by the abdomen to prevent rolling onto the stomach. Finally, a pillow can be placed between the legs with either the top leg bent up and the bottom leg straight or both legs bent up.

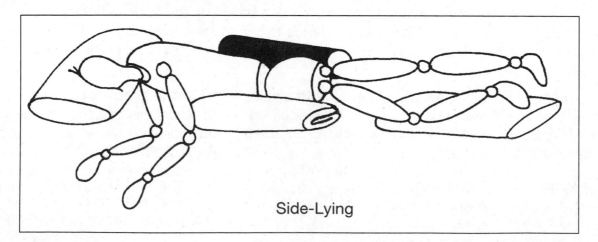

Side-Lying

continues

continued

Sitting

In the sitting position, children tend to be either:

- very floppy, where they demonstrate a very rounded back as well as forward head with their legs maintained wide apart or
- very stiff, where they tend to push backwards and straighten out.

To be properly positioned in the sitting position, children should be erect with their hips, knees, and feet all bent to 90°. A seat belt should be used to keep the hips back in the chair. This usage is for safety purposes and helping to prevent them from pushing out of their seats.

Note: The seat belt should be properly positioned at a 45° angle to the seat and back to allow it to cross the hips properly.

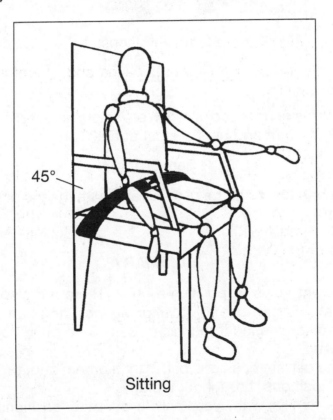

Sitting

If the child continues to push out of the chair, be sure the seat belt is properly and snugly positioned. Then, wedge the seat in the front by placing a towel roll under the knees. This placement will cause the hips to be bent more than 90°, which may decrease the spasticity and the tendency to push even more.

continues

continued

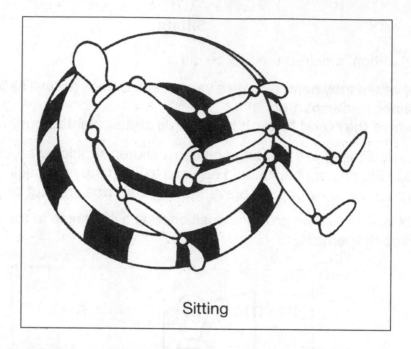

Sitting

If the child cannot hold his or her head up when sitting perfectly erect, tilt the child back *slightly*, trying to keep the back straight and hips at least at a 90° angle.

Semisitting

A tire tube and bean bag chair can be used as alternate means of positioning some children in a semisitting position.

SUMMARY

There are many different ways to position a child. There are also many different pieces of adapted equipment that you can use for positioning including hammocks, side-lyers, supine boards, corner chairs, roll chairs, adapted tricycles, molded bean bags, feeder seats, adapted home chairs, and so forth.

Each child will tolerate certain positions better than others and, therefore, should be allowed to assume a variety of positions throughout the day.

It is important to be familiar with your child's adapted positioning equipment and to be knowledgeable about its use. Questions about positioning and different pieces of adapted equipment should be directed to the child's physical and occupational therapists.

Source: Margaret Plack, "Positioning," *Parents as Respite Caregivers: A Training Manual*, United Cerebral Palsy Association of Nassau County, Inc., Roosevelt, New York, © 1985.

Proper Positioning and Handling for Premature Babies

YOUR BABY

Premature babies experience a very different environment than full-term infants in the first weeks of life. Studies suggest that premature infants in the nursery can benefit developmentally from appropriate sensorimotor input; that is, touch, visual input, movement, and sounds.

The guidelines that follow are general. It is very important to remember that each baby is different and will respond differently to input. So, your baby may not always respond in a predictable way to the activities suggested here. Each baby's medical condition will affect readiness and tolerance for these developmental activities. Therefore, It is important to consult your child's physician, nurse, or therapist regarding these activities. When presenting a development activity, it is important to consider your baby's state of alertness in order to benefit from the activity. Newborns require a great deal of quiet and sleep in these early weeks. Therefore, "more" activity is not "better."

POSITIONING AND HANDLING

"Muscle tone" is a concept that describes the tension or tightness in the muscles. Often, premature babies initially have low muscle tone and feel "floppy." Low tone gives them less control for holding positions and making movements. Most notable is their difficulty with holding flexed (bent toward body) postures.

Proper positioning and handling could compensate for the floppiness and help the baby to develop desirable movement patterns. It is important to change the baby's positions frequently.

Note: The baby's medical condition will determine the readiness for certain positions, particularly in regard to head positions.

Typical "low tone" postures include legs rolled out toward the bed surface, arms held away from the midline of the body, and head held to one side. The following are good ways to modify the baby's position in bed to reverse the above tendencies and encourage development of more desirable patterns of movement in the arms and legs. Medical conditions may require specific positioning that will take priority.

Side-Lying

Side-lying is a very good position for premature babies. When the baby is on his or her side, it is important to keep the legs bent with shoulders forward, hands toward midline. Use a rolled blanket to help keep the baby in position. If the newborn tends to arch backwards in the side-lying position, a long towel along the entire back surface and tucked into the mattress may help keep the baby curled. Remember to alternate sides. To facilitate gastric emptying, position on the right side down after feedings. Some babies may need to arch their necks to get air into their lungs. This action should not be interfered with.

continues

continued

Supine

Spending some time in a supine (back-lying) position is beneficial for premature infants. Use a rolled blanket arranged like a "U" to help keep head in midline, arms close to the chest, and legs curled up.

Avoid the supine position immediately after feeding. Remember, too, that it is important to change the baby's position frequently.

Swaddling

Swaddling helps newborns feel more secure. The swaddled baby is sometimes more able to receive sensory input, especially visual input, and to feed more easily. Use swaddling to help encourage flexion.

SENSORY INPUT

In the first months of life, babies learn to relate to the world through basic senses. Providing appropriate sensory input on the level at which your baby can benefit will help minimize certain aspects of any nursery environment, which can, at times, be noxious.

Some general guidelines for sensory input include:

- **Tactile** (touching). Generally, handle the baby firmly but gently. Light touch can be tickling or irritating. Stroking (going from the fingers to shoulders, and from toes to the hips, and from the nape of the neck down the back) is believed to be helpful in soothing the newborn and encouraging movement. Repeat some strokes.

- **Vestibular** (motion). Appropriate motion helps to develop balance centers in the inner ear. Motion can be very effective in determining your baby's behavioral state. Repetitive predictable movement is soothing to your baby.

    For example, for centuries rocking chairs have been used for this purpose. Moving the infant **gently** up and down in a linear pattern using adequate head support has also been found to be soothing. On the contrary, moving rapidly side to side will arouse the baby. It is very important to have the newborn in a well-supported flexed posture when providing motion as described above.

- **Auditory** (sound). Sound is another basic sense that can affect your baby's behavioral state. The ability to hear, even in the young baby, is developed to the extent that a whisper can be heard. Speak and sing to your baby using a soft, high-pitched voice, which is easiest to tune into. Avoid shrill, loud, or sudden noises.

- **Visual** (sight). As premature newborns approach term, they will show ability to focus on your face or on an object. Although newborns are able to perceive colors, it is easiest for them to

continues

continued

focus on patterns with the greatest contrast—that is, black and white designs. For example, they would prefer a panda bear to a brown teddy bear.

The black and white contrast of your eyes helps the baby to focus on the face and enjoy your interaction. It will be difficult for your baby to focus when the lighting in the room is too bright. Their immature eyes are not able to filter out a high degree of background light. When the baby is quiet and alert, and the lighting is softened, encourage the newborn to focus on your face. After the baby is focusing well on your face, move your head slowly to one side or the other to encourage the baby to track with his or her eyes. Sometimes talking softly to the baby will help keep his or her attention. Sometimes it will be too demanding for the newborn to attend to your voice and your face at the same time. Try to determine whether speaking helps him or her to focus better.

Notes:

Courtesy of Mary Saltez Sheahan and Joanne Valvano, The George Washington University Medical Center, Physical Therapy Department, and Georgetown University Medical Center, Child Development Center, Washington, DC.

What Your Child Needs To Do To Learn To Walk

Child's Name _____   Date _____

ACHIEVING EARLIER MOTOR (MOVEMENT) MILESTONES

(The therapist should check the skills a particular child needs to learn.)

___ Lift head while on stomach

___ Roll back to stomach

___ Sit leaning propped on arms

___ Sit propped on only one arm and reach with the other (weight shift)

___ Sit alone without falling. This skill requires having balance/parachute reactions of reaching out with the arms to prevent falling to the:

    ___ Front

    ___ Side

    ___ Back

___ Get onto hands and knees crawling position by self

___ Shift weight or crawl on hands and knees or hands and feet

    ___ Twisting at the waist (trunk rotation)

___ Kneel alone without falling: This skill requires having balance/parachute reactions of reaching out with the arms to prevent falling to the:

    ___ Front

    ___ Side

    ___ Back

___ Pull self to standing position using furniture

___ Walk sideways (cruise) around furniture

___ Stand alone about 3 seconds. Have balance/parachute reactions of reaching out with the arms to prevent falling to the:

    ___ Front

___ Have waist twisting (trunk rotation) and weight shifting skills

Note: Until the parachute reactions are also developed to the side and back, the child will be an unsafe walker.

continues

continued

BARRIERS TO WALKING

The therapist should check those barriers that apply to the specific child.

___ The brain sends signals to the muscles that makes them tight or stiff (spastic or hypertonic) so the child cannot control them well. This action prevents the child from developing protective parachute responses and/or trunk rotation.

___ The muscles are unusually weak and floppy (hypotonic) all over the body so the child does not have strength to hold a stable position.

___ Some muscles are unable to move at all (paralyzed), so the child does not have sufficient muscle strength around some joints to stand up.

___ Paralyzed muscles may also lack sensation or the ability to feel so the child does not know they are there.

___ The child's feeling in the legs may not be entirely normal. It is like walking on your legs when they have "gone to sleep."

___ The child may have an abnormal shape to the bones, or the joints may be malformed, too tight, too loose, or out of the joint socket.

___ The child may be visually impaired or blind so that he or she is afraid to move or walk.

___ The child may be overly sensitive to and afraid of movement such as swinging or spinning.

___ The child may have pain in some muscles, joints, tendons, or ligaments.

___ The child may show no interest in moving or walking.

Notes:

Courtesy of Caryl Semmler, PhD, OTR, Dallas, Texas.

Seat Cushions for People Who Use Wheelchairs

Nearly everyone who sits in a wheelchair can benefit from using a seat cushion. The right cushion can improve posture, increase comfort, distribute pressure to prevent skin breakdown, and enhance a person's functional ability and endurance in a wheelchair. Because there are many types of seat cushions and reasons to use them, it takes knowledge and experience to help someone select the proper cushion. Factors like the person's medical condition and history, motor and sensory function, previous skin breakdown, orthopedic problems, bowel and bladder function, and method of transfer in and out of the chair both affect and are affected by the type of cushion used.

SKIN BREAKDOWN

People who lack sensation or who have trouble shifting weight and changing positions are at risk for skin breakdown. Most people think of decubitus ulcers or pressure sores as resulting from excessive or prolonged pressure while sitting in a chair or lying in bed, but they can also occur because of skin shear from sliding, heat and moisture buildup from incontinence or perspiration, and repeated trauma during transfers. Poor nutrition, poor circulation, low muscle tone or bulk, age, and poor posture all make a person more susceptible to skin breakdown. Understanding someone's individual risk factors can help sort out what properties in a cushion are necessary to decrease pressure over bony prominences, maintain better postural alignment, dissipate heat and moisture, and ease transfers.

It is important to provide cushioning not only for the time spent sitting in a wheelchair, but also for use in bed, on a car seat, for toilet and bath activities, and even during recreational activities like weight lifting, horseback riding, and boating. Many researchers now examining skin breakdown are not only measuring pressures during normal sitting, but are also measuring dynamic patterns of peak pressures and weight-relieving behaviors over time. Studies show that people who shift weight frequently are able to tolerate much higher sitting pressures.

POSTURE

A cushion should be measured and fitted as carefully as the wheelchair in which it sits. Proper width and depth ensure pressure distribution over as much of the sitting surface as possible. The height and position of armrests and footrests can help the user bear weight on other parts of the body. The use of a firm base beneath a cushion, available directly from some cushion manufacturers, can improve pelvic positioning and help distribute pressure more evenly. While a firm seat provides much more stability for the pelvis than a sling seat, many people find the increased height of a firm seat causes problems with transfers, fitting under tables, and overall height while riding in a van. Knowing what type of cushion will be used when the wheelchair is first prescribed can allow compensation for the height difference.

continues

continued

The pelvis forms the primary weight-bearing area during sitting. Abnormal muscle tone and skeletal deformities can make the pelvis tilt forward to back, tip to the side, or rotate on the sitting surface. These positions can increase pressure on the bonier parts of the pelvis and raise the risk of skin breakdown. Additional support for the trunk or legs can help correct some of these postures and align the pelvis better, but there are times when a special cushion is needed to compensate for these problems.

TYPES OF CUSHIONS

Cushions can be classified by the materials used in construction or by the manner in which they function. For many years, people distinguished between cushions designed for pressure relief and those designed for postural control. In recent years, however, with the development of new materials and a greater understanding of the interaction between pressure and posture, many new cushions have been designed with properties that meet needs in both areas.

Foam

There are many types of foam cushions available to fit wheelchairs and their users. The properties of foam that must be considered in selecting a cushion are the density (as measured by indentation load deflection), the ability to spring back repeatedly over time, fire retardancy, air circulation or dissipation of heat, and water or urine resistance.

A flat foam cushion distributes weight by compressing to varying degrees beneath the person sitting on it. The more a piece of foam is compressed, the harder it pushes back, so a 4-inch-thick cushion will feel softer, or offer less resistance, when it is compressed 1 inch than when it is compressed 3 inches. Since people's "bottoms" are curved, the bony prominences of the pelvis will settle deeper into the cushion and show higher pressures than the sides of the thighs. It is important to be sure that the foam under the deepest part is not fully compressed, or "bottomed out," so that its cushioning effect is lost. Softer foams tend to provide better pressure relief than stiffer foams, but they offer less postural support or stability.

The composition of a foam determines how much surface resistance it offers. Some of the foams used in seating were developed to allow bony prominences to sink more deeply into the surface while still offering good support under the areas right next to them. They also tend to be sensitive to heat and cold, responding to the warmth of the body to mold around the person but getting very hard when exposed to cold. Some foams, like eggcrate, are convoluted or sliced to break up the surface resistance.

Many foam cushions are now being made with a contour molded into them to more closely match the shape of the user and reduce pressure. These contours can improve posture and stability by holding the pelvis back on the seat and keeping the legs adducted. Generically shaped cushions are adequate for many users, but people with asymmetrical postures or significant orthopedic problems may need custom contoured cushions. Some manufacturers provide the option of adding

continues

continued

extra support pads or cushioning components to customize the shape. Others allow carving of relief areas for postural asymmetries or bony prominences. Cutout areas to eliminate weight bearing on a specific area like the coccyx or the ischial tuberosities must be fitted very carefully. It is possible to restrict circulation even further by forming a ring of pressure around the relieved area.

Flotation

A flotation cushion has a sealed envelope filled with a movable substance like water, air, or gel. Since the cushioning or support is provided by a substance that moves, the cushion responds to changes in the user's posture by moving away from the area of greatest pressure or depth. While this feature can help to distribute weight more evenly, there is a risk that the substance could completely move out of the area needing support and "bottom out." The dynamic nature of a flotation cushion also tends to make it less stable for many users.

Air

Air-filled cushions can consist of a single or compartmentalized air bladder, a sealed foam cushion that contains air, or multiple air cells. The single bladder cushions are the least expensive, and they tend to be the most durable, but they don't distribute pressure as effectively as the other types. Foam and air cushions are self-inflating, and the foam serves as a safety feature if the cushion is punctured. Multiple air cell cushions distribute pressure more evenly, since each cell supports part of the body independently of the other. Some users complain of decreased stability on these cushions, but this can be improved with variations like multiple valve control of inflation, different cell heights, and a firm contoured base.

Air cushions are lighter weight than other flotation cushions, making it easier to move them during transfers. Users must be taught to inflate them properly and to monitor them carefully to ensure effective pressure management. If air cushions are inflated to the point of being firm, they lose their flotation properties and can be the source of high-pressure areas under bony prominences. Most air cushions come with their own hand pumps and patching kits.

An alternating pressure cushion uses a pump to vary the pressure within different areas of the seat continuously. This feature is intended to substitute for the user's inability to shift weight him- or herself. This type of system is more commonly used in beds than in wheelchairs, probably because of the need for an external power source and the size of the weight-bearing surface. Many people have found it more practical and versatile to vary the position of the wheelchair seat and back in order to shift weight, in some cases using a power recline or tilt system.

Gel

There is a variety of cushions that fall into this category, using "liquid" or "dry" gels to provide a flotation surface for sitting. Gel cushions tend to be heavy, and the gel eventually stiffens or

continues

continued

wears out and needs to be replaced. Most are sensitive to temperature and will freeze or harden in cold climates. The more fluid gels generally need to be contained within some type of base, and the gel may need to be repositioned before the user transfers into the chair.

Water

Water cushions are less expensive to purchase and maintain than gel cushions, but they are heavy to lift out of the chair. They help to dissipate heat in hot climates but are also susceptible to cold. Some users object to the noise of the water moving within the cushion, though this is decreased if the envelope is baffled. Leaks are easier to detect in water cushions than air or sometimes gel cushions, which can be an advantage where there are problems with monitoring.

Hybrid Cushions

Some manufacturers make hybrid cushions that combine several materials to provide the best characteristics while eliminating some of the drawbacks. For example, using a gel flotation pad only under the areas of highest pressure with foam supporting the rest of the person can reduce the cost and weight of a cushion considerably.

CUSHION COVERS

The cover of a cushion has a significant effect on its ability to relieve and distribute pressure. A non-stretchy cover will hammock or interfere with the ability of the cushion to conform to the shape of the user. A waterproof cover will protect the cushion from water or urine, but it traps heat and moisture against the body and interferes with air circulation. Slippery surfaces may make transfers easier and decrease skin shear but they also make it harder for the person to stay positioned all the way back on the seat. The ideal cover is stretchy to conform to body contours and breathable for air circulation. If water resistance is required, compromises may be necessary or one can use a cushion that is waterproof without a cover.

SHEEPSKIN PADS

The use of a natural or synthetic sheepskin pad on a wheelchair seat or other surface can help with skin shear, air circulation, and heat dissipation while providing some additional cushioning. Many people will use a fleece pad to insulate the top of a gel or water cushion during cold weather. Manufacturers are now making these pads to cover armrests, headrests, footplates, seat cushions, and other surfaces.

Source: "Seat Cushions," Fact Sheet #11, ABLEDATA, Silver Spring, Maryland, Revised February 1992.

Wheelchair Safety

IS IT DIFFICULT?

Some people are apprehensive about taking an individual who uses a wheelchair on an outing. Other people are overly confident. Both approaches are wrong. Once aware of the general rules, the actual act of pushing a wheelchair is no more difficult than pushing a baby carriage. On the other hand it is not quite as simple, for the person you are pushing may be cumbersome and may have ideas of his or her own.

BASIC PARTS OF STANDARD WHEELCHAIR

Arm Rests

Arm rests are usually removable. Many a novice has attempted to lift or fold a wheelchair by grabbing the arms and pulling upward, only to find the chair still stationary, and two arm rests in his or her hands mid-air. The surprise is often amusing, and sometimes dismaying. Any attempt to lift the arms of the wheelchair when a child is in it is most dangerous. The arms free themselves, and the child with a disability may not have the muscle control and balance to prevent a bad fall. The child may also be startled to have the source of support on both sides suddenly removed. *Never* lift a wheelchair by its arm rests.

Foot Rests

Some foot rests are removable. They are attached to each side of the chair, and usually swing outward and fold upward on hinges. When pushing a wheelchair, they are out of the pusher's vision, so take care to keep an ample distance between the wheelchair and any pedestrians in front of it. Being bumped by foot rests can be both annoying and painful to innocent pedestrians.

Some children do not have, or do not use foot rests. Always allow enough foot room for the child in the chair. Be careful not to run the child's feet into objects or cause them to get caught in the front wheels.

Brakes

There is a separate brake for each side of the chair. Be sure to find out how the brakes are applied. Some lock when pushed back in toward the chair, and others lock when pushed forward.

continues

continued

SAFETY SUGGESTIONS

Curbs

When getting a wheelchair from the curb to the street, turn yourself and the chair backwards. After stepping into the street, ease the chair down until the large wheels hit the pavement. To get the wheelchair onto the sidewalk from the street stay behind the chair, then tilt the chair back far enough so that the small wheels are on the sidewalk first. It will then be easy to lift the rest of the chair up onto the sidewalk.

Ramps

Descending a long ramp may be more difficult than is suspected. No matter how short or long a ramp is, always turn yourself and the chair around and *go down backward*. The pusher's body will then keep the chair from picking up momentum. A second person is sometimes needed to grasp the lower part of the chair to help keep the chair under control.

It is not difficult to push a wheelchair up a gradually sloped ramp, but a steep long ramp may be very difficult and require two people: one to push the chair and the other to back up and pull while grasping some secure part on the front of the chair.

Stairs

At least two people are needed to lift a child in a wheelchair up and down stairs.

Always take a wheelchair up a flight of stairs backwards. One person should hold onto the handgrips firmly, tilt the chair quite far back, and pull it up one step at a time, resting it on each step on the large back wheels. The second person should face the chair, grasp the rods to which the foot rests are attached, and lift the front of the chair. Although the wheels are the most accessible part of the chair, when the time comes for it to be lifted, the wheels should never be used for this purpose.

Always take a wheelchair down stairs forward (the chair faces the stairs). One person should firmly grasp the handgrips and tilt the chair quite far back. The second person goes down backward while grasping the rods to which the foot rests are attached. Gently ease the chair down one step at a time, resting the large back wheels on each step. Keep the chair tilted in the same position throughout the descent. The person in front should provide balance and help control speed.

If a very heavy child is being taken up or down stairs, it is advisable to use three people: one to hold the handgrips, and two to hold the front rods, with one person on each side of the chair. If three people are used, lifting up or down stairs is done with ease.

continues

continued

Automobile Trips

When removing a child who can sit in a regular automobile seat, it will be necessary to transfer the child from the wheelchair to the seat. Be sure the car is parked away from the curb. Place the wheelchair close to the car; in this way the lifter will be able to move the child from the chair into the car and not have to bend way over in doing so. The child who can move from the wheelchair into the car without help usually finds it easier if the car is parked closer to the curb. In either case it is best to place the child in the seat next to the driver; some support may be needed if the child does not have adequate balance. This support can be supplied by having someone sit next to the child. The driver should always be cautious in starting and stopping so there are no unnecessary jerks.

Always be sure to put the brakes on when stopping the chair, even for a brief pause, or when the child is being moved in or out of the wheelchair. The brakes must be locked into place when a child remains seated in the wheelchair while being transported in a motor vehicle.

When putting a wheelchair into the trunk of a car, grasp the rim or the center of one of the large wheels and any stationary part of the front of the chair. Lift like any other bulky object being sure to lift the chair high enough to clear the license plate and bumper, which often extend above the openings of a car trunk.

Wheels

Take care that nothing gets caught in the spokes of the wheels. Dangling ends of clothing worn by the child in the wheelchair, and objects hung onto the back side of the chair should all be kept away from the moving wheels.

Seat Belts

It is desirable for children who use wheelchairs to use a seat belt, although some say they feel more comfortable without one. Those children with a disability that does not allow them to make immediate, automatic adjustments of balance while moving should *always* use a seat belt.

Seat belts can be purchased at any surgical supply store. Good substitutes for the manufactured item are trunk or suitcase straps or regular leather belts. Any substitute must, of course, be large enough to go around the child's waist or lower chest and the back of the wheelchair. It should be comfortable, of strong material, and have a sturdy buckle.

In circumstances when improvisation becomes necessary, a large square scarf may be used. Fold the scarf diagonally and tie it securely to prevent sliding and sudden constriction, which can cause discomfort or pain.

Tilting Rods

Modern wheelchairs have two rods close to the ground in the rear. These rods serve as foot pedals for the pusher, and it is extremely important to know how to use them.

continues

continued

After getting a good grasp on the handle, the pusher puts one foot on one of the pedals; applies a downward pressure, which raises the front wheel of the chair from the ground; tilts the chair back slightly; and maneuvers safely over bumps and holes in the street, door sills, and over any other gradation in levels, such as from the street to a curb. Using the tilting rods may require more caution, but no more energy, on the part of the pusher. Occasionally, a child who uses a wheelchair may wish to negotiate differences in levels in another way, but in most cases the above method is safe and satisfactory.

HOW TO CLOSE A WHEELCHAIR

Do not try to close the wheelchair by lifting up on the arm rests. Lift the seat up by the leather handles that are attached to the seat of the chair, by the seat frame, or by lifting the seat at the front and back. Be sure that the foot rests are up, or the chair will not close.

If the wheelchair has a high back rest, always remember to unlock the bars behind it.

HOW TO OPEN A WHEELCHAIR

Grasp the seat frame on both sides. The seat will flatten by pushing down on the frame. Do not try to open it by pulling or pushing it apart by the arm rests. If there are foot rests, they should be upright when starting. Do not lower them until the chair is open and the child is seated in the wheelchair. Wheelchairs with high backs have two locking bars behind the back rest that must be locked in place when the chair is open, to keep the back rest firm.

MAJOR RULES: CONSIDERATION OF THE CHILD

First, consult with the child you are to push, as to the "dos" and "don'ts."

Ask the child exactly how the wheelchair works because each wheelchair is as different as the child who uses it.

Ask how the child wishes to be pushed, not only on level ground, but up and down the curbs, stairs, and so forth. Do not try to impose unfamiliar ways of doing things.

The child has developed routines that are safe and efficient and in which the child has the greatest confidence. This principle applies not only to pushing the chair, but also to moving an arm or a leg to a more comfortable position, or getting the person into and out of clothing, automobiles, and so forth.

Ask the above questions repeatedly if necessary. The child will not mind, but will in fact, welcome your questions. The child is aware that it is in his or her best interests to put the new pusher at ease.

continues

continued

Just one word of caution. Do not let your concern turn into overzealousness that results in doing more than is necessary. A child with a disability likes to be as independent as physical limitations allow.

In cold weather do not push too slowly, for children who use wheelchairs are apt to have poor circulation, and even when well wrapped up they may get chilled easily.

When pushing a wheelchair, rubber-soled, low-heeled shoes should be worn. This advice is especially appropriate when pushing a chair for some distance, or going up and down ramps or stairs.

If a person is not used to it, pushing a wheelchair for long distances can leave wrist muscles (ordinarily not used in this way) stiff and the palms of the hands sore. Not much can be done to ease the wrists, but pressure on the palms can be eased by wrapping a piece of foam rubber around the handles of the wheelchair, even though they may already have hard rubber covers.

Notes:

Source: Reprinted with the permission of the Easter Seal Society of Nebraska.

Mobility Equipment Basics

- **Walkers.** Walkers are used mainly by children who need maximum support to balance when walking. Types of walkers include wheeled or nonwheeled, those used in front of the child and those used behind, foldable or nonfoldable, and height-adjustable.

  Note: Walkers should not be used more than one step length in front of the child. All four legs should be in contact with the ground before stepping. Beware of obstacles that could cause tripping such as rugs, door jams, cracks in sidewalks, and stairs.

- **Crutches.** Crutches are used by children who need some support but desire greater mobility. Types of crutches include standard underarm and forearm, which allow freer use of the hands.

  Note: Children should not lean on underarm portion of crutches. Watch for tripping hazards such as pebbles. Water can cause rubber tips to slip. Check tips frequently.

- **Canes.** Canes are used by children who need minimal assistance with walking. Types of canes include single- and multitip canes.

  Note: Watch for tripping hazards. Canes may not provide adequate support on rough terrain.

- **Standing frames.** Through the use of a frame and straps, children can experience being upright even when they do not have the strength or ability to stand alone. Standing frames are ideal for use in the classroom or other areas that allow for socializing. Types of standing frames include prone stander, supine stander, and parapodiums as well as freedom standers, which provide less support and more movement.

  Note: Be sure straps are secure and that the child is well supported. Parapodiums and freedom standers can tip over.

- **Wheelchairs.** Often wheelchairs serve as a child's main means of positioning and mobility. Children may remain in them for most of their waking hours. It is *essential* that a child's wheelchair fit well and provide the necessary support for that particular child. There are dozens of types of wheelchairs available and, while similar, all have their own options or features. Especially note the following features:
  — Wheelchair frame. Does the wheelchair fold or come apart? Are the wheels removable? Do the frames tilt or recline?
  — Arm rests. Do they swing away or come off for easier transfers?
  — Leg rests. Do they swing away or remove for easier transfers?
  — Brakes. Where are they located? Are they high or low on the wheels? Do they have extensions for easier reach? Do they push forward to lock or pull back?

  Note: Be sure brakes are on during transfers.

continues

continued

— Support system. What kind of system is used—a single seat belt or a complex system that includes a chest harness, lateral supports, head support, abductor wedge, footstraps, and so on?

Note: Each system is individualized for each child.

— Seating system. Is the seating system adequate? (This system is one of the most important parts of a child's chair. Prolonged sitting can be uncomfortable and cause structural changes in a child if the seating system is inadequate. Even when designed properly if the child is positioned improperly there can be severe repercussions including decubiti, contractures, and scoliosis.)

Note: Know how each child should be properly seated and secured.

- **Power chairs.** Each power chair is as individual as its owner, more so when compared with a standard wheelchair. Power chairs are heavy and often difficult to maneuver for the inexperienced. They often contain attachments for communication devices and can be tricky when attempting transfers. Learn about these chairs before attempting to assist a child who uses a power chair.

- **Braces.** The majority of braces are now made of plastics, though heavier metal braces are still around. Depending on which joint or joints need support braces will vary significantly. Braces may be worn to provide support, prevent deformity, prevent injury, or limit motion. Braces can be used for almost any area of the body and are formed to fit a particular child. Observe how the braces are to be worn before putting braces on or taking them off.

Notes:

Source: *Developmental Disabilities Review Course*, Children's Association for Maximum Potential, San Antonio, Texas, 1992.

Types of Seating Systems

Approaches to seating can be broken down into three main categories, although most seating specialists will combine different techniques to meet their clients' needs.

Planar (or linear) seating refers to the use of flat planes or surfaces to support the user. These components are usually adjustable, and proponents of this approach claim it offers a greater ability to accommodate growth and change. A variety of foams and interchangeable hardware allows adaptation of these components to suit the user's needs.

Modular contoured seating uses components with generic contours, with a variety of sizes and configurations of support pads and hardware allowing the system to be fitted to the user. While there is often some adjustment for growth and change, contoured components probably need to be exchanged for different sizes sooner than properly prescribed planar components. Proponents of contoured seating claim a better distribution of pressure and increased comfort because it more closely matches the shape of the user's body contours.

Custom contoured or molded seating involves custom-forming the seating system around the user's body contours, often while applying specific support to correct or improve postural problems. This type of system provides greater surface contact for people who have significant skeletal or structural deformities like severe scoliosis because of the intimacy of the fit, but it is difficult to achieve a good fit in indoor clothing and then allow room for heavy sweaters and coats in cold weather. Custom molding also requires a higher level of fitting and fabrication technology and expertise on the part of the provider.

This handout describes seating components that fall into the first two categories.

SEATING COMPONENTS

Seats

The key point of control or stability in the sitting position is almost always the pelvis or hips. A good base of support can enhance a person's ability to balance, reach, propel, transfer, or perform any other tasks. A seating system usually begins with a *solid seat insert* that distributes pressure over as broad a sitting surface as possible, both to maximize the base of support and to minimize pressure in concentrated areas. It is generally acknowledged that the standard sling seat upholstery on most wheelchairs provides a poor base of support for the user and that, at the very least, the user should sit on a *cushion* with a firm level base. This cushion can be placed on top of the existing seat upholstery, or the upholstery can be removed and the seat hooked onto the wheelchair frame with hardware that allows easy removal to fold the chair. The size, angle, and shape of the sitting surface and the composition of the material used for cushioning all influence how well a seat works for a particular user. Seats should provide support under the full length of the thigh without causing pressure behind the knee. Users with leg-length discrepancies may require an *offset seat depth*.

continues

continued

Pelvic Supports

Proper alignment of the pelvis on the seat can be crucial to normalizing the user's muscle tone, preventing deformities, and maximizing stability on the seat. A lapbelt or pelvic strap can be a key to maintaining the hips all the way back in the seat, and the angle at which it crosses the pelvis can help to control anterior or posterior pelvic tilt. Lateral hip guides can be placed on the sides of the hips to help keep the pelvis centered on the seat. These may be used at the rear of the seat only to support the hips, or they can be extended the full length of the seat to control the position of the knees as well. Separate pads on the outsides of the knees are often called *abductors*. Support of the inner surface of the thighs to maintain abduction of the hips can be accomplished with an *abductor buildup* on the front edge of the seat surface or with a separate pad or pommel called an *abductor* or *abduction wedge*. Transfers are easier if the abductor is mounted with hardware that allows it to be removed or flipped down out of the way.

Foot and Leg Supports

Most wheelchairs or mobility bases come with some type of foot support, but it may not provide adequate support for the user with special positioning needs. Foot or leg rest height should be set to relieve some of the pressure on the under-surface of the thighs. Footrests often need to swing out of the way or be removed for transferring in and out of the wheelchair. The angle of knee flexion or extension can play a crucial role in the user's ability to stay seated back in the wheelchair; people with hamstring tightness will need to keep their knees flexed more or the muscle group will pull on the pelvis and extend the hips. At the same time, the knees may need to be extended slightly in order for the feet to clear the casters when they swivel around to the front to turn the chair. *One-piece footplates, adjustable angle footplates, posterior calf rests, heel loops,* and *ankle straps* are all used to help position the feet.

Backs

Sling back upholstery often encourages a wheelchair user to sit with a posterior pelvic tilt and kyphotic back. The addition of a *solid back insert*, whether flat or contoured, can provide better support for the sacrum and the spine and increase trunk stability. A solid back insert can be mounted in a wheelchair by placing it in front of the back upholstery with straps attaching to the push handles, or the upholstery can be removed and the back mounted with hardware that allows adjustment and easy removal to fold the chair for transporting. Careful examination of the user's spine and posture can help determine his or her tolerance for a flat or contoured surface and the type of foam selected. A flat back can be modified with additional pads on top of or underneath the upholstery to provide *lumbar support, shoulder protraction*, or gentle *lateral trunk support*, or a *contoured back* may be recommended.

continues

continued

Trunk Supports

People with trunk weakness or asymmetry often need lateral support to help them sit upright in their wheelchairs. *Lateral trunk supports* are made in a variety of shapes and sizes and can be attached to solid back inserts, wheelchair back uprights, or wheelchair arm rests with hardware that allows adjustment for growth and change. Some hardware allows them to swing out of the way or to be removed to make transfers easier. Anterior trunk support is sometimes needed for children who pull or fall forward. It can be provided with *swingaway lateral trunk supports* that curve around to the front, with wide straps that fasten across the front of the user's chest, or with a variety of *harnesses* or *anterior supports* that incorporate straps and pads to support the abdomen, sternum, and/or shoulders. *Rigid shoulder supports* or *retractors* that swing down in front of the shoulders may be necessary in some extreme situations. It may also be appropriate to consider mounting the whole seating system in a mobility base that *reclines* or *tilts back* in space to relieve the user from the forward pull of gravity on the spine and head.

Arm Supports

Standard *wheelchair arm rests* are available in various configurations that can make it easier to support the upper extremities. *Removable* or *flip-up* arms can make transfers easier, and *adjustable height* can enable the user or caregiver to set the arm rest at different heights for different activities. The seating evaluation must determine whether the arm rest is to support only the weight of the arm, or whether weight bearing on the forearm will be used to keep the person from leaning forward. Different *arm rest pads* or *troughs* can be added to support the forearm, and straps or additional pads can be used to keep the arm from moving to the rear or off the sides. *Laptrays* can be mounted on the arm rests in a variety of ways to provide more support surface for the arms or for feeding, fine motor, or other activities.

Head Supports

Many people with postural problems also need external support for their heads, particularly if their chairs recline or tilt back, or if they ride in wheelchair vans. Head rests are most easily mounted on chairs with solid backs, although hardware is available to equip sling back chairs with head rests. Simple headrests consist of flat panels, though some users may need specific neck or occipital support with adjustable pads or contoured foam. Removable hardware can make transfers easier, and adjustable hardware can help accommodate changes in growth or condition. Anterior support of the head is more difficult to accomplish without compromising safety or appearance. Anterior supports include *halos, forehead* or *chin straps, cervical collars,* and *overhead slings* such as those used for cervical traction.

Source: *"Modular Seating Components,"* Fact Sheet #10, ABLEDATA, Silver Spring, Maryland, Revised 1992.

Orthoses

WHAT IS AN ORTHOSIS?

An orthosis (brace) is a medically prescribed device applied to or around a body segment or manipulated by the body to aid function. The purposes of orthoses are as follows:

- relieve pain
- support the body weight or the weight of a body part
- increase function or capacity
- limit activity
- prevent or correct deformity
- reeducate muscles
- stabilize joints

Immobilization restricts motion in a joint. It is seldom complete. Immobilization is used:

- to allow healing
- to provide stability at proximal joints to allow effective muscular action at more distal joints
- as a preoperative testing measure before arthrodesis
- for pain relief

Restriction in a brace ordinarily limits the available range of motion by means of stops. Stabilization maintains the alignment of two parts of the body by preventing unwanted motion.

A static splint is an unhinged brace that is used for positioning. Night splints and resting splints are examples. A dynamic splint is an articulated device that has a provision to replace the motive action of a muscle. (An articulation is a joint between rigid parts.) A supportive orthosis has force characteristics to assist weak muscles with structural support. The inductive orthosis induces a reflex response to have the person voluntarily or involuntarily move the body into a corrective position. It produces a physiological change or response to counteract deformity. The mechanical forces exerted by the brace are insufficient by themselves to result in the desired response.

Serial casting, or bracing that stretches slowly, is much more effective than intermittent rapid stretch. Rapid stretch causes a reflex contraction of the muscles of the antagonist muscles, thus inhibiting stretching. Slow stretch fatigues the muscles on the contracted side, thereby allowing motion to the maximum that the joint is capable of at that time.

continues

continued

CARE OF ORTHOSES

Weekly Care

- Wash with an appropriate cleansing soap. Leather should be washed with saddle soap.
- Remove all dirt from joints. If the joints are metal, they should be oiled.
- Inspect for worn or missing parts and for parts that are starting to wear or break.
- Check alignment and check positioning of shoes and attachments.

General Care

- Do not bang the orthosis or allow the child to do so.
- Keep plastic braces away from sources of heat such as the trunk or back seat of an automobile.
- See the physician at least every 3 months to ensure that the orthosis is still the appropriate size for the growing child.

Notes:

Source: E. Marquardt, L.W. Friedmann, and G. Koester, "Amputations, Protheses, and Orthoses," in *Orthopedics*, Linda A. Karacoloff, ed., Aspen Publishers, Inc., © 1987.

Transporting Children Who Are Casted

CHILDREN WHO ARE UNABLE TO SIT UP

- Decide what type of vehicle will be used at discharge and whether the vehicle seat will meet the child's height and cast width requirements.

- Measure the child's length and the width of the leg spread created by the cast.

- Measure the length of the vehicle seat.

- Do not position a casted child into the rear seat of a two-door vehicle.

- Do not use a van with no seats in the back for transporting the casted child. Placing a child in a cast on a mattress on the floor provides no form of restraint, and places the child at high risk of further injury if he or she strikes objects or persons in the van's interior.

- Do not place the casted child in a reclined vehicle seat. The load of the seat belt is concentrated entirely on the child's abdomen and could place tremendous force on this area. In addition, the head and neck are also more exposed to crash forces and are unprotected.

- Do not position a casted child in a reclined wheelchair in a vehicle during travel. Wheelchairs are not designed for travel purposes. It is important to provide a tie-down system for the wheelchair and a separate securement system for the wheelchair occupant that have been dynamically crash tested. In a reclined wheelchair, it is impossible to provide a proper and secure means of separate restraint for the casted child and for the wheelchair.

- Ensure that the vehicle has at least two sets of working seat belts on the vehicle seat on which the child will lay. Two working sets of seat belts will allow use of a vest specifically modified to restrain the casted child. The vest allows the child to lay completely flat on the vehicle seat. Seat belts are then routed through vest side loops to secure the child to the vehicle seat. If lap/shoulder belts are present in the vehicle seat, check to see if the seat belt tongue is free-sliding. If so, a locking clip is necessary to maintain adjustment of seat belts.

- Check with the insurance company about coverage for ambulance transport if a child is unable to fit laying flat on a vehicle seat.

- Borrow or obtain an alternative vehicle if insurance does not cover ambulance travel.

CHILDREN WHO ARE ABLE TO SIT UP

- Even if your child is in a cast, providing proper and secure protection for them during travel is still important.

- Use of standard car safety seats or safety belts may still be possible.

continues

continued

- Position the safety belt low on the pelvis, on the stomach.

- Ensure the safety belt is tightened snugly at the child's hips.

- Position a child in a cast at a side angle, if necessary, for legs to fit on the vehicle seat. An ancillary seat belt can be used to wrap and secure legs on a vehicle seat.

- Never secure the child in a cast on a fully reclined bucket seat. The load of the seat belt is then concentrated entirely on the child's abdominal area and could cause injury. The child's head and neck are also not properly supported in the fully reclined position and are more exposed to crash forces.

- Build the floor area up with soft pillows positioned on top of a light-weight cardboard box (for example, diaper box) if the child's casted legs stretch out beyond the vehicle seat. Heavy objects, such as suitcases, should not be used; they could become dangerous projectiles in a crash.

- Do not place the shoulder belt underneath the arm or behind the back of the child. Position the child's buttocks toward the middle of the vehicle seat to lower the shoulder belt on the child's chest.

- Use only commercially available restraint devices for babies, toddlers, and older children in casts who are not able to sit up. Avoid homemade devices or modified restraints that have not been dynamically tested.

- Evaluate the child's needs for transportation with the orthopedic surgeon and nursing staff as far as possible in advance of discharge. Consider the dimensions of the child's cast and the set up of the vehicle (for example, size of seat, number of safety belts).

- Talk with the child's occupational and physical therapists about procedures for transferring the child from the wheelchair to the vehicle.

- Check with the insurance company about securing an ambulance transport if it is impossible to secure an appropriate vehicle to accommodate the child.

Notes:

Courtesy of Automotive Safety for Children Program, James Whitcomb Riley Hospital for Children, Indianapolis, Indiana.

Transporting Children Who Are Ventilator-Dependent and Who Have Tracheostomies

- Many babies and toddlers can use commercially available child safety seats that meet the following requirements for optimum safety, positioning, and comfort:

  — The car safety seat should not have a shield or arm rest. An arm rest or shield is a padded surface that the child's neck area could strike in a crash.

  — The car safety seat that has a five-point harness (that is, harness straps that contact on both shoulders, both hips, and between the legs) is preferred for a child with a tracheostomy. The major advantages are:

      (a) No feature could potentially serve as a contact point for the tracheostomy.

      (b) The parent has easy access to the child with the more open five-point harness system.

      (c) The five-point harness straps can be positioned more easily around additional tubing (for example, gastrostomy tubes).

      (d) The car safety seat should have several angles of recline that can accommodate the child in the forward- or rear-facing positions.

- For the older child with a tracheostomy who weighs more than 40 pounds and is taller than 40 inches:

  — Use a belt-positioning booster car safety seat that has a removable shield. The child is secured by the vehicle lap-shoulder belt. The child should be able to sit up independently to use a belt-positioning booster seat.

  — Use special restraint devices. There are a variety of safety-tested restraint systems for older children. Make certain you understand all the possible choices before determining one solution.

- Consider these questions:

  — Can the child tolerate a full upright position or is a variety of levels of recline necessary?

  — Is the harness for the device used for positioning only or has it been tested for transportation purposes?

  — Is a tether required? (A tether is a long strap that extends off the back of the restraint and must be bolted into solid metal. The tether helps to hold the restraint more upright against the vehicle seat.)

  — If the child has other ancillary medical equipment, how is this equipment secured during transport? (The best place for extra medical equipment is in a location where it is least likely to become dislodged during impact [that is, on the floor or underneath a wheel-chair]).

Courtesy of Automotive Safety for Children Program, James Whitcomb Riley Hospital for Children, Indianapolis, Indiana.

Infant Apnea Monitoring at Home

WHY DOES YOUR BABY NEED A MONITOR AT HOME?

Your child's physician (neonatologist or pediatrician) has determined that your newborn is at high risk for apnea and bradycardia, and/or sudden infant death syndrome (SIDS). Because there is no specific cause known, it is very important to monitor your baby, especially during sleep or when your child is alone.

A test called a "sleep pneumogram" (pronounced nu-mo-gram) is used to determine whether your baby needs a monitor at home. This test, which was performed while your baby was hospitalized, is just one tool that assesses the need for continued monitoring of your child's heart rate and respiratory rate at home.

WHO IS AT HIGH RISK?

Five groups of high-risk babies have been identified:

1. siblings of SIDS victims
2. twin of a SIDS victim
3. premature infants
4. child with apnea or cyanotic episodes
5. child with an abnormal sleep pneumogram

The occurrence of SIDS peaks between the ages of 4 to 6 months; the danger of SIDS is usually over by 1 year of age.

Home monitors help alleviate stress. You will be able to sleep at night knowing the alarm will sound if your baby is in trouble.

THE MONITOR AT HOME

Follow these ten guidelines at home:

1. Refer to your handbook frequently concerning how to operate the monitor and how to care for it. Your monitor representative is always available to answer questions.
2. Have a list of important telephone numbers next to each telephone, including:
   — ambulance service or rescue squad
   — hospital emergency department
   — physician's office
   — police department
   — fire department
   — emergency number of electric utility company
   — monitor representative

continues

continued

3. Notify your electric company that you have special medical equipment in your home and you should be placed on the priority repair list. Your monitor should have a built-in, battery-powered failure alarm.

4. Notify your nearest rescue squad or ambulance service. Let them know you have a baby on a home monitor and will be calling them in case of an emergency.

5. Notify a neighbor when you get home from the hospital.

6. Use the speaker available with your monitor. This feature allows your baby to be in one place and the parent or caregiver to be elsewhere in the home.

7. Arrange furniture so that there is easy access to your baby's room.

8. Be mindful that household chores such as vacuuming, washing, dishwashers, and so forth may result in noises that would not permit you to hear an alarm. These activities must be scheduled for a time when someone is available to watch the baby, or these chores can be done when the child is awake and can continually be observed.

9. Consider where the baby should sleep at night. Many parents feel more comfortable locating the baby's crib in their bedroom during the first few weeks of monitoring. As confidence in the monitor and your ability to deal with the alarm grows, consider returning your child to his or her own room.

10. You can take short trips. Do not travel in a car alone with your baby, but if absolutely necessary, travel should be scheduled when the infant is most likely to stay awake. Anytime your child is asleep or unattended, he or she should be monitored, including when traveling in a car. Always place the baby in a restraint device. Also, drive in the right lane where natural light on the child is best. This is valuable because skin color is one of the best indications of a problem.

MAINTAINING WRITTEN RECORDS

- Keep a monitor event sheet for recording episodes. Your monitor handbook may include such a chart.
- Keep a daily journal of the baby's activities and the medications given. See the monitor handbook.

THE BABY'S SKIN

The areas chosen for the placement of electrodes should be clean, dry, and free from powder, oils, and perspiration residue. Area with rashes or chafing should be avoided. Skin irritation occurs most commonly when disposable electrodes are used and then removed.

You should have instructions concerning electrodes, wires, placement, and so forth. For further questions, you may refer to your monitor handbook or contact your monitor representative.

continues

continued

RESPONDING TO AN ALARM

Concentrate on Your Baby and Not on the Monitor

1. Look and observe before touching:
   — Is your baby breathing?
   — Is your baby's color normal?
   — Check the position of your baby. Is his or her airway open?
2. If each question above can be answered with yes, there is no need to interrupt your baby's sleep. One good reason to observe before touching is that your baby's condition and progress are being evaluated by your physician by the number of apneic episodes and the severity of those episodes. If the baby is stimulated before ascertaining whether the baby is breathing, there will be no way of knowing if it was a real episode. Another reason to first observe and calmly think, is to learn not to overreact and panic. This lesson is not easy. It is a frightening situation at best. It might be helpful to learn a process to know what your actions are going to be when the monitor does alarm. The following instructions could be helpful in assisting you in planning.

Instructions If Alarm Sounds

1. If your baby is breathing and color is normal:
   — Wait a few seconds.
   — See if breathing and color remain normal.
   — Reset alarm lights.
2. If your baby is not breathing or the heart rate is low, but color is normal:
   — Wait.
   — Reset alarm lights if alarm ceases and the baby is breathing.
   — Note episode on event sheet.
3. If your baby is not breathing or the heart rate is low:
   — Observe 5 to 10 seconds.
   — Determine whether the baby is breathing or if the heart rate is low.
   — Try gentle stimulation (by lightly touching back, check feet moving under blanket). If no response . . .
   — Try moderate stimulation (flicking feet or skin on chest, gently stroking or patting body). If no response . . .
   — Try vigorous stimulation (support head and rub body, slap bottom or feet or pinch).
4. If stimulation is successful and your baby is breathing, notify your physician of episode. If stimulation fails to return heart rate, breathing, and color to normal, begin CPR. (Do not leave the hospital with your baby without first having CPR instruction.)

continues

continued

— Contact nearest ambulance or rescue squad. **Do not stop CPR** for more than 5 seconds.
— Contact your physician. This can be done *after* receiving help.

MEDICATIONS

It may be necessary for your baby to take medication for the apnea in addition to having a monitor. The medication most often prescribed is theophylline. It is usually given in two doses daily, and it should be given with a feeding. Possible side effects of theophylline include a fast heart rate and vomiting. Your child's physician should be notified if these occur.

Your baby will need to have blood drawn periodically to test the level of theophylline in his or her blood.

HOW ABOUT THE PARENTS?

Taking a break and getting away from it all is important to the health of family and marriage. It is important for you to get out even for short periods of time occasionally. Because finding a babysitter, especially one trained in CPR, is often difficult, below are a few suggestions.

- Have dinner or visit at a friend's home. The monitor is very mobile and can easily be taken along.
- Go to a drive-in movie in warm seasons.
- Check your area for a mother's support group of babysitters who will care for babies on home monitors.
- Involve other family members in the care of your baby.

WHEN CAN THE MONITOR BE DISCONTINUED?

Below is a list of criteria commonly used to determine when your baby no longer requires home monitoring.

- No monitored events requiring vigorous stimulation or full resuscitation for 3 months.
- No real alarms or self-resolved apnea for 2 months.
- No apnea during stress challenge (febrile illness, immunizations).
- Normal pneumogram.

SOME COMMON QUESTIONS

Will My Baby Receive a Shock or Electrical Charge as a Result of Monitoring?

No. The electrodes only pick up and transmit signals to the monitor that are generated by your baby. Of course, as with all electrical appliances, the monitor should not be attached to your baby while being bathed.

continues

continued

Will the Monitor Have Adverse Effects on My Baby's Growth and Development?

No. The fact that your baby is on a home monitor will not effect growth. Any problems with growth and development could be related to circumstances at birth, a disease your baby has had, nutrition, present condition, and so forth.

What about Feeding My Baby?

There are no special tasks or considerations for feeding a baby on a home monitor. Some physicians suggest removing the monitor while feeding since you are going to be constantly observing your baby.

GLOSSARY

Apnea. Episode of cessation of breathing for 15 seconds or longer.

Bradycardia. A heart rate of less than 80 beats per minute for 10 seconds. (Normal for babies is 110 to 150 beats per minute.)

Periodic breathing. Three or more pauses in breathing of 3 seconds duration with a breath interrupting the apnea within a 20 second period. (Common in premature babies.)

Sudden Infant Death Syndrome. The sudden and unexpected death of a baby, for reasons that are unclear. It is the most common manner of death in the first year of life following the neonatal period.

Sleep pneumogram. Tracing or graphic record of respiratory movements.

High risk. A term sometimes used to describe a child who is felt to be susceptible to conditions that may lead to a life-threatening event.

Cyanosis. Bluish discoloration of skin caused by lack of oxygen in the blood.

Source: "Sharing Information: Infant Apnea Monitoring," East Tennessee Children's Hospital, © 1993. East Tennessee Children's Hospital publishes pamphlets on a variety of topics related to children's health. For more information contact the Child Health Education Center, East Tennessee Children's Hospital, 2018 Clinch Avenue, PO Box 15010, Knoxville, TN 37901; 615–541–8262.

Safety for Infants and Toddlers

SAFETY FEATURES FOR AN INFANT'S ROOM

- Room should be painted with a nontoxic paint.
- Crib features should be checked for safety.
  - Bars should be no more than 2⅜ inches apart.
  - Railing should be at least 26 inches higher than the lowest level of the mattress support.
  - Mattress should fit snugly into crib.
  - All surfaces should be smooth.
  - A bumper guard should be installed to protect infant from the hard railing.
  - Crib should be placed away from hot radiators or cold drafts.
  - Pillow should not be used in crib.
- Changing table should be sturdy, with a strap. (Even with a strap, never turn your back while changing diaper.)

CAR SAFETY

- Children under 40 lbs should be placed in a car seat.
- Everyone over 40 lbs should wear a seat belt with a shoulder harness.

HOUSE PLANTS

- Be aware that some house plants are poisonous:
  - caladium
  - narcissus
  - daffodils
  - holly berries
  - philodendron
  - poinsettia leaves

BATH SAFETY

- The water temperature should be checked carefully.
- An infant or a toddler should never be left alone in the tub.

TOY SAFETY

- Toys should always be appropriate for your child's age.
- Toys with buttons or objects that can easily be pulled off and swallowed should be avoided.
- Toys with sharp edges or breakable toys should be avoided.

continues

continued

FIRE SAFETY

- Children should never be allowed to play with matches.
- Place totfinder sticker in child's bedroom window.
- Home should have both smoke alarms and fire extinguisher.

EMERGENCY NUMBERS

- Keep emergency numbers of the fire department, police, poison control center, ambulance, and doctor next to phone.

PRECAUTIONS WHEN FEEDING AN INFANT

- Temperature of food or formula should be checked carefully before feeding.
- Infant should be kept in an upright position to prevent choking.
- An infant's bottle should never be propped, and the infant should never be left unattended with a bottle.
- Parents should learn Heimlich maneuver.

GENERAL HINTS TO PROMOTE A SAFE ENVIRONMENT

- Keep electrical cords away from infants and toddlers.
- Cover electrical outlets with a special plug device.
- Keep hot irons away from infants and toddlers.
- Block stairs with a securely fitting folding gate to prevent falls.
- Hook all cupboards that contain dangerous kitchen, laundry, or bathroom chemicals.
- Turn pan handles to the back of the stove to prevent children from pulling pans down.
- Keep hot or sharp objects well out of child's reach.
- Keep small objects that could be swallowed out of child's reach.
- Watch pets closely when they are around children.
- Never leave small children alone close to a pool or pond.
- Teach children not to talk to strangers or accept anything from strangers.

Source: Donna Meyers, *Client Teaching Guides for Home Health Care*, Aspen Publishers, Inc., © 1989.

Preventing Poisoning

Each year, thousands of children find and swallow poisons. We can work to prevent poisoning and treat it as quickly as possible.

Keep all dangerous products out of children's reach! At around eight months, babies begin to move about the home and explore. Before that time, dangerous household items should be moved to places your children can't reach.

- Place poisonous items on high shelves, not under sinks. Remember, in the bathroom, children can stand on toilets and sinks to reach a medicine cabinet.
- Keep these things out of reach: cleaning supplies, kerosene, birth control pills, medicine, vitamins, iron pills, paint, nail polish, soap, hair dyes, fertilizer, alcohol, mothballs, and plants.
- Get cabinet locks for cabinets that your child is able to reach. Some health departments offer these for free, but you can also buy them at discount, toy, or department stores.

Medicines and vitamins are especially dangerous because children like their bright colors, sizes, and shapes. They often think medicines and vitamins are candy. Iron tablets that many women take after pregnancy are also dangerous for children.

- Don't call medicines or vitamins "candy"; children will become more interested in taking them.
- If you keep birth control pills or any other medications in your purse, keep your purse out of your child's reach.
- If a medicine must be refrigerated, put it in a bag and keep it in the back of the refrigerator where children can't see or reach it.
- When grandparents visit, they may bring more medicines into the home. Take extra care.
- If your child does take medicine or vitamins that he or she is not supposed to, call the Poison Control Center immediately. Call the Poison Control Center *before* giving Ipecac syrup!
- Look at the dates on medicine and vitamin containers. Check expiration dates before using them. Medicines and vitamins should not be used after they expire. Flush old medicine down the toilet or put it in a trash can children can't reach.

Poisonings can be very scary, but they are usually treatable. PREVENT poisoning by keeping dangerous things out of children's reach!

Source: Luanne G. Gardner Sheaffer, MPA et al., *Child Development Health and Safety: Educational Materials for Home Visitors and Parents*, Aspen Publishers, Inc., © 1996.

Basic Steps of Pressure Sore Care

PREPARE

1. Wash hands with soap and water.
2. Get supplies: saline, irrigation equipment (syringe or other device, basin, large plastic bag); dressings and tape; disposable plastic gloves and small plastic (sandwich) bag; towel; glasses, goggles, and plastic apron (optional).
3. Move patient into comfortable position.
4. Place large plastic bag on bed to protect bed linen.

REMOVE DRESSING

1. Place hand into small plastic bag.
2. Grasp old dressing with bag-covered hand and pull off dressing.
3. Turn bag inside-out over the old dressing.
4. Close the bag tightly before throwing it away.

IRRIGATE SORE

1. Put on disposable plastic gloves. (Wear glasses or goggles and plastic apron if drainage might splash.)
2. Fill syringe or other device with saline.
3. Place basin under pressure sore to catch drainage.
4. Hold irrigation device one to six inches from sore and spray the sore with saline.
5. Use enough force to remove dead tissue and old drainage but not to damage new tissue.
6. Carefully remove basin so fluid doesn't spill.
7. Dry the skin surrounding the sore by patting skin with soft, clean towel.
8. After assessing and dressing the sore, remove gloves by pulling them inside out. Throw gloves away properly.

ASSESS SORE

1. Assess healing. As sore heals, it will slowly become smaller and drain less. New tissue at the bottom of the sore is light red or pink and looks lumpy and glossy. Do not disturb this tissue.
2. Tell health care provider if the sore is larger, drainage increases, the sore is infected, or there are no signs of healing in two to four weeks.

continues

continued

DRESSING THE SORE

Place a new dressing over the sore as instructed by the doctor or nurse. Remember to:

- Use dressings only once.
- Keep dressings in the original package or other closed plastic package.
- Store dressings in a clean, dry place.
- Throw out the entire package if any dressings get wet, contaminated, or dirty.
- Wash your hands before touching clean dressings.
- Do not touch packaged dressings once you touch the sore.

Notes:

Source: "Treating Pressure Sores," Consumer Version, Clinical Practice Guideline Number 15, U.S. Department of Health and Human Services, Public Health Service, Agency for Health Care Policy and Research, Rockville, Maryland, AHCPR Publication No. 95-0654, December 1994.

Cleaning Pressure Sores

Pressure sores heal best when they are clean. They should be free of dead tissue (which may look like a scab), excess fluid draining from the sore, and other debris. If not, healing can be slowed, and infection can result.

A health care professional will show you how to clean and/or rinse the pressure sore. Clean the sore each time dressings are changed.

Cleaning usually involves rinsing or "irrigating" the sore. Loose material may also be gently wiped away with a gauze pad. It is important to use the right equipment and methods for cleaning the sore. Tissue that is healing can be hurt if too much force is used when rinsing. Cleaning may be ineffective if too little force is used.

Use only cleaning solutions recommended by a health care professional. Usually saline is best for rinsing the pressure sore. Saline can be bought at a drugstore or made at home.

Caution: Sometimes water supplies become contaminated. If the health department warns against drinking the water, use saline from the drugstore or use bottled water to make saline for cleaning sores.

Do not use antiseptics such as hydrogen peroxide or iodine. They can damage sensitive tissue and prevent healing.

Cleansing methods are usually effective in keeping sores clean. However, in some cases, other methods will be needed to remove dead tissue.

RECIPE FOR MAKING SALINE (SALT WATER)

1. Use one gallon of distilled water or boil one gallon of tap water for five minutes. **Do not use well water or sea water.**
2. Add eight teaspoons of table salt to the distilled or boiled water.
3. Mix the solution well until the salt is completely dissolved. Be sure storage container and mixing utensil are clean (boiled).

Note: Cool to room temperature before using. This solution can be stored at room temperature in a tightly covered glass or plastic bottle for up to one week.

Source: "Treating Pressure Sores," Consumer Version, Clinical Practice Guideline Number 15, U.S. Department of Health and Human Services, Public Health Service, Agency for Health Care Policy and Research, Rockville, Maryland, AHCPR Publication No. 95-0654, December 1994.

Removing Dead Tissue and Debris from Pressure Sores

Dead tissue in the pressure sore can delay healing and lead to infection. Removing dead tissue is often painful. You may want to give your child pain-relieving medicine 30 to 60 minutes before these procedures.

Under supervision of health care professionals, dead tissue and debris can be removed in several ways:

- **Rinsing** (to wash away loose debris).
- **Wet-to-dry dressings.** In this special method, wet dressings are put on and allowed to dry. Dead tissue and debris are pulled off when the dry dressing is taken off. This method is only used to remove dead tissue; it is never used on a clean wound.
- **Enzyme medications** to dissolve dead tissue only.
- **Special dressings** left in place for several days help the body's natural enzymes dissolve dead tissue slowly. This method should not be used if the sore is infected. With infected sores, a faster method for removing dead tissue and debris should be used.

Qualified health care professionals may use surgical instruments to cut away dead tissue.

Based on your child's general health and the condition of the sore, the doctor or nurse will recommend the best method for removing dead tissue.

Notes:

Source: "Treating Pressure Sores," Consumer Version, Clinical Practice Guideline Number 15, U.S. Department of Health and Human Services, Public Health Service, Agency for Health Care Policy and Research, Rockville, Maryland, AHCPR Publication No. 95-0654, December 1994.

Dressings for Pressure Sores

CHOOSING DRESSINGS

Choosing the right dressings is important for pressure sore care. The doctor or nurse will consider the location and condition of the pressure sore when recommending dressings.

The most common dressings are gauze (moistened with saline), film (see-through), and hydrocolloid (moisture- and oxygen-retaining) dressings. Gauze dressings must be moistened often with saline and changed at least daily. If they are not kept moist, new tissue will be pulled off when the dressing is removed.

Unless the sore is infected, film or hydrocolloid dressings can be left on for several days to keep in the sore's natural moisture.

The choice of dressing is based on:

- the type of material that will best aid healing
- how often dressings will need to be changed
- whether the sore is infected

In general, the dressing should keep the sore moist and the surrounding skin dry. As the sore heals, a different type of dressing may be needed.

STORING AND CARING FOR DRESSINGS

Clean (rather than sterile) dressings usually can be used, if they are kept clean and dry. There is no evidence that using sterile dressings is better than using clean dressings. However, contamination between patients can occur in hospitals. When clean dressings are used in institutions, procedures that prevent cross-contamination should be followed carefully.

At home, clean dressings may also be used. Carefully follow the methods given below on how to store, care for, and change dressings.

To keep dressings clean and dry:

- Store dressings in their original packages (or in other protective, closed plastic packages) in a clean, dry place.
- Wash hands with soap and water before touching clean dressings.
- Take dressings from the box only when they will be used.
- Do not touch the packaged dressing once the sore has been touched.
- Discard the entire package if any dressings become wet or dirty.

CHANGING DRESSINGS

Ask your doctor or nurse to show you how to remove dressings and put on new ones. If possible, he or she should watch you change the dressings at least once.

continues

continued

Ask for written instructions if you need them. Discuss any problems or questions about changing dressings with the doctor or nurse.

Wash your hands with soap and water before and after each dressing change. Use each dressing **only once**. You should check to be sure the dressing stays in place when changing positions. After the used dressing is removed, it must be disposed of safely to prevent the spread of germs that may be on dressings.

USING PLASTIC BAGS FOR REMOVAL

A small plastic bag (such as a sandwich bag) can be used to lift the dressing off the pressure sore. Seal the bag before throwing it away. If you use gloves, throw them away after each use.

Notes:

Source: "Treating Pressure Sores," Consumer Version, Clinical Practice Guideline Number 15, U.S. Department of Health and Human Services, Public Health Service, Agency for Health Care Policy and Research, Rockville, Maryland, AHCPR Publication No. 95-0654, December 1994.

Pain, Infection, and Pressure Sores

Even if you care for your child's pressure sore properly, problems may come up. Pain and infection are two such problems. Pain can make it hard to move or to participate in care. Infection can slow healing.

MANAGING PAIN

Your child may feel pain in or near the pressure sore. If so, tell your doctor or nurse. Covering the sore with a dressing or changing your child's body position may lessen the pain.

If your child feels pain during cleaning of the pressure sore or during dressing changes, medicine may help. It may be over-the-counter or prescription medicine. Give medicine to relieve pain 30 to 60 minutes before these procedures to give it time to work. Tell your child's doctor or nurse if the pain medicine does not work.

TREATING INFECTION

Healing may be slow if the sore becomes infected. Infection from the sore can spread to surrounding tissue (cellulitis), to underlying bone (osteomyelitis), or throughout the body (sepsis). These serious complications demand immediate medical attention. If you note any of the signs of infection listed below, **call your child's doctor right away.**

SIGNS OF INFECTION

Infected Sore

- Thick green or yellow drainage
- Foul odor
- Redness or warmth around sore
- Tenderness of surrounding area
- Swelling

Widespread Infection

- Fever or chills
- Weakness
- Confusion or difficulty concentrating
- Rapid heart beat

Source: "Treating Pressure Sores," Consumer Version, Clinical Practice Guideline Number 15, U.S. Department of Health and Human Services, Public Health Service, Agency for Health Care Policy and Research, Rockville, Maryland, AHCPR Publication No. 95-0654, December 1994.

Checking Pressure Sore Treatment Progress

A health care professional should check pressure sores regularly. How often depends on how well the sore is healing. Generally, a pressure sore should be checked weekly.

EXAMINING THE SORE

The easiest time to check pressure sores is after cleaning. Signs of healing include decreased size and depth of the sore and less drainage. You should see signs of healing in two to four weeks. Infected sores may take longer to heal.

SIGNS TO REPORT

Tell your child's doctor or nurse if:

- the pressure sore is larger or deeper
- more fluid drains from the sore
- the sore does not begin to heal in two to four weeks
- you see signs of infection

Also report if:

- your child cannot eat a well-balanced diet
- your child has trouble following any part of the treatment plan
- your child's general health becomes worse

CHANGING THE TREATMENT PLAN

If any of these signs exist, your child's health care professional may need to change the treatment plan. Depending on your child's needs, these factors may be changed:

- support surfaces
- how often your child changes how he or she sits or lies
- methods of cleaning and removing dead tissue
- type of dressing
- nutrition
- infection treatment

continues

continued

OTHER TREATMENT CHOICES

If sores do not heal, your child's doctor may recommend electrotherapy. A very small electrical current is used to stimulate healing in this procedure. This is a fairly new treatment for pressure sores. Proper equipment and trained personnel may not always be available.

If your child's pressure sore is large or deep, or if it does not heal, surgery may be needed to repair damaged tissue. You and your child's doctor can discuss possible surgery.

Notes:

Source: "Treating Pressure Sores," Consumer Version, Clinical Practice Guideline Number 15, U.S. Department of Health and Human Services, Public Health Service, Agency for Health Care Policy and Research, Rockville, Maryland, AHCPR Publication No. 95-0654, December 1994.

First Aid for a Seizure

Knowledge of first aid is important. In the event of a seizure, the following procedures should be followed.

TONIC CLONIC (GRAND MAL)

- Ease child to the ground.
- Turn the head to the side to keep the airway clear of saliva.
- Loosen any tight clothing.
- Remove any sharp or hard objects (such as glasses or heavy furniture) that may injure the child.
- Do not force anything between the teeth or try to hold the tongue. (The tongue cannot be swallowed.)
- Do not restrain the child.
- Place something soft under the head.
- Call a physician immediately if the seizure lasts more than 10 minutes, if the child seems to be having multiple seizures, or if the child appears to be having trouble breathing.
- If the child falls asleep after the seizure, allow him or her to rest.
- Keep the child warm. (Remember, when the child regains consciousness, he or she will be confused, so it is best to provide support and privacy.)

COMPLEX PARTIAL (PSYCHOMOTOR)

- Speak to the child in a calm, reassuring voice.
- Do not restrain but gently guide the child from hazards.
- Remain with the child until he or she is completely aware of surroundings.

ABSENCE (PETIT MAL)

- Do not administer first aid, none needed.

Courtesy of Indiana State Department of Health, Indianapolis, Indiana.

Giving Medicine

IMPORTANT THINGS TO REMEMBER

There are five important things to remember about giving medicines to your child:

1. Give only the medicines that the physician approves. Check with the physician or nurse before giving medicines that you can buy *without* a prescription (called over the counter [OTC]). More than one medicine at a time can cause the different medicines to work more or less or differently, so it is very important for the physician to know about *all* the medicines you give to your child. Keep a list of all your child's medicines. It is a good idea to bring this list when you take your child to the physician.
2. Know the names of your child's medicines and what they are supposed to do for him or her (for example, make the fever go down, cure the infection, prevent an infection).
3. Know the possible side effects of the medicines. Ask your physician, nurse, or pharmacist. Report side effects to your physician right away (for example, rash, vomiting, diarrhea). If your child has a problem with a medicine be sure it is put in your child's record and always tell any new physicians that may see your child.
4. Be very sure about how much of each medicine to give. Check with your nurse or pharmacist about the exact amount and how to measure it. Even a small mistake could be dangerous in a small child.
5. Be sure to know how often to give the medicine and for how long. If your child takes more than one or two medicines, ask your nurse or physician to help develop a schedule. Some medicines must be taken exactly the same number of hours apart around the clock to keep the amount of medicine in the blood exactly right. Others only have to be taken during the time your child is awake. Some are better if given before or after meals. Sometimes your child will need to keep taking a medicine for a time after he or she is better in order to be completely better. Some medicines cannot be stopped suddenly. Always finish the medicine as taught by your nurse or physician.

MEASURING MEDICINES

Always wash your hands before starting.

Liquid Medicines

Liquid medicines are measured by:

- teaspoon
- tablespoon
- cubic centimeter (cc) or milliliter (mL)

continues

continued

Spoons

Always use a *measuring* spoon like the ones used for cooking. The spoons used to eat with are not the same and are not as accurate.

If a measuring spoon is not available ask your physician, nurse, or pharmacist to give you something to use for measuring, such as a medicine cup or syringe.

Syringes or Measuring Cups

Syringes are usually measured in cubic centimeters or milliliters. Syringes come in different sizes—1 cc, 3 cc, 5 cc, 10 cc, 20 cc, 30 cc, and 60 cc. There are special syringes that are used to give medicines by mouth. These syringes cannot be used with needles.

The smallest syringes (1 cc, 3 cc, and 5 cc) can be used to measure small amounts, even less than 1 cc. To be safe, have your nurse, physician, or pharmacist demonstrate how to measure with a syringe.

Medicine cups often have both teaspoons and tablespoons on one side and cubic centimeters and milliliters on the other side. Always hold the cup on a flat surface and keep your eye level with the cup to be sure the right amount is given.

Dropper

Some medicines come with their own dropper. To use it, squeeze the top, put the dropper in the medicine, and stop squeezing. The medicine will come up in the dropper. Hold it at eye level to be sure the medicine is at the right line. Do not switch droppers from one medicine to another because often the measurements are only for the medicine with which the dropper came.

Tablets and Capsules

Some medicines only come in capsules or tablets. If a child is able to swallow one, there is no problem. If your child cannot swallow the tablet or capsule, then the medicine must be given another way.

Tablets

Breaking Tablets. If your child has to take one-half of a tablet it might be possible to break it if it has a line on it. Tablets with lines are called scored tablets. The line is actually like a dent. Place a knife blade (carefully please) flat into the line and press down carefully. The tablet should break into two pieces. Tablets that are not scored are harder to break evenly. A pharmacist may need to prepare this medicine. Some coated tablets should not be broken. Check with your pharmacist.

Crushing Tablets. Many children can take tablets if they are crushed into powder. Check to make sure it is okay to crush it. One way to do this is to take a spoon, place the tablet in it, place another

continues

continued

spoon (bottom side down) onto it, and squeeze or push the spoons together. Be sure to get all the powder off the spoon. The powder can be mixed with something your child likes to eat or drink.

Capsules

Capsules can usually be opened and the powder or beads (which is actually the medicine) put into something your child will ingest. Be sure to **check with the pharmacist** that it is okay to open the capsule.

HOW TO MIX MEDICINES WITH FOOD OR DRINK

Both liquid medicine and powders can be mixed with drinks or food. Remember not to put the medicine into a large amount of liquid or food because if your child does not drink or eat the whole amount then he or she will not get all the medicine (for example, do not add medicine to a whole bottle or an entire bowl of cereal or fruit). Use a smaller amount (1 or 2 oz of juice, 1 or 2 tablespoons of food). Mix with food that is not essential to your child (for example, formula). Good things to mix with are juice, jelly, ice cream, applesauce, chocolate syrup, or other flavorful foods.

The taste of some medicines is very hard to cover up. If your child really hates the taste and will not take the medicine when mixed, you can call your nurse or physician. Perhaps the medication can be switched to something else.

GIVING MEDICINE TO BABIES AND CHILDREN

Babies and toddlers are the hardest to give medicine to because they do not understand why they must take it. Try to cover or change the taste first as already discussed. Then the baby may take the medicine easily from a bottle nipple or a spoon. Sometimes it is necessary to make your child take the medicine even when he or she does not want to.

Technique for Babies and Toddlers

Prepare and measure the medicine. Use a syringe or soft plastic dropper, or a spoon for medicine mixed in food. Sit in a firm comfortable chair. Place medicine within reach. Have a bib or towel on the child.

Take the child in your lap. If right handed, put the child in your left arm. Hold the child's left arm with your left hand. Put the child's right arm under your left arm around your back. Brace the child's head and shoulder between your left arm and chest so the head stays still. Tilt the head back a little. Put the medicine into the corner of your child's mouth toward the back along the side of the tongue (this location makes it harder for child to spit).

Give little amounts at a time to prevent choking and spitting. Gently keep mouth closed until the child swallows. Never yell or show anger. Speak softly and say kind things. When all the

continues

continued

medicine is finished, hold the child sitting up for a few minutes and cuddle and comfort. Offer the child water or juice.

Technique for Older Children

Older children want to please their parents but they need encouragement and little tricks to help them.

- Keep trying different foods to cover the taste until you find one that works.
- Offer the child a choice about what he or she wants it mixed with (or maybe he or she wants it straight), or what kind of spoon or cup or juice he or she wants.
- Encourage the child to take the medicine the way he or she prefers. Some children do best when they take a deep breath and drink fast. Others take it a step at a time with a drink in between. Sometimes it helps to count for your child while he or she takes it.
- Offer a reward such as a sticker or star or maybe even something good to eat afterward. The bad taste of some medicine can be cut by eating plain crackers afterward.
- Never ask your child whether he or she wants or will take the medicine. Instead be firm and state that he or she must take the medicine but offer as many choices as possible.
- Keep your explanations about why the medicine is needed as simple as possible. Connect taking the medicine not only to feeling better or having the body work better, but also to a desired activity or outcome (for example, being able to run races again or play a sport, or being able to look better or wear certain kinds of clothes).
- Get other loved ones to help, encourage, or reward your child.

You should be matter-of-fact about it but should also let your child know that you understand what a drag it is to have to take medicine. Some children will always resist taking medicine. Do not threaten, punish, hit, or yell at your child if he or she has a hard time taking medicine. This type of action will only make the situation worse and could make your child feel bad. Talk the problem over with your nurse, physician, or social worker.

PHARMACIES OR DRUG STORES

Try to find a pharmacy where the pharmacist is friendly and helpful. Parents should introduce themselves and their child to the pharmacist and explain about having a chronically ill child. Find out whether the pharmacy is open on weekends or at night or if the pharmacy can be opened in an emergency. Find out whether the pharmacist accepts Medicaid or insurance. Be friendly. Give your pharmacist some warning when low on a medicine that needs to be specially prepared. Remember, Medicaid pays the pharmacist very little for the medicines. Try to always pick up the medicines ordered.

The better you and your pharmacist know one another, the easier it will be. Ask your nurse or physician for the names of pharmacies that are helpful and friendly.

Source: *Caring for Your Child with HIV/AIDS*, Children's Hospital AIDS Program, Children's Hospital of New Jersey, Newark, New Jersey.

Pain Control

RULES ABOUT PAIN CONTROL

One of the difficulties in having a chronic illness is that it can cause pain or other uncomfortable symptoms. Often, in children pain is not recognized or treated. It is hard for adults to think about children being in pain so sometimes they pretend to themselves that children's pain is not that bad or it is not real at all. This approach is a mistake. We know that children feel pain and that we can help decrease or get rid of their pain altogether. There is no need for children to suffer. Parents, physicians, nurses, and social workers can work to help children. There are some rules about this to keep in mind.

- Children, even babies, can suffer from pain.
- When children say they have pain it means that they have pain. Very few children lie about having pain.
- Children who do not tell about their pain may still have pain but may not talk about it because:
  — They do not know how to express it.
  — They think grown-ups already know about the pain.
  — They are afraid they will have to go to the hospital or get a needle.
  — They do not know that anything can be done to get rid of the pain.
- Young children who cannot talk may show that they are in pain by:
  — crying more, being more irritable, and being harder to console
  — pulling away when touched or crying when moved, held, or lifted
  — making sad faces or twisting faces
  — becoming very quiet, less playful and active, more withdrawn, or eating less
  — seeming to be sad and depressed, or turning away from others
- Older children may become:
  — quiet, withdrawn, depressed, or less active
  — irritable, cranky, or argumentative
  — less cooperative with procedures and exams
  — more easily frightened
- Children experience different kinds of pain:
  — the pain from *procedures and treatments* (for example, blood drawing, IVs, and spinal taps)
  — *acute pain* from an infection or disease (for example, an ear infection)
  — *chronic pain* that is always there or that comes and goes (for example, headaches, abdominal pain, muscle spasm)

HOW CAN CHILDREN BE HELPED?

- Listen and watch carefully for the signs of pain.
- Believe a child who says that he or she has pain.

continues

continued

- Help your child tell the nurses and physicians about the pain
  — where it is
  — how much there is or how strong it is
  — what it feels like—sharp, dull, sore, aching, burning
  Tell the physicians and nurses the words the child uses to talk about pain
- Learn about ways to help your child that can be used with pain medication:
  — holding and being with your child
  — stroking the skin above or below the pain
  — using cold or ice packs, sucking on popsicles
  — distracting activities such as reading stories, listening to music, looking at pictures (especially during painful procedures)
  — performing relaxation exercises like deep breathing or imagining some pleasant memory
  — telling your child the truth about procedures; prepare your child ahead of time for painful procedures

MEDICINES FOR PAIN

There are also some important things to know about medicines used for pain.

- Different kinds of pain need different kinds of medicine.
- Each child needs his or her own amount of medicine to get rid of pain. The amount that works for one child may not work or may be too much for another child.
- Pain is best controlled by keeping the amount of pain medicine in the blood at a steady level. Thus for continuous pain, it is better to take the pain medicine every so many hours all the time than to wait for the pain to get bad and then give the medicine.
- Some pain medicines work for a time and then the child becomes tolerant to them, which means that he or she needs more medicine to get the same amount of pain relief. Tolerance is not the same thing as being addicted. A child with pain will not get addicted to medicine.
- Some pain medicines can cause sleepiness, dizziness, strange behavior, nausea, vomiting, constipation, or other symptoms in the beginning. Once your child's body gets used to the medicines, these side effects go away. If they do not, the amount of medicine can be changed so that your child is comfortable without those problems. Do not stop the medicine but do let the physician or nurse know.
- The best ways to give medicine to children are by mouth or through an IV. Children hate and fear shots (plus they hurt too) so this method is to be avoided, if possible. If a child has a lot of pain all the time it is possible to give a continuous IV infusion of medicine, using a pump.

continues

continued

TYPES OF PAIN MEDICINE

Mild Pain

For mild pain, nonnarcotic and nonsteroidal antiinflammatory drugs are available. Over-the-counter (without a prescription) medicines include:

- acetaminophen (Tylenol)
- ibuprofen (Advil)

Prescription medicines include:

- ibuprofen (Motrin)
- naproxen (Naprosyn)
- tolmetin

Remember, not all medicines are safe for young children. **Always** check with your child's physician before giving any medicines, even the ones sold in drugstores without a prescription.

Mild–Moderate Pain

- The same medicines listed for mild pain plus weak narcotics (opioids).
- Codeine can be given alone or together with acetaminophen (Tylenol). In addition to being a good pain killer codeine also gets rid of a cough.

Moderate–Severe Pain

- Narcotics (opioids)
  — morphine
  — methadone

Narcotics are extremely good at relieving pain. Many people fear using them because they do not understand these medicines. Some of the more common misconceptions people have about narcotics include:

- *Fear of addiction.* Narcotics cause physical dependency. If a narcotic is stopped suddenly after a child has taken the drug for some time, the child will have withdrawal symptoms (restlessness, runny nose, sleeplessness, irritability, tremors, nausea, diarrhea, muscle

continues

continued

pain). If the drug is decreased slowly, withdrawal is prevented. Children who take narcotics for pain can develop physical dependency but it is very rare for them to become addicted. Addiction is a psychological dependence, a desire to use the drug for other than medical reasons. Addiction is very different from physical dependency.

- *Safety.* Because one of the side effects of narcotics is the slowing down of breathing, people fear giving narcotics. However, when the amount that is given is correct this side effect does not occur. If it does occur it can be corrected by giving a medicine called Narcan.
- *Being "doped up" or sleepy.* When narcotics are first started, children sometimes are a little drowsy for 1 to 3 days. Once the body becomes used to the drug, this side effect goes away. The amount of drug given can also be changed so that the child does not have pain but is awake.

OTHER MEDICINES

There are other types of medicines that are usually used for other problems, but can be given with pain medicines. For example, Valium might be given to relax tight muscles or antidepressants might be given to decrease anxiety.

The most important thing to remember about your child's pain and discomfort is that it can be relieved. Your child does not have to suffer. You can be a partner with the physicians, nurses, and social workers in helping to keep your child comfortable.

Notes:

Source: *Caring for Your Child with HIV/AIDS*, Children's Hospital AIDS Program, Children's Hospital of New Jersey, Newark, New Jersey.

Medications for Attention Deficit Disorder with or without Hyperactivity

WHAT MEDICATIONS ARE USED?

Methylphenidate (Ritalin), dextroamphetamine (Dexedrine), and pemoline (Cylert) are the medications most commonly prescribed for attention deficit disorder with or without hyperactivity. These three drugs are all categorized as stimulants. On occasion, other medications are used, such as antidepressants (for example, desipramine and imipramine), sedatives, and antihistamines (for example, diphenhydramine). The following discussion deals only with stimulant medications.

HOW DO MEDICATIONS HELP ATTENTION DEFICIT DISORDER WITH OR WITHOUT HYPERACTIVITY?

It is always surprising to learn that stimulant medications can help a restless inattentive child. The stimulant medications basically help by stimulating a child to be more alert and to concentrate more on the task or activities of importance. The child would be less distracted by irrelevant sights and sounds. These drugs do not improve basic intellectual ability, academic skills, or coordination. However, if the child is more attentive, he or she may listen, look, and thus learn more effectively; the child may seem more coordinated because he or she will now be concentrating more carefully on the precise movements involved. Similarly, a child's social skills (particularly the ability to make and keep friends) may improve on medication because the child will be more observant of friends' interests and activities, and less likely to say or do something inappropriate.

WHAT CAN NOT BE EXPECTED FROM STIMULANT MEDICATION TREATMENT?

- *The stimulant medications do not correct learning disabilities.* A carefully planned specialized educational program is always indicated if learning disabilities or other learning problems exlst. However, stimulant medication may make a child more responsive to educational programs.
- *The stimulant medications do not correct problems with organization and systematic sequential planning.* Other procedures, such as calendars, color-coded notebooks, charts, reminders by school staff, would still be necessary. Again, medication may help a child to concentrate on these needs.
- *The stimulant medications do not correct motor planning problems (awkwardness) or visual perceptual problems (difficulty analyzing visual material).* An occupational therapy program would be a more appropriate resource for such difficulties.
- *The stimulant medications do not correct auditory processing problems* (difficulty remembering and interpreting what is heard). Language therapy and specialized educational

continues

continued

programs are more appropriate for auditory processing problems, although medication may help a child listen more carefully.

- *The stimulant medications do not usually correct inappropriate behaviors that have resulted from long-standing frustrations or inconsistent behavior management.* The stimulant medications also do not correct emotional disturbances. Counseling would be strongly indicated in these situations.

Improvement with stimulant medication does not prove that a child's difficulty is only an attention deficit disorder or that medication is essential. Medication should not even be considered until a child has had sufficient evaluation to determine the factors contributing to inattention. If there are significant emotional problems, medication should definitely not be an initial form of treatment. In addition, medication should not be considered until a child is in a suitable classroom environment, is involved with an appropriate behavior management program, and is receiving other indicated remedial services.

HOW IS THE EFFECTIVENESS OF MEDICATION DETERMINED?

Because stimulant medications are often used for several years, it is important to be sure that the medication is truly helping. The effects are easiest to assess when the child is in a regularly scheduled program. A suggested method is to have a teacher observe the child's behavior for several weeks, during which time different drug conditions (lower dose, higher dose, no medication) are tried; the teacher is asked to use a behavior checklist and is not informed of the specific drug condition. The parents also carefully observe their child during this period. In older children, where the simple use of any pill might have a positive effect, a placebo (inactive pill) might also be used during one of the trial periods.

After an effective dose is roughly determined, it is continued for several weeks and a decision is made about a daily schedule. Although some children do well on only one early morning dose each day, many children require two to three doses of medication each day. There are also long-acting preparations (given once per day), but they are not always successful.

WHAT ARE THE PROBLEMS WITH STIMULANT MEDICATIONS?

Stimulant medications are quite safe, but as with all drug therapy, there can be side effects.

Poor Appetite

Poor appetite is the most common side effect and often becomes less evident with time. However, some children will continue to have no appetite for lunch, although later gorging themselves when the effect of medication has worn off. It is best to give medication with or after breakfast so that the breakfast appetite is not adversely affected.

continues

continued

Some children, especially if a later dose is given, become very hungry after the regular evening meal is over. Some families adjust to this effect by having supper later than they ordinarily would. Others allow the child to take a large evening snack.

Sleep Problems

Some children may not sleep as well and others may sleep far better. There may be less side effect on sleep if a later afternoon dose is not given.

Reduced Growth Rate

Reduced growth rate is a rare side effect if the recommended doses are followed. When it occurs, "catch up" growth can be expected if the medication is discontinued for periods of time—such as during summer vacations.

Tics

Tics are involuntary movements of small muscle groups, often involving the face. It is a rare side effect but an important one. Stimulant medication should probably not be given, or given with extra care, if there is a family history of tics or if the child already has demonstrated tics. Some experts now believe that a combination of medications can be given when both attentional problems and tics require medical management.

Excessive Aloofness/Disinterest in the Environment

This effect often reflects a dose which is too high for that particular child. It is very important that this effect not persist because it would be counterproductive for the child, both at home and at school. On occasion, even lower doses will result in this effect. Then, other medications may need to be considered.

Excessive Fussiness/Resistance to Change

On occasion, a child on stimulant medication will become quite fussy and rigid in ways of performing. This effect will also be counterproductive and may require a decreased dose or trials of other medications.

Increased Pulse and Increased Blood Pressure

These effects have not generally been of significance. They usually occur, if at all, just shortly after administration of the medication.

continues

continued

WHAT ARE THE LONG-TERM EFFECTS OF THESE STIMULANT MEDICATIONS?

Although these drugs do help self-esteem and classroom performance, long-term studies still suggest that medication alone is not the answer. Specialized educational programs, appropriate behavior management techniques, and counseling all continue to be most essential.

These drugs are not addicting, and they have not been shown to lead to abuse of other drugs.

HOW LONG IS MEDICATION GIVEN?

When a child is first on medication, drug holidays should be considered on a regular basis, partly to determine if there is really a difference on and off of medication and partly to allow some drug-free time. Weekends, Christmas holidays, and summer vacations are times when medication might be omitted. However, therapy may also need to be continued during these periods if the child is participating in activities that require sustained attention, such as tutoring programs or Sunday school. In addition, the social skills of some children are significantly improved on medication, and it is therefore helpful for them to be on medication even when they are not in school.

It is essential that the efficacy of medication be reassessed at least annually. Reassessment can often be done by discontinuing medication for about 1 week during the school year without forewarning the teacher. Teacher observations are then requested at the end of the period off of medication.

Stimulant medications can be given through adolescence and even into adulthood. However, many adolescents and adults prefer not to take medication, and they may regulate their personal and work lives in such a fashion that their attentional problems are not too troublesome. For instance, they might avoid jobs that require sustained attention on one task.

HOW IS STIMULANT MEDICATION OBTAINED?

Stimulant medication is a controlled substance and must be prescribed by a physician. Prior to prescription of medication, a child's general physical health should be evaluated. A physician cannot renew stimulant medication by a telephone call to the druggist. Rather, the physician must communicate with the family and determine the physical and behavioral status of the child on medication. The physician is only permitted to prescribe a limited amount of medication at a time.

SUMMARY

Stimulant medications are appropriate drugs for children with attention deficit disorder. However, they require careful monitoring, and they are not a substitute for specialized education, behavior management programs, and counseling. Stimulant medications should never be considered unless a child has had an adequate physical, neurological, and developmental assessment. The effects of stimulant medication should be reassessed on a regular basis.

Courtesy of Joanna Dalldorf, MD, Developmental and Behavioral Pediatrics, Chapel Hill, North Carolina.

Toilet Training through Task Analysis

WHAT IS TASK ANALYSIS?

The close examination of a skill to discover exactly what movements are required to perform it independently is called task analysis. People task analyze a skill not only to discover whether or not a child is ready to learn it, but also to tell just exactly what will be taught. It is nearly impossible to teach something that cannot be described in detail.

Task analysis can be used for the basic skill of toilet training. First of all, for successful toilet training your child must have a few prerequisite skills. These three prerequisite skills are:

1. the ability to wait about 90 minutes between eliminations
2. the ability to follow simple directions ("Come here." "Sit down." "Stand up.")
3. the ability to sit down in a chair for about 5 minutes

WHAT ARE THE BASIC SKILLS?

When these skills have been demonstrated, the basics of toileting can be taught. Toileting is made up of a large number of skills. A task analysis of toileting would include the following 12 skills:

1. recognizing the need to go
2. holding back before eliminating (to have a chance to get over to the potty)
3. traveling to the bathroom
4. pulling the pants down
5. sitting on the toilet correctly
6. eliminating in the toilet
7. properly using toilet paper
8. pulling pants up again
9. flushing the toilet
10. washing hands correctly
11. drying hands
12. leaving the bathroom when finished

All of these skills are needed for independent toileting and must be learned by the child. Of course, some children will have to learn slightly different actions to accomplish each skill, especially if the child has a physical handicap. In addition, each of these major skills can be further broken down into smaller steps for actual teaching. For example, pulling the pants down is actually made of such movements as finding the fastener, grasping, unfastening, inserting the hands to hold the fabric of the pants, pulling down, letting go when the pants are lowered, and

continues

continued

so on. Some of the overall skills may already be performed before toilet training begins and won't have to be taught again, but they will have to be performed in the right place, at the right time, and in the right sequence.

MAKING TEACHING EASY

Once the teaching plan is made up, conditions can be arranged that more or less set up the teaching situation for success. It is important to remember to make teaching as easy as possible for both the parent and child. This is done by reducing possible sources of distraction, selecting rewards that will function as positive reinforcement for the behavior to be taught, and teaching in small steps that are easy for the child to learn successfully.

For toilet training, parents want to make the desired behavior of eliminating more likely to occur at the time selected for teaching. This objective is accomplished in at least two ways. The first way is to have a pretty good idea of the times the child normally eliminates. Parents can find out when the need to eliminate normally occurs by making an hourly recording of whether or not the child has dry pants and noting the actual time of wet pants for several days before training begins. Also, it helps to have regular feeding and snack times that don't change much from day to day. The record of dry pants checks will tell you if the child meets the prerequisite of adequate bladder and bowel control (the ability to hold back), as well as the best time to schedule training sessions. Another method is to give the child large amounts of liquids on the days chosen for training, and even to use liquids as positive reinforcement during the actual training. The increased fluid intake will increase the number of times the child will have to eliminate, which will in turn provide more frequent opportunities to teach the skill of toileting.

BEGINNING TRAINING

When training begins, the child should be praised or otherwise rewarded for dry pants when checks are made. Then, at times when it is known that the child will have to eliminate, the child should be guided to the toilet with an adequate number of intermediate prompts to ensure that the entire sequence of behavior occurs. Prompts would include simple, verbal instructions and physical help in guiding the child's hands in any of the movements required. Some people recommend having the child wear little or very simple clothing during the first teaching sessions to avoid delay and distraction associated with undressing. The child can be allowed to sit on the toilet for about 5 minutes. If the child eliminates, the behavior should result in immediate enthusiastic praise, hugs, liquids, and perhaps a favorite food as reinforcement. Afterward, the child should be given an opportunity for play. If the child has had a large amount of liquid, another opportunity to use the toilet may be possible in about 10 or 15 minutes, when the steps can be repeated.

continues

continued

If the child does not eliminate while sitting on the toilet, he or she should still be praised enthusiastically for good sitting every 2 minutes or so. If elimination has not occurred after 5 or 6 minutes, the child can be rewarded for good sitting (with praise and liquids) and prompted to leave the toilet to play for 10 or 15 minutes before another attempt is made. During the early stage of intensive training, the child would be allowed to play quite close to the toilet area.

As the training progresses, more clothing can be worn by the child, and the child can be allowed to play farther away from the toilet area. Help with the toileting behavior would gradually be withdrawn as the child begins to require fewer prompts. Successful toileting should still be followed by much praise and hugging, but liquids or foods would not normally be continued beyond the initial intensive stage of training.

The way to handle inappropriate toileting may vary according to your preference and the advice you have received from professionals. However, the rewarding praise and hugging should never be associated with accidents. If the child wets in his or her pants, cleanup should not be made into a pleasant experience; just complete it quickly and follow it with a chance to toilet appropriately as described above. Some professionals recommend rushing the child immediately to the toilet when an accident occurs, because the act of running tends to stop the flow of urine until the child can be seated on the toilet. Others recommend telling the child that wetting the pants is incorrect, having the child help with cleanup, and then practicing walking over to the toilet area, sitting a few minutes, and then repeating the sequence a few times with no praise or encouragement. The main thing to remember is that the consequence following incorrect toileting should be different and less pleasurable than the consequence provided following correct toileting.

There are a number of manuals available for parents to guide toilet training of their child. Most manuals begin with daytime training. Nighttime and bowel training usually take a bit longer to refine.

Notes:

Courtesy of James A. Mulick, PhD, Professor, Department of Pediatrics, Division of Psychology, College of Medicine, The Ohio State University, and the Children's Hospital, Columbus, Ohio.

Bladder Management—Spina Bifida/Spinal Cord Injury

It is important that you discuss with the urologist specific goals for the urinary management of your child. Two such goals are preserving renal (kidney) function and achieving dryness. Frequent, regular urological evaluation to check the status of the kidneys and bladder is necessary to maintain healthy, well-functioning kidneys. Familiarity with and prompt attention to the signs and symptoms of a urinary tract infection may help preserve function. Also important are encouraging a good intake of fluids, good hygiene, and cleanliness.

Give thought to when you would like to see the goal of dryness accomplished. If a child is dry by the early school-age years, he or she may avoid being labeled or teased. Such negative labels have a tendency to stick throughout the school years. Being out of diapers is important for other reasons as well. Self-esteem is raised, the skin in that area is easier to keep in good condition, and the child does not get used to the feeling or the odor of wet diapers.

Urinary continence (dryness) may not be reached at a 100 percent level. It is still important for your child to be out of diapers, even if he or she has to wear a pad because of dampness.

A stepped approach is used when considering what to do to achieve dryness. It may be that your child needs only to go through "toilet training" as other children do, without additional measures. If some help is needed, medications may be given that relax the wall of the bladder and/or tighten the urinary sphincter. If this is not effective, the urologist may recommend your draining the bladder by clean, intermittent catheterization (CIC) at regular intervals throughout the day. If the above has been tried and the result has been poor, surgery may be indicated. It is helpful if you discuss options with the urologist and plan a course of action to accomplish your goals for your child before he or she begins school.

SELF-CARE

As soon as your child is able to help, even in a small way, encourage his or her participation in his or her care. The child may be instructed to tell you as soon as his or her diapers are wet or soiled, to bring you the clean diaper, and later to help clean himself or herself and change the diaper completely. As the child becomes older, it will help if he or she becomes increasingly responsible for a portion of his or her care. This includes helping with catheterization and accomplishing this task by school age.

PRIVACY, MODESTY

Keep in mind your child's need for privacy and modesty. It is important to keep bladder and bowel management as normal as possible, and one way to promote this is to catheterize and change diapers in the bathroom or bedroom. Preventing undue exposure and instructing your child regarding who may touch him or her in that area (for example, parent, doctor, nurse) are important for the child's safety. From an early age, your child needs to know what are appropriate actions from caregivers.

Source: Marjorie Szor, MA, MS, RNC, Myelomeningocele Clinical Nurse Specialist, Spina Bifida Center, Medical College Hospitals, Toledo, Ohio, © 1992.

Bowel Management—Spina Bifida/Spinal Cord Injury

Bowel function is almost always affected in persons with spina bifida or spinal cord injury, because the nerves that control this function leave the spinal cord at a very low level (S_2, S_3, S_4). The movement of food and wastes through the digestive system (peristalsis) is not affected, but the internal message relay system is. Two sphincter muscles are important in bowel control. Normally, the *internal sphincter* detects the presence of stool in the colon (large intestine) and relays this message to the brain. It also relaxes and lets stool move further down. The *external sphincter* receives messages from the brain to "hold everything" or "let go." When spinal nerves are not functioning well, these messages do not flow efficiently. The bowel *can* be trained, but it takes longer to establish control with a neurogenic bowel.

It is desirable for social, behavioral, and physical reasons that a child be out of diapers by the time he or she enters school. Bowel training needs to be started early enough for this to be well established. There are recommended guidelines to follow, but much of the success depends on trial and error and on tailoring the program to the individual. What works for one child may not for another. Timing, laxatives and their dosages, and so forth may need frequent adjustments. It is important to start this when the child will be home for a period of time without interruptions (such as scheduled surgeries or vacations). Bowel training requires your undivided attention.

The goal of bowel management is to have stool of a soft, well-formed consistency that is evacuated in the toilet at the same time every day or every other day. There will not be a need for diapers, and accidents will occur less than once a week. This will be accomplished by school age.

A thorough, step-by-step plan is available. Contact your doctor or nurse when you are ready to begin. You will need help and encouragement.

The following suggestions for preparing yourself and your child can be followed for some time before you actually begin toilet training.

- From infancy on, keep a mental note of what foods influence the frequency and consistency of your child's stool.
- Work on maintaining a normal stool consistency by adjusting food and fluids. Do this with the help of your pediatrician, family doctor, or clinical nurse specialist.
- Change diapers as soon as they are soiled, so that your child does not get used to the odor. Have your child help with changing and cleaning up.
- Encourage the bowel to move at the same time every day by using digital stimulation, rectal pressure, and/or abdominal massage. Refer to your doctor or nurse for help with this.
- Allow your young child to follow the parent of the same sex into the bathroom, so the child will know what to do.
- Don't wait until your child says "I'm ready to be out of diapers now" to begin training. However, some degree of cooperation is needed, so be sensitive to this mood. Don't wait too long for the "perfect time." After several years in diapers, children come to accept this as routine. They are comfortable with diapers and have no desire to work hard on establishing another habit. They even develop "nasal fatigue" as their noses no longer detect the unpleasant odor from a soiled diaper. By this time, they may already be labeled and

continues

continued

teased by their classmates and avoided socially. It is wise to begin bowel training a couple of years before school attendance.
- Parental guidance and commitment is necessary.
- Treat bowel management as an *expectation*, just as you would with a child with normal nerve control.
- A positive attitude is absolutely necessary for success.
- Reward your child with words of encouragement or special privileges, or use a star chart when the child sits on the toilet at the same time each day without complaining.
- Make this a pleasant time, perhaps by telling a special story or making it into a game.
- Avoid hassles, struggles, and negative feelings. Emphasize that sitting on the toilet is a normal action that is expected of your child, and that this is part of the process of growing up.
- Establish basic habits with your child:
  - Serve foods high in fiber daily. Know the list well. If your family is accustomed to white bread and flour, which are very poor in fiber and other nutrients, change to whole-grain breads, flours, and cereals when your child is still an infant. Children accept what they grow up with.
  - Make sure your child drinks plenty of fluids. Know the amount expected for the weight of the child.
- Have your child sit on the toilet at the same time each day after a meal (scheduled toileting). Never vary this time. The child's feet should rest on something solid, and he or she should be taught to bear down or push.
- Know what influences the bowels to move:
  - High-fiber foods
  - Fluids
  - Scheduled toileting
  - Exercise, activity
  - Eating
  - Certain medications
- Keep written records for a few weeks before starting to train. Notice correlations between mealtime and time of having a stool, as well as the consistency of the stool after your child eats certain foods. Look for correlations between medications and your child's stool pattern.

A strict regimen is necessary. There are many possible techniques to try, however. Help is available. Contact your doctor or nurse whenever you need someone to talk to about this and certainly when you start training in earnest. A written bowel-management program is available.

With some children, use of a star chart works well. Such a chart provides motivation and a positive, visual record of behavior and progress. This reward system can be used to make changes in other behavior and habits, as well.

Bowel management is an important part of your child's life, and it will take time and effort to find and maintain a workable program. Encourage yourself and your child. Have on hand plenty of patience, humor, consistency, and optimism. There are no easy solutions to neurogenic bowel control, but with a positive attitude it can be done!

Source: Marjorie Szor, MA, MS, RNC, Myelomeningocele Clinical Nurse Specialist, Spina Bifida Center, Medical College Hospitals, Toledo, Ohio, © 1992.

Influences on Bowel Management

INFLUENCE	REASON	YOUR ACTION
Timing	Toileting at same time every day trains the bowel.	Establish a regular time for toileting. This is most important. Strict timing trains the bowel. Use one or more of the following: • Stool softener (6 to 12 hours before bowel time) • Stimulant cathartic (time period varies) • Digital stimulation (at time of bowel movement) • Enema (only if necessary) Eating
Food stimulates	a reflex to have a bowel movement.	Eat meals at regular times. Include a warm drink.
Fluids	Fluids affect the consistency of the stool.	Take more than the minimum requirements of liquids each day.
Foods	Diet affects the consistency of the stool.	Include plenty of foods high in fiber.
Medicines	Some medicines affect movement of the stool.	Be aware of the action on the bowel of: • iron preparations—constipation • narcotic pain meds—constipation • laxatives—loose stools • antibiotics—loose stools
Activity	Exercise increases bowel activity.	Plan for daily periods of vigorous exercise.

Source: Marjorie Szor, MA, MS, RNC, Myelomeningocele Clinical Nurse Specialist, Spina Bifida Center, Medical College Hospitals, Toledo, Ohio, © 1992.

Bowel Management and Fluids

It is very important to drink enough liquids each day to make the stool soft enough to be passed easily. This is especially true if bulk-forming laxatives or very high-fiber foods are eaten. Most people don't realize how much fluid needs to be taken daily. The following is a guide. Your child should take *more* than is listed if he or she is constipated, is eating very high-fiber foods, or is taking bulk-forming laxatives.

Birth to 22 pounds	4¼ measuring cups (33 oz.)
23 to 44 pounds	4 measuring cups (32 oz.)—in addition to fluid in food
45 to 99 pounds	6 measuring cups (48 oz.)—in addition to fluid in food
100+ pounds	7 measuring cups (56 oz.)—in addition to fluid in food

Notes

Source: Marjorie Szor, MA, MS, RNC, Myelomeningocele Clinical Nurse Specialist, Spina Bifida Center, Medical College Hospitals, Toledo, Ohio, © 1992.

My Child Has an Ostomy

Child's Name _____   Date_____

My child, _____, has an ostomy. This handout contains information about ostomy surgery, the care that ostomies require, and other information that might be helpful while my child is in your care.

WHAT IS AN OSTOMY?

An *ostomy* is a surgical opening in the abdomen through which waste material is discharged when the normal function of the bowel or bladder has been lost. There are three basic types of ostomies. An ileostomy is an opening from the small intestine (ileum portion), and a *colostomy* is an opening from the large intestine (colon). Both types discharge feces. A *urostomy* is an opening to bypass the bladder and discharge urine. My child has _____.

WHAT CAUSES OSTOMY SURGERY?

Among the reasons for ostomy surgery for children are birth defects (such as spina bifida, exstrophy of the bladder, imperforate anus, etc.), ulcerative colitis, Crohn's disease, polyposis, malignancy, injury, and nerve damage or malfunction. The reason for my child's surgery was _____ _____.

WHAT DOES THE OSTOMY LOOK LIKE?

An ostomy is fashioned by bringing the opened portion of the remaining intestine or urinary outlet through the abdominal wall. It is red, and some people compare it to a rosebud because of the size and color, and because it has brought new life to the child. The technical term for it is stoma.

HOW IS THE OSTOMY CARED FOR?

The care and management of the ostomy depend on which type it is. Ileostomates, urostomates, and some colostomates can no longer control the particular type of elimination, but they can manage the discharge. In such cases, the ostomate wears a plastic or rubber collecting pouch, called an appliance, adhered to the abdomen at all times to protect the skin and collect the output. The appliance is emptied through a bottom opening at the ostomate's convenience. Some colostomies can be controlled by irrigation (enema) and only require a small gauze pad or plastic stick-on pouch to cover the stoma between irrigations. My child's method of management is as follows:

_____
_____
_____
_____

continues

continued

WHAT SHOULD I DO IF THE CHILD'S APPLIANCE COMES LOOSE OR BEGINS TO LEAK?

Some children can take care of their own appliances; others may need assistance. If my child's appliance needs removal and changing:

_____

_____

_____

_____

CAN THE CHILD CARE FOR THE OSTOMY OR IS HELP NEEDED?

_____

WHEN SPEAKING TO THE CHILD, HOW DO I REFER TO THE CHILD'S OSTOMY OR APPLIANCE?

Some children devise a cute name for the stoma, and some children simply call it "my ostomy" or "my appliance." My child calls it:

_____

_____

IS THE PHYSICAL ACTIVITY OF THE CHILD OSTOMATE LIMITED IN ANY WAY?

Most children who have an ostomy can participate in the normal activities of school or camp situations with the exception, in most cases, of harsh physical contact. Sometimes a child might have another problem, such as an orthopedic condition that may limit physical activities. However, the ostomy itself poses no limitations with the exception of rough contact sports. Otherwise, the child can swim, play ball, or take part in any activity chosen. My child has the following limitations:

_____

_____

DOES OSTOMY REQUIRE ANY SPECIAL MEDICATION FOR THE CHILD?

The ostomy itself does not require special medication, but some children may need to take medication, just as other children may need medication for a particular reason.

My child takes _____.

The prescribed dosage is _____.

continues

continued

I hereby give permission for _____ to administer the above medication to my child while in the care of the above named person(s).

_____   _____
(Signature of Parent)   (Date)

_____
(Prescribing Physician)

DOES THE CHILD REQUIRE A SPECIAL DIET?

The diet of the child who has an ostomy is usually not limited. However, sometimes certain foods need to be avoided because they may cause gas or odor. The foods that my child should avoid are:

_____

_____

WHAT ABOUT TAKING SHOWERS OR BATHING?

An ostomy does not preclude cleanliness and proper hygiene. However, sometimes a child who has an ostomy may feel embarrassed or shy about undressing in front of classmates or campmates who do not know about the ostomy. If my child expresses this feeling do not compel him or her to do so. Arrange a separate time or place for bathing. Allow the child to take the initiative in the matter of joining the group. In my child's case:

_____

_____

_____

WHAT SHOULD I DO ABOUT EMERGENCIES?

Follow the normal procedure for any emergency with any child. Contact me immediately by calling me collect at telephone number _____ or getting in touch with me at

_____.

If I am not available immediately, contact qualified medical help at once. Do not remove the appliance, except as described previously, or otherwise tamper with the ostomy without direction from myself or a physician. Special instructions are:

_____

_____

_____

_____

continues

continued

I hereby give my permission for _____
to seek and receive emergency medical or dental care for my child, _____,
during the time period of _____ to _____ .

_____   _____
(Signature of Parent)   (Date)

Our physicians' names and phone numbers are:_____
_____

Insurance information (if not covered by camp or school insurance) is:_____
_____

WHAT ELSE SHOULD I KNOW ABOUT CHILD OSTOMATES?

Please keep in mind that the child ostomate is first a child and second an ostomate. All children want to be included in the gang. Please treat my child as any other child, including discipline. Some teachers and counselors may be tempted to "go easy" on a child because of an ostomy. While this attitude is very kind, it can cause resentment among the other children in the group.

Also, keep in mind that ostomy surgery is not shameful, but sometimes the child may feel shy about it. My child might even be reluctant to discuss the ostomy, but if it is necessary to talk about it, take my child aside or choose a time when friends or classmates are not present. My child may not wish to let others hear about the ostomy until he or she knows them better. Respect these wishes and my child will be happier.

If a child with an ostomy is to stay overnight, special arrangements are sometimes needed for the child's comfort. Arrangements may include night drainage tubing for the child with a urostomy and plastic sheets. Special instructions for my child are:

_____
_____
_____

Source: Susan Hamilton, "My Child Has An Ostomy," United Ostomy Association, Inc., Irvine, California, 1–800–826–0826, © 1974.

Bathing and Toileting Concerns and Suggestions

Concerns	Suggestions
1. Making the bathtub area safe is of great importance. Most of these suggestions can be done easily. Special grab bars and seats are available for children with neuromuscular problems through catalogues, drug-stores, or medical supply companies.	• Use nonskid mats or strips in and around the bathtub and floor to decrease chances of slipping. • Purchase or make faucet covers to protect the child from accidental bumps. • Use safety rails and grab bars, transfer benches, tub seats, foam pads, shower chairs, bath pillows, etc., as needed. • Do not make the water too hot or cold. Besides any skin or thermoregulation changes that may occur, muscle tone is greatly affected by temperature and may make management of the child more difficult. • Choose tub toys carefully. Watch for mouthing of toys or soaps. • Don't *ever* leave the child alone in the bathtub. Monitor the water level as well. • Use "no tears" shampoos and soaps. • Use soap on a rope or wash mitts with soap holder pockets, or place soap in a nylon stocking that has one end tied to a fixed point so that soap does not get lost in the bathtub area.
2. Lifting, carrying, transferring, and/or holding a child for bath care can be a physical strain on the caregiver. Always follow good principles of body mechanics. Making the transition into and out of the water smoothly is important for both you and the child.	• Keep the child "collected." • Use special bath seats as needed. They can help main-tain a good seating posture to control tone and still leave a hand free for washing. They may also raise the child, reducing the amount of leaning or bending over into the tub. • Use an extended shower hose to ease washing and rinsing care. • Use a short stool to sit on during bath time. • Use transfer aids for bath time (for example, hydraulic or pump lifts and chairs, transfer benches). • Control the child's tone. Keep the child close. Do not lean over with the load. Bend knees and let the legs do the work. Half-kneeling may be a more comfortable transition position for you while transferring the child in and out of the tub. • Prepare the environment and the child. Have everything where you want it and within reach.

continues

continued

Concerns	Suggestions
3. Stimulating the senses can affect autonomic functions, behavior, and motor tone and control. The hypertonic child may become more spastic, or the hypotonic child may become more flaccid.	• Keep the water temperature moderate. • Try keeping the baby/child wrapped in towel or a T-shirt during the transition into the water. These can be removed and replaced as tolerated or needed during bathtime. • Have towels ready that are large enough for wrapping the child up. • Rub hands over the towel-wrapped body—rubbing the towel over the body may be too much stimulation. This action also helps maintain body warmth. Change to a dry towel to avoid chilling.
4. Training children with disabilities in toileting may require following a specialized program. Whatever method is used for bowel and bladder care, the toilet area must be a safe environment as well. Please consult an enterostomal nurse for specialized bowel and bladder concerns.	• Fasten or place safety rails over the standard toilet. • Make sure the feet are supported. • Use child-sized commodes with attachable positioning aids, safety bar, foot rests, and head supports. • Get assistance from occupational and physical therapists regarding the amount and types of support needed. • Use deflection shields for toilet seats or urinals; they can also be used for boys who will not be standing up.

Notes:

Source: Nancy J. Harris and Jill K. Martindale, "Physical Therapy and Occupational Therapy Interventions," in *Pediatric Home Care*, Patricia A. McCoy and Wendy L. Votroubek, eds., Aspen Publishers, Inc., © 1990.

Day Care Checklist

Name of Center or Family Day Care Provider

Address

Telephone Number   Date Visited

Instructions: *When you visit a child care program, take this checklist with you. Place a check mark in the "Yes" or "No" column for each item you observe. Compare the results of your checklists for each program you visit to see which program has the greatest number of checks in the "Yes" column. In addition, you should be able to answer "Yes" to the following questions about the day care setting that is your final choice:*

- *Do you feel that being in this setting will be a happy experience for your child?*
- *Do you feel that you will be able to develop a relaxed, sharing relationship with the provider?*

THE CARE PROVIDERS

Yes	No	
☐	☐	Is there a current license for operating a family day care home or day care center conspicuously posted?
☐	☐	Are there enough adults for the number and age of children?
☐	☐	Do the children receive the individual attention, warmth, and understanding that you would like for your child?
☐	☐	Are the children encouraged to make friends with other children?
☐	☐	Are the children happy and playing with each other? Talking to each other? Talking to adults?
☐	☐	Do caregivers recognize when a child is sad or upset or excited?
☐	☐	Do caregivers refrain from embarrassing any child?
☐	☐	Is an effort made to listen to and answer children's questions in ways they can understand?
☐	☐	Is discipline handled in a positive manner?
☐	☐	Do adults supervise the children at all times during naptime? If a child does not fall asleep, is the child engaged in a quiet activity?
☐	☐	Do you sense that the caregiver feels good about being with children? Has a sense of humor and enthusiasm?
☐	☐	Does the caregiver participate in training opportunities in child care child development?

continues

continued

HEALTH AND SAFETY

Yes   No

☐ ☐ Are sanitary arrangements made for diapering activities?

☐ ☐ Is the area for program activities well lit and ventilated?

☐ ☐ Are the indoor and outdoor spaces for children safe and free of hazards? (For example, radiators covered; stairways protected; windows protected; electrical outlets covered with safety caps; walkways free of ice and snow; outdoor space fenced and free from debris, broken glass, and so forth.)

☐ ☐ Are heavy pieces of furniture, such as storage shelves and bookcases, secure and stable so that they cannot tip over?

☐ ☐ Are detergents, household cleaners, and medicines kept in locked storage cabinets?

☐ ☐ Are smoke detectors and fire extinguishers provided?

☐ ☐ Are emergency fire drill and evacuation procedures posted in a conspicuous place in each room; and are emergency telephone numbers on each telephone?

☐ ☐ Are toys and equipment clean and in good repair (for example, free from sharp edges, splinters, paint chips, and loose parts)?

☐ ☐ Do caregivers get annual physical examinations?

☐ ☐ Is a written health record kept for each child?

☐ ☐ Are there written procedures for securing background checks on new caregivers?

☐ ☐ Are first aid supplies readily available and does at least one person have a current Red Cross first aid certificate?

☐ ☐ Does a registered nurse visit at least weekly in programs for children under 3 years old?

☐ ☐ Are there written procedures for reporting suspected cases of child abuse and neglect by parents or staff?

☐ ☐ Is there an adult responsible for receiving children when they arrive each day?

☐ ☐ At the end of the day, will your child be released to another person only if you have given written permission for this?

☐ ☐ Are there written procedures to follow when a child becomes sick?

☐ ☐ Is there a clearly written financial policy regarding a child's absence due to sickness or other causes?

☐ ☐ Are the meals and snacks prepared by the caregiver:

— sufficient to meet the needs of your work schedule?

— nutritious, attractive, and planned for the children served?

— inclusive of food items reflecting the children's age and cultural background?

continues

continued

Yes   No

— planned so that the children can be involved in meal and or snack preparation and cleanup?

— suitable to meet the needs of children on special diets?

☐   ☐   Is the area that is used for food preparation and eating clean?

☐   ☐   Do the caregivers eat with the children?

ENVIRONMENT

Yes   No

☐   ☐   Do the caregivers respect the children's rights to engage in activities by themselves and with other children?

☐   ☐   Is the space arranged so that children can freely select materials according to their own interests and abilities, and return them when they have finished?

☐   ☐   Do you hear adults in the program giving praise and encouragement to children to enhance their self-confidence?

☐   ☐   As you see children participating in the program, do they seem to be enjoying the activities?

☐   ☐   Do the caregivers help the children learn from a variety of activities?

☐   ☐   Is the program well supplied with equipment and supplies such as blocks, books, games, toys, and creative art materials?

☐   ☐   Is the space neat, clean, and attractively decorated?

☐   ☐   Is there space for active play and for quiet play?

☐   ☐   Is there a place for each child's personal belongings?

☐   ☐   Is there a special place away from the busy activities for a sick child to rest and yet allow for the caregiver to care for him or her?

☐   ☐   Can children reach the toilet and sink easily and safely?

PARENTS

Yes   No

☐   ☐   Did the caregiver adequately explain the program to you?

☐   ☐   Did the caregiver ask you about your family's cultural and language background so that activities can be planned that recognize each child's culture?

☐   ☐   Will the caregiver provide you with information on a regular basis about your child's activities and progress?

continues

continued

Yes   No

☐   ☐   Will opportunities be provided for you to be involved in making decisions about the program and your child's education?

☐   ☐   Were you encouraged to visit and observe the program at any time while your child is participating?

☐   ☐   Does the program give community resource information to parents and invite them to participate in educational activities?

☐   ☐   Is there a copy of the plans for children's daily activities available for parents?

☐   ☐   Will trips to local stores, building sites, parks, library, etc., be adequately supervised? Will your written permission be obtained for each trip?

Notes:

Source: *A Parent's Guide to Day Care*, New York State Department of Social Services, Albany, New York.

Making Your Yard and Garage Accessible

OUTDOORS

- Are walkways clear and wide enough to accommodate wheelchairs or walkers?
- Is there a ramp?
- Are doors at least 32 inches wide?
- Do sliding glass doors have low thresholds?
- Are railings installed on both sides of the front steps?
- Does the front door have a lever door handle rather than a doorknob?
- Is there a single-action deadbolt lock on the inside of the front door?
- Is the walkway/porch area well lighted?
- Is the mailbox in a location that makes it easy to retrieve mail?

GARAGE

- Is the garage wide enough to accommodate a wheelchair exiting from a van, or will the child have to get out of the van outdoors?
- Is the garage entrance high enough for a van?
- Is there an automatic garage door opener?
- Are the thresholds in the garage designed for wheelchairs, walkers, or children with limited mobility?

Note: The strategies above are for caregivers to use in modifying single-family, owner-occupied homes. If you live in public housing, contact your property manager to determine whether modifications can be made. If the public housing is federally subsidized, you may have certain rights under the Fair Housing Act. For more information, contact the Department of Housing and Urban Development (HUD).

Notes:

Source: "Assistive Technology and Home Modifications for Individuals with Disabilities," STAR Program, A System of Technology to Achieve Results, St. Paul, Minnesota.

Making the Indoors Accessible—General

- Are switches and thermostats located 44 inches from the floor for easy access?
- Do the switches have locator lights in them, for finding the switch in the dark?
- Can electrical outlets be placed at least 27 inches from the floor, to minimize bending?
- Will carpeting allow easy navigation with a wheelchair or walker? Is it securely fastened to the floor? (You may want to remove throw rugs, which can get in the way of wheelchairs, crutches, and walkers.)
- Do stairs have a sturdy, grippable hand rail and bannister?
- Is carpeting in good repair and tightly secured to the steps?
- Have ceiling lights been replaced with wall lights, to make it easier to replace light bulbs?
- Have light bulbs been replaced with long-life bulbs? (You might consider investing in a light-bulb changer, available at most hardware stores.)
- Do floor and table lamps have switches that are activated by touch or sound?
- Are smoke detectors installed low enough to allow ease in changing batteries, but high enough to provide proper protection?
- Is there a good location in which to keep a rechargeable flashlight in case of a power failure?
- Do doors have lever handles instead of round doorknobs?
- Are doorways at least 32 inches wide? If not, check to see whether doors can be mounted with swing-clear hinges. This will eliminate the need to tear out doorjambs and widen doorways.

One item that's a good idea in every room of the house is a personal security device that will provide help if someone falls or needs emergency assistance. There are a number of these devices on the market. Some, when activated, make a phone call to a central location that can dispatch help. Others are programmed to ring the home at prearranged times during the day; if the phone is not answered, emergency personnel are sent to the house.

Note: The strategies above are for caregivers to use in modifying single-family, owner-occupied homes. If you live in public housing, contact your property manager to determine whether modifications can be made. If the public housing is federally subsidized, you may have certain rights under the Fair Housing Act. For more information, contact the Department of Housing and Urban Development (HUD).

Source: "Assistive Technology and Home Modifications for Individuals with Disabilities," STAR Program, A System of Technology to Achieve Results, St. Paul, Minnesota.

Making Your Kitchen Accessible

- Do shelves roll out to minimize bending?
- Is there adequate storage space? (If not, you may want to modify a broom closet into an easily accessible pantry.)
- Does at least one shelf have cutouts that can hold bowls securely for one-handed stirring, at a level convenient to a child who is seated?
- Is there a scorch-proof shelf near the oven?
- Is lighting adequate and directed over the work areas?
- Do can openers, vegetable peelers, and other kitchen utensils have easy-grip handles?
- Is the sink easily accessible? (Some sinks have sloped fronts so that dishes can be slid into them. In addition, long-handled lever faucets and spray nozzles simplify dishwashing.)
- Does the refrigerator have a side-by-side refrigerator-freezer setup or a freezer on the bottom for easy access?
- Are burner controls mounted on the front of the stove, to eliminate the risk of burns from reaching over a heating element?
- Are fire extinguishers easily reached, lightweight, and easy to use?
- Do dishwashers, microwaves, washers, and driers have adequate labels for their settings? (Some manufacturers will provide Braille or tactile labels, or customized knob turners, on request.)

Besides these fairly major modifications, there are many inexpensive "tricks of the trade" that allow easier maneuvering in the kitchen:

- A small mirror mounted over the range allows seated cooks to see into the pans on back burners.
- Unbreakable glass pots let seated cooks see how the food is cooking.
- Clothespins can be attached to burner knobs to make turning easier, and can also be used to secure pots on a range so that one-handed stirring is possible.
- An old-fashioned potato masher or slotted spoon can be used to turn knobs on a clothes dryer.
- Tongs can help get cans or boxes off cabinet and refrigerator shelves.
- Oven rack handles can help cooks in wheelchairs or who have limited reach.
- A cart can be used to minimize carrying.

Note: The strategies above are for caregivers to use in modifying single-family, owner-occupied homes. If you live in public housing, contact your property manager to determine whether modifications can be made. If the public housing is federally subsidized, you may have certain rights under the Fair Housing Act. For more information, contact the Department of Housing and Urban Development (HUD).

Source: "Assistive Technology and Home Modifications for Individuals with Disabilities," STAR Program, A System of Technology to Achieve Results, St. Paul, Minnesota.

Making Your Bathroom Accessible

The bathroom presents challenges for safe modifications, to prevent falls and eliminate the hazards of using electrical appliances around water. In addition, privacy and dignity need to be considered along with accessibility and safety.

- Is the bathroom located in an accessible area of the home?
- Is the entry door adequate? (If the doorway is too narrow, sliding doors can add needed space. These doors recess into the wall and don't get in the way. A bathroom door also can be relocated—for instance, the wall of an adjoining closet can be knocked out to create a new doorway.)
- Will a commode or shower chair fit in the shower?
- Is a sturdy seat installed in the shower?
- Are grab bars around the toilet and tub?
- Is there a grab bar over the tub to assist the child in getting up and down?
- Is the faucet hardware easy to operate, with easy-to-turn knobs or levers?
- Does the shower have an antiscald mixer?
- Do the wet surfaces have antislip material?
- Can a wheelchair pull right up to the sink?
- Do combs, hair brushes, and toothbrushes have easy-grip handles?
- Does the linen closet or cabinet have adequate storage space? (You may want to consider installing extra shelves or organizers.)
- Are the electrical outlets located away from the sink and bathtub, to minimize the risk of electric shock?
- Is there a telephone or emergency alert device in the bathroom?

Note: The strategies above are for caregivers to use in modifying single-family, owner-occupied homes. If you live in public housing, contact your property manager to determine whether modifications can be made. If the public housing is federally subsidized, you may have certain rights under the Fair Housing Act. For more information, contact the Department of Housing and Urban Development (HUD).

Source: "Assistive Technology and Home Modifications for Individuals with Disabilities," STAR Program, A System of Technology to Achieve Results, St. Paul, Minnesota.

Making Your Living Room Accessible

- Are windows easy to open? (Windows that tilt out at the base making opening easy, and help keep out rain.)
- Do the TV and VCR have remote controls?
- Is a cordless phone installed? (This can be an important safety and communications device for children with mobility impairments.)
- Are phone jacks and phones installed throughout the house for safety and security?
- Are there remote control devices to allow control of appliances and lights from another room? (For instance, these devices can be used to turn lights on before entering a room.)
- Is there an intercom at the front door? (Another useful device is a wireless doorbell, which can be carried from room to room to ensure that ringing is heard.)

Note: The strategies above are for caregivers to use in modifying single-family, owner-occupied homes. If you live in public housing, contact your property manager to determine whether modifications can be made. If the public housing is federally subsidized, you may have certain rights under the Fair Housing Act. For more information, contact the Department of Housing and Urban Development (HUD).

Notes:

Source: "Assistive Technology and Home Modifications for Individuals with Disabilities," STAR Program, A System of Technology to Achieve Results, St. Paul, Minnesota.

Making the Bedroom Accessible

- Is the bed the right height for a minimally assisted wheelchair-to-bed transfer?
- Can lamps near the bed be turned on with a touch of the lamp base?
- Do closet lights turn on automatically when the door is opened?
- Are clothing rods easily adjustable for height?
- Are curtains of the easy-gliding type, rather than curtain rods and drawstrings?
- Is there a bedside caddy to keep magazines and other items within easy reach?
- Is there a phone next to the bed?
- Is the clock of sufficient brightness and volume for the child's needs? (Talking clocks are available for people with low vision, as are light alarms or bed vibrators for people with hearing impairments.)

Note: The strategies above are for caregivers to use in modifying single-family, owner-occupied homes. If you live in public housing, contact your property manager to determine whether modifications can be made. If the public housing is federally subsidized, you may have certain rights under the Fair Housing Act. For more information, contact the Department of Housing and Urban Development (HUD).

Notes:

Source: "Assistive Technology and Home Modifications for Individuals with Disabilities," STAR Program, A System of Technology to Achieve Results, St. Paul, Minnesota.

4
Care Coordination and Family-Professional Collaboration

Characteristics of Enabling and Empowering Families

1. The heart of the process for enabling and empowering families is the *relationship* established between the help seeker and the help giver.

2. Effective *communication* is the name of the game. The principal way to establish partnerships with families is to communicate in a way that individual members and the family unit are treated with respect and trust.

3. *Honesty* is the first and foremost requirement of effective communication and partnerships. Each and every interaction with the family must include a clear statement about the purpose of the exchange, what will be asked, and how the information will be used.

4. Effective help giving requires *understanding* the family's concerns and interests, not the minute details about every aspect of the family's life.

5. Emphasis should be placed on *solutions* rather than causes. Effective interactions that are both positive and proactive focus on identifying choices and options for meeting needs.

6. Effective interactive exchanges are ones in which listening promotes (help seeker) sharing, sharing promotes (help giver) understanding, understanding promotes (help seeker and help giver) exploration, and exploration promotes (help seeker) action.

7. *Confidentiality* must be maintained and preserved at all times. The help giver must communicate and reiterate to the help seeker that what is shared during interactions will be held in strictest confidence.

Notes:

Courtesy of Lilli Williams, PARENTS Project, Families First Coalition, Morganton, North Carolina.

Common Pitfalls in Breaking Diagnostic News

Breaking diagnostic news is difficult, for both parents and physicians. While there is no "cookbook" for breaking diagnoses, there are a few common pitfalls that should be considered.

PITFALL 1: FAILING TO RECOGNIZE THE POTENTIALLY DEVASTATING NATURE OF THE MEETING FOR PARENTS

Whether the disability or illness is mild or severe, it will alter the lives of the entire family. The child that the parents had wished for, planned for, and expected does not exist, and they must learn to accept a different child and perhaps a different set of hopes and expectations.

Be sensitive to parents' needs for privacy. Also be aware that acceptance is a process, and it may take repeated supportive efforts before they are able to assimilate fully the information you give them.

Rule of Thumb:	Remember, you may break this kind of news often, for parents this is a significant event that may alter their lives forever.

PITFALL 2: ALLOWING YOUR OWN DISCOMFORT TO GET IN THE WAY OF YOUR SENSITIVITY TO PARENTAL CUES

The diagnosis interview may be very uncomfortable for you, as well as for the parents. You may find yourself putting off delivery of the bad news by letting the conversation wander from the issue (talking at length about the weather, the parking situation, and so forth) or retreating into lengthy technical terminology and explanations. This kind of inadvertent avoidance may seem tempting, because it creates a more comfortable distance between you and your feelings of sadness, but most likely it will only raise parents' anxiety levels. Stay open and responsive to what parents need from you. Some may need a little time and emotional distancing, while others will need to sink into the immediate grief. Still others may want detailed medical information.

Rule of Thumb:	Share the diagnosis promptly and come *gently* but quickly to the point of the interview. Then support parents by following their lead.

PITFALL 3: BEING RELUCTANT TO ACKNOWLEDGE AND ADDRESS FEELINGS

It is important for you to acknowledge the emotionally charged nature of this event, even while you are gently steering the family to the business at hand. You will be most effective if you can

continues

continued

integrate the emotional aspects of the meeting with the informational ones. Some physicians avoid the issue by remaining cool and distant, or by rushing the interview, or by "ducking out" as soon as the diagnosis has been given. Remember, as uncomfortable as it may be for the physician, the discomfort is much greater for parents. You can ease their pain, and support them, just by being there.

Rules of Thumb: Acknowledge the parents' feelings: "You look very worried (upset, sad, angry. . .)."

Acknowledge your own feelings: "I'm worried (sad, concerned. . .)."

Reflect your concern with nonverbal as well as verbal communication. Touch parents if that feels appropriate, or lean forward. This show of concern will help to form a bond of trust between you and the parents that will facilitate more successful interactions later on.

PITFALL 4: AVOIDING FORMAL DIAGNOSIS

"Above all, do no harm" often serves as the guiding principle when a physician is considering early diagnosis, and you may attempt to put off parental pain by avoiding a formal diagnosis. Unfortunately, this kind of decision may help parents in the short term, only to make things more difficult for them in the long run.

Ignorance *isn't* bliss. The period of uncertainty between beginning to suspect a problem and getting a formal diagnosis (something concrete to deal with) is a traumatizing period of apprehension and anguish.

A formal diagnosis may be necessary for access to essential financial support, and badly needed services may depend on a formal diagnosis. Many insurance policies will not cover early intervention services or adaptive equipment unless a formal diagnosis is made. Support service agencies often have formal diagnosis as an entrance criterion. Before putting off the diagnosis, consider the practical ramification for the child and family.

When formal diagnosis is delayed, there is the risk that someone else may break the news to parents first. The diagnosis may be (and often is) presented to parents by other professionals or nonprofessionals who may lack complete information on the child's condition. Too often, parents must wait for a therapist or social worker willing to voice the unpleasant realities before they can find out what is wrong with their child. In sadder cases, relatives or well-meaning neighbors are the first to utter the words "cerebral palsy" or "mental retardation."

continues

continued

> **Rule of Thumb:** Discuss terminology, diagnosis, and causality with the family as clearly and as soon as possible. If no formal diagnosis can be made, explain why you are waiting. Analogies can be useful for this purpose. For example, instead of saying only that a child is developmentally delayed (which implies that the child will "catch up"), you might compare your ongoing monitoring of the child's development to watching a marathon race. In the beginning it is difficult to tell how the runners will do, but over time the gaps between runners grow larger and you can gauge their pace and outcome more accurately.

PITFALL 5: DISCOURAGING BONDING TO DECREASE PAIN

Sometimes the diagnosis is so severe that it seems as if it would be merciful if parents could be prevented from bonding with their child. The idea of helping parents by safeguarding them from falling in love with a child with a disability is fantasy. Experience and research show that it doesn't matter if a child dies prenatally, is stillborn, or is born with severe problems, parents will feel a tremendous loss, for they are *already* in love with their child.

> **Rule of Thumb:** Parents must grieve over the loss, no matter the degree of disability. It is important to remember that love and hope for their child is a parent's job. Through love they find hope and through the hope, survival and the ability to cope. Respect and acknowledge the parents' loss.

PITFALL 6: LIMITING REFERRALS TO SAVE PARENTS TIME AND MONEY

The doctor wants to avoid unnecessary expenses and practical hassles for the family, but must recognize that the best decisions about the value of various procedures and therapies include both clinical judgment and parents' personal priorities. Parents initially depend on the doctor to educate and orient them to their child's needs. Over time, however, they become more and more capable of taking responsibility for the needs of their child. The most successful partnership between parents and doctor allows the parents maximum participation in decision making. When the parents become participating members in the treatment process, assessing the family's needs will become easier and less time consuming for the doctor.

> **Rule of Thumb:** Offer parents a complete "menu" of options for support services. Encourage them to choose what is right for their family, and respect their choices.

Source: *The Pediatrician and the New Morbidity: A CME Training Program for the Practicing Physician*, Hawaii Medical Association, Honolulu, Hawaii, © 1989.

Working with Professionals

Parents and professionals have different relationships with children who have disabilities. The parents' relationship is personal, lifelong, and caring. Professionals' involvement is time-limited and objective. Neither relationship is better, they are simply different. As with most partnerships, bringing people together with different skills and perspectives can develop a successful relationship. Key points for working with professionals follow.

- Seek out professionals and parents who demonstrate concern for you and your family through their actions.
- Learn about child development in general, the nature of your child's disability, and possible implications for your child's development.
- Learn your rights and the rights of your child regarding:
  — service eligibility
  — confidentiality and access to services
  — informed consent and decision making
  — grievance procedures and rights of appeal
  — policies, principles, and standards for providing services
- Keep a record of all contact with professionals and agencies. Include the date and type of contact; the person's name and title, agency, telephone number (and address where necessary); a summary of important points discussed; and details worth recording.
- Keep copies of all information you gather or provide.
- Develop a file of all material related to your child's development and services.
- If access to a professional is difficult:
  — Discuss with the professional at the outset your expectations for access.
  — If you have difficulty setting up an appointment with a professional, request to meet by a certain date and specify how much time you think you will need.
  — Let the professional know you have problems reaching him or her and ask what to do to avoid delays.
- Tell the professional what kind of help you want, if you can. If you are not sure what kind of help you want, let the professional know you reserve the right to decide later.
- Tell the professional you want and expect to be involved in decisions about your child. You may need to anticipate upcoming decisions and request to be involved.
- If a professional uses terms you do not understand, ask for an explanation in simple terms.
- Do not give up responsibility for your child or advocating for your child's best interest.
- Know about available resources for you and your child. Be specific with your case manager about your child's and family's needs.

continues

continued

- Learn about the admission criteria, programs, and service goals of all relevant agencies.
- You are your child's best advocate; collect information, stay involved, and participate.
- Clarify the date, time frame, place, purpose, participants, and whether you need to bring materials when scheduling meetings with professionals. If you feel unsure about attending a meeting, arrange for another parent or advocate to go with you. Consider meeting at a neutral site, if your setting or the professional's setting could interfere with agreeing to the best results for your child.
- Write down points to be discussed, questions to be answered, and decisions to be made before the meeting.
- Be on time for all meetings. You may want to make notes of your discussion.
- Record the date, place, names, and affiliations of all participants; information discussed; decisions or disagreements; and the date and details of any future meetings after attending meetings and conferences.
- Make sure all commitments include a target deadline and identify the persons responsible.
- Remember professionals are people who choose to provide services of a particular nature. For this exchange to be useful, the professional should be a resource to you and your family.
- Involve your child in choosing services when appropriate, and respect the child's point of view.
- Develop relationships with professionals before you need them.
- Believe that all problems have solutions. Allow time to help. Don't give up.
- Remember you are the final decision maker.

Notes:

Source: *Working with Professionals: A Guide for Families with Special Needs*, South Carolina Mental Retardation Foundation, Columbia, South Carolina, © 1991.

The Neonatal Intensive Care Unit

Many hospitals have a separate nursery for babies needing constant attention and very special equipment to keep them alive. It is called a neonatal intensive care unit (NICU), or a high risk nursery. Babies born too small, too soon, or with severe birth defects often risk death or permanent disability that may be prevented by immediate intensive care.

TEAM CARE

A team of medical professionals watches over your baby every moment. Each member of the team is specially trained for NICU work.

- **Neonatologist.** The physician in charge of the neonatal unit. He or she is a pediatrician trained in the care of newborns.
- **Residents.** Physicians in training who are on 24-hour hospital call and manage your child's primary minute-to-minute care.
- **Consultants.** Medical specialists who are called in to examine and treat your baby if he or she has problems involving surgery, medication, or needs special attention for a particular problem.
- **Neonatal nurses.** Nurses who have completed special courses in the care of sick newborns and premature babies. Your baby is in the direct care of one of these nurses 24 hours a day. When you call or visit, the nurse caring for your baby will discuss progress with you and direct you to the physician caring for your child. There is always a nurse in charge of all neonatal nursing care.
- **Respiratory technicians.** Therapists with special knowledge in breathing problems and the equipment used to help babies breathe. These technicians take care of the respiratory equipment in the NICU and are always there.
- **Neonatal social worker.** The social worker who is specially trained to help you and your family with the questions and problems that may arise during your baby's hospital stay. If you have not been contacted by a social worker, please ask one of the physicians or nurses to introduce you.
- **Occupational or physical therapist.** Therapist who provides your baby with a stimulation program to help develop senses and muscular activities.
- **Unit secretary.** The unit secretary team is on 24-hour duty to do clerical work, order supplies, and act as receptionists.

YOU AND THE NURSERY

Most nurseries are open for parent visiting 24 hours a day. When you go in, you will be asked to put on a gown to cover your street clothes. You also may be asked to remove your jewelry and scrub your hands and arms. This request is to help control infection within the nursery.

continues

continued

You can touch your baby from the first visit, and as your child grows you will be encouraged to help feed, diaper, hold, rock, and love the baby. This helps form an important attachment between you and your baby, which may even assist the child's development. You will be asked to leave only when physicians are making routine checkups, or when your baby is receiving special treatment.

You may bring in small washable toys (with no buttons or parts that might be pulled off), and a small religious symbol if you wish. You may take snapshots and decorate your baby's area with pictures from home. Other immediate family members may visit on occasion. When you are not visiting, do not hesitate to telephone for progress reports.

NICU SIGHTS AND SOUNDS

Try not to be alarmed at the strange equipment you see and the noises they make. Try not to be frightened if you see your baby under a large light in a glass case or with tubes attached to parts of his or her body. The nurses and physicians will explain what each piece of equipment and each tube will do for your baby. Here is what you may see:

- Open beds with overhead heaters. These beds are to keep your baby's temperature regulated. A thermometer is attached to the skin, and once the heater is set for your baby's need, it cools or heats automatically as the room temperature changes.
- Incubators. Enclosed, see-through beds with portholes for reaching your baby. This machine, too, helps maintain your baby's temperature.
- Heart and breathing monitors. Above each baby's care area is a television screen that shows the heart rate and breathing. A buzzer sounds if there is a problem. Monitoring occurs by means of tiny wires attached to your baby's chest.
- "Bili lights" over an open bed. These lights are used to correct jaundice, yellowed skin caused by a blood reaction, which is common to premature babies. The baby is placed, unclothed and eyes covered, under the lights for a short while.
- Oxygen hood. A clear, plastic, box-type hood that is placed over the baby's head to give the necessary percentage of oxygen during some breathing difficulties.
- Continuous positive airway pressure (CPAP). Air is forced into the baby's nose through short tubes. CPAP helps the baby breathe better without actually breathing for the baby.
- Respirator. A machine that breathes for the baby when unable to breathe for himself or herself. One end of a tube is placed through the baby's mouth, into the windpipe. The other is attached to a machine that pumps in oxygen according to the baby's needs. The child is "weaned" from the machine as soon as possible.
- Chest tubes. Sometimes needed when a baby's lung collapses. A tube is inserted into the baby's chest to help expand the lung back to normal size. The tube is removed when the lung heals.

continues

continued

INFORMED CONSENT

While your baby is in the NICU, it may be necessary for medical specialists to use complicated treatments. These require a parent's consent. You have the right, as well as the responsibility, to help decide what is done to care for your baby. Ask questions in order to understand what is being planned. The physicians and nurses in the NICU will answer your questions and explain what is happening. Don't be embarrassed if you need to ask the same questions many times. Staff members are used to that. They know you are unfamiliar with medical words and treatments.

BREASTFEEDING

You may nurse your premature or sick baby. Before your baby is ready to nurse at your breast it is possible to pump the milk out by hand or machine and feed it to your baby by bottle or tube. Eventually this method can lead to natural breastfeeding.

PARENT SUPPORT GROUPS

Members of parent support groups who have experienced similar reactions may be able to help you by suggesting ways to minimize the stresses you feel at this time. Suggestions may include care of other children in the family, concern about economic matters, private time for yourself, ways to handle inquiries from concerned friends and relatives, and other day-to-day problems. If you join an organization in your area made up of parents who have or have had babies in a hospital high risk nursery, you may find such parents have something very special to share with you, and you with them.

FOLLOW-UP CARE

Your NICU staff will lead you to the hospital and community services that can ease your baby's move to the home environment. Many hospitals notify the community public health nurse in your area when your baby is about to be discharged. Some offer classes in infant CPR, or cardiopulmonary resuscitation. Many have a special clinic where babies who have been in the NICU are examined regularly from 6 months until school age, to evaluate growth.

It is important to remember you can call the NICU nursing staff for any questions or fears you have even after discharge. Be sure that your baby's pediatrician contacts the NICU pediatrician who has been caring for your baby in the hospital nursery. He or she will know the kinds of treatment your baby has had and will be able to answer many of your questions.

Source: *When Your Baby Needs Early Extra Care*, March of Dimes Birth Defects Foundation, White Plains, New York, 1986.

Cleft Palate Teams

With proper treatment, your child's cleft lip and/or palate can be repaired. Your child can look normal, eat without difficulty, and speak clearly. However, the treatment is complex, and many specialists need to work together to develop and carry out a plan that will meet your child's individual needs.

THE TEAM

Most states have at least one cleft palate team located at a major medical center. Populous states such as New York and California have many cleft palate teams. Your child's physician may be able to refer you to the cleft palate team nearest your home. Or you can contact the Cleft Palate Foundation. The center in which the team works may be called a cleft palate center, craniofacial center, or orofacial center.

An advantage of the team approach is that team members cooperate to develop a systematic, comprehensive treatment plan for your child. The expertise of team members is based on experience with large numbers of children who have this condition. They treat many more children with cleft lip and palate than most other professionals, and they have a major commitment to this specialty area of medicine.

If you seek treatment for your child at a cleft palate center in another city, you may need to travel there several times in the first year. After that, though, visits are likely to become less frequent. Members of the cleft palate team will be glad to call or write to your child's local physicians and specialists to supply information about the treatment plan. It will be especially important for your child's pediatrician to understand the phases of treatment, so he or she can be on the lookout for problems that need attention.

TEAM MEMBERS

- audiologist—evaluates hearing
- coordinator—oversees coordination of care
- dietitian—specialists in nutrition and feeding
- geneticist—studies inherited conditions
- orthodontist—corrects the position of teeth
- oral surgeon—specialists in mouth and jaw surgery
- otolaryngologist—treats ear, nose, and throat problems
- pediatrician—treats diseases in children
- pediatric surgeon—performs surgery on children
- pedodontist—provides dental care to children
- plastic surgeon—improves appearance and function by surgical means
- prosthodontist—makes artificial teeth and mouth prostheses
- psychologist—evaluates mental development and counsels
- social worker—helps with adjustment and finances
- speech pathologist—treats speech problems
- radiologist—performs special X-ray studies

Note: Not all these specialties are represented on all cleft palate teams.

Source: *Looking Forward: A Guide for Parents of the Child with Cleft Lip and Palate*, Mead Johnson & Company, Evansville, Indiana, © 1991.

General Information on Cleft Palate Surgery

PURPOSE

The surgery restores the barrier between the mouth and nose. The tissues that cover the roof of the mouth are loosened surgically, pulled together, and stitched in the middle of the mouth, eliminating the hole or cleft. The surgical area takes about 3 weeks to heal. Dissolving stitches are used for the operation so they do not need to be removed later.

The amount of the cleft to be closed in the operation depends on the extent of the cleft your child has. The soft palate, or muscular part at the back of the mouth, will be closed. This part is important for speech. The front bony part, or hard palate, is often closed at the same time as the soft palate. If your child has a complete cleft through the lip and gum, the gum is usually left open to allow for early growth of the dental arch and may be closed when the child is older and the teeth are starting to erupt.

PREOPERATIVE CARE

No aspirin-containing medicines should be given to the child for 2 weeks prior to surgery because they can interfere with blood clotting. Tylenol (acetaminophen) may, however, be used.

Children are admitted to the hospital the day of surgery. They must not be fed prior to surgery per the instructions of the anesthesiologist in the preoperative testing and examination.

POSTOPERATIVE CARE

Your child will be kept on his or her stomach rather than back for a few days so that fluids can drain from the surgical area out of the mouth. There will be some bloody discharge. There may be a small rubber breathing tube in the child's nostril and a stitch through the tongue that is taped to the child's cheek. Although these may appear quite unattractive, they are used to keep stress off the surgical area and make the child's breathing easier. They are usually removed the day after surgery.

Your child will be admitted to the intensive care unit for close observation the night of surgery. Usually he or she will be transferred to a regular floor the following day.

Your baby will have to wear small elbow cuffs on the arms for 3 weeks after surgery to keep fingers away from the mouth. These cuffs, which may be removed for supervised exercise periods, do not restrict movements of the hands or shoulders. They only prevent bending at the elbows.

To avoid putting tension on the repair site by sucking, babies should *not* be fed by nipple for 3 weeks after the operation. A cup is the preferable method and should be introduced to your child before surgery. You do not need to wean the baby completely from bottle or breast before the

continues

continued

operation, but the child should have some experience with drinking from a cup. If the baby is resistant to a cup, alternatives can be used. A cross-cut nipple can be used that minimizes the suction required for the baby to feed. Breastfeeding mothers may use an electric breast pump to express milk for the baby while he or she is hospitalized.

An IV will be in place until the baby is taking adequate nourishment by mouth, usually within 3 to 5 days of the surgery.

Spoon feeding is also permitted, but the child must not be allowed to feed himself or herself. The tip of the spoon should be inserted just inside the lips and the food dropped into the mouth so that the spoon cannot contact the healing palate.

A liquid diet will be allowed for 1 week after surgery, and a soft diet with foods the consistency of strained baby food will be adhered to for another 2 weeks. *No* solid foods, "sticky" foods, or hard objects such as toys are permitted in the child's mouth until after the 3 week postoperative physician visit.

If your child is experiencing pain or discomfort after the operation, medication will be given to alleviate the discomfort.

Your child will be discharged from the hospital as soon as he or she is taking enough food by mouth, is comfortable, and has no fever. Usually these conditions are met 2 to 3 days after the operation.

COMPLICATIONS

As in any surgery, complications can occur including bleeding, infection, breakdown of the repair, fistula formation, and adverse reactions to medications. Complications are uncommon, and most of the time the palate repair surgery yields positive results without difficulty.

RESULTS

With the soft palate intact and the major muscles of the palate connected, the child should be able to develop speech at the usual time for children. The barrier between the mouth and nose should make feeding easier once healing has occurred and should minimize or eliminate the leakage of food into the nose. Your child will be evaluated on a regular basis to assess his or her speech development.

QUESTIONS AND CONCERNS

If you have further questions and concerns about the operation, hospital procedures, or related areas, please call your child's doctor or the nurse coordinator.

Courtesy of Kant Lin, MD, Division of Craniofacial Surgery, Department of Plastic Surgery, University of Virginia Health Sciences Center, Charlottesville, Virginia.

General Information on Cleft Lip Repair Surgery

PURPOSE

Cleft lip repair surgery closes the cleft lip and attaches the major muscles within the upper lip in a functional fashion. A suture line that blends in as much as possible with the contours of the lip is used. The repair leaves a scar on the lip after the edges of the cleft are brought together, but the redness of the scar will fade with time and blend better with surrounding tissue. Clefts on both sides of the lip or extremely wide one-sided clefts may be repaired in two operations instead of one.

PREOPERATIVE CARE

No aspirin-containing medicines should be given to the child for 2 weeks prior to surgery because they can interfere with blood clotting. Tylenol (acetaminophen) may, however, be used.

Children are admitted to the hospital the day of surgery. They must not be fed prior to surgery per the instructions of the anesthesiologist in the preoperative testing and examination.

POSTOPERATIVE CARE

When you see your baby for the first time after surgery, you may think that he or she looks like a completely different child. You have gotten used to the cleft, which is now pulled together with small stitches and is usually covered with a bandage. There may be bruises on your baby's face from the attachment of the big muscles in the upper lip. There will be swelling around the surgical area as well as the tip of the nose if your baby's cleft extended into the nose. Sometimes there will be a yellow bolster held by a stitch through the nostril that holds the nose upright. Occasionally, there is some residual yellow or brown soap from the operating room on your child's face, but this soap will be washed off shortly. Finally, there is often a minimal amount of bloody discharge around the repair site.

Your baby may be fussy or sleepy the day of the surgery. An IV will be attached to provide needed nourishment until the baby feels like drinking again. Whenever your baby does wish to resume eating, however, he or she can be fed by whatever method was used before the surgery, either bottle or breastfeeding. If your baby is experiencing discomfort after the operation, medication (such as acetaminophen) will be given to alleviate this pain.

Your baby will have to wear small elbow cuffs on the arms for 3 weeks after surgery to keep fingers away from the suture line. These cuffs, which can be removed for supervised exercise periods, do not restrict movement of the hands or shoulders, but only prevent bending at the elbows.

Your baby will need to stay on his or her back to avoid rubbing the new stitches. A baby seat might be helpful in keeping him or her comfortable and slightly elevated. When you carry your baby after the operation, you need to make sure that he or she does not bump the upper lip on your shoulder. Facing the baby away from you is a good precaution.

continues

continued

The suture line will need to be cleaned several times a day with water. The nurses will show you how to do this procedure so that you can continue to clean the area when your baby goes home. Although it may be a little frightening at first, you will soon be able to cleanse the area without difficulty.

When you have mastered lip care and your baby has resumed feeding well by mouth, you may take him or her home. Usually discharge occurs the morning after the operation, as children are very resilient and heal quickly. You will be asked to bring your baby back to see the physician about 4 to 7 days after the surgery to have the stitches removed. Please bring a baby seat, if possible. You should guard against direct sun exposure on the suture line for several months after the operation because the sensitive healing skin is more susceptible to the harmful effects of the sun.

COMPLICATIONS

As in any surgery, complications can occur including bleeding, infection, breakdown of the repair, and adverse reactions to medications. Occasionally, for unforeseen reasons, the lip repair will pull apart a couple of days after the surgery and will have to be repaired again a few months later. Complications are uncommon, and most of the time lip repair surgery yields positive results without difficulty.

RESULTS

Your baby's appearance will be greatly improved by the cleft lip repair. Some scarring will remain, and the ultimate results cannot be accurately predicted because each child's face, skin, and healing capacity is slightly different. Generally, the outcome is very pleasing. Some children need minor revisions of the lip repair in later years to refine cosmetic details.

QUESTIONS AND CONCERNS

If you have further questions and concerns about the operation, hospital procedures, or related areas, please call your child's doctor or nurse coordinator.

Notes:

Courtesy of Kant Lin, MD, Division of Craniofacial Surgery, Department of Plastic Surgery, University of Virginia Health Sciences Center, Charlottesville, Virginia.

Treatment Team for Speech and Language Disorders

Once a child has been identified as having a speech or language disorder, most successful diagnoses and treatment involve a team of experts. The *audiologist*, an expert in the process of hearing, evaluates and assists those with hearing disorders. The audiologist may work in consultation with an *otolaryngologist*, a physician who specializes in ear, nose, and throat disorders. These two health professionals determine which hearing conditions can be treated—and perhaps corrected—medically or surgically, and which require rehabilitative techniques such as hearing aids or lip reading.

The *speech-language pathologist*, also called a speech therapist, studies the normal and abnormal processes of speech and language and measures and diagnoses speech and language problems. The pathologist can also enhance early learning of language, teach the correct production of speech and language, and help a child learn to understand words and sentences.

The *neurologist* is a physician with expertise in the workings of the brain and nervous system. The neurologist may use modern brain imaging techniques to "see" through the skull and detect brain abnormalities in a child with speech or language delay. A range of pencil-and-paper and physical tests have also been devised to help diagnose any underlying brain disorder that might account for the language problem.

The *psychologist* studies the science of human development and personality, and can administer tests to evaluate the child's cognitive capabilities. Such tests can help determine how the child's language age compares to his or her mental and chronological ages.

Notes:

Source: *Developmental Speech and Language Disorders*, Office of Scientific and Health Reports, National Institute of Neurological and Communicative Disorders and Stroke, National Institutes of Health, Public Health Service, U.S. Department of Health and Human Services, 1988.

Speech-Language Pathologists

WHO IS QUALIFIED TO HELP PEOPLE WITH SPEECH OR LANGUAGE DISORDERS?

Speech-language pathologists are specialists in human communication, its development, and its disorders. They are professionally educated to evaluate and treat people with communication problems.

The speech-language pathologist will have a master's degree or doctoral degree in speech-language pathology and should hold a Certificate of Clinical Competence (CCC) from the American Speech-Language-Hearing Association. In many states a license is also required.

HOW CAN THE SPEECH-LANGUAGE PATHOLOGIST HELP?

The clinical methods used will vary depending on the nature and severity of the problem, the age of the person, and the individual's awareness of the problem. Speech-language pathologists provide many specialized professional services that include:

- helping people with articulation disorders learn proper production of speech sounds
- assisting people with voice disorders to develop proper control for correct production
- assisting people who stutter to increase the amount of fluent speech, and to cope with this disorder
- assisting people with aphasia to re-learn language and speech skills and sentence order or to compensate for lost language and speech skills
- counseling people with speech and language disorders and their families to understand their disorder and to achieve normal communication in educational, social, and vocational settings
- advising individuals and the community on how to prevent speech and language disorders
- helping people understand the types and severity of communication disorders

WHERE CAN YOU FIND A SPEECH-LANGUAGE PATHOLOGIST?

Speech-language pathologists provide professional services in many different types of facilities such as:

- public and private schools
- hospitals
- rehabilitation centers
- nursing care facilities
- community clinics
- colleges and universities
- private offices
- state and local health departments
- state and federal governmental agencies

Courtesy of the American Speech-Language-Hearing Association, Rockville, Maryland.

5
Nutrition and Feeding

Parenteral and Enteral Feeding

Food Guide Pyramid:
A Guide to Daily Food Choices

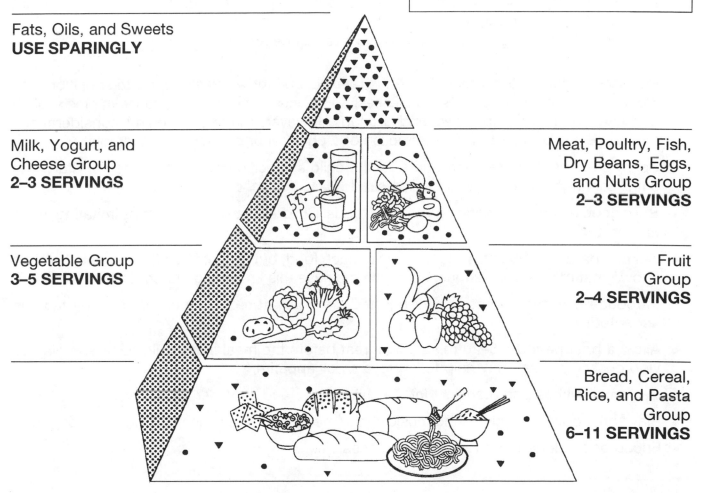

KEY
● Fat (naturally occurring and added)　▼ Sugars (added)

These symbols show fats, oils, and added sugars in foods.

Fats, Oils, and Sweets
USE SPARINGLY

Milk, Yogurt, and Cheese Group
2–3 SERVINGS

Meat, Poultry, Fish, Dry Beans, Eggs, and Nuts Group
2–3 SERVINGS

Vegetable Group
3–5 SERVINGS

Fruit Group
2–4 SERVINGS

Bread, Cereal, Rice, and Pasta Group
6–11 SERVINGS

Source: *FDA Consumer*, Vol. 26, No. 6, U.S. Department of Health and Human Services, July–August 1992.

Mealtime Goals and Guidelines

Mealtime is an important socializing influence in a child's development. Families who enjoy meals together are likely to have better appetites and digestion. Meals should be served in a relaxed, unhurried atmosphere at approximately the same time each day. Meals served at irregular times may result in hungry, irritable children, thereby making mealtime an unpleasant experience for all.

It is wise to understand that children's appetites vary from day to day as well as from meal to meal. During periods of rapid growth, appetite is normally increased and, conversely, as growth slows, appetite decreases. However, if a decreased appetite persists and growth is not occurring, a physician should be consulted.

Suggestions for making mealtime a positive experience are as follows:

- Position the child with motor difficulty in a relaxed, upright, and well-supported position. The ideal position is for the child's hips, knees, and ankles to be in 90° flexion with hips slightly abducted and feet supported and aligned. However, major positioning considerations should be performed under the direction of a physical or occupational therapist.

- Serve portions that are appropriate for the child's specific needs and appetite. Start with small servings and give seconds if desired.

- Set a good example by eating a variety of foods. Children learn what to eat by imitating those around them.

- Set standards, such as tasting one bite of each food, but do not force the issue. If the child knows that others are anxious, he or she may use this knowledge to control the situation.

- Introduce new foods gradually. If rejected, try again at regular intervals until the taste is accepted.

- Allow a brief period (15–20 minutes) for rest before the meal if the child has been playing vigorously. The rest may help to improve a dull appetite.

- Use small dishes and utensils that the child enjoys and consider his or her own.

- Play soft, soothing background music during meals to create a pleasant, calm atmosphere.

- Encourage independent feeding when possible.

Source: Tina Shaddix, "Meal Planning for the Childhood Years," Nutritional Care for the Child with Developmental Disabilities series, United Cerebral Palsy of Greater Birmingham, Birmingham, Alabama, © 1986.

Iron Deficiency Anemia

WHAT IS IRON?

Iron, an essential nutrient, is critical to the formation of red blood cells, which carry oxygen to all parts of the body. If iron is not received in adequate amounts, iron deficiency anemia may result. Iron deficiency is the most common nutritional deficiency in children. It may be caused by the following factors:

- periods of rapid growth
- excessive milk intake
- pica (the ingestion of nonedible substances such as dirt, paint, clay, paper, and so forth)
- inadequate intake of foods high in iron
- certain medical conditions

Symptoms of iron deficiency anemia include:

- irritability
- listlessness
- lack of energy
- poor appetite
- shortness of breath
- frequent illness

It is important that foods high in iron be included in the child's daily diet. It is equally important that foods high in vitamin C be served each day, because vitamin C aids in the body's utilization of iron and cannot be stored in the body as other vitamins are.

Iron supplements are sometimes prescribed if the level of iron in the blood is extremely low. Side effects of these supplements include constipation, diarrhea, and nausea. Check with the child's physician if these problems persist.

IRON-RICH FOODS

The following foods are rich sources of iron:

- liver
- organ meats, such as kidney
- meat, fish, or poultry

continues

continued

- enriched breads and cereals (especially dry baby cereals and cereals fortified with extra iron), wheat germ
- dried beans and peas, such as chili, navy, or pinto beans and split peas
- peanut butter
- dark green leafy vegetables, such as spinach, broccoli, chard, kale, beets, turnips, and dandelion greens
- dried fruits, such as raisins, prunes, dates, figs, and apricots

VITAMIN C–RICH FOODS

The following fruits and vegetables are rich in vitamin C:

- oranges/juice
- grapefruit/juice
- lemons
- tangerines
- strawberries
- cantaloupe
- watermelon
- tomato juice
- turnip greens
- turnips
- green pepper
- broccoli

Notes:

Source: Tina Shaddix, "Meal Planning for the Childhood Years," Nutritional Care for the Child with Developmental Disabilities series, United Cerebral Palsy of Greater Birmingham, Birmingham, Alabama, © 1986.

Helpful Hints for Weight Control

WHAT TO DO

- Plan ahead. Plan meals and snacks several days in advance to eliminate "hasty" or unwise food choices. Planned meals and snacks served at consistent times are better than allowing the child to eat throughout the day. Don't keep in the house high-calorie food that may tempt the child.

- Limit the use of artificial sweeteners such as saccharine or aspartame. Also limit dietetic foods such as cookies, cakes, candy, sodas, gelatin, etc., because these foods are not necessarily low in calories and the child needs to learn that these foods should be eliminated.

- Use thinly sliced bread for sandwiches or serve open-faced sandwiches with one slice of bread. Use mustard in place of mayonnaise. Limit ketchup to 1 to 2 tablespoons daily.

- Do not allow the child to skip meals. This action usually leads to unplanned between-meal snacks.

- Give smaller portions to begin the meal if second helpings are usually desired.

- Avoid foods high in fat and sugar, such as sugar-coated cereals, cookies, cake, candy, ice cream or sherbet, chips, fried foods, peanut butter, sauces, gravy, creamed soup, Kool-Aid, Hi-C, and other drinks with added sugar. Limit butter, margarine, mayonnaise, and salad dressing, if possible.

- Prepare foods without adding extra fat (butter, margarine, oil). Cut all visible fat from meats. Remove skin from chicken or turkey. Cook foods by baking, broiling, roasting, or steaming.

- Serve fruits and vegetables raw whenever possible. They are more filling than when cooked.

- Avoid breading and flouring foods before cooking. Breading and flouring only add extra calories.

- Avoid giving appetite suppressants or diuretics ("water pills") that may endanger the health of the child.

- Steer clear of fad diets. These diets may jeopardize the child's health.

- Consult the child's physician about the need for a multivitamin supplement when calories must be restricted, because it may be difficult to receive enough nutrients—especially iron—from the foods eaten.

A "WEIGH" OF LIFE

In order to help the child accomplish the goal of weight control, you must not only encourage wise food choices, but you must help change the behaviors that initially led to the weight problem. Utilize any of the following suggestions that are appropriate for the child:

continues

continued

- Examine the child's (and even the entire family's) eating patterns in order to identify problem areas. Keep a "diary" of all foods eaten. Record the type of food eaten, the time, and reason for consumption (boredom, hunger, and so forth). This record will help you recognize problem foods or behaviors.

  Once you have identified the problem, you can find a way to solve it. For example, if your child is eating a large snack at bedtime, find another activity to do, such as reading or telling a bedtime story.

- Avoid using food as a reward. Use alternatives—praise, a favorite activity, and so on.

- Select only one room in which the child may eat. Make sure the child is comfortably seated without distractions. Don't allow the child to watch television while eating.

- Encourage interest in activities other than eating. This may aid in avoiding moods or situations such as boredom, anger, or depression, which may trigger overeating.

- Encourage active exercise whenever possible. Exercise helps decrease (not increase) appetite and "burn" calories.

- Don't keep high-calorie foods in the house, or serve forbidden foods to other family members. Dietary compliance will be much easier with help from the entire family. The recommendations in this handout form the framework for a healthy diet that may be utilized by the entire family.

- Limit eating at fast food restaurants, which generally serve high-calorie foods. If eating out is a necessity, a cafeteria is a better choice because more appropriate food choices may be made.

Notes:

Source: Tina Shaddix, "Weight Control for the Overweight Child," Nutritional Care for the Child with Developmental Disabilities series, United Cerebral Palsy of Greater Birmingham, Birmingham, Alabama, © 1986.

Promoting Weight Gain

Optimal nutrition is essential for all children to achieve their physical and developmental potential. The well-nourished child is likely to grow at an expected rate, have an increased capacity for learning and cognitive ability, have resistance to infections, and have the energy to take advantage of opportunities that are offered. The nutritional well-being of the child with a developmental disability is of prime importance, but, due to a variety of medical and physical problems, it may be difficult to achieve.

One of the most common nutritional problems of the child with developmental disabilities is that of inadequate weight gain, which may become a concern shortly after birth or at any time during the child's development. The causes vary according to the individual child, but the five major ones include:

1. Impaired oral-motor function (difficulty in sucking or chewing, drooling food and liquids, and tongue thrust), which may limit food and nutrient intake.

2. Athetosis (uncontrolled, excessive movement), which greatly increases caloric requirement. This characteristic is common in some types of cerebral palsy.

3. Frequent illness or infections, including colds, pneumonia, and other respiratory ailments, which place stress on the body and increase caloric requirements.

4. Heavy bracings or other orthotic devices designed to improve motor ability, which increase energy expenditure. The child who becomes more ambulatory due to these devices may have an increased energy expenditure that results in weight loss.

5. Decreased appetite usually resulting from certain medications, which interferes with adequate caloric intake. (Food may be better tolerated if medication is not given just prior to mealtime.) The child should also be given several smaller meals throughout the day instead of three larger ones. If this problem exists, the child's physician should be consulted.

The energy (calorie) requirement needed to promote a weight gain of 1 pound is approximately 3,500 calories in addition to calories expended (utilized) by the child. There are commercially prepared high-calorie supplements that are designed to promote weight gain, but they should be used only after consultation with a physician or nutritionist. However, more commonly used foods such as milk powder, eggs, or oil may facilitate weight gain when used as supplements to the child's favorite foods and/or regular meals.

Source: Tina Shaddix, "Promoting Weight Gain," Nutritional Care for the Child with Developmental Disabilities series, United Cerebral Palsy of Greater Birmingham, Birmingham, Alabama, © 1986.

Snacks To Promote Weight Gain

Snacks may supply the important nutrients and additional calories that the child needs if ingestion is inadequate at main meals. Therefore, special emphasis should be placed on serving nutritious and interesting foods to supplement the principal meals.

FIVE THINGS TO REMEMBER

1. Choose snack foods from the basic food groups. Commercially prepared foods, such as potato chips and candy bars, do not provide enough nutrients to promote good health.

2. Serve snacks no less than 2 hours before a main meal. Otherwise, the child's appetite may be decreased at the main meal, which provides the majority of the child's nutrient requirements.

3. Limit the use of sugar. Use it with foods such as milk (in puddings and ice cream), oatmeal, and peanut butter (in cookies), which supply essential nutrients as well. Although sugar does supply calories, it does not provide any nutrients needed for health. An overabundance of sugar may actually have an adverse effect on the child's health.

4. Allow the child to help in preparing the snack when possible. Children will usually eat what they have prepared. Also allow them to serve themselves from small bowls, pour liquids from a child-sized pitcher, etc.

5. Relax. Encourage the child to eat, but do not force the issue. Appetites normally vary from day to day and are dependent on the child's growth, activity level, and emotions. Negative attitudes and inappropriate mealtime behavior can easily develop if the child is forced to eat. However, if a decreased appetite persists, the child may need a complete medical examination.

EXCELLENT SNACKS

Excellent snack suggestions include:

- milkshakes or eggnogs fortified with high-calorie supplements
- whole milk (1 cup) blended with baby rice cereal (½ cup), fruit (½ cup), and corn oil (2 teaspoons)
- sliced cheese with crackers
- buttered cheesetoast

continues

continued

- creamy peanut butter on crackers (make sure the child can effectively chew this snack)
- small sandwiches (egg salad, tuna, ham)
- fruit and cottage cheese with wheat germ topping
- yogurt with wheat germ topping
- cereal and milk fortified with high-calorie supplements

POOR SNACKS

Poor snack choices include:

- soda
- potato chips
- candy
- cakes and pies
- iced tea
- sugar cookies

Notes:

Source: Tina Shaddix, "Promoting Weight Gain," Nutritional Care for the Child with Developmental Disabilities series, United Cerebral Palsy of Greater Birmingham, Birmingham, Alabama, © 1986.

High-Calorie Food Fortifiers

WAYS TO ADD CALORIES

The following list contains eight high-calorie foods that may be added to the child's favorite foods, thereby increasing caloric and nutrient intake without significantly increasing the volume of foods.

1. Egg yolk, which supplies approximately 60 calories per yolk, may be added to foods such as meat loaf, mashed potato, cooked cereal, or macaroni and cheese before cooking. Cooked egg may be added to mashed potatoes, casseroles, salads, or sandwich spreads. Due to the danger of salmonella infection, never add raw egg to foods that do not need to be cooked. The American Heart Association recommends that, due to the high cholesterol content, egg yolks be limited to three per week in an attempt to minimize the risk of heart disease.
2. Wheat germ, which supplies 25 calories per tablespoon, may be added to meat dishes, casseroles, cereals, salads, yogurt, or fruits.
3. Vegetable oils, margarine, or mayonnaise, which supply approximately 35 to 40 calories per teaspoon, may be added to casseroles, soups, cooked cereals, puddings, or sandwiches. Mayonnaise may be used as a dressing on vegetables or gelatin salads.
4. Baby cereals (dry), which supply 9 calories per tablespoon, may be added to beverages, mashed potatoes, cooked cereals, or yogurt.
5. Powdered nonfat milk, which supplies 25 calories per tablespoon, may be added in the following proportions:
   — ¼ cup to 1 cup fluid milk
   — ¼ cup to 1 cup cooked cereal, such as oatmeal or wheat cereal
   — 2 tablespoons to ½ cup mashed potatoes
   — ½ cup to 1 pound ground meat
   — ¼ cup to milkshakes or yogurt

   Note: In children under 2 years of age, it is not recommended that powdered nonfat milk be used in large amounts because the high protein content may place an unnecessary burden on the developing kidneys.

6. Undiluted evaporated milk, which supplies 25 calories per tablespoon, may be used in place of whole milk in desserts, baked goods, meat dishes, cooked cereals, and cream soups.

   Note: In children under 2 years of age, it is not recommended that powdered nonfat milk be used in large amounts because the high protein content may place an unnecessary burden on the developing kidneys.

continues

continued

7. Peanut butter (creamy), which supplies 100 calories per tablespoon, may be spread on toast, bread, crackers, or used in desserts such as puddings, custards, cookies, or milkshakes.

   Note: For the young child or the child with oral-motor impairment, peanut butter may be too difficult to manage and should therefore be avoided.

8. Cheese, which supplies approximately 100 calories per ounce, may be served melted over meat or potatoes, in casseroles, or grated into eggs, pasta, rice, soups, and cooked cereals.

OTHER CALORIE-BOOSTING IDEAS

In addition to fortifying the child's favorite foods with the high-calorie supplements previously listed, the following six suggestions may also be utilized to increase caloric and nutrient intake.

1. Serve vegetables creamed, such as creamed peas or carrots; top favorite vegetables with cheese sauce.
2. Serve meat with extra sauce or gravy when possible.
3. Use less water than recommended when reconstituting frozen juices.
4. Bread or flour meat before cooking.
5. Use whole milk instead of water in condensed cream soups or instant cooked cereals.
6. Add a packet of powdered breakfast mix to milk or shakes.

Notes:

Source: Tina Shaddix, "Promoting Weight Gain," Nutritional Care for the Child with Developmental Disabilities series, United Cerebral Palsy of Greater Birmingham, Birmingham, Alabama, © 1986.

Nutritional Management of Constipation

One of the most common nutritional problems of the child with developmental disabilities, particularly in children with motor dysfunction, is that of chronic constipation.

WHAT IS CONSTIPATION?

Constipation is the passage of hard, dry, sometimes painful stools. It does not mean irregular bowel movements or lack of a movement in a 24-hour period.
The causes vary according to the individual child, but the five major ones include:

1. inadequate texture or fiber, which may be restricted due to impaired oral function (difficulty in chewing, drooling food and liquids, and tongue thrust)
2. inadequate intake of fluids, which may be the result of such things as impaired oral function, illness, or lack of energy
3. abnormal muscle tone, either too high or too low, which prohibits the gastrointestinal tract from functioning optimally
4. decreased activity level due to motor impairment, which either decreases or eliminates normal physical activity that aids proper elimination
5. poor sitting position, due to lack of trunk control, which crowds the intestinal tract and inhibits normal intestinal movement

WHAT CAN BE DONE TO HELP CONTROL CONSTIPATION?

Symptoms may often be controlled or alleviated by the following three simple changes:

1. Increase dietary fiber or roughage.
2. Increase intake of fluids, especially juice and water.
3. Establish a schedule for regular exercise and toileting.

HELPFUL HINTS

Six helpful hints are as follows:

1. Remember to include generous amounts of high-fiber foods and liquids in the child's daily diet.
2. Make sure the child gets adequate rest each day.

continues

continued

3. Use laxatives, suppositories, or enemas only if prescribed and under the supervision of a physician or nurse practitioner. Mineral oil should never be used because it decreases the absorption of fat-soluble vitamins.

4. Increase intestinal movement (peristalsis) through exercise. This recommendation is essential to the management of constipation. Therefore, physical activity or exercise should be encouraged when possible. Organizations that promote special activities for the disabled, such as Special Olympics, or schools that provide adapted physical education programs will assist in planning an individualized program to meet the child's special needs. A physical or recreational therapist can suggest ways to increase activity levels.

5. Make sure the child is properly positioned during meals to minimize the danger of aspiration or choking. Also, children are often unable to consume adequate fluid or fiber due to head and neck hyperextension or a feeling of insecurity during feeding. A physical therapist can suggest ways to position the child properly.

6. Establish a schedule for elimination by placing the child on the toilet at regular times each day. Sitting on the toilet increases the intraabdominal pressure, which aids in elimination.

   - Begin by placing the child on the toilet for 3- to 5-minute intervals and gradually increasing the time to 10 to 15 minutes. Immediately after meals is an excellent time for this activity because there is increased bowel activity.

   - Have the child grunt or blow balloons, if possible, to increase pressure.

   - Use an adapted potty chair if the child has difficulty with balance or trunk control. A physical therapist can assist in the design or construction of an appropriate chair.

   - Maintain the schedule for elimination and allow the child's body to adapt to the routine. Consistency is the key.

Notes:

Source: Tina Shaddix, "Management of Constipation," Nutritional Care for the Child with Developmental Disabilities series, United Cerebral Palsy of Greater Birmingham, Birmingham, Alabama, © 1986.

Increasing Fiber

Remember:

Fiber absorbs water and increases peristalsis, or intestinal movement, thereby moving waste through the digestive system to be excreted from the body. Therefore, it is very important that the child's diet be high in fiber.

GUIDELINES

Chronic constipation is often a result of inadequate fiber intake, especially in the child with oral-motor impairment. For the child who has no difficulty in chewing or swallowing foods, the necessary dietary changes outlined here are relatively simple. However, for the child who does not adequately chew or swallow, an increased dietary fiber content may be more difficult to achieve. For these children, the following four general guidelines should apply:

1. Progress from blended, pureed, or baby foods to table foods as rapidly as possible. Commercial baby foods contain very little fiber, and the texture of these foods does not facilitate improved oral skills. The child's therapist (physical, occupational, or speech) will be able to determine readiness skills for textured foods.

2. For the child with oral-motor impairment, use a baby food grinder or food processor to obtain an appropriate food texture. This method retains some of the fiber content.

3. Serve bran cereal for breakfast or mix unprocessed bran in the child's food each day. This technique will supply additional fiber in a form that the child can tolerate.

4. Include in the daily diet generous amounts of the high-fiber foods listed in the next section.

HIGH-FIBER FOODS

Whole Grain Cereals and Breads

Cereals

- Bran Flakes
- Bran Buds
- Raisin Bran
- All Bran
- Crispy Wheats and Raisins
- Fruit'n Fiber Cereal
- Granola
- Grape-Nuts
- Most
- Nutri-Grain
- oatmeal
- Quaker 100% Natural Cereal
- Shredded Wheat

continues

continued

Breads

- whole wheat bread
- bran muffins
- cornbread

Raw Fruits

- prunes
- pears
- apples
- strawberries

- dried peaches
- raisins
- figs

Vegetables

Cooked

- broccoli
- collard greens
- sweet potatoes
- spinach
- cabbage

- turnip greens
- mustard greens
- dried peas or beans (legumes)
- corn

Raw

- cabbage (slaw)
- carrots

- tomato
- lettuce

Unprocessed Bran

Unprocessed bran may be purchased at most grocery stores, may be mixed with foods if the above suggestions do not lessen the problem. Begin by mixing 1 to 2 teaspoons daily and slowly increase the amount to no more than 2 tablespoons daily. Bran may be easily mixed with such foods as cereals, mashed potatoes, and applesauce, or combined with hamburger or other ground meats.

HIGH-FIBER DIET

- Breakfast
  applesauce
  high-fiber cereal
  milk

continues

continued

- Lunch or dinner
  sandwich made with whole wheat bread
  vegetable
  fruit or vegetable salad
  milk

  or

  meat
  potato with skin
  vegetable
  whole grain bread
  fruit or vegetable salad
  milk

- Snacks
  fruit or vegetable juice
  fruit or vegetable
  whole wheat crackers with peanut butter

Note: Whole milk (1 cup) blended with baby rice cereal (½ cup), fruit (½ cup), and corn oil (2 teaspoons) may be substituted for milk in the diet of the child with oral-motor problems who has difficulty in consuming thinner liquids.

Notes:

Source: Tina Shaddix, "Management of Constipation," Nutritional Care for the Child with Developmental Disabilities series, United Cerebral Palsy of Greater Birmingham, Birmingham, Alabama, © 1986.

Increasing Fluid Intake

Remember:

Adequate fluid intake is essential to soften the stool so it is more easily passed.

Chronic constipation is often a result of inadequate fluid intake. Most children need approximately 1 to 2 quarts of fluid each day. To ensure adequate fluid intake, follow these five guidelines.

1. Limit sweetened drinks such as carbonated beverages, tea, and fruit juices with added sugar. Excellent alternatives are unsweetened juice and water.

Recommended Fluid Intake

Child's Weight (Pounds)	Total Fluids Needed in 24 Hours (Cups)
7	2
12	3⅓
21	5
26	6
36	7
44	8

2. Increase the intake of prune juice, which has a natural laxative effect, by combining it with another fruit juice that is more readily accepted by the child. Prune juice may be especially beneficial if served at bedtime.

3. Increase the amount of liquid consumed by the child with oral-motor problems by thickening the liquids with baby cereals, blended fruit, or unflavored gelatin. The thickened consistency of the beverage flows into the child's mouth more slowly than thinner liquids, thereby allowing for improved oral-motor function as well as increased fluid intake.

continues

continued

4. Use a jaw control technique in the child who does not independently feed when giving liquids. This technique should also help increase the amount of liquid actually consumed. When using this technique, the person feeding the child is positioned on the child's side, with his or her arm coming from behind the child's head. The middle finger is placed under the chin and the index finger is placed between the chin and the lower lip. The thumb is placed in the palm of the hand. Upward pressure is then applied to the child's chin to assist with jaw closure. Slight inward pressure should be applied to the lower lip (Illustration A). If the child must be fed from the front, the thumb is placed on the chin with the middle or index finger under the chin (Illustration B). These assists should be maintained until after the child has swallowed.

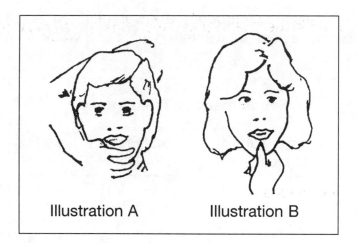

Illustration A   Illustration B

5. Serve whole milk (1 cup) blended with baby rice cereal (½ cup), fruit (½ cup), and corn oil (2 teaspoons). This drink increases fluid intake and alleviates the symptoms of constipation.

Notes:

Source: Tina Shaddix, "Management of Constipation," Nutritional Care for the Child with Developmental Disabilities series, United Cerebral Palsy of Greater Birmingham, Birmingham, Alabama, © 1986.

Dietary Management of Urinary Tract Infections

The child with a mobility-limiting disability frequently has urinary tract infections because of muscle weakness, paralysis of the lower extremities, and loss of proper bladder functioning. Urine may back up and be stored in the bladder too long, which may result in infections. Because the urine tends to be alkaline in these children, kidney stones may form. If the urine is made less alkaline (or more acidic) the chance for infections and the formation of stones may be lessened.

The child's diet should include plenty of fluid (1 to 2 quarts) each day in the form of water and fruit juices. Prune juice and cranberry juice are good choices because they have a tendency to acidify the urine. Do not give your child carbonated beverages or sweetened fruit drinks.

Other foods to be included in the diet to make the urine more acidic are:

- meats
- eggs
- fish
- poultry
- cheese
- whole grain cereals and breads
- prunes
- plums
- cranberries

It is important to watch for the presence of urinary tract infections and to contact your child's physician immediately if such an infection is suspected. Because diet alone may not acidify the urine sufficiently, the physician may need to prescribe a medication for this purpose. Still, these diet principles will help to increase the effectiveness of the medication.

Notes:

Courtesy of the Chauncey Sparks Center for Developmental and Learning Disorders, Division of Nutrition, Birmingham, Alabama.

Nutrition for Children with HIV

TO IMPROVE APPETITE

- Plan small, frequent meals. Keep snacks on hand. Leftovers, held at safe temperatures, make great snacks.
- Provide nutrient-dense foods, such as instant breakfast drinks, puddings, or shakes.
- Have your child sip on dietary supplements throughout the day.
- Have your child drink fluids at the end of meals rather than during meals. Broths are filling without adding extra calories.
- Feed your child in pleasant surroundings, in the company of family or friends.
- Rely on favorite foods only during times when your child's appetite is very good, so your child will not associate those foods with feeling ill.
- Select satisfying, nutritious meals when your child feels good, to make up for times when his or her appetite is poor.
- Serve your child the heaviest meal at noon, when his or her appetite may be better, rather than at night.

TO PREVENT OR COPE WITH NAUSEA AND VOMITING

- Be sure that your child eats and drinks meals slowly.
- Serve your child small, frequent meals.
- Serve dry foods such as toast, crackers, or bagels, especially after your child gets up in the morning.
- Avoid high-fat, greasy, or fried foods.
- Do not let your child consume liquids until at least 30 minutes after meals.
- Have your child sip cool liquids between meals, such as noncarbonated beverages (flat colas or ginger ale, and fruit juices); avoid liquids that are lukewarm.
- Avoid serving spicy foods; serve bland foods, such as rice.
- Try serving cold foods or foods at room temperature.
- Try serving salty foods, which your child may tolerate better than those that are sweet.
- Be sure that your child eats in well-ventilated areas, away from food aromas.

TO COPE WITH TASTE AND SMELL CHANGES

- Experiment with your child's favorite seasonings. Cinnamon, mint, basil, oregano, or bacon bits are some ideas; use lemon juice in food preparation.
- Encourage your child to sip liquids or suck on hard candies or fresh fruits to reduce off-flavors in his or her mouth.

continues

continued

- If your child finds that meat tastes bitter, try marinating it in sweet-and-sour sauce, dressings, or teriyaki sauce; or try protein alternates (eggs, cheese, nuts, fish, milk, tofu).
- Disguise the taste of medications with juice, lemonade, milk, or applesauce.
- Help your child to practice good oral hygiene; use sugarless gum or lemon juice to cleanse the mouth.

TO COPE WITH DISORDERS OF THE ORAL/ESOPHAGEAL CAVITY

Swallowing

- Serve your child soft-textured foods, and avoid sticky or coarse ones.
- Add gravies and sauces to meat and starches, or encourage your child to sip fluids with them.
- Cut food into small pieces or blenderize.
- Serve milkshakes or prepared dietary supplements.
- Try serving cold items, as they can be soothing.

Mouth Sores

- Avoid irritants such as spices or citrus, or acidic, rough, or coarse foods.
- Encourage your child to drink liquids or blenderized food through a straw to bypass sores.
- Stimulate saliva with sour candy.

Dry Mouth

- Stimulate saliva with sour candy.

Mucus Production

- Serve citrus juices or encourage your child to suck on lemon and sugar to cut mucus.

TO REDUCE DIARRHEA

- Serve smaller, more frequent meals to aid in preventing stomach distention.
- Serve liquids between meals and at room temperature.
- Avoid lactose (milk products), substituting lactose-free milk (such as Lactaid) or milk products.
- Avoid fatty foods, which may be malabsorbed.
- Avoid foods high in insoluble fiber, such as whole grains (for example, bran) or raw fruits or vegetables with skins or seeds.

continues

continued

- Try a bulking agent, such as Metamucil, or serve foods high in soluble fibers (pectins and gums), including oatmeal, pears, and potatoes.
- Avoid corn, garlic, and nuts, which may not be well tolerated.
- If your child is gassy, avoid gas-producing foods, such as citrus fruits or juices, carbonated beverages, excessive sweets, chewing gum, dried beans, onions, broccoli, cauliflower, and vegetables from the cabbage family.
- Avoid caffeine, which may act as a gastrointestinal stimulant.
- To help replace electrolytes, include high-potassium foods and fluids such as bananas, orange juice, peaches, or apricot nectar, or sports drinks, such as Gatorade.

If diarrhea persists, particularly if it is frequent, watery, or in large amounts, contact your physician.

TO IMPROVE CALORIE AND PROTEIN INTAKE

- Add milk,* honey, sugar, margarine, or butter to hot cereals, soups, and gravies. Use fat in cooking and at the table.
- Add dry milk powder* to mashed potatoes, casseroles, soup, pudding,* and milk* drinks.
- Serve whole milk* or half and half* rather than low-fat milk.
- Spread peanut butter* on toast, waffles, bananas, or apples.
- Use sour cream, mayonnaise, whipped cream, jelly, honey, and syrup.
- Add a slice of cheese* to scrambled eggs, sandwiches, hamburgers,* and apple pie.
- Serve nuts,* cheese,* hard-boiled eggs,* and hard candies as snacks.
- Try instant breakfast drinks* or commercially prepared supplements.*

OTHER POINTERS

- If you lack refrigeration or cooking facilities, many foods that are high in protein and/or calories require little storage or preparation, including peanut butter, jelly, nuts, canned or dried fruits, candy, chocolate, crackers or bread with toppings such as honey, and single servings of canned fish and juices.
- To avoid food-borne illness, always clean food, hands, and work space well. Keep cold foods cold and hot foods hot!
- Each person will tolerate foods differently. Your child's diet must be planned to meet his or her individual needs in order to provide the best nutritional care.
- Questions regarding this and other nutrition information may be answered by contacting your nutritionist.

*These foods are high in protein as well as calories.

Source: Carol Sherman et al., *Quality Food and Nutrition Services for AIDS Patients*, Aspen Publishers, Inc., © 1990.

Tips for Food Safety

WASH

- Hands thoroughly in hot, soapy water before and after preparing and eating meals, and after using the toilet.
- Fresh fruits and vegetables thoroughly with cold water before and after peeling.
- All utensils, cutting boards, and appliances thoroughly with soap and hot water. If they have been in contact with raw meat, fish, or poultry, wash after use and before exposure to cooked products or other foods.
- Dishes in hot, soapy water with clean cloth or sponge. Then soak the cloth or sponge in a mixture of household bleach and water (1 part to 10 parts) for 5 minutes. Use this solution to clean counters, floors, and appliances.

REFRIGERATE

- Foods containing protein such as fish, poultry, lean meat, cheese, eggs, and ready-made salads or sandwich fillings immediately. Keep all foods covered.
- Foods to defrost rather than leaving them on a counter at room temperature to defrost. Do not refreeze food that has been defrosted or partially thawed.

COOK

- Foods thoroughly especially fish, poultry, eggs, and meats.

AVOID

- Raw foods that are usually cooked before serving or raw (unpasteurized) milk.

Notes:

Source: Catherine Cowell and Karen W. Rubin, "Children with AIDS Living at Home: A Challenge for a Community Support Team," *Nutrition Focus*, Vol. 4:5, Child Development and Mental Retardation Center, University of Washington, Seattle, Washington, © 1989.

Breastfeeding

BREASTFEEDING IS BEST

Your milk is the best start you can give your baby, because:

- Breast milk has everything your baby needs to grow up strong and healthy.
- Breast milk helps keep your baby from getting sick.
- Breast milk tastes good! Breastfeeding your baby is good for you too. It helps tighten up your stomach and gets you back in shape. As your baby grows, you will save time and money. You do not have to buy anything. Your milk is always fresh and ready to use.

BREASTFEEDING IS SPECIAL

Mother's milk is special for a baby. It does not matter if your breasts are large or small. Your body makes plenty of milk for your baby.

The more your baby nurses, the more milk your body makes. And it makes the right kind and amount of milk at the right time for your baby. Your milk changes as the baby grows. It changes to meet the baby's needs.

The first milk from your breast is called **colostrum**. Colostrum:

- Is good for your baby
- Helps protect your baby from sickness
- Looks yellow and thick or may look clear and watery
- Changes color in a few days

Each time you breastfeed your baby, you will have two types of milk. During the first few minutes, your milk may look bluish and thin like water. Later, it may get thick and creamy.

Breast milk is all your baby needs for four to six months.

TO PUT BABY TO YOUR BREAST

1. Hold your baby close with mouth in front of your nipple.
2. Put your hand behind the brown area and lift up your breast.
3. Touch your baby's lips with your nipple and squeeze out a little milk (see Figure A).

Figure A

continues

continued

4. When your baby opens its mouth wide, pull your baby close so that your baby can get as much of the brown part of the breast as possible inside mouth (see Figure B).
5. Hold your baby close while nursing (see Figure C).
6. Burp your baby before changing to your other breast. Next time, start your baby feeding on the second breast.

Figure B

Figure C

TO TAKE BABY AWAY FROM YOUR BREAST

Gently break the suction by placing a clean finger in the corner of your baby's mouth between the gums.

WASH UP! IT'S IMPORTANT!

Rinse breasts at least twice a day.

- Splash clear water on your nipples. Do not use soap or anything else on your nipples—just plain water.
- Pat your breasts dry with a clean cloth. This will help keep your nipples from getting sore.

Remember, washing is important. Always pick up your baby with clean hands. Be sure to wash your hands with soap and water after you change your baby's diaper or after you go to the bathroom.

continues

continued

WHEN TO FEED YOUR BABY

A new baby needs to eat often, about every two to three hours during both day and night (eight or more times in 24 hours). Feeding often is also important to you. It helps give you a good milk supply and keeps your breasts from becoming too full.

Sometimes your baby will need to eat more often than every two hours. This is normal and should be allowed. It is also alright for you to nurse your baby if your breasts are becoming too full.

If you are careful about the way your baby nurses and make sure that your nipple and the brown area are pulled well into your baby's mouth, you can allow your baby to nurse eight to ten minutes from the first day. This gives your baby colostrum and helps get your milk started. Within a few days, your baby will probably want to nurse the usual 15 to 20 minutes at each feeding.

IS YOUR BABY GETTING ENOUGH TO EAT?

Your body makes as much milk as your baby needs. You can ask yourself these questions to tell if your baby is getting enough to eat.

- Does my baby have six, seven, or eight wet diapers each day?
- Does my baby sleep some between feedings?
- Is my baby gaining weight?

If you answer "no" to any of these questions, try feeding more times each day. Also, let your baby feed longer.

WHAT ABOUT BABY'S DIRTY DIAPERS?

The breastfed baby's dirty diapers may be:

- Bright yellow to dark brown in color
- Very soft and a little lumpy
- Without a strong smell
- As many as ten in one day
- None at all for three or four days

All are normal. It just depends on your baby.

continues

continued

TO TAKE CARE OF YOUR BREASTS

If your nipples get sore, try these suggestions:

- When you nurse, try to hold your baby closer and try to allow your baby to hold more of the brown area inside the mouth (especially the bottom side near your baby's tongue).
- Hold your baby differently when you nurse. Put your baby's feet under your arm like a football or lie down beside your baby in bed. Changing positions keeps you from getting too sore in one place.
- Feed your baby for a shorter time than usual (but more often, if your baby seems hungry).
- Wrap an ice cube in a cloth, wet it, and put it on the sore nipple before you breastfeed. Leave it on for 10 to 30 seconds.
- Splash clear water over the nipple after each breastfeeding. Pat dry with a clean cloth or paper towel. Do not use soap or alcohol.
- Give your nipples some fresh air for about 15 minutes after nursing.

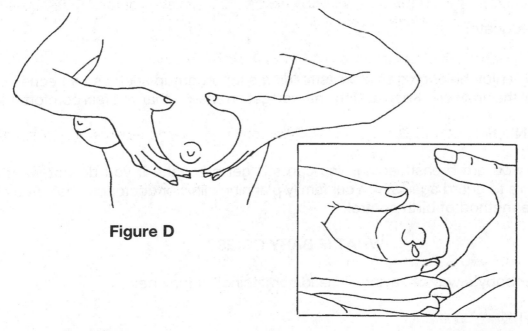

Figure D

Figure E

If your breasts are hard and swollen, try these suggestions:

- Feed your baby more often to keep breasts soft and empty.
- Soak a cloth in warm water and put it on your breasts, or take a warm shower. Squeeze out some milk to make your breasts softer so your baby can get a good hold (see Figures D and E).
- Feed your baby in more than one way. Try sitting up and lying down.

continues

continued

- Gently massage your breasts from under the arm and down to the nipple. This will help reduce soreness you may feel in your breasts.
- Keep breastfeeding. When your breasts are swollen, you may not feel well. You should feel better in one or two days. Drink lots of liquids. Take no medicine. If you have a fever, call your clinic or physician.

Do not stop breastfeeding.

WHO CAN HELP?

During the first few months of breastfeeding, you may have ups and downs. If you have a question, ask a:

- nurse
- nutritionist/dietitian
- nursing mother
- midwife
- childbirth educator
- physician

Some women enjoy belonging to a breastfeeding support group such as La Leche League. No one has all the answers. Keep asking until you get an answer that you feel comfortable with.

FAMILY PLANNING

Even though you are breastfeeding, you can still get pregnant! If you do not want to get pregnant, be sure to guard against it. Your family planning clinic or doctor can help you choose a safe, effective method of birth control.

WHAT IF BABY CRIES?

Crying is your baby's way of saying, "I need something!" It may be:

- A clean diaper
- A burp
- A hug and kiss
- A nap
- More or less covers to be comfortable

If you have recently breastfed, try giving your baby these things first. If nothing helps, your baby may still be hungry. So try breastfeeding more often until your body makes more milk.

continues

continued

BREASTFEEDING WHEN YOU ARE SICK

You can keep breastfeeding even with most illnesses, such as coughs, colds, fever, or diarrhea. Your milk is good, and it still protects your baby from many illnesses. If you have questions about breastfeeding when sick, call your clinic.

When you breastfeed, you are eating for both you and your baby, so you will need to eat more than usual. Eat well and eat a healthy diet.

Each day you should eat:

- 3 servings of milk, yogurt, and cheese products
- 4 servings of fruits and juices (at least one serving should be from the citrus, melon, and berries group)
- 5 servings of vegetables (at least one serving each of dark green, deep yellow, and starchy vegetables)
- 11 servings of grains, breads, and cereals (include whole-grain products often)
- 2 to 3 servings of meat, fish, poultry, eggs, dried beans, and peas (for a total of 7 ounces per day)

Be sure to finish your prenatal vitamins. If you have a question about the foods you eat, ask your dietitian.

BREASTFEEDING—THE GIFT OF LOVE

Your breastmilk is the very best food for your baby. So any and all breastfeeding is good. But try to breastfeed for at least four months. Six months is even better!

Remember, it's worth it! Your milk gives your baby the very best start in life. And only you can give it!

Notes:

Courtesy of Iowa Department of Health and U.S. Department of Agriculture, Women, Infants, and Children (WIC) Special Supplemental Food Program.

Oral-Motor Development and Feeding Skills

ORAL-MOTOR DEVELOPMENT AND NUTRITION

Optimal nutrition is essential for all children to achieve their physical and developmental potential. The well-nourished child is likely to grow at an expected rate, have an increased capacity for learning and cognitive ability, have resistance to infections, and have the energy to take advantage of opportunities that are offered. The nutritional well-being of the child who has a developmental disability is of prime importance but, due to a variety of medical and physical problems, it may be difficult to achieve.

One of the most common causes of diminished nutritional health in the child with a developmental disability is abnormal oral-motor development, which may actually limit food and nutrient intake. While the development of oral-motor skills is important to the feeding process, it is also important for the development of prespeech and language skills, as well as social interaction.

NORMAL ORAL-MOTOR DEVELOPMENT

A working knowledge of oral-motor development and feeding skills is necessary for the caregiver of the child to develop realistic expectations within the child's capacity for development. The following overview consists of the progression of skills necessary for bottle and cup drinking, spoon feeding of semisolids, and the development of chewing skills.

Bottle and Cup Drinking

- **Suckling**, an early method of sucking, is normally observed in the first 5 to 6 months of life and is characterized by a forward-backward movement of the tongue. The rhythmical licking action of the tongue on the nipple is combined with jaw opening and closing, and there is usually loose approximation of the lips. Suckling is gradually replaced by sucking.
- **Sucking**, a pattern that occurs gradually, is usually achieved by 6 to 8 months of age. It is characterized by a rhythmical raising and lowering of the tongue to obtain liquid. There is firmer approximation of the lips and less jaw movement observed in sucking than in suckling. Suckling and sucking trigger the swallowing mechanism, resulting in the smooth coordination of suckling-sucking, swallowing, and breathing.
- **Cup drinking** is usually introduced between 4 and 6 months of age. The baby responds either by attempting the sucking procedure or by allowing small amounts to be poured into the mouth. There are 3 stages of jaw control development involved in cup drinking.

continues

continued

Guidelines for Jaw Control Development Involved in Cup Drinking

1. Age 4 to 6 months through 12 months of age:
   - wide up and down movement of jaw resulting in liquid loss
   - poor or inconsistent lip activity
   - combination of suckling and sucking used by the tongue
2. Age 15 through 18 months:
   - jaw stabilization achieved externally by biting down on cup, resulting in less liquid loss
   - lip function improves
3. By 24 months of age:
   - jaw stabilization achieved through active muscle control
   - intake of liquid controlled with cup between lips with little jaw opening

---

Spoon Feeding of Semisolids

- **Spoon feeding** is usually introduced between 4 and 6 months of age. Initially, when food is presented, the baby sees it, anticipates, and begins to suckle with initial difficulty in grading jaw movement. Food is scraped off onto the upper teeth, and lips do not help remove it. At 4 to 5 months of age, the tongue is quiet in anticipation of the food, and the lips may reach forward for the spoon. At 6 months, the lips actively participate in removing food from the spoon. Lip pressure and coordination improve with increasing age. The child initially uses wide jaw opening and closing but learns to grade jaw movements.

Development of Chewing

Chewing involves the development of jaw, tongue, and lip control. It is characterized by phasic bite, munching, tongue lateralization, and vertical, lateral, and rotary jaw movement.

- **Phasic bite**, a rhythmical bite and release with jaw opening and closing, can be observed from birth to 3 to 5 months of age.
- **Munching**, the flattening and spreading of the tongue combined with up and down movement of the jaw, begins around 5 months of age and develops as a combination of two primitive patterns: phasic bite and sucking.
- **Tongue lateralization**, a rolling movement of the tongue toward the side of the mouth to project food between the molars, occurs around 5 to 6 months of age when food is placed on or near the molars. Then, around 10 to 11 months of age, the child transfers food from

continues

continued

the center of the tongue to the side of the mouth. Finally, at 15 to 18 months, food can be transferred from one side of the mouth to the other.

- **Tongue thrust** is the forceful protrusion of the tongue from the mouth that may interfere with the insertion of a nipple or spoon. Food may be pushed out of the mouth during feeding.

- **Tonic bite reflex** is the tight closure of the jaw in response to oral-tactile stimulation, resulting in difficulty with opening the mouth. (*Note:* The tonic bite reflex is different from jaw clenching in which the child uses a firm bite on the spoon or cup due to jaw instability. Jaw clenching occurs due to a child's difficulty with grading jaw movement and is more readily released than the tonic bite.)

- **Lip retraction** is the drawing back of the lips so that they form a tight line over the mouth. The lips cannot assist in sucking or removing food from the spoon.

- **Tongue retraction** is the pulling back of the tongue, often toward the roof of the mouth, which may interfere with breathing or with placing the nipple or spoon in the mouth (or both).

- **Exaggerated or abnormal gag reflex** is elicited by stimulation to the front of the tongue or lips, which results in the forward and downward movement of the tongue and extension of the jaw. It may be caused by increased hypersensitivity or by difficulty with swallowing.

Notes:

Source: Tina Shaddix and Nancy Barnacastle, "Oral-Motor Development and Feeding Techniques," Nutritional Care for the Child with Developmental Disabilities series, United Cerebral Palsy of Greater Birmingham, Birmingham, Alabama, © 1986.

Enhancing Oral-Motor Skills

Treatment techniques for oral-motor dysfunction stress the importance of correct positioning and handling techniques as well as increasing the texture of food that is consumed by the child. These techniques can be incorporated by caregivers into the feeding experience to promote and enhance the development of oral-motor skills.

When attempting to make changes in the feeding procedure, it is important to follow these guidelines in an orderly sequence:

- Provide correct positioning.
- Increase food texture.
- Provide oral treatment and appropriate feeding techniques. (For more information, see handouts on Oral Treatment Techniques and Feeding Treatment Techniques.)

POSITIONING

The positioning that a child with a developmental disability assumes can affect oral-motor skills and interfere with the success of a feeding program. Problems that may interfere with proper positioning include: hypertonic (high) or hypotonic (low) muscle tone, asymmetries, head and neck hyperextension, shoulder elevation, shoulder retraction, poor trunk control, posterior pelvic tilt, increased flexor tone of the upper extremities, increased extensor tone, and adduction of the lower extremities.

Furthermore, head and neck hyperextension may result in tongue retraction, jaw extension, cheek and lip retraction, or choking. Poor head and trunk control may result in the child feeling posturally insecure and unstable, thus requiring increased effort on the part of the child to maintain stability. Consequently, oral-motor control is decreased. Therefore, a good sitting posture that provides stability and support for the child is imperative to the development of oral-motor skills.

Adapted seating equipment has proven useful to help achieve proper positioning for the child with developmental disabilities. Three-layered cardboard as well as wooden chair inserts with lap trays are practical alternatives for this population.

For some children, regular car seats, highchairs, wheelchairs, and travel chairs may be adapted to provide proper positioning for feeding. However, major positioning considerations should be performed under the direction of a physical or occupational therapist.

Components of good sitting posture for feeding aim for:

- neutral head and neck alignment, with head in midline
- stable and relaxed shoulders

continues

continued

- symmetrical upper and lower trunk, extended and aligned
- neutral and stable pelvis
- 90° flexion for hips, knees, and ankles, with hips slightly abducted
- supported and aligned feet

INCREASING FOOD TEXTURE

One of the most important aspects to consider in feeding a child with oral-motor dysfunction is the texture of food that is offered. This texture plays a major role in the type of tongue, lip, and jaw movements that are exhibited by the child. Certain textures serve to enhance proper oral development while others only facilitate additional abnormal patterns. Furthermore, if the child is not offered foods to chew, he or she may never acquire this important skill. Therefore, it is critical that the child's diet include as much texture as possible, and that the texture be gradually increased in a progressive manner.

The progression from liquids to strained foods and then to a greater variety of textures may be a slower process in children with developmental disabilities. Problems with abnormal muscle tone, poor postural alignment, hypersensitivity, and other difficulties may interfere with the addition of appropriate foods. It is extremely important to encourage this process as soon as possible because the longer the child goes without learning to manage solid foods, the more resistant he or she will become. If resistance becomes a persistent problem, a therapist (physical, occupational, or speech) should be consulted.

Notes:

Source: Tina Shaddix and Nancy Barnacastle, "Oral-Motor Development and Feeding Techniques," Nutritional Care for the Child with Developmental Disabilities series, United Cerebral Palsy of Greater Birmingham, Birmingham, Alabama, © 1986.

Guidelines for the Progression of Food Textures

The guidelines below will assist in the identification of various stages of oral-motor development and in the selection of foods appropriate for each stage. The child's therapist (physical, occupational, or speech) may also be of assistance in determining readiness skills for increased texture.

LEVEL 1—PUREED FOODS

- Avoid the use of commercially prepared strained (baby) foods. The taste difference will make the transition to table foods more difficult.
- Puree regular table foods to the consistency of strained foods by using a household blender. Allow several weeks for the child to adapt to the change in taste.
- Progress to level 2 when the child displays a predominant sucking action during feeding, but cannot move food to the sides of the mouth using the tongue.

LEVEL 2—THICKENED PUREED FOODS

- Thicken pureed foods in order to facilitate certain tongue and jaw movements that are unnecessary to ingest thinner foods. Nutritious thickeners include mashed potato flakes, wheat germ, bread crumbs, or dry baby cereals. Thicker pureed foods may also be produced by using less blender action.
- Include other nutritious foods such as oatmeal or hot wheat cereal, mashed potatoes, mashed banana, applesauce, or yogurt.
- Progress to level 3 when the child begins to display vertical (up and down) chewing.

LEVEL 3—GROUND FOODS

- Grind regular table foods by using a small baby-food grinder, or a food chopper, both of which can be purchased at most department stores. A household food processor may be used for grinding larger quantities of food.
- Include ground meats with broth or gravy, ground or mashed cooked vegetables and fruits, scrambled egg, mashed soft-boiled egg, egg salad, cottage cheese, pimento cheese, or prepared meat salads.
- Offer foods designed to stimulate biting and chewing.
- Progress to level 4 when the child begins to move foods from side to side by using the tongue.

continues

continued

LEVEL 4—CHOPPED FOODS

- Obtain textures for this stage by chopping meats, fruits, and vegetables into small bite-size pieces by using a knife rather than the blender, food processor, or baby-food grinder. Meats, fruits, and vegetables should be cut into bite-size pieces.

- Include chopped meats and casseroles, chopped cooked vegetables, chopped fruits, grilled cheese or chopped meat sandwiches, and finely chopped slaw or salad.

- Progress to level 5 when the child has a mature rotary chew and freely moves food from side to side in the mouth. However, some children with developmental disabilities may never progress to this advanced level.

LEVEL 5—COARSELY CHOPPED FOODS

- Include small pieces of chopped meats, crispy fruits and vegetables, coarsely chopped salad and slaw, and cornbread.

HELPFUL HINT

Do not mix foods together unless it is necessary. Mixing foods deprives the child of sensory cues of color, texture, and taste necessary for normal feeding.

Level of Oral Development	Desired Food Texture
• Child tolerates only commercially prepared strained foods.	• Level 1—pureed table foods
• Child handles food through a sucking action and cannot move food to sides of mouth.	• Level 2—thickened pureed foods
• Child begins to show vertical (up and down) chewing motions.	• Level 3—ground foods
• Child begins to move food from side to side by using the tongue.	• Level 4—chopped foods
• Child displays mature rotary chew.	• Level 5—coarsely chopped foods

Source: Tina Shaddix and Nancy Barnacastle, "Oral-Motor Development and Feeding Techniques," Nutritional Care for the Child with Developmental Disabilities series, United Cerebral Palsy of Greater Birmingham, Birmingham, Alabama, © 1986.

Introducing Liquids from a Cup

Just as the texture of food plays an important role in the oral-motor development of the child, the consistency of liquid offered is also critical to this same development.

When a child first begins to drink from a cup, he or she often does not have the mature swallow pattern or adequate jaw control (or both) necessary to manage extremely runny liquids such as water and milk. This difficulty is especially true for some children with developmental disabilities. In addition to the immature swallow, the child may also have difficulty getting a complete seal with the lips on the cup and may therefore lose a great deal of the liquid.

Some children with oral-motor difficulties are often able to handle thicker liquids more efficiently than thinner ones. This difference may be due in part to the greater tactile stimulation provided by the thicker, heavier liquids and to the slower passage of the liquid to the throat. Therefore, in order to ensure an adequate intake of fluid from the cup as well as facilitation of a more mature swallowing pattern, liquids from level 1 should be offered initially, with a gradual progression to level 4 as oral skills improve.

Recommended Fluid Intake	
Child's Weight (Pounds)	Total Fluids Needed in 24 Hours (Cups)
7	2
12	3⅓
21	5
26	6
36	7
44	8

Weaning from the bottle to the cup is usually completed by 12 months of age in babies without disabilities. With regard to the child with developmental disabilities, early weaning is even more critical to the development of oral skills.

continues

continued

Comparative Difficulties of Liquids

Easiest

Level 1: heavy, milky liquids

— milk thickened with baby cereal, blenderized fruit, or yogurt

— milkshakes

— whole milk (1 cup), blended with baby rice cereal (½ cup), fruit (½ cup), and corn oil (2 teaspoons)

— cooked cereals thinned with milk, such as oatmeal, hot wheat cereals, and so forth

Level 2: heavy, clear liquids

— fruit blended in own juice

— blended fruit drinks, such as fruit slush and sherbets

Level 3: thin, milky liquids

— milk

— cream soup (thinned)

Level 4: thin, clear liquids

— water

— bouillon/broth

— fruit juices

— soft drinks

Most Difficult

— tea

Source: Tina Shaddix and Nancy Barnacastle, "Oral-Motor Developmental and Feeding Techniques," Nutritional Care for the Child with Developmental Disabilities series, United Cerebral Palsy of Greater Birmingham, Birmingham, Alabama, © 1986.

Oral Treatment Techniques

The following techniques are effective in developing a proper sensitivity around the face and for increasing oral awareness. It is recommended that these techniques be incorporated into daily activities such as playtime or bathtime. It is especially important that the child not be overstimulated prior to mealtime. Individual children have their own level of sensitivity, and some may react adversely to these techniques. Therefore it is important that these procedures be recommended and demonstrated by a professional who works with the child.

TOWELING

Toweling provides firm sensory input and elongation of the musculature of the child's facial-oral area.

The procedure for toweling is as follows. Using a washcloth or other material that the child can tolerate, provide deep pressure with graded movement to the following areas:

- temporomandibular joints (below cheekbones) to corners of the mouth (Illustration A)
- below eyes to above upper lip (Illustration B)
- below the nose, pressing downward to upper lip (Illustration C)
- below lower lip, pressing upward (Illustration D)

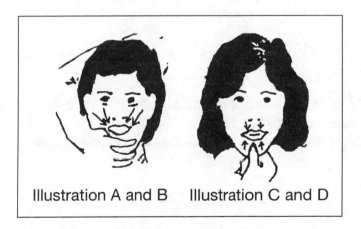

Illustration A and B   Illustration C and D

Relative to the toweling technique, it is helpful to:

- Begin with deep pressure sensory input on the child's body (legs, trunk, arms) and then progress to facial area if the child is especially hypersensitive.
- Perform toweling techniques whenever it is necessary to wipe the child's face, such as mealtime, bathtime, playtime, or when the child has drooled.

continues

continued

RUBBING TEETH AND GUMS

Rubbing the biting surfaces of the teeth or gums may aid in developing normal oral sensitivity. A commercially available toothbrush trainer system may be used initially for this procedure because it may be easier for the child to tolerate. A wash cloth or towel wrapped around an adult's finger or fingers may also be used.

The procedure is as follows:

- Talk to the child and let him or her know what you are doing.
- Rub the biting surface of the teeth and gums, using deep pressure. A small amount of bleeding from the gums may occur. If this problem persists, a dentist should be consulted.
- Go slowly and be cautious as you may elicit a tonic bite reflex.
- Guide the child's own fingers or a pacifier through the above procedures as an alternative method.

ELONGATION

Elongation of the tongue musculature is useful in inhibiting tongue retraction and providing stability and sensory input to the tongue. The procedure is as follows:

- Press down on tongue and stroke slightly forward, using deep pressure.

DEEP PRESSURE

Deep pressure applied to the hard palate is useful in providing sensory input. The procedure is as follows:

- Rub the hard palate (area in the roof of the mouth directly behind the teeth).
- Rub forward, backward, and side to side.
- Do not rub the soft palate (area behind the hard palate) because it is an especially hypersensitive area.

LIP FLICKING

Lip flicking is useful for a child with lip retraction to help release the tone in the upper lip. The procedure is as follows:

- Use oral control.
- Place index or little finger in the mouth halfway along upper lip; rapidly turn finger causing upper lip to come forward.

Source: Tina Shaddix and Nancy Barnacastle, "Oral-Motor Development and Feeding Techniques," Nutritional Care for the Child with Developmental Disabilities series, United Cerebral Palsy of Greater Birmingham, Birmingham, Alabama, © 1986.

Feeding Treatment Techniques

ORAL/JAW CONTROL

Oral control is used to provide jaw stability so the child may actively use the tongue, lips, and cheeks. This procedure may also be used for the following reasons:

- to obtain neutral head and neck alignment and midline orientation
- to provide a base for tongue movement that inhibits tongue retraction and thrusting
- to stimulate up and out movement of the lower lip and to provide better lip activity and closure
- to inhibit exaggerated opening of the mouth by preventing jaw thrusting and biting
- to monitor abnormal suck and swallow
- to reduce predominant suck pattern
- to facilitate munching and chewing

Note: As the child develops more active jaw control, the oral control procedure may gradually be discontinued.

Five specific oral/jaw control techniques should be utilized during cup drinking, spoon feeding, and biting and chewing.

1. The feeder sits beside the child and comes from behind with the arm. This technique helps to position the child for improved shoulder stabilization, neck elongation, and neutral head flexion.
2. The side of the middle finger is placed under the chin at the base of the tongue musculature. Upward pressure is applied to assist with closure and to inhibit tongue retraction and thrust as well as jaw extension and retraction.
3. The index finger is placed in the depression between the chin and lower lip to assist with opening the mouth. Slight inward pressure is applied to stimulate the lower lip in coming up and out.
4. The thumb should be in the palm or away from face. Do not place thumb on the mandible. (Illustration A).
5. If the child is fed from the front, place the thumb on the chin with middle or index finger under chin, being careful not to force head and neck hyperextension (Illustration B).

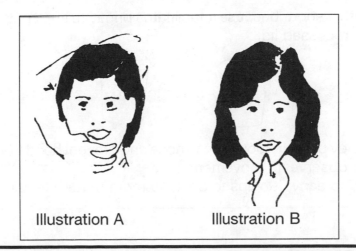

Illustration A   Illustration B

continues

continued

Helpful Hints

- Use a mirror to help monitor the following undesirable positions: (1) pulling mandible to one side; (2) lateral head turn; (3) pulling chin forward; and (4) head and neck hyperextension.
- Never use intermittent pressure when using jaw control. Simply apply firm, continuous pressure on the lower jaw. Intermittent pressure results in abnormal chewing patterns.
- Maintain jaw control until the child has swallowed.

CUP DRINKING

Six specific techniques may be utilized when the child is having difficulty drinking from a cup:

1. Use oral/jaw control to provide stability and to reduce predominant suck patterns.
2. Check to make sure child has enough head and neck flexion (head and neck are not hyperextended).
3. Place the rim of the cup on the lower lip rather than between the teeth. Placing the cup between the teeth tends to stimulate the bite reflex.
4. Lift the cup so that the liquid just touches the upper lip, forcing active involvement of the upper lip in the drinking process.
5. Let the cup remain between the lips after each swallow. Removal of the cup after each swallow may result in an inefficient and abnormal drinking pattern.
6. Begin cup drinking with a slightly thickened liquid, which stimulates swallowing and is less likely to spill.

Helpful Hints

- Do not use a cup with a spout because it facilitates primitive suck patterns. Use a cut-out cup or a cup with a recessed lid.

- Use cut-out cups. They provide room for the nose and prevent head from tilting back. They also allow feeder to observe lip movements.
- Introduce cup drinking early; it helps to develop more mature feeding skills.

---

continues

continued

BITING AND CHEWING

Two specific techniques may be utilized to stimulate chewing and adequate biting:

1. Place food on the molars or in between gum and cheek to stimulate chewing motions and tongue lateralization. Use jaw control if needed. (Remember to alternate sides of the mouth.)
2. Stimulate biting and chewing by including toasted bread strips or crusts, dried fruits, cheese strips, cooked vegetable pieces, and strips of meat in the diet. Note that the child may have difficulty with raisins, grapes, or meats that require shearing and tearing.

Helpful Hints

- Avoid foods with mixed textures (such as vegetable soup) that require swallowing part of the food while continuing to hold the remainder in the mouth.
- Avoid chewable foods that break apart into firm and diffuse pieces (for example, crackers, chips, and so forth). The child may find it impossible to put together a mass to be chewed.
- Give the child as much texture as he or she is able to handle. The child will never learn to chew if all foods are blended or mashed.
- Do not passively move jaw in rotary or chewing motion. This manipulation may interfere with coordination between movements of lips, tongue, and jaw.

SPOON FEEDING

Five specific techniques should be utilized when introducing food from the spoon:

1. Present food from the front of the child with spoon below eye level.
2. Place the spoon in the child's mouth and apply firm pressure on the middle of the tongue. This action stimulates spontaneous use of the lips and tongue and inhibits tongue thrusting.
3. Withdraw the spoon as soon as lips begin closing. Do not scrape the upper lip or teeth with the spoon. Scraping tends to result in lip retraction and requires no action on the part of the child to remove food from the spoon.
4. Maintain lip and jaw closure by using oral/jaw control until the child swallows. With the lips closed, the tongue can push food around in the mouth rather than thrusting it out. If lip movement is poor, do not passively pull down on upper lip. This action may increase spasticity in the child who is hypersensitive. Lip closure is elicited more successfully through proper oral/jaw control techniques.

continues

continued

5. Do not excessively wipe food from the child's chin. When you desire to wipe, use a blotting motion with firm pressure. Use proper jaw control to eliminate an excessive amount of food leakage.

Helpful Hints

- Choose a spoon that enables the child to easily use the lips to remove food. The bowl of the spoon should be shallow, short, and rounded on the end. Long, pointed spoons may stimulate a gag reflex.

- Choose a soft plastic or rubber-coated spoon for children with hypersensitivity or a bite reflex.

- Begin spoon feeding by placing a small amount of food on the front of the spoon. This placement makes removal easier.

- Do not place spoon too far into the mouth. This action may elicit the gag reflex.

- Do not attempt to remove or pull the spoon from the mouth when a bite reflex has been elicited. Wait until the child releases the bite.

- Avoid using an infa-feeder. It only serves to prolong immature oral-motor patterns.

Notes:

Source: Tina Shaddix and Nancy Barnacastle, "Oral-Motor Development and Feeding Techniques," Nutritional Care for the Child with Developmental Disabilities series, United Cerebral Palsy of Greater Birmingham, Birmingham, Alabama, © 1986.

Swallowing Problems

BASICS OF SWALLOWING

Swallowing of food and liquid requires coordination of a large number of muscles in the mouth, throat (pharynx), and esophagus (a tube that leads from the pharynx to the stomach). As food is placed in the mouth, the lips are closed to prevent drooling. Muscles of the tongue and jaw move food around in the mouth for chewing. When chewing is finished, the food is collected into a ball by movements of the tongue.

The swallow begins as the tongue pushes the food upward and backward toward the back of the mouth and the throat (pharynx). As the tongue pushes the food or liquid toward the back of the mouth, the muscles in the pharynx begin to move to receive the food. The top of the windpipe (larynx) begins to lift, move forward, and close to keep food from going into the lungs. The soft part of the roof of the mouth (the soft palate) lifts to close off the entrance to the nose.

As food passes over the back of the tongue and enters the pharynx, muscles in the pharynx contract to squeeze the food through the pharynx and into the esophagus. As the food approaches the entrance to the esophagus, the valve at the top of the esophagus opens to allow the food to pass. Muscles in the esophagus then contract to push the food from the top of the esophagus through the valve at the bottom of the esophagus and into the stomach.

Normal swallowing is a very fast process, taking less than 2 seconds to move the food from the mouth, through the pharynx, and into the esophagus. Normal swallowing is safe because the larynx (the entrance to the windpipe) is closed as the food passes. The food is normally moved efficiently through the mouth and pharynx, with very little trace of food or liquid left behind.

If larger amounts of food are swallowed at one time, the swallow takes slightly longer, and the muscles of the mouth and pharynx work simultaneously, rather than in a sequence. At times, the breath is held to protect the windpipe in anticipation of a very large swallow. Though normal swallowing changes at times with the types of food swallowed, the safety and efficiency of the swallow do not change.

TYPES OF SWALLOWING PROBLEMS

There are a large number of possible swallowing problems. There may be difficulties closing the lips, moving the tongue to control food during chewing, or moving the tongue to push food from the front to the back of the mouth. Muscles of the face may be weak and may allow food to collect in the cheeks. There may be a problem with sensation in the mouth so that the person cannot feel where food is located, or even be aware that there is any food in the mouth. Some people have a problem triggering the pharyngeal stage of swallowing so that the muscles in the pharynx do not begin to work fast enough. Other people may have difficulty coordinating the muscles that close and protect the windpipe (larynx) or with muscles that close the valve into the nose (the soft palate). Sometimes there are difficulties lifting the windpipe (larynx) or opening the valve into the esophagus.

continues

continued

Moreover, the control of muscles that push food through the pharynx may be damaged, causing food to be left behind in the throat. The muscles of the esophagus may also be damaged so that they cannot contract and put pressure on the food as it enters the esophagus. Any one of these problems can occur by itself or in combination with other abnormalities.

SIGNS OF A SWALLOWING PROBLEM

In some people, there is no outward sign or symptom of a swallowing problem. However, other people give clear signals that they are having difficulty swallowing. Most common signs of a swallowing problem include:

- coughing while eating or drinking or very soon after eating or drinking
- wet sounding voice during or after eating
- increased congestion in the chest after eating or drinking
- slow eating
- multiple swallows on a single mouthful of food
- obvious extra effort or difficulty while chewing or swallowing
- fatigue or shortness of breath while eating
- temperature rise 30 minutes to an hour after eating
- weight loss associated with increased slowness in eating
- repetitive pneumonias

If you see any of these signs or symptoms of a swallowing problem, you should bring it to the attention of the child's physician or seek a swallowing therapist, usually a speech-language pathologist, for evaluation.

DANGERS OF A SWALLOWING PROBLEM

If a swallowing problem remains untreated, the person can become dehydrated because of the inability to swallow liquids. The person's alertness level may change. Or, the person may lose weight and become malnourished because of difficulty eating foods that require a lot of chewing or foods of a particular thickness.

Pneumonia may also result from a swallowing problem if food or liquid gets into the lungs while swallowing. Or, the person may have increased secretions as the lungs clean themselves of food or liquid. In order to prevent these medical problems, people with suspected swallowing problems should receive careful evaluation, followed by carefully planned treatment.

continues

continued

CAUSES OF SWALLOWING PROBLEMS

Many different medical problems can cause swallowing difficulties. People with sudden damage to the nervous system, such as stroke, head injury, or spinal cord injury, may have difficulty swallowing. People with diseases affecting muscle strength or coordination may have swallowing problems. For example, people with the various types of muscular dystrophy, cerebral palsy, or even diabetes may have difficulty swallowing. People who have progressive neurological diseases such as motor neuron disease (amyotrophic lateral sclerosis [ALS]), myasthenia gravis, or multiple sclerosis (MS) may also have problems swallowing. Tumors of the head and neck and their treatment can cause swallowing problems, as can injuries to the neck or head. Other medical problems such as arthritis or scleroderma can cause swallowing difficulties, as can drying of the mouth (for example, as a side effect of taking certain drugs).

These various medical problems cause swallowing difficulties because they either damage sensation or weaken or discoordinate one or more of the muscles involved in swallowing. As a result, food enters the lungs or stays in the mouth or pharynx after the swallow. In this latter case, repeated swallows and increased effort are required.

Though each of these diseases or types of damage may cause different types of swallowing problems, people have one thing in common: They have difficulty eating safely and efficiently.

HOW CAN THE SWALLOWING PROBLEM BE EVALUATED?

There are many ways to evaluate a person's swallowing ability. One of the most common methods is an X-ray study known as a modified barium swallow. This test is a simple one in which the person sits comfortably in his or her usual position for eating and is given a variety of foods and liquids to swallow in different amounts. During the test, the person's mouth and pharynx are examined to determine whether each structure is moving normally and whether various muscles are operating normally. Not only can the structures be seen, but the food can also be observed as it moves through the mouth and pharynx to find out if it stays in the mouth or throat after attempts to swallow. During this X-ray study, the swallowing therapist can also introduce treatment techniques to improve the person's swallow. In this way, the swallowing therapist can determine the best types of treatment for the person.

Other ways to examine swallowing use a small fiberoptic tube to look down the person's throat as he or she swallows or use other imaging techniques to view the mouth, the larynx, or the pharynx during swallowing. All of these procedures are comfortable and should not cause the person any difficulty.

WHAT TREATMENTS ARE AVAILABLE?

No two people are alike in their swallowing problem. Each person must have an individual treatment plan developed for him or her after careful, detailed evaluation of swallowing.

continues

continued

There is a wide range of treatments for swallowing problems. Some treatments are as simple as changing the person's head or body position when swallowing, or changing the kinds of foods the person eats. Others involve the person's learning new ways to swallow. Some procedures exercise muscles that are not working properly.

WHAT CAN YOU DO TO HELP?

First, you can help identify the person with a swallowing problem and tell the person's physician. Or, you can schedule an appointment with a swallowing therapist for an evaluation.

Once the person's swallow has been evaluated and a therapy program has been outlined, you are very important in helping the person follow the treatment plan. You can remind the person about the exercises or swallowing techniques, and perhaps work with the person at home to practice these techniques. Assist the person during meals to assure that he or she is following directions correctly and eating the correct types of foods.

If you must feed the person, it is important that you place the correct amount of food in the person's mouth in the area where the person has the best sensation. You may need to watch the person carefully to be sure that one spoonful of food has been swallowed before presenting another. Some people need to swallow two or three times on a single mouthful of food before more food is introduced. Other people need to take a swallow of liquid between every one or two swallows of solid food. Some people need to have food positioned in a certain place on the tray or on the table so they can see the food adequately.

The swallowing therapist will advise you about the best ways to help the person. The swallowing therapist will also show you how to best position the person's head or body, and will tell you which food consistencies the person can swallow safely, and what to watch for as the person swallows to be sure the person is a safe and efficient swallower.

The prediction for improvement of a swallowing problem is excellent if the person receives a detailed evaluation and an individual treatment plan, which may include therapy. As a caregiver you are critical to improvement by providing support in the home and by encouraging the person to practice and use the treatment provided by the swallowing therapist. You are an important part of the person's recovery.

Source: Jeri Logemann, PhD, *Swallowing Problems: How Can They Be Identified and Treated?*, Menu Magic, Indianapolis, Indiana, © 1991. The *Swallowing Problems* brochure is available in professional and caregiver editions. For free copies contact Menu Magic, PO Box 22236, Indianapolis, IN 46222; 800–572–5888.

Behavior Management at Mealtime

Some conflict is inevitable at mealtime, but if conflicts are managed within firm limits, mealtime is likely to be a satisfying experience.

Many mealtime conflicts arise when the child learns that misbehavior causes parents to give in to demands due to fear that the child will not receive adequate nourishment. The following eight guidelines may prove helpful when behavior problems arise at mealtime:

1. Serve appropriate foods to all family members. Do not cater to the child by serving foods not offered to other family members.

2. Make no comments about the amount of food eaten.

3. Set a reasonable time limit for completion of the meal. For some children a timer (bell) signaling the end of the meal establishes an objective end and seems less like punishment.

4. Refuse to become involved in a power conflict with the child. By praising appropriate behavior and ignoring the inappropriate, the child will be more likely to eat when hungry.

5. Do not threaten or scold the child for refusing to eat. Give no foods until the next scheduled meal or snack.

6. Ignore the child if a tantrum is thrown, or place the child in another room. Return attention only when calm is established.

7. Do not force-feed the child who does not feed independently. When inappropriate behavior occurs, turn away. After a few seconds try again. If food is again refused, wait several minutes and offer the food again. If it is still refused, remove the child from the table and withhold food until the next scheduled meal or snack.

8. Praise the child often for behavior compliance.

Notes:

Source: Tina Shaddix, "Meal Planning for the Childhood Years," Nutritional Care for the Child with Developmental Disabilities series, United Cerebral Palsy of Greater Birmingham, Birmingham, Alabama, © 1986.

Feeding the Newborn with Cleft Lip/Palate

A newborn baby with a cleft lip and/or palate may have feeding difficulties. Although the baby possesses the suck-swallow reflex, the sucking may not be adequate because the structure of the mouth does not permit strong suction. The most common problems noted in babies are taking in a great deal of air while feeding, feeding very slowly, and bringing milk or formula back up through the nose. Do not be alarmed by these incidents, but continue to be patient as you and the baby adjust to the situation.

Special nipples and bottles are usually needed. Using a squeeze bottle allows control of the rate of milk flow. A pulsing action throughout the entire feed is required with this bottle. Coordinating the squeeze with the baby's suck will be helpful. Some babies may be able to use a regular glass bottle with a special nipple. Experiment with several types of bottles and nipples to find the combination best suited to you and your baby.

You can make feeding easier by holding your baby upright on your lap. This position prevents the formula from coming back up through the baby's nose. Limit the feeding period to 45 minutes, as your baby may tire. If your baby uses too much energy, he or she may not gain weight as recommended. If you have any questions about the amount of formula required, please contact your family physician or pediatrician, who can provide you with guidelines for adequate nutrition.

When your baby sucks, too much air may be taken into the stomach. Frequent burping will help solve this problem. Because food may get trapped in the cleft in the roof of the mouth, clean your baby's mouth after feeding. You can remove excess food using a small amount of sterile water. If this doesn't work, the remaining milk solids can be removed with moistened gauze. Also, since your baby breathes through the mouth, the lips may become dry and crusted. Coat lips lightly with Vaseline to relieve dryness.

Breastfeeding may be possible with your baby. However, you are advised to discuss this with the child's plastic surgeon, because it may not be possible to breastfeed immediately following the lip repair. A baby with just a cleft lip (not palate) should have little difficulty because the breast tissue molds to the unrepaired cleft in the lip. Breastfeeding may also be possible in babies with a less severe cleft in the palate. If the cleft is too large, the breast milk could be expressed either manually or with a breast pump.

Although feeding may seem complicated at first, you will gain confidence and skill as your baby develops. If difficulties continue, you can discuss them with the occupational therapist, who is a feeding specialist.

Courtesy of The Hospital for Sick Children Foundation, Toronto, Ontario, Canada.

Feeding Instructions Following Cleft Palate Repair

FIRST WEEK AFTER SURGERY—LIQUIDS

Give your child liquids using a cup or cross-cut nipple with squeeze bottle.

- formula or breast milk
- apple juice
- white grape juice
- sweetened drink mixes
- fruit juices

SECOND AND THIRD WEEK AFTER SURGERY—LIQUIDS AND SOFT FOODS

Carefully feed your child with a spoon (with a nonstick coating) in a sideways position.

- applesauce
- mashed fruits
- yogurt
- puddings
- creamed cereals (rice and wheat)
- baby foods (all strained)
- cooked vegetables, mashed (for example, mashed potatoes)
- mashed macaroni and cheese

FOLLOWING THIRD WEEK

Resume regular diet for child's age.

Notes:

Courtesy of Kant Lin, MD, Division of Craniofacial Surgery, Department of Plastic Surgery, University of Virginia Health Sciences Center, Charlottesville, Virginia.

Feeding Instructions Following Posterior Pharyngeal Flap (PPF) Surgery

FIRST WEEK AFTER SURGERY—LIQUIDS

Give your child liquids using a cup or cross-cut nipple with squeeze bottle.

- milk shakes
- yogurt shakes
- milk or chocolate milk
- ginger ale
- fruit punch
- all fruit juices (pear, apple, apricot, white grape, grape; citrus juices may be irritating to your child's mouth)

SECOND AND THIRD WEEK AFTER SURGERY—LIQUIDS AND SOFT FOODS

Carefully feed your child with a spoon (with a nonstick coating) in a sideways position.

- all liquids mentioned above
- cooked vegetables, mashed
- scrambled eggs
- frozen yogurt
- pureed fruit
- applesauce
- gelatin desserts
- macaroni and cheese
- creamed cereals
- creamed chicken soup
- vegetable and beef soup, mashed
- puddings
- cheerios
- custards

FOLLOWING THIRD WEEK

Resume regular diet for child's age.

Courtesy of Kant Lin, MD, Division of Craniofacial Surgery, Department of Plastic Surgery, University of Virginia Health Sciences Center, Charlottesville, Virginia.

Feeding Children with Fetal Alcohol Syndrome

Many children with fetal alcohol syndrome (FAS) have a difficult time eating or being fed. Some children are considered to be suffering from failure to thrive. Because these children are often small in comparison with other children, parents of children with FAS worry about whether they are getting enough to eat. They seem to have smaller-than-average appetites and may take a longer time to eat. By age 4 or 5 years, most children will be eating a small, but nutritionally adequate, diet. Pediatricians and relatives may not understand the unique difficulties of feeding a child with FAS and may tell parents to "just feed the child more."

HOW DO I KNOW IF MY CHILD IS GETTING ENOUGH FOOD TO GROW PROPERLY?

Children who continue to gain weight and height, even if very slowly, are probably eating enough. Your child's weight and height should be in similar percentiles on growth charts. Consult with your child's physician or a nutritionist if you are concerned.

WHY DOES IT TAKE MY CHILD SO LONG TO EAT?

Babies have difficulty coordinating sucking and swallowing. Milk may dribble out of their mouths because of the delay in swallowing. They tire easily and may slow down or abandon the effort of eating altogether. Their tendency to be easily distracted further lengthens mealtimes. As children grow older, their reflexes improve. They may, however, continue to eat slowly because of poor muscle control or sensitivity to texture of foods.

WILL CERTAIN FOODS MAKE EATING EASIER FOR MY CHILD?

Some children with FAS have sensory hyperactivity or tactile defensiveness. They don't like the feeling of nipples, spoons, or certain foods in their mouths. Foods that are warm (neither hot nor cold) and have some texture (neither smooth nor very lumpy) are easier for children to tolerate. If you find that your child puts food in his or her mouth but doesn't swallow, try adding a little texture to it (for example, add wheat germ or bacon bits to mashed potatoes). Finger foods may be easier for your child to handle.

ARE MEDICAL TESTS NECESSARY TO MAKE SURE THERE IS NO PHYSICAL REASON MY CHILD EATS SO LITTLE?

Children who have small appetites but who grow steadily—even if slowly—probably do not need specialized medical examinations or tests. If your child does not grow, loses a substan-

continues

continued

tial amount of weight for no obvious reason (children may temporarily lose weight during a cold or other illness), or has persistent vomiting or diarrhea, a medical examination should be conducted.

ARE SOME FOODS BETTER FOR MY CHILD?

Meat, grains, fruits, vegetables, and dairy products should be the major foods in your child's diet. Foods with little nutritional value (soda, donuts, or candy) should be used only as occasional treats. These foods fill your child up without providing essential vitamins.

WHY IS MY CHILD SUCH A SLOPPY EATER (GULPING FOOD, DROPPING FOOD ON THE FLOOR)?

Children with poor muscle control or with perceptual or spatial difficulties may lack the eye-hand coordination required for eating neatly. Hypersensitivity to the feeling of food in their mouths may cause them to chew over and over or to play with food in their fingers. Serving meals in a shallow bowl rather than a flat plate and allowing the use of a spoon over a fork may make eating easier. For children who have difficulty drinking out of a glass or cup, use straws or a cup that has a lipped cover.

TIPS

- Reduce distractions (turn off the television, don't talk to the child too much, try to have a calm and quiet mealtime).
- Allow ample time for meals.
- Recognize that children may stop and start eating many times during a meal.
- Give your child small servings.
- Give your child a chair with arms and in which his or her feet are touching either a footrest or the floor (being surrounded by surfaces that come in contact with the body can reduce fidgeting).
- Let your child stand at the dinner table if he or she has trouble sitting for a long time.
- Avoid using mealtimes to discuss stressful topics, such as discipline, with children.

Source: Barbara A. Morse and Lyn Weiner, "FAS: Parent and Child," Fetal Alcohol Education Program, Boston University School of Medicine, Brookline, Massachusetts, © 1992.

Hyperalimentation for Hospitalized Children

WHAT IS HYPERALIMENTATION?

Hyperalimentation is a means of meeting most of a child's needs for food and fluids through a vein. This technique delivers more calories and essential nutrients, such as amino acids, vitamins, and minerals, than normal IV fluids. Hyperalimentation is used in babies and children who are unable to tolerate feedings by mouth for various reasons.

HOW IS HYPERALIMENTATION GIVEN?

Hyperalimentation must be given through a large vein. A plastic catheter is inserted Into a superior vena cava, one of the largest veins in the body. This vein delivers blood to the heart. In order to properly place the catheter, the child may be taken to surgery and placed under general anesthesia. In babies, the catheter is inserted through the scalp or neck and threaded through the internal jugular vein, which is in the neck, into the superior vena cava. In children, the catheter is inserted into the left side of the chest into the subclavian vein, which lies under the collar bone, and threaded into the superior vena cava. The child will have a dressing over the site where the catheter enters the body.

CARE OF THE CHILD

There are special things that must be done while a child is receiving hyperalimentation in order to prevent infection, keep the catheter in place, and monitor the child's response to treatment. Five things you might expect are:

1. Fluid will be given through tubing that goes into a machine called an infusion pump. The pump assures that the child gets the proper amount of fluid. If something is not functioning properly, the pump will alarm. Tell the nurse immediately when the machine alarms.

2. The bottle of hyperalimentation fluid and tubing will be changed every day to prevent infection.

3. The dressing will be changed every 2 to 3 days by the physician or nurse. Again, this action helps to prevent infection.

4. A urine specimen may be needed every day to test the urine for sugar. For babies and toddlers who are not toilet trained, a wet diaper is sufficient.

5. It will sometimes be necessary for babies and toddlers to have their hands restrained in order to prevent them from pulling the catheter out.

continues

continued

HOW PARENTS CAN HELP

A parent's cooperation with the physician and nurse's plan of care is very important if the hyperalimentation is to succeed. It will be hard not to care for your child as you do at home, but staff members are willing to help you care for your child in the hospital. The following are things you can do to help:

1. Never leave the baby or toddler unrestrained if you leave the bedside. It is okay to remove the restraints while you are holding the child or standing at the bedside. In fact, there are times when it is good to take the restraints off so the child can play with his or her toys.

2. You may hold or bathe your child, but only with assistance from the nursing staff. Lifting or holding the child improperly can cause the catheter to pull out.

3. For babies who will not be allowed to have a bottle, a pacifier might be helpful in satisfying their need to suck.

4. Favorite small toys from home are often helpful in entertaining the child while in the hospital. For babies, mobiles and busy toys that attach to the crib provide stimulation and entertainment.

5. If the infusion pump begins to alarm, tell the nurse immediately. Never try to turn the alarm off.

6. Save wet diapers or urine specimens for the staff when requested.

7. Keep a record when your child urinates or has a stool. If your child wears diapers, save the wet and soiled diapers for the nurse.

Notes:

Source: "Sharing Information: Hyperalimentation," East Tennessee Children's Hospital, Knoxville, Tennessee, © 1988. East Tennessee Children's Hospital publishes pamphlets on a variety of topics related to children's health. For more information contact the Child Health Education Center, East Tennessee Children's Hospital, 2018 Clinch Avenue, PO Box 15010, Knoxville, TN 37901; 615–541–8262.

Tube Feedings: Nasogastric Tubes and Gastrostomy Tubes

SPECIAL FEEDINGS

Because your child has special care needs, he or she will need to be fed in a different way in order to receive good nutrition for body functioning and development. Your child will receive nourishment in liquid form through tube feedings.

You are a very important asset to your child's growth and development. Answers to your questions and assistance will be provided as you prepare to manage a tube feeding program at home. This handout was developed to help you learn the technique. Nurses will assist you in feeding your child by this method before you take your child home.

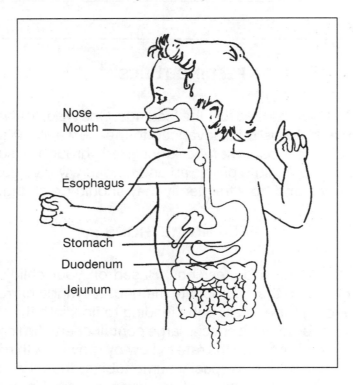

EQUIPMENT NEEDED

The following equipment is needed:

- syringes
- stethoscope
- formula or fluid as ordered by your child's physician (Prepare enough formula for 1 day only. Discard any unused refrigerated formula after 24 hours. Always use standard measuring cups and spoons.)

continues

continued

- sterile water (Sterile water is made by boiling tap water for 10 minutes then cooling to room temperature. This water is sterile for 24 hours stored in a closed sterile container.)
- tube
- lubricant
- tape

The tube feeding your child will be receiving is _____

The scheduled feeding times are _____

The amount of formula your child needs each day is _____

The amount of formula needed for each feeding is _____

Recipe:

_____

_____

_____

FEEDING TUBES

There are different types of tubes used for tube feedings. One type, the *nasogastric tube*, enters the body through the nose. Its tip is then advanced to the stomach. This tube is taped to your child's nose or cheek. The *gastrostomy tube* is inserted through a surgical opening in the abdomen to the stomach. Your child's physician and nurses will give you specific instructions about the care of these tubes and how frequently they should be changed.

FEEDING METHODS

There are different methods for tube feedings. Based on your child's specific needs, your child's physician will recommend the appropriate method. A syringe barrel (without the plunger) can be attached to the feeding tube to allow the feeding to flow into the stomach by gravity; or, the feeding tube may be connected to a special large container and tubing. A roller clamp on the container tubing can be used to regulate the rate of flow by gravity. A third method is infusion by pump. The feeding tube is connected to special pump tubing; then the pump is set to flow at a certain rate and volume. Once again, you will be given specific instructions, as well as an opportunity to ask questions about the method of tube feeding chosen for your child.

INSERTING THE NASOGASTRIC TUBE

Gather your equipment. Wash your hands for 2 minutes with soap and water. Prepare your child as appropriate for his or her age. You might suggest that the older child think about swallowing a "lump" in the back of the throat. The baby and younger child may need to be gently restrained

continues

continued

until he or she develops a tolerance to this procedure. Position your child with head and shoulders up slightly. Determine how much of the tube needs to be inserted by measuring, with the tube, from your child's nose to his or her ear lobe to a point midway between the xiphoid process of the sternum and umbilicus (belly button). Mark the length with tape.

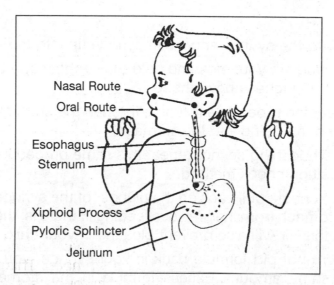

Lubricate the tube by moistening the tip with sterile water or water-soluble lubricant. Insert the tube by passing the tube gently through the nostril, aiming down and back toward the ear. Proceed slowly. Swallowing will help advance the tube. Stop if there is any resistance to passage of the tube. Do not use force. As soon as the marker tape reaches the nostril, stop advancing the tube and lightly tape tube to nose. Check for proper tube placement.

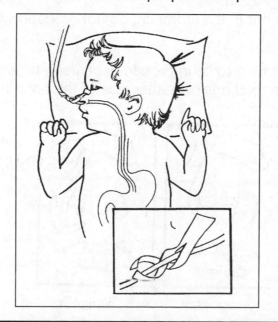

continues

continued

IS THE TUBE IN THE STOMACH?

Before any fluids or feedings are given, the feeding tube must be checked to be sure that its tip is in the proper position in the stomach. Check tube placement by following seven steps:

1. Draw 1 to 2 cc/ml air into the syringe and insert syringe tip into the feeding tube.
2. Place stethoscope earplugs in your ears and hold the stethoscope bell over the stomach area, approximately 1 to 2 inches above the navel.
3. Inject the air into the feeding tube while listening through the stethoscope for the gurgling or "whooshing" sound of air going into the stomach.
4. If you do not hear the whooshing sound, repeat this same procedure and listen carefully. Proceed to second position check method.
5. For the second position check, pull back on the plunger of the syringe to see if there is any old formula left in the stomach from the previous feeding. If there is, the tube is in the correct position. Withdrawing this air will also prevent bloating in your child's small stomach.
6. If you draw 5 to 10 cc/ml of old formula back in your syringe, you should decrease the next feeding by that same amount. Excess formula in the stomach is only an occasional occurrence; it is a signal that your child has not been able to digest fully the last feeding.
7. If the tube is in the trachea or windpipe, your child may be coughing, gasping, choking, dusky in color, and unable to speak. Remove the tube immediately without alarming your child. Allow for rest and try again.

    If tests show the tube is not in the stomach, do not proceed with the feeding, withdraw the tube and try again.

When the tube is checked and found to be in proper placement, tape it to your child's cheek or nose, being careful not to rub or pull against either side of the nostril.

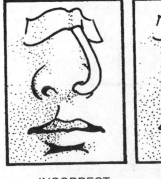

INCORRECT   CORRECT

continues

continued

GIVING THE TUBE FEEDING

The next step is to place your child in the feeding position. Your child needs to be laying on his or her back or right side with the shoulders and head slightly elevated. This position, which aids the formula flow through the tube to his or her stomach, can best be done in a baby seat or by propping with a pillow.

Syringe Method

Take the plunger out of the syringe, attach the syringe to the tube, and pour the room temperature formula into the syringe. Hold the syringe about 6 to 8 inches above your child allowing the formula to flow through the tubing by gravity. Never force the formula into the tube. The feeding should last 15 to 20 minutes. If your child gets the formula too fast, he or she may vomit or feel bloated and uncomfortable. After the formula has been given, pour ___ cc/ml of sterile water into the syringe to clear the feeding tube and prevent clogging. Remove the syringe. Cap the feeding tube or remove the tube—whichever your nurses or physicians recommend. Lay your child on his or her right side with a blanket or towel roll behind. This will help him or her digest the food better and if he or she were to spit up, the formula would flow out the side of his or her mouth, decreasing the chances of choking.

Gravity Drip or Pump Method

This setup should be prepared prior to tube insertion and tube placement checks. Gather needed equipment: formula, feeding set, large-volume container, IV pole, water, and pump (if used). Attach the feeding set and tubing to the large-volume container and close the flow regulator clamp on the feeding set. Hang the feeding container on the IV pole about 2 feet above your child. Fill the container with room temperature formula. Remove the cap on the end of the feeding tube and open the flow regulator allowing formula to fill the tubing. Then tighten the flow regulator clamp and replace the cap on the end of the tubing. If you are using a pump for infusion, follow the specific pump instructions to attach the tubing setup to the pump and to set the proper rate and volume. Next, remove syringe from feeding tube after checking for proper stomach placement. Attach feeding set tubing and proceed with feeding as instructed. When feeding is completed, give ___ cc/ml water for flush through feeding tube.

CARE OF EQUIPMENT

Only clean equipment should be used for your child's feedings. Your measuring equipment, blender used to mix the formula, and syringes should be cleaned thoroughly with hot, soapy water

continues

continued

then rinsed thoroughly with boiling water after each use. Use a clean bag with tubing every 24 hours and discard used ones. Clean the outside of your pump once a week with a mild detergent and warm water.

GASTROSTOMY TUBE SITE CARE

You will need to cleanse the skin around the gastrostomy tube site every day. Carefully cleanse around the tube with mild soap and water, rinsing well with warm tap water. Allow to dry. Observe for redness, swelling, tenderness, or an unusual yellow or green drainage from around the tube. The gastrostomy tube should be clamped or capped at all times, except during feedings. You may need to daily apply a small split gauze around the tube and tape in place.

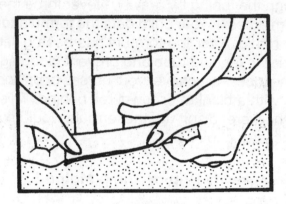

TROUBLE-SHOOTING

If any of the following problems occur, notify your child's physician or home health care nurse:

- vomiting, persistent nausea, or stomach upset
- diarrhea continuing over 1 to 2 days
- constipation continuing over 3 to 5 days
- symptoms of dehydration (excessive thirst, dry mouth, dry cracked lips, fever, weakness, dry, warm skin, weight loss, decreasing amount of urine)
- weight loss
- concerns or questions you have related to your child's condition or tube feeding

If the pump malfunctions or will not operate, notify the pump supplier at _____.

Source: "Sharing Information: Tube Feeding," East Tennessee Children's Hospital, Knoxville, Tennessee, © 1993. East Tennessee Children's Hospital publishes pamphlets on a variety of topics related to children's health. For more information contact the Child Health Education Center, East Tennessee Children's Hospital, 2018 Clinch Avenue, PO Box 15010, Knoxville, TN 37901; 615–541–8262.

Nutrition for Your Gastrostomy-Fed Child

ROLES OF SOME IMPORTANT VITAMINS

- Vitamin A—promotes growth, healthy skin, good vision, and helps the body resist infection.
- B vitamins—help form blood cells, maintain nervous system, maintain appetite, and aid the body in digestion and use of food.
- Vitamin C—helps build healthy gums, tissues, bones, and teeth, heals wounds, and helps resist infection.
- Vitamin D—helps build bones and teeth.

ROLES OF SOME IMPORTANT MINERALS

- Calcium—builds bones and teeth, maintains muscles and cells.
- Iron—builds red blood cells.
- Fluoride—forms strong teeth and bones.

VITAMIN AND MINERAL REQUIREMENTS

The Recommended Dietary Allowance (RDA) is a good guideline for the vitamin and mineral needs of babies, children, and adults. Although the RDA provides a good starting point, your child's medical condition or the drugs he or she is taking can increase or decrease nutrient needs. Vitamin and mineral requirements can usually be met by a well-planned gastrostomy diet. However, once your child is no longer only on baby formula, it takes more planning to make sure he or she is getting all of the nutrients required.

Some vitamins and minerals deserve special attention for the child who is fed by gastrostomy tube. Here are some reasons why.

- Vitamin D—Adult formulas may not meet a child's vitamin D needs. Fortified milk contains vitamin D while other dairy products such as yogurt and cottage cheese do not.
- Calcium—Most adult formulas are lower in calcium than baby formulas.
- Iron—The iron needs of children with chronic medical conditions can be high. Tube feedings may be low in iron-containing foods such as meat, baby cereal, and iron-fortified baby formula.
- Fluoride—Fluoride is not in formulas, only some water supplies. Some water supplies are fluoridated while others are not.

FLUID

Your child's fluid needs must be met every day to prevent dehydration. Although fluid needs vary from child to child, most children need about 1½ ounces of fluid per pound of body weight

continues

continued

daily. This requirement can increase to 2 to 3 ounces per pound in very hot weather and during bouts of fever, vomiting, or diarrhea.

Semisolid foods such as strained fruits and vegetables, Jello, and yogurt contain some fluid, but the best sources of fluid are formula, milk, juice, and water. Water can be used as part of a feeding or to flush the tube after a feeding. If your child needs more fluid than his or her typical feeding provides, you may find it easier to give water in between the feedings.

When water is softened, the minerals are removed by replacing them with salt. Usually cold kitchen tap water is not softened, so it can be used to help avoid excess salt intake. Check with your local health department if you have well water or are concerned for any other reason about the amount of bacteria or nitrate in your water. The health department can easily and inexpensively test your water for safety.

Children usually regulate their own fluid intake by drinking more when they are thirsty and less when they are not. Because your child is gastrostomy-fed, he or she may be less able to control fluid intake, which places your child at greater risk for dehydration or fluid overload. To reduce this risk, ask your child's doctor to help you determine your child's fluid needs when well or ill.

Symptoms of Dehydration

- Weight loss
- Extreme thirst
- Small amount of urine (less than usual amount of wet diapers)
- Dry skin (does not bounce back when pressed or pushed by finger)
- Sunken eyes
- Dry lips
- Headache, dizziness, listlessness

Symptoms of Fluid Overload

- Puffy looking
- Trouble breathing (rapid breathing)
- Rapid weight gain

Call Your Physician If These Symptoms Occur

Body salts, as well as fluids, are lost during vomiting or diarrhea. Potassium, sodium, and chloride are the most important of these body salts and are in your child's diet. However, when your child is sick, he or she may not be able to tolerate feedings and will need fluid and body salts from another source, such as Pedialyte or Lytren (an electrolyte solution). Low-calorie electrolyte solutions are easy for children to digest during illness and provide the necessary fluid and

continues

continued

body salts. These products are better than water, sweetened drinks, or juices when your child has a short-term illness.

It is important to remember that your child can go for a few days without receiving the ideal diet, but fluid needs must be met every day. If your child is sick for more than a few days, you will need to consult your child's doctor to ensure that your child is reintroduced to a diet providing calories and other important nutrients.

CHOOSING A GASTROSTOMY FEEDING

There are many things you and your child's doctor need to consider in choosing the best feeding for your child. Unfortunately, there is no perfect feeding. You may have to try several feedings or combinations of feedings, before you find the one that works best. Considering the following factors can help:

- age and size of your child
- child's fluid, calorie, protein, vitamin, and mineral needs
- what feeding your child tolerates best
- cost, convenience, and availability of the feeding
- size and type of the feeding tube
- how much of your child's feeding is given through the tube
- your family's typical diet and schedule

Several feeding choices are available, including baby formulas, pediatric formulas, adult formulas, and homemade, blenderized formulas. Similarities and differences among the feedings follow.

COMMON FORMULAS

Formula Type	Name	Amount	Calories	Use
Baby, cow milk–based	Enfamil, Similac, SMA, Similac with Whey	1 ounce	20 or 24	Full-term baby or sick baby without special nutritional needs (SMA is the lowest in sodium)
Baby, soy-based	Prosobee, Isomil, Isomil-SF, Nursoy	1 ounce	20 or 24	Full-term baby with family history of documented cow's milk or protein sensitivity; lactose intolerance following common diarrhea

continues

continued

Formula Type	Name	Amount	Calories	Use
Baby, predigested	Nutramigen	1 ounce	20 or 24	Baby or child with soy and cow's milk intolerance, allergies, severe or persistent diarrhea; digestive enzyme deficiency
	Pregestimil, Alimentum	1 ounce	20 or 24	Baby or child with chronic diarrhea, multiple food allergies, digestive enzyme deficiency, cystic fibrosis, short gut, severe malnutrition
Baby, partially predigested, milk-based	Good Start HA	1 ounce	20 or 24	Soy and cow's milk sensitivity or allergy
Pediatric formula	Pediasure	1 ounce	30	Child aged 1–6 years without special nutritional needs; lactose intolerance
Adult formula	Ensure, Osmolite, Isocal, Sustacal Resource, Nutren, Precision Isotonic	1 ounce	30–31	Child or adult without special nutritional needs, with lactose intolerance, or in need of complete feeding or calorie supplement
Adult, high-fiber formula	Ensure with Fiber, Sustacal with Fiber, Jevity, Compleat Modified, Profiber	1 ounce	30–33	Child or adult who needs additional fiber, has lactose intolerance, or needs total or partial feeding
Adult, high-calorie	Pulmocare, Ensure Plus, Sustacal HC, Magnacal	1 ounce	45–60	Child or adult who needs a high-calorie supplement for oral or gastrostomy tube feeding; not to be used as only source of diet

continues

continued

	Name	Amount	Calories	Use
Adult, partially predigested	Vital HN, Tolerex Travasorb, Isotein, Peptamen	1 ounce	30	Child or adult with chronic diarrhea, multiple food allergies, cystic fibrosis, short gut, severe malnutrition

BABY FORMULAS

Breast milk or baby formulas are the preferred feedings for most children under 1 year of age and for some gastrostomy tube-fed children older than 1 year, because they are rich in nutrients and are easy to digest.

Milk-based baby formulas are most frequently used because they contain nutrients in amounts similar to breast milk. These formulas are available in low iron or iron-fortified varieties. Iron-fortified formulas are recommended for most babies to prevent anemia. Other formulas have been developed for babies with special nutritional or physical needs.

A common concern in feeding a baby or child with a gastrostomy tube is providing enough calories for growth within the volume of feeding the child can tolerate. To achieve this goal, you may need to increase the calories in baby formula by either mixing it differently or adding "calorie boosters." There is a limit to the concentration of formula a baby can tolerate, so these changes should be made with the guidance of a dietitian.

Baby formulas are usually mixed to 20 calories per ounce; however, they can be mixed to provide more calories per ounce if necessary. Babies and children are at risk for dehydration when the concentration of formula is greater than 24 calories per ounce. For this reason, concentrating formula to more than 24 calories per ounce is recommended only when under close medical supervision.

High-Calorie Formula

Instructions for mixing formula to 24 calories per ounce to obtain high-calorie formula follow.

Ready-to-Feed Formula

Do not use this form of the formula because it only has 20 calories per ounce.

Concentrate Formula

This formula comes in 13-ounce cans. To make 24-calories-per-ounce formula, mix one 13-ounce can of concentrate with 8½ ounces of water.

continues

continued

Powder Formula

A measuring scoop is provided in each 1-pound can of formula powder. Mix five level scoops of powder in 8 ounces (1 cup) of water. (The formula manufacturer will state whether a particular formula powder is to be packed or unpacked when measuring; these instructions should be followed when mixing formula.) The formula mixes more easily if you first add a small amount of water to the powder to make a paste before adding the rest of the measured water.

To make larger volumes of formula, mix ½ cup plus 2 scoops of powdered formula with 2 cups of water. Blend. Refrigerate in covered container for 1 to 2 days.

Packed	Unpacked
SMA	Enfamil
Nursoy	Prosobee
Pregestimil	Similac
Portagen	Isomil
Nutramigen	Good Start

Using Calorie Boosters

A variety of other products, such as oils, sugars, starches, or dehydrated (dried) baby foods, can be added to baby formulas to help increase calories. These calorie boosters are tolerated by most children and do not put your child at risk for dehydration unless diarrhea or vomiting occurs. Starting with a small amount and gradually increasing the amount added to your child's feeding will improve your child's ability to handle the calorie boosters added to his or her feeding. It may take several days to weeks to work up to a higher calorie formula that your child can tolerate.

Oils and sugars supply important calories but none of the protein, vitamins, and minerals your child needs to maintain his or her health. Your child's dietitian will help you make sure that your child continues to get essential nutrients when you increase the caloric content of the feedings by various methods.

Here are some calorie boosters and guidelines.

Source	Product	Calories per Teaspoon	Considerations
Fats	Vegetable oil	40	Inexpensive, readily available, difficult to mix, sticks to tubing
	Lipomul	30	Expensive, obtain through pharmacy or hospital supply, mixes easily, contains saccharine
	Microlipid	10	Fewer calories than the oils, mixes well, expensive

continues

continued

Source	Product	Calories per Teaspoon	Considerations
	MCT	40	Expensive, obtain through pharmacy or hospital supply, can dissolve plastic tubing, use only for special fat requirements
Sugars	Table sugar (sucrose)	15	Inexpensive, mixes easily, too much causes diarrhea
Starches	Corn syrup	20	Inexpensive, mixes easily, too much causes diarrhea
	Polycose	7.5	Mixes easily, more similar to starch than sugar, less likely to cause diarrhea than sugar, expensive, readily available
	Dehydrated baby cereal	3–5	Inexpensive, thickens formula, readily available, lower in calories, contains iron

The following example shows three ways to change formula from 24 calories per ounce to 26 calories per ounce by adding calorie boosters.

1. Choice 1:   Mix 3 cc/ml of Lipomul with 8 ounces of 24-calories-per-ounce formula.
2. Choice 2:   Mix 2 teaspoons (10 cc/ml) of Polycose powder with 8 ounces of 24-calories-per-ounce formula.
3. Choice 3:   Mix 1 cc/ml of corn oil and 2 cc/ml of corn syrup with 8 ounces of 24-calories-per-ounce formula.

PEDIATRIC FORMULAS

As your child grows, he or she needs more calories. You could increase his or her calories by giving more baby formula, but at some point the volume of formula your child needs will become so great that he or she can no longer tolerate it. Because calorie boosters do not provide nutrients, there is a limit to the amount of calories your child should get from this source. For this reason, a pediatric formula named Pediasure was recently developed. Pediasure has 30 calories per ounce, similar to some adult formulas, yet provides the vitamins and minerals needed for most children ages 1 through 6 years. You may choose to switch your child to this formula if the amount of baby formula he or she needs to grow is more than your child can handle.

continues

continued

Because there is only one pediatric formula available and it was developed so recently, it is still costly.

ADULT FORMULAS

An adult formula may be the best choice for your child when he or she is older than 1 year, especially if additional calories are needed. These products vary widely in their calorie content, providing from 30 to 60 calories per ounce. Formulas containing 60 and 45 calories per ounce are too rich and should not be used without additional water.

The vitamin and mineral content of adult formulas is intended to meet the needs of adults who ordinarily consume more than a child. For this reason, adult formulas may not provide enough vitamins and minerals to meet your child's needs, especially calcium and vitamin D. Your child's dietitian can help determine if these nutrients needs as well as others are being met and can suggest appropriate supplementation if necessary.

Adult formulas can be used for children with special needs. These formulas include predigested formulas for children with malabsorption, lactose-free formulas for children unable to digest milk sugar, and high-fiber for children who are suffering from constipation.

It can require time for your child to adjust to an adult formula. A gradual change from a baby or pediatric formula will help in the transition.

BLENDERIZED DIETS

Many recipe options are available for blenderized diets. You can simply use a formula with a jar of baby food added daily or blenderize a full-course meal. Strained baby foods or blenderized table foods can be combined with milk, formula, juice, and other liquids to provide a well-balanced tube feeding diet for children over 1 year of age. Points for consideration in choosing a blenderized diet are listed in the table.

Advantages	Disadvantages
• Lower cost	• Longer preparation time
• High fiber decreases constipation and diarrhea	• Requires larger size feeding tube
• Greater variety	• Requires more planning to ensure good nutrient intake
• Can have some psychosocial benefit— sharing food with family gives personal touch	• May require larger volume of total fluid
	• Difficult to give continuous drip because of thickness

Your child's dietitian can help you plan recipes that meet your child's special nutritional needs. You can work together to select the combination of ingredients that your child thrives on and can handle.

continues

continued

Transition from Formula to Blenderized Feedings

Although uncommon, any child can develop a food allergy or sensitivity that could cause nausea, vomiting, bloating, diarrhea, or rash. For this reason, give one new food at a time and offer small amounts (½ to 2 ounces) of a single food for 3 days in a row. This way, you can identify the particular food if your child is having problems. If symptoms occur, discontinue use and try again at a later date.

The following list provides typical foods and fluids for blenderized diets.

Food	Amount	Calories
Whole milk	4 ounce (oz)	75
2 percent milk	5 oz	60
Skim milk	4 oz	45
Condensed milk	4 oz	120
Evaporated milk—skim	4 oz	120
Evaporated milk—whole	4 oz	170
Yogurt—plain	4 oz	60
Yogurt—fruited	4 oz	130
Liquid yogurt	4 oz	100
Powdered breakfast mix	1 package	130
Dry milk powder	¼ cup	80
Cooked cereal	4 oz	62
Baby cereal (dry)	4 tablespoons (T)	60
Baby foods, jarred		
Cereal with fruit	4.5-oz jar	100
Strained fruit	4.5-oz jar	80
Fruit juice	4.5-oz jar	60
Fruit dessert	4.5-oz jar	110
Strained vegetables	4.5-oz jar	50
Vegetables with meat	4.5-oz jar	80
Strained meat	4.5-oz jar	80
High-meat dinner	4.5-oz jar	115
Egg yolk	4.5-oz jar	190
Prunes	4.5-oz jar	100
Dehydrated baby food		
Fruit	1 T (dry)	16

continues

continued

Food	Amount	Calories
Vegetables	1 T (dry)	12
Cereals with fruit	1 T (dry)	12
Fruit combinations	1 T (dry)	12
Dinners	1 T (dry)	10
Table sugar	1 T	45
Corn syrup	1 T	60
Molasses	1 T	45
Honey (can cause infant botulism)	1 T	65
Vegetable oil	1 T	120

Choosing Ingredients

The main ingredient in a blenderized diet is the fluid portion or liquid base. Baby, pediatric, and adult formulas contain all of the major nutrients and make an excellent liquid-base choice. Milk or liquid yogurt can be used as the fluid portion if you combine them with other ingredients to meet your child's nutrient needs.

It is helpful to use the four food groups in planning your child's blenderized diet. A discussion of the food groups, the most important vitamins and minerals they provide, and some examples of foods to use follow.

1. Dairy
   Good sources of protein, calcium, phosphorus, and vitamin D.
   Examples: Skim milk
   2 percent milk
   Whole milk (do not use raw milk due to risk of food poisoning)
   Powdered breakfast mix
   Yogurt (does not provide vitamin D)
   Reconstituted condensed milk or evaporated milk
   Cottage cheese

2. Meats and meat alternatives
   Good sources of protein, minerals such as iron and zinc, and B vitamins.
   Examples: Dehydrated baby meats, poultry
   Jarred baby meats, poultry
   Soft-cooked meats, poultry, fish
   Cooked, dried beans and legumes (lower in iron than meats)
   Tofu (low in iron)
   Cooked egg (do not use raw egg due to risk of salmonella)

continues

continued

3. Fruits and vegetables
   Good sources of vitamin A, vitamin C, and fiber.
   Examples: Jarred baby fruits and vegetables
   Dehydrated baby fruits and vegetables
   Cooked vegetables
   Frozen, canned vegetables (canned may be high in salt)
   Frozen, canned, dried fruits
   Fruit or vegetable juice

4. Grains and cereals
   Good sources of B vitamins, some iron, and other minerals.
   Examples: Cooked cereal
   Dehydrated or jarred infant cereal
   Soft-cooked noodles or rice

(*Note:* It is difficult to include many foods from this group because of the thick consistency. Essential nutrients can be obtained from other food groups.)

Example—Johnny's Diet

Johnny is 3½ years old and weighs 38 pounds. He seems interested in sharing food with his family. His parents want to change his feeding to a blenderized diet using foods similar to what his family is eating. They hope this change will encourage him to want "real food." They also think the added fiber of a blenderized diet will help relieve Johnny's constipation.

Johnny's health care providers have determined that he needs about 1,300 calories, 26 grams of protein, and 45 ounces (1,350 cc/ml) of fluid each day. His parents worked together with the health care providers to plan a daily recipe that is best for Johnny and his family. They have the option of buying baby food or blenderizing their own table food. Either way, this combination of ingredients provides him with enough vitamins and minerals so no additional supplementation is necessary. They will try the following recipe and contact their health care providers if any feeding changes are needed.

Johnny's Daily Recipe #1		*Date: July*

3 cups whole milk
5 ounces strained meat (two 2½-ounce jars)
13½ ounces strained fruit (three 4½-ounce jars)
4½ ounces strained vegetable (one 4½-ounce jar)
4 tablespoons rice cereal (dry)
2 tablespoons corn oil

Total Volume:	45 ounces	1,350 cc
Total Calories:	1,300	

continues

continued

Johnny can tolerate larger feedings, so his parents decide to give him five 9-ounce feedings each day. Each feeding is followed by a small amount of water (½ ounce [15 cc]) to clean out the tube. Let's look at Johnny's feeding schedule.

Feeding Plan (blenderized feeding)

Time	Feeding	Amount	Flush	Meds
7:00 A.M.	Daily Recipe #1	9 oz	15 cc (½ ounce)	
11:00 A.M.	Daily Recipe #1	9 oz	15 cc (½ ounce)	
3:00 P.M.	Daily Recipe #1	9 oz	15 cc (½ ounce)	
6:00 P.M.	Daily Recipe #1	9 oz	15 cc (½ ounce)	
9:00 P.M.	Daily Recipe #1	9 oz	15 cc (½ ounce)	

Johnny's parents prefer a simpler recipe for the weekends during the summer because they like to go camping. At those times another recipe would be helpful. Ensure with fiber was chosen because it is an adult formula with additional fiber that should help relieve Johnny's constipation.

Johnny's Daily Recipe #2   *Date: July*

40 ounces (5 cans) Ensure with fiber
5 ounces of water as flush
1 drop multivitamin (liquid)

Total Volume: 45 ounces   1,350 cc
Total Calories: 1,300

Preparing the Blenderized Feeding

Preparation

It is very important for the blenderized food or feeding to be prepared with clean hands and equipment and refrigerated immediately to reduce the risk of contamination.

- Wash hands.
- Wash counter or tabletop with warm soapy water.
- Assemble:
  — clean utensils
  — blender or food processor
  — measuring cups and spoons

continues

continued

- — ladle and mixing spoons
- — storage containers with lids
- — recipe
- Assemble ingredients:
  - — cooked or fresh foods for blending, cut in small pieces
  - — jarred or dried baby foods (listen for "pop" when opening jars)
  - — liquid base (formula, milk, water)
  - — previously blenderized meat or vegetables that have been frozen, then thawed in the refrigerator when ready for use

Blending

You will need a blender or food processor.

- Cut up whole foods.
- Blend "solid" foods first.
- Blend on low speed initially, gradually increasing speed as necessary.
- Avoid blending yogurt or dry milk on "high," because they may become "frothy."
- Add fluids gradually to full volume of recipe.
- If you are blending more than 1 day's recipe or blending 2 days worth at once, then:
  - — Blend solids first.
  - — Divide into two equal containers.
  - — Return one half of solid mixture to blender and add half the fluid.
  - — Blend, pour into storage container.
  - — Put remaining half of solid mixture and second portion of fluid in the blender.
  - — Blend and pour into second storage container.

Storage

- Cover feedings and store in refrigerator. Refrigerated feedings should be used within 24 to 48 hours.
- You can store blenderized feedings in a small, closed freezer container or bag. These will keep in a non self-defrosting freezer for up to 3 months.

Cleanup

- Wash counter or tabletop and utensils with hot, soapy water and rinse.
- Take blender or processor apart so all parts are cleaned with hot, soapy water and rinse.
- Be sure to clean storage containers in hot, soapy water and rinse before reusing.

continues

continued

ADDRESSING SOME PROBLEMS

Constipation

Constipation usually refers to hard, difficult to pass bowel movements. It can be caused by a low-fiber diet, inadequate fluid intake, inactivity, or medications. Changes in diet help relieve constipation.

- Increase total fluid content during or between feedings.
- Add some warm prune juice in water to the first morning feeding.
- Increase the fiber content of the feeding. Fiber is the indigestible part of the food available in fruits, vegetables, grains, and some specialized formulas. Ideas for increasing fiber in the gastrostomy tube diet are:
  — Bran can be added to very "thick," blenderized feedings given by syringe.
  — Fruit can be added to the feeding or given between feedings.
  — High-fiber, adult formulas can be used for children over 1 year of age.
- Concentrated sugar, such as corn syrup, honey, and molasses, added to the diet may pull water into the intestine, thus easing constipation. However, this method should not be used if your child is fluid-restricted.
- Do not give honey to children less than 1 year of age, because it can cause a serious illness, infant botulism.

If dietary changes are not practical or not working, your child's nurse or physician may recommend a stool softener, gentle laxative, or bulking agent. Examples of these are Citrucel, Fibercon, Maltsupex, and Senukot.

Diarrhea

Diarrhea refers to frequent, loose, watery stools. Diarrhea can be caused by an infection, medications, or diet. Some ideas that can help in finding out if feedings are the cause of diarrhea are:

- Switch from a milk-based to a soy-based formula.
- Stop or cut back on calorie boosters, such as fats and sugars, in feedings.
- Dilute the strength of the formula by adding more water if your child is not fluid-restricted.
- Reduce the amount of feeding given at one time by giving smaller amounts more frequently.
- Give feedings more slowly.
- Increase dietary fiber (see ideas previously given under Constipation).
- Warm the feeding to room temperature.

If diarrhea becomes excessive or severe, call your child's physician. The physician may recommend taking your child off feedings for a couple of days to allow the stomach to rest. As

continues

continued

discussed earlier, Pedialyte, Lytren, or other electrolyte solutions can be given for a few days to provide the salts and fluid your child loses in the stool. Electrolyte solutions should **not** be used to mix formulas unless recommended.

If any changes are made that lower the calorie or other nutrient content of the formula for a long time, contact your child's physician, nurse, or dietitian. They can tell you if other ways of increasing calories or needed nutrients are possible.

Vomiting

Vomiting is of concern when it makes your child uncomfortable, interferes with your child's feeding, or is a medical risk. If your child vomits and breathes food particles into the lungs, pneumonia can result. Frequent vomiting of fluid can also lead to dehydration. Several factors can cause vomiting, including medications, allergies or food sensitivities, or medical conditions such as rapid breathing, coughing, or infection.

Changes in the amount, number, or ingredients of feedings can help reduce or prevent vomiting. These changes should be made in a step-by-step fashion so the solution to the problem can be identified. Examples of feeding manipulations are:

- Remember to "burp" younger children during and after feedings.
- Reduce rate of tube feeding; give at a slower rate over a longer period.
- Reduce volume of the feeding by giving more frequent, smaller feedings.
- Rearrange feeding times if your child has a particular time of day when vomiting occurs.
- Use small feedings during the day and a "continuous drip" feeding overnight (not possible with thick, blenderized diet).
- Reduce concentration of the formula or feeding. For example, decrease 24-calorie-per-ounce formula to 20 calories per ounce.
- Remove calorie boosters, such as fats or sugars, from the feedings temporarily; check for improvement.
- Place your child in an upright position during feeding and up to 1 hour following the feeding.
- Thicken the feeding with a baby cereal, potato buds, or commercial thickeners.

For any changes that lower the calories or other nutrient content of the formula or feeding for a long time, contact your child's physician, nurse, or dietitian for advice on other ways of increasing calories or needed nutrients.

Vitamin and Mineral Supplementation

Vitamin and mineral requirements can usually be met by a well-planned gastrostomy diet. Sometimes vitamin or mineral supplementation is necessary. Vitamins are available as liquid or chewables. Drops usually contain only a few select vitamins. If your child needs multiple vitamins,

continues

continued

a chewable can be crushed into the feeding. A few products contain both vitamins and select minerals. These are harder to crush so should be used only when necessary.

It is important to remember that too much of a vitamin or mineral can be as dangerous as too little. Your child's dietitian will help make sure your child's nutrient needs are met.

PROGRESS RECORD

Children do change. As they do, their nutrient and feeding needs also change. It is wise to have your child's diet evaluated by your child's health care professionals on a routine basis. The younger your child is, the more frequently his or her diet should be reviewed.

It is helpful for you to keep an ongoing record of your child's growth and feeding goals and any concerns you may have. On a day-to-day basis, it can be difficult to see change, but looking back over your child's record can help illustrate progress.

_____ Progress					
Date	Age	Height	Weight	Current Feedings	Concerns/Goals

Source: *Nutrition for Gastrostomy-Fed Child: A Parent Handbook*, Copyright 1989 Board of Regents of the University of Wisconsin System, University Hospital and Clinics, all rights reserved.

6
Oral Health

Tooth Eruption Pattern

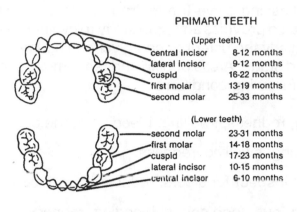

PRIMARY TEETH

(Upper teeth)

central incisor	8-12 months
lateral incisor	9-12 months
cuspid	16-22 months
first molar	13-19 months
second molar	25-33 months

(Lower teeth)

second molar	23-31 months
first molar	14-18 months
cuspid	17-23 months
lateral incisor	10-15 months
central incisor	6-10 months

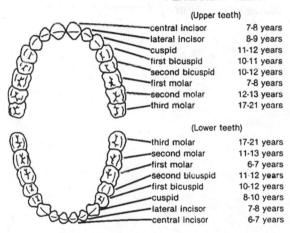

PERMANENT TEETH

(Upper teeth)

central incisor	7-8 years
lateral incisor	8-9 years
cuspid	11-12 years
first bicuspid	10-11 years
second bicuspid	10-12 years
first molar	7-8 years
second molar	12-13 years
third molar	17-21 years

(Lower teeth)

third molar	17-21 years
second molar	11-13 years
first molar	6-7 years
second bicuspid	11-12 years
first bicuspid	10-12 years
cuspid	8-10 years
lateral incisor	7-8 years
central incisor	6-7 years

The drawing shows the usual eruption dates for the primary (baby) and permanent (adult) teeth. The actual eruption of teeth, however, can be delayed, especially if there is a developmental disability (for example, Down syndrome). Some conditions include genetically missing teeth. If you have a question about whether or not a tooth is erupting on time, consult your family dentist.

Source: *Special Care for Special Needs: A Dental Education Booklet for Clients, Caregivers and Parents*, Office of Dental Health, Division of Family Services, Arizona Department of Health Services, Phoenix, Arizona, © 1992.

Examining the Mouth

While daily brushing and flossing serve the main purpose of maintaining oral hygiene and health, examining the mouth also provides an opportunity to evaluate a child's overall oral health. By examining the mouth regularly the parent or caregiver can notice the beginning of a problem before it reaches an advanced stage. Areas of pain and tenderness should be noted. The mouth should be inspected for the following conditions:

- **Lips:** Look for chapping, redness, swelling, bleeding at the corners of the mouth.

- **Tongue:** Check for coating, swelling, redness.

- **Cheeks, throat, palate:** Inspect for ulcers, redness, swelling.

- **Gums:** Look for swelling, pus, food debris, bleeding, redness.

- **Teeth:** Check for decay, calculus, staining, fractures.

Notes:

Source: *Special Care for Special Needs: A Dental Education Booklet for Clients, Caregivers and Parents*, Office of Dental Health, Division of Family Services, Arizona Department of Health Services, Phoenix, Arizona, © 1992.

Positioning for Daily Oral Care

COOPERATIVE CHILD

A baby or small child may be seated in a familiar chair. A baby seat allows face-to-face contact with the child. Your smiles and talking will help the baby feel happy and comfortable about the oral care. The introduction of cleaning the gums with a washcloth should be short and pleasant. Work each day on cleaning a bit more of the mouth. Soon the baby will accept this daily experience.

A toddler may be seated facing you in your lap or seated on a chair or counter. This position allows easy access to the newly erupting teeth. Using the toothbrush you can brush the child's teeth for him or her and also allow the child to brush his or her own teeth. You may guide the child's hand to brush all the teeth. You may brush your teeth at the same time, modeling proper oral care. Keep this session relaxed and happy with lots of smiles and encouragement. Short positive sessions are best while gradually lengthening the session to complete oral care.

UNCOOPERATIVE CHILD

People with disabilities may need a unique position that is more comfortable in order to perform their oral care. Consider the positions you and your child have already discovered that are comfortable (for example, inclining or flex position; sitting in the wheelchair or on bean bags or pillows). Use your personal experience and the recommendations of the child's physical therapist to select a position for performing daily oral care.

You have already discovered how cooperative your child is in receiving a bath, home therapies, hair combing, dressing, and oral care. When your child understands the need for oral care—but due to the disability (such as cerebral palsy) may be unable to control his or her response to stimulation—the physical therapist, occupational therapist, dental professional, or medical professional will be able to recommend strategies for you to use in positioning and stabilizing for oral care.

Combativeness during oral care can arise from a variety of reasons. Some are from the disabling condition, the strategy used to perform oral care, the products used, or the learned response. The child may not understand oral care or why you are doing the procedure. The feeling may be uncomfortable to the child, due to sensitivity of his or her face and mouth. The child may not be able to control his or her muscle response to stimulation. The oral tissues, teeth, and gums may hurt during brushing. Pain may be from oral lesion, infection, or tooth decay. Biting or gagging reflexes may be strong, making oral care uncomfortable. The toothpaste may have an unpleasant flavor or sensation. The toothpaste can stimulate extra salivation.

The following positions have been successfully used to accomplish daily oral care.

continues

continued

Position of Child Receiving Oral Care	Position of Person Delivering Oral Care
Seated (in chair, in wheelchair, on counter, in bean bag)	Facing child
Lying down (on couch, on bed, in bean bag, or on foam pad)	Sitting next to child or with child's head in your lap
Flexed position (on pillows, in bean bag, or on foam pads)	Sitting next to child or with child's head in your lap
Control head moving (position noted above)	Position behind the child, cradle head in arm
Control arms moving (position noted above or loosely wrap in a sheet or blanket)	Second person helps hold hands

Notes:

Source: John N. Dane and Lynn C. Schuchman, *Oral Health Education Project: A Manual for Families and Case Managers of Persons with a Disability*, School of Dentistry, University of Missouri-Kansas City, © 1990.

How To Brush

Place the bristles at a 45° angle to the teeth, with *the brush resting on the gums.* Moving slowly in a circular motion, count to ten without taking the brush from the teeth. Repeat this motion for every two or three teeth, moving to the inside, outside, and chewing surfaces until you have cleaned all your child's teeth.

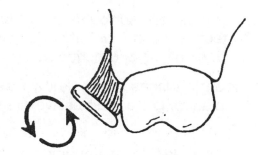

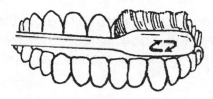

Brush the outside surfaces of the upper teeth using a vibrating motion.

Brush the outside surfaces of the lower teeth using the same motion.

Brush all inside surfaces as well.

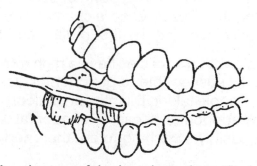

Use the toe of the brush to clean the inside of the front teeth.

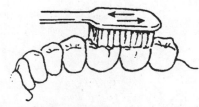

Brush chewing surfaces with a back and forth motion.

Source: John N. Dane and Lynn C. Schuchman, *Oral Health Education Project: A Manual for Families and Case Managers of Persons with a Disability*, School of Dentistry, University of Missouri-Kansas City, © 1990.

Periodontal Disease

Healthy teeth are surrounded by healthy gums and bone. These structures are needed to provide teeth a solid foundation for good function. When routine care of teeth and gums is neglected, gingivitis and periodontal disease begin.

Periodontal disease, also known as gum disease or "pyorrhea," is caused by bacteria found in plaque. It is a progressive illness affecting most adults. There are three stages of gum disease.

Gingivitis (meaning inflammation of the gums) is the first stage marked by redness, swelling, tenderness, and, most importantly, bleeding of the gums. When the teeth are kept plaque-free, the gums will become healthy and the condition will reverse itself.

The second stage is early periodontitis. In this stage plaque actively moves below the gum line and permanently destroys the supporting bone. When the bone is lost, the gums are likely to recede. Recession is harmful because it increases the risk of root decay and tooth sensitivity.

Advanced periodontitis is the last stage. There is continued recession of the gums and loss of bone. The teeth may become loose and pus may be discharged from the gums.

There is a less common form of periodontal disease that affects adolescents known as juvenile periodontitis. This disease is characterized by specific areas of severe bone and gum loss, most commonly involving the first molars and front (incisor) adult teeth.

People with disabilities have a high rate of periodontal disease. People with cerebral palsy are especially susceptible to periodontal disease because of poor oral hygiene and tooth-grinding habits. People taking Dilantin, an anticonvulsant drug, will have overgrowth of the gums that can lead to periodontal disease. Periodontal disease can be prevented by diligent oral hygiene efforts or by possibly switching to another medication.

Notes:

Source: *Special Care for Special Needs: A Dental Education Booklet for Clients, Caregivers and Parents*, Office of Dental Health, Division of Family Services, Arizona Department of Health Services, Phoenix, Arizona, © 1992.

Adapting Oral Hygiene Aids

Certain factors must be evaluated when determining the need for modifications:

- The child must be motivated to perform his or her own oral care procedures.
- Hand strength of the child must be measured. A standard test, usually performed by an occupational therapist or physical therapist, determines whether the child has a deficit in hand strength and function.
- New instruction must accompany the introduction of a modified oral hygiene tool. Even if the child has been able to accomplish oral care procedures in the past with the standard tools, the introduction of a new tool requires adjustment. If a child is not motivated to accept the new toothbrush, it will most likely be abandoned quickly.

Consult with the child's physician or occupational or physical therapist for advice on which adaptation would most benefit your child.

- **Toothpaste cap.** If an enlarged handle is helpful on the toothbrush, the toothpaste cap will need to be enlarged also. You may find a style of toothpaste that is easier for your child to open and dispense. Some options are the flip cap, pump, or a wall dispenser.
- **Floss aid.** A floss holder or aid can assist children who cannot hold the floss in their fingers. This aid can also make it easier for parents or caregivers to floss the child's teeth.
- **Bending the brush.** Changing the angle of the toothbrush handle can assist a child to reach his or her mouth. This adaptation will aid children who cannot easily bend their wrist.
- **Longer toothbrush handle.** Adding material to the end of a toothbrush handle allows the child with a limited range of motion at the elbow or wrist to reach the mouth.
- **Enlarged toothbrush handle.** When a child cannot close his or her fingers around the toothbrush handle, the handle can be enlarged to the size of the child's grip.
- **Toothbrush cuff.** If the child cannot close his or her fingers around the toothbrush handle, a "universal" cuff can hold the brush for the child. These cuffs are available from an occupational or physical therapist.
- **Electric toothbrush.** An electric toothbrush can aid the child who has weak muscle strength or difficulty in moving the toothbrush. It can also aid the parent or caregiver who is brushing the teeth of the child.

  The electric toothbrush can help a child to brush his or her own teeth. Several brands of brushes are available. Follow the manufacturer's instructions for charging the battery, cleaning, and maintaining the brush.

When selecting an electric toothbrush, consider the child's needs and the type of brush available.

continues

continued

— weight of the toothbrush: can be held in position in the mouth long enough for the child to brush his or her teeth

— size of the handle: fits the child's hand comfortably

— on/off switch: style of switch that can be managed by the child

— style of brush action:

    (a) up and down motion brush: brush head moves in an up-and-down motion

    (b) elliptical or oval motion brush: brush head moves in an oval; some brushes combine both actions

    (c) rotating bristles: the bristles rotate in circles; the head of the brush does not move

Notes:

Source: John N. Dane and Lynn C. Schuchman, *Oral Health Education Project: A Manual for Families and Case Managers of Persons with a Disability*, School of Dentistry, University of Missouri-Kansas City, © 1990.

Preparing Your Child for the First Dental Visit

There are no fast and sure rules for how to prepare a child with a disability for a dental appointment. Depending on the intellectual level at which your child is functioning, you may be able to explain in simple terms what is going to happen. Remember, your child is able to feel your anxiety, so if you are anxious about the appointment be sure you don't pass on your fear.

BASIC STRATEGIES

- If your child will sit and listen to you read, try reading him or her a book about a dental visit. There are several titles available.

- Play a game about going to the dentist. Include opening your mouth and looking around inside. Getting a child with a disability to open his or her mouth is sometimes quite difficult, especially if the child hasn't been receiving routine oral care. Practice mouth opening.

- Bring the child to a routine dental visit that you or another member of the family is having. Let the child watch. This visit will familiarize the child with the office and make it less threatening.

If communication with your child is difficult, playing games and reading stories about a dental visit may be long-range goals and may require a lot of preparation. You may wish to ask an occupational therapist about working with your child on this matter. If you have the time and the will to provide the experiences, you should do so. Because a visual examination of the mouth will be of primary importance, work on your child's ability to open his or her mouth.

MOUTH-OPENING STRATEGIES

Toothbrushing

If you are brushing your child's teeth regularly, this will help. If not, then you can use this as an excuse to gain access to the mouth. If you cannot gain access then seek assistance from your dentist at the appointment or ask an occupational therapist for help.

Mouth Prop

A simple mouth prop, comprised of a stack of tongue blades taped together or a folded washcloth, can be used to hold the mouth open. Once open, let your child become more familiar with the presence of the mouth prop before you remove it. Once your child is accustomed to it, you may then wish to start gently brushing the teeth. This action may cause some reaction by your child, but repeated efforts in a gentle manner will be reassuring over a period of time.

continues

continued

If you are unsuccessful in opening your child's mouth, then expect that the dentist will have some difficulty too. With your help and permission the dentist may wish to use some form of rigid mouth prop, either rubber or metal covered with rubber to stabilize your child's mouth. Reassure your child that this prop is only to help and it is not a punishment.

The dentist may request to use other forms of restraint to provide care. If restraint is necessary, be sure that the dentist explains the procedure fully and that you are comfortable with the procedure.

PREPARING FOR AN APPOINTMENT

Tips that may help include:

- Don't make the visit the high point of the day. Your child will suspect something is up.
- Avoid using bribery or threats in an attempt to encourage good behavior.
- Avoid saying negative words such as "hurt," "shot," "pull," or "drill."
- Don't try to describe exactly what will happen. The dentist and dental hygienist have special words and ways of explaining the procedures to a child.
- Don't expect perfect behavior. Your child may be shy or fearful and misbehave. If your child throws a tantrum, end the visit and try again another day. Especially with a child with a disability, "acting out" behavior may require reinforcement of the reasons for being at the dentist. With an older child, over 3 years old, the dentist may try to handle the situation without you.
- Don't make the dentist the villain. Dental treatment is something *you* want for the child.

Unfortunately, children sometimes require restorative dental treatment to repair dental decay that has occurred due to lack of good preventive care. In these circumstances, if the decay is extensive, the teeth will need to be put to sleep (anesthetized). Many children with disabilities have had multiple visits to physicians' offices, and some may have had repeated surgery. These children have been sensitized to health care and the "physician's office experience." These children will require more patience and reassurance than children that have not had the previous experiences. Opinions vary on how to explain this to your child. But a few principles should be adhered to:

- If you have not had good personal experiences in the dentist's office, you may not be the best person to explain dental treatment to the child. Even though your explanation may be good, if you are anxious about dental care you will communicate your anxiety through your actions. Consider if someone with a good dental treatment history might be a better person to explain the dental visit to your child.

continues

continued

- Have another child who has had a good visit describe a successful dental visit.

- Try to tell your child in words and ideas that he or she can understand. Playing a simple game or acting out a dental visit with a doll or toy may help.

- Be honest, but be sure not to provide too much information too quickly. If your child doesn't understand, it may frighten him or her. Remember, calm reassurance is the best way to provide support for what your child will experience. If your child has a strong negative or fearful reaction to a dental injection, you may have to participate in a "desensitizing" experience to help your child overcome his or her fear of the dentist.

Notes:

Source: John N. Dane and Lynn C. Schuchman, *Oral Health Education Project: A Manual for Families and Case Managers of Persons with a Disability*, School of Dentistry, University of Missouri-Kansas City, © 1990.

Oral Health and Autism

There are no unique problems related to the dentition and perioral structures associated with autism. The child is at risk for dental diseases associated with incomplete daily oral hygiene or infrequent professional cleanings. Teaching oral care procedures should complement the strategies established by parents or teachers. Some children may have difficulty adjusting to the dental office environment, so care should be taken to prepare the child for in-office procedures.

- Common dental problems associated with poor or incomplete oral hygiene and/or infrequent professional cleanings:
  — increased dental decay
  — increased gingival and periodontal disease
- Preventive management concerns and strategies:
  — daily oral hygiene
    (a) Child able to provide independent daily oral care: teach, support, and reinforce as needed.
    (b) Child provides incomplete daily oral care: teach and reinforce to become as independent as possible; complete daily oral care by family or caregiver.
    (c) Child unable to provide daily oral care: complete daily oral care by family or caregiver.
  — orientation to the dental office environment
  — sealants
  — diet and nutrition
    (a) fluoride supplementation
    (b) cariogenic food as reinforcers

Notes:

Source: John N. Dane and Lynn C. Schuchman, *Oral Health Education Project: A Manual for Families and Case Managers of Persons with a Disability*, School of Dentistry, University of Missouri-Kansas City, © 1990.

Oral Health and Mental Retardation

The degree of cognitive impairment varies with each child. In general, the communication and learning strategies already in use by parents or teacher are recommended for teaching the dental oral care procedures. Research shows the child with mental retardation is able to perform adequate home oral hygiene procedures, and is therefore able to prevent dental diseases of tooth decay and periodontal disease. Mental retardation occurs with other disabilities and is part of other developmental syndromes; both conditions may have an impact on the dental condition of the child.

- Common dental problems associated with poor or incomplete oral hygiene and/or infrequent professional cleanings:
  — increased dental decay
  — increased gingival and periodontal disease
- Dental problems associated with the child who has mental retardation as part of other syndromes and conditions:
  — malocclusion, associated with craniofacial syndromes
  — developmental anomalies of the enamel
- Common dental problems associated with falls or medications containing phenytoin:
  — fractured teeth
  — hyperplasia of the gingiva (increases with poor oral hygiene)
- Other conditions may include:
  — pica (eating nonfood substances such as chalk or soil)
  — tongue thrusting habit
  — clenching and bruxing teeth
  — drooling
  — self-injurious behavior
- Preventive management concerns and strategies:
  — daily oral hygiene
    (a) Child able to provide independent daily oral care: teach, support, and reinforce as needed.
    (b) Child provides incomplete daily oral care: teach and reinforce to become as independent as possible; complete daily oral care by family or caregiver.
    (c) Child unable to provide daily oral care: complete daily oral care by family or caregiver.
  — dietary or nutritional factors
    (a) special diet (prolonged bottle feeding, tube feeding)
    (b) inadequate diet
    (c) cariogenic food as behavioral reinforcers
    (d) fluoride supplements
  — oral effects of medications
  — sealants
  — stabilize during daily oral care due to ability to cooperate and control of muscle movements

Source: John N. Dane and Lynn C. Schuchman, *Oral Health Education Project: A Manual for Families and Case Managers of Persons with a Disability*, School of Dentistry, University of Missouri-Kansas City, © 1990.

Oral Health and Down Syndrome

Although a unique set of dental conditions is associated with Down syndrome, the risk to dental diseases is associated with the child's age, degree of mental disability, home environment, and ability to provide daily oral care.

- Common dental problems include these developmental changes in the teeth:
  — small teeth
  — malocclusion
  — delayed loss of primary teeth, delayed eruption of permanent teeth
  — congenitally missing teeth
  — enamel anomalies
  — large furrowed tongue
- Common dental problems associated with poor or incomplete oral hygiene and/or infrequent professional cleanings:
  — tooth decay (several studies show lower incidence of decay)
  — increased gingival and periodontal disease
- Other conditions may include:
  — pica (eating nonfood substances such as chalk or soil)
  — tongue thrusting habit
  — clenching and bruxing teeth
  — drooling
  — self-injurious behavior
- If the child has a heart defect, a consultation is needed with a physician concerning premedication with antibiotic therapy prior to dental treatment
- Preventive management concerns and strategies:
  — daily oral hygiene
    (a) Child able to provide independent daily oral care: teach, support, and reinforce as needed.
    (b) Child provides incomplete daily oral care: teach and reinforce to become as independent as possible; complete daily oral care by family or caregiver.
    (c) Child unable to provide daily oral care: complete daily oral care by family or caregiver.
  — dietary or nutritional factors
    (a) special diet (prolonged bottle feeding, tube feeding)
    (b) inadequate diet
    (c) cariogenic food as behavioral reinforcers
    (d) fluoride supplements
  — oral effects of medications
  — sealants
  — ability to cooperate varies, but is usually good

Source: John N. Dane and Lynn C. Schuchman, *Oral Health Education Project: A Manual for Families and Case Managers of Persons with a Disability*, School of Dentistry, University of Missouri-Kansas City, © 1990.

Oral Health and Cerebral Palsy

The variation in the degree of severity and the manifestation makes it difficult to predict the dental impact of cerebral palsy. The motor dysfunction of the muscles of chewing and speech can contribute to several dental problems. The motor skill development can also impair or delay the individual's ability to provide daily oral care independently. The following dental conditions may occur more frequently with the person with cerebral palsy.

- Poor control of the muscles of speech and chewing (includes the muscles of the cheek, lips, and tongue) may contribute to:
  - tissue biting
  - drooling
  - tooth loss or bruxism
  - mouth breathing
  - malocclusion (open bite)
- Poor control of the muscles of the arm and hand may contribute to:
  - poor or incomplete oral hygiene (brushing, flossing)
  - tissue trauma
- Other conditions associated with cerebral palsy are:
  - enamel hypoplasia
  - periodontal disease
  - perioral sensitivity
  - involuntary movements during dental treatment
- Common dental problems associated with falls or medications containing phenytoin:
  - fractured teeth
  - hyperplasia of the gingiva (over growth of the gums—increases with poor oral hygiene)
- Preventive management concerns and oral strategies:
  - daily oral hygiene
  - adaptations of oral care products
  - fluoride supplements
  - sealants
  - stability of involuntary movements
  - desensitization of perioral tissues

Source: John N. Dane and Lynn C. Schuchman, *Oral Health Education Project: A Manual for Families and Case Managers of Persons with a Disability*, School of Dentistry, University of Missouri-Kansas City, © 1990.

Oral Health and Cleft Palate

Dental care is especially important for children born with clefts. Children with cleft palate have more problems with the way their teeth grow in than most other children, and they need special dental care. One or more of the teeth may be misshapen or be missing, or there may be two of the same kind of tooth. Usually, some of the teeth come through in a poor position. If your child has dental problems, they can be treated by dental specialists on the cleft palate team.

Although dental treatment may not begin for a while, dental evaluations in infancy are essential to your child's overall treatment plan. Periodically, dental impressions may be made of your child's mouth. X-rays will be taken of teeth that haven't come through yet.

Care of your child's teeth is very important. Strong, healthy teeth are needed to anchor prostheses and appliances in the mouth and to hold braces later. So, start brushing your child's teeth after meals with a child-size toothbrush when they first come in. Teach your child good techniques for brushing teeth as soon as the child is old enough.

Six-month checkups should be scheduled with a children's dentist from the time the child is 2 to 3 years old. Any cavities should be filled right away. When your child gets older, braces may be needed. Your child's dental needs will require careful attention from infancy onward.

Notes:

Source: *Looking Forward: A Guide for Parents of the Child with Cleft Lip and Palate*, Mead Johnson & Company, Evansville, Indiana, © 1991.

Oral Health and Sensory Disorders

The impact on dental care is in the child's ability to communicate and learn proper dental care. Some children with sensory disorders may have difficulty adjusting to the dental office environment. Care should be taken to prepare the child for in-office procedures.

- Common dental problems associated with poor or incomplete oral hygiene and/or infrequent professional cleanings:
  — increased dental decay
- Other dental problems that may occur include:
  — enamel hypoplasia due to prematurity (interrupted development)
  — increased oral sensitivity
  — bruxism and tooth loss (children with hearing impairments)
  — tooth fractures, oral trauma due to falls (children with visual impairments)
- Preventive management:
  — daily oral hygiene
    (a) Child able to provide independent daily oral care: teach, support, and reinforce as needed.
    (b) Child provides incomplete daily oral care: teach and reinforce to become as independent as possible; complete daily oral care by family or caregiver.
    (c) Child unable to provide daily oral care: complete daily oral care by family or caregiver.
  — fluoride supplementation
    (a) sealants
- Orientation to the dental office environment

Notes:

Source: John N. Dane and Lynn C. Schuchman, *Oral Health Education Project: A Manual for Families and Case Managers of Persons with a Disability*, School of Dentistry, University of Missouri-Kansas City, © 1990.

Oral Health and Spina Bifida

Dental problems arise due to the limited joint movement, muscular weakness or atrophy, and cerebral shunts associated with spina bifida. Dental problems also occur due to the child's inability to provide his or her own oral care and tolerate dental treatment.

- Common dental problems associated with spina bifida:
  — enamel hypoplasia
- Common dental problems associated with incomplete daily oral care. May be associated with limited joint movements and muscular weakness or atrophy:
  — dental decay
  — gingival and periodontal disease
- If the child has a cerebral shunt, a consultation with the physician is needed because premedication with antibiotic therapy may be required prior to dental treatment.
- Preventive management:
  — daily oral hygiene
    (a) Child able to provide independent daily oral care: teach, support, and reinforce as needed.
    (b) Child provides incomplete daily oral care: teach and reinforce to become as independent as possible; complete daily oral care by family or caregiver.
    (c) Child unable to provide daily oral care: complete daily oral care by family or caregiver.
  — dietary or nutritional factors
    (a) special diet (prolonged bottle feeling, tube feeding)
    (b) inadequate diet
    (c) cariogenic food as behavioral reinforcers
    (d) suboptimal fluoride supplements
  — sealants
  — stabilize during oral care due to muscle weakness

Notes:

Source: John N. Dane and Lynn C. Schuchman, *Oral Health Education Project: A Manual for Families and Case Managers of Persons with a Disability*, School of Dentistry, University of Missouri-Kansas City, © 1990.

Oral Health and Seizure Disorders

The dental problems associated with seizure disorders are related to the trauma received during a seizure. The oral effects of the anticonvulsive medication phenytoin are related to this drug. Other anticonvulsants are not known to cause gingival overgrowth. Poor oral hygiene or the presence of plaque appears to stimulate the overgrowth reaction. There are no dental problems associated from the brain dysfunction itself.

- Oral facial trauma result from seizures:
  - soft tissue trauma to the lips, tongue, and cheeks
  - trauma to the hard palate, facial or jaw bones
  - fractures of the teeth (most frequently anterior teeth)
- Common dental problems associated with gingival overgrowth:
  - increased gingival inflammation
  - malpositioned teeth
  - impaired chewing function
  - poor appearance because tissue most frequently covers anterior teeth
- Preventive management:
  - daily oral hygiene
    - (a) Child able to provide independent daily oral care: teach, support, and reinforce as needed.
    - (b) Child provides incomplete daily oral care: teach and reinforce to become as independent as possible; complete daily oral care by family or caregiver.
    - (c) Child unable to provide daily oral care: complete daily oral care by family or caregiver.
  - fluorides to reduce plaque and gingival diseases
  - trauma management
    - (a) Recommend mouthguards for children with uncontrolled seizures (especially if wearing a helmet).
    - (b) Repair or replace damaged teeth, consider the possibility of future damage.

Source: John N. Dane and Lynn C. Schuchman, *Oral Health Education Project: A Manual for Families and Case Managers of Persons with a Disability*, School of Dentistry, University of Missouri-Kansas City, © 1990.

7
Educational Issues

Developing a School Program for a Child with Fragile X Syndrome

1. **Learn as much as possible about fragile X syndrome and sensory integration dysfunction.**

   Also, fragile X conferences can keep parents up to date on treatment issues. If it is not possible for you to attend conferences, contact the organizers and/or presenters for tapes or the latest written information about fragile X.

2. **Become familiar with state and national laws and know your rights.**

   Obtain a copy of your state's special education law book. Contact your protection and advocacy, child advocacy, The Arc, or other advocacy groups for written materials and advocacy training courses.

3. **Be involved in your child's program.**

   Visit your child's class regularly and have open communication with the teacher and support personnel. Observe your child's therapy sessions. When your child is scheduled to have a program change (or when you can feel he or she needs a change from the current program), visit all other program possibilities, even if they weren't suggested by your school district.

4. **Ensure the program for your child is multidisciplinary.**

   While you are working to create an optimal multidisciplinary program appropriate for your child, try to obtain the best possible services in the interim. It may mean obtaining public or private schooling and therapies while working to make the school program fit your child's needs.

5. **Set goals when looking for or creating a program for your child.**

   Even though there is a vast range of functioning levels in children with fragile X syndrome, there are many common characteristics and needs. Here is a list of sample goals for a child named Nathan:

   - The program must be multidisciplinary.
   - The program must provide for Nathan's sensory integration needs. This goal would require an occupational therapist trained and experienced in sensory integration therapy several times a week, an appropriate location for the therapy, equipment to meet Nathan's needs (which also can be used by other students), and provisions for the occupational therapist to educate other staff members working with Nathan about his sensory needs.

continues

continued

- The program must address Nathan's strengths. Almost all parents of children with fragile X syndrome and many professionals working with them agree that the present assessment tools do not adequately demonstrate the strengths of the child with fragile X syndrome. Parents must make sure when placing and teaching children with fragile X syndrome that their strengths (often demonstrated through informal means of assessment) are taken into account.

- The program must help remediate Nathan's weaknesses. As typical with many children with fragile X syndrome, Nathan has weaknesses in math, sequencing, abstract reasoning, and fine motor skills. His program needs to address these weaknesses, using his strengths as much as possible to help remediate them.

- His program needs to be in a school where he could stay throughout his elementary years and where he would have nondisabled role models.

6. **Plan the Individualized Education Program (IEP) early enough in the spring so you can work out any difficulties.**

7. **Make sure you have copies of all your child's reports and make sure the sources of them are familiar with your child.**

   People need to spend a good deal of time with children with fragile X syndrome to be able to properly understand them.

8. **Try to avoid due process if at all possible, but do not hesitate to file for it if the school district does not meet your child's needs.**

   You may choose to retain a private attorney who specializes in special education law. Legal services may also be available through protection and advocacy, The Arc, and other advocacy groups.

9. **When your child's IEP is developed, get everything in writing.**

   Put everything in writing: goals, therapists' names, the length and frequency of therapy, and so forth. The IEP is your legal document that ensures services are provided for your child so that he or she can be successful in the educational environment. Make sure everything is in writing.

Source: Mary Ann Fischer, "Fighting for a School Program for a Child with Fragile X Syndrome," *National Fragile X Foundation Newsletter*, National Fragile X Foundation, © Summer 1990.

Education Techniques for Preschool Children with Fetal Alcohol Syndrome/Fetal Alcohol Effects

ENVIRONMENT

1. Maintain a calm and quiet environment.
   - Use soft music as a calming technique.
   - Tone down classroom so the room is not overly stimulating.
     — Keep a minimal number of objects hanging from the ceiling and on the walls.
     — Use calm paint colors on the walls.
   - Dim the lights for nap time.
   - Use headphones for quiet time.
2. Establish structure.
   - Enforce the same rules in the same way.
3. Establish a routine for smooth transition from one activity to another activity.
   - Tell the children what they will be doing (for example, "We'll finish painting then we'll eat a snack").
   - Give the children objects associated with the next activity (for example, "When we finish our snack, we will brush our teeth." The teacher then gives the child his or her toothbrush at this time so the child has an easier time making the transition.).
   - Involve the child in preparations for the next activity (for example, the child could carry the book to reading area or carry the puppet to the puppet show).

LANGUAGE DEVELOPMENT

For children who are not talking:

1. Begin with simple story books.
2. Touch an object and name the object for the child (for example, the teacher touches a table and says to the child "table").
3. Use real objects such as "trees," "cars," and "dog" and name the objects.

For children who are talking using single words:

1. Stimulate more words in the child's vocabulary (for example, if the child says "drink" say to the child "more drink").
2. Expand the child's vocabulary slowly (for example, when the child starts using two words at a time, start using three words "want more drink").
3. Talk with the child at the child's level (for example, use short sentences; avoid using long sentences).

continues

continued

For children who articulate poorly:

1. Obtain the services of a speech therapist.
2. Use proper pronunciation—a good role model is important.
3. Go around the classroom, touch objects, and name the object. Then have the child do the same thing.
4. Have the child say what he or she wants at mealtime rather than just giving the child food.
5. Use musical activities to help teach vocabulary.
   - Sing a good morning song.
   - Sing a song before the children eat.
   - Learn and sing name songs.
   - Play circle game songs involving sitting down, standing up, and name games.

Use sign language to teach children with fetal alcohol syndrome (FAS) even when they do not have a hearing loss. Sign language is a concrete and visible language that can be used along with verbal language.

MATH

1. Remember that memorized counting from one to ten does not mean the child understands the numbers.
2. Teach the child to learn what the number "1" means before any more numbers are taught to the child (e.g., "Give me one crayon"; "Put one napkin on the table").
3. Cut numbers out of paper and then glue on oatmeal, rice, glitter, and so forth so the child can see, feel, and hear the number.
4. Touch and count objects.

ALPHABET

1. Cut letters from paper and then glue other objects to the letter.
2. Match letters.
3. Match words.
4. Use the sounds of the letters repeatedly (for example, "J" is for juice, jump, jacket, and so on).
5. Cut letters out of sandpaper and have the child follow the sandpaper letters with his or her finger.
6. Write a letter on the blackboard and have the child trace the letter on the blackboard.
7. Make dots on a paper in the shape of a letter and have the child connect the dots to make the letter, gradually decreasing the number of dots to connect to make the letter.
8. Make letters out of gelatin.
9. Have the child use all capital letters when first writing his or her name. Sometimes it makes it easier for the child.

continues

continued

SENSORY STIMULATION

1. Use as much sensory stimulation as possible to teach each concept. For example, when teaching the color "orange":
   - Wear orange clothes.
   - Paint with orange paint.
   - Use orange construction paper for projects.
   - Serve oranges for a snack.
   - Sit on an orange rug.
2. Use objects as much as possible to teach concepts.
   - Teach children about "circles" by
     — laminating polka dot fabric
     — using a cookie cutter to cut circle sandwiches
     — cutting circles from construction paper and gluing circular cereal bits to the paper
3. Use teaching activities that are "concrete."
   - Do not give vague commands. For example, one child, even though told to stay in the yard, continued to wander into the street. Parents obtained four large orange cones and had the child stay inside the four cones. Parents gradually expanded the cones.
   - Do not ask abstract questions (for example, "What do you want?"). Give the child choices he or she can see, feel, touch, and hear.

MANAGEMENT OF HYPERACTIVITY

1. Keep the environment structured.
2. Make a picture calendar.
   - Make a board with hooks.
   - Laminate pictures of activities for the whole day.
     — Have a picture of a child taking off a jacket and hanging it up.
     — Have a picture of a child putting a puzzle together.
   - Have the child take the picture off the hook, turn it over, and hang the picture back on the hook as the child completes each activity during the day. This way, the child knows that he or she has completed the activity.
3. Allow the child to choose from two or three toys. Give the child plenty of time to make the choice. If the child seems to have difficulty making a choice, watch the child to see if he or she looks longer at a particular toy or makes a movement toward a certain toy.
4. Place each activity in two baskets.
   - Have two baskets for a puzzle, two baskets for a pegboard, two baskets for a matching activity, two baskets for lacing cards, two baskets for scissors and paper activity, and so forth. Having one activity in one set of baskets will keep the child's attention on the activity for a longer period of time.

continues

continued

- Take the activity out of the "start" basket and when the child has finished the activity, have the child put the activity into the "finish" basket.

5. Keep the designated activities in the same place. The child will know where to return the activity when he or she is finished.

6. Have children sit on a chair rather than on the floor. The chair keeps the child from leaning backward, forward, and sideways. The chair helps keep the child in a specific space.
   - Demonstrate to children how to sit in the chair. Place feet flat on the floor, hands on the side, and sit up straight.
   - Have the activity at the table ready for the child when the child is sitting properly. The child probably will not sit at the table very long waiting for the teacher to bring an activity.

7. Structure the day alternating quiet time, active time, quiet time, active time, and so forth.

8. Adhere to a routine when tantrums occur.
   - Take the child to a different room. Play lullaby music to help calm the child.
   - Hold the child.
   - Talk in a calm voice; walk slowly. If the teacher is relaxed, it will help the child relax. A teacher's body language should not get the child excited.
   - Determine what happened before the tantrum occurred. Look for the antecedents to the behavior. Antecedents are the events or things that happen that help the child lose his or her temper.
   - Look at different ways to eliminate the chances of the child throwing a tantrum. If the child has an extremely difficult time with loud noises and lots of activity, the child should be taught in a relatively quiet and calm area.
   - Teach the child new ways of dealing with stress as another means to eliminate tantrums. Teach the child to say "I'm mad."

9. Review the child's diet. It could be a contributing factor for the behavior.

10. Observe the child for any health problems.
    - Look for a child pulling at his or her ears. It may signal an ear infection.
    - Ask the child to "Show me where you hurt."

11. Ignore negative behavior whenever possible. Avoid overreacting to negative behavior.

12. Build in positive reinforcement.
    - Hug the child as he or she finishes each activity on the picture calendar. When the child does a good job on a project, let the child know he or she will get a hug. Children with FAS or fetal alcohol effects (FAE) often like to be hugged.

13. Be flexible. If a child does not need sleep at nap time, the child may benefit from having active activities. Allow him or her to ride a tricycle in the hall.

SHORT ATTENTION SPAN

1. Determine how long the child is working on an activity.

continues

continued

2. Expand the child's attention span gradually. For example, if the child is drawing circles on a paper and the child decides to quit have the child draw "one more" circle. Never make the child do the activity more than once if the instruction was to "draw one more circle."

SOCIAL BEHAVIOR

1. Show the child how to share toys. If necessary, use a timer to share the most popular toys.
2. Teach the child how to be a friend through the use of puppets or dolls.
3. Teach the child how to sit with a friend at the table.
4. Pair children for a week so the child with developmental disabilities can learn from children who do not have developmental disabilities.

EYE-HAND COORDINATION ACTIVITIES

1. Use puzzles with knobs on the pieces.
2. Use lace cards.
   • Make larger lace cards from cardboard to facilitate use.
   • Use masking tape on the end of the lace to make it easier for the child to sew on the card.
3. Use squeeze clothes pins.
4. Be prepared to demonstrate the activity. The teacher may need to show the child the object, show the child how to do the activity, guide the child through the activity, and then encourage the child to do the activity on his or her own. The teacher could pick up the puzzle piece for the child to put in the right place in the puzzle. The teacher could lace the first two holes of a lacing card.
5. Have the child put pegs in a board.
6. Have the child pound a peg board.

EVALUATIONS

1. Have the following evaluations performed to learn more about the child's development and assist in planning the activities:
   • speech and language evaluations
   • psychological evaluations
   • motor evaluations
2. Remember that children with FAS/FAE usually need more one-to-one teaching. The number of staff available relative to the number of children who have FAS/FAE in each center needs to be evaluated.

Source: South Dakota University Affiliated Program, University of South Dakota, School of Medicine, 414 E. Clark, 208 Julian Hall, Vermillion, SD 57069, 1–800–658–3080.

Education Techniques for Elementary School Students with Fetal Alcohol Syndrome/Fetal Alcohol Effects

ENVIRONMENT

1. Maintain a calm and quiet environment.
   - Play soft calm music during breaks.
   - Tone down classroom so the room is not overly stimulating.
     — Keep a minimal number of objects hanging from the ceiling and on the walls.
     — Use calm paint colors on the walls.
     — Reduce classroom clutter.
     — Use bulletin boards as teaching tools, use soft colors. (Bulletin boards can be covered when not in use.)
   - Use headphones for quiet time.
   - Remember that students with fetal alcohol syndrome (FAS)/fetal alcohol effects (FAE) are not always able to block out other noises.
2. Establish structure.
   - Develop a few simple rules.
   - Enforce the same rules in the same way.
   - Use the same language when enforcing the rules.
3. Establish a routine for smooth transition from one activity to another activity.
   - Give the student reminders for ending and beginning of activities. Use tactual and verbal signals (touch shoulder, tap elbow, say "The bell will ring in five minutes, you need to finish up" or "We will go to lunch when the bell rings").
   - Adhere to a consistent routine every day.
   - Provide notebooks for students that have all their classroom activities in order for the day. The notebook gives the student a concrete item with which to structure his or her day. Class periods should not exceed 20 minutes.
   - Involve the student in preparations for the next activity. The child can carry the book to the reading area or the puppets to the puppet show.
   - Schedule several breaks during the day. Students with FAS/FAE may need sleep during the day. They may need to get up and move around more frequently than other students. Plan activities to facilitate movement and creativity between seat work assignments. Students with FAS/FAE may also need food snacks during the day.

LANGUAGE DEVELOPMENT

1. Talk with the student at the student's level. Use short sentences; avoid long sentences.
2. Help improve poor articulation.
   - Use the services of a speech therapist to help both the student and teacher.
   - Use proper pronunciation at all times. A good role model is important.

continues

continued

- Remember that articulation errors are common. Accept communications without correcting them. Repeat the sounds correctly.
- Use music activities to help students learn vocabulary.
  — Sing a good morning song.
  — Sing a song before the student eats.
  — Learn and sing name songs.
  — Play circle game songs that require the child to sit down and stand up; play name games.
3. Be aware of quantity versus quality of speech issues.
  - Remember that quantity does not indicate quality. Students with FAS/FAE often use a large quantity of speech.
  - Listen for the number of words per sentence.
  - Listen for the number of new words that the student uses.
  - Stress concept development through concrete examples encouraging the student to demonstrate understanding. For example, to demonstrate an understanding of "temperature," ask the child what he or she would wear on a hot day and on a cold day.
4. Use sign language.
  - Use sign language to teach students with FAS even when they do not have a hearing loss.
  - Remember that sign language is concrete and visible and can be used along with verbal language.

ELEMENTARY MATHEMATICS

1. Stress concept development of numbers encouraging students to demonstrate knowledge. Memorized counting from one to ten does not mean the student understands numbers.
2. Teach the student to learn what the number "one" means before any more numbers are taught to the student. Ask the child to "Give me one crayon" or "Put one card on the table."
3. Cut numbers out of paper. Glue oatmeal, rice, glitter, and the like to the number. The student can see, feel, and hear the number as well as manipulate objects that represent the number.
4. Touch and count objects.
5. Teach functional mathematics (that is, money, time, addition, subtraction).
6. Allow the student to use his or her fingers for addition and subtraction or a calculator. These techniques should not be the first choice but they should not be ruled out if the child can benefit from them. A calculator may be necessary for the student with FAS/FAE to do multiplication and division.

ALPHABET

1. Make letters out of paper and glue other objects to the letters.
2. Match letters to objects (for example, A is for apple).
3. Match letters to pictures.

continues

continued

4. Match letters to letters.
5. Follow the above sequence with words. Match words to words (for example, Apple-apple).
6. Generalize new words into other activities, other class work, and home activities. Have a "Letter for the Day." Use the sounds of the letter repeatedly. "J" is for juice, jump, jacket, and so on. Continue same objectives with words.
7. Use green and red clues to indicate the beginning and ending of a letter to facilitate proper writing of letters.

READING

1. Help students overcome difficulties with focusing their eyes on the left side of the page and moving their eyes to the right.
   - Allow student to use a piece of paper to follow the line across the page.
   - Use green marker at the left side changing to red at the right side for written work.
   - Use colored arrows to signal starting points and direction from left to right.
2. Use books with simple, plain pictures. Small detailing marks in a picture can distract the student.
3. Provide the student with books that follow the student's interest and independent reading levels. Independent reading levels means the student can read 90% of the words in the book.
4. Read aloud to the students daily and provide uninterrupted silent reading periods.

SENSORY STIMULATION

1. Use as much sensory stimulation as possible to teach each concept. For example, when teaching the color "orange":
   - Wear orange clothes.
   - Paint with orange paint.
   - Use orange construction paper for projects.
   - Serve oranges for a snack.
   - Sit on an orange rug.
2. Use objects as much as possible to teach concepts. For example, when teaching children about "circles":
   - Laminate polka dot fabric.
   - Use a cookie cutter to cut circle sandwiches.
   - Cut circles from construction paper and glue circular cereal bits to the paper.
3. Use teaching activities that are "concrete."
   - Do not give vague commands. For example, one child, even though told to stay in the yard, continuously wandered into the street. To be more "concrete" four, the parents obtained large orange cones and told the child to stay inside the four cones. Gradually the parents expanded the area covered by the cones until the concept was learned.
   - Tie concepts to concrete objects. For example, the teacher can set a work-play schedule by using pictures, nesting cups, or similar objects. The teacher could set out six nesting cups to show the student that he or she has six activities to complete before taking a break.

continues

continued

- Do not ask abstract questions (for example, "What do you want?"). Give the child choices he or she can see, feel, touch, and hear.

MANAGEMENT OF HYPERACTIVITY

1. Keep the environment structured.
2. Have as few rules as possible and enforce rules consistently. (Never make a rule that will not be enforced. Avoid threats.)
3. Make a picture calendar.
   - Make a board with hooks.
   - Laminate pictures or take Polaroid pictures of child doing activities to occur during the day or during a work time.
     — Have a picture of a student taking off a jacket and hanging it up.
     — Have a picture of a student putting a puzzle together.
   - Have the child take the picture off the hook, turn it over, and hang the picture back on the hook as the student completes each activity during the day. The child then knows that he or she has completed the activity.
4. Make lists for the student to follow during the day (for example, "Read the story starting on page 30 in the reading book"; "Do the worksheet on page 10 in the reading workbook"; "Read about rocks starting on page 15 in the science book").
   - Tape the list to the student's desk. Some students with FAS/FAE have difficulty relating instructions on the chalkboard to their own behavior.
5. Place each activity in two baskets.
   - Have two baskets for a puzzle, two baskets for a pegboard, two baskets for a matching activity, two baskets for lacing cards, two baskets for scissors and paper activity, and so on. Having one activity in one set of baskets will keep the student's attention on the activity for a longer period of time.
   - Take the activity out of the "start" basket and when the student has finished the activity, the student can put the activity into the "finish" basket.
6. Keep the designated activities in the same place. The child will know where to return the activity when he or she is finished with the activity.
7. Enclose shelves and bookcases to eliminate visual distraction.
8. Use vivid colors to emphasize important concepts. Emphasize with sound and movement the factors that complement the learning objectives.
9. Give structure to organized activities.
   - Provide the sequence of activity.
   - Explain what is expected of the child.
   - Explain what behaviors will be acceptable (for example, "During this activity we will stay in our chairs. There will be no talking. Keep your eyes on your own paper. If you want help, raise your hand and I will come to help you.").

continues

continued

10. Balance loosely structured activities with highly structured activities to give the student the opportunity to move about, visit, relax, and so forth.
11. Structure the day alternating quiet time, active time, quiet time, active time, and so on.
12. Adhere to a routine when tantrums occur.
    - Remain calm and quiet. Talk in a calm voice; walk slowly. If the teacher is relaxed, it will help the student relax. A teacher's body language should not get the student excited.
    - Let the student know there is a protocol for loss of control. Taking the student's hand and holding it a short time will give the student a signal that the teacher thinks the student is losing control. If restraint is necessary, the teacher needs to exercise care and control. Talk to the student, telling him or her that you are helping him or her to control behavior (for example, "I am going to hold on to you until you are calm. Are you feeling better? Let me know when you are ready for me to let go.").
    - Take the student to a different room if necessary. Soft music and soft colors in the room may help calm the student. Talk to the student in a calm, soft voice. Ask the student to tell the teacher when he or she is ready to go back to the classroom.
    - Determine what happened before the tantrum occurred. Look for the antecedents to the behavior. Antecedents are the events that happen that precipitate the loss of temper.
    - Look at different ways to eliminate the chances of the student throwing a tantrum. If the student has an extremely difficult time with loud noises and lots of activity, the student should be taught in a relatively quiet and calm area.
    - Teach the student new ways of dealing with stress as another means of eliminating tantrums. Teach the student to say "I'm mad."
13. Review the child's diet. It could be a contributing factor for the behavior.
14. Observe the student for any health problems.
    - Observe to see if the student is pulling at his or her ears. It may signal an ear infection.
    - Ask the student to "Show me where it hurts."
    - Look for behaviors that may signify visual problems (for example, abnormal head posturing, squinting, holding paper close to face, obvious errors made when working from the chalkboard).
15. Ignore negative behavior whenever possible. Avoid overreacting to negative behavior.
16. Build in positive reinforcement.
    - Give the student positive reinforcement for his or her efforts in completing an activity as the student finishes each activity on the picture calendar.
    - Tell the student when he or she does a good job on a project (for example, "I really like the way you wrote the letter 'k' ").

SHORT ATTENTION SPAN

1. Determine how long the student is able to work on a given activity.
2. Expand the length of time by "one more try" and reinforce the student.

continues

continued

3. Determine what activity the student can attend to longest. What is it about that activity that allows him or her to attend? Generalize these features to other activities.

SOCIAL BEHAVIOR

1. Show the student how to share playground equipment. It may be necessary to use a timer to share the most popular equipment.
2. Teach the student how to be a friend.
   - Use puppets or dolls.
   - Emphasize feelings of others.
   - Practice using manners, consideration statements, and apologies.
3. Teach the student how to sit with a friend at the table.
   - Emphasize interaction, sharing, courtesy, etc.
4. Use peer tutoring.
   - Pair children for a week so the child with FAS/FAE can learn from children who do not have FAS/FAE.
   - Allow students with FAS/FAE to help other students (for example, "Jane will bring the basket around to pick up your papers. Have them ready when she gets to your desk.").
   - Capitalize on academic strengths of the student with FAS/FAE.

EYE-HAND COORDINATION ACTIVITIES

1. Use puzzles with knobs on the pieces.
2. Use lace cards.
   - Make larger lace cards from cardboard to facilitate use.
   - Put masking tape on the end of the lace to make it easier for the child to lace the card.
3. Let the student help with tasks that require sorting, stapling, putting things in place, and similar activities.
4. Show the student the object, show the student how to do the activity, guide the student through the activity, and then encourage the student to do the activity on his or her own. The teacher could pick up the puzzle piece for the student to put in the right place in the puzzle or the teacher could lace the first two holes of a lacing card.

EVALUATIONS

1. Arrange for the following evaluations. They may be helpful in learning more about the student's development and assist in planning teacher activities:
   - speech and language evaluations
   - psychological evaluations
   - motor evaluations
2. Remember that students with FAS/FAE usually need more one-to-one teaching. The students with FAS/FAE usually need repetition of the information. Both the student/teacher ratio and the number of times information is repeated need to be evaluated.

Source: South Dakota University Affiliated Program, University of South Dakota, School of Medicine, 414 E. Clark, 208 Julian Hall, Vermillion, SD 37069, 1–800–658–3080.

Early Intervention Programs for Children with Hearing Impairments

Child's Name _____ Date _____

GENERAL GUIDELINES

Parents who have just discovered that their child is deaf or severely hard of hearing often don't know where to turn for support and assistance. Families need encouragement and the kind of information that will help them understand deafness, meet their child's needs, and integrate deafness in the family.

Kind of Program

The American Society for Deaf Children recommends parent-infant programs that are specifically for families with children who are deaf or severely hard of hearing, not mainstream programs. Only specialized programs can enable parents to provide their child and their family with an environment that encourages natural and open communication; offer specialized information and assistance from specialized, qualified staff; and provide the opportunity to share their experiences with other parents facing similar challenges. A home visiting program that can assist the family and the child who is deaf in his or her natural home setting is also an important component of supportive early intervention.

Communication Characteristics

A developing child needs a natural communication, language, and social environment. Families and children who are deaf can relate to each other most naturally when they use communication modes that allow their children to communicate and acquire language easily and efficiently. For children with any significant degree of hearing loss, language will need to be accessed visually, and thus sign language will need to be used for communication, language acquisition, and optimal development. Speech and audition are areas that also need to be addressed for the full spectrum of communication modes and will be most useful for children who have the most hearing.

Special Skills for Families

Families need programs that teach them sign language. Aside from learning sign language, parents need no special skill to be the parent of a child who is deaf. Living and relating naturally to their child using the communication that works best and meeting some adults who are deaf are perhaps the most effective forms of early intervention.

Information and Exposure

Families need information about community resources, educational options, and laws that guarantee their child's rights. Families need to know about language acquisition, sign language, interpreters, deaf

continues

continued

culture, amplification, and other technology, and other areas that will affect the well-being of their child and family. Families can benefit from meeting a variety of professionals, who are both deaf and hearing, who can provide them information and encouragement.

Support for Families

The most effective parent-infant programs sponsor a variety of support groups. Parents need to share their experiences with each other and have a forum for their successes and their concerns. Groups composed of fathers, siblings, and grandparents all help families meet the challenge of deafness. The American Society for Deaf Children suggests linking with larger parent groups like The American Society for Deaf Children and the national PTA for a broader perspective about deaf issues and parent issues generally. Of course, The American Society for Deaf Children is also a resource for parent issues and deaf issues. An opportunity to talk with adults who are deaf or hard of hearing also helps parents better understand and meet their child's needs.

CHECKLIST FOR PARENTS

Programs where parents are encouraged to look on their child as first and foremost a child and themselves as parents who are capable of bringing up their child who is deaf are the kind of programs most parents find beneficial for themselves and their child.

The following checklist can assist parents in evaluating parent-infant programs. Checklists, however, cannot include all factors or evaluate attitudes. Remember, a positive attitude about deafness is a key feature of any program.

If deafness is looked on as an affliction or as a family tragedy, and signing as "a last resort" rather than as an appropriate accommodation for deafness, children and families cannot prosper. On the other hand, if deafness is looked on as another way of being a person, and signing as an effective, valuable means of communication, families can thrive. In programs where children who are deaf or severely hard of hearing are viewed as having the same needs, capabilities, and rights as their hearing peers, parents and their child are provided the first critical step to a productive future.

The checklist that follows presents questions parents can ask about the program.

What Kind of Program Is This?

1. Is the program specifically for families with children who are deaf and
   severely hard of hearing?   Yes___ No___
2. Is the program total communication (TC)?   Yes___ No___
3. What communication mode and languages are used?
   American sign language ____ Signed English ____ Pidgin Signed English ____ Speech ____
   Other _____

continues

continued

Who Are the Staff?

Does the professional staff sign fluently?	Yes___ No___
Are there any staff members who are deaf?	Yes___ No___
Are parents of children who are deaf on the staff?	Yes___ No___
Are staff qualified in child development?	Yes___ No___
Are staff trained in deafness specifically?	Yes___ No___
Is there a clear curriculum for the children?	Yes___ No___
Are there specialists and/or referrals for children who are deaf with additional disabilities?	Yes___ No___

How many children per staff? _____

What Services Are Offered to the Children?

Are there developmental evaluations?	Yes___ No___
Are there TC play groups with other children who are deaf?	Yes___ No___
Is there a TC parent-child group with staff who are deaf?	Yes___ No___
Is there a TC parent-child group with hearing staff?	Yes___ No___
Is there audiological testing and evaluation?	Yes___ No___
Is there audiological training, as appropriate?	Yes___ No___
Is there speech awareness and training, as appropriate?	Yes___ No___
Is there physical therapy, when appropriate?	Yes___ No___
Is there teaching or referral for other disabilities?	Yes___ No___

Is This a Center-Based or a Home-Based Program?

Are there center-based services?	Yes___ No___
Are there home-based services?	Yes___ No___
How often are home visits included?	Weekly___ Monthly___

What Services Are Offered Parents and Families?

Is there individual parent counseling?	Yes___ No___
Are there parent groups?	Yes___ No___
Is there sign language instruction?	Yes___ No___
—In the center?	Yes___ No___
—In the home?	Yes___ No___
—Once weekly?	Yes___ No___
—More than once weekly?	Yes___ No___
—Are grandparents welcome?	Yes___ No___
Are there services and/or sign classes for siblings?	Yes___ No___

continues

continued

Are there information classes for families?	Yes___ No___
—Are they weekly?	Yes___ No___
—Are they monthly?	Yes___ No___
Are there social opportunities for families?	Yes___ No___
Are there direct linkages with community resources?	Yes___ No___
Are there structured opportunities to meet people who are deaf?	Yes___ No___
Is transportation to the center provided for families?	Yes___ No___

How often? _____

CONCLUSION

This checklist addresses in general terms program characteristics that fill the needs of families with children who are deaf or severely hard of hearing. Appropriate programs will offer most of these services. For a child with additional needs, additional staff and referral is crucial.

The best parent-infant program is a program that starts a family on the path to communication and normal family life. Such a program encourages family communication that allows each child to take a proud place in the family. This beginning increases the probability that the child who is deaf or severely hard of hearing will succeed as an adult "who can do anything but hear."

Notes:

Courtesy of the American Society for Deaf Children, Silver Spring, Maryland.

Hints for Teaching Children with Hearing Impairments

The following list contains 14 helpful hints you might want to share with your child's classroom teachers.

1. Assign the student a favorable seat, removed from noise sources and close to the area where instruction occurs. Avoid moving around excessively in class. A hearing aid helps only partially and cannot be expected to make this student hear as well as nondisabled students—the optimal distance of a hearing aid is less than 10 feet.

2. Establish positive attitudes toward the child with a hearing impairment. Remember, the teacher is a model for all the students in the class.
   - Help the class to understand hearing and hearing loss by having specialists discuss the ear, hearing, hearing loss, hearing conservation, hearing aids, FM trainers, effects of noise, famous people with hearing impairments, and so on.
   - Encourage the student who is deaf or hard of hearing to participate in class activities. Do not expect less work or achievement from this student.

3. Speak naturally, at a moderate pace, and face the student. The child may rely heavily on visual cues to aid understanding.
   - If you are aware that the student has a better ear, try to instruct from that side. Discuss the student's current audiogram with the school audiologist.
   - Be careful not to "talk to the blackboard."
   - Do not exaggerate mouth movements or shout. Shouting often results in distortion of speech and, if the child is wearing amplification (hearing aids or FM trainer), may hurt the student's ears.
   - Do not stand or sit in front of a bright light or window. It makes speechreading difficult if not impossible.
   - Introduce new topics clearly with a short sentence or key word so the student can follow changes in activities.
   - Use visual aids whenever possible, such as blackboard, overhead projector, or handouts.
   - Indicate that another student is speaking by pointing to the speaker or saying the student's name.
   - Remember that moustaches and beards limit the amount of information that can be obtained from speechreading.

4. Recognize that trying "to hear" demands concentration and can be both frustrating and stressful. The student will hear and understand less when tired or ill. When possible, give "listening breaks."

continues

continued

5. Provide written instructions and summaries to help the student keep in touch with lesson content.
   - Place a simple lesson outline on the blackboard.
   - Write key words or phrases on the blackboard as the lesson progresses.
   - Write new vocabulary on the blackboard and make the pronunciations clear.
   - Write homework assignments on the blackboard, including date due and other important information.

6. Restate or write down important announcements made over the public address system.

7. Remember, the student with a hearing impairment may have speech and language problems.
   - If you have difficulty understanding the student, ask him to repeat.
   - Do not call attention to the student's speech errors in the classroom. Record and share them with the speech pathologist.
   - Realize that the student may have limited vocabulary and syntax, both receptively and expressively. A failure to understand may be related to this language deficit as well as the hearing impairment. If the student does not understand what you said, rephrase it.
   - Be sure the student understands when questions are being asked.
   - Give written tests whenever possible, making sure that they are written at a level the student can read and comprehend. When preparing an academic test, ensure that it tests knowledge of the subject and not reading or writing skills.

8. Remember, the amplification used by the student is essential to success.
   - Check the hearing aids and batteries each morning for clarity and power.
   - Keep extra hearing aid batteries at school.
   - Encourage the student to tell you if the aid is not working properly.
   - If the child uses an FM trainer, ascertain that he or she charges the device at home each evening. Pass the microphone to other students when they are speaking. If that idea is not practical, the teacher should revocalize student statements.

9. Use captioned films and filmstrips whenever possible. When films are being used, there is an attachment that can be plugged into the audio output of the projector and into the FM trainer. This device is of great assistance because the student receives the message directly rather than having to hear the rattling of the projector, which may mask the message.

10. Recognize that some allowances may be needed. Depending on the student's hearing loss, amplification, and use of residual hearing, some tutoring after class and notetaking during class may be necessary. For older students, it is often helpful to have another student take notes. It is difficult to speechread and take notes at the same time.

continues

continued

11. Ensure that the sound quality of tape and record players and film projectors is optimal and the student is seated in close proximity to the speaker.

12. Encourage the school and city administration to treat acoustically the classrooms used by students with hearing impairments (for example, install carpeting, draperies, and acoustical ceiling tile; test the heater, air conditioner, and flourescent lights for excessive noise).

13. Communicate regularly with the child's other teachers. The student will probably receive itinerant services (for example, from a speech and language pathologist and a certified teacher of children with hearing impairments). There should be regular communication between the mainstreaming teacher and the itinerant teachers, and one teacher should be designated as the liaison among the teachers and with the parents.

14. Communicate regularly with parents. Consider sending home advance notice of material to be covered. Parents are willing and able to assist with drills and pre- and post-review work.

Notes:

Source: "Teaching Hard of Hearing Students: Some Helpful Hints," SHHH Information Series #161, Self Help for Hard of Hearing People, Inc., Bethesda, Maryland, © 1989.

Adaptations in Instruction for Young Children with Visual Impairments

Suggestions here concern basic considerations for children with visual impairments. Where questions arise, consult an ophthalmologist to aid in identifying the extent of probable vision loss or confer with professionals who have worked with children who are visually impaired.

1. Introduce activities that require manipulation of objects with various textures. Teach the child to discriminate among textures.

2. Teach the child to recognize where sounds are located and how far away the sounds are.

3. Teach the child to reach for an object by a sound cue. This concept will aid the child in exploring and learning about objects. Attach bells to objects you want the child to explore. Use this sound cue consistently when a new object is being introduced.

4. Emphasize crawling, creeping, cruising, and walking. Encourage the child to be confident in self-initiating body movement.

5. Use finger walking to aid the child in locating parts of his or her body or objects nearby.

6. Watch the child's hands for information. When responding to a child's gesture, squeeze the hand lightly to acknowledge this gesture. Also, a similar gesture can be used to alert the child to a change in activity.

Notes:

Source: *Resource Kit: Handicapped Children Birth to Five—Social*, Maryland State Department of Education.

Braille Alphabet

The six dots of the braille cell are arranged and numbered:

```
1 ● ● 4
2 ● ● 5
3 ● ● 6
```

The capital sign, dot 6, placed before a letter makes a capital letter:

```
1   4
2   5
3 ● 6
```

The number sign, dots 3, 4, 5, 6 placed before the characters a–j, makes numbers 1 through 0 (for example, a preceded by the number sign is 1, b is 2, and so on):

```
1 ● 4
2 ● 5
3 ● ● 6
```

a	b	c	d	e	f	g	h	i	j
●	● · ● ·	● ● · ·	● ● · ●	● · · ●	● ● ● ·	● ● ● ●	● · ● ●	· ● ● ·	· ● ● ●

k	l	m	n	o	p	q	r	s	t
● · ● ·	● · ● · ● ·	● ● · · ● ·	● ● · ● ● ·	● · · ● ● ·	● ● ● · ● ·	● ● ● ● ● ·	● · ● ● ● ·	· ● ● · ● ·	· ● ● ● ● ·

u	v	w	x	y	z	capital sign	number sign	period	comma
● · · · ● ●	● · ● · ● ●	· ● ● · · ●	● ● · · ● ●	● ● · ● ● ●	● · · ● ● ●	· · · · · ●	· ● · ● ● ●	· · ● ● · ●	· · ● · · ·

Source: National Library Service for the Blind and Physically Handicapped, The Library of Congress, Washington, DC.

Adaptations in Instruction for Young Children with Speech/Language Disorders

The following list contains nine basic considerations for children who have language and speech impairments. Where questions arise, consultation with a speech and language pathologist should be requested.

1. Combine the word or phrase being taught by presenting it in a meaningful situation. (Content may be chosen according to the child's interest and participation.)

2. Use real objects and experiences.

3. Repeat the response you desire three times when a child does not respond to your question.

4. Repeat what the child says and also expand on what the child says when the child makes efforts to speak.

5. Observe how a child processes language input.

6. Model new words and sounds. Use many contexts, both structured and informal, such as free-play times, for generalization of concepts.

7. Sit in front of a mirror with the child when teaching new sounds. Also, you may hold thin paper in front of the child's mouth to show the child the air puff produced from the sound.

8. Help the child learn to recognize the source of a sound. Move the child to the source of the sound and place the child's hand on the object.

9. Use a tape recorder for immediate playback of sounds that the child has made. Allow the child time to respond to the tape. This activity should cease if it becomes stressful.

Notes:

Source: *Resource Kit: Handicapped Children Birth to Five—Social*, Maryland State Department of Education.

Use of "Information for Teachers—
Children with Spina Bifida"

The following pages include useful background information for your child's teachers and others. This is a short, concise overview of some of the difficulties that children with spina bifida may experience. Below each item there is space for you to write, if you like, a description of your child's particular strengths, weaknesses, needs, equipment used, assistance required, and bowel and bladder regimens.

Make copies of these pages. Each year give them to your child's current teacher. Be sure to retain your original for future use.

This information may also be given to other persons who have contact with your child, such as a babysitter, Girl Scout leader, Sunday school teacher, physical therapist, occupational therapist, early intervention specialist, or school bus driver. Use your judgment regarding their interest. Some people ask questions directly; others avoid discussing issues, yet may be quite interested in having more understanding.

It is recommended that you offer this to your child's teacher during the summer before school begins. He or she will have more time to review it then. After school begins, teachers have many demands on their time and may not be able to spend the time reading this important information.

Notes:

Source: Marjorie Szor, MA, MS, RN, C, Clinical Nurse Specialist—Myelomeningocele, © Medical College Hospitals, Toledo, Ohio.

Information for Teachers—Children with Spina Bifida

Children with spina bifida are similar to their classmates in most ways, but due to nerve damage may experience *varying degrees* of difficulty in the following areas:

LOSS OF STRONG MOVEMENT OF LEGS AND/OR FEET

May use braces, special shoes, crutches, a walker, or a wheelchair or may need none of the above.

LOSS OF SENSATION IN LEGS AND/OR FEET

Need protection of skin from

- Excessive heat
- Excessive cold
- Pressure: Every 15 minutes the child should shift weight (if in a wheelchair) and every 15 minutes the child should do pressure releases (wheelchair pushups) by raising off the seat and holding this position for 15 seconds.
- Dampness: Soiled or damp diapers or underwear needs to be changed as soon as possible.

BOWEL MANAGEMENT

Because the nerves from the spinal cord to the bowel are not working properly, a strict regimen needs to be followed.

Though most children receive few signals from the bowel, the bowel can be trained. This requires toileting once a day at the same time every day. A diet high in fiber and fluids helps keep the stool the right consistency.

Several other management methods can be used as well. However, occasional accidents do happen, even when management methods are generally successful.

URINARY CONTINENCE

Because the nerves from the spinal cord to the bladder are not working properly, complete dryness is usually difficult. To accomplish continence, children may take bladder medicines and/or catheterize their bladder.

If they "cath" themselves, they need to do this one to three times during the school day. It is important that they have sufficient time to do this, so that they remove all the urine from their

continues

continued

bladder. They may or may not need help/supervision in accomplishing this. Privacy is important to maintain while cathing.

Urinary tract infections are common and need to be treated with antibiotics. Infection can cause the urine to have a strong odor, and it can cause wetness, even though the child is usually dry.

SHUNT

Ninety percent of babies born with spina bifida also have hydrocephalus ("fluid on the brain"). To correct this, a tube called a shunt is placed in a ventricle of the brain. The other end of this tubing is usually placed in the abdomen, though sometimes in the heart. This allows drainage of the fluid off the brain.

Occasionally, this shunt system malfunctions. Parents are aware of the signs and symptoms and would be in contact with the neurosurgeon, if they occur. If, however, over a period of time you notice the child's school performance deteriorating or that he or she does not act as alert as previously, it would be helpful to report this to the parents.

LATEX SENSITIVITY

Children with spina bifida are at high risk for developing an allergic reaction to latex (natural rubber). If they are positive reactors already, they should not come in contact with anything made of latex. If they have not yet developed a sensitivity, it is recommended that they also not have contact with latex items, with the intent that with decreased exposure they may never develop such a sensitivity. Some of these reactions are very serious.

INDEPENDENCE

It is easy for children with spina bifida to rely on others for many things they could do themselves. If this is allowed to happen, a pattern of "learned helplessness" develops. It is useful if they are encouraged to break down tasks into small steps and to be praised for accomplishing these. To perform their own self-care, to problem solve, and to have their share of classroom responsibilities will promote the important development of healthy self-esteem.

EMOTIONAL GROWTH

The teacher has a powerful role in influencing emotional health and growth in these children.

Close communication with the parents can help not only to identify potential problems but also to reinforce each other's endeavors, with maturation the intended result.

continues

continued

LEARNING

The neurological sequelae of spina bifida, hydrocephalus, shunts, shunt infection, and Chiari hindbrain malformation are not completely understood. It is apparent, however, that those children with spina bifida, though they may have good verbal fluency, frequently have perceptual-motor problems with below-average eye-hand coordination.

Organizational skills, including sequencing, may also need support. Lately, there has been a focus on the higher-than-average incidence of attention deficit disorder. Because of the frequent occurrence of learning disabilities in students with spina bifida, testing and appropriate services are recommended.

Notes:

Source: Marjorie Szor, MA, MS, RN, C, Clinical Nurse Specialist—Myelomeningocele, © Medical College Hospitals, Toledo, Ohio.

Planning for the Child Who Is Dependent on Medical Technology

When a child who is dependent on medical technology enters school, he or she is taking a major step toward achieving his or her maximum potential. When a private duty nurse must accompany the child to school, the child's safe and successful integration into the school program hinges on the combined efforts of the family, school, and private duty nursing agency. The guidelines below suggest appropriate responsibilities for the family, school, and nursing agency.

RESPONSIBILITIES OF PRIVATE DUTY NURSING AGENCY

Transportation

Prior to the child's admission to school, a transportation plan should be in place as agreed upon by the family, school, and nursing agency. The plan should include:

- method of transportation and who accompanies the child
- parental responsibilities related to transportation
- methods of dealing with emergencies during transport
- parental responsibilities for notifying the school and transporter when the child will be absent

Licensure

The agency must maintain active licensure files and provide evidence of licensure to family and school representatives when requested.

Ongoing Communication

The agency must provide the school with the name of the private duty nurse, the agency name and phone number, and a designated contact person at the agency. The contact person will be available to discuss issues or concerns regarding agency personnel.

Daily Notification

The private duty nurse notifies the principal or school nurse upon arrival each morning.

Medical Equipment and Supplies

The private duty nurse arrives at school with properly functioning equipment and medical supplies needed for the day.

Monitoring

Because the child's safety is of primary importance, the private duty nurse should be in attendance or in close proximity to the child at all times, including during therapy and recreational sessions.

If scheduled breaks are taken, the private duty nurse must inform school personnel and ensure proper monitoring of the child until the nurse returns.

Emergency Planning

The nursing agency participates in the development of emergency plans that will be

continues

continued

signed by the family, the agency, and the school. The emergency plan should include the following items as well as who is responsible for notification:

- doctor's name and phone number
- paramedic phone number
- hospital emergency room phone number
- evacuation plan with equipment necessary for life support
- method of transporting child home in an emergency

The nurse ensures that the emergency plan and patient care plan accompany the child at all times.

Care Plan

The nurse is responsible for the nursing care of the child at school and for implementing the agreed upon patient care plan. The nurse may discuss variances from the Individualized Education Program (IEP) with school personnel, parents, and the nursing agency supervisor.

Continuity of Care

The private duty nurse works collaboratively with school therapies and treatment programs to ensure continuity of care.

School Conferences

The nurse and/or nursing supervisor may attend routine school conferences at the discretion of the parents.

Documentation

A document should be drawn up by the family, nursing agency, and school including all the above items. It should be signed and dated by these three parties, and copies should be provided to all parties.

All documents should be revised at the beginning of the school year or whenever there is a change in care, school building, or agency.

Child's Privacy

The private duty nurse should adhere to the American Nurses' Association's code for nurses, with special emphasis on safeguarding the student's right to privacy by protecting information of a confidential nature.

continues

continued

RESPONSIBILITIES OF THE SCHOOL DISTRICT

Transportation

Prior to the child's admission to school, a transportation plan should be in place as agreed upon by the family, school, and nursing agency. The plan should include:

- method of transportation and who accompanies the child
- parental responsibilities related to transportation
- methods of dealing with emergencies during transport
- parental responsibilities for notifying the school and transporter when the child will be absent

Licensure

The school may request a copy of the nursing license from each private duty nurse.

Ongoing Communication

The school must provide the nursing agency with the name and telephone number of a contact person at the school.

Daily Notification

School staff facilitates the daily notification process.

Medical Equipment and Supplies

Any equipment or supplies provided by the school should be properly maintained and made available as needed.

Monitoring

The school allows and facilitates the private duty nurse to be in attendance at all times, including during therapy and recreational sessions.

The school cooperates in the monitoring of the child during scheduled breaks.

Emergency Planning

The school has a specific plan of emergency care for each child, including medical, fire, and natural disaster emergencies as agreed to by the family, nursing agency, and school.

The school will attach to the IEP a copy of the emergency plan and the current patient care plan. A second copy should be submitted to the school nurse.

The school will ensure that the emergency plan and patient care plan accompany the child at all times.

Care Plan

The school will provide the appropriate education in the least restrictive environment, develop and implement the child's IEP, be aware of the patient care plan, and advise the parent of any academic or medical concerns.

Continuity of Care

The school works collaboratively with the private duty nurse, family, and doctor to ensure continuity of care.

continues

continued

School Conferences

The school will invite the nurse and/or supervisor to routine school conferences at the discretion of the parents.

Documentation

A document should be drawn up by the family, nursing agency, and school including all the above items. It should be signed and dated by these three parties, and copies should be provided to all parties.

All documents should be revised at the beginning of the school year or whenever there is a change in care, school building, or agency.

Child's Privacy

School personnel will observe the usual and customary protection of the rights of privacy of students.

RESPONSIBILITIES OF THE FAMILY

Transportation

A transportation plan should be in place prior to the child's admission to school as agreed upon by the family, school, and nursing agency. The plan should include:

- method of transportation and who accompanies the child
- parental responsibilities related to transportation
- methods of dealing with emergencies during transport
- parental responsibilities for notifying the school and transporter when the child will be absent

Licensure

The family has knowledge of the credentials of caregivers providing nursing care in school.

Ongoing Communication

The family should initiate and maintain a dialogue among appropriate school and nursing agency personnel.

Medical Equipment and Supplies

The family is responsible for providing and maintaining equipment and supplies coming from home.

Monitoring

The family participates in planning of monitoring arrangements between school and private duty nurses.

Emergency Planning

The family participates in the development of plans that address medical and transportation emergencies involving the child.

The family will learn from the school how the child will be evacuated during a fire or natural disaster.

The family will immediately inform the nursing agency and school personnel of any changes in the medical or nursing care of the child.

Care Plan

The family collaborates with the school and the nursing agency in developing the IEP and the patient care plan.

continues

continued

Continuity of Care

The family will collaborate with the school and the private duty nurse to facilitate continuity of care.

School Conferences

The family may ask that the nurse and/or supervisor attend routine school conferences to ensure continuity of care.

Documentation

A document should be drawn up by the family, nursing agency, and school including all the above items. It should be signed and dated by these three parties, and copies should be provided to all parties.

All documents should be revised at the beginning of the school year or whenever there is a change in care, school building, or agency.

Child's Privacy

Parents will provide the necessary permission for agency and school personnel to share information as it relates to the safety and well-being of the child.

Notes:

Courtesy of Laura Frost, Vice President, CM Healthcare Resources, Inc., Chicago, Illinois; Rosemary Manago, MSN, RN, Assistant Director, DSCC Home Care Program, Division of Specialized Care for Children, The University of Illinois at Chicago, Chicago, Illinois; Joan Reilly, MSN, RN, Chicago Board of Education, Chicago, Illinois; Kim Rzab, RN, Chicago, Illinois.

Appendix—Patient Information Sheets Grouped by Diagnosis

Many patient information sheets in this manual apply to a wide variety of disabilities. This appendix lists only those patient information sheets that are disability-specific.

Index